G U I D E   T O

Genealogical Research

IN THE NATIONAL ARCHIVES OF THE UNITED STATES

THIRD EDITION

Edited by

ANNE BRUNER EALES & ROBERT M. KVASNICKA

National Archives and Records Administration

Washington, DC

2000

PUBLISHED FOR THE NATIONAL ARCHIVES AND RECORDS ADMINISTRATION
BY THE NATIONAL ARCHIVES TRUST FUND BOARD

LIBRARY OF CONGRESS CATALOGING-IN-PUBLICATION DATA

United States. National Archives and Records Administration.
    Guide to genealogical research in the National Archives/edited by Anne Bruner Eales
  and Robert M. Kvasnicka.– 3rd ed.
     p. cm.
  Includes bibliographical reference and index.
  ISBN 1-880875-24-1
    1. United States–Genealogy–Bibliography–Catalogs. 2. Registers of births,
  etc.–United States–Bibliography–Catalogs. 3. United States. National Archives and
  Records Administration–Catalogs. I. Eales, Anne Bruner. II. Kvasnicka, Robert M.,
  1935– III. Title

Z5313.U5 U54 2000
[CS68]
016.929'1'072073–dc21
00-055905

DESIGNED BY JANICE HARGETT, NATIONAL ARCHIVES

CONTENTS

LIST of TABLES

PREFACE

The fascination of family history has spread across America. Millions of individuals are now tracing their ancestry, and we at the National Archives and Records Administration (NARA) work hard to be of help. One major result is this new edition of the *Guide to Genealogical Records in the National Archives.*

Part of the interest of this guide, however, is in what it reveals about us. The National Archives is often thought of as the place that displays the Declaration of Independence, the U.S. Constitution, and the Bill of Rights. Thousands of people come yearly to see those great Charters of Freedom in the Rotunda of our original building. But our holdings are now housed in more than 30 buildings across the country, from Washington, DC, to the West Coast, and from Atlanta to Anchorage, where we preserve and provide access to literally billions of paper records, along with photographs, films, audio and video tapes, drawings, blueprints, museum objects, and—increasingly—computer-generated records.

Genealogists know this because they find useful records in our regional as well as our Washington, DC, area archives, and the treasures they find are less in the celebrated historical documents than in our thousands of pension files, passenger lists, census records, and other materials that shed light on the lives of the humble as well as the renowned, the immigrant as well as the early settler, and those who came in bondage as well as those who sought a freer, better life. We display the Charters of Freedom because they created a government for "We the People." We preserve many other historical records because they document who "we the people" were and are. And every day, family historians flock to our research rooms, use our microfilm publications, and explore our online resources to find out.

NARA is the nation's recordkeeper, safeguarding records of all three branches of the Federal Government. Our mission is to provide ready access to essential evidence that documents the rights, identities, and entitlements of citizens; the actions for which Federal officials are responsible; and the national experience. NARA meets an almost unlimited range of information needs, ensuring access to records on which both the credibility of government and the accuracy of history depend.

To help researchers, we prepare various kinds of finding aids that describe the nature and content of Federal records. For example, the *Guide to Federal Records in the National Archives of the United States* (1995), available in print or on the NARA web site at *www.nara.gov*, gives a broad picture of the materials in our custody. Popular older guides include *A Guide to Federal Records Relating to the Civil War* and *A Guide to the Archives of the Confederate States of America*, both of which were reprinted in 1998.

This publication, *Guide to Genealogical Research in the National Archives*, supersedes the 1985 edition. A complete revision and enlargement, this new guide covers records not described in the earlier version and includes references to information available through the NARA web site. This guide also contains illustrations and photographs, citations to many new and previously cited microfilm publications, and expanded and clarified descriptions of the relevant records held by the National Archives and Records Administration.

Many NARA staff members contributed to this revision by evaluating and verifying descriptions of records, compiling new information, reviewing text, and designing and printing the final product. Special thanks are due to Margaret Adams, Eileen Bolger, Eric Bittner, John Butler, Stuart Butler, Tod Butler, John Celardo, Suzanne Dewberry, Diana Duff, Robert Ellis, Sandra Glasser, Milton Gustafson, Janice Hargett, Suzanne Harris, Mary Ann Hawkins, Walter Hickey, Walter Hill, Donald Jackanicz, Joyce Justice, Susan Karren, Brenda Kepley, Maureen MacDonald, Michael Meier, Mary Frances Morrow, Dan Nealand, Diane Nixon, Jean Nudd, Kathleen O'Connor, James Owens, Bruce Parham, Alan Perry, Michael Pilgrim, Claire Prechtel-Kluskens, Trevor Plante, Constance Potter, Charles Reeves, Barbara Rust, Ronnie Saunders, Richard Smith, Sharon Thibodeau, John Vandereedt, Rebecca Warlow, Reginald Washington, Thomas Wiltsey, and Mitchell Yockelson. Susan Carroll prepared the index. By explaining the research potential of genealogical materials in the National Archives of the United States, the cooperative effort of these individuals makes this guide a valuable resource for family historians.

JOHN W. CARLIN
Archivist of the United States

INTRODUCTION

I.1 Value and Limitations of Federal Records

Today more and more people are discovering the rewards of genealogy—the study of family history. The National Archives and Records Administration (NARA), keeper of the historically valuable records of the Federal Government, can aid genealogical research in many ways. Some of the records in NARA help to establish lines of ancestry, with relationships between generations of a family often given or implied. Genealogists can use pension applications and later census records for this purpose. Other Federal records also give information about individuals—physical descriptions, places of birth and residence, and activities and occupations—thereby expanding the researcher's picture of an ancestor's life.

However, genealogists should be aware of three important limitations to doing research in these archives. First, NARA keeps only Federal records, and these are useful for genealogical purposes only when they reflect interaction between individuals and the Federal Government. The best information about birth, marriage, and death, the milestones of life and the backbone of genealogy, can more often be found in family, local, and state records.

Second, the colonial period of American history is not documented in the National Archives, and very few records predate the Revolutionary War. Most of the records described in this guide pertain to the 19th century, a time when government did not touch the lives of Americans to the extent that it does today.

The third limitation arises from the nature of an archives. Records are arranged to reflect their original purpose, usually maintained just as they were kept by the agencies that created them. Their future use for family history was not a consideration. As a result, records frequently are not presented in a way that might seem most helpful to genealogists. For example, names are not listed alphabetically in census records. The records are arranged geographically because the primary reason for taking the census was to determine a state's representation in the U.S. House of Representatives.

Because of these limitations, a researcher must come to the archives with information about when, how, and where an ancestor came into contact with the Federal Government. Indeed, the more detailed a researcher's knowledge of American history and geography, the more effective will be their use of Federal records. A general understanding of patterns of immigration, migration, and settlement, and how an individual fitted into these patterns is helpful.

This introduction contains only a few suggestions about getting started in genealogical research, with remarks about the organization of records in general, finding aids to Federal records, and research facilities and special programs that are available to genealogists through various NARA facilities. The introduction is followed by chapters describing records that are grouped according to broad subject areas. Each chapter contains specific information about a particular group of records—why they were created, how they are arranged, how they can be used, and what one can expect to find. Additional information about the availability of microfilm, finding aids, and help with research on the subject is included where applicable. Cross-references and related index entries are to paragraph numbers rather than page numbers. Researchers will find some chapters are more helpful and pertinent to their projects than others. The reader should note that the order of chapters is not indicative of their relative research value for genealogists.

I.2 Research Methods and Aids

It is recommended that the beginning genealogist consult basic guidebooks about how to conduct genealogical research. These should be available at most libraries. An excellent source of relevant publications is NARA's *Aids to Genealogical Research Catalog*, which is listed on the National Archives and Records Administration web site at *www.nara.gov.*

Successful use of archival records depends on a carefully planned research strategy. Before coming to the National Archives, genealogists should thoroughly research information by consulting family members and records in regional and local institutions, including material in libraries, historical and genealogical societies, and local archival depositories.

Genealogists should start with themselves and work backwards toward the unknown, finding all available vital information about parents, grandparents, and other relatives. The place to begin is at home, with such things as family Bibles, newspaper clippings, military paperwork, birth and death certificates, marriage licenses, school records, diaries, letters, scrapbooks, identifying information on photographs, and baby books. These often provide four key elements that are the basic building blocks for a family historian: names, dates, places, and relationships. If available, older relatives, who may already have gathered genealogical data or are able to provide input from personal memory, can be important sources. Advertisements placed in genealogical bulletins in a city, county, or state where ancestors lived may also result in valuable contacts.

State, county, and church records are particularly useful. Some states began to keep birth and death records earlier than others, but in most of the United States, registration of these milestones became a government requirement between 1890 and 1915. Before that time evidence of births and deaths were usually maintained in county records, some dated as early as the establishment of the county. Since property acquisition and disposition frequently are good sources of genealogical information, deeds, wills, and other such records normally found in the county should also be researched. Often the earliest county records, or copies of them, are available in state archives. Some churches also have records of important events in the lives of their members, and a few denominations even have their own archives and archivists. Genealogists should investigate the possibility of locating information about an ancestor in the records of the church to which they belonged. Only after this background research has been completed should a trip to a National Archives facility be considered.

Advice on planning a research visit to NARA can be obtained from the National Archives web site at *www.nara.gov*, which lists such things as locations, hours, and guidelines for using Federal records. NARA's web page for genealogists, "The Genealogy Page," also at *www.nara.gov*, includes information such as genealogical resources on the internet, listings of genealogy workshops and courses, and genealogical material in the NARA Archival Information Locator (NAIL). NAIL is an emerging source of descriptive information about records of genealogical interest held by NARA and is the prototype for an agency-wide Archival Research Catalog (ARC) slated for debut in 2001. Although NAIL currently contains only a limited portion of NARA's descriptions, plans call for approximately 80 percent of NARA's archival holdings to be described at the series level in ARC by 2007.

I.3 Records at the National Archives

Based on its origin, every document in the National Archives has been assigned to a numbered record group (RG). Most commonly, a record group consists of the records of a single bureau, such as Records of the Bureau of the Census, Record Group (RG) 29. Often the records of the head of an executive department and units with department-wide responsibility are assigned to a general record group, as in General Records of the Department of State, RG 59. In some instances, the functions of a particular office or other administrative unit of an agency were important or unique enough to warrant the establishment of a separate record group; an example is Records of the War Department Collection of Confederate Records, RG 109. Appendix I contains a list of all the record groups cited in this publication.

Record groups are measured in cubic feet. In the year 2000 more than 2 million cubic feet of materials held by the National Archives and Records Administration are divided among 545 record groups. The holdings include billions of pages; millions of photographs, motion pictures, aerial photographs, maps, and charts; thousands of sound recordings and architectural and engineering drawings; and thousands of data sets of electronic records.

In this guide the unit of description is usually the series, a subset of a record group, filed together because they relate to the same subject, function, or activity, or have some other relationship arising from their origin and use. Within most series, records are kept in the order that best served

the need of the creating agency. This arrangement can make finding specific genealogical facts difficult and often determines the information a researcher must have to frame a research question that can be answered. The nature of the additional information varies from series to series; it will be discussed in the chapters with descriptions of the records in that chapter.

Many of the records that are useful to a genealogist are in the general correspondence series of various agencies, so taking a few minutes to learn the arrangement of a 19th-century government office file will prove helpful. Throughout most of the 19th century, government agencies usually filed correspondence in two series: "letters sent" for outgoing communications, and "letters received" for incoming communications. Often the letters were folded in thirds by a government clerk, and an endorsement was written across one of the three sections. The endorsement usually consisted of the letter's date, correspondent's name, subject, and sometimes a list of enclosures and the action taken. The letters were then filed so that the endorsements could be examined without taking the letters out of the file.

In other cases, letters received or copies of letters sent may have been bound into a volume that might or might not have an index. It was also customary to make a register entry for each letter sent or received. Letters could be assigned an identifying symbol, perhaps alphanumerical, consisting of the first letter of the surname of the correspondent and a number assigned serially in order of dispatch or receipt. If the letters were filed chronologically, the entry in the register might be made thereunder in alphabetical sections. Registers contain varying information, consisting of some or all of the following: correspondent's name, date of communication, abstracts of contents and reply or other note of action taken, and possibly a cross-reference to other letters on the same subject or to the symbol of the reply or incoming letter in the correspondence series. Registers therefore serve as finding aids to the correspondence series.

I.4 NARA Finding Aids

The National Archives and Records Administration publishes several different kinds of finding aids to assist researchers in using its vast holdings. These include guides, reference information papers (RIP), and special lists (SL) relating to particular subjects. Such finding aids may cover many record groups—as guides do—or focus on a specific type of document within one record group—as some special lists do. Detailed descriptions of the contents of some record groups are provided in inventories (INV) or preliminary inventories (PI). These finding aids contain a history of the organization and functions of the agency that created the records and descriptions of the series that make up the record group. The finding aids especially valuable for genealogical research are cited in this guide at appropriate points in the text. A typical citation is *Records of the Bureau of Indian Affairs*, Preliminary Inventory (PI) 163, compiled by Edward E. Hill (Washington: National Archives and Records Service, 1965).

This guide describes series most valuable for genealogy, but researchers may wish to consult finding aids for record groups not cited in this guide to find other documents related to their research. The *Select List of Publications of the National Archives and Records Administration*, General Information Leaflet (GIL) 3, provides a complete list of finding aids, ordering instructions, and, where applicable, prices. This select list and the *Aids to Genealogical Research Catalog* are available from Customer Service Center, National Archives and Records Administration, NWCC1, Room 406, 700 Pennsylvania Ave., NW, Washington, DC 20408-0001.

I.5 NARA Microform Publications

The National Archives reproduces records in two forms: microfilm and microfiche. NARA's extensive microform program, which has been assisted by the generous sharing of film produced by other groups, such as the Genealogical Society of Utah, has been underway since the 1940s. This program has resulted in two notable achievements: preservation of material held by the National Archives and enhanced access to records. Generally, if a series has been filmed, the film is used for research rather than the original. Priceless, fragile, and awkwardly bound documents thus can be removed from reference circulation in order to avoid damage and deterioration from ordinary use. Filming also makes valuable records available to researchers in many parts of the country. NARA microform publications are available for use in the National Archives Building in Washington, DC, and the National Archives at College Park, MD. Many important microform publications—including microfilm of Federal census schedules, 1790–1920—are available in NARA's regional archives. Addresses for these facilities are listed in Table 1. Appendix II contains a list of all the microform publications cited in this publication.

In 1999 the National Archives placed on its web page at *www.nara.gov* a microfilm locator. The locator is an inventory of the microfilm available in NARA research rooms across the country and thus will include microfilm publications acquired from other sources. Many of these publications are not for sale by the National Archives. The locator provides the publication number, title, number and size of microfilm rolls, a citation as to the location and type of any relevant finding aid, and whether or not NARA sells the publication.

In addition, many state and local archives, historical and genealogical societies, libraries, and research institutions have purchased copies of National Archives microfilm and make it available to their patrons. Individuals can buy rolls from NARA to use on a microfilm reading machine at home or with permission at a local library. (*See* ordering instructions below.) Because microfilmed records are widely distributed, researchers should explore their own community resources completely before planning research trips to National Archives facilities.

Series that have been microfilmed are cited in this guide by title and number. A typical citation is M694, *Index to Compiled Service Records of Volunteer Soldiers Who Served from 1784 to 1811*, 9 rolls. These microfilm citations are divided into five categories: M, A, T, P, and C. Most "M" publications reproduce an entire series of records; A, T, P, and C publications are numbered in the same sequence and do not always reproduce a complete series. They may contain only segments, by date or subject, of a larger series. "A" and sometimes "T" publications may be copies of microfilm produced by other Federal agencies and later accessioned by the National Archives. "A" and "T" publications are reproduced and sold exactly as they were filmed by the originating agency; sometimes introductory material has been added. "P" publications are reproduced for preservation purposes, and "C" are those produced by private contractors and available through NARA 7 years after their original publication date. Many introductions and tables of contents are printed as accompanying descriptive pamphlets (DP). Not all microfilm publications have them.

NARA microform publications are listed in the *National Archives Microfilm Resources for Research, A Comprehensive Catalog* (rev. 2000). This catalog groups microform products by record group, publication number, and subject. Federal population census records are described in the following catalogs: *The 1790–1890 Federal Population Censuses* (rep. 2001), *1900 Federal Population Census* (rep. 2000), *The 1910 Federal Population Census* (rep. 2000), and *The 1920 Federal Population Census* (1992). "The 1930 Federal Population Census" will be available by 2002. Other National Archives select catalogs that describe microfilm publications of interest to genealogists are *Immigrant & Passenger Arrivals* (rev. 1991), *Military Service Records* (1985), *American Indians* (rev. 1998), and *Black Studies* (1984). To purchase any of these catalogs, contact Fee Publications, National Archives Trust Fund (NWCC2), P.O. Box 100793, Atlanta, GA 30384-0793.

For costs and more information about purchasing rolls of microfilm or fee publications, call 1-800-234-8861, or fax 1-301-713-6169.

Certain microfilm publications useful to genealogists are also available through the National Archives Microfilm Rental Program. These include the Federal population census schedules and Soundexes from 1790–1920, American Revolutionary War service records and index, and Revolutionary War pension and bounty-land-warrant application files. By participating in this program, you get the best clarity and readability available through any genealogical source. Most orders are mailed out the same day they are received. If the roll you request cannot be mailed within 10 days of receipt of the order, NARA will notify you of the date we expect to fill it. You will never have to wait more than 60 days. For more information about microfilm rental or to learn whether a library near you is one of the 6,000 nationwide that participates in the NARA rental program, call 301-604-3699 or write to the National Archives Microfilm Rental Program, P.O. Box 30, Annapolis Junction, MD 20701-0030.

I.6 Government Publications

Many Federal records have been published as government documents that are available in most large libraries throughout the United States. These printed records are identified in this guide. By using these printed materials as much as possible, researchers may be able to save the expense of a trip to one of NARA's facilities if the information they seek is available in print at a nearby library. In some cases, the citation of a published document in this guide will be followed by a "SuDocs No.," such as "Z4.14/1:HD4," an example of a Superintendent of Documents Number assigned by the Government Printing Office to documents printed for an agency. Reference may also contain a serial number for a document printed for one of the houses of Congress, such as "Ser. 4535"; or a library call number, such as DS711.W6. These numbers are helpful to librarians who are asked to locate one of these publications for a researcher.

I.7 Research Facilities at the National Archives

National Archives Building and National Archives at College Park

The historic National Archives Building (NAB) is located at 700 Pennsylvania Ave., NW, Washington, DC. The Archives/Navy Memorial stop on the Yellow and Green Lines of the Metro, Washington's subway, is across Pennsylvania Avenue from the NAB, and several commercial parking lots are also located nearby.

The National Archives at College Park (NACP) is located at 8601 Adelphi Road in College Park, MD. As of this date, the R3 Metrobus runs between the NACP and the Greenbelt, Fort Totten, and Prince George's Plaza Green Line Metro stations. Researcher parking is also available at the College Park facility in an adjacent, three-level parking garage. A staff shuttle bus between the NAB and NACP is accessible to researchers on a space-available basis and runs on the hour from 8:00 a.m. to 5:00 p.m., Monday through Friday.

NARA maintains libraries at both the Washington and College Park facilities. These libraries have extensive reference collections, complete sets of up-to-date finding aids, and holdings in U.S. history, Federal agency administrative history, and archival theory and practice. While the majority of the library's collection is housed at College Park,

materials from one library can be transferred to the other within one day.

National Personnel Records Center

The National Personnel Records Center (NPRC) in St. Louis, MO, holds both civilian and military personnel files. Release of information from records held at the NPRC is governed by the Freedom of Information Act of 1967 and the Privacy Act of 1974, as well as directives from the Department of Defense and other Federal agencies. Copies of most military and medical records on file at NPRC, including DD Form 214, Report of Separation (or equivalent), can be made available upon request to the veteran who is the subject of the file. Only limited information from official military personnel files of living veterans can be released to the general public without the consent of the veteran.

Further information about requesting military records can be obtained by contacting the National Personnel Records Center (NPRC), Military Records Facility, 9700 Page Ave., St. Louis, MO 63132-5100, or by calling 1-314-538-4261 (Army records); 1-314-538-4243 (Air Force records); and 1-314-538-4141 (Coast Guard, Marines, or Navy records). This facility holds military personnel records, and military and retired military medical records from all services, as well as selected dependent medical records, morning reports, rosters, and Philippine army and guerilla records.

Military service files for the following groups date approximately from:

Air Force Enlisted and Officers: September 1947
Army Enlisted: November 1912
Army Officers: July 1917
Coast Guard Enlisted and Officers: January 1898
Marine Corps Enlisted and Officers: January 1905
Navy Enlisted: January 1886
Navy Officers: January 1903

Unfortunately a 1973 fire destroyed nearly all records pertaining to persons discharged from the Army before 1960 and two-thirds of those discharged from the Air Force before 1964. Alternate sources are used when possible.

For information about civilian personnel records from Federal agencies nationwide and selected military dependent medical records, inquiries should be sent to National Personnel Records Center (NPRC), Civilian Records Facility, 111 Winnebago St., St. Louis, MO 63118-4199, or phoned to 1-314-538-5761.

The NARA web site at *www.nara.gov* also contains a link to the National Personnel Records Center.

Presidential Libraries

Presidential libraries serve as repositories for the papers, records, and historical materials of Presidents from Herbert Hoover to George Bush. Their use to the genealogist will be extremely limited, but those wishing more

TABLE 1
NARA's Regional Archives

Anchorage
NARA's Pacific Alaska Region
654 W. Third Ave.
Anchorage, AK 99501-2145
907-271-2441
alaska.archives@nara.gov
Archival holdings from Federal agencies
and courts in Alaska; extensive holdings
of NARA microfilm publications

Atlanta
NARA's Southeast Region
1557 St. Joseph Ave.
East Point, GA 30344-2593
404-763-7474
atlanta.archives@nara.gov
Archival holdings from Federal agencies
and courts in Alabama, Florida, Georgia,
Kentucky, Mississippi, North Carolina,
South Carolina, and Tennessee; extensive
holdings of NARA microfilm publications

Boston
NARA's Northeast Region
380 Trapelo Rd.
Waltham, MA 02452-6399
781-647-8104
waltham.archives@nara.gov
Archival holdings from Federal agencies
and courts in Connecticut, Maine,
Massachusetts, New Hampshire, Rhode
Island, and Vermont; extensive holdings
of NARA microfilm publications

Chicago
NARA's Great Lakes Region
7358 S. Pulaski Rd.
Chicago, IL 60629-5898
773-581-7816
chicago.archives@nara.gov
Archival holdings from Federal agencies
and courts in Illinois, Indiana, Michigan,
Minnesota, Ohio, and Wisconsin; extensive holdings of NARA microfilm publications

CONTACT THE INDIVIDUAL REGIONAL
ARCHIVES OR CONSULT THE NARA
WEB SITE AT *www.nara.gov* FOR
UP-TO-DATE INFORMATION ABOUT THE
LOCATIONS, HOURS, AND RESEARCH
PROCEDURES AT THE FACILTIES.

Denver
NARA's Rocky Mountain Region
Building 48–Denver Federal Center
W. 6th Avenue and Kipling Street
Denver, CO 80225-0307
Mailing address: P.O. Box 25307
Denver, CO 80225-0307
303-236-0817
denver.archives@nara.gov
Archival holdings from Federal agencies
and courts in Colorado, Montana, New
Mexico, North Dakota, South Dakota,
Utah, and Wyoming; extensive holdings
of NARA microfilm publications

Fort Worth
NARA's Southwest Region
501 W. Felix Street, P.O. Box 6216
Fort Worth, TX 76115-3405
817-334-5525
ftworth.archives@nara.gov
Archival holdings from Federal agencies
and courts in Arkansas, Louisiana,
Oklahoma, and Texas; extensive holdings of NARA microfilm publications

Kansas City
NARA's Central Plains Region
2312 E. Bannister Rd.
Kansas City, MO 64131-3011
816-926-6272
kansascity.archives@nara.gov
Archival holdings from Federal agencies
and courts in Iowa, Kansas, Missouri,
and Nebraska; extensive holdings of
NARA microfilm publications

Laguna Niguel
(Referred to in some NARA publications
as Los Angeles)
NARA's Pacific Region
24000 Avila Rd., First Floor–East Entrance
Laguna Niguel, CA 92677-3497
Mailing address: P.O. Box 6719
Laguna Niguel, CA 92607-6719
949-360-2641
laguna.archives@nara.gov
Archival holdings from Federal agencies
and courts in Arizona, southern California, and Clark County, NV; extensive
holdings of NARA microfilm publications

New York City
NARA's Northeast Region
201 Varick St.
New York, NY 10014-4811
212-337-1300
newyork.archives@nara.gov
Archival holdings from Federal agencies
and courts in New Jersey, New York,
Puerto Rico, and the U.S. Virgin Islands;
extensive holdings of NARA microfilm
publications

Philadelphia
NARA's Mid Atlantic Region
900 Market St.
Philadelphia, PA 19107-4292
215-597-3000
philadelphia.archives@nara.gov
Archival holdings from Federal agencies
and courts in Delaware, Maryland,
Pennsylvania, Virginia, and West Virginia;
extensive holdings of NARA microfilm
publications

Pittsfield
NARA's Northeast Region
10 Conte Dr.
Pittsfield, MA 01201-8230
413-445-6885
pittsfield.archives@nara.gov
Extensive holdings of NARA microfilm
publications

San Francisco
NARA's Pacific Region
1000 Commodore Dr.
San Bruno, CA 94066-2350
650-876-9001
sanbruno.archives@nara.gov
Archival holdings from Federal agencies
and courts in northern California,
Hawaii, Nevada (except Clark County),
the Pacific Trust Territories, and American Samoa; extensive holdings of NARA
microfilm publications

Seattle
NARA's Pacific Alaska Region
6125 Sand Point Way, NE
Seattle, WA 98115-7999
206-526-6501
seattle.archives@nara.gov
Archival holdings from Federal agencies
and courts in Idaho, Oregon, and Washington; extensive holdings of NARA
microfilm publications

information on the libraries, as well as a list of their holdings, should access the NARA web site at *www.nara.gov*, or contact the Office of Presidential Libraries, Room 2200, National Archives at College Park, 8601 Adelphi Rd., College Park, MD 20740-6001.

NARA's Regional Archives

The regional archives of the National Archives and Records Administration are listed on page 7 in Table 1. The holdings in these facilities, with the exception of Pittsfield, document Federal operations at the state and local level and include records of the U.S. district courts and appeals courts, the Corps of Engineers, the Bureau of Indian Affairs, the Bureau of Customs, and naval districts and shore establishments. Regional archives have microfilm copies of many records of high genealogical value. These include the Federal population census and selected military service records, pension applications, immigration and naturalization records, and bounty land warrant files and indexes. Each regional archives has a variety of finding aids associated with genealogy that are available upon request to Customer Service Center, National Archives and Records Administration, NWCC1, Room 406, 700 Pennsylvania Ave., NW, Washington, DC 20408-0001, or through the NARA web site at *www.nara.gov/regional*.

I.8 Reference Services at the National Archives

The National Archives makes records available to researchers at all of its facilities and provides information and assistance through its web site at *www.nara.gov*, but it does not perform research for patrons. NARA does not trace family lineage or attempt genealogical conclusions, nor does it maintain files or publications about specific families. The National Archives does not maintain a list of persons who do genealogical research for a fee, but researchers may obtain the names of professional genealogists from the Board for Certification of Genealogists, P.O. Box 14291, Washington, DC 20044, or the Association of Professional Genealogists, P.O. Box 40393, Denver, CO 80204-0393. Genealogists also advertise their services in the *Genealogical Helper* and *Heritage Quest*.

When exact identifying information is given in a mail request, the National Archives can furnish photocopies of records **for a fee**. Copies of compiled service records, bounty land warrant application files, pension application files, passenger arrival records, public land entry files/homestead, and census pages are examples of records that may be photocopied. Details about use of special orders and the exact information they require will be found in the guide chapters relating to particular kinds of records.

CHAPTER 1
Census Records

1.1 Introduction

As required by Article 1, Section 2, of the Constitution, a census has been taken in the United States every 10 years since 1790 to enumerate (count) the population for apportioning representatives to the lower house of Congress. Information about households and individuals was collected by house-to-house canvass. The filled-in forms constitute the population schedules for each decennial census. The census records for many states are incomplete, particularly those before 1850. Different information was recorded in each census year. The questions asked for each census are listed in section 1.2.2.

To protect the privacy of people enumerated in the census, population schedules are restricted and are not available for 72 years after the census is taken. For example, the 1930 census will be released on April 1, 2002. Access to censuses before their release is restricted to the person to whom the information is related, their authorized representative, or in the case of deceased individuals, their heirs or administrators. For information from these censuses, contact the Bureau of the Census, P.O. Box 1545, Jeffersonville, IN 47131, and request a copy of the "Application for Search of Census Records," BC Form 600. The Census Bureau's records containing individual names are not on a computer; they are on microfilm, arranged according to the individual's address at the time of the census.

Arrangement of the Records

The population and nonpopulation schedules are part of the Records of the Bureau of the Census, Record Group (RG) 29. The 1890 special census of Civil War veterans and widows, which is cited frequently in this chapter, is part of Records of the Veterans Administration, RG 15.

The schedules are arranged by census year; thereunder, alphabetically by name of state; then, with a few exceptions, alphabetically by name of county. Researchers must know the county in which the subject of their research lived during the census year and may need to know an exact address.

Usually a microfilm roll contains all the schedules for one county or several small counties. The arrangement of surnames on a page of the schedules is normally in the order in which the enumerator visited the households. To search for a particular name in the schedules—once the year, the state, and the county have been established—necessitates scanning each page from top to bottom. This process is tedious, but the method is simple.

The census taker numbered the pages of the schedules; when the schedules were arranged later, they were often renumbered. It is possible, therefore, for some volumes to have two or more series of page numbers. A hand stamp was used for numbering the pages in many of the volumes, and it is this number that is used in published indexes.

Microfilm Copies of Census Schedules

The National Archives has reproduced as microfilm publications all of the available Federal population census schedules. They can be purchased (*see* section I.5) or used in the microfilm reading room in the National Archives Building and in the research rooms of the National Archives regional records services facilities. The microfilm publication numbers are cited in this chapter as the schedules are discussed by census year.

Microfilm Rental Program

Federal population census schedules (including slave schedules) from 1790 to 1920 and Soundex indexes from 1880 to 1920 are available through the National Archives Microfilm Rental Program, which is described in section I.5 of the introduction to this volume. For additional information about microfilm rental, call 301-604-3699 or write to the National Archives Microfilm Rental Program, P.O. Box 30, Annapolis Junction, MD 20701-0030.

Locations of Federal Population Schedules

The National Archives and its regional facilities are not the only depositories of population census schedules. The law often required the preparation of more than one set of schedules. The duplicate sets for the 1800, 1810, 1820, 1830, and 1840 censuses were filed with the Federal district or superior courts. The duplicate sets for 1850, 1860, and 1870 were filed with county courts. Many schedules filed with county courts have been deposited in state libraries or state archives. The original 1880 schedules were so fragile that they were transferred to various non-Federal depositories in 1956 after they were microfilmed. Many state and local libraries have sets of the published 1790 schedules and microfilm copies of some of the population and mortality schedules.

Occupation Codes

In the 1900, 1910, and 1920 censuses, the Bureau of the Census tabulated occupations. To help in this process, each occupation had a particular number. These numbers are frequently noted in the right-hand column or margin of the census form. In the 1910 census, 9-3-0-0 means ranch laborer and 2-1-0-0 stands for farm laborer. The occupation codes can be distinguished because they are written by someone other than the enumerator. The National Archives has not located master lists for the occupation codes.

Enumeration Districts and Helpful Maps

County boundaries of the areas in which the 1790 census was taken and the same areas in 1900 are shown on maps on pages 61-70 of *A Century of Population Growth From the First Census of the United States to the Twelfth* (Washington: Bureau of the Census, 1909; reprinted by the Genealogical Publishing Co., Baltimore, 1967).

Census enumeration district maps and enumeration subdivision and district descriptions are discussed generally in section 19.2. Some descriptions of the districts are available on microfilm under the title *Descriptions of Census Enumeration Districts, 1830-1890 and 1910-1950*, T1224, 146 rolls.

TWELFTH CENSUS

SCHEDULE N

State _New York_

County _Franklin_

Township or other division of county _Brighton Town_

Name of incorporated city, town, or village, within the above-named division, _X_

Enumerated by me on the _Eleventh_ day of June

	LOCATION.			NAME	RELATION.	PERSONAL DESCRIPTION.										Place of b
	IN CITIES.	Number of dwelling-house, in the order of visitation.	Number of family, in the order of visitation.	of each person whose place of abode on June 1, 1900, was in this family. Enter surname first, then the given name and middle initial, if any. INCLUDE every person living on June 1, 1900. OMIT children born since June 1, 1900.	Relationship of each person to the head of the family.	Color or race.	Sex.	DATE OF BIRTH.		Age at last birthday.	Whether single, married, widowed, or divorced	Number of years married.	Mother of how many children.	Number of these children living.	Place of
	Street.	Home Number.							Month.	Year.						
				3	4	5	6		7		8	9	10	11	12	
51		27	6td	Daly, Catherine	Servant	w	7	Aug	1846	16 20	S					New
52				MLicense, Margarett	Servant	w	7	Dec	1830	40	S					New
53				Menchinn, Elizabeth	Servant	w	7	Oct	1870	30	S					New
54				Clark, Henry	boarder	w	m	June	1888	12	S					New
55				Carr, Robert	Servant	w	m	June	1877	21	S					New
56				Donaldson, William	Servant	w	m	Aug	1875	24	S					New
57		28	28	Wardner, Charles A	Head	w	m	Jan	1878	22	m					New
58				—, Mary A.	Wife	w	7	Oct	1876	24	m		0	0		New
59				Fuller, Hattie	Servant	w	7	July	1881	18	S					New
60		29	29	Prellwitz, Levine W	Head	w	7	Mar	1873	27	w	6	2	2		New
61				—, James R.	son	w	m	Oct	1895	4	S					New
62				—, William R	son	w	m	Aug	1898	1	S					New
63				Flanders, Hiram	Servant	w	m	Dec	1859	40	m	14				New
64				—, Lillie	Servant	w	7	July	1861	39	m	14	0	0		New
65				Noaker, Riza	Servant	w	7	Mar	1844	56	w	2	1	1		New
66				Torf, Fred	Servant	w	m	Mar	1880	20	S					New
67				Moore, McMartin	Boarder	w	m	July	1877	22	S					New
68				—, John R	Boarder	w	m	Feb	1862	37	S					New

Upper part of a page from the 1900 Census Population
Schedules. Records of the Bureau of the Census, RG 29.
National Archives Microfilm Publication T623.

Supervisor's District No. **5** Sheet No. **1**

Enumeration District No. **65** **2**

Name of Institution, **X**

Ward of city, **X**

Arthur C Davis, Enumerator.

61

NATIVITY.		CITIZENSHIP.			OCCUPATION, TRADE, OR PROFESSION		EDUCATION.				OWNERSHIP OF HOME.				
parents of each person enumerated. If born in the United territory; if of foreign birth, give the Country only.					of each person TEN YEARS of age and over.										
Place of birth of FATHER of this person.	Place of birth of MOTHER of this person.	Year of immigration to the United States.	Number of years in the United States.	Naturalization.	OCCUPATION.	Months not employed.	Attended school (in months).	Can read.	Can write.	Can speak English.	Owned or rented.	Owned free or mortgaged.	Farm or home.	Number of farm schedule.	
14	15	16	17	18	19	20	21	22	23	24	25	26	27	28	
Ireland	Ireland				Kitchen Girl	4		yes	yes	yes					51
Ireland	Ireland				Table waiter	4		yes	yes	yes					52
New York	New York				Laundress			yes	yes	yes					53
New York	New York				At School	10	yes	yes	yes						54
New York	New York				Farm Laborer			yes	yes	yes					55
New York	New York				Farm Laborer			yes	yes	yes					56
New York	New York				Boarding House Keeper			yes	yes	yes	O	M	H	1	57
New York	New York							yes	yes	yes					58
Vermont	Vermont				Domestic			yes	yes	yes					59
New York	New York				Boarding House Keeper			yes	yes	yes	O	M	F	21	60
New York	New York														61
New York	New York														62
New York	New York				Farm Laborer	4		yes	yes	yes					63
New York	New York				Chambermaid			yes	yes	yes					64
Vermont	New York				Nurse			yes	yes	yes					65
New York	New York				Chore boy	6		yes	yes	yes					66
Vermont	Virginia	Home in Elizabeth N.J. Has been here one year						yes	yes	yes					67
New York	New York	Home at mechanicsville Has been here since July 1878.						yes	yes	yes					68

Ordering Copies of Census Records by Mail

The National Archives does not search census indexes, nor does it provide census research services by mail. Copies of individual census pages, however, can be ordered through the mail by using a National Archives Trust Fund form, which may be obtained from the Customer Service Center, National Archives and Records Administration, Room 406, 700 Pennsylvania Ave., NW, Washington, DC 20408-0001, or from one of NARA's regional archives facilities. (*See* Table 1 in the introduction to this volume for locations.)

To complete the form, the following information is required: the name of the person, page number, census year, state; for 1880 through 1920 the enumeration district should be included.

A Note About Native Americans

Census enumerators did not count Indians not taxed, that is, Indians who lived on reservations or who roamed individually or in bands over unsettled tracts of land. Indians who lived among the non-Indian population or on the outskirts of towns were often included in the general population schedules under their anglicized name rather than their Indian name.

In 1880 the Bureau was authorized to conduct a special census of all Native Americans living on reservations under the jurisdiction of the United States. Available schedules are very limited and include only those taken at Tulalip Agency in Washington Territory, Yakima Agency near Fort Simcoe in Washington Territory, Standing Rock Agency near Fort Yates in Dakota Territory, and Round Valley in California. They are reproduced on microfilm as *Schedules of a Special Census of Indians, 1880,* M1791, 5 rolls.

In the 1920 Soundex index, reservations (but not individuals living on the reservations) are included in the Institutions section, which is found on the last roll for each state. Individuals can be located in the Soundex index.

The records of the Bureau of Indian Affairs (BIA), RG 75, include many tribal census rolls that are completely unrelated to the decennial census schedules. BIA records are described in Chapter 11 of this guide.

Other Censuses

The organic act establishing a territory or state usually contained provision for taking an enumeration of the inhabitants. The records of these enumerations are especially helpful if there are gaps in the decennial Federal census for a state at or near the year of a territorial or state census. For the locations of the schedules of such censuses taken as a result of state legislation, *see* Ann S. Lainhart, *State Census Records* (Baltimore: Genealogical Publishing Co.; revised 1997).

1.2 Population Schedules

1.2.1 Indexes to Population Schedules

The existing schedules for the 1790 census were published by the Federal Government in the early 1900s, with the schedules for each state in a separate, indexed volume. They have since been privately reprinted. The Government has not published other schedules or indexes, but many privately published abstracts and indexes are available. Although these private publications vary considerably in format, geographic scope, and accuracy, they frequently save researchers from fruitless searches and facilitate the location of specific entries in the schedules. Some of these publications are available in the research rooms at the National Archives Building and the regional archives.

Soundex Indexes: 1880-1920

Beginning with the 1880 census, the censuses are indexed by the Soundex system. To locate a person with the Soundex index, it is necessary to know the name, the name of the head of the household, and the state or territory in which the person lived at the time of the census.

The Soundex is a coded surname (last name) index based on the way a surname sounds rather than the way it is spelled. Surnames that sound the same but are spelled differently, like Schafer and Schaeffer, have the same code and are filed together. The Soundex coding system was developed so that a name can be found even though it may have been recorded under various spellings.

To search for a surname, it is necessary to work out the code. Every Soundex code consists of a letter and three numbers. The letter is always the first letter of the surname. The numbers are assigned to the remaining letters of the surname according to the Soundex guide. The Soundex indexes are organized by state, thereunder by Soundex code number, and thereunder alphabetically by first name. It is important to remember that names can be spelled in different ways that may lead to a different Soundex code. For example, Klausen would be K425, but Clausen is C425. Lee is L000, but Leigh is L200. Variant spellings should always be checked.

Soundex Coding Guide/Code Key Letters and Equivalents

1	b, p, f, v
2	c, s, k, g, j, q, x, z
3	d, t
4	l
5	m, n
6	r

To create the Soundex code, use the following steps:

Step 1: Bring down the first letter of the last name.

Step 2: Disregarding the first letter, omit the remaining letters A, E, I, O, U, W, Y, and H.

Step 3: Write down the numbers found on the Soundex

TABLE 2
Checklist of National Archives Publications Relating to Census Records

THE CATALOGS OF *FEDERAL POPULATIONS CENSUSES,*
WHICH LIST THE AVAILABILITY OF CENSUS SCHEDULES AND SOUNDEX INDEXES,
ARE ALSO AVAILABLE ONLINE AT *www.nara.gov/genealogy.*

Federal Population Censuses, 1790–1890: A Catalog of Microfilm Copies of the Schedules. Washington: National Archives Trust Fund Board, reprinted 2001.

1900 Federal Population Census: A Catalog of Microfilm Copies of the Schedules. Washington: National Archives and Records Service, reprinted 2000.

1910 Federal Population Census: A Catalog of Microfilm Copies of the Schedules. Washington: National Archives Trust Fund Board, reprinted 2000.

1920 Federal Population Census: A Catalog of Microfilm Copies of the Schedules. 2nd edition. Washington: National Archives Trust Fund Board, 1992.

Blake, Kellee. "First in the Path of the Firemen: The Fate of the 1890 Population Census." *Prologue: Quarterly of the National Archives*, 28, No. 1 (Spring 1996): 64-81.

Blake, Kellee. "The Fourteenth Numbering of the People: The 1920 Federal Census." *Prologue: Quarterly of the National Archives*, 23, No. 2 (Summer 1991): 131-143.

Carpenter, Bruce. "Using Soundex Alternatives: Enumeration District, 1880-1920." *Prologue: Quarterly of the National Archives*, 25, No. 1 (Spring 1993): 90-93.

Davidson, Katherine H. and Charlotte M. Ashby, comps. *Records of the Bureau of the Census.* Preliminary Inventory 161. Washington: National Archives and Records Service, 1964; reprinted 1997.

Fishbein, Meyer H. *The Censuses of Manufacturers, 1810-1890.* Reference Information Paper 50. Washington: National Archives and Records Service, 1973.

Lawson, Sarah. "The Census and Community History: A Reappraisal." *Our Family, Our Town.* Washington: National Archives and Records Administration, 1987.

Newman, Debra L., comp. *List of Free Black Heads of Families in the First Federal Census*, *1790.* Special List 34. Washington: National Archives and Records Service, revised 1974.

Publications of the Bureau of the Census, *1790-1916*, T825, 42 rolls. This National Archives microfilm publication reproduces many of the early census reports and is a particularly useful source of statistical information.

Rhoads, James B. and Charlotte M. Ashby, comps., *Cartographic Records of the Bureau of the Census.* Preliminary Inventory 103. Washington: National Archives and Records Service, 1958.

ADDITIONAL SOURCES

Wright, Carroll D., and William C. Hunt. *The History and Growth of the United States Census.* 56th Cong., 1st sess., S. Doc 194, serial 3856; reprinted by Johnson Reprint Corp., New York, 1966.

Thorndale, William, and William Dollarhide. *Map Guide to the U.S. Federal Census, 1790–1920.* Baltimore: Genealogical Publishing Co., 1978.

Two Hundred Years of Census Taking: Population and Housing Questions, 1790–1990 (Washington: 1989) U.S. Department of Commerce, Bureau of the Census. The booklet is for sale by the Superintendent of Documents, U.S. Government Printing Office, Washington, DC 20402 (Stock No. 003-024-01874-8.)

Typical Soundex card from the index to the 1900 Census Population Schedules for Ohio. Records of the Bureau of the Census, RG 29. National Archives Microfilm Publication T1065.

Series of Soundex cards from the index to the 1900 Census Population Schedules for Illinois, showing several names bearing the same Soundex code. Records of the Bureau of the Census, RG 29. National Archives Microfilm Publication T1043.

Coding Guide for the first three remaining unslashed letters. Add zeros for any empty spaces. Disregard any additional letters.

ADDITIONAL RULES

Names with double letters: If the surname has any double letters, they should be treated as one letter. For example, the two "t"s in Ritter are coded with one "3" (R360).

Names with letters side-by-side that have the same number on the Soundex coding system: A surname may have different letters side-by-side that have the same number on the Soundex Coding Guide. For example, PF in Pfister (1 is the number for both P and F [P236]); CKS in Jackson (2 is the number for C, K, and S [J250]). These letters should be treated as one letter.

Names with prefixes: Mc and Mac are not considered prefixes. If the surname has a prefix, such as Van, Con, De, Di, La, or Le, code the name both with and without the prefix because it might be listed under either code.

Mixed codes: If several surnames have the same code, the cards for them are arranged alphabetically by given name. There are divider cards showing most code numbers, but not all. For instance, one divider may be numbered 350 and the next one 400. Between the two divider cards there may be names coded 353, 350, 360, 364, 365, and 355, but instead of being in numerical order they are interfiled alphabetically by first name.

The following names are examples of Soundex coding and are given only as illustrations.

Name	Letters Coded	Code No.
Allricht	l, r, c	A 462
Eberhard	b, r, r	E 166
Heimbach	m, b, c	H 512
Hanselmann	n, s, l	H 524
Kavanagh	v, n, g	K 152
Lind, Van	n, d	L 530
Lukaschowsky	k, s, s	L 222
McDonnell	c, d, n	M 235
McGee	c	M 200
O'Brien	b, r, n	O 165
Oppenheimer	p, n, m	O 155
Riedemanas	d, m, n	R 355
Schafer	f, r	S 160
Shaeffer	f, r	S 160
Zita	t	Z 300
Zitzmeinn	t, z, m	Z 325

1880: The 1880 census is indexed only for families with children aged ten years or younger. This applies only to the index; the populations schedules cover the whole population.

1890: Although no Soundex index exists, an alphabetical index is available for the small percentage of population schedules that survived the 1921 Department of Commerce fire.

1900: A Soundex index is available for all states.

1910: A Soundex index is available only for the following 21 states: Alabama, Arkansas, California, Florida, Georgia, Illinois, Kansas, Kentucky, Louisiana, Michigan, Mississippi, Missouri, North Carolina, Ohio, Oklahoma, Pennsylvania, South Carolina, Tennessee, Texas, Virginia, and West Virginia. Although they are not Soundexed, population schedules are available for the other states.

1920: A Soundex index exists for all states. At the end of each state schedule is a separate listing for institutions.

1.2.2 Descriptions of Population Schedules by Year

Each time the Federal census was taken, additional questions were asked and more information was gathered. The following section describes each census year by year. The records are arranged by census year, state, and county, then by city, township, or minor civil division (MCD). The counties, cities, townships, and MCDs are not always arranged in alphabetical order within the state. After 1880 the records are arranged by state; supervisors district; county; city, township, or MCD; and enumeration district (ED). The EDs are not always in numerical order.

1790 Census

Date census taken: first Monday in August 1790 [August 2, 1790]

Population schedules. (Original schedules—*First Census of the United States, 1790,* M637, 12 rolls; Published schedules—*Publications of the Bureau of the Census: 1790 Census, Printed Schedules,* T498, 3 rolls)

Census questions. The 1790 census generally includes the following information:

Name of the head of household
Number of free white males age 16 and upwards
Number of free white males under age of 16
Number of free white females
Number of slaves
Number of all other free persons

Although there were only 13 states in the Union in 1790, the census was taken in an area constituting 17 present-day states. Schedules survive for two-thirds of those states. There are microfilmed schedules (original and printed) for Connecticut, Maine, Maryland, Massachusetts, New Hampshire, New York, North Carolina, Pennsylvania, Rhode Island, South Carolina, and Vermont. The schedules for Delaware, Georgia, Kentucky, New Jersey, Tennessee, and Virginia did not survive. The 1790 schedules for Virginia that appear on T498 were reconstructed from state enumerations and tax lists.

In the early 1900s, the Bureau of the Census published these schedules in a single indexed volume for each state. These volumes have been privately reprinted.

1800 Census

Date census taken: first Monday in August 1800 [August 4, 1800]

Population schedules. *(Second Census of the United States, 1800, M32, 52 rolls)*

Entries are usually arranged in the order of enumeration; in rare cases they are arranged in rough alphabetical order by initial letter of surname.

Census questions. The 1800 census generally includes the following information:

Name of town

Name of head of household

Number of free white males in these age categories:
    Under 10 years of age
    10 and under 16
    16 and under 26, including heads of families
    26 and under 45, including heads of families
    45 and upwards, including heads of families

Number of free white females in these age categories :
    Under 10 years of age
    10 and under 16
    16 and under 26, including heads of families
    26 and under 45, including heads of families
    45 and upwards, including heads of families

Number of other free persons, except Indians not taxed ("Indians not taxed" refers to Indians remaining in their tribes and not living among the general population.)

Number of slaves

1810 Census

Date census taken: first Monday in August 1810 [August 6, 1810]

Population schedules. *(Third Census of the United States, 1810, M252, 71 rolls)*

Census questions. The 1810 census generally includes the following information:

Name of town

Name of head of household

Number of free white males in these age categories:
    Under 10 years of age
    10 and under 16
    16 and under 26, including heads of families
    26 and under 45, including heads of families
    45 and upwards, including heads of families

Number of free white females in these age categories:
    Under 10 years of age
    10 and under 16
    16 and under 26, including heads of families
    26 and under 45, including heads of families
    45 and upwards, including heads of families

Number of other free persons, except Indians not taxed ("Indians not taxed" refers to Indians remaining in their tribes and not living among the general population.)

Number of slaves

1820 Census

Date census taken: first Monday in August 1820 [August 7, 1820]

Population schedules. *(Fourth Census of the United States, 1820, M33, 142 rolls)*

Census questions. The 1820 census generally includes the following questions:

Name of head of household

Number of free white males in these age categories:
    Under 10 years
    10 and under 16
    Between 16 and 18 [males age 16–18 were probably counted in both this and 16–26 category]
    16 and under 26, including heads of families
    26 and under 45, including heads of families
    45 and upwards, including heads of families

Number of free white females in these age categories:
    Under 10 years
    10 and under 16
    16 and under 26, including heads of families
    26 and under 45, including heads of families
    45 and upwards, including heads of families

Number of foreign born, not naturalized [whites only]

Number of persons, including slaves, engaged in agriculture

Number of persons, including slaves, engaged in commerce

Number of persons, including slaves, engaged in manufacturing

Number of free colored persons in these age categories:
    Males under 14 years
    Males 14 and under 26
    Males 26 and under 45
    Males 45 and upwards
    Females under 14 years
    Females 14 and under 26
    Females 26 and under 45
    Females 45 and upwards

Number of all other persons except Indians not taxed ("Indians not taxed" refers to Indians remaining in their tribes and not living among the general population.)

1830 Census

Date census taken: June 1, 1830

Population schedules. *(Fifth Census of the United States, 1830, M19, 201 rolls)*

Census questions. The 1830 census generally includes the following information:

Name of county, city, ward, town, township, parish, precinct, hundred, or district

Name of head of household

Number of free white males in these age categories:
    Under 5 years of age
    5 and under 10
    10 and under 15

15 and under 20

20 and under 30

30 and under 40

40 and under 50

50 and under 60

60 and under 70

70 and under 80

80 and under 90

90 and under 100

100 and upwards

Number of free white females in these age categories:

Under 5 years of age

5 and under 10

10 and under 15

15 and under 20

20 and under 30

30 and under 40

40 and under 50

50 and under 60

60 and under 70

70 and under 80

80 and under 90

90 and under 100

100 and upwards

Number of male slaves in these age categories:

Under 10 years of age

10 and under 24

24 and under 36

36 and under 55

55 and under 100

100 and upwards

Number of female slaves in these age categories:

Under 10 years of age

10 and under 24

24 and under 36

36 and under 55

55 and under 100

100 and upwards

Number of free colored males in these age categories:

Under 10 years of age

10 and under 24

24 and under 36

36 and under 55

55 and under 100

100 and upwards

Number of free colored females in these age categories:

Under 10 years of age

10 and under 24

24 and under 36

36 and under 55

55 and under 100

100 and upwards

Total number of all persons

Number of white persons included in the following categories:

deaf and dumb, under 14 years of age

deaf and dumb, of the age of 14 and under 25

deaf and dumb, of the age of 25 and upwards

Number of foreign born, not naturalized

Aliens—foreigners not naturalized

Number of slaves and colored persons in the following categories:

deaf and dumb, under 14 years of age

deaf and dumb, of the age of 14 and under 25

deaf and dumb, of the age of 25 and upwards

The 1830 schedules are on printed forms of uniform size. Each entry spans two facing pages; the left-hand page contains chiefly family data, and the right-hand page contains slave data.

1840 Census

Date census taken: June 1, 1840

Population schedules. *(Sixth Census of the United States, 1840, M704, 580 rolls)*

Census questions. The 1840 census generally includes the following information:

Name of head of household

Number of free white males in these age categories:

Under 5 years of age

5 and under 10

10 and under 15

15 and under 20

20 and under 30

30 and under 40

40 and under 50

50 and under 60

60 and under 70

70 and under 80

80 and under 90

90 and under 100

100 and older

Number of free white females in these age categories:

Under 5 years of age

5 and under 10

10 and under 15

15 and under 20

20 and under 30

30 and under 40

40 and under 50

50 and under 60

60 and under 70

70 and under 80

80 and under 90

90 and under 100

100 and older

Number of free colored males in these age categories:

Under 10 years of age

10 and under 24

24 and under 36

36 and under 55

55 and under 100

100 and upwards
Number of free colored females in these age categories:
   Under 10 years of age
   10 and under 24
   24 and under 36
   36 and under 55
   55 and under 100
   100 and upwards
Number of slave males in these age categories:
   Under 10 years of age
   10 and under 24
   24 and under 36
   36 and under 55
   55 and under 100
   100 and upwards
Number of slave females in these age categories:
   Under 10 years of age
   10 and under 24
   24 and under 36
   36 and under 55
   55 and under 100
   100 and upwards
Number of persons in each family employed in:
   Mining
   Agriculture
   Commerce
   Manufactures and trades
   Navigation of the oceans
   Navigation of canals, lakes, and rivers
   Learned professions and engineers
Names and ages of pensioners for Revolutionary War or
   military services
Deaf and dumb white persons in these categories:
   Under 14
   14 and under 25
   25 and upwards
Blind and insane white persons in these categories:
   Blind
   Insane and idiots at public charge
   Insane and idiots at private charge
Blind and insane colored persons in these categories:
   Deaf and dumb
   Blind
   Insane and idiots at public charge
   Insane and idiots at private charge
Schools, etc.
Universities or colleges
Number of students
Academic and grammar schools
Number of scholars
Primary and common schools
Number of scholars
Number of scholars at public charge
Number of white persons over 20 years of age in each
   family who cannot read or write

The names and ages of the military pensioners listed in the 1840 schedules were printed in A Census of Pensioners for Revolutionary or Military Services; With Their Names, Ages, Places of Residence . . . . (Washington: Department of State, 1841). This publication has been microfilmed at the end of roll 3 of T498, and has been reprinted by the Southern Book Co., Baltimore, 1954, and by the Genealogical Publishing Co., Baltimore, 1967. Also available is A General Index to a Census of Pensioners . . . 1840, compiled by the Genealogical Society (Baltimore: Genealogical Publishing Co., 1965).

The population schedules are on printed forms of uniform size. Each entry spans two facing pages; the left-hand page contains chiefly family data, and the right-hand page contains slave, employment, and pension data. Entries are usually arranged in order of enumeration.

1850 Census

Date census taken: June 1, 1850
Population schedules. *(Seventh Census of the United States, 1850, M432, 1,009 rolls)*
Often called "the first modern census," the 1850 census gathered more comprehensive information than its predecessors. Before 1850 only the name of the head of the household was recorded. In the 1850 schedules, the name of each free person in a household is given for the first time. Separate slave schedules exist for those states where slavery was protected by law (see below).
Census questions. The 1850 census generally includes the following information:
   Dwelling house number (numbered in order of visitation)
   Family number (numbered in order of visitation)
   Name of every person whose usual place of abode on
      the first day of June 1850 was in this family
   Description:
      Age
      Sex
      Color (white, black, or mulatto)
      Profession, occupation, or trade for each person over
         15 years of age
   Value of real estate owned:
      Value of real estate
      Value of personal property
   Place of birth (state, territory, or country)
   Married within the year (June 1849–June 1850)
   At school within the last year
   Persons over 20 years of age who cannot read and write
   Whether deaf and dumb, blind, insane, idiotic, pauper, or
      convict

On separate slave schedules, the name of each slave owner or person with whom the slave is living appears with number of slaves owned, and number of slaves manumitted. Under the slave holder's name, a line for each slave shows:

Age

Color (black or mulatto)

Sex

Whether deaf-mute, blind, insane, or idiotic

Whether a fugitive from the state

The names of the slaves were not entered.

1860 Census

Date census taken: June 1, 1860

Population schedules. (*Eighth Census of the United States, 1860, M653, 1,438 rolls*)

Census questions. The 1860 census generally includes the following information:

Dwelling house number (numbered in order of visitation)

Family number (numbered in order of visitation)

Name of every person whose usual place of abode on the first day of June 1860 was in this family

Description:

Age

Sex

Color (white, black, or mulatto)

Profession, occupation, or trade of each person over 15 years of age

Value of estate owned:

Value of real estate

Value of personal estate

Place of birth (state, territory, or country of birth)

Married within the year

Attended school within the year

Persons over 20 years of age who cannot read or write

Whether deaf and dumb, blind, insane, idiot, pauper, or convict

The information in the slave schedules is the same as the 1850 slave schedules.

1870 Census

Date census taken: June 1, 1870

Population schedules. (*Ninth Census of the United States, 1870, M593, 1,748 rolls*)

Census questions. The 1870 census generally includes the following information:

Dwelling house number (numbered in order of visitation)

Family number (numbered in order of visitation)

Name of every person whose place of abode on the first day of June 1870 was in this family

Description:

Age at last birthday. If under 1 year, give months in fractions, thus ³⁄₁₂

Sex—Males (M.), Females (F.)

Color—White (W.), Black (B.), Mulatto (M.), Chinese (C.), Indian (I.)

Profession, occupation, or trade of each person, male or female

Value of real estate owned:

Value of real estate

Value of personal property

Place of birth, naming state or territory of U.S., or the country, if of foreign birth

Parentage:

Father of foreign birth

Mother of foreign birth

If born within the year, month of birth (Jan., Feb., etc.)

If married within the year, month of marriage (Jan., Feb., etc.)

Attended school within the year

Education:

Cannot read

Cannot write

Whether deaf and dumb, blind, insane, or idiotic

Constitutional relations:

Male citizen of the U.S. of 21 years of age and upwards

Male citizen of U.S. of 21 years of age and upwards whose right to vote is denied or abridged on other grounds than rebellion or other crime

Constitutional relations does not refer to men who fought in or supported the Confederacy, but to former male slaves. The instructions to the enumerators include the following language:

"As the fifteenth amendment to the Constitution, prohibiting the exclusion from the suffrage of any person on account of race, color or previous condition of servitude has become the law of the land, all state laws working such exclusion have ceased to be of virtue. If any person is, in any state, still practically denied the right to vote by reason of any such state laws not released, that denial is merely an act violence, of which the courts may have cognizance, but which does not come within the view of marshals and their assistance in response to the census."

The Minnesota census schedules are reproduced as a separate microfilm publication, *Minnesota Census Schedules for 1870,* T132, 13 rolls.

1880 Census

Date census taken: June 1, 1880

Populations schedules. (*Tenth Census of the United States, 1880, T9, 1,454 rolls*)

Census questions. The 1880 census generally includes the following information:

In cities:

Name of street

House number

Dwelling house numbered in order of visitation

Families in order of visitation

Name of each person whose usual place of abode on June 1, 1880, was in this family

Personal description:

Color—White (W.), Black (B.), Mulatto (M.), Indian (I.), or Chinese (C.)

Sex—Male (M.), Female (F.)

Age at last birthday prior to June 1, 1880. If under 1 year, give months in fractions, thus, $\frac{3}{12}$

If born within the census year, month of birth

Relationship of each person to the head of this family—whether wife, son, daughter, servant, boarder, or other

Civil condition:

Single

Married

Widowed /divorced

Married during census year

Occupation:

Occupation, profession, or trade of each person, male or female

Number of months this person has been unemployed during this census year

Health:

Is the person [on the day of enumerator's visit] sick or temporarily disabled, so as to be unable to attend to ordinary business or duties; if so, what was the sickness or disability?

Blind

Deaf and dumb

Idiotic

Insane

Education:

Attended school within the census year

Cannot read

Cannot write

Nativity:

Place of birth of this person, naming state or territory of U.S., or the county, if of foreign birth

Place of birth of the father of this person, naming state or territory of U.S., or the country, if of foreign birth

Place of birth of the mother of this person, naming state or territory of U.S., or the country, if of foreign birth

Indexes. The National Archives has a microfilm copy of the Soundex index cards for those entries that relate to households containing a child aged 10 or under. (*See* 1.2.1 for an explanation of the Soundex.) The cards show the name, age, and birthplace of each member of such households, and there is a separate cross-reference card for each child aged 10 or under whose surname is different from that of the head of the household in which he or she is listed.

The cards are arranged by state or territory. A microfilm publication is available for each state or territory and the District of Columbia. North and South Dakota were combined as Dakota Territory, and no census was taken in Indian Territory (later Oklahoma).

1890 Census

Date census taken: first Monday in June 1890

Population schedules. (*Eleventh Census of the United States, 1890*, M407, 3 rolls)

The original 1890 population schedules were destroyed or badly damaged by a fire in the Department of Commerce in Washington in 1921. Less than 1 percent of the schedules still exist. The surviving fragments are reproduced as follows:

Roll 1. Alabama, Perry County (Perryville Beat No. 11 and Severe Beat No. 8).

Roll 2. District of Columbia, Q, 13th, 14th, R, Corcoran, 15th, S, R, and Riggs Streets, and Johnson Avenue.

Roll 3. Georgia, Muscogee County (Columbus); Illinois, McDonough County (Mound Twp.); Minnesota, Wright County (Rockford); New Jersey, Hudson County (Jersey City); New York, Westchester County (Eastchester) and Suffolk County (Brookhaven Twp.); North Carolina, Gaston County (South Point Twp. and River Bend Twp.) and Cleveland County (Twp. No. 2); Ohio, Hamilton County (Cincinnati) and Clinton County (Wayne Twp.); South Dakota, Union County (Jefferson Twp.); and Texas, Ellis County (J.P. No. 6, Mountain Peak, and Ovilla Precinct), Hood County (Precinct No. 5), Rusk County (No. 6 and J.P. No. 7), Trinity County (Trinity Town and Precinct No. 2), and Kaufman County (Kaufman).

Census questions. The 1890 census generally includes the following information:

Number of dwelling house in order of visitation; number of families in this dwelling house; number of persons in this dwelling house; number of family in the order of visitation; number of persons in this family

Christian name in full, and initial of middle name

Surname

Whether a soldier, sailor, or marine during the Civil War (U.S. or Conf.) or widow of such person

Relationship to head of family

Whether white, black, mulatto, quadroon, octoroon, Chinese, Japanese, or Indian

Sex

Age at nearest birthday. If under one year, age in months

Whether single, married, widowed, or divorced

Whether married during the census year (June 1, 1889–May 31, 1890)

Mother of how many children, and number of those children living

Place of birth

Place of birth of father

Place of birth of mother

Number of years in the United States

Whether naturalized

Whether naturalization papers have been taken out

Profession, trade, or occupation

Months unemployed during the census year (June 1, 1889–May 31, 1890)

Attendance of school (in months) during the census year (June 1, 1889–May 31, 1890)

Able to read

Able to write

Whether suffering from acute or chronic disease, with name of disease and length of time afflicted

Whether defective in mind, sight, hearing, or speech, or whether crippled, maimed, or deformed, with name of defect

Whether a prisoner, convict, homeless child, or pauper

Supplemental schedule and page [not available]

Is the home you live in hired, or is it owned by the head or by a member of the family?

If owned by head or member of family, is the home free from mortgage incumbrances?

If the head of the family is a farmer, is the farm which he cultivates hired, or is it owned by him or by a member of his family?

If the home or farm is owned by head or member of family, and mortgaged, give the post office address of the owner

Indexes. A card index to the 6,160 names on the surviving 1890 schedules is filmed on *Index to the Eleventh Census of the United States, 1890,* M496, 2 rolls.

Special Schedule—Surviving Soldiers, Sailors, and Marines, and Widows, etc. The National Archives has some schedules of a special census of Union veterans and widows of veterans in 1890. They are on microfilm under the title *Schedules Enumerating Union Veterans and Widows of Union Veterans of the Civil War, 1890,* M123, 118 rolls. The schedules are those for Washington, DC, about half of Kentucky, and Louisiana, Maine, Maryland, Massachusetts, Michigan, Minnesota, Mississippi, Missouri, Montana, Nebraska, Nevada, New Hampshire, New Jersey, New Mexico, New York, North Carolina, North Dakota, Ohio, Oklahoma and Indian Territories, Oregon, Pennsylvania, Rhode Island, South Carolina, South Dakota, Tennessee, Texas, Utah, U.S. ships and navy yards, Vermont, Virginia, Washington, West Virginia, Wisconsin, and Wyoming.

Census questions. The 1890 veterans schedules generally include the following information:

House number

Family number

Names of surviving soldiers, sailors, and marines, and widows

Rank

Company

Name of regiment or vessel

Date of enlistment

Date of discharge

Length of service (years, months, days)

The schedules are arranged by state or territory, thereunder by county, and thereunder by minor subdivision. Each entry shows the name of a Union veteran of the Civil

War; name of his widow, if appropriate; veteran's rank, company, regiment, or vessel; dates of enlistment and discharge and length of service in years, months, and days; post office address; nature of any disability; and remarks.

Unlike the other census records described in this chapter, these schedules are part of the Records of the Veterans Administration, RG 15.

1900 Census

Date census taken: June 1, 1900

Population schedules. *(Twelfth Census of the United States, 1900, T623, 1,854 rolls)*

Census questions. The 1900 census generally includes the following information:

Location:

In cities:

Name of street

House number

Number of dwelling house, in the order of visitation

Number of the family, in order of visitation

Name of each person whose usual place of abode on June 1, 1900, was in this family

Relation:

Relationship of each person to the head of the family

Personal description:

Color or race

Sex

Date of birth—month and year

Age at last birthday

Whether single, married, widowed, or divorced

Number of years married

Mother of how many children

Number of those children living

Nativity: Place of birth of each person and parents of each person enumerated

Place of birth of this person

Place of birth of father of this person

Place of birth of mother of this person

Citizenship [if not born in the United States]:

Year of immigration into the United States

Number of years in the United States

Naturalization status

Occupation, trade, or profession of each person 10 and older:

Occupation

Number of months not employed

Education:

Attended school (in months)

Can read

Can write

Can speak English

Ownership of home:

Owned or rented

Owned free or mortgaged

Farm or home

Number of farm schedule (these schedules have not survived)

Separate military schedules for military personnel, including those at U.S. bases overseas and on naval vessels, are reproduced on rolls 1838–1842 of T623, with a Soundex index on T1081, *Index (Soundex) to the 1900 Federal Population Census Schedules for Military and Naval*, 32 rolls.

Indexes. The National Archives has a microfilm copy of a card index to all heads of households in the 1900 schedules, with cross-reference cards for persons in the household whose surname is different from that of the head of the household. The cards show the name, age, and birthplace of each member of the household. The cards are arranged by state or territory and thereunder by the Soundex system (*see* 1.2.1 for an explanation of the Soundex).

Separate military schedules were compiled for army personnel overseas and all navy personnel. Army personnel stationed in the United States were enumerated in the geographical area where they were stationed. There is no index for the military schedules.

1910 Census

Date census taken: April 15, 1910

Population schedules. (*Thirteenth Census of the United States, 1910, T624, 1,784 rolls*)

Census questions. The 1910 census generally includes the following information:

Location:
Street, avenue, road, etc.
House number (in cities and towns)
Number of dwelling house, in order of visitation
Number of family, in order of visitation
Name of each person whose usual place of abode on April 15, 1910, was in this family
Relation:
Relationship of this person to the head of the family
Personal description:
Sex
Color or race
Age at last birthday
Whether single, married, widowed, or divorced
Number of years of present marriage
Mother of how many children—number born and number now living
Citizenship:
Year of immigration into the United States
Whether naturalized or alien
Whether able to speak English; or if not, give language spoken
Occupation:
Trade or profession of, or particular kind of work done by the person
General nature of industry, business, or establishment

in which this person works
Whether an employer, employee, or working on own account
If an employee—whether out of work on April 15, 1910, and number of weeks out of work during 1909
Education:
Whether able to read
Whether able to write
Attended school any time since Sept. 1, 1909
Ownership of home:
Owned or rented
Owned free or mortgaged
Farm or house
Number of farm schedule [these schedules have not survived]
Whether a survivor of the Union or Confederate Army or Navy
Whether blind (both eyes)
Whether deaf and dumb

Indexes. Soundex indexes are available for the following states: Alabama, Georgia, Louisiana, Mississippi, South Carolina, Tennessee, and Texas. There are Miracode indexes for the following states: Arkansas, California, Florida, Illinois, Kansas, Kentucky, Michigan, Missouri, North Carolina, Ohio, Oklahoma, Pennsylvania, Virginia, and West Virginia. No indexes exist for the remaining 29 states and territories. Although the format of Soundex and Miracode indexes is different, the method for using them is basically the same.

The *Cross Index to Selected City Street and Enumeration Districts, 1910 Census* (M1283, 50 fiche) lists the enumeration districts for selected cities based on the address. The cities are: Akron, OH; Atlanta, GA; Baltimore, MD; Canton, OH; Chicago, IL; Cleveland, OH; Dayton, OH; Denver, CO; Detroit, MI; District of Columbia; Elizabeth, NJ; Erie, PA; Gary and Wayne, IN; Grand Rapids, MI; Indianapolis, IN; Kansas City, KS; Long Beach, CA; Los Angeles and Los Angeles County, CA; New York City (Manhattan, the Bronx, Brooklyn, and Richmond); Newark, NJ; Oklahoma City, OK; Omaha, NE; Patterson, NJ; Peoria, IL; Philadelphia, PA; Phoenix, AZ; Reading, PA; San Diego, CA; San Antonio, TX; and San Francisco, CA.

1920 Census

Date census taken: January 1, 1920

Population schedules. (*Fourteenth Census of the United States, 1920, T625, 2,076 rolls*)

Census questions. The 1920 census generally includes the following information:

Place of abode:
Street, avenue, road, etc.
House number or farm
Number of dwelling house, in order of visitation
Number of family, in order of visitation
Name of each person whose usual place of abode on

January 1, 1920, was in this family

Relation:

Relationship to the head of the family

Tenure:

Home owned or rented

If owned, free of mortgage

Personal description:

Sex

Color or race

Age at last birthday

Single, married, widowed, or divorced

Citizenship:

Year of immigration to the United States

Naturalized or alien

If naturalized, year of naturalization

Education:

Attended school any time since Sept. 1, 1919

Whether able to read

Whether able to write

Nativity and mother tongue: Place of birth of each person and parents of each person enumerated.

Person—place of birth and mother tongue

Father—place of birth and mother tongue

Mother—place of birth and mother tongue

Whether able to speak English

Occupation:

Trade, profession, or particular kind of work done

Industry, business, or establishment in which at work

Employer, salary, or wage worker, or working on own account

Number of farm schedule (these schedules have not survived)

Index. *Index (Soundex) to the 1920 Federal Population Census Schedules for Institutions,* M1605, 1 roll.

1.2.3 Special Schedules and Problems by State

This section provides information about census records arranged alphabetically by state and notes special conditions peculiar to each state.

Alabama

1830, M19, Rolls 1–4

1840, M704, Rolls 1–16; Census of pensioners, T498, Roll 3

1850, Free schedules, M432, Rolls 1–16; Slave schedules, M432, Rolls 17–24

1860, Free schedules, M653, Rolls 1–26; Slave schedules, M653, Rolls 27–36

1870, M593, Rolls 1–45

1880, T9, Rolls 1–35; Soundex index, T734, 74 rolls

1890, M407, Roll 1, Perry Co. (Perryville Beat No. 11 and Severe Beat No. 8); alphabetical index, M496, 2 rolls

1900, T623, Rolls 1–44; Soundex index, T1030, 177 rolls

1910, T624, Rolls 1–37; Soundex index, T1259, 140 rolls

1920, T625, Rolls 1–45; Soundex index, M1548, 159 rolls

Remarks:

1820. The extant part of the Alabama territorial census for 1820 is in the Alabama Department of Archives and History, Montgomery. The National Archives has a copy as it was printed in the *Alabama Historical Quarterly,* 6 (Fall 1944): 333–515.

Alaska

1900, T623, Rolls 1828–1832; Soundex index, T1031, 15 rolls

1910, T624, Rolls 1748–1750; no index

1920, T625, Rolls 2030–2031; Soundex index, M1597, 6 rolls

Remarks:

The only available census before 1900 is the Special Census of Sitka, Alaska, taken by the War Department, printed in 1871 as 42nd Congress, 1st sess., H. Ex. Doc. 5, serial 1470: 13–26.

American Samoa: *see* Guam and Samoa

Arizona

1860, M653, Roll 712 [enumerated with New Mexico]

1870, M593, Roll 46

1880, T9, Rolls 36–37; Soundex index, T735, 2 rolls

1900, T623, Rolls 45–48; Soundex index, T1032, 22 rolls

1910, T624, Rolls 38–42; no index

1920, T625, Rolls 46–52; Soundex index, M1549, 30 rolls

Remarks:

1850, 1860. The schedules for 1850 and 1860 that relate to the present state of Arizona are included among the schedules for New Mexico. *Federal Census—Territory of New Mexico and Territory of Arizona* (89th Cong., 1st sess., S. Doc. 13, serial 12668-1) includes the 1860 census.

1864. The National Archives has photostats in two volumes and typed and mimeographed copies of the Arizona schedules of 1864. The schedules are arranged by judicial district, thereunder by minor subdivision. For each person in a household, an entry shows name, age, sex, and marital status; number of years and months of residence in Arizona; brief naturalization data, if appropriate; place of residence of the family; occupation; and value of real and personal estate. *Federal Census—Territory of New Mexico and Territory of Arizona* (cited above) contains the 1864 special territorial census.

1866, 1867, and 1869. Photostats of Arizona schedules of 1866, 1867, and 1869 are available in one volume. The schedules are arranged by county. For each person in a household, an entry shows name; place of residence; whether head of family; and whether under 10, 10 but under 21, or over 21. The following list identifies by census year the names of the counties for which schedules are available:

1866. Pahute, Mohave, Pima, Yuma, and Yavapai

1867. Mohave, Pima, and Yuma

1869. Yavapai

1870. Federal Census—*Territory of New Mexico and*

Territory of Arizona (cited above) contains the 1870 census.

Arkansas
1830, M19, Roll 5
1840, M704, Rolls 17-20; Census of pensioners, T498, Roll 3
1850, Free schedules, M432, Rolls 25-31; Slave schedules, M432, Roll 32
1860, Free schedules, M653, Rolls 37-52; Slave schedules, M653, Roll 53-54
1870, M593, Rolls 47-67
1880, T9, Rolls 38-60; Soundex index, T736, 48 rolls
1900, T623, Rolls 49-80; Soundex index, T1033, 135 rolls
1910, T624, Rolls 43-68; Soundex index, T1260, 139 rolls
1920, T625, Rolls 53-86; Soundex index, M1550, 131 rolls

Remarks:
1860. The 1860 schedules for Little River County are missing.

California
1850, M432, Rolls 33-36
1860, M653, Rolls 55-72
1870, M593, Rolls 68-93
1880, T9, Rolls 61-86; Soundex index, T737, 34 rolls
1900, T623, Rolls 81-116; Soundex index, T1034, 198 rolls
1910, T624, Rolls 69-111; Soundex index, T1261, 272 rolls
1920, T625, Rolls 87-154; Soundex index, M1551, 327 rolls

Remarks:
1850. The 1850 schedules for Contra Costa, San Francisco, and Santa Clara Counties are missing from the schedules at the National Archives.

Canal Zone: see Panama

Colorado
1860, enumerated with Kansas
1870, M593, Rolls 94-95
1880, T9, Rolls 87-93; Soundex index, T738, 7 rolls
1900, T623, Rolls 117-130; Soundex index, T1035, 69 rolls
1910, T624, Rolls 112-126; no index
1920, T625, Rolls 155-173; Soundex index, M1552, 80 rolls

Remarks:
1885. Colorado was one of five states and territories to elect to take an 1885 census with Federal assistance pursuant to an act of 1879 (20 Stat. 480). The unbound population and mortality schedules are in the National Archives, and they have been microfilmed as *Schedules of the Colorado State Census of 1885*, M158, 8 rolls. The schedules show the same type of information as the 1880 schedules, but in many cases the initial letters of the given names of enumerated persons appear instead of the names.

Connecticut
1790, Original schedules, M637, Roll 1; Published schedules, T498, Roll 1

1800, M32, Rolls 1-3
1810, M252, Rolls 1-3
1820, M33, Rolls 1-3
1830, Ml9, Rolls 6-11
1840, M704, Rolls 21-32; Census of pensioners, T498, Roll 3
1850, M432, Rolls 37-51
1860, M653, Rolls 73-93
1870, M593, Rolls 96-117
1880, T9, Rolls 94-110; Soundex index, T739, 25 rolls
1900, T623, Rolls 131-152; Soundex index, T1036, 107 rolls
1910, T624, Rolls 127-144; no index
1920, T625, Rolls 174-199; Soundex index, M1553, 111 rolls

Dakota Territory
1860, M653, Roll 94
1870, M593, Roll 118
1880, T9, Rolls 111-115; Soundex index, T740, 6 rolls

Remarks:
For later censuses, *see* North Dakota or South Dakota

Delaware
1800, M32, Roll 4
1810, M252, Roll 4
1820, M33, Roll 4
1830, M19, Rolls 12-13
1840, M704, Rolls 33-34; Census of pensioners, T498, Roll 3
1850, M432, Rolls 52-55
1860, Free schedules, M653, Rolls 95-99; Slaves schedules, M653, Roll 100
1870, M593, Rolls 119-122
1880, T9, Rolls 116-120; Soundex index, T741, 9 rolls
1900, T623, Rolls 153-157; Soundex index, T1037, 21 rolls
1910, T624, Rolls 145-148; no index
1920, T625, Rolls 200-204; Soundex index, M1554, 20 rolls

Remarks:
1790. The missing 1790 census has been reconstructed from local real estate tax lists and published as *Reconstructed 1790 Census of Delaware*, National Genealogical Society Genealogical Publication 10, by Leon de Valinger, Jr. (Washington: National Genealogical Society, 1954).

District of Columbia
1800, M32, Roll 5
1820, M33, Roll 5
1830, M19, Roll 14
1840, M704, Roll 35; Census of pensioners, T498, Roll 3
1850, M432, Rolls 56-57
1860, Free schedules, M653, Rolls 101-104; Slave schedules, M653, Roll 105
1870, M593, Rolls 123-127
1880, T9, Rolls 121-124; Soundex index, T742, 9 rolls
1890, M407, Roll 2, Q, 13th, 14th, R, Corcoran, 15th, S, R, and Riggs Sts., and Johnson Avenue; alphabetical index M496, 2 rolls; Special census of Civil War veterans and widows, M123, Roll 118

1900, T623, Rolls 158-164; Soundex index, T1038, 42 rolls
1910, T624, Rolls 149-155; no index
1920, T625, Rolls 205-213; Soundex index, M1555, 49 rolls

Remarks:

1790. Schedules that relate to the parts of Montgomery and Prince Georges Counties that now form the present District of Columbia are among the schedules of Maryland for 1790. Schedules for that part of Virginia that was formerly a part of the District of Columbia were enumerated as part of the schedules of Virginia. The 1790 census schedules for Virginia have not survived but published reconstructed schedules appear on T498.

1800. Entries for the existing 1800 schedules have been alphabetized and printed in Artemas C. Harmon, "U.S. Census of the District of Columbia in Maryland for the Year 1800," in *The National Genealogical Society Quarterly*, vols. 38 (Dec. 1950): 105-110, and 39 (Mar. 1951): 16-19 and (June 1951): 56-59. They cover only the present District of Columbia, which is on the Maryland side of the Potomac River.

1820, 1830, and 1840. Schedules include Alexandria County, the part of the District of Columbia that was retroceded to Virginia in 1846. For the location of the ward boundaries of Washington City and Georgetown for each of the decennial years 1820-70, *see* Laurence F. Schmeckebier's "Ward Boundaries of Washington and Georgetown," *Records of the Columbia Historical Society* (1955): 51-52 and 66-77, with maps. The National Archives has large-scale copies of these maps.

Florida

1830, Ml9, Roll 15
1840, M704, Roll 36; Census of pensioners, T498, Roll 3
1850, Free schedules, M432, Rolls 58-59; Slave schedules, M432, Roll 60
1860, Free schedules, M653, Rolls 106-109; Slave schedules, M653, Roll 110
1870, M593, Rolls 128-133
1880, T9, Rolls 125-132; Soundex index, T743, 16 rolls
1900, T623, Rolls 165-177; Soundex index, T1039, 62 rolls
1910, T624, Rolls 156-169; Soundex index, T1262, 84 rolls
1920, T625, Rolls 214-232; Soundex index, M1556, 74 rolls

Remarks:

1825. The National Archives has photostatic copies of two pages of the territorial census for Leon County, 1825. The originals are in the Florida State Library, Tallahassee.

1885. Florida was one of five states and territories to elect to take an 1885 census with Federal assistance pursuant to an act of 1879 (20 Stat. 480). The unbound population and mortality schedules are in the National Archives, and they have been microfilmed as *Schedules of the Florida State Census of 1885*, M845, 13 rolls. The schedules show the same type of information as the 1880 schedules, but in many cases the initial letters of the given names of enumerated persons appear instead of the names.

Georgia

1820, M33, Rolls 6-10
1830, M19, Rolls 16-21
1840, M704, Rolls 37-53; Census of pensioners, T498, Roll 3
1850, M432, Rolls 61-96
1860, Free schedules, M653, Rolls 111-141; Slave schedules, M653, Rolls 142-153
1870, M593, Rolls 134-184
1880, T9, Rolls 133-172; Soundex index, T744, 86 rolls
1890, M407, Roll 3, Muscogee Co. (Columbus); alphabetical index, M496, 2 rolls
1900, T623, Rolls 178-230; Soundex index, T1040, 214 rolls
1910, T624, Rolls 170-220; Soundex index, T1263, 174 rolls
1920, T625, Rolls 233-286; Soundex index, M1557, 200 rolls

Remarks:

1790, 1820. Tax lists for various years for a few of the counties have been published in *Some Early Tax Digests of Georgia,* edited by Ruth Blair, 2 vols. (Atlanta: Georgia Department of Archives and History, 1926). This publication is used as a substitute for missing 1790, 1800, 1810, and 1820 schedules. Also available is *Substitute for Georgia's Lost 1790 Census* (Albany, GA: Delwyn Associates, 1975). Wills, deeds, tax digests, court minutes, voter lists, and newspapers were searched to compile this list.

1800. The only schedules known to exist are for Oglethorpe County. These have been published in *1800 Census of Oglethorpe County, Georgia,* by Mary B. Warren (Athens, GA, 1965).

1820. The 1820 schedules for Franklin, Rabun, and Twiggs Counties are missing.

Guam and Samoa

1920, T625, Roll 2032; Guam Soundex index, M1602, 1 roll; American Samoa Soundex index, M1603, 2 rolls

Hawaii

1900, T623, Rolls 1833-1837; Soundex index, T1041, 30 rolls
1910, T624, Rolls 1751-1755; no index
1920, T625, Rolls 2033-2039; Soundex index, M1598, 24 rolls

Remarks:

1900. In this first census taken in Hawaii, schedules for some of the enumeration districts on islands of Hawaii and Kauai are missing.

Idaho

1870, M593, Roll 185
1880, T9, Roll 173; Soundex index, T745, 2 rolls
1900, T623, Rolls 231-234; Soundex index, T1042, 19 rolls
1910, T624, Rolls 221-228; no index
1920, T625, Rolls 287-295; Soundex index, M1558, 33 rolls

Illinois

1820, M33, Rolls 11-12

1830, M19, Rolls 22-25
1840, M704, Rolls 54-73; Census of pensioners, T498, Roll 3
1850, M432, Rolls 97-134
1860, M653, Rolls 154-241
1870, M593, Rolls 186-295
1880, T9, Rolls 174-262; Soundex index, T746, 143 rolls
1890, M407, Roll 3, McDonough Co. (Mound Twp.), alphabetical index, M496, 2 rolls
1900, T623, Rolls 235-356; Soundex index, T1043, 475 rolls
1910, T624, Rolls 229-337; Soundex index, T1264, 491 rolls
1920, T625, Rolls 296-419; Soundex index, M1559, 510 rolls

Remarks:

1810. Some of the 1810 schedules, together with 1818 schedules for Illinois Territory, were transcribed and published in *Illinois Census Returns, 1810, 1818, Collections of the Illinois State Historical Library*, vol. 24, edited by Margaret Cross Norton (Springfield, IL, 1935). This volume was reprinted by the Genealogical Publishing Co., Baltimore, 1969.

1820. The 1820 state schedules, which differ slightly from the 1820 Federal schedules, have been published in *Illinois Census Returns, 1820, Collections of the Illinois State History Library*, vol. 26, edited by Margaret Cross Norton (Springfield, IL, 1934). This volume was reprinted by the Genealogical Publishing Co., Baltimore, 1969.

1850. The 1850 schedules for Edgar County show the county of birth of each person enumerated. *See* O. Kenneth Baker's "Virginia (and West Virginia) Origins of Settlers in Edgar Co., Illinois, as Revealed by the 1850 Census," *National Genealogical Society Quarterly*, 36 (Sept. 1948): 73-76, and his "Migration From Virginia to Edgar County, Illinois, as Revealed by the 1850 Census Schedules for 200 Families," *National Genealogical Society Quarterly*, 38 (Mar. 1950): 1-5 and (June 1950): 41-46.

Indiana

1820, M33, Rolls 13-15
1830, M19, Rolls 26-32
1840, M704, Rolls 74-100; Census of pensioners, T498, Roll 3
1850, M432, Rolls 135-181
1860, M653, Rolls 242-309
1870, M593, Rolls 296-373; City of Indianapolis, first enumeration, M593, Rolls 340-341; City of Indianapolis, second enumeration, M593, Rolls 338-339
1880, T9, Rolls 263-324; Soundex index, T747, 98 rolls
1900, T623, Rolls 357-414; Soundex index, T1044, 253 rolls
1910, T624, Rolls 338-389; no index
1920, T625, Rolls 420-475; Soundex index, M1560, 230 rolls

Iowa

1840, M704, Rolls 101-102; Census of pensioners, T498, Roll 3
1850, M432, Rolls 182-189

1860, M653, Rolls 310-345
1870, M593, Rolls 374-427
1880, T9, Rolls 325-371; Soundex index, T748, 78 rolls
1900, T623, Rolls 415-468; Soundex index, T1045, 212 rolls
1910, T624, Rolls 390-430; no index
1920, T625, Rolls 476-521; Soundex index, M1561, 181 rolls

Remarks:

1850-80. The regional archives in Kansas City has non-population schedules on microfilm, A1156, 61 rolls.

Kansas

1860, M653, Rolls 346-352
1870, M593, Rolls 428-443
1880, T9, Rolls 372-400; Soundex index, T749, 51 rolls
1900, T623, Rolls 469-505; Soundex index, T1046, 148 rolls
1910, T624, Rolls 431-461; Soundex index, T1265, 145 rolls
1920, T625, Rolls 522-556; Soundex index, M1562, 129 rolls

Remarks:

1855, 1856, 1857, 1858, and 1859 Territorial Censuses. The National Archives has microfilmed copies of these censuses under the title *Kansas Territorial Censuses, 1855-1859*, M1813, 2 rolls. This microfilm publication includes the 1857 Shawnee Census. The originals are in the Kansas State Historical Society, 6425 SW Sixth Street, Topeka, KS 66615-1099.

1860. The Kansas City regional archives has a microfilm copy of the schedules of the 1860 Kansas territorial (non-Federal) census on XC-4, 5 rolls. The originals are in the Kansas State Historical Society. *See above* for address.

1865. The Kansas City regional archives has a microfilm copy of the 1865 Kansas state census on XC-5, 8 rolls. The originals are in the Kansas State Historical Society in Topeka. *See above* for address.

1875. The Kansas City regional archives has a microfilm copy of the 1875 Kansas state census on XC-6, 20 rolls. The originals are in the Kansas State Historical Society in Topeka. *See above* for address.

Kentucky

1810, M252, Rolls 5-9
1820, M33, Rolls 16-29
1830, M19, Rolls 33-42
1840, M704, Rolls 103-126; Census of pensioners, T498, Roll 3 [Carter Co. at end of the roll]
1850, Free schedules, M432, Rolls 190-222; Slave schedules, M432, Rolls 223-228
1860, Free schedules, M653, Rolls 353-400; Slave schedules, M653, Rolls 401-406
1870, M593, Rolls 444-504
1880, T9, Rolls 401-446; Soundex index, T750, 83 rolls
1890, Special census of Civil War veterans and widows, M123, Rolls 1-3
1900, T623, Rolls 506-555; Soundex index, T1047, 200 rolls
1910, T624, Rolls 462-506; Soundex index, T1266, 194 rolls
1920, T625, Rolls 557-602; Soundex index, M1563, 180 rolls

Remarks:

1790, 1800. Schedules for 1790 and 1800 have been reconstructed from local tax returns. Entries have been alphabetized and printed in two separate volumes: *"First Census" of Kentucky, 1790,* by Charles Brunk Heinemann and Gaius Marcus Brumbaugh (Washington: G.M. Brumbaugh, 1940), and *"Second Census" of Kentucky, 1800,* compiled by Garrett Glenn Clift (Frankfort, 1954). Both volumes were reprinted by the Genealogical Publishing Co. of Baltimore, the first in 1965, and the second in 1966.

Louisiana

1810, M252, Roll 10
1820, M33, Rolls 30-32
1830, M19, Rolls 43-45
1840, M704, Rolls 127-135; Census of pensioners, T498, Roll 3
1850, Free schedules, M432, Rolls 229-241; Slave schedules, M432, Rolls 242-247
1860, Free schedules, M653, Rolls 407-426; Slave schedules, M432, Rolls 427-431
1870, M593, Rolls 505-535
1880, T9, Rolls 447-474; Soundex index, T751, 55 rolls
1890, Special census of Civil War veterans and widows, M123, Rolls 4-5
1900, T623, Rolls 556-586; Soundex index, T1048, 146 rolls
1910, T624, Rolls 507-535; Soundex index, T1267, 132 rolls
1920, T625, Rolls 603-636; Soundex index, M1564, 135 rolls

Maine

1790, Original schedules, M637, Roll 2; Published schedules, T498, Roll 1
1800, M32, Rolls 6-8
1810, M252, Rolls 11-12
1820, M33, Rolls 33-39
1830, M19, Rolls 46-52
1840, M704, Rolls 136-155; Census of pensioners, T498, Roll 3
1850, M432, Rolls 248-276
1860, M653, Rolls 432-455
1870, M593, Rolls 536-565
1880, T9, Rolls 475-492; Soundex index, T752, 29 rolls
1890, Special census of Civil War veterans and widows, M123, Rolls 6-7
1900, T623, Rolls 587-603; Soundex index, T1049, 80 rolls
1910, T624, Rolls 536-548; no index
1920, T625, Rolls 637-651; Soundex index, M1565, 67 rolls

Remarks:

1800. Some of the 1800 schedules for York County are missing.

Maryland

1790, Original schedules, M637, Roll 3; Published schedules, M637, Roll 1

1800, M32, Rolls 9-12
1810, M252, Rolls 13-16
1820, M33, Rolls 40-46
1830, M19, Rolls 53-58
1840, M704, Rolls 156-172; Census of pensioners, T498, Roll 3
1850, Free schedules, M432, Rolls 277-299; Slave schedules, M432, Rolls 300-302
1860, Free schedules, M653, Rolls 456-483; Slave schedules, M653, Rolls 484-485
1870, M593, Rolls 566-599
1880, T9, Rolls 493-518; Soundex index, T753, 47 rolls
1890, Special census of Civil War veterans and widows, M123, Rolls 8-10
1900, T623, Rolls 604-630; Soundex index, T1050, 127 rolls
1910, T624, Rolls 549-570; no index
1920, T625, Rolls 652-678; Soundex index, M1566, 126 rolls

Remarks:

1800. There are no schedules for Baltimore Co., only for the City of Baltimore.

1830. The 1830 schedules for Montgomery, Prince Georges, St. Marys, Queen Annes, and Somerset Counties are missing.

Massachusetts

1790, Original schedules, M637, Roll 4; Published schedules, T498, Roll 1
1800, M32, Rolls 13-19
1810, M252, Rolls 17-22
1820, M33, Rolls 47-55
1830, M19, Rolls 59-68
1840, M704, Rolls 173-202; Census of pensioners, T498, Roll 3
1850, M432, Rolls 303-345
1860, M653, Rolls 486-534
1870, M593, Rolls 600-659
1880, T9, Rolls 519-568; Soundex index, T754, 70 rolls
1890, Special census of Civil War veterans and widows, M123, Rolls 11-16
1900, T623, Rolls 631-697; Soundex index, T1051, 318 rolls
1910, T624, Rolls 571-633; no index
1920, T625, Rolls 679-752; Soundex index, M1567, 326 rolls

Michigan

1820, M33, Roll 56 (includes present-day Wisconsin)
1830, M19, Roll 69 (includes present-day Wisconsin)
1840, M704, Rolls 203-212; Census of pensioners, T598, Roll 3
1850, M432, Rolls 346-366
1860, M653, Rolls 535-566
1870, M593, Rolls 660-715
1880, T9, Rolls 569-614; Soundex index, T755, 73 rolls
1890, Special census of Civil War veterans and widows, M123, Rolls 17-21

1900, T623, Rolls 698-755; Soundex index, T1052, 257 rolls

1910, T624, Rolls 634-688, Soundex index, T1268, 253 rolls

1920, T625, Rolls 753-821, Soundex index, M1568, 291 rolls

Minnesota

1850, M432, Roll 367

1860, M653, Rolls 567-576

1870, M593, Rolls 716-719; T132, Rolls 1-13

1880, T9, Rolls 615-638; Soundex index, T756, 37 rolls

1890, M407, Roll 3, Wright Co. (Rockford); alphabetical index, M496, 2 rolls; Special census of Civil War veterans and widows, M123, Rolls 22-25

1900, T623, Rolls 756-798; Soundex index, T1053, 180 rolls

1910, T624, Rolls 689-730; no index

1920, T625, Rolls 822-867; Soundex index, M1569, 174 rolls

Remarks:

1849. The National Archives has a copy of the 1849 census of the Territory of Minnesota, published as Appendix D of the *Journal of the House of Representatives, First Session of the Legislative Assembly of the Territory of Minnesota* (St. Paul, 1850).

1857. The National Archives has a microfilmed copy of *Schedules of the Minnesota Territory Census of 1857*, T1175, 5 rolls. The 1857 schedules for Minnesota Territory were created pursuant to Section 4 of an act of 1857 (11 Stat. 167) to enable Minnesota Territory to become a state. The schedules are on printed forms in five volumes. They are arranged alphabetically by county, thereunder by minor subdivision. The enumeration was taken as of September 21, 1857. For each inhabitant of a household, an entry shows name; age; sex; color; state, territory, or country of birth; if a voter, whether native or naturalized; and occupation.

1870. A large part of the 1870 schedules formerly in the possession of the Bureau of the Census was destroyed by fire in 1921; others that were damaged were destroyed by authorization of Congress in 1933. The destroyed schedules pertain to the counties with names running alphabetically from Aitkin to Sibley. The *Minnesota Census Schedules for 1870*, T132, 13 rolls, is a copy of the duplicate set of the 1870 schedules in the custody of the Minnesota Historical Society, St. Paul.

Mississippi

1820, M33, Rolls 57-58

1830, M19, Rolls 70-71

1840, M704, Rolls 213-219; Census of pensioners, T498, Roll 3

1850, Free schedules, M432, Rolls 368-382; Slave schedules, M432, Rolls 383-390

1860, Free schedules, M653, Rolls 577-594; Slave schedules, M653, Rolls 595-604

1870, M593, Rolls 720-754

1880, T9, Rolls 639-670; Soundex index, T757, 69 rolls

1890, Special census of Civil War veterans and widows, M123, Roll 26

1900, T623, Rolls 799-835; Soundex index, T1054, 156 rolls

1910, T624, Rolls 731-765; Soundex index, T1269, 118 rolls

1920, T625, Rolls 868-901; Soundex index, M1570, 123 rolls

Remarks:

1816. The Mississippi Department of Archives and History, Jackson, has the territorial schedules for 1816 and some other years. The National Archives has a copy of the 1816 schedules as published in *Early Inhabitants of the Natchez District*, by Norman E. Gillis (Baton Rouge, 1963). Persons residing outside the Natchez District in 1816 are listed in an appendix.

1830. The 1830 schedules for Pike County are missing.

1860. The 1860 schedules for free and slave inhabitants for Hancock and Washington Counties and the 1860 schedules for free inhabitants for Tallahatchie County are missing.

Missouri

1830, M19, Rolls 72-73

1840, M704, Rolls 220-233; Census of pensioners, T498, Roll 3

1850, Free schedules, M432, Rolls 391-421; Slave schedules, M432, Rolls 422-424

1860, Free schedules, M653, Rolls 605-660; Slave schedules, M653, Rolls 661-664

1870, M593, Rolls 755-826

1880, T9, Rolls 671-741; Soundex index, T758, 114 rolls

1890, Special census of Civil War veterans and widows, M123, Rolls 27-34

1900, T623, Rolls 836-908; Soundex index, T1055, 300 rolls

1910, T624, Rolls 766-828; Soundex index, T1270, 285 rolls

1920, T625, Rolls 902-966; Soundex index, M1571, 269 rolls

Montana

1870, M593, Roll 827

1880, T9, Roll 742; Soundex index, T759, 2 rolls

1890, Special census of Civil War veterans and widows, M123, Roll 35

1900, T623, Rolls 909-915; Soundex index, T1056, 40 rolls

1910, T624, Rolls 829-837; no index

1920, T625, Rolls 967-978; Soundex index, M1572, 46 rolls

Remarks:

1860. The 1860 schedules that relate to the eastern part of the present state of Montana are included in the volume for the unorganized part of Nebraska Territory; those for the western part are included in the schedules of Washington Territory.

Nebraska

1860, M653, Roll 665

1870, M593, Rolls 828-833

1880, T9, Rolls 743-757; Soundex index, T760, 22 rolls

1890, Special census of Civil War veterans and widows, M123, Rolls 36-38

1900, T623, Rolls 916-942; Soundex index, T1057, 107 rolls

1910, T624, Rolls 838-857; no index

1920, T625, Rolls 979-1003; Soundex index, M1573, 96 rolls

Remarks:

1885. Nebraska was one of five states and territories to elect to take an 1885 census with Federal assistance pursuant to an act of 1879 (20 Stat. 480). The unbound population and mortality schedules are in the National Archives, and they have been microfilmed as *Schedules of the Nebraska State Census of 1885*, M352, 56 rolls. The schedules show the same type of information as the 1880 schedules, but in many cases the initial letters of the given names of enumerated persons appear instead of the names.

Nevada

1870, M593, Rolls 834-835

1880, T9, Rolls 758-759; Soundex index, T761, 3 rolls

1890, Special census of Civil War veterans and widows, M123, Roll 39

1900, T623, Roll 943; Soundex index, T1058, 7 rolls

1910, T624, Rolls 858-859; no index

1920, T625, Rolls 1004-1005; Soundex index, M1574, 9 rolls

Remarks:

1860. The 1860 schedules that relate to the present state of Nevada are included among the schedules for Utah. For Elko County, *see* St. Marys County, UT; for Douglas, Lyon, Ormsby, and Storey Counties, *see* Carson County, UT, on roll 1314.

New Hampshire

1790, Original schedules, M637, Roll 5; Published schedules, T498, Roll 1

1800, M32, Roll 20

1810, M252, Rolls 23-25

1820, M33, Rolls 59-61

1830, M19, Rolls 74-78

1840, M704, Rolls 234-246; Census of pensioners, T498, Roll 3

1850, M432, Rolls 425-441

1860, M653, Rolls 666-681

1870, M593, Rolls 836-850

1880, T9, Rolls 760-769; Soundex index, T762, 13 rolls

1890, Special census of Civil War veterans and widows, M123, Roll 40

1900, T623, Rolls 944-952; Soundex index, T1059, 52 rolls

1910, T624, Rolls 860-866; no index

1920, T625, Rolls 1006-1014, Soundex index, M1575, 41 rolls

Remarks:

1800. Some of the 1800 schedules for Rockingham and Strafford Counties are missing.

1820. The 1820 schedules for Grafton County are missing.

New Jersey

1830, M19, Rolls 79-83

1840, M704, Rolls 247-262; Census of pensioners, T498, Roll 3

1850, Free schedules, M432, Rolls 442-465; Slave schedules, M432, Roll 466

1860, M653, Rolls 682-711

1870, M593, Rolls 851-892

1880, T9, Rolls 770-801; Soundex index, T763, 49 rolls

1890, M407, Roll 3, Hudson Co. (Jersey City); alphabetical index, M496, 2 rolls; Special census of Civil War veterans and widows, M123, Rolls 41-43

1900, T623, Rolls 953-998; Soundex index, T1060, 204 rolls

1910, T624, Rolls 867-912; no index

1920, T625, Rolls 1015-1073; Soundex index, M1576, 253 rolls

Remarks:

1790. Substitutes for the missing 1790 census of New Jersey are: *New Jersey in 1793: An Abstract and Index to the 1793 Militia Census of the State of New Jersey*, by James S. Norton (Salt Lake City: Institute of Family Research, 1973) and *Revolutionary Census of New Jersey*, by Kenn Stryker Rodda (New Orleans: Polyanthos, 1972), which covers 1773-84.

1800–1820. No population schedules for New Jersey in these years have survived.

New Mexico

1850, M432, Rolls 467-470

1860, M653, Rolls 712-716

1870, M593, Rolls 893-897

1880, T9, Rolls 802-804; Soundex index, T764, 6 rolls

1890, Special census of Civil War veterans and widows, M123, Roll 44

1900, T623, Rolls 999-1003; Soundex index, T1061, 23 rolls

1910, T624, Rolls 913-919; no index

1920, T625, Rolls 1074-1080; Soundex index, M1577, 31 rolls

Remarks:

1790, 1823, and 1845. *Spanish and Mexican Colonial Censuses of New Mexico, 1790, 1823, 1845,* by Virginia L. Olmsted (Albuquerque: New Mexico Genealogical Society, Inc., 1975) is the best record of New Mexico's early censuses.

1885. New Mexico was one of five states and territories to elect to take an 1885 census with Federal assistance pursuant to an act of 1879 (20 Stat. 480). The unbound population and mortality schedules are in the National Archives, and they have been microfilmed as *Schedules of the New Mexico Territory Census of 1885*, M846, 6 rolls. The schedules show the same type of information as the 1880 schedules, but in many cases the initial letters of the given names of enumerated persons appear instead of the names.

New York

1790, Original schedules, M637, Roll 6; Published schedules, T498, Roll 2

1800, M32, Rolls 21-28

1810, M252, Rolls 26-37

1820, M33, Rolls 62-79

1830, M19, Rolls 84-117

1840, M704, Rolls 263-353; Census of pensioners, T498, Roll 3

1850, M432, Rolls 471-618

1860, M653, Rolls 717-885

1870, M593, Rolls 898-1120; New York City, first enumeration, rolls 975-1013; New York City, second enumeration, rolls 1014-1053

1880, T9, Rolls 805-949; Soundex index, T765, 187 rolls

1890, M407, Roll 3, Westchester Co. (Eastchester), Suffolk Co. (Brookhaven Twp.); alphabetical index, M496, 2 rolls; Special census of Civil War veterans and widows, M123, Rolls 45-57

1900, T623, Rolls 1004-1179; Soundex index, T1062, 768 rolls

1910, T624, Rolls 920-1094; no index

1920, T625, Rolls 1081-1281; Soundex index, M1578, 885 rolls

Remarks:

Information about state schedules, 1825-1925, for New York is available as *An Inventory of New York State and Federal Census Records,* revised edition, compiled by Edna L. Jacobson (Albany: New York State Library, 1956).

North Carolina

1790, Original schedules, M637, Roll 7; Published schedules, T498, Roll 2

1800, M32, Rolls 29-34

1810, M252, Rolls 38-43

1820, M33, Rolls 80-85

1830, M19, Rolls 118-125

1840, M704, Rolls 354-374; Census of pensioners, T498, Roll 3

1850, Free schedules, M432, Rolls 619-649; Slave schedules, M432, Rolls 650-656

1860, Free schedules, M653, Rolls 886-919; Slave schedules, M653, Rolls 920-927

1870, M593, Rolls 1121-1166

1880, T9, Rolls 950-988; Soundex index, T766, 79 rolls

1890, M407, Roll 3, Gaston Co. (South Point Twp. and River Bend Twp.), Cleveland Co. (Twp. #2); alphabetical index, M496, 2 rolls; Special census of Civil War veterans and widows, M123, Roll 58

1900, T623, Rolls 1180-1225; Soundex index, T1063, 168 rolls

1910, T624, Rolls 1095-1137; Soundex index, T1271, 178 rolls

1920, T625, Rolls 1282-1329; Soundex index, M1579, 166 rolls

Remarks:

1790. The 1790 schedules for Caswell, Granville, and Orange Counties no longer exist. As a substitute in the published 1790 index, local tax records were used.

1810. The 1810 schedules for Craven, Greene, New Hanover, and Wake Counties are missing.

1820. The 1820 schedules for Currituck, Franklin, Martin, Montgomery, Randolph, and Wake Counties are missing.

North Dakota

1860, *See* Dakota Territory

1870, *See* Dakota Territory

1880, *See* Dakota Territory

1890, Special census of Civil War veterans and widows, M123, Roll 59

1900, T623, Rolls 1226-1234; Soundex index, T1064, 36 rolls

1910, T624, Rolls 1138-1149; no index

1920, T625, Rolls 1330-1343; Soundex index, M1580, 48 rolls

Remarks:

1900. Schedules for the first time were designated "North Dakota" and "South Dakota," rather than "Dakota."

Ohio

1820, M33, Rolls 86-95

1830, M19, Rolls 126-142

1840, M704, Rolls 375-434; Census of pensioners, T498, Roll 3

1850, M432, Rolls 657-741

1860, M653, Rolls 928-1054

1870, M593, Rolls 1167-1284

1880, T9, Rolls 989-1079; Soundex index, T767, 143 rolls

1890, M407, Roll 3, Hamilton Co. (Cincinnati), Clinton Co. (Wayne Twp.); alphabetical index, M496, 2 rolls; Special census of Civil War veterans and widows, M123, Rolls 60-75

1900, T623, Rolls 1235-1334; Soundex index, T1065, 397 rolls

1910, T624, Rolls 1150-1241; Soundex index, T1272, 418 rolls

1920, T625, Rolls 1344-1450; Soundex index, M1581, 476 rolls

Remarks:

1800. The National Archives has a microfilm copy of the 1800 and 1803 censuses for Washington County on M1804, 1 roll.

1810. The National Archives has a microfilm copy of the 1810 census for Washington County on M1803, 1 roll.

Oklahoma

1890, Special census of Civil War veterans and widows, M123, Roll 76 (includes both Oklahoma and Indian Territories)

1900, T623, Rolls 1335-1344 (Oklahoma Territory); Soundex index, T1066, 42 rolls

1900, T623, Rolls 1843-1854 (Indian Territory); Soundex index, T1082, 42 rolls

1910, T624, Rolls 1242-1277; Soundex index, T1273, 143 rolls

1920, T625, Rolls 1451-1490; Soundex index, M1582, 155 rolls

Remarks:

1860. The 1860 schedules that relate to the present state of Oklahoma are included with schedules for Arkansas. They appear on roll 52 of M653. The persons enumerated were living on Indian lands.

1890. The National Archives has a microfilm copy of the *First Territorial Census for Oklahoma, 1890,* M1811, 1 roll. The census is comprised of schedules for Logan, Oklahoma, Cleveland, Canadian, Kingfisher, Payne, and Beaver Counties.

1900. The 1900 schedules are the first to list Oklahoma.

1907. For Seminole County special agents were employed to take a census as of July 1, 1907. The census is reproduced on *1907 Census of Seminole County, Oklahoma,* M1814, 1 roll. The schedules contain name, age, sex, color, and relationship to head of the family for each person enumerated.

Oregon

1850, M432, Roll 742

1860, M653, Rolls 1055-1056

1870, M593, Rolls 1285-1288

1880, T9, Rolls 1080-1084; Soundex index, T768, 8 rolls

1890, Special census of Civil War veterans and widows, M123, Roll 77

1900, T623, Rolls 1345-1353; Soundex index, T1067, 54 rolls

1910, T624, Rolls 1278-1291; no index

1920, T625, Rolls 1491-1506; Soundex index, M1583, 69 rolls

Overseas Military and Naval Forces

1920, T625, Rolls 2040-2041; Soundex index, M1600, 18 rolls

Remarks:

1920. Page numbers are repeated within the volumes.

Panama

1920, T625, Roll 2042; Soundex index ("Panama Canal Zone"), M1599, 3 rolls

Pennsylvania

1790, Original schedules, M637, Rolls 8-9; Published schedules, T498, Roll 2

1800, M32, Rolls 35-44

1810, M252, Rolls 44-57

1820, M33, Rolls 96-114

1830, M19, Rolls 143-166

1840, M704, Rolls 435-503; Census of pensioners, T498, Roll 4

1850, M432, Rolls 743-840

1860, M653, Rolls 1057-1201

1870, M593, Rolls 1289-1470; Philadelphia, first enumeration, Rolls 1387-1414, 1445; Philadelphia, second enumeration, Rolls 1415-1444

1880, T9, Rolls 1085-1208; Soundex index, T769, 168 rolls

1890, Special census of Civil War veterans and widows, M123, Rolls 78-91

1900, T623, Rolls 1354-1503; Soundex index, T1068, 612 rolls

1910, T624, Rolls 1292-1435; Soundex index, T1274, 688 rolls

1920, T625, Rolls 1507-1669; Soundex index, M1584, 712 rolls

Remarks:

1870. The National Archives has accessioned the "state" copy of the original population schedule.

Philippines

1910, T624, Roll 1784 (Hospital ships and stations)

Puerto Rico

1910, T624, Rolls 1756-1783; no index

1920, T625, Rolls 2043-2075; Soundex index, M1601, 165 rolls

Remarks:

1899. A census was taken in this year, but the schedules were destroyed.

Rhode Island

1790, Original schedules, M637, Roll 10; Published schedules, T498, Roll 3

1800, M32, Rolls 45-46

1810, M252, Rolls 58-59

1820, M33, Rolls 115-117

1830, M19, Rolls 167-168

1840, M704, Rolls 504-506; Census of pensioners, T498, Roll 3

1850, M432, Rolls 841-847

1860, M653, Rolls 1202-1211

1870, M593, Rolls 1471-1480

1880, T9, Rolls 1209-1216; Soundex index, T770, 11 rolls

1890, Special census of Civil War veterans and widows, M123, Roll 92

1900, T623, Rolls 1504-1513; Soundex index, T1069, 49 rolls

1910, T624, Rolls 1436-1445; no index

1920, T625, Rolls 1670-1681; Soundex index, M1585, 53 rolls

Samoa

1920, T625, Roll 2032; Soundex index, M1603, 2 rolls

South Carolina

1790, Original schedules, M637, Roll 11; Published schedules, T498, Roll 3

1800, M32, Rolls 47-50

1810, M252, Rolls 60-62

1820, M33, Rolls 118-121

1830, Ml9, Rolls 169-173

1840, M704, Rolls 507-516; Census of pensioners, T498, Roll 3

1850, Free schedules, M432, Rolls 848-860; Slave schedules, M432, Rolls 861-868

1860, Free schedules, M653, Rolls 1212-1228; Slave schedules, M653, Rolls 1229-1238

1870, M593, Rolls 1481-1512

1880, T9, Rolls 1217-1243; Soundex index, T771, 56 rolls

1890, Special census of Civil War veterans and widows, M123, Roll 93

1900, T623, Rolls 1514-1545; Soundex index, T1070, 124 rolls

1910, T624, Rolls 1446-1474; Soundex index, T1275, 93 rolls

1920, T625, Rolls 1682-1713; Soundex index, M1586, 112 rolls

Remarks:

1820–50. The schedules for Clarendon County for 1820, 1830, 1840, and 1850 are missing.

South Dakota

1860, *See* Dakota Territory

1870, *See* Dakota Territory

1880, *See* Dakota Territory

1890, M407, Roll 3, Union Co. (Jefferson Twp.); alphabetical index, M496, 2 rolls; Special census of Civil War veterans and widows, M123, Roll 94

1900, T623, Rolls 1546-1556; Soundex index, T1071, 44 rolls

1910, T624, Rolls 1475-1489; no index

1920, T625, Rolls 1714-1727; Soundex index, M1587, 48 rolls

Tennessee

1810, M252, Roll 63

1820, M33, Rolls 122-125

1830, Ml9, Rolls 174-182

1840, M704, Rolls 517-537; Census of pensioners, T498, Roll 3

1850, Free schedules, M432, Rolls 869-901; Slave schedules, M432, Rolls 902-907

1860, Free schedules, M653, Rolls 1239-1280; Slave schedules, M653, Rolls 1281-1286

1870, M593, Rolls 1513-1572

1880, T9, Rolls 1244-1287; Soundex index, T772, 86 rolls

1890, Special census of Civil War veterans and widows, M123, Rolls 95-98

1900, T623, Rolls 1557-1606; Soundex index, T1072, 188 rolls

1910, T624, Rolls 1490-1526; Soundex index, T1276, 142 rolls

1920, T625, Rolls 1728-1771; Soundex index, M1588, 162 rolls

Remarks:

1800. Some of the 1800 schedules have been reconstructed from local tax records. *See Early East Tennessee Tax Payers*, compiled by Pollyanna Creekmore (Easley, SC: Southern Historical Press, 1980), which is a reprint of material originally published by the East Tennessee Historical Society.

1810. The National Archives has the 1810 schedules for Rutherford County. The 1810 schedules for Grainger County have been transcribed and published in *Grainger County, Tennessee, Federal Census of 1810, Population Schedule (Third Census) and County Tax Lists for 1810*, edited by Pollyanna Creekmore (Knoxville: Lawson McGhee, 1956).

1820. The National Archives has the 1820 schedules for 26 of the 48 counties.

Texas

1850, Free schedules, M432, Rolls 908-916; Slave schedules, M432, Rolls 917-918

1860, Free schedules, M653, Rolls 1287-1308; Slave schedules, M653, Rolls 1309-1312

1870, M593, Rolls 1573-1609

1880, T9, Rolls 1288-1334; Soundex index, T773, 77 rolls

1890, M407, Roll 3, Ellis Co. (J.P. No. 6, Mountain Peak, and Ovilla Precinct); Hood Co. (Precinct No. 5); Rusk Co. (No. 6 and J.P. No. 7); Trinity Co. (Trinity Town and Precinct No. 2); Kaufman Co. (Kaufman); alphabetical index, M496, 2 rolls; Special census of Civil War veterans and widows, M123, Rolls 99-102

1900, T623, Rolls 1607-1681; Soundex index, T1073, 286 rolls

1910, T624, Rolls 1527-1601; Soundex index, T1277, 262 rolls

1920, T625, Rolls 1772-1860; Soundex index, M1589, 373 rolls

Remarks:

1829–36. The Texas State Archives, Austin, has Texas census schedules, 1829-36. These were published as *The First Census of Texas, 1829-1836*, National Genealogical Society Special Publication 22, by Marion Day Mullins (Washington: National Genealogical Society, 1976).

U.S. Vessels and Navy Yards

1890, Special census of Civil War veterans and widows, M123, Roll 104

Utah

1850, M432, Roll 919

1860, M653, Rolls 1313-1314

1870, M593, Rolls 1610-1613

1880, T9, Rolls 1335-1339; Soundex index, T774, 7 rolls

1890, Special census of Civil War veterans and widows,

M123, Roll 103

1900, T623, Rolls 1682–1688; Soundex index, T1074, 29 rolls

1910, T624, Rolls 1602–1611; no index

1920, T625, Rolls 1861–1869; Soundex index, M1590, 33 rolls

Vermont

1790, Original schedules, M637, Roll 12; Published schedules, T498, Roll 3

1800, M32, Rolls 51–52

1810, M252, Rolls 64–65

1820, M33, Rolls 126–128

1830, MI9, Rolls 183–188

1840, M704, Rolls 538–548; Census of pensioners, T498, Roll 3

1850, M432, Rolls 920–931

1860, M653, Rolls 1315–1329

1870, M593, Rolls 1614–1629

1880, T9, Rolls 1340–1350; Soundex index, T775, 15 rolls

1890, Special census of Civil War veterans and widows, M123, Roll 105

1900, T623, Rolls 1689–1696; Soundex index, T1075, 41 rolls

1910, T624, Rolls 1612–1618; no index

1920, T625, Rolls 1870–1876; Soundex index, M1591, 32 rolls

Remarks:

1800. The 1800 schedules have been printed and indexed in *Heads of Families at the Second Census of the United States Taken in the Year 1800: Vermont* (Montpelier: Vermont Historical Society, 1938; reprinted by the Genealogical Publishing Co., Baltimore, 1972).

Virginia

1810, M252, Rolls 66–71

1820, M33, Rolls 129–142

1830, M19, Rolls 189–201

1840, M704, Rolls 549–579; Census of pensioners, T498, Roll 3

1850, Free schedules, M432, Rolls 932–982; Slave schedules, M432, Rolls 983–993

1860, Free schedules, M653, Rolls 1330–1385; Slave schedules, M653, Rolls 1386–1397; Free and Slave schedules (Northern Halifax County only), M1808, 1 roll

1870, M593, Rolls 1630–1682

1880, T9, Rolls 1351–1395; Soundex index, T776, 82 rolls

1890, Special census of Civil War veterans and widows, M123, Rolls 106–107

1900, T623, Rolls 1697–1740; Soundex index, T1076, 174 rolls

1910, T624, Rolls 1619–1652; Soundex index, T1278, 183 rolls

1920, T625, Rolls 1877–1919, Soundex index, M1592, 168 rolls

Remarks:

1790. The 1790 schedules have been reconstructed and published in two volumes that supplement each other: *Heads of Families at the First Census of the United States Taken in the Year 1790: Records of the State Enumerations, 1782 to 1785, Virginia* (Washington: Bureau of the Census, 1908), and Augusta B. Fothergill and John Mark Naugle, *Virginia Tax Payers, 1782–87, Other Than Those Published by the United States Census Bureau* (Richmond, 1940). The first volume was reprinted by the Reprint Co., Spartanburg, SC, 1961, and by the Genealogical Publishing Co., Baltimore, 1966 and 1970. The Fothergill and Naugle volume was reprinted by the Genealogical Publishing Co. in 1966.

1810. The 1810 schedules for the following counties are missing: Grayson, Greenbrier, Halifax, Hardy, Henry, James City, King William, Louisa, Mecklenburg, Nansemond, Northampton, Orange, Patrick, Pittsylvania, Russell, and Tazewell. A card index for 1810 census schedules for Virginia is reproduced as *Index to the 1810 Population Census for Virginia*, T1019, 35 rolls.

1820, 1830, and 1840. Schedules for Alexandria County are included with schedules for the District of Columbia.
1810, 1820, 1830, 1840, 1850, and 1860. These schedules include present-day West Virginia.

Virgin Islands

1920, T625, Roll 2076; Soundex index, M1604, 3 rolls

Washington

1860, M653, Roll 1398

1870, M593, Roll 1683

1880, T9, Rolls 1396–1398; Soundex index, T777, 4 rolls

1890, Special census of Civil War veterans and widows, M123, Roll 108

1900, T623, Rolls 1741–1754; Soundex index, T1077, 69 rolls

1910, T624, Rolls 1653–1675; no index

1920, T625, Rolls 1920–1946; Soundex index, M1593, 118 rolls

Remarks:

1860. The 1860 schedules for Benton, Columbia, San Juan, and Snohomish Counties are missing.
1870. The 1870 schedules for Benton and Columbia Counties are missing.

Washington, DC: *See* District of Columbia

West Virginia

1870, M593, Rolls 1684–1702

1880, T9, Rolls 1399–1416; Soundex index, T778, 32 rolls

1890, Special census of Civil War veterans and widows, M123, Rolls 109–110

1900, T623, Rolls 1755–1776; Soundex index, T1078, 93 rolls

1910, T624, Rolls 1676–1699; Soundex index, T1279, 108 rolls

1920, T625, Rolls 1947-1974; Soundex index, M1594, 109 rolls

Wisconsin

1840, M704, Roll 580; Census of pensioners, T498, Roll 3

1850, M432, Rolls 994-1009

1860, M653, Rolls 1399-1438

1870, M593, Rolls 1703-1747

1880, T9, Rolls 1417-1453; Soundex index, T779, 51 rolls

1890, Special census of Civil War veterans and widows, M123, Rolls 111-116

1900, T623, Rolls 1777-1825; Soundex index, T1079, 189 rolls

1910, T624, Rolls 1700-1744; no index

1920, T625, Rolls 1975-2024; Soundex index, M1595, 196 rolls

Remarks:

1820, 1830. The schedules for 1820 and 1830 are included in the schedules for Michigan.

1836, 1838, 1842, 1846, and 1847. The National Archives has microfilm copies of these Wisconsin territorial censuses on M1809, 3 rolls. Original schedules are in the State Historical Society of Wisconsin, Madison, WI 53706.

Wyoming

1870, M593, Roll 1748

1880, T9, Roll 1454; Soundex index, T780, 1 roll

1890, Special census of Civil War veterans and widows, M123, Roll 117

1900, T623, Rolls 1826-1827; Soundex index, T1080, 15 rolls

1910, T624, Rolls 1745-1747; no index

1920, T625, Rolls 2025-2029; Soundex index, M1596, 17 rolls

Remarks:

1860. The 1860 schedules for present-day Wyoming are among the schedules for Nebraska.

1.3 Nonpopulation Census Schedules

Nonpopulation census schedules consist of agricultural, mortality, industry/manufacturers, and defective, dependent, and delinquent classes schedules as well as social statistics. The Bureau of the Census did not take all of these censuses in all years. All but social statistics include names.

The Bureau of the Census distributed the original nonpopulation schedules to non-Federal repositories in 1918 and 1919, long before the establishment of the National Archives. The National Archives and Records Administration (NARA) has acquired microfilm or published copies of many of these schedules, including copies of some 1820 industry schedules, and many of the 1850–1880 nonpopulation schedules listed in the sections above. NARA holds no nonpopulation schedules for some states and does not hold complete nonpopulation schedules for others. Those schedules that are available on microfilm at the National Archives Building in Washington, DC, are listed by state following explanations of the various schedules. For schedules not listed, contact the appropriate state archives or historical society. To verify the availability of nonpopulation schedules at NARA's regional archival facilities, check the online microfilm locator at *www.nara.gov.*

Agricultural, 1850-80

The Department of the Interior directed that census enumerators gather agricultural information in the course of conducting the census. The enumerators gathered data about farms that met certain dollar value production thresholds.

1850. For the year ending June 1, 1850, every farm with an annual produce worth $100 or more was enumerated, giving the name of the owner, agent, or tenant, and the kind and value of acreage and machinery and amounts of livestock and produce.

1860. For the year ending June 1, 1860, the schedules show the name of the owner, agent, or tenant for farms with an annual produce worth $100 or more. The enumerators recorded the kind and value of acreage and machinery and amounts of livestock and produce.

1870. For the year ending June 1, 1870, the schedules show the name of the owner, agent, or tenant of farms of three acres or more or with an annual produce worth $500. The enumerators recorded the kind and value of acreage and machinery and amounts of livestock and produce.

1880. For the year ending June 1, 1880, the schedules show the name of the owner, agent, or tenant of farms of three acres or more or with an annual produce worth $500. The enumerators recorded the quantity and value of acreage and machinery and amounts of livestock and produce.

Defective, dependent, and delinquent—1880 only

In 1880, the Superintendent of the Census collected information about "defective, dependent, and delinquent classes," using the following schedules: No. 1, Insane Inhabitants; No. 2, Idiots; No. 3, Deaf-Mutes; No. 4, Blind Inhabitants; No. 5, Homeless Children (in institutions); No. 6, Inhabitants in Prison; and No. 7, Pauper and Indigent Inhabitants.

Prior to the 1880 census, the only inquiries about mental and physical defects were part of the population schedules. Individuals in institutions are listed in the regular population schedule.

In 1880 those who were blind, deaf, idiotic, insane, or permanently disabled were recorded in the population schedules, with further information about their condition on supplemental schedules of dependent classes, which are extant for some states among the nonpopulation schedules.

Manufacturers Schedules, 1810, 1820, and 1880; Industrial Schedules, 1850-70

1810. Congress authorized the taking of "an account of the several manufacturing establishments and manufacturers" for the first time in section 2 of an act of May 1, 1810 (2 Stat. 605). The marshals and assistants took this census under the direction of the Secretary of the Treasury and forwarded the completed schedules and abstracts to him. These schedules apparently have been lost except for fragments that appear in the volumes of 1810 population schedules.

The results of the 1810 manufacturing schedules were published as *A Statement of the Arts and Manufacturing of the United States of America . . . ,* prepared by Tench Coxe (Washington: P. Cornman, Jr., 1814); reprinted in *American State Papers: Finance* (Washington: Gales and Seaton, 1832), 2:425–439, and also reprinted by Maxwell Reprint Co., Elmsford, NY, 1971.

For each manufacturing establishment, the schedules contain the name of the owner, kind of establishment, quantity and estimated value of the goods manufactured, and, in some cases, quantity of raw materials used. Mining, fisheries, mercantile, and trading enterprises also appear in the 1850 through 1870 schedules. The fragments of schedules that exist are among the population schedules.

1820. The 1820 enumeration records 14 items relating to the nature and names of articles manufactured, including market value of article annually manufactured; kind, quantity, and cost of raw materials annually consumed; number of men, women, boys, and girls employed; quantity and kinds of machinery; amount of capital invested; amount paid annually in wages; amount of contingent expenses; and general observations. The surviving schedules are on microfilm as *Records of the 1820 Census of Manufacturers,* M279, 27 rolls.

1850. For the year ending June 1, 1850, the enumerators recorded information about manufacturing, mining, fisheries, and every mercantile, commercial, and trading business with an annual gross product of $500 or more. The schedules show the name of the company or owner; kind of business; amount of capital invested; and quantity and value of materials, labor, machinery, and products.

1860. For the year ending June 1, 1860, the enumerator recorded information about manufacturing, mining, fisheries, and all kinds of mercantile, commercial, and trading businesses if the annual gross product amounted to $500. The schedules show the name of the company or owner; kind of business; capital investment; and quantity and value of material, labor, machinery, and products.

1870. The enumerators recorded information about manufacturing, mining, and fisheries if the annual gross product amounted to $500 for the year ending June 1, 1870. The schedules show the name of the company or owner, kind of business, amount of capital invested, and information about the quantity and value of materials, labor, machinery, and products.

1880. Special agents, rather than the regular enumerators, recorded information for certain large industries and in cities of more than 8,000 inhabitants. These schedules no longer exist. The regular enumerators continued to collect information on general industry schedules and special schedules for the production of cereals, cotton, forest products, fruit growing, meat production, and tobacco. The schedules show the name of the company or owner and much specific information about the kind, quantity, and value of materials, labor, machinery, and products.

Mortality, 1850-80

As part of the census reforms for the 1850 census, enumerators gathered information on the deaths of individuals for the year preceding the census. The 1850, 1860, 1870, and 1880 mortality schedules contained information on persons who had died during the 12 months prior to the date the census was taken. (There is no information on deaths occurring in the nine years outside of the census year.) The entries in most of these schedules give the cause of death.

1850. The mortality schedules give the following information for each person who died during the year ending June 1, 1850: name, age, sex, color (white, black, or mulatto), whether married or widowed, place of birth, occupation, month of death, cause of death, and number of days ill.

1860. The mortality schedules give the following information about each person who died during the year ending June 1, 1860: name, age, sex, color (black, white, mulatto), whether slave or free, whether married or widowed, place of birth, occupation, month of death, cause of death, and number of days ill.

1870. The schedules show the following information about each person who died within the year ending June 1, 1870: name, age, sex, color (white, black, mulatto, Chinese, or Indian), whether married or widowed, place of birth, whether father and mother foreign born, occupation, month of death, and cause of death.

1880. The schedules give the following information about each person who died during the year ending June 1, 1880: name, age, sex, color, marital status, occupation, place of birth, length of residence in the United States, place of birth of father and mother, month of death, cause of death, place cause of death was contracted, and name of attending physician.

Social Statistics, 1850-80

Social statistics generally provide data on crime, real estate, wages, churches, schools, newspapers, libraries, and public debt. These schedules provide statistical information only and do not give names.

Alabama

Industry/Manufacturers
    1820, M279, Roll 27

Arizona

Mortality

1870, schedules, T655, Roll 1

1880, schedules, T655, Roll 2

Arkansas

Industry/Manufacturers

1820, M279, Roll 27

Colorado

Agricultural

1885, State Census, M158, Rolls 1–8*

Industry/Manufacturers

1885, State Census, M158, Rolls 1–8*

Mortality

1870, schedules, T655, Roll 3

1880, schedules, T655, Roll 4

1885, State Census, M158, Rolls 1–8*

*The Schedules of the Colorado State Census of 1885 are arranged alphabetically by county, thereunder numerically by enumeration district. Within each enumeration district, the schedules appear in the following order: population, agriculture, manufacturers, mortality. The schedule for social statistics was authorized but not taken. The census was taken June 1, 1885.

Connecticut

Industry/Manufacturers

1820, M279, Roll 4

Delaware

Manufacturers

1820, M279, Roll 17

District of Columbia

Agricultural

1850, M1793, Roll 1

1860, M1793, Roll 1

1870, M1793, Roll 1

1880, M1794, Roll 1

Dependent, Defective, and Delinquent

1880, M1795, Roll 1

Industry/Manufacturers

1820, M279, Roll 17

1850, M1793, Roll 1

1860, M1793, Roll 1

1870, M1793, Roll 1

1880, M1795, Roll 1

Mortality

1850, index and schedules, T655, Roll 5; schedules, M1793, Roll 1

1860, index and schedules, T655, Roll 5

1870, index and schedules, T655, Roll 5

1880, index and schedules, T655, Roll 6

Social Statistics

1850, M1793, Roll 1

1860, M1793, Roll 1

1870, M1793, Roll 1

Florida

Agricultural

1850, T1168, Roll 1

1860, T1168, Roll 3

1870, T1168, Roll 5

1880, T1168, Rolls 7–8

1885, State Census, M845, Rolls 1–13*

Industry/Manufacturers

1850, T1168, Roll 2

1860, T1168, Roll 4

1870, T1168, Roll 6

1880, T1168, Roll 9

1885, State Census, M845, Rolls 1–13*

Mortality

1885, State Census, M845, Rolls 1–13*

*The schedules of the Florida State Census of 1885 are arranged alphabetically by county, thereunder by the type of schedule—population, agriculture, manufacturers, and mortality—and thereunder by enumeration district, precinct, or city. Population schedules exist for all but Alachua, Clay, Columbia, and Nassau Counties. For some of the counties there are no schedules for agriculture, manufacturers, or mortality. A schedule for social statistics was authorized but not taken. The census was taken June 1, 1885.

Georgia

Agricultural

1850, T1137, Rolls 1–3

1860, T1137, Rolls 4–6

1870, T1137, Rolls 7–9

1880, T1137, Rolls 10–20

Defective, Dependent, and Delinquent Classes

1880, T1137, Roll 26

Industry/Manufacturers

1820, M279, Roll 19

1880, T1137, Rolls 21–22

Mortality

1850, index and schedules, T655, Roll 7

1860, index and schedules, T655, Roll 8

1870, index and schedules, T655, Roll 9

1880, schedules, T655, Rolls 10–12

Social Statistics

1850, T1137, Roll 23

1860, T1137, Roll 24

1870, T1137, Roll 25

Illinois

Agricultural

1850, T1133, Rolls 1–4

1860, T1133, Rolls 5–11

1865, T1133, Rolls 12–13

1870, T1133, Rolls 13–23

1880, T1133, Rolls 32–56

Industry/Manufacturers

1820, M279, Roll 27

1860, T1133, Roll 30

1870, T1133, Rolls 30–31

1880, T1133, Rolls 24–29

Mortality

1850, T1133, Roll 58

1860, T1133, Rolls 58-59
1870, T1133, Roll 59-60
1880, T1133, Rolls 60-64
Social Statistics
1860, T1133, Roll 57
1870, T1133, Roll 15

Indiana
Manufacturers
1820, M279, Roll 20

Iowa
Agricultural
1850, T1156, Roll 1
1860, T1156, Rolls 2-5
1870, T1156, Rolls 6-14
1880, T1156, Rolls 15-36
Industry/Manufacturers
1850, T1156, Roll 37
1860, T1156, Roll 38
1870, T1156, Rolls 39-41
1880, T1156, Rolls 42-45
Mortality
1850, T1156, Roll 54
1860, T1156, Roll 55
1870, T1156, Rolls 56-58
1880, T1156, Rolls 59-62
Social Statistics
1850, T1156, Roll 46
1860, T1156, Rolls 47-48
1870, T1156, Roll 49
1880, T1156, Rolls 50-53

Kansas
Agricultural
1860, T1130, Roll 1
1870, T1130, Rolls 4, 8-12
1880, T1130, Rolls 13-38
Defective, Dependent, and Delinquent Classes
1880, T1130, Rolls 45-48
Industry/Manufacturers
1860, T1130, Roll 1
1870, T1130, Roll 4
1880, T1130, Rolls 39-41
Mortality
1860, T1130, Roll 1
1870, T1130, Rolls 3, 5*
1880, T1130, Rolls 6-7, 42-44
Social Statistics
1860, T1130, Roll 1
1865, T1130, Roll 2
1870, T1130, Roll 5
*Includes social statistics data.

Kentucky
Agricultural
1850, M1528, Rolls 1-5
1860, M1528, Rolls 6-10
1870, M1528, Rolls 11-16
1880, M1528, Rolls 17-31

Defective, Dependent, and Delinquent Classes
1880, M1528, Rolls 41-42
Industry/Manufacturers
1820, M279, Roll 20
1850, M1528, Roll 32
1860, M1528, Roll 33
1870, M1528, Roll 34
1880, M1528, Rolls 35-37
Mortality
1850, index and schedules, T655, Roll 13
1860, index and schedules, T655, Roll 14
1870, index and schedules, T655, Roll 15
1880, index and abstracts, T655, Rolls 16-17
1880, schedules, T655, Rolls 18-20
Social Statistics
1850, M1528, Roll 38
1860, M1528, Roll 39
1870, M1528, Roll 40

Louisiana
Agricultural
1850, T1136, Roll 5
1860, T1136, Roll 6
1870, T1136, Rolls 7-8, 14
1880, T1136, Rolls 9-13
Defective, Dependent, and Delinquent Classes
1880, T1136, Roll 4
Industry/Manufacturers
1820, M279, Roll 27
1880, T1136, Roll 15
Mortality
1850, index and schedules, T655, Roll 21
1860, index and schedules, T655, Roll 22
1870, index and schedules, T655, Roll 23
1880, index, abstracts, schedules, T655, Roll 24
1880, schedules, T655, Roll 25
Social Statistics
1850, T1136, Roll 1
1860, T1136, Roll 2
1870, T1136, Roll 3

Maine
Industry/Manufacturers
1820, M279, Roll 1

Maryland
Agricultural
1850, City and County of Baltimore, M1799, Roll 1;
Worcester Co., M1793, Roll 1
1860, City of Baltimore, M1799, Roll 1
Industry/Manufacturers
1820, M279, Roll 16
1850, City and County of Baltimore, M1799, Roll 1
1860, City of Baltimore, M1799, Roll 1
Social Statistics
1850, City and County of Baltimore, M1799, Roll 1

Massachusetts
Agricultural
1850, T1204, Rolls 1-4

1860, T1204, Rolls 11–14
1870, T1204, Rolls 18–20
1880, T1204, Rolls 24–29
Defective, Dependent, and Delinquent Classes
1880, T1204, Rolls 33–36
Industry/Manufacturers
1820, M279, Roll 2
1850, T1204, Rolls 5–6
1860, T1204, Roll 15
1870, T1204, Roll 21
1880, T1204, Rolls 30–32
Mortality
1850, T1204, Rolls 9–10
1850, T1204, Roll 10
1860, T1204, Roll 17
1870, T1204, Rolls 22–23
1880, T1204, Rolls 37–40
Social Statistics
1850, T1204, Rolls 7–8
1860, T1204, Roll 16
1870, T1204, Roll 22

Michigan
Agricultural
1850, T1164, Rolls 1–4
1860, T1164, Rolls 7–12
1870, T1164, Rolls 16–23
1880, T1164, Rolls 28–63
Industry/Manufacturers
1820, M279, Roll 27
1850, T1164, Roll 5
1860, T1164, Roll 13
1870, T1164, Rolls 24–25
1880, T1164, Rolls 64–68
Mortality
1850, T1163, Roll 1
1860, T1164, Roll 15
1870, T1164, Rolls 26–27
1880, T1164, Rolls 74–77
Social Statistics
1850, T1164, Roll 6
1860, T1164, Roll 14
1870, T1164, Roll 25
1880, T1164, Rolls 69–73

Minnesota
Agricultural
1860, M1802, Roll 1

Missouri
Industry/Manufacturers
1820, M279, Roll 27

Montana
Agricultural
1870, M1806, Roll 1
1880, M1794, Roll 1
Defective, Dependent, and Delinquent Classes
1880, M1806, Roll 1
Industry/Manufacturers

1870, M1806, Roll 1
1880, M1806, Roll 1
Mortality
1870, M1806, Roll 1
1880, M1806, Roll 1
Social Statistics
1870, M1806, Roll 1

Nebraska
Agricultural
1860, T1128, Roll 2 [Roll 1 of T1128 is a population schedule.]
1870, T1128, Rolls 3–4
1880, T1128, Rolls 5–12
1885, State Census, M352, Rolls 1–56*
Defective, Dependent, and Delinquent Classes
1880, T1128, Roll 16
Industry/Manufacturers
1860, T1128, Roll 2
1870, T1128, Roll 4
1880, T1128, Roll 13
1885, State Census, M352, Rolls 1–56*
Mortality
1860, T1128, Roll 2
1870, T1128, Rolls 3–4
1880, T1128, Rolls 14–15
1885, State Census, M352, Rolls 1–56*
Social Statistics
1860, T1128, Roll 2
1870, T1128, Roll 4
*The schedules for the Nebraska State Census of 1885 are arranged alphabetically by county, thereunder numerically by enumeration district. Within each enumeration district, the schedules appear in the following order: population, agriculture, manufacturers, mortality. A schedule for social statistics was authorized but not taken. The census was taken August 19, 1885.

Nevada
Agricultural
1880, M1794, Roll 1

New Hampshire
Industry/Manufacturers
1820, M279, Roll 1

New Jersey
Industry/Manufacturers
1820, M279, Roll 17
Mortality
1850, M1810, Roll 1
1860, M1810, Roll 1
1870, M1810, Rolls 1–2
1880, M1810, Rolls 2–4

New Mexico
Agricultural
1885, M846, Rolls 1–6
Industry/Manufacturers
1885, M846, Rolls 1–6
Mortality

1885, M846, Rolls 1–6

The schedules for the New Mexico State Census of 1885 are arranged alphabetically by county, thereunder by the type of schedule—population, agriculture, manufacturers, and mortality—and thereunder numerically by enumeration district. A schedule for social statistics was authorized but not taken. The census was taken June 1, 1885.

New York

Industry/Manufacturers

    1810, M1792, Roll 1

    1820, M279, Rolls 5–11

North Carolina

Industry/Manufacturers

    1820, M279, Roll 19

    1850, M1805, Roll 6

    1860, M1805, Roll 2

    1870, M1805, Roll 7

    1880, M1805, Rolls 8–9

Mortality

    1850, M1805, Roll 1

    1860, M1805, Roll 2

    1870, M1805, Roll 3*

    1880, M1805, Rolls 4–5

*Roll 3 includes retakes of the following: 1870 Agricultural schedules, Duplin Co., Faison's Twp., pp. 6–7, and Columbus Co., Whiteville Twp., pp. 2–3; 1870 Mortality schedules, McDowell Co., Dysartsville Twp., p. 447, and Yadkin Co, Fanbush Twp., p. 788.

Ohio

Agricultural

    1850, T1159, Rolls 1–11

    1860, T1159, Rolls 16–27

    1870, T1159, Rolls 31–43

    1880, T1159, Rolls 49–92

Defective, Dependent, and Delinquent Classes

    1880, T1159, Rolls 99–101

Industry/Manufacturers

    1820, M279, Rolls 21–25

    1850, T1159, Rolls 12–13

    1860, T1159, Roll 28

    1870, T1159, Rolls 44–48

    1880, T1159, Rolls 93–98

Mortality

    1850, T1159, Rolls 14–15

    1860, T1159, Rolls 29–30

    1880, T1159, Rolls 102–104

Pennsylvania

Agricultural

    1850, T1138, Rolls 1–9

    1860, T1138, Rolls 10–19

    1870, T1138, Rolls 20–30A

    1880, T1138, Rolls 31–57

Defective, Dependent, and Delinquent Classes

    1880, M597, Rolls 10–23

Industry/Manufacturers

    1820, M279, Rolls 12–15

    1850, T1157, Rolls 1–5

    1860, T1157, Rolls 6–9

    1870, M1796, Rolls 1–4

    1880, M1796, Rolls 4–9

Mortality

    1850, M1838, Rolls 1–2

    1860, M1838, Rolls 3–4

    1870, M1838, Rolls 5–7

    1880, M1838, Rolls 8–11

Social Statistics

    1850, M597, Rolls 1–5

    1860, M597, Rolls 6–8

    1870, M597, Rolls 9

Rhode Island

Industry/Manufacturers

    1820, M279, Roll 2

South Carolina

Industry/Manufacturers

    1820, M279, Roll 19

Tennessee

Agricultural

    1850, T1135, Rolls 1–5

    1860, T1135, Rolls 6–10

    1870, T1135, Rolls 11–16

    1880, T1135, Rolls 17–29

Defective, Dependent, and Delinquent Classes

    1880, T1135, Rolls 39–40

Industrial/Manufacturers

    1820, M279, Rolls 26–27

    1850, T1135, Roll 30

    1860, T1135, Roll 31

    1870, T1135, Roll 32 [No Roll 33 for T1135.]

    1880, T1135, Rolls 34–35

Mortality

    1850, index and schedules, T655, Roll 26

    1860, index and schedules, T655, Roll 27

    1880, schedules, T655, Rolls 28–30

Social Statistics

    1850, T1135, Roll 36

    1860, T1135, Roll 37

    1870, T1135, Roll 38

Texas

Agricultural

    1850, T1134, Rolls 2–3 [No Roll 1 for T1134.]

    1860, T1134, Rolls 3–7

    1870, T1134, Rolls 7–12

    1880, T1134, Rolls 13–44

Defective, Dependent, and Delinquent Classes

    1880, T1134, Roll 49–53

Industry/Manufacturers

    1850, T1134, Roll 45

    1860, T1134, Rolls 45–46

    1870, T1134, Rolls 47–49

Mortality

    1850, T1134, Rolls 53–54

1860, T1134, Rolls 54-55
1870, T1134, Rolls 55-56
1880, T1134, Rolls 56-60
Social Statistics
1850, T1134, Roll 44
1860, T1134, Rolls 44-45
1870, T1134, Roll 45

Utah
Mortality
1870, M1807, Roll 1

Vermont
Agricultural
1850, M1798, Rolls 1-2
1860, M1798, Rolls 3-4
1870, M1798, Rolls 5-6
Industry/Manufacturers
1820, M279, Roll 3
1850, M1798, Roll 7
1860, M1798, Roll 8
1870, M1798, Roll 8
Mortality
1870, M1807, Roll 1

Virginia
Agricultural
1850, T1132, Rolls 1-3
1860, T1132, Rolls 5-8; M1808 (Northern District of Halifax County only), Roll 1
1870, T1132, Rolls 11-14, 17
1880, T1132, Rolls 20-30
Defective, Dependent, and Delinquent Classes
1880, T1132, Rolls 33-34
Industry/Manufacturers
1820, M279, Roll 18
1850, T1132, Roll 4
1860, T1132, Roll 8; M1808 (Northern District of Halifax County only), Roll 1
1870, T1132, Roll 15
1880, T1132, Rolls 31-32
Mortality
1850, T1132, Roll 1
1860, T1132, Roll 5; M1808 (Northern District of Halifax County only), Roll 1
1870, T1132, Roll 10
1880, T1132, Rolls 18-19
Social Statistics
1850, T1132, Roll 4
1860, T1132, Roll 9; M1808 (Northern District of Halifax County only), Roll 1
1870, T1132, Roll 16

Washington
Agricultural
1860, A1154, Roll 1
1870, A1154, Roll 4
1880, A1154, Roll 6
Defective, Dependent, and Delinquent Classes
1880, A1154, Roll 8

Industry/Manufacturers
1860, A1154, Roll 2
1870, A1154, Roll 5
1880, A1154, Roll 7
Mortality
1860, A1154, Roll 3
1870, A1154, Roll 3
1880, A1154, Roll 3
Social Statistics
1860, A1154, Roll 2
1870, A1154, Roll 5

Wyoming
Agricultural
1880, M1794, Roll 1

2.1 Introduction

The records of arrivals of persons entering the United States at seaports and at the U.S.-Canadian and U.S.-Mexican land borders are a rich, widely used source of genealogical information. Immigration records available from NARA consist of customs passenger lists, transcripts and abstracts of customs passenger lists, immigration passenger lists, crew lists, lists and/or card records of land border crossings, and indexes to some of these lists and/or card records. Captains or masters of vessels primarily created passenger and crew lists prior to arrival at the ports of entry in order to comply with Federal laws; U.S. immigration officials mostly created records at U.S. land borders. These records are an important genealogical resource because they document a high percentage of the immigration during the century between 1815 and 1914, the period during which the majority of immigrants came to the United States.

Most of these records are in Records of the U.S. Customs Service, Record Group (RG) 36, or in the Records of the Immigration and Naturalization Service, RG 85. Table 3 shows the ports with existing lists and indexes that are available as NARA microfilm publications.

2.1.1 Limitations of Immigration Records

Most immigration records document the period between 1820 and 1957. NARA has no records relating to immigration during the colonial period. A few early lists are dated 1798, but the lists before 1819 are primarily baggage lists or cargo manifests that also happen to include the names of passengers. Although such manifests are very fragmentary, some have been included in the microfilm publications to make coverage for a particular port as complete as possible. For only a very few ports do the records span the entire 1820–1957 period; for most ports, records cover only parts of that period. In Table 3 the lists are not necessarily complete for the years shown; there may be gaps in coverage.

Contributing to the difficulty of using the records of passenger arrivals are their physical characteristics. They were written by several different individuals over many years, and the conditions of their preservation before they were placed in NARA were not ideal. For this reason researchers must use microfilm copies of the lists if they have been prepared. In addition, many of the original customs lists are no longer in NARA but have been transferred to Balch Institute for Ethnic Studies, 18 South 7th St., Philadelphia, PA 19106. Also, many 20th-century immigration records were destroyed by the Immigration and Naturalization Service (INS) after they filmed them, and those records now exist only on microfilm.

Finally, records of ship passenger and land border arrivals are voluminous. As a result, the researcher must have basic information about the immigrant and their arrival in order to undertake a successful search for the arrival record.

2.1.2 Search Strategy

In order to locate an individual's immigration record, the researcher must have five basic pieces of information:

(1) The immigrant's full name at the time of immigration. This name may or may not be different from the one the immigrant used later in the United States. The immigrant's name was recorded on the ship passenger list by a ship employee prior to departure from the port of embarkation or later aboard ship. The researcher should be aware that the name recorded on the ship passenger list may be spelled differently due to one or more causes: the immigrant may not have been able to spell their own name; the ship employee may not have been able to speak or write the immigrant's language and consequently misunderstood and miswrote the name; or it could have been simple carelessness by the ship employee. The researcher should also have a basic understanding of the spelling of names in the immigrant's language and other relevant languages. For example, a Bohemian immigrant known in the United States as John Polak might have his first name recorded on a passenger list as Jan (from his native Czech language) or as Johan, Johannes, or Hans (from the German ship employee's native language).

(2) The immigrant's date of birth. At the very least, the researcher must know the immigrant's actual or approximate year of birth in order to distinguish between immigrants of the same name.

(3) The immigrant's ethnic group. The researcher must know the immigrant's ethnic group, such as English, Polish, German, Jewish, Mexican, or Russian. In addition, the researcher must have a basic understanding of the political history of the area from which the immigrant came. For example, if the immigrant was Polish, the researcher should know that during the 19th and early 20th centuries Poland, or parts of it, were claimed by the Austro-Hungarian Empire, Germany, and Russia. Thus, a 1912 passenger list could record the "race" (ethnic group) of a Polish immigrant from Galicia as "Polish" and the "country of origin" as "Austria." Earlier passenger lists might simply record such a Polish immigrant as being from "Austria." A researcher who lacks an understanding of such political history is more likely to fail to locate the desired immigration record. Census records, described in Chapter 1, will indicate the person's country of birth, ethnic group, and/or native tongue. In addition, knowing the immigrant's ethnic group and/or country of origin may assist in narrowing the search for the immigrant's vessel, as described in the next section under "Vessel Registers."

(4) The immigrant's date of immigration. The more specific information the researcher has, the more likely the immigration record will be found. For ports of arrival for which indexes exist, the researcher should know the

LIST OF ALL THE PASSENGERS

Taken on board the *Brig Henry Clay* — of *New York* — in any foreign Port or Place.

Names of Passengers.	Ages.	Sex.	Occupation.	Country to which they belong.	Country of which they intend to become inhabitants	Died on the Voyage
John Leget	32 years	Male	Painter & Glazier	England	State of Indiana	
Hannah Leget	28 "	Female	None	"	"	
John Alford	25 "	Male	Sails Maker	"	"	
Ann Alford	25 "	Female	none	"	"	
John Elston	25 "	Male	Paper Maker	"	"	
Sarah Elston	30 "	Female	None	"	"	
Hannah Jones	48 "	"	"	"	"	
Jacob Jones	22 "	Male	Labourer	"	"	
Elizabeth Jones	14 "	Female	none	"	"	
Mary Jones	12 "	"	"	"	"	
Charlotte Jones	6 "	"	"	"	"	
William Jones	8 "	Male	"	"	"	
Jacob Alford	2 "	"	"	"	"	
Israel Alford	7 months	"	"	"	"	
John Elston Junr	6 "	"	"	"	"	
Sand Rogers	35 years	Female	"	"	"	
Sarah Rogers	14 "	"	"	"	"	
Elizabeth Rogers	12 "	"	"	"	"	
Stephen Rogers	10 "	Male	"	"	"	
Thomas Rogers	8 "	"	"	"	"	
Wm Rogers	6 "	"	"	"	"	
Mary Rogers	3 "	Female	"	"	"	
John Rogers	6 months	Male	"	"	"	
Richard Seamore	50 years	"	Mariner	"	"	
Elizabeth Seamore	50 "	Female	None	"	"	
George Seamore	20 "	Male	Mariner	"	"	
Sand Seamore	14 "	Female	None	"	"	
Richard Seamore Jr	9 "	Male	"	"	"	
Henry Seamore	7 "	"	"	"	"	
Solomon Seamore	2 "	"	"	"	"	
Wm Hardy	30 "	"	Mariner	"	"	
Sarah Hardy	30 "	Female	None	"	"	
John Hardy	7 "	Male	"	"	"	
Sarah Hardy Jr	5 "	Female	"	"	"	
John Lander	34 "	Male	Cabinett Maker	"	"	
Sarah Lander	38 "	Female	None	"	"	
Thomas Lander	9 "	Male	"	"	"	
Mary Lander	1 "	Female	"	"	"	
Louiza Cudliss	38 "	"	"	"	"	
Frederick Cudliss	11 "	Male	"	"	"	
Louiza Cudliss Jr	13 "	Female	"	"	"	
John Cudliss		Male	"	"	"	
George Cudliss	4 "	"	"	"	"	
Eliza Cudliss	17 "	Female	"	"	"	
Elizabeth Lander	25 "	"	"	"	"	
Michael Labera	35 "	Male	Physician	Paris France	Philada	
Flora Langsley	60 "	Female	none	"	"	
Thomas Medford	45 "	Male	Farmer	England	"	

Havre de Grace

signed Wm Bedell Jr

Sept. 4. 1820.

immigrant's approximate year of immigration. For ports of arrival for which no index exists, the researcher should at least narrow the search to a particular month and year. The 1900 and 1920 censuses, described in Chapter 1, indicate the year of immigration. Naturalization records, described in Chapter 3, may provide the alien's full name and the date and port of arrival in the United States. Other sources, such as family information, newspaper obituaries, and 19th-century county histories, may also indicate an immigrant's month and year of immigration.

(5) The immigrant's port of arrival. The researcher can guess the port of entry. If the port of entry is not known, the researcher should begin their search in the indexes for indexed ports before attempting to search the records of unindexed ports. For example, if the immigrant arrived between 1847 and June 1896, the researcher should first search indexes of passenger arrivals at the ports of Baltimore, Boston, New Orleans, Philadelphia, and the miscellaneous Atlantic and Gulf Coast ports before attempting to locate an individual in the passenger lists for the port of New York, since there is no comprehensive index for arrivals at New York, 1847-June 1896. Available indexes are discussed in greater detail in the next section.

2.1.3 Indexes and Research Aids

Microfilmed Indexes

Many of the records are indexed. For example, alphabetical card indexes to customs passenger lists were compiled in the mid-1930s for the INS by the Work Projects Administration (WPA) and the National Youth Administration. Microfilmed WPA indexes exist for lists to Baltimore, 1820-97; Boston, 1848-91; New York, 1820-46; and Philadelphia, 1800-1906. In addition, M334, *Supplemental Index to Passenger Lists of Vessels Arriving at Atlantic and Gulf Coast Ports (Excluding New York), 1820-1874*, 188 rolls, provides an incomplete index to arrivals at 75 more ports. Indexes also exist for some Canadian and Mexican land border ports.

In general, microfilmed indexes consist of cards that show the following information for each person: name, age, sex, marital status, occupation, nationality, last permanent residence, destination, port of entry, name of vessel, and date of arrival. The indexes may contain all the information sought about the arrival of a passenger, but they are not necessarily complete or infallible. An indexer may have made errors in transcribing information from the lists. When possible, the information should be verified by examination of the microfilmed immigration record.

Published Indexes and Finding Aids

A growing number of published indexes, created by private individuals and organizations, supplement the microfilmed indexes noted above and in Table 3. These can be found in libraries with genealogical collections. They are

especially helpful for the period before January 1, 1820, which has few Federal passenger lists, and for the period 1847-June 1896, which has no comprehensive index for arrivals at the port of New York.

One comprehensive annotated bibliography of sources that is particularly useful is *Immigrant Arrivals: A Guide to Published Sources*, revised edition, by Virginia Steele Wood (Washington: Library of Congress, 1997).

Colonial Period through 1819

Among the many finding aids for the colonial period through 1819 and some later years, *see* P. William Filby, *Passenger and Immigration Lists Bibliography, 1538-1900, Being a Guide to Published Lists of Arrivals in the United States and Canada*, 2nd edition (Detroit: Gale Research Co., 1988). This is a revision and enlargement of Harold Lancour, *A Bibliography of Ship Passenger Lists*, 3rd edition (New York: New York Public Library, 1963). In the 1980s P. William Filby and Mary K. Meyer launched a project to consolidate all known published passenger and naturalization lists, as well as other lists of American residents of foreign birth, which they have published as *Passenger and Immigration Lists Index: A Guide to Published Arrival Records of ... Passengers Who Came to The United States and Canada in the Seventeenth, Eighteenth, and Nineteenth Centuries* (Detroit: Gale Research Co., 1981-), 3 volumes plus annual supplements totalling over 2.25 million names to date. In addition, some finding aids to pre-1819 Irish passengers include Brian Mitchell, *Irish Passenger Lists, 1803-1806: Lists of Passengers Sailing from Ireland to America Extracted from the Hardwicke Papers* (Baltimore: Genealogical Publishing Co., 1995), and Donald M. Schlegel, *Passengers from Ireland: Lists of Passengers Arriving at American Ports Between 1811 and 1817* (Baltimore: Genealogical Publishing Co., 1980).

19th Century

In addition to Filby and Meyer's *Passenger and Immigration Lists Index*, useful indexes to 19th-century arrivals at New York and elsewhere include:

Glazier, Ira A., and P. William Filby. *Germans to America: Lists of Passengers Arriving at U.S. Ports, 1850-*. 60 vols. to date, through May 1891. Wilmington, DE: Scholarly Resources, 1988- .

Glazier, Ira A. *Migration from the Russian Empire: Lists of Passengers Arriving at the Port of New York, 1875-*. 6 vols. to date, through June 1891. Baltimore: Genealogical Publishing Co., 1995- .

Glazier, Ira A., and P. William Filby. *Italians to America: Lists of Passengers Arriving at U.S. Ports, 1880-1899*. 9 vols. Wilmington, DE: Scholarly Resources, 1992.

Glazier, Ira A., and Michael Tepper. *The Famine Immigrants: Lists of Irish Immigrants Arriving at the Port of New York, 1846-1851*. 7 vols. Baltimore: Genealogical Publishing Co., 1983.

Mitchell, Brian. *Irish Emigration Lists, 1833-1839: Lists of Emigrants Extracted from the Ordnance Survey Memoirs for Counties Londonderry and Antrim.* Baltimore: Genealogical Publishing Co., 1989.

Olsson, Nils William, and Erik Wiken. *Swedish Passenger Arrivals in U.S. Ports, 1820-1850.* Stockholm: Schmidts Boktryckeri AB, 1995.

Swierenga, Robert P., comp. *Dutch Immigrants in U.S. Ship Passenger Manifests, 1820-1880:An Alphabetical Listing by Household Heads and Independent Persons.* 2 vols.Wilmington, DE: Scholarly Resources, 1983.

Vessel Registers

If the name of the port of entry and the approximate arrival date are known, it may be possible to determine the exact date and the name of the vessel from records of vessel entrances maintained at the ports. These records, which are in RG 36, show the name of each vessel, its captain, the port of embarkation, and date of arrival. For some ports there are two series, one with entries arranged alphabetically by name of vessel, and the other with entries arranged chronologically. If, in addition to the port of entry and approximate date of arrival, the port of embarkation is known, the search for the vessel's name and exact date of arrival may be facilitated. For example, if a passenger embarked from Stockholm for New York in a year in which 500 passenger vessels arrived in New York, the search could be narrowed to the relatively few passenger lists for vessels sailing from Stockholm. Sometimes the port listed as the port of embarkation was the last foreign port at which the vessel called, not necessarily the port at which the immigrant boarded.

NARA has lists of vessel arrivals for most U.S. seaports. Arrangement varies from list to list, but the most common are alphabetically by name of vessel or chronologically by date of arrival. Often more than one type of list exists for a specific period. Most lists contain at least the date of entry, the name, country of origin, type and rig of vessel, the master's name, and the last port of embarkation. The lists for the port of New York have been microfilmed as M1066, *Registers of Vessels Arriving at the Port of New York From Foreign Ports 1789-1919,* 27 rolls.

The *Morton Allan Directory of European Passenger Steamship Arrivals* (New York: Immigrant Information Bureau, Inc., 1931; reprinted Baltimore: Genealogical Publishing Co., 1979) contains information concerning vessels arriving at the ports of New York, 1890-1930, and at Baltimore, Boston, and Philadelphia, 1904-26. It lists by year the name of the steamship company and by exact date the names of vessels arriving at these ports. Note, however, that Morton Allan shows some dates of arrival a day or two earlier or later than the actual arrival date, and not all ship arrivals are listed.

2.1.4 Obtaining Copies of Immigration Records from NARA

Obtaining copies from NARA

Copies of immigration records can be ordered through the mail by using a National Archives Trust Fund form, which may be obtained from the Customer Service Center, National Archives and Records Administration, Rm. 406, 700 Pennsylvania Ave., NW, Washington, DC 20408-0001. Copies of this form can also be requested by email at *inquire@nara.gov.*

Research facilities

Microfilmed immigration records are available for inspection during regular research hours at the National Archives Building, 700 Pennsylvania Ave., Washington, DC 20408. Consult the National Archives web site at *www.nara.gov* for the hours of operation. Selected microfilmed records are also available at NARA regional facilities and at many public libraries and other facilities with genealogical collections. *See* Table 1 in the introduction to this volume for the location of NARA's regional archives.

2.2 Types of Immigration Records

2.2.1 Customs Passenger Lists

An act of 1819 (3 Stat. 489) and later acts required the master of a ship entering an American port from a foreign port to file a list of passengers with the district collector of customs. The records, known as customs passenger lists, may be in the form of original lists or copies, abstracts, or transcripts of these lists. They are part of the Records of the U.S Customs Service in RG 36.

Original lists exist only for a few ports. The general date span for original lists is 1820-1902, but New Orleans is the only port for which every year of the entire period is covered. An original list was prepared on board ship, sworn to by the master of the vessel, and filed with the collector of customs when the ship arrived at the port. It usually contains the following information: name of vessel, name of master, port of embarkation, date of arrival, port of arrival, and for each passenger, their name, age, sex, occupation, country of origin, country of intended settlement, and date and circumstances of death en route, if applicable. The information about passengers was recorded for immigrants, tourists, and U.S. citizens returning from abroad.

Copies and abstracts of original customs passenger lists were made in the offices of the collectors of customs and were usually sent once each quarter to the Secretary of State in accordance with the 1819 act that generated the original lists. Some collectors prepared copies of the individual lists, and other prepared abstracts, which are consolidated lists of names of all passengers who arrived at a given port during the quarter. The practice at each port varied from time to time. The general date span for copies and abstracts is 1820-1905, but for no port do these exist for every year of that period.

The copies of the customs passenger lists usually contain the vessel's name, port of embarkation, port of arrival, and sometimes name of master and date of arrival. The abstracts usually contain the name of the district or port, quarter-year of arrival, and sometimes the port of embarkation. Copies and abstracts contain for each passenger the same information that is found in the original lists, but some information may be abbreviated. For example, some copies and abstracts show only the initials of the given names of passengers.

State Department Transcripts of lists, 1819-32 (8 vols.), were apparently prepared at the Department of State from copies or abstracts sent to the Secretary of State by the collectors of customs. At one time there were 9 volumes, but volume 2 is missing.

Entries are arranged by the quarter-year of arrival, thereunder by district or port (apparently randomly arranged), thereunder by name of vessel, and thereunder by name of passenger. Each entry typically shows the name of the custom house (district or port), ending date of the quarter, name of ship or vessel, and the following information about each passenger: name, age, sex, occupation, "country to which they belong," "country of which they intend becoming inhabitants," and whether the person died on the voyage. The bulk of the records are for 1820-27. Fewer records were transcribed in 1828-32; and no transcript was made for the period October 1831-September 1832. Less than 30 passengers were recorded for 1819.

All entries in volume 1 and some entries from the missing volume 2 were printed in *Letter from the Secretary of State, with a Transcript of the List of Passengers Who Arrived in the United States from the 1st October, 1819, to the 30th September, 1820* (S. Doc. 118, 16th Cong., 2d sess., serial 45).

Entries in volumes 5, 8, and 9 (excluding those for New York City) were indexed as part of M334, *Supplemental Index to Passenger Lists of Vessels Arriving at Atlantic and Gulf Coast Ports (Excluding New York), 1820-1874*, mentioned above. Volume 5 contains the quarters ending December 31, 1824, through September 30, 1825, and part of the transcript for the quarter ending September 30, 1824. Volumes 8 and 9 contain the quarters ending June 30, 1827, through December 31, 1832, and part of the transcript for the quarter ending March 31, 1827.

A card index prepared by NARA staff before 1960, which is arranged alphabetically by port or district of arrival, identifies the date of arrival (given as the ending date of the quarter-year of arrival), volume number, and beginning page number upon which the district or port's arrivals are found in the volumes.

The State Department transcripts are not entirely free from errors. They are, however, especially useful when they include information from lists not otherwise in existence.

For example, information about New York arrivals during the second quarter of 1820 is not otherwise available; nor are there any original lists or copies for 1819, except for New Orleans. The law providing for the creation of customs passenger lists did not go into effect until January 1, 1820, but a few collectors apparently reported arrivals beginning on October 1, 1819.

The eight volumes of State Department Transcripts, the card index, and the *Letter from the Secretary of State* have all been reproduced as T1219, *State Department Transcripts of Passenger Lists, ca. October 1819-ca. December 1832*, 2 rolls.

2.2.2 Immigration Passenger Lists

An act of 1882 (22 Stat. 214) established procedures for recording the arrival of immigrants in the United States. The records maintained by Federal immigration officials are often called **immigration passenger lists or manifests.** NARA has microfilm copies of these lists, dated generally 1883-1957. The INS began enforcing Federal immigration acts after its creation in 1891; the 1882 act was enforced by state governments under contract to the Customs Service. Some of these pre-1891 lists were inherited by the INS and were subsequently transferred to NARA as a part of the Records of the Immigration and Naturalization Service in RG 85.

Microfilm copies of the immigration passenger lists vary in informational content. For the earliest lists, which are for Philadelphia in 1883, immigration officials used Pennsylvania state forms. They contain the following information: name of master, name of vessel, ports of arrival and embarkation, date of arrival, and, for each passenger, name, place of birth, last legal residence, age, occupation, sex, and remarks. Forms prescribed by Federal law soon came into use, and by 1893 an immigration passenger list included name of master, name of vessel, ports of arrival and embarkation, date of arrival, and the following information for each passenger: full name; age; sex; marital status; occupation; nationality; last residence; final destination; whether in the United States before, and if so, when and where; and whether going to join a relative, and if so, the relative's name, address, and relationship to the passenger. The format of the immigration passenger list was revised in 1903 to include race, in 1906 to include a personal description and birthplace, and in 1907 to include the name and address of the nearest relative in the immigrant's home country.

Immigration passenger lists include the names not only of immigrants but also of visitors and U.S. citizens returning from abroad. For some ports, there are separate lists for aliens and for citizens; such a distinction is shown in Table 3, if appropriate. For the most part, lists of aliens include the same information as that discussed above. Lists of citizens show for each passenger, name, age, sex, and marital status; date and place of birth if born in the United

SALOON, CABIN, AND STEERAGE ALIENS MUST BE COMPLE
THIS SHEET IS FOR SECOND-CABIN PASSENG

LIST OR MANIFEST OF ALIEN PASSENGERS FOR THE U. S. IMMIGR

Required by the regulations of the Secretary of the Treasury of the United States, under Act of Congress approved March 3
Officer of any vessel having such passengers on board upon arrival at a p

S.S. _St. Louis_ sailing from _Cherbourg_, _9th Mar_, 1907 Arriving a

No. on List	NAME IN FULL	Age. Yrs. Mos.	Married or Single.	Sex.	Calling or Occupation.	Able to— Read.	Write.	Nationality. (Country of last permanent residence.)	*Race or People.	Last Residence. (Province, City, or Town.)	Final Destination. (State, City, or Town.)	Whether having a ticket to such final destination.	By whom was passage paid?	Whether in possession of $50, and if less, how much?
1	Michael Kulganus	25	m.	S	Restauranteur	yes		Greek	Greek	Chicago	Chicago Il.	no	self	$30
2	Angeliki A. Poulitsa	20	F	S	—	yes	yes	do	do	Geraki, Sparta	Dayton Ohio	no	do	$50
3	Helen A. Poulitsa	20	F	S	—	no	no							$40
4	Anastasia G. Geralon	25	M	S	—	yes	yes	—	—	Sparta	New York	yes	"	$10
5	John P. Trempelis	19	M	S	labourer			—	—	—	Harriburg Penn	"		$20
6	Antonio G. Scarvounis	20	M	S				—	—	—	Cincinnati O.	yes	"	$20
7	Catingo Courlas	30	F	M	Confectioner	no	no	U.S.A						
8	Nikitas Courlas	30	M	M	"			"	—	—	—			
9	Metaxon J. Drivaki	35	F	M	—	"	"	Greek	Greek	Sparta	Cincinnati	no	self	$25
10	Caterina J. Drivaki	10	F	S	—	"	"	—	—	—	Oh.	"		
11	Geo. N. Rasmoulos	19	M	S	labourer	yes	yes	—	—	—	Chicago Ill.	"		$20
12	Demetrios C. Gianes	15	M	S	schoolboy			—	—	—				$15
13	Athanassios N. Varlas	25	M	M	labourer			NON IMMIGRANT ALIEN. Ohio	—	—		"	"	$20
14	Demetrios N. Courlas	19	M	S				—	—	—	Cincinnati	yes		$15
15	Jean G. Caramichas	20	M	S				—	—	—	O.	"		$10
16	John M. Guinis	30	M	M				—	—	—		no		$15
17	Michel N. Catirtzis	42	M	M		no	no	—	—	NON IMMIGRANT ALIEN.	—	"		$15
18	Nicolas P. Sinnis	11	M	S	schoolboy	yes	yes	—	—	—	Springfield O.	"		$15
19	Critieon Polukaenon	38	F	M		no	no	—	—	Piraeus	Chicago Ill.	"		$20
20	Nicolas P. Kayorge	11	M	S	schoolboy	yes	yes	—	—	Tinos	Cincinnati	yes	mother	$15
21	Nicolas Paradisinon	25	M	S	Confectioner	yes	yes	—	—	Patmo	NON IMMIGRANT ALIEN Peoria	no	Self	$40
22	Jean Doufacopoulos	23	M	S	Merchant	yes	yes	—	—	Tripoli	NON IMMIGRANT ALIEN Columbus Ohio	no	Self	$20
23	Elefano Megazine	46						Suias	Italian					$60
24														
25														
26														
27	John Butler	28	M	M				Citizen USA						
28														
29														
30														

* " Race or People " is to be determined by the stock from which they sprang and the language they speak. List of races wi

...red to the U. S. Immigration Officer by the Commanding
...kates.

...York March 19th, 1907   4

NOTE.—This slip must be attached to the right side of each manifest of alien passengers, Cat. Nos. 500, 500-A, and 500-B, and the information indicated by the headings given by the masters of vessels.

7

PERSONAL DESCRIPTION.

16	17		22			Height		Color of—		Marks of Identification	PLACE OF BIRTH
...ther going to join a relative or friend; and if so, ...ative or friend, and his name and complete address.	Ever in prison or institution of institution	Whether a Polyg-amist.	Whether an An-archist.	Whether able...	Condition of Health, Mental and Physical.	Deformed or Crippled. Nature, length of time, and cause.	Feet	Inches	Hair	Eyes		
business in Chicago ...taurant keeper, 17... Chicago Ill (diocese makers)	no	no	no	no	good	no	5	6	dark	dark brown	none	Athens, Greece
...her A. Poulitsas, Dayton	id	id	id	id	id	id	5	4	brown	black brown	—	Geraki Greece
...her John Poulitsa, Dayton	"	"	"	"	"	"	5	3	light	chest black	——	
...ney ...sto Gerakon, 48	"	"	"	"	"	"	5	3	brown	black brown	——	
...St. New York ...n Costas Trompelys	"	"	"	"	"	"	5	6	——	" chest	——	
Margat Str. Harrisburg Pa ...Peter Mitrin, 39 East	"	"	"	"	"	"	5	7	——	" black	——	
...street Cincinnati Ohio	"	"	"	"	"	"	5	1	——	" chest	——	
							5	7	——	" "	——	
...and John Drivaki ...oast 6th Str. Cincinnati ...er	no	no	no	no	good	no	5	0	——	" black	——	
							4	2	light	light chest	——	
...er Alex Rasmoulos, ...entworth av. Chicago Ill.	"	"	"	"	"	"	5	5	brown	black "	—	
..." "	"	"	"	"	"	"	5	0	light	chest black	—	
...er Nick Varlas, 130.-132	"	"	"	"	"	"	5	8	brown	black "	—	
...an St. Pique Ohio ...Ath N. Courlas	"	"	"	"	"	"	5	5	light	" chest	—	
...ati Ohio 419 Central str. ...Peter Courlas 507	"	"	"	"	"	"	5	8	brown	" black	—	
...str. Cincinnati Ohio ...e-in-law Gust. Courlas,	"	"	"	"	"	"	5	8	"	chest gray	—	
...ut str. Cincinnati Ohio ...in-law Jas. Mercpoulos	"	"	"	"	"	"	5	8	"	black chest	—	
...al av. Cincinnati Ohio ...Peter Jennis, High Fountain	"	"	"	"	"	"	4	10	"	" gray	—	
...ngfield Ohio ...and 39 Cottage Grove Av.	"	"	"	"	"	"	5	5	dark	dark brown	none	Sparta.
...ago Ill ...er Peter Kayorge, Walnut	"	"	"	"	"	"	4	2	brown	chest chest	—	Athens Greece
...07 Cincinnati Ohio ...d James Petrakos	"	"	"	"	"	"	5	8	"	" "	—	Patmos Turkey
...nton St. Peoria Ill ...Louis Scanto	"	"	"	"	"	"	5	1	"	Black "		Trifili
...mth High St Columbus Oh. ...near ...elita ...ury Co. California	"	"	"	"	"	"	5	4	"	" "		Switzerland

57

States; date of naturalization and name and location of court, if applicable; and current address.

Immigration passenger lists are arranged by port, thereunder chronologically. To find information about a particular individual in these voluminous records, the researcher should have the information described above in "Search Strategy" in 2.1.2.

To some extent, the immigration passenger lists are covered by microfilmed card indexes. For the ports of Boston; New York; Philadelphia; Portland, ME; and Providence, RI, there are also microfilmed book indexes, arranged by ship, thereunder in rough alphabetical order by the first letter of the passenger's surname. The book indexes are described more specifically in the special notes below.

2.2.3 Canadian and Mexican Land Border Crossing Immigration Records

When records of arrivals began to be kept at the Canadian border in 1895 and at the Mexican border, ca. 1903, immigration authorities found it impractical to collect arrival information on lists as they did for ship passengers. Therefore, separate cards or "card manifests" for each person were used instead. These cards contained the same information as that collected on traditional ship passenger arrival lists, such as full name, age, sex, marital status, occupation, point of arrival in the United States, and final destination.

In addition, the statistical treatment of Canadian and Mexican border immigrants at times has differed from that of other immigrants. Understanding the difference between "statistical" and "nonstatistical" arrivals is useful in locating a person's land border arrival record, particularly for those persons crossing the U.S.-Mexican land border. In general, immigrants will be statistical; nonimmigrants (visitors) will be nonstatistical arrivals.

Also, it is important to know that prior to September 30, 1906, records of arrivals at the Canadian and Mexican borders, respectively, consist solely of non-Canadians and non-Mexicans, respectively; after that date, all arrivals, both Canadians and non-Canadians and Mexicans and non-Mexicans, were recorded.

Immigration Statistics and Definitions

Beginning in 1895, immigrants who arrived at Canadian seaports with the declared intention of proceeding to the United States were recorded and included in immigration statistics. Other alien arrivals at land borders began to be reported in 1906, and reporting was fully established in 1908 under authority of an act of February 20, 1907 (34 Stat. 898).

Not all aliens entering via the Canadian and Mexican borders were necessarily counted for inclusion in the immigration statistics. Before approximately 1930, no count was made of residents of Canada, Newfoundland, or Mexico who had lived in those countries for a year or more if they planned to enter the United States for less than 6 months. However, from about 1930 to 1945, the following classes of aliens entering via the land borders were included in immigration statistics:

(1) Those who had not been in the United States within 6 months, who came to stay more than 6 months;

(2) Those for whom straight head tax was a prerequisite to admission, or for whom head tax was specially deposited and subsequently converted to a straight head tax account;

(3) Those required by law or regulation to present an immigration visa or reentry permit, and those who surrendered either, regardless of whether they were required by law or regulation to do so;

(4) Those announcing an intention to depart from a seaport in the United States for Hawaii or other insular possession of the United States or for a foreign country, except arrivals from Canada intending to return there by water; and

(5) Those announcing an intention to depart across the other land boundary.

These classes were revised in 1945 so that the statistics of arriving aliens at land border ports of entry for 1945–52 included arriving aliens who came into the United States for 30 days or more, and returning alien residents who had been out of the country more than 6 months. Arriving aliens who came into the United States for 29 days or less were not counted, except for those who were certified by public health officials, held for a board of special inquiry, excluded and deported, or individuals in transit who announced an intention to depart across another land boundary or by sea.

From 1953 to at least 1957, all arriving aliens at land border ports of entry were counted for statistical purposes except Canadian citizens and British subjects resident in Canada who were admitted for 6 months or less; Mexican citizens who were admitted for 72 hours or less; and returning U.S. residents who had been out of the country for more than 6 months. Beginning in February 1956, residents returning from stays of less than 6 months in Western Hemisphere countries also were not counted. Because of regulation changes in 1957, returning residents without reentry permits or visas who had been abroad for 1 year or less were not counted.

Summary. Statistical arrivals were immigrants or nonimmigrants who were subject to the head tax and generally not from the Western Hemisphere. By contrast, nonstatistical arrivals were immigrant or nonimmigrants who usually were natives of the Western Hemisphere and not subject to the head tax. Although arrival of the latter was not included in immigration statistics, a record of that arrival may still have been made. It cannot be said with certainty that the definitions of statistical and nonstatistical arrivals were applied uniformly at any particular port on the Canadian or Mexican borders.

Definitions of Immigrants and Nonimmigrants

Since 1906, arriving aliens were divided into two classes: immigrants, or those who intended to settle in the United States; and nonimmigrants, those admitted aliens who declared an intention not to settle in the United States and all aliens returning to resume domiciles formerly acquired in the United States. Since 1924 aliens arriving to settle in the United States were further classified as quota or nonquota immigrants. **Quota immigrants** were those admitted under quotas established for countries in Europe, Asia, Africa, the Pacific Basin, and the colonies, dependencies, and protectorates belonging to those nations. **Nonquota immigrants** were spouses and unmarried children of U.S. citizens; natives from the independent countries of the Western Hemisphere, their spouses, and unmarried children under 18 years of age; and members of the clergy who entered with their families to carry on their profession. From 1933 to 1952, professors and their spouses and children were also classified as nonquota immigrants. **Nonimmigrants** were alien residents of the United States returning from a temporary visit abroad, or nonresident aliens admitted to the United States for a temporary period, such as tourists, students, foreign government officials, those engaged in business, people representing international organizations, the spouses and unmarried children of all these individuals, and agricultural laborers from the West Indies.

For more information about the keeping of immigration statistics and definitions used therein, see *The Statistical History of the United States from Colonial Times to the Present* (Stamford, CT: Fairfield Publishers, Inc., ca. 1965): 48–52, or *Historical Statistics of the United States, Colonial Times to 1970*, Bicentennial Edition, Part I (Washington: U.S. Bureau of the Census, 1975): 97–120 (H. Doc. 93–78 [Part I]). For further information about immigration and naturalization laws prior to 1953, see *Laws Applicable to Immigration and Nationality*, Edwina A. Avery and Catherine R. Gibson, eds., U.S. Immigration and Naturalization Service (Washington: Government Printing Office, 1953).

Head Tax Collections

As mentioned above, some aliens were subject to **head taxes**. As a result, some of the records were annotated (H.T.) or segregated into special series to meet particular recordkeeping needs of the particular port. For example, the records of arrivals at San Ysidro, CA, include a series of "head taxes transferred to the regular fund," which refers to "special" head tax collections later designated as "general" head tax collections. The difference between "general" and "special" is explained in paragraph G of Rule 1, Collection of Head Tax, in U.S. Department of Labor, Bureau of Immigration, *Immigration Laws and Rules of July 1, 1925* (Washington: Government Printing Office, 1925): 86, as follows:

Subdivision G.—Tax designated general and special—Disposition.

Paragraph 1. Head tax is hereby designated as "general" and "special." The term "general" tax shall apply to the tax collected on account of every alien entering the United States, either directly or from the Canal Zone or any insular possession, and alien seamen regularly admitted, unless such aliens are by the provisions of the law exempt from the payment of such tax. The moneys so collected shall be deposited in the Treasury of the United States in the manner provided by law.

Paragraph 2. The term "special" tax shall apply to the tax collected on account of (1) every alien held for special inquiry and (2) every alien making unsatisfactory claim to exemption for any one of the following reasons:

(a) That he is passing in transit through the United States.

(b) That he is under 16 years of age and accompanied by either father or mother.

(c) That he is entering for temporary stay after an uninterrupted residence of at least one year immediately preceding in Canada, Newfoundland, Mexico, or Cuba.

(d) That he is a resident or citizen of a possession of the United States; i.e., the Philippine Islands, Virgin Islands, Puerto Rico, Hawaii, or Guam.

(e) That he is a citizen of the United States.

(f) That he is a seaman regularly admitted and returning from continuous round-trip voyage.

Records of "head taxes refunded" refers to head taxes collected from persons held for boards of special inquiry or collected for reasons (a)-(f) above. These persons could apply, within 90 days after entry into the United States, for a refund and submit proof of entitlement to such refund.

Forms Used

As noted above, most records of persons crossing the Canadian and Mexican land border were primarily made on "card manifests" that largely contained the same information found on traditional ship passenger lists. However, different types of card manifests were used for different purposes. This section describes the **most common forms**.

All of the forms described below usually include the person's name, age or date of birth, gender, date and port of entry into the United States, and the country of which they were a citizen ("nationality") and/or "race" (i.e., Mexican, Japanese, etc.). If the person's physical description is given, this usually includes height, complexion, hair color, eye color, and identifying marks. The reverse side of the cards may include instructions for the form's use, annotations noting dates of subsequent entries into the United States, or, in some cases, an attached individual or family photograph. Usually both the front and reverse sides of each card were microfilmed.

Form 257D, *Record of Alien Admitted for Temporary Stay*, see Form I-94.

Forms 500, 500A, and 500B, *List* or *Manifest of Alien Passengers for the U.S. Immigration Officer at Port of Arrival*, include the person's marital status, occupation, ability to read and write, town and country of last permanent residence, birthplace, physical description, final destination, and whether the individual possesses a ticket to final destination. They also include the name and address of the friend or relative the alien intends to join. If the alien was ever in the United States in the past, the dates and places of such residence or visitation are indicated. These forms were traditionally used by vessel masters to record information about ship passengers in advance of arrival at U.S. ports. The INS discontinued using them at land border ports since the lack of opportunity for advance completion made them impractical.

Form 502, an index card, includes the names of persons accompanying the individual and the port of entry. These cards are an index to "long form" (i.e., Form 548) manifests that contain additional information; thus the cards also indicate the manifest number ("list number") and line number on the manifest ("group number") where that person may be found.

Form 521, a pre-entry examination form, includes the person's place of birth, home address, and the names of any accompanying children under age 16. For aliens, the person's occupation, destination in the United States, name of the person to whom destined, and intended length of stay are also recorded. The reverse side of the card states, in part, that "This form is intended to facilitate the entry into the United States of returning United States citizens, aliens lawfully resident in the United States returning from a temporary visit to Canada, and aliens coming from Canada for a temporary visit. It should be filled out, signed, and presented to a United States immigration officer at Halifax, Yarmouth, St. John (N.B.), Quebec, Montreal, Winnipeg, Vancouver, Victory, or Sidney (B.C.)."

Form 548, 548-B, or I-448, *Manifest*, was the most commonly-used form. It generally includes the person's marital status, place of birth, physical description, occupation, ability to read and write and in what language, place of last permanent residence, destination, purpose for entering the United States, intention of becoming a U.S. citizen or of returning to country of previous residence, head tax status, and previous citizenships. It also includes the name and address of the friend or relative the alien intended to join, persons accompanying the alien, and the name and address of the alien's nearest relative or friend in the country from which they came. If the alien was ever in the United States in the past, the dates and places of such residence or visitation are indicated. Additional information may be recorded if the alien appealed a decision deporting or barring him from entering the United States. Form 548 or I-448 is generally a card manifest. However, during some periods at some ports, the INS used an entire sheet of paper for the Form 548 manifest. Both sizes generally include the same information. The reverse side of the card manifest Form 548 sometimes includes the alien's photograph, occasionally with spouse and minor children. The sheet (long form) manifests may have a manifest number handwritten or mechanically stamped near the upper right-hand corner of the form, or the manifest number may be the so-called "serial number" annotated near the upper right-hand corner.

Form 621, *Statistical*, is a detailed statistical index card that includes the person's marital status ("conj. cond"), occupation, ability to read and write, last place of residence, future place of residence, date and place of admission to the United States, place of birth, and physical description. These cards also indicate who paid the immigrant's passage, the amount of money the person brought, and the names of individuals accompanying them. The manifest number in the upper right-hand corner of these cards is used, along with the date of arrival, to locate the person's statistical manifest. In some record series, the manifest number is located to the right of the person's sex, such as F-127 (female, manifest no. 127).

Form 629, *Nonstatistical*, see Form Spl. 442.

Form 657, *Record of Registry*, includes the following information about the alien as of the alien's date of arrival: name; age; occupation; race or people; place of last residence before entry; and date, port, place, and means (i.e., ship or railway) of arrival in the United States. This form also includes the following information about the alien as of the alien's date of registry: name, age, occupation, physical description, place of residence, and place of birth. It also includes the alien's photograph, date of approval of registry, certificate of registry number, district file number, and bureau file number. Sometimes "homemade" typewritten versions of this official INS form were used; these do not indicate the form number.

Form 680 or I-480, *List* or *Manifest of Aliens Employed on the Vessel as Member of Crew*, varied over time but generally includes the name of the vessel, shipmaster or captain, ports of arrival and embarkation, date of arrival, and the following information about each crew member: position in ship's company, whether able to read, and physical description. The form also indicates the date and place at which the individual was engaged for employment and whether they were to be paid off or discharged at the port of arrival. The I-480 also generally indicates whether the immigrant inspector admitted the crew member or detained him on board the vessel. If the alien had another identification document, such as a passport or declaration of intention to become a citizen ("first papers"), that may be noted in the "remarks" column. Although the primary purpose of this form was to record pertinent information about aliens, many U.S. citizen crew members are included on these lists. Sometimes copies of Canadian immigration service forms were used in lieu of this form.

Form "Spl. 187A," *Primary Inspection Memorandum*, which was used for alien arrivals, includes person's marital status, occupation, ability to read and write and in what language, place of last permanent residence, destination, citizenship before becoming a citizen of Canada, purpose for entering United States, intention of becoming a U.S. citizen, head tax status, and previous citizenships. It also includes the name and address of the friend or relative the alien intended to join, persons accompanying the alien, and the name and address of the alien's nearest relative or friend in the country from which they came. If the alien was ever in the United States, the dates and places of such residence or visitation are indicated. Additional information may be recorded on the reverse side of the card if the alien appealed a decision barring them from entering the United States.

Form "Spl. 222," *Departure*, includes the following information about each person: marital status, occupation, ability to read and write, country of future permanent residence, country of birth, country where the person lived before coming to the United States, date and port of last arrival in United States, town and state of last residence in United States, and date and port of departure. If the person was a native-born U.S. citizen, the person's birthplace was to be noted. If the person was a naturalized U.S. citizen, the date and place of naturalization was to be noted.

Form "Spl. 259," "statistical," is a less detailed statistical index card that includes the person's last place of residence, destination, and status as immigrant or nonimmigrant. The cards also provide a BSI (Board of Special Inquiry) number. Although a manifest (list) and line number are noted at the bottom of the card, the number that is annotated to the right of the person's name is generally the "real" manifest number that is used, along with the date of arrival, to locate the person's statistical manifest. In some record series, the manifest number is located to the right of the person's sex, such as F-127 (female, manifest no. 127).

Form "Spl. 442" or Form 629, *Nonstatistical*, includes the person's marital status, occupation, ability to read and write, place of last permanent residence, and destination. It also indicates individuals accompanying the alien, the amount of money the alien is carrying, and if they have ever been in the United States. The reverse side of some cards may be annotated with dates of subsequent admissions to the United States, destination, and purpose for visiting, such as "6 days to Mission, TX, visiting."

Form I-94, I-94(C), I-94(E), or 257D, *Record of Alien Admitted for Temporary Stay*, includes the alien's date and place of birth, marital status, occupation, physical description, names of accompanying alien children under age 14, name and address of nearest relative at home, name and address of person to whom destined, purpose and intended length of U.S. visit, and means of arrival. The purpose of U.S. visit may be described in English (such as "pleasure 1 month") or as the applicable section of U.S.

immigration law (such as "B-2 72 hours" or "P1/3/2/3/8 days"). The "manifest number" is handwritten or mechanically stamped in the upper right-hand corner; it is not the "T" number in the upper right-hand corner in some record series.

Form I-189, *Application for Resident Alien's Border Crossing Identification Card*, includes the person's permanent U.S. address, date and place of birth, marital status, occupation, ability to read and write, physical description, and the means of lawful entry into the United States for permanent residence. It has the alien's signature and fingerprint or photograph. Also included are the border crossing identification card number and its date of issuance.

Form I-190, *Application for Nonresident Alien's Border Crossing Identification Card*, includes the alien's date and place of birth, marital status, occupation, ability to read and write, place of residence, physical description, purpose of U.S. visit, and fingerprint or photograph. The number, date of issuance, and place of issuance of the person's passport may be noted. Also included are the border crossing identification card number and its date of issuance.

Form I-196, *Application for U.S. Citizen Seaman's Identification Card*, includes the person's means of U.S. citizenship, i.e., birth in United States, birth abroad to U.S. citizen parent(s), or naturalization of self or parent(s); permanent home address; date and place of birth; physical description; date of application for the U.S. Citizen Seaman's Identification Card and date when it was approved; documents submitted in support of the application; U.S. Citizen Seaman's Identification Card number; and fingerprint.

Form I-407, *Land Border Departure Record*, records an alien's abandonment of lawful domicile in the United States. The form includes the person's name; age; sex; race; marital status; occupation; ability to read and write; country of citizenship; country of residence before coming to the United States; place of last permanent residence in the United States; place of intended permanent residence; alien registration number; port, date, and means (i.e., auto or railroad) of departure; date and port of most recent arrival in the United States; and place, date, and certificate number of naturalization. For aliens, certain "facts of last recorded admission for permanent residence" were to be noted, including the person's name and the port, date, and means of arrival. Other arrival dates and places or visa numbers may be noted.

Form I-448, *Manifest, see* Form 548.

Form I-480, *List* or *Manifest of Aliens Employed on the Vessel as Member of Crew, see* Form 680.

Form I-481, *List* or *Manifest of all Persons Employed on a Great Lakes Vessel*, was most used from 1946-54. This form usually contains the names of the vessel, shipmaster, ship owner, and local agent; port of embarkation; and the following information about each crew member: position in crew, whether to be discharged at the port of arrival, whether medically examined during the current season or year, and identification card number or alien registration number. It also generally indicates whether the immigrant inspector admitted the crew member or detained him on board the vessel. If the alien had another identification document, such as a passport or declaration of intention to become a citizen ("first papers"), that may be noted in the "remarks" column.

Form I-489, *Statement of Master of Vessel Regarding Changes in Crew Prior to Departure*, sometimes accompanies the Form I-480. This form indicates names and other information of any crewmen who deserted, were discharged, were left in a hospital at the port of arrival, or signed on at the port of arrival.

Arrangement of the Records

The arrangement of Canadian and Mexican land border crossing arrival records varies according to the type of record. Those records kept on traditional ship passenger lists may be arranged by port and then by date or by date and then by port.

Those records kept on card manifests are usually arranged by port, then alphabetically by soundex code, or chronologically with or without a manifest number. Chronologically arranged records usually also have a related index. In addition, card manifests for busier ports are often arranged by record series (type of record), which are usually entitled or described using one or more of these terms: statistical, nonstatistical, permanent, and temporary. Statistical and nonstatistical are defined above. "Permanent" refers to aliens intending to permanently stay in the United States; "temporary" refers to alien visitors to the United States. In general it can be said that permanent arrivals were "statistical" and temporary arrivals were "nonstatistical," but, as indicated above, the definitions of those terms were not necessarily uniformly applied.

For arrivals at Mexican border ports, alphabetically arranged card manifest records follow special rules. Generally the card manifests are arranged alphabetically by surname, thereunder by given name. Double names are filed as if the second part of the double name were not there. For example, *Jiminez De San Miguel, Petra* is filed among other persons named *Jimenez, Petra*; *Castro, Maria de los Angeles* is filed among other persons named *Castro, Maria*; and *Montalvo-Hernandez, Jose* is filed among other persons named *Montalvo, Jose*.

In addition, "special rules" may also govern arrangement of particular record series. For example, M1756, *Application for Nonresident Alien's Border Crossing Identification Cards Made at El Paso, Texas, ca. July 1945–December 1952*, 62 rolls, shows some alphabetical disarrangement due to human error and three variations in the filing scheme: similar-sounding surnames may be filed together; within a surname, first names that start with the same letter may be filed together; and within a surname, there may have been no attempt to alphabetize by

first name. There are numerous instances of similar-sounding names being filed together. For example, Spanish surnames containing the letter "s" may be filed as if the letter were "z." Thus, persons surnamed *Dias* might be filed among those named *Diaz*, and those surnamed *Espinosa* might be filed among those named *Espinoza*. Other names, such as *Arreola* and *Arriola*, *Anima* and *Animas*, *Cordova* and *Corboda*, and *Luevan*, *Luevano*, *Luevanos*, and *Luevand* are filed together in M1756.

As another example, in M2041, *Temporary and Nonstatistical Manifests of Aliens Arriving at Eagle Pass, Texas, July 1928–June 1953*, 14 rolls, surnames like *De La Huerta* are filed under *Huerta*. Within a particular surname, first names like *Antonia* and *Antonio* may be filed together.

The descriptive material reproduced on the beginning of each roll of Mexican border crossing microfilm publications attempts to alert researchers to special rules or problems concerning arrangement but may not indicate all of them. Alphabetical disarrangement of the records is common, particularly in larger record series, and may cause overlap within or between rolls.

2.2.4 Records Relating to Chinese Immigrants

As a general rule, immigration records are not arranged or segregated by ethnic group. However, due to the first Chinese Exclusion Act (22 Stat. 58) and subsequent legislation, special attention was given to the admissibility of Chinese aliens. As a result, lists, registers, case files, and other records resulting from the Chinese Exclusion Act were maintained separately from other records. Note, however, that Chinese prosecuted under the provisions of the general immigration laws are not so segregated but will be found in the general INS records. Among the microfilmed records relating to Chinese immigrants are: M1144, *Case Files of Chinese Immigrants, 1895–1920, from District No. 4 (Philadelphia) of the Immigration and Naturalization Service*, 51 rolls; M1364, *Lists of Chinese Passengers Arriving at Seattle (Port Townsend), Washington, 1882–1916*, 10 rolls; M1413, *Registers of Chinese Laborers Returning to the U.S. through the Port of San Francisco, 1882–1888*, 12 rolls; M1414, *Lists of Chinese Passenger Arrivals at San Francisco, 1882–1914*, 32 rolls; M1476, *Lists of Chinese Applying for Admission to the United States Through the Port of San Francisco, 1903–1947*, 27 rolls; and M1638, *Immigration and Naturalization Service Case Files of Chinese Immigrants, Portland, Oregon, 1890–1914*, 15 rolls. Some NARA regional facilities contain additional unmicrofilmed records.

2.2.5 Departure Records

The INS recorded departures at ports since 1917, but most of those records were not permanently kept. However, some departure records do exist, such as M1778, *Passenger and Crew Lists of Vessels Departing the Trust Territory of the Pacific Islands for Arrival at Guam,*

1947-1952, and Related Records, 1 roll, and M2021, *Passenger Lists of Citizens (June 1924-Aug. 1948) and Aliens (March 1946-Nov. 1948) Arriving at Pensacola, Florida, and Passenger Lists of Vessels Departing from Pensacola, Florida (Aug. 1926-March 1948)*, 1 roll, which includes lists that indicate departure from Charleston, SC (12 ships), and Panama City, FL (1 ship).

Some records of departure of specific persons may be found interfiled in Canadian and Mexican border arrival records on INS Form "Spl. 222," *Departure*, or INS Form I-407, *Land Border Departure Record*, both described above, but these records are relatively rare. However, rolls 5-6 of M1462, *Alphabetical Index to Canadian Border Entries through Small Ports in Vermont, 1895-1924*, 6 rolls, includes both arrivals and departures at Canaan and St. Albans, VT.

2.3 Special Notes by Port of Entry

Baltimore, MD. In addition to passenger lists required by Federal law, an 1835 Maryland state law required masters of vessels to submit to the mayor of Baltimore lists of passengers arriving in that port. These "city lists" were borrowed by NARA when M255, *Passenger Lists of Vessels Arriving in Baltimore, 1820-1891*, 50 rolls, was microfilmed to fill gaps in the Federal records for the years 1833-66. Although M255 contains both the Federal record and the borrowed city lists, the two parts are indexed separately. M327, *Index to Passenger Lists of Vessels Arriving at Baltimore, 1820-1897 (Federal Passenger Lists)*, 171 rolls, is the index to the lists made in compliance with Federal law and covers mainly the period 1832-97. M326, *Index to Passenger List of Vessels Arriving at Baltimore, 1833-1866 (City Passenger Lists)*, 22 rolls, covers the "city lists" only. Both indexes are arranged by the Soundex code, which is explained in section 1.2.1 of this guide. M334 also indexes some arrivals at Baltimore.

Blaine, WA. Roll 10 of M1365, *Certificates of Head Tax Paid by Aliens Arriving at Seattle [Washington] from Foreign Contiguous Territory, 1917-1924*, 10 rolls, contains such certificates (receipts) surrendered at Blaine, WA, March-April 1929.

Boston, MA. M265, *Index to Passenger Lists of Vessels Arriving at Boston, 1848-1891*, 282 rolls, is an alphabetical card index to passenger lists made in compliance with an 1848 Massachusetts state law. The related state-law passenger lists are in the Massachusetts State Archives, 220 Morrissey Blvd., Boston, MA 02125; the Federal-law passenger lists are reproduced in M277, *Passenger Lists of Vessels Arriving at Boston, Massachusetts, 1820-1891*, 115 rolls. M334 also indexes some arrivals at Boston. In T790, *Book Indexes, Boston Passenger Lists, 1899-1940*, 107 rolls, entries are arranged chronologically by date of vessel arrival, thereunder by class of passenger, and thereunder for the most part in rough alphabetical order by initial letter of passenger's surname.

Eagle Pass, TX. Nonstatistical manifests and statistical index cards are interfiled in M1754, *Nonstatistical Manifests and Statistical Index Cards of Aliens Arriving at Eagle Pass, Texas, June 1905-November 1929*, 27 rolls. The M1754 statistical index cards serve as an index to the June 1905-November 1929 statistical manifests on rolls 1-27 of M1755, *Permanent and Statistical Manifests of Alien Arrivals at Eagle Pass, Texas, June 1905-June 1953*, 30 rolls. The statistical index cards on M2040, *Index to Manifests of Permanent and Statistical Arrivals at Eagle Pass, Texas, December 1, 1929-June 1953*, 2 rolls, serve as an index to the statistical manifests on rolls 27-30 of M1755.

El Paso, TX. Applications for nonresident alien's border crossing identification cards in M1756, mentioned above, are alphabetically arranged in four separate subseries: (1) main series, rolls 1-62; (2) students attending all approved schools *except* Lydia Patterson Institute, roll 62; (3) students attending Lydia Patterson Institute, roll 62; and (4) persons inadvertently omitted from the main series, roll 62.

Galveston, TX. M1359, *Passenger Lists of Vessels Arriving at Galveston, Texas, 1896-1948*, 36 rolls, includes passenger lists for vessels arriving at Brownsville, Houston, Port Arthur, Sabine, and Texas City, TX. Roll 1 also includes several lists from 1893 but none for 1894 or 1895.

Gloucester, MA. M1321, *Passenger Lists of Vessels Arriving at Gloucester, Massachusetts, October 1906-March 1942*, 1 roll, contains lists consisting primarily of one alien fisherman per vessel, although some vessels have several crew members or passengers.

Laredo, TX. Most alien arrivals recorded in M2008, *Lists of Aliens Arriving at Laredo, Texas, from July 1903 to June 1907, via the Mexican National Railroad or the Laredo Foot Bridge*, 1 roll, were Europeans, but there were also a number of Mexican, Japanese, Turkish, Syrian, Guatemalan, and Korean citizens, as well as several foreign diplomatic personnel.

New Orleans, LA. M2009, *Work Projects Administration Transcript of Passenger Lists of Vessels Arriving at New Orleans, Louisiana, 1813-1849*, 2 rolls, contains volumes 1, 2, and 3 of typewritten volumes prepared by the Work Projects Administration of Louisiana entitled, "Passenger Lists Taken From Manifests of the Customs Service, Port of New Orleans." These volumes, along with volumes 4 and 6, which have not been microfilmed, are in the NARA Library. Volume 5 is missing. Each volume includes an alphabetical index to the names of passengers.

New York, NY. Most 19th-century immigrants came through the port of New York. M261, *Index to Passenger Lists of Vessels Arriving at New York, 1820-1846*, 103 rolls, serves the customs passenger lists for that period, and T519, *Index to Passenger Lists of Vessels Arriving at New York, 1897-1902*, 115 rolls, serves the immigration passenger lists of the later period, July 1, 1897-June 30, 1902. Unfortunately, there is no comprehensive index for New York arrivals for the period 1847-June 1897.

Photographs of immigrants arriving at Angel Island, San Francisco Bay (top), and Ellis Island. Photographs Nos. 90-G-2038, 90-G-125-3, and 90-G-125-42. Records of the Public Health Service, 1912-1968, RG 90.

In T612, *Book Indexes to New York Passenger Lists, 1906-42,* 307 rolls, entries are arranged chronologically by year, thereunder by vessel line or group of vessel lines, thereunder chronologically by date of vessel arrival, and thereunder in rough alphabetical order by initial letter of passenger's surname. T621, *Index (Soundex) to Passenger Lists of Vessels Arriving at New York, New York, July 1, 1902-Dec. 31, 1943,* 744 rolls, is an index to immigrant aliens but does not index nonimmigrants.

Pascagoula, MS. M2027, *Admitted Alien Crew Lists of Vessels Arriving at Pascagoula, Mississippi, July 1903-May 1935,* 1 roll, primarily consists of alien crew members admitted to the United States, but a few U.S. citizens, alien passengers who were not vessel crew members, and "stowaways" are also included. A large number of the alien crew members were noted to be deserters or discharged seamen. Some seamen had arrived at other ports; these men are included in crew arrivals at Pascagoula because, after working on vessels engaged in coastwise trade or otherwise living in the United States for some length of time, they presented themselves to INS alien inspectors at Pascagoula in order to legalize their admission to the United States. In these cases of delayed legal admittance, the date and circumstances of admission are typically noted on the passenger list.

Pensacola, FL. M2021, *Passenger Lists of Citizens (June 1924-Aug. 1948) and Aliens (March 1946-Nov. 1948) Arriving at Pensacola, Florida, and Passenger Lists of Vessels Departing from Pensacola, Florida (Aug. 1926-March 1948),* described above, includes some lists indicating arrival at Destin, FL (1 ship); Port St. Joe, FL (3 ships); or Charleston, SC (5 ships), and lists indicating departure from Charleston, SC (12 ships), and Panama City, FL (1 ship).

Philadelphia, PA. The earliest original customs lists for Philadelphia are those for 1820. Cargo manifests for 1800-19, and a few later ones that contain names of passengers that do not appear on the customs passenger lists, were filmed with the custom lists in M425, *Passenger Lists of Vessels Arriving in Philadelphia, 1800-1882,* 108 rolls, to make the coverage as complete as possible. M360, *Index to Passenger Lists of Vessels Arriving at Philadelphia, Pennsylvania, 1800-1906,* 151 rolls, contains names from cargo manifests, 1800-19; names from passenger lists, 1820-82; and names from some passenger lists, 1883-1906. M334 also serves as an index to some arrivals at Philadelphia. In T791, *Book Indexes, Philadelphia Passenger Lists, 1906-26,* 23 rolls, entries are arranged by vessel line, thereunder by date of vessel arrival, thereunder in part by class of passenger, and thereunder in rough alphabetical order by initial letter of passenger's surname.

Portland, ME. In T793, *Book Indexes, Portland, Maine, Passenger Lists, 1907-1930,* 10 rolls, entries are arranged chronologically by date of vessel arrival, thereunder in rough alphabetical order by initial letter of passenger's surname.

Providence, RI. In T792, *Book Indexes, Providence Passenger Lists, 1911-34,* 15 rolls, entries are arranged chronologically by date of vessel arrival, thereunder in rough alphabetical order by initial letter of passenger's surname.

St. Petersburg, FL. M1959, *Passenger Lists of Vessels Arriving at St. Petersburg, Florida, December 1926-March 1941,* 1 roll, includes many Canadians traveling on vacation; Cuban citizens, including teenage Cuban boys who were students at the Florida Military Academy in St. Petersburg; U.S. citizens; and aliens from various European countries.

Salem and Beverly, MA. In RG 36 NARA has customs lists of aliens arriving in about 10 ships at the ports of Salem and Beverly, MA, 1798 and 1800. The lists were made in accordance with an act of 1796 that required masters of ships coming into U.S. ports to file lists of aliens aboard with the collector of customs. Such lists for other ports are not among the records in NARA. These lists contain some or all of the following information: name of vessel, name of master, date of arrival, names of ports of embarkation and arrival, and, for each alien, name, age, birthplace, name of country of emigration, name of country of allegiance, occupation, and personal description. They were were transcribed and published by Mrs. Georgie A. Hill, "Passenger Arrivals at Salem and Beverly, Mass., 1798-1800," *New England Historical and Genealogical Register* 106 (July 1952): 203-209.

San Francisco, CA. M1389, *Indexes to Passenger Lists of Vessels Arriving at San Francisco, California, 1893-1934,* 28 rolls, contains three indexes: (1) general index to non-Chinese passengers; (2) index to persons arriving from the Philippines, Honolulu (Sept. 30, 1902-June 12, 1907), and insular possessions (May 28, 1907-Oct. 28, 1911); and (3) index to persons arriving from the East Indies. A3361, *Register of Citizen (1943-1947) and Alien (1936-1949) Arrivals by Aircraft at San Francisco, California,* 1 roll, is arranged by record series, thereunder chronologically. M1387, *Minutes of the Boards of Special Inquiry at the San Francisco Immigration Office, 1899-1909,* 2 rolls, includes the names of aliens, members of the BSIs, charges on which each alien was detained, and a summary of each hearing, including the board's decision. Hearings were held to determine if detained aliens suspected of being contract laborers or those "likely to become a public charge" should be excluded from or admitted to the United States.

See 2.5 for description of Board of Special Inquiry process.

San Pedro/Wilmington/Los Angeles, CA. M1763, *Index to Passenger Lists of Vessels Arriving at San Pedro/Wilmington/Los Angeles, California, 1907-1936,* 7 rolls, serves as an index to part of M1764, *Passenger Lists of Vessels Arriving at San Pedro/Wilmington/Los Angeles, California, June 29, 1907-June 30, 1948,* 118 rolls. M1763 contains more than 94,000 index cards to passenger arrivals at this port and includes many U.S. citizens,

TABLE 3
Available Immigration Records

EXPLANATION OF CODE PHRASES USED IN "TYPE" COLUMN

admitted alien crew	Alien ship crew members granted permanent admission to the United States.
air-alien	Airplane passenger lists of aliens.
air-citizen	Airplane passenger lists of U.S. citizens.
air-pass/crew	Lists of airplane passengers and crew.
alien arrivals	Card or sheet manifests of alien arrivals.
alien index	Index cards providing arrival information used to locate alien in related alien list.
alien list	Lists of alien arrivals at land border ports made on Form 500B or equivalent "sheet manifests" traditionally used to record ship passengers arriving at seaports.
alien/citizen arr.	Card or sheet manifests of alien and citizen arrivals.
app. nonres. alien BCIC	INS Form I-190, Applications for Nonresident Alien's Border Crossing Identification Cards, used to speed processing of alien visitors, primarily Mexican nationals, who frequently visited the United States.
BSI list	List of persons held for hearings before Boards of Special Inquiry (BSI).
BSI minutes	Minutes of hearings before Boards of Special Inquiry (BSI).
BSI records	Records of Boards of Special Inquiry (BSI).
Chinese admission	Record arranged chronologically, then by vessel, then by an assigned serial number. Indicates the person's name, residence, and class of eligibility for admission, such as merchant, merchant's son, son of native, wife of native, etc.
Chinese imm. case files	Case files relating to the admission or exclusion of Chinese immigrants.
Chinese laborers	Lists of Chinese laborers.
Chinese landing record	Record of Chinese arriving in the United States.
Chinese passengers	Lists of Chinese passengers of various occupations.
Chinese returning record	Record of Chinese departing the United States.
Japanese landing record	Record of Japanese arriving in the United States.
misc. head tax manifests	Card or sheet manifests upon which special action was taken concerning the collection of head tax; these were segregated from other manifests.
nonstat. manifests/ Nonstatistical Manifests	Card manifests of aliens whose arrival was *recorded* for the purposes of U.S. immigration law, but not *counted* for the purposes of immigration statistics.
nonstat./temp. manifests	Nonstatistical/Temporary Manifests. Card manifests of aliens whose arrival was *recorded* for the purposes of U.S. border control but not *counted* for the purposes of immigration statistics. Typically, these aliens were temporary visitors to the United States.
paid head tax certs.	Duplicate of certificates (receipts) issued to aliens who had paid head tax. Prior to 1924 these were often used as a kind of "reentry permit."
perm. manifests	Permanent Manifests. Card or sheet manifests of aliens who intended to permanently reside in the United States.
permanent admission	Card or sheet manifests of aliens who intended to permanently reside in the United States.

TABLE 3
Available Immigration Records

returning aliens	Card or sheet manifests of aliens readmitted as returning U.S. residents.
ship/air-pass/crew	Interfiled lists of passengers and crew members from both ships and airplanes. Lists of crew members may predominate.
ship-aliens	Lists of alien passengers on ships. Occasionally, U.S. citizens may also be included.
ship-book index	Typically, an index arranged chronologically, then by ship, then roughly alphabetically by the first letter of the passenger's surname. Usually indicates page and line number where the passenger's immigration record may be found.
ship-citizens	Lists of U.S. citizen ship passengers.
ship-copies/abstracts	Copies or abstracts of the original records, as described above.
ship-crew lists	Lists of crew members of ships. Usually, lists of alien crew members predominate, but U.S. citizen crew members may also be listed.
ship-customs	Passengers lists, 1820–ca. 1890 or later, submitted to U.S. customs officials, as described above.
ship-departure	Passenger lists of persons departing the United States.
ship-Hawaiian passengers	Passengers who departed from Hawaii.
ship-immigration	Ship passenger lists, ca. 1890–1957, which may include both aliens and U.S. citizens; some crew lists may also be included.
ship-insular passengers	Passengers from a U.S. possession, i.e., Philippine Islands, Virgin Islands, Puerto Rico, Hawaii, or Guam.
ship-pass./crew	Lists of ship passengers and crew.
ship-passenger index	Index to names of passengers on related passenger lists.
ship-Phil. pass. index	Index to names of Philippine passengers on related passenger lists.
ship-qtrly. abstracts	Abstracts arranged by quarter-year, described above under copies and abstracts.
ship-State Dept. trans.	State Department Transcript, described above.
ship-WPA index	Index to names of passengers on related WPA transcript.
ship-WPA transcript	Transcript of original record created by WPA.
stat. index	Card index to related statistical manifests.
stat. manifests	Statistical Manifests. Card or sheet manifests of aliens whose arrival was recorded for the purposes of U.S. border control, and also counted for the purposes of immigration statistics. Typically, these aliens intended to remain permanently in the United States.
stat./nonstat. index	Index to related interfiled statistical and nonstatistical manifests.
stat./nonstat. manifests	Interfiled statistical and nonstatistical manifests.
stat./perm. index	Index to related statistical/permanent manifests.
stat./perm. manifests	Card or sheet manifests of aliens whose arrival was recorded for the purposes of U.S. border control, and also counted for the purposes of immigration statistics. Typically, these aliens intended to remain permanently in the United States.
temporary visitors	Card manifests of aliens who intended to temporarily visit the United States.
vessel index	Index to arrivals by vessels; does not contain names of passengers.

TABLE 3
Available Immigration Records

PORT OR DISTRICT	TYPE	ARRANGEMENT	MICROFILM	DATES
Alabama				
Mobile	ship-copies/abstracts	chronological	M575	1832, 1849-52
	ship-passenger index	alphabetical	M334	1832, 1849-52
	ship-passenger index	alphabetical	T517	1890-1924
Alaska				
Eagle	alien index	alphabetical	M2016	Jun 1906-Aug 1946
	ship-immigration	chronological	M2018	Dec 1910-Oct 1938
Hyder	alien index	alphabetical	M2016	Jun 1906-Aug 1946
Ketchikan	alien index	alphabetical	M2016	Jun 1906-Aug 1946
Nome	alien index	alphabetical	M2016	Jun 1906-Aug 1946
Skagway	alien index	alphabetical	M2016	Jun 1906-Aug 1946
	alien list	chronological	M2017	Oct 1906-Nov 1934
White Pass, *see* Skagway, M2016 and M2017				
Arizona				
Douglas	nonstat. manifests	alphabetical	M1759	Jul 1908-Dec 1952
	stat. index	alphabetical	M1759	Jul 1908-Dec 1952
San Luis	permanent admission	alphabetical	M1504	Jul 24, 1929-Dec 1952
	temporary visitors	alphabetical	M1504	Jul 24, 1929-Dec 1952
San Fernando, *see* Sasabe, M1850				
Sasabe	nonstat./temp. manifests	alphabetical	M1850	1927-1952
	returning aliens	alphabetical	M1850	Jul 1, 1924-1952
	stat./perm. index	alphabetical	M1850	Jan 1, 1919-Jun 30, 1924
	stat./perm. manifests	unarranged	M1850	1919
	stat./perm. manifests	chronological	M1850	Jan 14, 1919-Jun 30, 1924
California				
Andrade	stat./nonstat. index	alphabetical	M2030	Aug 30, 1911-Jun 30, 1924
	stat./nonstat. manifests	chronological	M2030	Aug 30, 1911-Jul 6, 1924
	stat./nonstat. manifests	alphabetical	M2030	Jul 1, 1924-Dec 24, 1952
Campo	app. nonres. alien BCIC	alphabetical	M2030	Jul 1, 1946-Dec 24, 1952
	nonstat. manifests	alphabetical	M2030	ca. Sep 2, 1912-Jul 1, 1924
	stat./nonstat. index	alphabetical	M2030	ca. May 1911-Jul 7, 1924
	stat./nonstat. manifests	alphabetical	M2030	Sep 2, 1910-Dec 24, 1952
	stat./nonstat. manifests	chronological	M2030	Jul 2, 1912-Jul 7, 1924
El Capitan, *see* Ventura, A3363				
Ellwood, *see* Ventura, A3363				
Los Angeles, *see* Ventura, A3363; San Pedro, M1763 and M1764				
Port Hueneme, *see* Ventura, A3363				
San Diego	ship/plane index	alphabetical	M1761	ca. 1904-ca. 1952
San Francisco, *see also* Ventura, A3363				
	ship-customs	chronological	M1412	Jan 2, 1903-Apr 18, 1918
	ship-immigration	chronological	M1410	May 1, 1893-May 31, 1953
	ship-insular passengers	chronological	M1438	May 28, 1907-Oct 28, 1911
	ship-Hawaiian passengers	chronological	M1494	Sep 30, 1902-May 17, 1907
	ship-pass./crew	chronological	M1411	Dec 1, 1954-Feb 28, 1957
	ship-citizen	chronological	M1439	Jun 27, 1930-Jan 19, 1949
	ship-crew lists	chronological	M1416	Dec 28, 1905-Oct 30, 1954
	admitted alien crew	chronological	M1436	Sep 1, 1896-Sep 24, 1921
	ship-passenger index	alphabetical	M1389	May 1, 1893-May 9, 1934
	ship-Hawaiian pass. index	alphabetical	M1389	Sep 30, 1902-Jun 12, 1907
	ship-Phil. pass. index	alphabetical	M1389	May 1, 1893-May 9, 1934
	vessel index	alphabetical	M1437	1882-1957
	air-alien	chronological	A3361	Sep 29, 1936-Apr 30, 1949

TABLE 3
Available Immigration Records

PORT OR DISTRICT	TYPE	ARRANGEMENT	MICROFILM	DATES
	air-citizen	chronological	A3361	Mar 10, 1943–Sep 5, 1947
	Chinese admission	chronological	M1476	Jul 7, 1903–Jan 7, 1947
	Chinese laborers	chronological	M1413	Jun 6, 1882–Oct 9, 1888
	Chinese passengers	chronological	M1414	Aug 9, 1882–Dec 25, 1914
	BSI minutes	chronological	M1387	Mar 29, 1899–Jul 12, 1904
San Pedro, *see also* Ventura, A3363				
	BSI list	chronological	M1852	Nov 3, 1930–Sep 27, 1936
	ship-passenger index	alphabetical	M1763	1907–36
	ship-immigration	chronological	M1764	Jun 29, 1907–Jun 30, 1948
San Ysidro	misc. head tax manifests	chronological	M1767	Dec 7, 1923–Feb 1925
	nonstat. manifests	chronological	M1767	Apr 21, 1908–Jun 30, 1924
	nonstat. manifests	alphabetical	M1767	Apr 21, 1908–Dec 1952
	stat. index	alphabetical	M1767	Apr 21, 1908–Jun 30, 1924
	stat. manifests	chronological	M1767	Apr 21, 1908–Jun 30, 1924
	stat. manifests	alphabetical	M1767	Apr 21, 1908–Dec 1952
Tecate, *see* Campo, M2030				
Tia Juana, *see* San Ysidro, M1767				
Ventura	ship/air-pass/crew	chronological	A3363	May 1929–Dec 1956
Wilmington, *see* San Pedro, M1763 and M1764				
Connecticut				
Bridgeport	ship-copies/abstracts	chronological	M575	1870
	ship-passenger index	alphabetical	M334	1870
	ship-pass/crew	chronological	M1320	Feb 1929–Feb 1959
	air-pass/crew	chronological	M1320	Apr 1946–Feb 1959
Fairfield	ship-copies/abstracts	chronological	M575	1820–21
	ship-State Dept. trans.	chronological	T1219	1820
	ship-passenger index	alphabetical	M334	1820–21
Groton, *see* New London				
Hartford	ship-copies/abstracts	chronological	M575	1837
	ship-passenger index	alphabetical	M334	1837
	air-pass/crew	chronological	M1320	Apr 1946–Feb 1959
New Haven	ship-copies/abstracts	chronological	M575	1820–73
	ship-State Dept. trans.	chronological	T1219	1820, 1822–31
	ship-passenger index	alphabetical	M334	1820–73
	ship-pass/crew	chronological	M1320	Feb 1929–Feb 1959
	air-pass/crew	chronological	M1320	Apr 1946–Feb 1959
New London	ship-copies/abstracts	chronological	M575	1820–47
	ship-State Dept. trans.	chronological	T1219	1820, 1823–27, 1829, 1831
	ship-passenger index	alphabetical	M334	1820–47
	ship-pass/crew	chronological	M1320	Feb 1929–Feb 1959
	air-pass/crew	chronological	M1320	Apr 1946–Feb 1959
Saybrook	ship-copies/abstracts	chronological	M575	1820
	ship-passenger index	alphabetical	M334	1820
Delaware				
Delaware District	ship-State Dept. trans.	chronological	T1219	1820
Wilmington	ship-copies/abstracts	chronological	M575	1820, 1830–31, 1833, 1840–49
	ship-passenger index	alphabetical	M334	1820, 1830–31, 1833, 1840–49
District of Columbia, *see also* Alexandria, VA				
Georgetown	ship-copies/abstracts	chronological	M575	1820–21
	ship-State Dept. trans.	chronological	T1219	1820
	ship-passenger index	alphabetical	M334	1820–21

TABLE 3
Available Immigration Records

PORT OR DISTRICT	TYPE	ARRANGEMENT	MICROFILM	DATES
Florida				
Apalachicola	ship-immigration	chronological	M1842	Sep 4, 1918
Boca Grande	ship-immigration	chronological	M1842	Oct 28, 1912–Oct 19, 1939
	ship-passenger index	alphabetical	T517	1890–1924
Boynton	ship-immigration	chronological	M1842	May 9, 1942
Carrabelle	ship-immigration	chronological	M1842	Nov 7, 1915
Destin, *see* Pensacola, M2021				
Fernandina	ship-immigration	chronological	M1842	Aug 29, 1904–Mar 12, 1935
Fort Pierce	ship-immigration	chronological	M1842	May 27, 1939, May 6, 1942
Hobe Sound	ship-immigration	chronological	M1842	May 4, 1942
Jacksonville	ship-passenger index	alphabetical	T517	1890–1924
Key West	ship-copies/abstracts	chronological	M575	1837-52, 1857-68
	ship-immigration	chronological	T940	Nov 2, 1898–Dec 14, 1945
	ship-passenger index	alphabetical	M334	1837-52, 1857-68
	ship-passenger index	alphabetical	T517	1890–1924
Knights Key	ship-passenger index	alphabetical	T517	1890–1924
Lake Worth	ship-immigration	chronological	M1842	May 8, 1942
Mayport	ship-immigration	chronological	M1842	Nov 16, 1902, Feb–Apr 1916
Miami	ship-passenger index	alphabetical	T517	1890–1924
Millville	ship-immigration	chronological	M1842	Jul 4, 1916
Panama City, *see also* Pensacola, M2021				
	ship-aliens	chronological	M1840	Nov 10, 1927–Dec 12, 1939
	ship-citizens	chronological	M1840	Sep 10, 1933–Dec 12, 1939
Pensacola	ship-citizens	chronological	M2021	Jun 21, 1924–Aug 7, 1948
	ship-aliens	chronological	M2021	Mar 1, 1946–Nov 22, 1948
	ship-departure	chronological	M2021	Aug 3, 1926–Mar 2, 1948
	ship-passenger index	alphabetical	T517	1890–1924
Port Inglis	ship-immigration	chronological	M1842	Mar 29, 1912–Jan 2, 1913
Port St. Joe, *see also* Pensacola, M2021				
	ship-immigration	chronological	M1842	Jan 18, 1923–Mar 21, 1923, Oct 13, 1939
St. Andrews	ship-immigration	chronological	M1842	Jan 2, 1916–May 13, 1926
St. Augustine	ship-copies/abstracts	chronological	M575	1821-22, 1824, 1827, 1870
	ship-State Dept. trans.	chronological	T1219	1822-24, 1827
	ship-passenger index	alphabetical	M334	1821-22, 1824, 1827, 1870
St. Johns	ship-copies/abstracts	chronological	M575	1865
	ship–passenger index	alphabetical	M334	1865
St. Petersburg	ship-immigration	chronological	M1959	Dec 15, 1926, Mar 28, 1936–Mar 1, 1941
Stuart	ship-immigration	chronological	M1842	May 6, 1942
Tampa	ship-passenger index	alphabetical	T517	1890–1924
	ship-immigration	chronological	M1844	Nov 2, 1898–Dec 31, 1945
Georgia				
Darien	ship-copies/abstracts	chronological	M575	1823, 1825
	ship-passenger index	alphabetical	M334	1823, 1825
Savannah	ship-copies/abstracts	chronological	M575	1820-26, 1831, 1847-51, 1865-68
	ship-State Dept. trans.	chronological	T1219	1820-23, 1825-26, 1831
	ship-passenger index	alphabetical	M334	1820-26, 1831, 1847-51, 1865-68
	ship-passenger index	alphabetical	T517	1890–1924
	ship-immigration	chronological	T943	Jun 5, 1906–Dec 6, 1945

TABLE 3
Available Immigration Records

PORT OR DISTRICT	TYPE	ARRANGEMENT	MICROFILM	DATES
Idaho				
Eastport, *see* St. Albans Dist., VT, M1461and M1464				
Porthill, *see* St. Albans Dist., VT, M1461 and M1464				
Louisiana				
Lake Charles	vessel index	alphabetical	M1514	May 1, 1908–Nov 30, 1954
New Orleans	ship-customs	chronological	M259	Jan 1, 1820–Jan 31, 1903
	ship-qtrly. abstracts	chronological	M272	Jan 1, 1820–Jun 30, 1875
	ship-State Dept. trans.	chronological	T1219	1820–27
	ship-WPA transcript	chronological	M2009	1813–49
	ship-immigration	chronological	T905	Jan 8, 1903–Dec 31, 1945
	ship-crew lists	chronological	T939	Jan 1910–Dec 1945
	ship-WPA index	alphabetical	M2009	1813–49
	ship-passenger index	alphabetical	M334	*See* note on M334
	ship-passenger index	alphabetical	T527	1853–99
	ship-passenger index	alphabetical	T618	1900–52
Maine				
Bangor	ship-copies/abstracts	chronological	M575	1848
	ship-passenger index	alphabetical	M334	1848
Bath	ship-copies/abstracts	chronological	M575	1825, 1827, 1832, 1867
	ship-passenger index	alphabetical	M334	1825, 1827, 1832, 1867
Belfast	ship-copies/abstracts	chronological	M575	1820–31, 1851
	ship-State Dept. trans.	chronological	T1219	1820, 1822–24, 1827, 1829, 1831
	ship-passenger index	alphabetical	M334	1820–31, 1851
Calais, *see also* St. Albans Dist., VT, M1461 and M1464				
	alien/citizen arr.	alphabetical	M2042	ca. 1906–52
Eastport, *see* St. Albans Dist., VT, M1461 and M1464				
Falmouth, *see* Portland, M334 and M575				
Fort Fairfield, *see also* St. Albans Dist., VT, M1461 and M1464				
	alien & citizen manifest	alphabetical	M2064	ca. 1909–Apr 1953
Fort Kent, *see* St. Albans Dist., VT, M1461 and M1464				
Frenchman's Bay	ship-copies/abstracts	chronological	M575	1821, 1826–27
	ship-State Dept. trans.	chronological	T1219	1822, 1825–27
	ship-passenger index	alphabetical	M334	1821, 1826–27
Houlton, *see* St. Albans Dist., VT, M1461 and M1464				
Jackman, *see* St. Albans Dist., VT, M1461 and M1464				
Kennebunk	ship-copies/abstracts	chronological	M575	1820–42
	ship-State Dept. trans.	chronological	T1219	1820, 1822–25, 1827
	ship-passenger index	alphabetical	M334	1820–42
Lowelltown, *see* St. Albans Dist., VT, M1461 and M1464				
Madawaska, *see* St. Albans Dist., VT, M1461 and M1464				
Old Town, *see* St. Albans Dist., VT, M1461 and M1464				
Passamaquoddy	ship-copies/abstracts	chronological	M575	1820–59
	ship-State Dept. trans.	chronological	T1219	1822–23, 1825–26, 1831
	ship-passenger index	alphabetical	M334	1820–59
Penobscot	ship-copies/abstracts	chronological	M575	1851
	ship-passenger index	alphabetical	M334	1851
Portland and Falmouth	ship-copies/abstracts	chronological	M575	1820–24, 1826–53, 1856–Mar 1868
	ship-State Dept. trans.	chronological	T1219	1820–32
	ship-passenger index	alphabetical	M334	1820–24, 1826–53, 1856–Mar 1868

TABLE 3
Available Immigration Records

PORT OR DISTRICT	TYPE	ARRANGEMENT	MICROFILM	DATES
Portland	ship-immigration	chronological	A1151	Nov 29, 1893–Mar 1943
	ship-passenger index	alphabetical	T524	Nov 29, 1893–Mar 1943
	ship-book index	chronological	T793	Apr 1907–Apr 6, 1930
Vanceboro	alien arrivals	alphabetical	M2071	1906–52; a few for 1888–1905
Waldoboro	ship-copies/abstracts	chronological	M575	1820–21, 1833
	ship-State Dept. trans.	chronological	T1219	1820–21
	ship-passenger index	alphabetical	M334	1820–21, 1833
Wiscasset	ship-State Dept. trans.	chronological	T1219	1819, 1829
	ship-passenger index	alphabetical	M334	See note on M334
Yarmouth	ship-copies/abstracts	chronological	M575	1820
	ship-passenger index	alphabetical	M334	1820
Maryland				
Annapolis	ship-copies/abstracts	chronological	M575	1849
	ship-passenger index	alphabetical	M334	1849
Baltimore	ship-customs	chronological	M255	Sep 2, 1820–Dec 28, 1891
	ship-qtrly. abstracts	chronological	M596	Jan 1, 1820–Jun 30, 1869
	ship-State Dept. trans.	chronological	T1219	1820, 1822–26, 1829
	ship-immigration	chronological	T844	Jun 2, 1892–Jun 30, 1948
	ship-immigration	chronological	M1477	Dec 1, 1954–May 7, 1957
	ship-passenger index	alphabetical	M334	See note on M334
	ship-passenger index	Soundex	M327	1820–97
	ship-passenger index	Soundex	M326	1833–66
	ship-passenger index	Soundex	T520	1897–Jul 1952
Havre de Grace	ship-copies/abstracts	chronological	M575	1820
	ship-passenger index	alphabetical	M334	1820
Massachusetts				
Barnstable	ship-copies/abstracts	chronological	M575	1820–26
	ship-State Dept. trans.	chronological	T1219	1820–26
	ship-passenger index	alphabetical	M334	1820–26
Beverly, see Salem				
Boston	ship-customs	chronological	M277	Jan 1, 1883–Jul 29, 1891
	ship-copies/abstracts	chronological	M277	Sep 22, 1820–Mar 31, 1874
	ship-State Dept. trans.	chronological	T1219	1820–27
	ship-immigration	chronological	T843	Aug 1, 1891–Dec 31, 1943
	ship-crew lists	chronological	T938	May 1, 1917–Oct 1930
	ship-passenger index	alphabetical	M334	See note on M334
	ship-passenger index	alphabetical	M265	1848–91
	ship-passenger index	alphabetical	T521	Jan 1, 1902–Jun 30, 1906
	ship-passenger index	alphabetical	T617	Jul 1, 1906–Dec 31, 1920
	ship-book index	chronological	T790	Apr 1, 1899–Sep 14, 1940
Charlestown, see also Boston, T1219				
	ship-passenger index	alphabetical	M334	See note on M334
Dighton	ship-copies/abstracts	chronological	M575	1820–36
	ship-State Dept. trans.	chronological	T1219	1819, 1823, 1826, 1828
	ship-passenger index	alphabetical	M334	1820–36
Edgartown	ship-copies/abstracts	chronological	M575	1820–70
	ship-State Dept. trans.	chronological	T1219	1820–28, 1831–32
	ship-passenger index	alphabetical	M334	1820–70
Fall River	ship-copies/abstracts	chronological	M575	1837–65
	ship-passenger index	alphabetical	M334	1837–65
Gloucester	ship-copies/abstracts	chronological	M575	1820, 1832–39, 1867–68, 1870
	ship-crew lists	chronological	T941	Mar 1918–Dec 1943

PORT OR DISTRICT	**TYPE**	**ARRANGEMENT**	**MICROFILM**	**DATES**
	ship-passenger index	alphabetical	M334	1820, 1832-39, 1867-68, 1870
	ship-immigration	chronological	M1321	Oct 14, 1906–Mar 11, 1942
Hingham	ship-copies/abstracts	chronological	M575	1852
	ship-passenger index	alphabetical	M334	1852
Marblehead	ship-copies/abstracts	chronological	M575	1820-36, 1849
	ship-State Dept. trans.	chronological	T1219	1820-23, 1825-27
	ship-copies/abstracts	alphabetical	M334	1820-36, 1849
Nantucket	ship-copies/abstracts	chronological	M575	1820-51, 1857-62
	ship-State Dept. trans.	chronological	T1219	1820, 1822-25, 1829, 1831
	ship-passenger index	alphabetical	M334	1820-51, 1857-62
New Bedford	ship-copies/abstracts	chronological	M575	1826-52
	ship-State Dept. trans.	chronological	T1219	1822, 1825-27, 1830-31
	ship-immigration	chronological	T944	Jul 1, 1902–Jul 1942
	ship-crew lists	chronological	T942	May 1917–Dec 1943
	ship-passenger index	alphabetical	M334	1826-52
	ship-passenger index	alphabetical	T522	Jul 1, 1902–Nov 18, 1954
Newburyport	ship-copies/abstracts	chronological	M575	1821-39
	ship-State Dept. trans.	chronological	T1219	1821-31
	ship-passenger index	alphabetical	M334	1821-39
Plymouth	ship-copies/abstracts	chronological	M575	1821-36, 1843
	ship-State Dept. trans.	chronological	T1219	1822, 1824, 1826-27, 1829-30
	ship-passenger index	alphabetical	M334	1821-36, 1843
Salem and Beverly	ship-copies/abstracts	chronological	M575	1865-66
	ship-State Dept. trans.	chronological	T1219	1823
	ship-passenger index	chronological	M334	1865-66; *see* note on M334
Michigan				
Detroit, *see also* St. Albans Dist., VT, M1461 and M1464				
	alien/citizen arr.	alphabetical	M1478	1906-54
	ship-pass./crew	chronological	M1479	Jan 29, 1946–Mar 31, 1957
Port Huron, *see* St. Albans Dist., VT, M1461 and M1464				
Saint Clair, *see* St. Albans Dist., VT, M1461 and M1464				
Saint Mary, *see* St. Albans Dist., VT, M1461 and M1464				
Minnesota				
Duluth, *see* St. Albans Dist., VT, M1461 and M1464				
International Falls, *see* St. Albans Dist., VT, M1461 and M1464				
Ranier, *see* St. Albans Dist., VT, M1461 and M1464				
Warroad, *see* St. Albans Dist., VT, M1461 and M1464				
Mississippi				
Gulfport	ship-passenger index	alphabetical	T523	Aug 27, 1904–Aug 28, 1954
Pascagoula	admitted alien crew	chronological	M2027	Jul 15, 1903–May 21, 1935
	ship-passenger index	alphabetical	T523	Jul 15, 1903–May 21, 1935
Montana				
Gateway, *see* St. Albans Dist., VT, M1461 and M1464				
Sweet Grass, *see* St. Albans Dist., VT, M1461 and M1464				
New Hampshire				
Portsmouth	ship-copies/abstracts	chronological	M575	1820-22, 1824, 1826-33, 1835-37, 1842-52, 1857-61
	ship-State Dept. trans.	chronological	T1219	1820, 1822, 1824-31
	ship-passenger index	alphabetical	M334	1820-22, 1824, 1826-33, 1835-37, 1842-52, 1857-61
New Jersey				
Bridgeton	ship-copies/abstracts	chronological	M575	Jul 1828

TABLE 3
Available Immigration Records

PORT OR DISTRICT	TYPE	ARRANGEMENT	MICROFILM	DATES
	ship-State Dept. trans.	chronological	T1219	1828
	ship-passenger index	alphabetical	M334	Jul 1828
Cape May	ship-copies/abstracts	chronological	M575	1828
	ship-passenger index	alphabetical	M334	1828
Little Egg Harbor	ship-copies/abstracts	chronological	M575	1831
	ship-passenger index	alphabetical	M334	1831
Newark	ship-copies/abstracts	chronological	M575	1836
	ship-passenger index	alphabetical	M334	1836
Perth Amboy	ship-copies/abstracts	chronological	M575	1820, 1829–32
	ship-State Dept. trans.	chronological	T1219	1829
	ship-passenger index	alphabetical	M334	1820, 1829–32
New York				
Alexandria Bay	alien/citizen arr.	alphabetical	M1481	Jul 1929–Apr 1956
Black Rock, *see* St. Albans Dist., VT, M1461 and M1464				
Buffalo, *see* St. Albans Dist., VT, M1461 and M1464				
Cape Vincent, *see also* St. Albans Dist., VT, M1461 and M1464				
	alien/citizen arr.	alphabetical	M1481	Jul 1929–Apr 1956
Champlain	alien/citizen arr.	alphabetical	M1481	Jul 1929–Apr 1956
Charlotte, *see* St. Albans Dist., VT, M1461 and M1464				
Clayton	alien/citizen arr.	alphabetical	M1481	Jul 1929–Apr 1956
Fort Covington, *see also* St. Albans Dist., VT, M1461 and M1464				
	alien/citizen arr.	alphabetical	M1481	Jul 1929–Apr 1956
Hogansburg	alien/citizen arr.	Soundex	M1482	Jul 1929–Apr 1956
Lewiston, *see* St. Albans Dist., VT, M1461 and M1464				
Louisville Landing, *see* St. Albans Dist., VT, M1461 and M1464				
Malone, *see also* St. Albans Dist., VT, M1461 and M1464				
	alien/citizen arr.	Soundex	M1482	Jul 1929–Apr 1956
Mooers	alien/citizen arr.	alphabetical	M1481	Jul 1929–Apr 1956
Morristown, *see also* St. Albans Dist., VT, M1461 and M1464				
	alien/citizen arr.	Soundex	M1482	Jul 1929–Apr 1956
New York City	ship-customs	chronological	M237	Jan 7, 1820–Jun 17, 1897
	ship-State Dept. trans.	chronological	T1219	1820–27
	ship-immigration	chronological	T715	Jun 16, 1897–Jul 3, 1957
	ship-passenger index	alphabetical	M261	1820–46
	ship-passenger index	alphabetical	T519	Jun 16, 1897–Jun 30, 1902
	ship-book index	ship line/chron.	T612	1906–42
	ship-passenger index	Soundex	T621	Jul 1, 1902–Dec 31, 1943
	ship-passenger index	Soundex	M1417	1944–48
	vessel index	chron./alpha.	M1066	Aug 5, 1789–Dec 31, 1919
Niagara Falls, *see* St. Albans Dist., VT, M1461 and M1464				
Nyando, *see also* St. Albans Dist., VT, M1461 and M1464				
	alien/citizen arr.	Soundex	M1482	Jul 1929–Apr 1956
Ogdensburg, *see also* St. Albans Dist., VT, M1461 and M1464				
	alien/citizen arr.	Soundex	M1482	Jul 1929–Apr 1956
Oswegatchie	ship-copies/abstracts	chronological	M575	1821–23
	ship-State Dept. trans.	chronological	T1219	1821–23
	ship-passenger index	alphabetical	M334	1821–23
Rochester, *see also* St. Albans Dist., VT, M1461 and M1464				
	ship-copies/abstracts	chronological	M575	1866
	ship–passenger index	alphabetical	M334	1866
Rooseveltown, *see* Nyando				
Rouses Point, *see also* St. Albans Dist., VT, M1461 and M1464				

TABLE 3
Available Immigration Records

PORT OR DISTRICT	TYPE	ARRANGEMENT	MICROFILM	DATES
	alien/citizen arr.	alphabetical	M1481	Jul 1929–Apr 1956
Sag Harbor	ship-copies/abstracts	chronological	M575	1829, 1832, 1834
	ship-State Dept. trans.	chronological	T1219	1829
	ship-passenger index	alphabetical	M334	1829, 1832, 1834
Thous. Is. Bridge	alien/citizen arr.	alphabetical	M1481	Jul 1929–Apr 1956
Trout River	alien/citizen arr.	alphabetical	M1481	Jul 1929–Apr 1956
Waddington	alien/citizen arr.	Soundex	M1482	Jul 1929–Apr 1956
North Carolina				
Beaufort	ship-copies/abstracts	chronological	M575	1865
	ship-passenger index	alphabetical	M334	1865
Edenton	ship-copies/abstracts	chronological	M575	1820
	ship-State Dept. trans.	chronological	T1219	1820
	ship-passenger index	alphabetical	M334	1820
New Bern	ship-copies/abstracts	chronological	M575	1820-45, 1865
	ship-State Dept. trans.	chronological	T1219	1820-30
	ship-passenger index	alphabetical	M334	1820-45, 1865
Plymouth	ship-copies/abstracts	chronological	M575	1820, 1825, 1840
	ship-State Dept. trans.	chronological	T1219	1820, 1823
	ship-passenger index	alphabetical	M334	1820, 1825, 1840
Washington	ship-copies/abstracts	chronological	M575	1828-31, 1836-37, 1848
	ship-State Dept. trans.	chronological	T1219	1828-29, 1831
	ship-passenger index	alphabetical	M334	1828-31, 1836-37, 1848
North Dakota				
Hannah, *see* St. Albans Dist., VT, M1461 and M1464				
Neche, *see* St. Albans Dist., VT, M1461 and M1464				
Northgate, *see* St. Albans Dist., VT, M1461 and M1464				
Pembina, *see* St. Albans Dist., VT, M1461 and M1464				
Portal, *see* St. Albans Dist., VT, M1461 and M1464				
Ohio				
Cleveland, *see* St. Albans Dist., VT, M1461 and M1464				
Sandusky	ship-copies/abstracts	chronological	M575	1820
	ship-State Dept. trans.	chronological	T1219	1820
	ship-passenger index	alphabetical	M334	1820
Oregon				
Astoria	Chinese admission	chronological	M1638	1893-1903
	Chinese laborers	chronological	M1638	1882-93
Portland	Chinese admission	chronological	M1638	1898-1903
	Chinese landing record	chronological	M1638	1890-1914
	Chinese returning record	chronological	M1638	1891-1913
	Japanese landing record	chronological	M1638	1897-1900
Pennsylvania				
Philadelphia	ship-customs	chronological	M425	Jan 1, 1800–Dec 29, 1882
	ship-State Dept. trans.	chronological	T1219	1820-22, 1824-27, 1829
	ship-immigration	chronological	T840	Jan 1, 1883–Dec 31, 1945
	ship-passenger index	alphabetical	M360	1800-1906
	ship-passenger index	alphabetical	M334	*See* note on M334
	ship-passenger index	Soundex	T526	Jan 1, 1883–Jun 28, 1948
	ship-book index	chronological	T791	May 14, 1906–Jun 17, 1926
	BSI records	chronological	M1500	Aug 29, 1893–Nov 16, 1909
	Chinese imm. case files	chronological	M1144	1900-23
Rhode Island				
Bristol & Warren	ship-copies/abstracts	chronological	M575	1820-26, 1828, 1843-71

TABLE 3
Available Immigration Records

PORT OR DISTRICT	TYPE	ARRANGEMENT	MICROFILM	DATES
	ship-State Dept. trans.	chronological	T1219	1820–28
	ship-passenger index	alphabetical	M334	1820–26, 1828, 1843–71
Newport	ship-copies/abstracts	chronological	M575	1820–52, 1857
	ship-State Dept. trans.	chronological	T1219	1820–28, 1830–31
	ship-passenger index	alphabetical	M334	1820–52, 1857
Providence	ship-copies/abstracts	chronological	M575	1820–67
	ship-State Dept. trans.	chronological	T1219	1820, 1822–31
	ship-immigration	chronological	A1188	Jun 17, 1911–Jan 1943
	ship-passenger index	alphabetical	M334	1820–67
	ship-passenger index	alphabetical	T518	Jun 18, 1911–Oct 5, 1954
	ship-book index	chronological	T792	Dec 13, 1911–Jun 26, 1934
Warren, see Bristol, M334 and M575				
South Carolina				
Charleston, see also Pensacola, FL, M2021				
	ship-copies/abstracts	chronological	M575	1820–28
	ship-State Dept. trans.	chronological	T1219	1820–29
	ship-passenger index	alphabetical	M334	1820–29
	ship-passenger index	alphabetical	T517	1890–1924
Georgetown	ship-immigration	chronological	M1842	Jun 17, 1923–Oct 24, 1939
Port Royal	ship-copies/abstracts	chronological	M575	1865
	ship-passenger index	alphabetical	M334	1865
S. Carolina Dist.	ship-State Dept. trans.	chronological	T1219	1822–23, 1828
Texas				
Beaumont	vessel index	alphabetical	M1514	May 1, 1908–Nov 30, 1954
Brownsville, see also Galveston, M1359				
	nonstat. manifests	alphabetical	M1502	Feb 1905–Jun 1953
	stat. manifests	chronological	M1502	Feb 1905–Mar 1952
	stat. index	alphabetical	M1502	Feb 1905–Mar 1952
	vessel index	chronological	M1514	1935–55
Eagle Pass	nonstat. manifests	alphabetical	M1754	Jun 1, 1905–Nov 30, 1929
	nonstat./temp. manifests	chronological	M2041	Jul 1, 1928–Mar 21, 1929
	nonstat./temp. manifests	alphabetical	M2041	Mar 22, 1929–Jun 1953
	stat. index	alphabetical	M1754	Jun 1, 1905–Nov 30, 1929
	stat./perm. index	alphabetical	M2040	Dec 1, 1929–Jun 1953
	stat./perm. manifests	chronological	M1755	Jun 1905–Jun 1953
El Paso	app. nonres. alien BCIC	alphabetical	M1756	ca. Jul 1945–Dec 1952
	temp. manifests	alphabetical	M1757	ca. Jul 1924–1954
Fabens	app. nonres. alien BCIC	alphabetical	M1768	ca. 1945–Dec 24, 1952
	perm. manifests	alphabetical	M1768	Jul 1, 1924–Jul 27, 1952
	temporary visitors	alphabetical	M1768	Jul 1, 1924–54
Fort Hancock	app. nonres. alien BCIC	alphabetical	M1766	ca. 1945–Dec 24, 1952
	temporary visitors	alphabetical	M1766	1924–54
Galveston	ship-copies/abstracts	chronological	M575	1846–71
	ship-immigration	chronological	M1359	1893, Jan 14, 1896–Oct 25, 1948
	ship-passenger index	alphabetical	M334	1846–71
	ship-passenger index	alphabetical	M1357	1896–1906
	ship-passenger index	alphabetical	M1358	1906–51
Houston, see also Galveston, M1359				
	vessel index	alphabetical	M1514	Jul 1948–Nov 1954
Laredo	alien list	chronological	M2008	Jul 1903–Jul 1904, May 1905–Jun 1907

TABLE 3
Available Immigration Records

PORT OR DISTRICT	TYPE	ARRANGEMENT	MICROFILM	DATES
	temp. manifests	alphabetical	M1771	Dec 1, 1929–Apr 8, 1955
Port Arthur, *see also* Galveston, M1359				
	vessel index	alphabetical	M1514	May 1, 1908–Nov 30, 1954
Progreso	nonstat./temp. manifests	alphabetical	M1851	Oct 1928–May 27, 1955
	stat. index	alphabetical	M1851	Oct 6, 1928–Nov 19, 1952
	stat. manifests	chronological	M1851	Oct 6, 1928–Nov 19, 1952
Rio Grande City	nonstat. manifests	alphabetical	M1770	Mar 22, 1916–May 30, 1955
	stat. index	alphabetical	M1770	Nov 16, 1908–Jan 15, 1952
	stat. manifests	chronological	M1770	Nov 16, 1908–Jan 15, 1952
Roma	nonstat./temp. manifests	alphabetical	M1503	Mar 1, 1928–May 30, 1955
	stat. index	alphabetical	M1503	Aug 13, 1929–Aug 19, 1954
	stat./nonstat. manifests	alphabetical	M1503	Mar 1, 1928–Nov 30, 1929
	stat. manifests	chronological	M1503	Aug 13, 1929–Aug 19, 1954
Sabine, *see* Galveston, M1359				
San Antonio	stat. manifests	alphabetical	M1973	May 17, 1944–Mar 1952
Texas City, *see* Galveston, M1359				
Thayer, *see* Progreso, M1851				
Yseleta	stat./perm. manifests	alphabetical	M1849	Jul 1, 1924–Jul 27, 1952
	temp. manifests	alphabetical	M1849	1924–1954
	app. nonres. alien BCIC	alphabetical	M1849	ca. 1945–Dec 24, 1952
Zapata	app. nonres. alien BCIC	alphabetical	M2024	Apr 29, 1945–Sep 15, 1953
	nonstat./stat. manifests	alphabetical	M2024	Aug 18, 1923–Nov 30, 1929
	nonstat./temp. manifests	alphabetical	M2024	Apr 25, 1929–Sep 10, 1952
	stat. index	alphabetical	M2024	Dec 1, 1929–Jun 7, 1950
	stat. manifests	chronological	M2024	Aug 18, 1923–Jun 7, 1950
Vermont				
Alburg, *see also* St. Albans Dist., VT, M1461 and M1464				
	perm./temp. manifests	alphabetical	M1462	1895–1924
Beecher Falls, *see also* St. Albans Dist., VT, M1461 and M1464				
	perm./temp. manifests	alphabetical	M1462	1895–1924
Canaan	perm./temp. manifests	alphabetical	M1462	1895–1924
Highgate Springs	perm./temp. manifests	alphabetical	M1462	1895–1924
Island Pond, *see also* St. Albans Dist., VT, M1461 and M1464				
	perm./temp. manifests	alphabetical	M1462	1895–1924
Newport, *see* St. Albans Dist., VT, M1461 and M1464				
Norton	perm./temp. manifests	alphabetical	M1462	1895–1924
Richford, *see also* St. Albans Dist., VT, M1461 and M1464				
	perm./temp. manifests	alphabetical	M1462	1895–1924
St. Albans, *see also* St. Albans Dist., VT, M1461 and M1464				
	perm./temp. manifests	alphabetical	M1462	1895–1924
	ship-immigration	chronological	M1465	Jul 9, 1929–Jun 24, 1949
St. Albans Dist.	ship-immigration	chron./alpha.	M1464	Jan 11, 1895–Nov 30, 1954
	index-land arrivals	Soundex	M1461	1895–1924
	index-seaport arrivals	Soundex	M1463	1924–52
Swanton, *see also* St. Albans Dist., VT, M1461 and M1464				
	perm./temp. manifests	alphabetical	M1462	1895–1924
Virginia				
Alexandria	ship-copies/abstracts	chronological	M575	1820–65
	ship-State Dept. trans.	chronological	T1219	1820–31
	ship-passenger index	alphabetical	M334	1820–65
East River	ship-copies/abstracts	chronological	M575	1830
	ship-State Dept. trans.	chronological	T1219	1830

TABLE 3
Available Immigration Records

PORT OR DISTRICT	TYPE	ARRANGEMENT	MICROFILM	DATES
	ship-passenger index	alphabetical	M334	1830
Hampton	ship-copies/abstracts	chronological	M575	1820–21
	ship-passenger index	alphabetical	M334	1820–21
Norfolk and Portsmouth	ship-copies/abstracts	chronological	M575	1820–57
	ship-State Dept. trans.	chronological	T1219	1820–32
	ship-passenger index	alphabetical	M334	1820–57
Petersburg	ship-copies/abstracts	chronological	M575	1820–21
	ship-State Dept. trans.	chronological	T1219	1819–20, 1822
	ship-passenger index	alphabetical	M334	1820–21
Portsmouth, *see* Norfolk, M334, M575, and T1219				
Richmond	ship-copies/abstracts	chronological	M575	1820–24, 1826–30, 1832, 1836–37, 1844
	ship-State Dept. trans.	chronological	T1219	1820–24, 1828, 1830
	ship-passenger index	alphabetical	M334	1820–24, 1826–30, 1832, 1836–37, 1844
Washington				
Blaine, *see also* St. Albans Dist., VT, M1461 and M1464				
	paid head tax certs	chronological	M1365	Mar 1929–Apr 1929
Ferry, *see* St. Albans Dist., VT, M1461 and M1464				
Marcus, *see* St. Albans Dist., VT, M1461 and M1464				
Oroville, *see* St. Albans Dist., VT, M1461 and M1464				
Port Townsend, *see* Seattle, M1364, and Tacoma, M1484 and M1638				
Seattle	ship-immigration	chronological	M1398	Jan 4, 1949–Nov 29, 1954
	pass./crew lists	chronological	M1383	Aug 29, 1890–Mar 6, 1957
	crew lists	chronological	M1399	Sep 16, 1903–Mar 8, 1917
	insular passengers	chronological	M1485	Apr 27, 1908–Mar 10, 1917
	Chinese passengers	chronological	M1364	Jun 23, 1882–Nov 16, 1916
	paid head tax certs.	chronological	M1365	1917–Apr 1929
Sumas, *see* St. Albans Dist., VT, M1461 and M1464				
Tacoma	ship-customs	chronological	M1484	Nov 10, 1894–Nov 12, 1909
	Chinese admission	chronological	M1638	1896–1901
Wisconsin				
Ashland	ship-crew lists	chronological	M2005	Aug 1922–Jun 1934, Jun 1938–Oct 1954
Guam				
Guam	ship-pass./crew	chronological	M1778	1947–52
Trust Territory of the Pacific Islands				
See Guam, M1778				
Mexico				
Veracruz	ship-copies/abstracts	chronological	M2032	1921–23

TABLE 4
Immigration Records Destroyed by the Immigration and Naturalization Service
Prior to Preservation on Microfilm
(i.e., these records do not exist).
Similar gaps exist for airplane arrival records.

PORT OR DISTRICT	TYPE	ARRANGEMENT	MICROFILM	DATES
Florida				
Jacksonville	ship-alien	chronological	none	Jul 8, 1948–Dec 31, 1954
	ship-citizen	chronological	none	Sep 24, 1948–Dec 31, 1954
Miami	ship-alien	chronological	none	Jul 7, 1948–Dec 31, 1954
	ship-citizen	chronological	none	Jan 26, 1949–Dec 31, 1954
Pensacola	ship-alien	chronological	none	Jul 2, 1948–Dec 31, 1954
	ship-citizen	chronological	none	Aug 10, 1948–Dec 31, 1954
Port Everglades	ship-alien	chronological	none	Dec 11, 1945–Dec 31, 1954
	ship-citizen	chronological	none	Dec 6, 1945–Dec 31, 1954
	ship-immigration	chronological	none	Jan 10, 1949–Dec 31, 1954
Tampa	ship-immigration	chronological	none	Jun 30, 1948–Dec 31, 1954
Key West	ship-immigration	chronological	none	Jul 1, 1948–Dec 31, 1954
Georgia				
Savannah	ship-immigration	chronological	none	Jun 30, 1948–Dec 31, 1954
Louisiana				
New Orleans	ship-immigration	chronological	none	Jul 1, 1948–Nov 30, 1954
Maryland				
Baltimore	ship-immigration	chronological	none	Jul 1, 1948–Nov 30, 1954
New York				
New York	ship-citizen	chronological	none	Jan 1, 1944–May 20, 1944
	ship-aliens & citizens	chronological	none	Jan 1, 1949–Sep 17, 1949
	ship-aliens & citizens	chronological	none	Dec 1, 1954–Dec 31, 1954
Pennsylvania				
Philadelphia	ship-immigration	chronological	none	Jul 1, 1948–Nov 30, 1954
Puerto Rico				
San Juan	ship-immigration	chronological	none	Jul 1, 1948–Nov 30, 1954
Virgin Islands				
St. Thomas	ship-immigration	chronological	none	Jul 1, 1948–Dec 31, 1954

foreign-born U.S. nationals such as Filipinos, British citizens, several Canadians, and citizens of Mexico, Japan, and various European and Central and South American countries. M1852, *Record of Persons Held for Boards of Special Inquiry at the San Pedro, California, Immigration Office, November 3, 1930–September 27, 1936*, 1 roll, is a list of persons detained for boards of special inquiry. Most of the persons listed were detained due to questions about their U.S. citizenship or prior U.S. residency.

San Ysidro (Tia Juana), CA. In M1767, Manifests of *Alien Arrivals at San Ysidro (Tia Juana), California, April 21, 1908–December 1952*, 20 rolls, the index to statistical manifests, April 21, 1908–June 30, 1924, may also serve as an index to the nonstatistical manifests, April 21, 1908–June 30, 1924; *see* series description on microfilm for further details. The miscellaneous head tax manifests, also in M1767, include records of special head tax collections, later designated general head tax collections, and head taxes refunded.

Tampa, FL. M1844, *Passenger Lists of Vessels Arriving at Tampa, Florida, November 2, 1898–December 31, 1945*, 65 rolls, includes two major gaps for which no passenger lists exist: December 21, 1902–September 2, 1904, and May 1, 1915–November 30, 1915.

Vanceboro, ME. M2071, *Alphabetical Manifest Cards of Alien Arrivals at Vanceboro, Maine, ca. 1906–December 24, 1952*, 13 rolls, also includes a few manifest cards that document arrivals between 1888 and 1905.

Ventura, CA. A3363, *Passenger and Crew Lists of Vessels Arriving at Ventura, California, May 1929–December 1956*, 1 roll, primarily consists of ship and airplane crew lists, although some passengers are also included. While these lists were filed at Ventura, CA, the port of arrival is frequently indicated as El Capitan, Ellwood, Los Angeles, Port Hueneme, San Francisco, or San Pedro, all in California.

2.4 Special Notes for Microfilm Publications Containing Records of Multiple Ports

M334, *Supplemental Index to Passenger Lists of Vessels Arriving at Atlantic and Gulf Coast Ports (Excluding New York), 1820–1874*, mentioned above, contains 75 ports, of which 68 are included in M575, *Copies of Lists of Passengers Arriving at Miscellaneous Ports on the Atlantic and Gulf Coasts and at Ports on the Great Lakes, 1820–1873*, 16 rolls. The lists on M575 are arranged by port, thereunder by date of arrival. The seven ports on M334 which are not part of M575 are Baltimore, MD; Beverly, MA (grouped with Salem, MA); Boston and Charlestown, MA; New Orleans, LA; Philadelphia, PA; and Wiscasset, ME. Charleston, SC, is sometimes shown as the "District of South Carolina." Index cards for these seven ports undoubtedly refer to entries in volumes 5, 8, and 9 of T1219, *State Department Transcripts of Passenger Lists, ca. October 1819–ca. December 1832*, 2 rolls, described above.

M1464, *Manifests of Passengers Arriving in the St. Albans, Vermont, District Through Canadian Pacific and Atlantic Ports, 1895–1954*, 639 rolls, includes arrivals at Canadian Pacific and Atlantic seaports who entered the United States at 53 Canadian land border ports. These records are arranged by year, thereunder by month, thereunder by port, and thereunder by ship. These records are indexed by M1461, *Soundex Index to Canadian Border Entries Through the St. Albans, Vermont, District, 1895–1924*, 400 rolls, and by M1463, *Soundex Index to Entries into the St. Albans, Vermont, District Through Canadian Pacific and Atlantic Ports, 1924–1952*, 98 rolls.

M2016, *Alphabetical Index of Alien Arrivals at Eagle, Hyder, Ketchikan, Nome, and Skagway, Alaska, June 1906–August 1946*, 1 roll, is an index of aliens who crossed the Canadian border into Alaska, usually by railroad but occasionally on foot or by steamship. The majority of arrivals occurred before 1920, some were in the 1930s, and a few are dated 1941, 1942, and 1946. The arriving aliens were primarily citizens of Canada, Russia, Austria, Great Britain, Montenegro, Italy, Greece, Japan, Norway, Sweden, and various other European countries. M2016 serves as an index to alien arrivals in M2017, *Lists of Aliens Arriving at Skagway (White Pass), Alaska, October 1906–November 1934*, 1 roll, and to M2018, *Lists of Aliens Arriving at Eagle, Alaska, December 1910–October 1938*, 1 roll. Note, however, that citizen arrivals included in M2017 and M2018 are not indexed.

T517, *Index to Passenger Lists of Vessels Arriving at Ports in Alabama, Florida, Georgia, and South Carolina, 1890–1924*, 26 rolls, primarily serves as an index to arrivals at Tampa and Key West, FL, but other ports indexed include Mobile, AL; Boca Grande, Jacksonville, Knights Key, Miami, and Pensacola, FL; Savannah, GA; and Charleston, SC.

2.5 Miscellaneous Records

American Samoa. Immigration and emigration records of American Samoa are described in 18.10.

Boards of Special Inquiry. *The Process.* Each arriving person faced a "primary inspection" to determine their status, a process which consisted of questioning by an immigration official, usually a single inspector. The inspector followed defined lines of questioning concerning age, birthplace, amount of money, occupation, and U.S. citizenship or prior U.S. residence, if applicable, to determine whether the person was admissible. If doubt existed about the person's admissibility, the person was referred to a board of special inquiry (BSI). Each board consisted of three members who were appointed by the commissioner of immigration in charge of the local immigration station. Permanent boards were maintained in larger ports of entry.

The administrative law hearing before a BSI began with the presentation of evidence. The detainee was called before a table or bench to face the seated members of the board, placed under oath, and subjected to questioning by the chairman of the board. The first phase of the interrogation was routine. Basic facts were put into the record: age, birthplace, port of departure for the United States, destination in this country, amount of money in the individual's possession, trade or calling, purpose of migration, and applicable evidence of U.S. citizenship or prior U.S. residency. Any documents the person brought to the hearing were examined. Witnesses who came to testify on behalf of the detained person were secluded in a separate room. They were not called to testify until after the detainee had completed their testimony. Usually the board rendered its decision immediately at the end of the hearing. Two out of three board members prevailed. If the decision was to admit, the person was immediately released from detention. If the decision was to deport, the person was kept in detention until deported or until an appeal was completed.

Microfilmed Records. M1387, *Minutes of the Boards of Special Inquiry at the San Francisco Immigration Office, 1899-1909,* listed above, provides the names of aliens and members of the board, the charges on which each alien was detained, and a summary of each hearing, including the board's decision. The records are chronologically arranged in bound volumes, each having its own index.

M1500, *Records of the Special Boards of Inquiry, District No. 4 (Philadelphia), Immigration and Naturalization Service, 1893-1909,* 18 rolls, is likewise chronologically arranged and has information content similar to that reproduced in M1387.

M1852, *Record of Persons Held for Boards of Special Inquiry at the San Pedro, California, Immigration Office, November 3, 1930-September 27, 1936,* listed above, contains a chronological listing of persons detained for BSI, most of whom were detained due to questions about their U.S. citizenship or prior U.S. residency. The case file numbers shown to the left of each person's name refer to stenographers' notebooks in which BSI proceedings were recorded; these notebooks no longer exist.

Inspection cards. Most 20th-century immigrants arriving by steamship would carry an "inspection card" that was issued to passengers by steamship lines and used by the ship's surgeon to monitor the passenger's health. The cards typically bear daily check marks made by the surgeon showing he checked each passenger each day. They were later used by U.S. Public Health Service and U.S. immigration inspectors at the port of New York (Ellis Island) and other locations. Only a few marks or stamps might be added to the inspection cards at the ports of departure and arrival. These cards were not created or retained by U.S. immigration officials and are not in NARA.

"Passenger Acts," 1852–57. M2010, *Correspondence Relating to Enforcement of the "Passenger Acts," 1852-57,* 1 roll, contains correspondence of the Attorney General from the General Records of the Department of Justice, RG 60, about alleged violations on over 30 specific vessels

of acts of Congress regulating the health and safety conditions aboard vessels carrying passengers in foreign or interstate commerce. These vessels are named in the descriptive material reproduced at the beginning of M2010.

2.6 Records in the Custody of the Immigration and Naturalization Service (INS)

"A-File" (Alien File). An INS A-File case file contains all records (except naturalization) relating to an individual immigrant since April 1, 1944, and including naturalization records since April 1, 1956. Any immigrant who arrived or whose case was opened after April 1, 1944, should have records filed within the A-File system. A-Files were decentralized between 1950 and 1955 and thereafter maintained by the various INS Files Control Offices (FCO's). In 1999 INS began to re-centralize A-Files at a National INS Records Center. A-Files are identified by Alien Registration Number; are indexed by name, date of birth, and place of birth; and remain subject to INS Freedom of Information/Privacy Act restrictions.

C-File. An Immigration and Naturalization Service (INS) C-File case file contains a duplicate copy of naturalization papers and records relating to all U.S. naturalizations dated September 27, 1906, to April 31, 1956, as well as records of renunciation and resumption of citizenship and applications for certificates of derivative citizenship since 1929. These files are maintained on microfilm by the INS in Washington, DC, and are indexed by name, date of birth, and place of birth. C-Files remain subject to INS Freedom of Information/Privacy Act restrictions. Beginning April 1, 1956, all naturalization and citizenship records were filed in an INS A-File.

Alien Registration Cards. In response to distant threats of war, the United States enacted the Alien Registration Act of June 28, 1940 (54 Stat. 670), and most resident aliens registered at a Post Office between July–December 1940. Records relating to the issuance of such cards will be found in the alien's A-File, described above.

Record of Registry/Lawful Entry. An act of March 2, 1929 (45 Stat. 1512), which became effective July 1, 1929, and was amended on August 7, 1939 (53 Stat. 1243), allowed a record of lawful arrival—called a record of registry—to be made for certain aliens who had entered the United States at an earlier time but for whom the INS could find no record of arrival. In particular, if an alien had entered the United States before July 1, 1924, resided in the country continuously since that entry, was of good moral character, and was not subject to deportation, they could obtain a record of registry by making application to the INS and paying the requisite fee. The registry program was reauthorized by the Nationality Act of 1940 (54 Stat. 1137) under the name "Lawful Entry." Registry files cover the years 1929 to 1944; Lawful Entry paperwork after

April 1, 1944, was placed in an alien's individual "A-File." As of 1999 both Registry/Lawful Entry Files and A-Files remain in the legal custody of the Immigration and Naturalization Service, and researchers interested in examining those records should direct a Freedom of Information Act request to that agency only if they can provide Registry File (Bureau File) number (i.e., R-#####). Some Canadian and Mexican border crossing microfilm publications include registry records made on Form 657, *Record of Registry,* described above.

Records Destroyed by INS Prior to Preservation Microfilming. A change in INS microfilming procedure in the late 1940s resulted in the destruction of ship and airplane arrival manifest records for various ports, ca. July 1, 1948–ca. December 31, 1954, prior to preservation on microfilm; known destroyed ship arrival records are listed in Table 4 (destroyed airplane arrival records have similar gaps). Thus, these records do not exist in any form, but researchers seeking an immigration record may find evidence of the alien's date and ship or airplane of arrival in the alien's "A-File" described above.

World War II Refugees. NARA does not have passenger lists of World War II refugees who arrived in the United States on a U.S. military transport ship. However, evidence of the date and ship of arrival of such persons may be found in the alien's "A-File" described above. The names of such persons may appear either in the INS "Master Index" or in the INS "Central Index System" held by the Washington, DC, office of the Immigration and Naturalization Service.

Requesting Copies of Records in INS custody. Requests for copies of records in INS custody should be submitted to Immigration and Naturalization Service, Attn: FOIA/PA Office, 425 Eye St., NW, Washington, DC 20536. The FOIA request should include the arriving individual's name, year of birth (exact date if available), and country of birth (exact place if available). If the person was born less than 100 years ago, some evidence of death (i.e., a newspaper death notice, copy of a death certificate, or picture of a gravestone) would be helpful toward securing release of relevant records. If the person is still living, that individual should sign their own letter of request, submitted pursuant to the Privacy Act (instead of the Freedom of Information Act).

2.7 Bibliography

Wood, Virginia Steele. *Immigrant Arrivals: A Guide to Published Sources.* Revised edition. Washington: Library of Congress, 1997. Bibliography of published indexes and works on the ships, the immigration experience, and immigrants' personal narratives.

Immigration Statistics

Bromwell, William Jeremy. *History of Immigration to the United States, Exhibiting the Number, Sex, Age, Occupation, and Country of Birth, of Passengers Arriving in the United States by Sea from Foreign Counries, from September 30, 1819 to December 31, 1855: Compiled Entirely from Official Data . . . .* New York: Redfield, 1856; reprinted New York: Arno Press & A.M. Kelley, 1969. Statistical data in yearly tables.

U.S. Bureau of the Census. *Historical Statistics of the United States: Colonial Times to 1970.* Washington: Government Printing Office, 1975.

Methodology and Sources

Colletta, John P. *They Came in Ships: A Guide to Finding Your Immigrant Ancestor's Arrival Record.* Revised edition. Salt Lake City: Ancestry Publishing, 1993.

Smith, Marian L. "The Creation and Destruction of Ellis Island Immigration Manifests." Two parts. *Prologue: Quarterly of the National Archives* 28. Part 1, No. 3 (Fall 1996): 240–245; Part 2, No. 4 (Winter 1996): 314–318.

Smith, Marian L. "Jewish Immigration to the U.S. via Mexico and the Caribbean, 1920–1922." *Generations* (Jewish Genealogical Society of Michigan) 14, No. 2 (Spring 1999): 8–13.

Smith, Marian L. "The RMS Titanic Passenger Manifest: Record of Survivors—and Revival of a Record." *Voyage* (Titanic International Society) 29 (1999): 4–9.

Smith, Marian L. "Certificates of Arrival and the Accuracy of Arrival Information Found in U.S. Naturalization Records." *Avotaynu: The International Review of Jewish Genealogy* XIV, No. 2 (Summer 1998): 18–23; reprinted *FGS Forum* 10, No. 3 (Fall 1998): 9–12.

Smith, Marian L. "Interpreting U.S. Immigration Manifest Annotations." *Avotaynu: The International Review of Jewish Genealogy* XII, No. 1 (Spring 1996): 10–13.

Ports of Arrival

Bolino, August C. *The Ellis Island Source Book.* 2nd edition. Washington: Kensington Historical Press, 1990.

Natale, Valerie. "Angel Island: 'Guardian of the Western Gate.'" *Prologue: Quarterly of the National Archives* 30, No. 2 (Summer 1998): 125–135.

Voices from Ellis Island: An Oral History of American Immigration: A Project of the Statue of Liberty-Ellis Island Foundation. Frederick, MD: University Publications of America, 1987. 185 microfiche; 8 reels microfilm.

Ships

Anuta, Michael J. *Ships of Our Ancestors.* Baltimore: Genealogical Publishing Co., 1993; reprinted 1999. Over 880 illustrations of ships.

Bonsor, N.R.P. *North Atlantic Seaway: An Illustrated History of the Passenger Services Linking the Old World with the New.* 4 vols. Revised edition. Vols. 1–2, Newton Abbot, England: David & Charles, 1975; vols. 3–4, Jersey, Channel Islands: Brookside Pub., 1979. Discusses American, British, and European steamship lines, 1829–1957, with brief comments on each vessel; 200 illustrations.

*Immigrants at Ellis Island. Photograph No. 90-G-125-16,
Records of the Public Health Service, 1912–1968, RG 90.*

CHAPTER 3   *Naturalization Records*

3.1   *Introduction*

3.1.1   *Federal Court Records*

3.1.2   *Primary Types of Naturalization Records*

3.1.3   *Naturalization Records by State*

3.2   *Naturalization Information in Other Federal Records*

3.3   *Naturalization Records Not in the National Archives*

3.1 Introduction

The first naturalization act, passed in 1790 (1 Stat. 103), provided that an alien who desired to become a citizen of the United States should apply to "any common law court of record, in any one of the states wherein he shall have resided for the term of one year at least." Under this and later laws, and under varying requirements, aliens were naturalized in Federal, state, and local courts. Before 1906 aliens were more likely to go to a state or local court close to their home to take the naturalization oath. After 1906 they usually went to the Federal court. However, records of aliens taking naturalization oaths in local or state courts have been found as late as the 1930s.

3.1.1 Federal Court Records

Records of naturalization proceedings in Federal courts are usually among the records of the district court for the district in which the proceedings took place. These records may still be in the custody of the court, they may have been transferred to a regional records services facility of the National Archives and Records Administration (NARA), or they may have been transferred to the National Archives Building, Washington, DC. They are all part of Record Group (RG) 21, Records of District Courts of the United States.

A Federal naturalization record usually consists of a declaration of intention, petitions, a record of the oath of naturalization, and occasionally depositions. The nature of the information found in these types of documents is discussed first in this chapter, followed by a listing by state of those naturalization records held by NARA's regional archives facilities. Some indexes are available, but the researcher should know where and when the subject of research became a citizen before beginning to look for documentation of naturalization.

3.1.2 Primary Types of Naturalization Records

Declarations of intention are instruments by which applicants for U.S. citizenship renounced allegiance to foreign sovereignties and declared their intention to become U.S. citizens. Early declarations of intention usually show the following for each applicant: name, country of birth or allegiance, date of the application, and signature. Some show the date and port of arrival in the United States.

After 1906 a longer and more detailed form was used, including such information as the applicant's name, age, occupation, and personal description; date and place of birth; citizenship; present address and last foreign address; vessel and port of embarkation for the United States; port and date of arrival in the United States; and date of application and signature.

A declaration of intention normally preceded proof of residence or a petition to become a citizen by two or more years, but the declaration was sometimes not required if the person had been honorably discharged from certain military service or had entered the country when a minor or was married to a citizen of the United States.

Naturalization petitions are instruments by which persons who had declared their intention to become U.S. citizens and who had met residency requirements and made formal application for U.S. citizenship. Through September 26, 1906, information on the petitions was limited to names of the petitioner and sovereign to whom he is foreswearing allegiance, and occasionally the petitioner's residence, occupation, date and country of birth, and port and date of arrival in this country. The amount of information given in these early petitions varies but is typically quite limited. Starting on September 27, 1906, information includes name, residence, occupation, date and place of birth, citizenship, and personal description of applicant; date of emigration; ports of embarkation and arrival; marital status; names, dates, places of birth, and residence of applicant's spouse and children; date at which U.S. residence commenced; time of residence in state; name changes; and signature. Copies of declarations of intention and certificates of arrival are often interfiled with petitions. After 1930 declarations of intention may include the applicant's photograph.

Naturalization depositions are formal statements made by witnesses in support of the applicant's petition. The records indicate the period of the applicant's residence in a certain locale and other information, including the witnesses' appraisals of the applicant's character. The witnesses were designated by the applicant.

Records of naturalization and oaths of allegiance document the granting of U.S. citizenship to petitioners. The early orders of admission to citizenship are often available only in the minute books of the court. In fact, entries for administration of oaths of allegiance have been found in unlikely places, such as a criminal minute book that happened to be on a clerk's desk at the time. Daily minutes are recorded chronologically, and most minute books have alphabetical indexes showing names of individuals appearing in the minutes. Later records of naturalization are in the form of certificates, often unnumbered but chronologically arranged in bound volumes with indexes to surnames.

In some cases all records for one person have been gathered together in a **petition and record**, which usually includes the petition for naturalization, affidavits of the petitioner and witnesses, the oath of allegiance, and the order of the court admitting the petitioner to citizenship.

3.1.3 Naturalization Records by State

Alabama

NARA's Southeast Region in Atlanta has records of the U.S. district courts in Alabama. Unless otherwise indicated, all of the records discussed below are indexed.

Naturalization records of the **U.S. District Court for the Southern District of Alabama** for the Mobile Division include petitions for naturalization, 1906-69, and declarations of intention, 1855-62 and 1885-1986. Records for the Selma Division include petitions for naturalization, 1909-43, and declarations of intention, 1909-41.

Records of the **U.S. District Court for the Middle District of Alabama** for the Northern Division at Montgomery include petitions for naturalization, 1912-60; declarations of intention, 1907-60; and military naturalization petitions, 1917-18.

Records of the **U.S. District Court for the Northern District of Alabama** for the Southern Division at Birmingham include petitions for naturalization, 1909-63, and related index, 1911-63; declarations of intention, 1911-59; and unindexed military naturalization petitions, 1918-24. Records for the Northeastern Division at Huntsville include petitions for naturalization, 1924-26, and declarations of intention, 1923-25; those for the Northwestern Division at Florence include petitions for naturalization, 1922-26, and declarations of intention, 1923-29.

Naturalization records from the district courts in Birmingham, Mobile, Montgomery, and Selma are available on rolls 1-17 of M1547, *Naturalization Records of U.S. District Courts in the Southeast, 1790-1958*, 106 rolls.

Alaska

NARA's Pacific Alaska Region (Anchorage) has records of the first, third, and fourth judicial divisions of the **U.S. District Court for the District of Alaska and for the Territory of Alaska, 1900–60,** and the **U.S. District Court for the District of Alaska**, 1960-91. Records relating to naturalization include, for Juneau, indexed declarations of intention, 1900-29, microfilmed as part of M1539, *Naturalization Records of the U.S. District Courts for the State of Alaska, 1900-1924*, 5 rolls; special court orders, 1914-32; and a "Schedule C & miscellaneous cashbook, 1954-60," which includes names of applicants for citizenship, declarations of intentions, and fees paid. Records for Ketchikan include certificates of naturalization, 1903-9; declarations of intention, 1906-72; and petitions, 1913-86; and for Skagway, declarations of intention, 1901-17, microfilmed on M1539. The indexes to declarations of intention for Juneau and Skagway have been microfilmed as M1241, *Indexes to the Naturalization Records of the U.S. District Court for the District and Territory of Alaska, 1900-1929*, 1 roll.

Records relating to naturalization from the **U.S. District Court for the District of Alaska** at Anchorage include declarations of intention and petitions for naturalization, 1903-91; hearing records, 1930-58; naturalization order books, 1960-79; and indexes, 1903-91 (for Cordova, Seward, Valdez, and other towns). Other naturalization records include, for Cordova, petition and record files, 1910-59; for Kodiak, indexes to naturalization actions, 1931-60; for Seward, petition files, 1911-57; and for Valdez, petition and record documents, 1902-28, and indexes to naturalization actions, 1930-44. Naturalization petition files at Anchorage also include declarations and petitions for residents of Adak, Amchitka, Cordova, Homer, Kodiak, Seward, Valdez, and other towns and cities throughout Alaska. Indexes have been reproduced as M1788, *Indexes to Naturalization Records of the U.S. District Court for the District, Territory, and State of Alaska (Third Division), 1903-1991*, 22 rolls.

NARA's regional facility at Anchorage also holds naturalization records accessioned from the **U.S. District Court** in Fairbanks, including indexes to certificates of arrival and certificates of naturalization, 1900-73; naturalization case files, declarations of intention, petitions, and other naturalization records, 1900-91; naturalization certificate stubs, 1908-26; depositions for petitions, 1908-91; transferred petitions, 1946-54, 1960-80; and administrative files, 1959-86. Also available are a small number of miscellaneous naturalization records for Bethel, 1927-32; Eagle, 1901-5 and 1927-29; Flat, 1926; Iditarod, 1911-26; McGrath, 1927-32; Ruby, 1908-30; Wiseman, 1927-32, and other towns. Included on M1539, discussed above, are the naturalization case files for Fairbanks, 1910-24; Iditarod, 1913-16; and Ruby, 1908-20, and a small number of naturalization records from Circle City and Nome.

The Alaska State Archives, 141 Willoughby Ave., Juneau, AK 99801-1720, holds some naturalization records for the **First Division,** at Juneau, 1900-60; Petersburg, 1930-55; and Wrangell, 1915-47; and for the **Second Division**, at Nome, 1900-72.

Arizona

NARA's Pacific Region (Laguna Niguel) has records relating to the naturalization process during the territorial and early statehood years for all five judicial districts. They include declarations of intention, 1881-1912; petitions and certificates for naturalization, 1870-1915; and indexes from 1864-1990, though inclusive dates for the territorial years differ for Cochise, Maricopa, Pima, and Yavapai counties. Many of these records for the years 1864-1911 appear with their indexes on M1615, *Naturalization Records of the U.S. District Court for the Territory of Arizona, 1864-1915*, 5 rolls. Additionally, 22 bound and indexed volumes of "WPA Records of Naturalization" include copies of certificates of citizenship, final naturalizations, naturalization petitions, minute books of naturalization, and affidavits for the years 1882-1915. The volumes were assembled by the Arizona Work Projects Administration (WPA).

The Laguna Niguel facility also has naturalization records for the **U.S. District Court,** Tucson, including declarations of intention, 1915-88, with index, 1915-29; petitions for naturalization, 1915-91, with index, 1915-31; military petitions for naturalization, 1918-46, with index, 1918; certificates of naturalization, 1915-26; naturalization orders granted or denied, 1929-89, and 1949-55; and naturalization actions of the **Superior Court of Pima County**, 1912-15, with index. All of these records have been microfilmed as M1616, *Naturalization Records of the U.S. District Court for the District of Arizona, 1912-1915*,

7 rolls. Not available on microfilm are: petitions for naturalization transferred, 1953-90; naturalization depositions, 1915-19; naturalization repatriations, 1936-64; and overseas military naturalization petitions, 1954-55.

The Laguna Niguel facility also has, for the **U.S. District Court**, Phoenix, naturalization records including petitions for naturalization, 1929-91; declarations of intention, 1929-72; petitions for naturalization transferred, 1953-74; records relating to repatriations, 1929-68; and petitions recommended to be continued, granted, denied, 1935-83.

Arkansas

NARA's Southwest Region in Fort Worth has records of the **U.S. District Court for the Western District of Arkansas**. The records relating to naturalization include, for El Dorado, indexed declarations of intention, 1925-51, and lists of granted, denied, and continued petitions, 1929-52; for Harrison, indexed declarations of intention, 1907-50; indexed petitions, 1909-50; and lists of granted, denied, and continued petitions, 1935-52; for Hot Springs, indexed declarations of intention, 1940-82; indexed petitions, 1941-81; petitions by military servicemen, 1954; transferred petitions, 1954-88; applications to regain citizenship and repatriation oaths, 1963; and lists of granted, denied, and continued petitions, 1941-91; for Texarkana, indexed declarations of intention, 1908-80; indexed petitions, 1907-80; transferred petitions, 1954-81; stubs of naturalization certificates, 1907-68; applications to regain citizenship and repatriation oaths, 1941-68; and lists of granted, denied, and continued petitions, 1926-92. The records of the **U.S. District Court**, Fort Smith, include declarations, petitions, and oaths of admission, 1872-1906; indexed declarations of intention, 1907-87; indexed petitions, 1911-64; transferred petitions, 1954-84; stubs of naturalization certificates, 1907-26; and lists of granted, denied, and continued petitions, 1938-73. The records of the **U.S. Circuit Court**, Fort Smith, include naturalization orders, 1900-6, and petitions, 1906-11.

California

NARA's Pacific Region (San Francisco) has the records of the **U.S. Circuit and District Courts for the Northern District of California**, San Francisco. Circuit court records relating to naturalization include an index, 1855-1911; declarations of intention, 1855-1911; naturalization petitions and affidavits, 1903-6; petition and record of naturalization, 1907-11; and certificates of naturalization, 1855-1906. District court records relating to naturalization include an index, 1852-ca. 1989; records of naturalization, 1852-1906; petition and record of naturalization; 1907-72; and petitions for naturalization from military personnel, 1918-55. The index to naturalization records is microfilmed as M1744, *Index to Naturalization [Records] in the U.S. District Court for the Northern District of California., 1852-ca. 1989*, 165 rolls. Also available is T1220, *Selected Indexes to Naturalization Records of the U.S. Circuit and District Courts, Northern District of California, 1852-1928*, 3 rolls. Naturalizations recorded in court minutes can be found in minute books reproduced as part of T717, *Records of the U.S. District Court for the Northern District of California and Predecessor Courts, 1851-1950*, 125 rolls. Such naturalizations are arranged by date and provide only the name of the person naturalized.

NARA's Pacific Region (San Francisco) also has the records of the **U.S. District Court for the Eastern District of California**, Sacramento. Records relating to naturalization include declarations of intention, 1917-56; petition and record of naturalization, 1917-29; petitions for naturalization, 1922-56; and naturalization petitions from military personnel, 1944-46.

NARA's Pacific Region (Laguna Niguel) has the records of the **U.S. District Court for the Southern District of California**. Records relating to naturalization for the Southern District, Central Division, Los Angeles, include an index, 1887-1931; declarations of intention, 1887-1966; petitions for naturalization, 1887-1973; naturalization petitions of military personnel, 1918-46; petitions for repatriation, 1936-52; petitions for repatriation of military personnel, 1922-46; naturalization petitions of overseas military personnel, 1942-54; a court order book, 1926-31; and a civil order book, 1938-54. Some records for this jurisdiction are available on microfilm under the following titles: M1524, *Naturalization Records of the United States District Court for the Southern District of California, Central Division, Los Angeles, 1887-1940*, 244 rolls; M1525, *Naturalization Index Cards of the United States District Court for the Southern District of California, Central Division, Los Angeles, 1915-1976*; M1606, *Index Cards to Overseas Military Petitions of the U.S. District Court for the Southern District of California, Central Division (Los Angeles), 1943-1945, 1954, 1955-1956*, 2 rolls; and M1607, *Index to Naturalization Records of the U.S. District Court for the Southern District of California, Central Division, Los Angeles, 1887-1937*, 2 rolls.

For the Southern District, Southern Division, San Diego, naturalization records include petitions for naturalization, 1955-66; declarations of intention, 1955-66; naturalization depositions, 1955-66; naturalization court orders, 1955-66; and naturalization repatriations, 1966-73.

The records of the **U.S. Circuit Court for the Southern District of California** include an index to declarations of intention and petitions for naturalization, 1887-1911, and naturalization depositions and case files, 1925-61, located in district court records.

Donated materials include naturalization records received from the **Superior Court of Los Angeles County**, including a naturalization index, 1850-1915; naturalization records, 1850-88; certificates of citizenship, 1876-1906; declarations of intention, 1887-1915; and petitions for naturalization, 1907-15. Some of these records are available as the following microfilm publications: M1608, *Naturalization Index of the Superior Court for Los Angeles County, California, 1852-1915*, 1 roll, and M1614,

Naturalization Records of the Superior Court of Los Angeles County, California, 1876-1915, 28 rolls.

Naturalization records donated by the **Superior Court of San Diego County** include indexes to declarations and naturalized citizens, 1853-1956; certificates and records of naturalization, including petitions, 1883-1906; petitions for naturalization, 1906-56; naturalization petitions for military personnel, 1918-19; declarations of intention, 1941-55; petitions granted and denied, 1929-58; transferred petitions, 1953-55; and petitions for repatriation, 1936-55. Some of these records are available on these microfilm publications: M1526, *Naturalization Index Cards from the Superior Court of San Diego County, California, 1929-1956*, 5 rolls; M1609, *Index to Citizens Naturalized in the Superior Court of San Diego, California, 1853-1956*, 1 roll; M1612, *Index to Declarations of Intention in the Superior Court of San Diego County, California, 1853-1956*, 1 roll; and M1613, *Naturalization Records in the Superior Court of San Diego County, California, 1883-1958*, 19 rolls.

Colorado

NARA's Rocky Mountain Region in Denver has naturalization case files, declarations of intention, and petition and record books, 1876-1969, for the **U.S. District Courts** at Denver and Pueblo. Additional records for the Denver court include petitions and certificates of soldiers, 1918-46; court orders, 1942-66; transfers and repatriations, 1947-69; and overseas petition docket, 1954-55. Some records and accompanying indexes have been microfilmed on M1192, *Naturalization Records Created by the U.S. District Courts in Colorado, 1877-1952*, 79 rolls. Additional indexes are available in the regional facility's microfilm research room.

Connecticut

NARA's Northeast Region in Boston has records of the **U.S. District Court for the District of Connecticut**. Records relating to naturalization include declarations of intention for the New Haven office, 1911-63, and the Hartford office, 1911-55, and records of naturalization for both offices, 1842-1903. Also available are petitions and records of naturalization for the New Haven office, 1911-65, with an index for 1906-49; petitions and records of naturalization for the Hartford office, 1911-73; and military petitions, 1919 and 1942-56. Naturalization records of the **U.S. Circuit Court** for the district include declarations of intention for the New Haven office, 1906-11, and for the Hartford office, 1906-11; and petitions and records of naturalization for both offices, 1893-1911.

Some naturalization records from **local courts in Connecticut** are available as well. These records came into the custody of the Federal district court and are therefore now part of RG 21. Records from the **City Court of New Haven** consist of declarations of intention, with index cards, 1907-23, and petitions and records of naturalization,

with index cards, 1906-23; from the **City Court of Hartford**, records of naturalization, 1875-76; from the **City Court of Meriden**, declarations of intention, 1928-39, and petitions and records of naturalization, 1903-29; and from the **City Court of Ansonia**, declarations of intention filed 1893-1906, and petitions and records of naturalization, 1893-1906.

The Northeast Region also holds some records, 1790-1975, donated by non-Federal courts, including courts of common pleas, district courts, municipal courts, and superior courts.

Delaware

NARA's Mid Atlantic Region (Center City Philadelphia) has petitions for naturalization, 1797-1963, and declarations of intention, 1817-1967, for the **U.S. District Court for the District of Delaware** and petitions for naturalization, 1828-1902, for the **U.S. Circuit Court for the District of Delaware**. The U.S. District Court records include military petitions filed at Fort DuPont, 1918-19, and repatriation petitions filed between 1938-68. The facility also has a combined index to the petitions for naturalization and the declarations of intention for both the District and Circuit Courts for Delaware, 1797-1929. Microfilmed records include petitions for naturalization, 1840-1930, on M1644, *Naturalization Petitions of the U.S. District and Circuit Courts for the District of Delaware, 1795-1930*, 19 rolls; index to petitions, 1795-1929, on M1649, *Index to Naturalization Petitions for the U.S. Circuit Court, 1795-1928, for the District of Delaware*, 1 roll; and declarations of intention, 1842-1936 (reference microfilm). Note: the date spans of the microfilm publications may reflect the overall dates of the series and not necessarily the dates of the material that was actually filmed.

District of Columbia

Naturalization papers were issued chiefly by the U.S. Circuit Court for the District of Columbia from 1802 to 1863 and after that date by the Supreme Court of the District of Columbia. Since all the records from 1802 were maintained as a single series, these records are all filed with the records of the **Supreme Court of the District of Columbia** in RG 21. Included are three volumes that are useful in locating an individual's naturalization records. They consist of a single volume index to most series of naturalization records, which is reproduced as M1827, *Index to Naturalization Records of the U.S. Supreme Court for the District of Columbia, 1802-1909*, 1 roll; a volume of naturalization index stubs, 1906-26; and a volume of military naturalization index stubs, 1918-24.

For the most part, the naturalization records fall into two chronological periods, 1802-1906 and 1907 forward. The pre-1907 records include unbound declarations of intention with supporting papers, such as proofs of residence, arranged chronologically, 1802-1903; a bound volume containing transcripts for 1818 and abstracts of declarations of intention, 1819-65; bound volumes of declarations of intention, 1866-1906; and bound volumes labeled "naturalization records," consisting in part of orders of admission, 1824-1906. The information found in these bound naturalization records varies over time. For the period 1824-39, the records provide basically the same information for each petitioner as that contained in the declaration of intention, plus the date of admission to citizenship and proof of age; for the years 1839-65, the name of each person and the term and year of admission, arranged by initial letter of a surname; for 1866-1906, the name, place of birth, age, date of declaration of intention, statement of honorable military discharge, or statement of arrival as a minor (at first, before the age of 18, and later 21); and from 1903, the date of arrival.

Records for the post-1906 years include petitions received from the Bureau of Immigration and Naturalization Service, 1906-23, and military petitions, 1918-20, issued under the act of May 9, 1918. The Court records also include applications for naturalization, 1903-10, and depositions taken in support of petitions for naturalization under the act of June 29, 1906. Bound volumes contain naturalization records issued after 1906, arranged by certificate number. The files for each petitioner typically contain a certificate of arrival, a declaration of intention, and a petition for nationalization plus supporting documents. The documents usually show the name of the petitioner, port of entry, date of arrival, name of the vessel, occupation, address at time of petition, personal description, and names of wife and children and their birth dates.

Naturalization records are also located in the minutes of the District of Columbia Circuit Court, 1801-37 and 1847-63, reproduced on M1021, *Minutes of the U.S. Circuit Court for the District of Columbia, 1801-63,* 6 rolls; District Court Minutes, 1801-63; and the Special Term Minutes of the Criminal Court, the Law Court, and the General Term Minutes of the Supreme Court of the District of Columbia. Each volume of the minutes usually contains an alphabetical index.

Florida

All of the naturalization records discussed below are indexed unless otherwise indicated.

NARA's Southeast Region in Atlanta has the records of the **U.S. District Court for the Southern District of Florida.** Records relating to naturalization for the Key West Division include petitions, 1847-1969, with an index to May 1959; declarations of intention, 1867-1956; and military petitions, 1945-54. Naturalization records for the Miami Division include petitions, 1913-70, indexed to Jan. 1959; declarations of intention, 1913-67, indexed to Sept. 1950; and naturalization petition transfers, 1953-60.

Naturalization records of the **U.S. District Court for the Middle District of Florida,** Tampa Division, include petitions, 1907-60; a naturalization index, 1906-60; and declarations of intention, 1909-63, indexed to 1960. Tampa

was in the Southern District from 1879-1962. The records for the Jacksonville Division include petitions, 1895-1975, indexed to Sept. 1954; declarations of intention, 1892-1975, indexed to Feb. 1961; and military petitions, June 1918-Dec. 1923, with index. Jacksonville was in the Southern District until 1962. Naturalization records for the Orlando Division include petitions for naturalization, 1932-73. Those for the Ocala Division include petitions, 1940-65. The Ocala Division was part of the Southern District of Florida from 1900-62.

The records of the **U.S. District Court for the Northern District of Florida,** Pensacola Division, include petitions, 1903-72; declarations of intention, 1906-45; and unindexed military petitions, 1918-22.

Naturalization records from the district courts in Key West, Miami, and Tampa are available on rolls 17-42 of M1547, cited in the Alabama entry.

Georgia

All of the naturalization records discussed below are indexed unless otherwise indicated.

NARA's Southeast Region in Atlanta has records of the **U.S. District and Circuit Courts for the Southern District of Georgia,** Savannah Division, including an index to naturalizations in district minutes, 1790-1886, and in circuit minutes, 1794-1886; declarations of intention, 1825-86 and 1908-77; petitions for naturalization, 1790-1861 and 1909-73, indexed through 1970; and military petitions, 1918-23 and 1945-54. Some naturalization oaths are recorded in five volumes of general minute books, 1789-1857, which are reproduced on rolls 1 and 2 of M1172, *Index Books, 1789-1928, and Minutes and Bench Dockets, 1789-1870, for the U.S. District Court, Southern District of Georgia,* 3 rolls.

The records of the **U.S. District Court for the Middle District of Georgia,** Athens Division, include declarations of intention, 1907-28, and petitions for naturalization, 1910-25. Records of the Macon Division include declarations of intention, 1906-29; petitions for naturalization, 1906-29; and military petitions, eight volumes for 1918.

Records of the **U.S. District Court for Northern District of Georgia,** Rome Division, include declarations of intention, 1907-64; petitions for naturalization, 1909-26; and unindexed military petitions for March-November 1918. Records of the Atlanta Division include declarations of intention, 1907-61, indexed to 1950; petitions for naturalization, 1907-64, indexed to 1950; and unindexed military petitions, 1918-24.

Some naturalization proceedings are recorded in the seven volumes of minutes reproduced on M1184, *Minutes of the U.S. Circuit Court for the District of Georgia, 1790-1842, and Index to Plaintiffs and Defendants in the Circuit Court, 1790-1860,* 3 rolls. Naturalization records from the district courts in Athens, Atlanta, Rome, and Savannah are available on rolls 43-61, 100-102, and 104-105 of M1547, cited in the Alabama entry.

Hawaii

NARA's Pacific Region (San Francisco) has the records of the **U.S. District Court for the District of Hawaii**, Honolulu. Records relating to naturalization include an index, microfilmed as M2074, *Index to Naturalization in the U.S. District Court for the District of Hawaii, 1900-1976*, 23 rolls; declarations of intention, 1900-91; petitions for naturalization, 1910-60; and naturalization petitions from military personnel, 1918-55.

Idaho

NARA's Pacific Alaska Region (Seattle) has records of the **U.S. District Court for the District of Idaho**. Naturalization records include, for the court in Boise, declarations of intention, 1901-90; naturalization records, 1903-6; petitions, 1907-81; transferred petitions, 1953-78; and a list of persons naturalized in Superior Court, 1866-1907; for the court in Coeur d'Alene, declarations of intention, 1912-65; naturalization orders, 1930-67; petitions, 1912-67; transferred petitions, 1958-73; and repatriation oaths, 1939-54; and for the court in Moscow, declarations of intention, 1907-67; journal of admissions, 1892-1903; naturalization orders, 1940-64; petitions, 1907-67; transferred petitions, 1955-65; and an index to naturalization records, 1930-64.

Naturalization records for the court in Pocatello include declarations of intention, 1921-41; naturalization orders, 1929-45; and petitions, 1915-41. Those for the court in Twin Falls include declarations of intention, 1907-80; petitions, 1907-80; transferred petitions, 1958-73; and memorandums of naturalization proceedings, 1908-14.

Illinois

NARA's Great Lakes Region in Chicago has records of the **U.S. District Court for the Northern District of Illinois**, Eastern Division, Chicago. Court records before 1871 were destroyed in the 1871 Chicago fire. Existing naturalization records include declarations of intention, 1872-1982; an index to declarations of intention, 1906-60; orders, 1872-1903 and 1921-76; petitions, 1906-75, and an index to petitions, 1906-60; petitions based on military service, 1918-26; and repatriations, 1936-69. Naturalization records of the **U.S. Circuit Court for the District** include declarations of intention, 1906-11, and petitions, 1906-11.

The records of the **U.S. District Court for the Southern District of Illinois**, Southern Division, Springfield, include declarations of intention, 1903-50; naturalization record volumes, 1856-1903; and petitions, 1906-66. Records of the Northern Division, Peoria, include declarations of intention, 1905-51; an index to declarations of intention and petitions, 1905-54; stubs from certificates of naturalization, 1903-26; petitions, 1908-54; a naturalization order book, 1929-57; and overseas naturalizations, 1943-55. Naturalization records for the **U.S. Circuit Court for the District** include declarations of intention, 1856-1902, and naturalization record volumes, 1862-1903.

The records of the **U.S. District Court for the Eastern District of Illinois**, Danville, include declarations of intention, 1906-51; naturalization petitions and records, 1906-62; repatriations, 1938-50; and military petitions, 1944-54.

Indiana

NARA's Great Lakes Region in Chicago has records of the **U.S. District Court for the Southern District of Indiana**, Indianapolis. Records relating to naturalization include certificates of naturalization, 1917-24, not inclusive; declarations of intention, 1906-48; petitions, 1907-45; and petitions based on military service, 1918.

Naturalization records of the **U.S. District Court for the Northern District of Indiana**, Hammond, include declarations of intention, 1906-21.

Iowa

NARA's Central Plains Region in Kansas City has records of the **U.S. District Court for the Northern District of Iowa**. Records relating to naturalization include, for the Cedar Rapids Division, declarations of intention, 1910-81; petitions for naturalization, 1913-78; and certificate stubs, 1917-27; for the Fort Dodge Division, declarations of intention, 1917-77; petitions for naturalization, 1909-77; and other naturalization records, including oaths of allegiance, continuances, and denials, 1929-63; and for the Mason City Division, declarations of intention, 1944-58; petitions for naturalization, 1944-61; military petitions, 1954; and other naturalization records, including oaths of allegiance, continuances, and denials, 1944-61. Records of the Dubuque Division include declarations of intention, 1914-65; petitions for naturalization, 1915-62; and miscellaneous naturalization records, 1937-63; and those for the Waterloo Division include declarations of intention, 1944-58; petitions for naturalization, 1944-62; and miscellaneous naturalization records, 1944-62. Also held are **U.S. Superior Court records** for Linn County including declarations of intention, 1886-1947, and petitions for naturalization, 1891-1947.

NARA's Central Plains Region also has **U.S. District Court records for the Southern District of Iowa**. Records relating to naturalization include, for the Keokuk Division, declarations of intention, 1949-88, and petitions for naturalization, 1853-74; for the Ottumwa Division, declarations of intention, 1916-51; petitions for naturalization, 1916-51; certificate stubs, 1921-26; and miscellaneous naturalization records, 1938-51; for the Creston Division, declarations of intention, 1930-51, and petitions for naturalization, 1931-51; and for the Des Moines Division, declarations of intention, 1915-88, and petitions for naturalization, 1915-84.

Kansas

NARA's Central Plains Region in Kansas City has records of the **U.S. District Court for the District of Kansas**. Records relating to naturalization include, for the First Division, Topeka, an index to naturalization cases, 1856-97;

declarations of intention, 1862-1942; petitions for naturalization, 1868-1984; certificate stubs, 1908-21; and repatriation and military petitions, 1940-55; for the Second Division, Wichita, declarations of intention, 1909-91; petitions for naturalization, 1909-91; transfers of petitions, 1954-91; certificate stubs, 1909-91; and military petitions, 1942-56; for the Fort Scott Division, declarations of intention, 1915-64; petitions for naturalization, 1915-67; certificate stubs, 1916-29; and naturalization record volumes, 1937-66; and for the Kansas City Division, petitions for naturalization, 1939-70.

Kentucky

All of the records discussed below are indexed except where otherwise indicated.

NARA's Southeast Region in Atlanta has records of the **U.S. District Court for the Western District of Kentucky**. Naturalization records for the Louisville Division include declarations of intention, 1906-51; petitions for naturalization, 1906-57; and unindexed military petitions, 1918-21. Records of the Bowling Green Division include declarations of intention, 1915-78, and petitions for naturalization, 1915-76.

NARA's Southeast Region also has records of the **U.S. District Court for the Eastern District of Kentucky**. Records relating to naturalization include, for the Catlettsburg/Ashland Division, petitions for naturalization, 1913-29; for the Covington Division, declarations of intention, 1911-56, and petitions for naturalization, 1910-56; for the Frankfort Division, declarations of intention, 1910-28 and 1931-52, and petitions for naturalization, 1912-29 and 1931-73; for the Lexington Division, declarations of intention, 1922-29, and petitions for naturalization, 1922-43; for the London Division, declarations of intention, 1913-72, and petitions for naturalization, 1913-73, indexed to 1949; for the Pikeville Division, declarations of intention, 1938-42, and petitions for naturalization, 1942-59; and for the Richmond Division, petitions for naturalization, 1913-28.

Naturalization records from the district court in Louisville are available on rolls 62-75 of M1547, cited in the Alabama entry.

Louisiana

NARA's Southwest Region in Fort Worth has records of the **U.S. District Court for the Western District of Louisiana**. Records relating to naturalization for the Alexandria Division include indexed declarations of intention, 1919-20; indexed petitions, 1922-64; stubs of naturalization certificates, 1918-28; and lists of granted, denied, and continued petitions, 1930-59; for the Opelousas Division, indexed declarations of intention, 1918-56; indexed petitions, 1922-64; and lists of granted, denied, and continued petitions, 1930-55; and for the Shreveport Division, declarations of intention and petitions, 1885-91; indexed declarations of intention, 1906-42; indexed petitions, 1902-67; and lists of granted, denied, and continued petitions, 1929-56.

NARA's Southwest Region also has records of the **U.S. District Court for the Eastern District of Louisiana**. Records relating to naturalization for the Baton Rouge Division include indexed declarations of intention, 1907-51; indexed petitions, 1908-91; transferred petitions, 1956-75; lists of granted, denied, and continued petitions, 1929-87; applications to regain citizenship and repatriation oaths, 1939-54; an index to naturalization petitions, 1971-90; and an index to naturalization certificates, 1939-92. The records for the New Orleans Division include letters received, 1912-26; letters received from the Bureau of Immigration and Naturalization, 1906-22; letters sent, 1906-24; indexed orders admitting aliens to citizenship, 1836-1903; indexed declarations of intention, 1813-1906 and 1906-77; questionnaires for declarations of intention, 1906-28; petitions and applications, 1898-1903; oaths of applicants, 1876-98; indexed petitions, 1906-59; questionnaires for petitions, 1911-29; depositions of witnesses, 1908-27; transferred petitions to and from the New Orleans court, 1953-87; lists of granted, denied, and continued petitions, 1929-86; petitions by military servicemen, 1943-55; applications to regain citizenship and repatriation oaths, 1940-70; abandoned certificates of arrival, questionnaires, and declarations, 1926-27; index to naturalization petitions and orders, ca. 1837-1988; and an index to naturalization certificates, ca. 1920-88. The names of some individuals who were certified as naturalized citizens during the period November 1808 to December 1814 are found in the court minutes reproduced on roll 1 of M1082, *Records of the U.S. District Court for the Eastern District of Louisiana, 1806-1814*, 18 rolls.

Records for the **U.S. Circuit Court**, New Orleans Division, include letters received from the Bureau of Immigration and Naturalization, 1906-11; letters sent, 1901-11; indexed orders admitting aliens to citizenship, 1839-98; oaths of applicants, 1863-98; indexed declarations of intention, 1892-1903 and 1906-11; questionnaires for declarations of intention, 1908-11; declarations of intention filed in state and local courts, ca. 1886-1911; petitions, 1838-61 and 1906-11; questionnaires for petitions, 1909-11; and depositions of witnesses, 1909-11.

Maine

NARA's Northeast Region in Boston has naturalization records of the **U.S. District and Circuit Courts for the District of Maine**. These include declarations of intention, 1849-1955, with an index for 1906-55; petitions and records of naturalization, 1790-1945, with an index for 1851-1944; military petitions, 1918-19 and 1942-45, and naturalization record books, 1851-1906.

Maryland

NARA's Mid Atlantic Region (Center City Philadelphia) has petitions for naturalization, 1903-72, and declarations of intention, 1911-67, for the **U.S. District Court for the District of Maryland** and declarations of intention, 1906-11, for the **U.S. Circuit Court for the District of**

File clerks, typists, stenographers, and general clerical assistants from the National Youth Administration (NYA) learned jobs at the Bureau of Immigration in an atmosphere of strict attention to the serious implications of their work. NYA workers and the regular Civil Service staff worked side by side. NYA assistance increased the clerical output of the Bureau by 50 percent. Photographs Nos. 119-G-144-D, 119-G-138D, 119-G-133-D, and 119-G-130-D in box 25. Records of the National Youth Administration, RG 119.

Maryland. The U.S. District Court records include military petitions filed at Fort Meade, 1918-23. Microfilmed records include petitions for naturalization, 1906-31, on M1640, *Naturalization Petitions of the U.S. District Court for the District of Maryland, 1906-1930*, 43 rolls; indexes to naturalization petitions, 1797-1951, on M1168, *Indexes to Naturalization Petitions to the U.S. Circuit and District Courts for Maryland, 1797-1951*, 25 rolls; and declarations of intention, 1906-31 (reference microfilm). Some naturalization proceedings are recorded in the court minutes microfilmed on M931, *Minutes of the U.S. Circuit Court for the District of Maryland, 1790-1911*, 7 rolls.

Massachusetts

NARA's Northeast Region (Boston) has records of the **U.S. District Court for the District of Massachusetts**. Records relating to naturalization include declarations of intention, 1798-1950; petitions and records of naturalization, 1790-1970, with an index, 1790-1966; military petitions and records of naturalization, 1919; naturalization case dockets and files, 1908-55; and women's applications for repatriation, 1936-69. Naturalization records of the **U.S. Circuit Court** include declarations of intention, 1845-1911, and petitions and records of naturalization, 1845-1911, with an index, 1845-1906. Some indexes are reproduced on M1545, *Index to Naturalization Petitions and Records of the U.S. District Court, 1906-1966, and the U.S. Circuit Court, 1906-1911, for the District of Massachusetts*, 115 rolls. Select records are reproduced on M1368, *Petitions and Records of Naturalization of the U.S. District Court and Circuit Courts of the District of Massachusetts, 1906-1929*, 330 rolls.

Michigan

NARA's Great Lakes Region in Chicago has early petitions and orders of naturalization processed by the **U.S. Territorial Court**. They are recorded in a journal reproduced on roll 9 of M1111, *Records of the Territorial Court of Michigan, 1815-1836*, 9 rolls.

Records of the **U.S. District Court for the Eastern District of Michigan**, Southern Division, Detroit, relating to naturalization include declarations of intention, 1856-1984; naturalization depositions, 1909-70; naturalization petitions, 1837-1980; and register of declarations of intention, 1837-1916. Naturalization records of the **U.S. Circuit Court** for the district include declarations of intention, 1874-1912, and naturalization petitions, 1837-1911.

Naturalization records of the **U.S. District Court for the Western District of Michigan** include for the Northern Division, Marquette, declarations of intention and petitions, 1887-1915, and an index, 1887-1915; and for the Southern Division, Grand Rapids, naturalization petitions, 1868-1972, and declarations of intention, 1907-78.

Minnesota

NARA's Central Plains Region in Kansas City has records of the **U.S. District Court for the District of Minnesota.**

Records relating to naturalization include, for the First Division, Winona, naturalization certificate stubs, 1909-20; declarations of intention, 1895-1924; naturalization petitions, 1896-1920; declarations of intention, 1895-1924; and naturalization petitions, 1896-1920; for the Second Division, Mankato, naturalization papers, 1893-1919; declarations of intention, 1906-40; and petitions for naturalization, 1897-1944; and for the Third Division, St. Paul, a naturalization index, 1859-97; naturalization certificates, 1859-97; declarations of intention, 1859-1955; naturalization petitions, 1897-1951; military naturalization petitions, 1918; and overseas naturalization petitions, 1943-56. Records for the Fourth Division, Minneapolis, include declarations of intention, 1890-1962; naturalization petitions, 1897-1965; military naturalization petitions, 1918; naturalization repatriation cases, 1919-42; naturalization order books, 1929-60; naturalization certificate stubs, 1907-27; and soldiers' naturalization certificate stubs, 1918-19; and for the Sixth Division, Fergus Falls, declarations of intention, 1890-1947; naturalization petitions, 1897-1946; and repatriation applications and orders, 1938-46.

U.S. Circuit Court records relating to naturalization include, for the First Division, Winona, declarations of intention, 1910, and naturalization petitions, 1897-99; for the Second Division, Mankato, declarations of intention, 1900-11, and naturalization petitions, 1897-1911; for the Third Division, St. Paul, declarations of intention, 1864-1911, and naturalization petitions, 1897-1911; for the Fourth Division, Minneapolis, declarations of intention, 1890-1911; naturalization petitions, 1897-1911; and naturalization certificate stubs, 1907-12; and for the Sixth Division, Fergus Falls, declarations of intention, 1890-1911, and naturalization petitions, 1897-1911.

NARA's Great Lakes Region in Chicago also has records of the **U.S. District Court for the District of Minnesota**. Records relating to naturalization include, for the Third Division, St. Paul, declarations of intention, 1894-1943, and petitions, 1897-1955; and for the Sixth Division, Fergus Falls, declarations of intention, 1947-50, and petitions, 1944-78.

Mississippi

All of the Mississippi records are indexed unless otherwise indicated.

NARA's Southeast Region in Atlanta has records of the **U.S. District Court for the Southern District of Mississippi**, which include, for the Biloxi Division, declarations of intention, 1906-45; petitions for naturalization, 1908-65, indexed to 1960; and transfer petitions, 1953-56; and for the Jackson Division, declarations of intention, 1911-58, and petitions for naturalization, 1911-53.

Records of the **U.S. District Court for the Northern District of Mississippi**, Western Division, Oxford, include petitions for naturalization, 1914-29. Included for the Delta Division, Clarksdale, are declarations of intention, 1913-55, and petitions for naturalization, 1913-55; and for the Eastern Division, Aberdeen, petitions for naturalization, 1914–43.

Naturalization records from the district courts in Biloxi and Jackson are available on rolls 75–79 and 103 of M1547, cited in the Alabama entry.

Missouri

NARA's Central Plains Region in Kansas City has records of the **U.S. District Court for the Eastern District of Missouri**. Records relating to naturalization include declarations of intention, petitions for naturalization, and certificate stubs for all divisions of the Eastern District, 1855–1991, and repatriations, oaths of allegiance, and admission certificates of minors, 1855–1946. **U.S. Circuit Court** records relating to naturalization for St. Louis include declarations of intention, 1849–1911; declarations of intention, 1907–9, that were surrendered to the court when petitions were filed; admission certificates, 1855–1903; admission certificates of minors, 1855–90; and papers pertaining to the issue of new certificates, 1908–11.

NARA's Central Plains Region also has records of the **U.S. District Court for the Western District of Missouri**. Records relating to naturalization include, for the Central Division, Jefferson City, an index to petitions, 1876–1980; declarations of intention, 1938–80; petitions for naturalization, 1938–82; transfers of petitions for naturalization, 1955–82; and an index to naturalization entries appearing in the court journals, 1876–1906; for the Northern Division, St. Joseph, declarations of intention, 1907–76; petitions for naturalization, 1907–76; transfers of petitions, 1959–63; military petitions, 1943–55; and certificate stubs, 1912–26; and for the Southern Division, Springfield, declarations of intention, 1895–1985; petitions for naturalization, 1911–83; transfers of petitions, 1946–83; and certificate stubs, 1916–27. Records for the Western Division, Kansas City, include declarations of intention, 1911–91; petitions for naturalization, 1913–91; military petitions, 1918 and 1942–46; repatriations, 1937–42; and transfers of petitions, 1989–91. Declarations of intention, petitions, and certificate records for all divisions were eventually consolidated with the Western Division records.

U.S. Circuit Court records for the Northern Division include declarations of intention, 1906–10; petitions for naturalization, 1907–11; and certificate stubs, 1907–12. Records for the Western Division include declarations of intention, 1906–11.

Montana

NARA's Rocky Mountain Region in Denver has naturalization records for the **U.S. Territorial Court for Montana**. Those relating to naturalization include journals of proceedings for the First Judicial District, Bozeman, 1868–89; for the Second District, Deer Lodge, 1871–89; for the Third District, Helena, 1868–88; and for the Fourth District, Miles City, 1886–87.

Records relating to naturalization from the **U.S. District Court for the District of Montana** include, for the Butte Division, declarations of intention, 1894–1902; an index to declarations of intention, 1894–1902; records of citizenship, 1894–1903; an index to records of citizenship, 1894–1903; and petition and record books, 1910–29; for Great Falls Division, declarations of intention, 1924, and petition and record books, 1926; and for the Helena Division, declarations of intention, 1892–1929; naturalization records, 1894–1906; an index to naturalization records, 1894–1906; naturalization petitions, 1907–27; and certificate stub books, 1900–27.

Indexes to naturalization records for Montana courts are microfilmed on M1236, *Indexes to Naturalization Records of the Montana Territorial and Federal Courts, 1868-1929*, 1 roll. Records from the Butte, Great Falls, and Helena Divisions are reproduced on M1538, *Naturalization Records of the U.S. District Courts for the State of Montana, 1891-1929*, 3 rolls.

Naturalization records from the **U.S. Circuit Court for the District of Montana** include declarations of intention, 1891–93; an index of naturalization, 1891–98; and records of citizenship, 1891–98.

Nebraska

NARA's Central Plains Region in Kansas City has records of the **U.S. District Court for the District of Nebraska**. Naturalization records include, for the Chadron Division, declarations of intention, 1930–49; petitions for naturalization, 1930–47; and repatriations, 1941; for the Grand Island Division, declarations of intention, 1930–51; petitions for naturalization, 1932–50; repatriations, 1941; and copies of certificates of naturalization, 1931–51; for the Hastings Division, declarations of intention, 1931–51; petitions for naturalization and related records, 1931–51; repatriations, 1941–42; and copies of certificates of naturalization; for the Lincoln Division, petitions for naturalization and related records, 1932–78; orders of court regarding petitions granted, 1932–57; and applications to take oath of allegiance, 1938–53; and for the McCook Division, declarations of intention, 1932–42; petitions for naturalization, 1940–42; petitions for naturalizations denied, continued, and granted and repatriations, 1941–42. Naturalization records available for the Norfolk Division include declarations of intention, 1930–41; petitions for naturalization and related records, 1930–51; applications to take oath of allegiance, 1940–51; and petitions for naturalizations denied, continued, and granted, 1930–51; for the North Platte Division, declarations of intention, 1931–51; petitions for naturalization and related records, 1930–47; petitions for naturalizations denied, continued, and granted and repatriations, 1937–44; for the Omaha Division, declarations of intention, 1876–1968; index to petitions for naturalization, 1930–40; petitions for naturalization and related records, 1876–1901 and 1930–81; certificate stubs, 1918–29; naturalization petitions granted, continued, and denied, 1930–61; transfers of naturalizations, 1954–83; and overseas naturalizations (OS series), 1955.

Nevada

NARA's Pacific Region (San Francisco) has declarations of intention, 1877-1951, and petitions for naturalization, 1908-56, for the **U.S. District Court for the District of Nevada**, First District, Fallon. Naturalization records for the Second District, Reno, include declarations of intention, 1853-1944; petitions for naturalization, 1907-49; and final naturalization papers, 1877-1906.

New Hampshire

NARA's Northeast Region (Boston) has records of the **U.S. District and Circuit Courts for the District of New Hampshire**. Records relating to naturalization include declarations of intention and records of naturalization, 1873-1977; petitions and records of naturalization for military personnel overseas, 1942-55; women's applications for repatriation, 1952-67; and a list of persons naturalized or filing declarations, 1849-71. Scattered records of naturalization from 1790 to 1850 can be found among the term papers of the courts.

New Jersey

NARA's Northeast Region (New York City) holds naturalization records of the **U.S. District Court for the District of New Jersey.** They include, for the Newark Office, petitions, 1914-82, with an alphabetical index on microfiche, and declarations of intention, 1914-68; for the Trenton Office, petitions, 1838-1906, with an alphabetical index; and, for the Camden Office, unindexed petitions, 1932-81. The facility also holds military petitions for World War I, 1918-19, from Fort Dix, with an alphabetical index; from Port Newark, arranged in numerical order with no index; and from Picatinny Arsenal. Also included are overseas military petitions for World War II and the Korean conflict; an alphabetical index to these petitions is available. Other naturalization records may be found in court minutes reproduced as part of T928, *Records of the U.S. District Court for the District of New Jersey and Predecessor Courts, 1790-1950*, 186 rolls.

The minutes of the U.S. Circuit Court, 1790-1911, are on rolls 1-4; minutes of the U.S. District Court, December 12, 1789-1950, are on rolls 5-62.

New Mexico

NARA's Rocky Mountain Region in Denver has records of the First through Seventh Judicial Districts of the **court for the Territory of New Mexico** located in Alamogordo, Albuquerque and Las Cruces, Fernandez de Taos and Albuquerque, Las Vegas, Roswell, Santa Fe, and Socorro. Records relating to naturalization include certificates of naturalization, 1907-11; declarations of intention, 1882-1917; and petitions for naturalization, 1906-17. Indexes are available in the regional facility's microfilm research room.

New York

NARA's Northeast Region (New York City) has naturalization petitions, 1824-1991; declarations of intention, 1842-1991; and naturalization certificate stubs, 1903-89, from the **U.S. District Court for the Southern District of New York**, New York City. Indexes to the records are available on microfilm: M1675, *Alphabetical Index to Declarations of Intention of the U.S. District Court for the Southern District of New York, 1917-50*, 111 rolls, and M1676, *Alphabetical Index to Petitions for Naturalization of the U.S. District Court for the Southern District of New York, 1824-1941*, 102 rolls. Naturalization documents found in the court's minute books, 1789-1841, are microfilmed as M886, *Minutes and Rolls of Attorneys of the U.S. District Court for the Southern District of New York, 1789-1841*, 9 rolls.

Records for the **U.S. Circuit Court for the Southern District of New York** include naturalization petitions, 1906-11; declarations of intention, 1845-1911; and naturalization certificate stubs, 1907-11. Minute books, including aliens' oaths of intention to become citizens of the United States and orders for the naturalization of aliens, 1790-1841, are reproduced on M854, *Minutes, Trial Notes, and Rolls of Attorneys of the U.S. Circuit Court for the Southern District of New York, 1790-1841*, 3 rolls.

Naturalization records for the **U.S. District Court for the Eastern District of New York**, Brooklyn, include petitions, 1865-1990; indexes to petitions, 1865-1977, microfilmed as M1164, *Index to Naturalization Petitions of the United States District Court for the Eastern District of New York, 1865-1957*, 142 rolls; declarations of intention, 1865-1979; indexes to declarations of intention, 1909-49; and naturalization certificate stubs, 1907-25 and 1958-77.

Records of the **U.S. District Court for the Western District of New York** consist of declarations of intention and petitions for naturalization, 1906-66. An index covering both series of records is available on M1677, *Alphabetical Index to Petitions for Naturalization of the U.S. District Court for the Western District of New York, 1906-1966*, 20 rolls.

Photocopies and an index to naturalization records, 1792-1906, from Federal, state, and local courts in New York City, that were produced by the Work Projects Administration (WPA), are discussed in 3.2.

North Carolina

NARA's Southeast Region in Atlanta has records of the **U.S. District Court for the Eastern District of North Carolina**, which include, for the Wilson Division, declarations of intention, 1929-45; petitions for naturalization, 1928-47; and unindexed military petitions from Camp Lejeune; for the Raleigh Division, petitions for naturalization, 1906-65, and one volume of unindexed military petitions, 1918-23; for the New Bern Division, petitions for naturalization, 1920-January 1927; for the Elizabeth City Division, petitions for naturalization, December 1909-August 1927; and for the Washington Division, declarations of intention, 1912-29, and petitions for naturalization, 1915-29.

Records of the **U.S. District Court for the Western District of North Carolina**, Asheville Division, include declarations of intention, 1918-71; petitions for naturalization, 1912-46; military petitions, 1918-23; and one volume of naturalization petitions for the **U.S. Circuit Court**, 1907-11.

Minute books from the various courts include declarations of intention and naturalization oaths. Some of these have been microfilmed under the following titles: M1425, *Minute Books, U.S. District Court, Eastern District of North Carolina, Albemarle Division at Edenton, 1807-70, and at Elizabeth City, 1870-1914,* 1 roll; M1426, *Minute Books, U.S. District Court, Eastern District of North Carolina, Cape Fear Division at Wilmington, 1795-96 and 1858-1911,* 2 rolls; M1427, *Minute Books, U.S. District Court, Eastern District of North Carolina, Pamlico Division at New Bern, 1858-1914,* 2 rolls; and M1428, *Minute Books, U.S. Circuit Court, Eastern District of North Carolina, Raleigh, 1791-1866,* 2 rolls. Naturalization records from the district courts in Wilson and Raleigh are available on rolls 79-82 of M1547, cited in the Alabama entry.

North Dakota

NARA's Central Plains Region in Kansas City has records of the **U.S. District Court for the District of North Dakota.** Records relating to naturalization include, for the Minot Division, declarations of intention, 1912-14; for the Fargo Division, declarations of intention, 1913-18; petitions for naturalization, 1906-24; and certificate stubs, 1907-24; and for the Bismarck Division, declarations of intention, 1912-17.

The records of the **U.S. Circuit Court** include, for the Minot Division, declarations of intention, 1906-11; for the Fargo Division, declarations of intention, 1896-1911, and petitions granted, 1896-1911; for the Grand Forks Division, declarations of intention, 1892-1909, and petitions granted, 1894; and for the Devils Lake Division, declarations of intention, 1891-1906, and petitions for naturalization, 1892-1901.

Ohio

NARA's Great Lakes Region in Chicago has records of the **U.S. District Court for the Northern District of Ohio.** Naturalization records of the Eastern Division, Cleveland, include certificates of naturalization, 1907-18; declarations of intention, 1855-91 and 1906-41; an index, 1855-1903; petitions, 1855-1901; and naturalization record volumes, 1856-80. Relevant records of the Western Division, Toledo, consist of declarations of intention, 1869-1929; an index to declarations of intention, 1869-84; and a naturalization index, 1875-1940.

Naturalization records of the **U.S. District Court for the Southern District of Ohio,** Western Division, Cincinnati, include depositions, 1918-35: petition books, 1906-59; declarations of intention, 1906-56; an index to declarations of intention and petitions, 1906-42; final

papers, 1859-1906; and an indexed naturalization journal, 1858-1906. Other records from the Southern District include declarations of intention, 1906-30, and certificates of naturalization, 1916-27, from Dayton, and certificates of naturalization, 1916-25, from Columbus.

The Great Lakes Region facility also has naturalization records from the **U.S. Circuit Court for the Southern District,** 1852-1905, including two journals that are indexed.

Oklahoma

NARA's Southwest Region in Fort Worth has records of the **U.S. District Court for the Western District of Oklahoma,** Oklahoma City, which include correspondence and notices, 1909-60, relating to naturalization. The records of the **U.S. District Court for the Eastern District of Oklahoma,** Muskogee, include indexed declarations of intention, 1909-88; indexed petitions, 1908-87; an index to declarations of intention and petitions, ca. 1908-36; petitions of military servicemen, 1944-45; transferred petitions, 1954-78; stubs of naturalization certificates, 1894-1929; and applications to regain citizenship and repatriation oaths, 1940-44.

NARA's Southwest Region also has records of the **U.S. District Court for the Northern, Southern, and Central Districts of the Indian Territory.** Naturalization records include, for Muskogee, indexed certificates of naturalization, 1889-1906; and for Ardmore, a naturalization record book, 1896-1906. Naturalization records for South McAlester include indexed declarations of intention, 1891-1906; indexed petitions, oaths of witnesses, and orders granting citizenship, 1904-6; indexed orders granting citizenship, 1890-1903; and indexed petitions and orders of naturalization for persons who arrived in the United States as minors, 1891-1903.

Oregon

NARA's Pacific Alaska Region (Seattle) has records of the **U.S. District Court for the District of Oregon.** Naturalization records include journals of admission to citizenship, 1877-1906; declarations of intention, 1918-62; unindexed petitions based on military service, 1868-1906 and 1918; petitions, 1930-70; and depositions, 1929-53 and 1958-73. Also included are certificate stubs, 1906-26; naturalization orders, 1926-60; index to declarations on intention, 1859-92; an index to declarations and petitions, 1935-56; and a card index to naturalization, 1920-1992. Some of these records have been microfilmed as M1540, *Naturalization Records of the U.S. District Court for the District of Oregon, 1859-1941,* 62 rolls. An index to the records has been filmed as M1242, *Index to the Naturalization Records of the U.S. District Court for Oregon, 1859-1956,* 3 rolls.

Records of the **U.S. Circuit Court for District of Oregon** relating to naturalization include journals of admission to citizenship, 1877-1906; declarations of intention, 1859-1907; petitions for naturalization, 1906-29; petitions based on military service, 1904-6; and an index to declarations of intention, 1859-1907.

Pennsylvania

NARA's Mid Atlantic Region (Center City Philadelphia) has records of the **U.S. District Court for the Eastern District of Pennsylvania**, Philadelphia. Records relating to naturalization include petitions for naturalization, 1795-1991; an index to declarations of intention, 1915-69; and declarations of intention, 1795-1967. Microfilmed records include declarations of intention, 1834-1929 (reference microfilm), and some petitions for naturalization, 1795-1929, reproduced on M1522, *Naturalization Petitions for the Eastern District of Pennsylvania* [1795-1931], 369 rolls, with related indexes on M1248, *Indexes to Naturalization Petitions to the U.S. Circuit and District Courts for the Eastern District of Pennsylvania, 1795-1951*, 60 rolls. **Records of the U.S. Circuit Court for the Eastern District** include petitions for naturalization, 1790-1911, and declarations of intention, 1815-1911. Naturalization proceedings are also recorded in the court's minutes, which are reproduced on M932, *Minutes of the U.S. Circuit Court for the Eastern District of Pennsylvania, 1790-1844*, 2 rolls.

Naturalization records of the **U.S. District Court for the Middle District of Pennsylvania** include an index for petitions for naturalization and declarations of intention filed in all Middle District divisions for the District and Circuit Courts, 1901-91; and for Scranton, declarations of intention, 1910-79; petitions for naturalization, 1901-90; and repatriation petitions, 1943-70; for Wilkes-Barre, declarations of intention, 1942-66; petitions for naturalization, 1943-71; and repatriation petitions, 1943-60; for Harrisburg, declarations of intention, 1910-16, and petitions for naturalization, 1911-17; and for Williamsport, declarations of intention, 1908-11, and petitions for naturalization, 1909-13.

Records for the **U.S. Circuit Court for the Middle District** include, for Scranton, declarations of intention, 1906-11, and petitions for naturalization, 1906-11; and for Harrisburg, declarations of intention, 1906-11, and petitions for naturalization, 1906-11. Records of the Middle District include petitions for naturalization in the Scranton Division, 1901-29; declarations of intention for the Williamsport Division, 1908-11; declarations of intention for the Harrisburg Division, 1912-16; declarations of intention for Scranton, 1906-31; and an index for all divisions, 1901-91.

Naturalization petitions received by the courts in Scranton, Harrisburg, and Williamsport are available as M1626, *Naturalization Petitions of the U.S. Circuit and District Courts for the Middle District of Pennsylvania, 1906-1930*, 123 rolls. The Scranton petitions actually begin in 1901.

Naturalization records of the **U.S. District Court for the Western District of Pennsylvania**, Pittsburgh Division,

include petitions for naturalization, 1820-1979, and declarations of intention, 1820-1972. Records of the **U.S. Circuit Court for the Western District of Pennsylvania**, Pittsburgh Division, include petitions for naturalization, 1820-99 and 1910-12, and declarations of intention, 1859-1911. (Circuit court petitions, 1820-1899, are interfiled with the district court records.) Naturalization records for the Erie Division include petitions for naturalization, 1940-72, and declarations of intention, 1940-52. Records of the Pittsburgh Division available on reference microfilm include declarations of intention, 1859-1931, and an index to petitions for naturalization, 1906-90. Petitions are available on M1537, *Naturalization Petitions of the U.S. District Court, 1820-1930, and Circuit Court, 1820-1911, for the Western District of Pennsylvania*, 437 rolls. A name index to declarations of intention and petitions for naturalization is reproduced on M1208, *Indexes to Registers and Registers of Declarations of Intention and Petitions for Naturalization of the U.S. District and Circuit Courts for the Western District of Pennsylvania, 1820-1906*, 3 rolls.

Puerto Rico

NARA's Northeast Region (New York City) has naturalization records of the **U.S. District Court of Puerto Rico**, consisting of petitions, 1898-1972, and an index, 1917-29.

Rhode Island

NARA's Northeast Region (Boston) has records of the **U.S. District Court for the District of Rhode Island**. Records relating to naturalization include declarations of intention, 1835-1950; petitions and records of naturalization, 1842-1950, with gaps; a name index to petitions and records of naturalization, 1796-1991; a name index to military petitions, 1918-45; women's applications for repatriation, 1944-71; naturalization record books, 1842-1903; and naturalization certificate stubs, 1911-57. Records of the **U.S. Circuit Court for the District of Rhode Island** include a record of declarations, 1888-97; petitions and records of naturalization, 1843-1911; naturalization record books, 1842-1901; and naturalization certificate stubs, 1907-11.

South Carolina

All of the South Carolina records are indexed unless otherwise indicated.

NARA's Southeast Region in Atlanta has records of the **U.S. District Court for the Eastern District of South Carolina**, Charleston Division, that include an index to naturalization proceedings, 1790-1906; declarations of intention, 1907-65; petitions for naturalization, 1866-1953; and military petitions, 1918-24. The **U.S. Circuit Court** records from the Charleston Division include a naturalization index, 1790-1906; declarations of intention, 1906-11; and petitions for naturalization, 1867-1911. Records for the Columbia Division include declarations of intention,

1910-41; petitions for naturalization, 1910-53; and military petitions for Camp Jackson, 1918-20, with an index.

Naturalization records for the U.S. District Court for the Eastern District also include, for the Florence Division, declarations of intention, 1910-56, and petitions for naturalization, 1917-43; for the Aiken Division, petitions for naturalization, 1917-26; and for the Orangeburg Division, declarations of intention, 1938-55, and petitions for naturalization, 1939-41.

Records of the **U.S. District Court for the Western District of South Carolina**, Greenville Division, include petitions for naturalization, 1911-65.

Naturalization records from the district courts in Aiken, Columbia, Charleston, and Florence are available on rolls 83-92 and 106 of M1547, cited in the Alabama entry. Some declarations of intention and naturalization oaths are found in the minutes of the courts reproduced on M1181, *Minutes, Circuit and District Courts, District of South Carolina, 1789-1849, and Index to Judgments, Circuit and District Courts, 1792-1874*, 2 rolls. Four volumes of annotated lists of names of persons admitted to U.S. citizenship by the U.S. courts in South Carolina from 1790 through 1906 are reproduced on M1183, *Record of Admissions to Citizenship, District of South Carolina, 1790-1906*, 1 roll. One volume lists aliens admitted as citizens, 1790-1860, and the other three volumes record "citizenships" and notices of intention, 1866-1906.

South Dakota

NARA's Central Plains Region in Kansas City has records of the **U.S. District Court for the District of South Dakota**. In general, records from the territorial courts and the district court divisions relating to naturalization consist of declarations of intention dating from 1876 and certificates of naturalization from 1892. Included for the Deadwood Division is a naturalization record book containing declarations of intention and petitions, 1890-1900; for the Pierre Division, declarations of intention, 1892; and for the Sioux Falls Division, declarations of intention, 1894-1924; petitions for naturalization, 1906-28; and certificates of naturalization, 1907-23.

The records for the **U.S. Circuit Court** for the Deadwood Division include declarations of intention, 1892-1900.

Tennessee

All of the Tennessee records discussed below are indexed unless otherwise indicated.

NARA's Southeast Region in Atlanta has records of the **U.S. District Court for the Eastern District of Tennessee**. Naturalization records include, for the Knoxville Division, declarations of intention, 1891-1988, and petitions for naturalization, 1908-70, indexed to December 1957; and, for the Greenville Division, declarations of intention, 1914-74, and petitions for naturalization, 1911-64. Records for the Chattanooga Division include petition index cards, 1890-1955; declarations of intention, 1907-57;

petitions for naturalization, 1907-74; and military petitions, August-December 1918 and 1941-45. An index to these records is available on M1611, *Index to Naturalization Records of the U.S. District Court for the Eastern District of Tennessee at Chattanooga, 1888-1955*, 1 roll.

Records of the **U.S. District Court for the Western District of Tennessee**, Memphis Division, include declarations of intention, 1906-61; petitions for naturalization, 1907-63, indexed except for December 1940-November 1954; and military petitions, 1918-19 and 1953-55. Naturalization records for the Jackson Division include declarations of intention, 1909-42, and petitions for naturalization, 1921-29. After March 1929 only declarations of intention were filed at Jackson; petitions for naturalization were all filed at the Memphis Division of the Western District of Tennessee.

Naturalization records from the district courts in Chattanooga, Greenville, and Knoxville are available on rolls 93-100 of M1547, cited in the Alabama entry. Some declarations of intention and naturalization oaths can be found in the minute books reproduced on M1214, *Minute Books of the U.S. Circuit Court for West Tennessee, 1803-1839, and of the U.S. Circuit Court for the Middle District of Tennessee, 1839-1864*, 4 rolls. A few can also be found in the volumes reproduced on M1213, *Minute Books of the U.S. District Court for West Tennessee, 1797-1839, and of the U.S. District Court for the Middle District of Tennessee, 1839-1865*, 1 roll.

Texas

NARA's Southwest Region in Fort Worth has records of the **U.S. District Court for the Northern District of Texas**. The naturalization records include, for Abilene, indexed declarations of intention, 1909-83; indexed petitions, 1911-84; indexed transferred petitions, 1955-84; indexed petitions of military servicemen, 1943-44; stubs of naturalization certificates, 1918-29; lists of granted petitions, 1929-87; and indexed applications to regain citizenship and repatriation oaths, 1941-61; for Amarillo, indexed declarations of intention, 1919-85; indexed petitions, 1913-88; petitions of military servicemen, 1944-55; and lists of granted, denied, and continued petitions, 1929-64; for Dallas, indexed declarations of intention, 1906-75; indexed petitions, 1908-79; indexed transferred petitions, 1959-76; indexed petitions of military servicemen, 1918-55; stubs of naturalization certificates, 1901-25; lists of granted and denied petitions, 1930-79; indexed applications to regain citizenship and repatriation oaths, 1940-67; and a card index to declarations and petitions, ca. 1908-89; for Fort Worth, indexed declarations of intention, 1907-59; indexed petitions, 1906-82; indexed petitions of military servicemen, 1918-28; stubs of naturalization certificates, 1914-24; and lists of granted petitions, 1930-67; for Lubbock, indexed declarations of intention, 1929-54; indexed petitions, 1930-62; petitions of military servicemen, 1942-54; and lists of granted petitions, 1931-59; for San Angelo, indexed declarations of intention, 1908-29; indexed petitions, 1910-59; and stubs of naturalization certificates, 1913-25; and for Wichita Falls, indexed declarations of intention, 1917-59; indexed petitions, 1917-80; indexed transferred petitions, 1955-84; petitions of military servicemen, 1918-20; stubs of naturalization certificates, 1919-26; lists of granted petitions, 1930-78; and applications to regain citizenship and repatriation oaths, 1940-61.

NARA's Southwest Region also has records of the **U.S. District Court for the Southern District of Texas**. The naturalization records include, for Brownsville, declarations of intention, 1874-84, and indexed declarations of intention, 1907-29; orders granting citizenship, 1875-95; indexed petitions, 1909-17; an index to petitions of military servicemen, 1918-26; and petitions by military servicemen, 1918-26; for Corpus Christi, indexed declarations of intention, 1913-55; indexed petitions, 1913-54; transferred petitions, 1953-71; petitions of military servicemen, 1918-45; stubs of naturalization certificates, 1907-27; lists of granted and denied petitions, 1953-77; indexed applications to regain citizenship and repatriation oaths, 1940-71; and an index to declarations of intention and petitions, ca. 1913-55; for Houston, dockets, 1927-45; declarations of intention, 1906-80; petitions, 1908-82; transferred petitions, 1953-83; petitions of military servicemen, 1918-28; stubs of naturalization certificates, 1983-91; applications to regain citizenship and repatriation oaths, 1936-68; an undated card index to naturalization certificates and declarations of intention; a card index to persons who received naturalization certificates and persons who petitioned for naturalization, 1926-81; and an index to declarations and petitions, ca. 1906-55; for Laredo, indexed declarations of intention, 1908-85; indexed petitions, 1907-88; stubs of naturalization certificates, 1908-28; indexed transferred petitions, 1955-90; petitions of military servicemen, 1918-24; stubs of naturalization certificates for military servicemen, 1918; and applications to regain citizenship and repatriation oaths; and for Victoria, indexed declarations of intention, 1907-54; indexed petitions, 1907-55; transferred petitions, 1953; stubs of naturalization certificates, 1911-23; lists of granted, denied, and continued petitions, 1929-55; and applications to regain citizenship and repatriation oaths, 1939-53.

For the **U.S. District Court**, Galveston Division, the records include an index to declarations of intention, 1871-1905; declarations of intention, 1871-1905 and 1906-7; an index to aliens granted citizenship, ca. 1871-1905; orders granting citizenship to adult aliens, 1871-1905, and to minor aliens, 1872-1901; petitions, 1907-20; stubs of naturalization certificates, 1908-21; and petitions by military servicemen. Records for the **U.S. Circuit Court for the Southern District**, Galveston Division, include an index to declarations of intention, ca. 1872-74; declarations of intention, 1867-74; an index to aliens granted citizenship, ca. 1872-76; orders granting citizenship to adult aliens, 1872-76, and minor aliens, 1872; and oaths of witnesses

and petitioners, 1871-96.

NARA's Southwest Region also has records of the **U.S. District Court for the Western District of Texas**. The naturalization records include, for Austin, minutes, 1871-77; term docket, 1908-18; indexed declarations of intention, 1907-70; indexed petitions, 1907-81; indexed transferred petitions, 1953-76; petitions by military servicemen, 1918-24 and 1943-55; stubs of naturalization certificates, 1907-26; lists of granted, denied, and continued petitions, 1936-73; indexed applications to regain citizenship and repatriation oaths; and an index to petitions, ca. 1907-70; for Del Rio, indexed declarations of intention filed in state court, 1908-14, and declarations of intention filed in Federal court, 1907-51; indexed petitions, 1908-76; indexed petitions of military servicemen, 1918-21; stubs of naturalization certificates, 1909-27; and copies of witness affidavits, 1918; for El Paso, term dockets, 1907-18; declarations of intention, 1890-1906 and 1906-80; petitions, 1907-72; indexed transferred petitions, 1953-73; petitions of military servicemen, 1917-56; stubs of naturalization certificates, 1907-26; lists of granted, denied, and continued petitions, 1926-73; and records relating to denied petition of labor leader Hubert Silex, 1947-50; and for Waco, orders granting citizenship, 1880; term dockets, 1907-41; indexed declarations of intention, 1906-80; indexed petitions, 1906-81; indexed transferred petitions, 1948-80; an index to petitions by military servicemen, ca. 1918-44; petitions of military servicemen, 1918-55; lists of granted petitions, 1928-82; and applications to regain citizenship and repatriation oaths, 1940-70.

For the **U.S. District Court**, San Antonio Division, the records include term dockets, 1907-17; indexed declarations of intention, 1906-74; indexed petitions, 1907-87; indexed transferred petitions, 1953-87; petitions by military servicemen, 1918-56; stubs of naturalization certificates, 1918-26; lists of granted petitions, 1983-88; applications to regain citizenship and repatriation oaths, 1937-70; and a card index to naturalization petitions, ca. 1933-85. Records of the **U.S. Circuit Court for the Western District**, San Antonio Division, include declarations of intention, 1881-1888.

NARA's Southwest Region has records of the **U.S. District Court for the Eastern District of Texas**. Naturalization records for Paris include indexed petitions, 1908-28; and for Texarkana, indexed declarations of intention, 1908-60; indexed petitions, 1930-60; indexed transferred petitions, 1954-57; and lists of granted, denied, or continued petitions, 1931-60.

Vermont

NARA's Northeast Region in Boston has records of the **U.S. District Court for the District of Vermont**. Records relating to naturalization consist of declarations of intention, 1859-1945, and petitions and records of naturalization, 1801-35 and 1842-1972. An index to the records is available.

Utah

NARA's Rocky Mountain Region in Denver has records of the **U.S. District Court for the District of Utah**, Salt Lake City, including petitions for naturalization and naturalization records, 1906-30, and declarations of intention, 1924. An alphabetical index to these records is available in the region's microfilm research room.

Virginia

NARA's Mid Atlantic Region (Center City Philadelphia) has records of the **U.S. District Court for the Eastern District of Virginia**. Records relating to naturalization for the Richmond Division include declarations of intention, 1911-60; petitions for naturalization, 1870-1953 (there are no petitions for the years 1875, 1878-79, 1881, 1884, 1887, and 1890-1911); and military petitions filed at Camp Lee, 1918-24. Records for the Alexandria Division include petitions for naturalization, 1909-81; declarations of intention, 1911-73; military petitions filed at Camp Humphreys, 1918-19; and repatriation petitions, 1940-68. Records of the **U.S. Circuit Court** for the Richmond Division include declarations of intention, 1906-11, and petitions for naturalization, 1906-12. Some records for the district and circuit courts for the Richmond Division are reproduced on M1647, *Naturalization Petitions of the U.S. District Court for the Eastern District of Virginia (Richmond), 1906-1929*, 10 rolls. Some petitions for naturalization, including military petitions, from the Alexandria Division are on M1648, *Naturalization Petitions of the U.S. District Court for the Eastern District of Virginia (Alexandria), 1909-29*, 5 rolls.

Naturalization records for the **U.S. District Court for the Western District of Virginia**, Abingdon Division, consist of petitions for naturalization, 1910-30, and declarations of intention, 1908-29. Some of these records are reproduced on M1645, *Naturalization Petitions of the U.S. District Court for the Western District of Virginia (Abingdon), 1914-1929*, 2 rolls. Records for the Charlottesville Division include petitions for naturalization, 1910-37, some of which are on M1646, *Naturalization Petitions of the U.S. District Court for the Western District of Virginia (Charlottesville), 1910-1929*, 1 roll. Petitions for naturalization are available for the Danville Division, 1907-66, and for the Roanoke Division, 1906-90.

Washington

NARA's Pacific Alaska Region (Seattle) has records for the U.S. District Courts for Eastern and Western Washington. Relevant records of the **U.S. District Court for the Eastern District of Washington**, include, for the Northern Division, Spokane, declarations of intention, 1890-1964; depositions, 1908-57; petitions, 1906-60; naturalization records for adults, 1903-6; naturalization records for minors, 1904-5; an index to declarations of intention, 1906-60; a naturalization index, 1880-1988; and other naturalization records, 1882-1903. Records for the Southern Division include, for Walla Walla, declarations of intention, 1907-50, and petitions, 1907-23; and, for Yakima, declarations of intention, 1907-72; petitions, 1907-72; repatriation petitions, 1936-60; and transferred petitions, 1954-71. Some of the records mentioned above have been filmed on M1541, *Naturalization Records of the U.S. District Court for the Eastern District of Washington, 1890-1972*, 40 rolls.

Records of the **U.S. District Court for the Western District of Washington**, for the Northern Division, Seattle, include naturalization indexes, 1890-1953; declarations of intention 1890-1954; petitions, 1906-70; military petitions, 1943-46; naturalization records of adults, 1890-1903; naturalization records of minors, 1892-1906; depositions, 1918-76; naturalization certificate stubs, 1907-25; statements of fact for petitions, 1908-26; and repatriation petitions, 1918-72. Relevant records of the Western District, Southern Division, include, for Tacoma, declarations of intention, 1907-57; naturalization records, 1896-1900; petitions, 1912-70; naturalization court orders, 1929-59; military petitions, 1918-19; overseas naturalization petitions, 1954-55; repatriation petitions, 1936-43; soldiers' repatriation petitions, 1936-43; depositions, 1937-57; an index to declarations and petitions, 1912-53; an index to military petitions, 1918-19; and naturalization stub books, 1913-26.

Many of the records for the Western Division of the U.S. District Court, District of Washington, have been filmed on M1542, *Naturalization Records of the U.S. District Court for the Western District of Washington, 1890-1957*, 153 rolls; M1232, *Indexes to Naturalization Records of the U.S. District Court for Western Washington, Northern Division (Seattle), 1890-1952*, 6 rolls; and M1237, *Indexes to Naturalization Records of the U.S. District Court, Western District of Washington, Southern Division (Tacoma), 1890-1953*, 2 rolls.

Records of the **U.S. Circuit Court for the Western District of Washington**, Southern Division, Tacoma, include declarations of intention, 1892-1906, and other naturalization records, 1890-1904.

Also available are records relating to naturalization from the Territorial and Superior Courts in King, Pierce, Snohomish, and Thurston Counties. For the **King County Territorial Court**, the records include declarations of intention, 1854-89, and an index of naturalization, 1864-81. For the **King County Superior Court**, the records include deposition case files, 1866-1924; declarations of intention, 1889-1924; declaration stub books, 1893-1906; petitions, 1906-28; final certificates, 1889-1906; naturalization journal for minors, 1903-6; and naturalization fee books, 1899-1906. An index to these records has been filmed on M1233, *Indexes to Naturalization Records of the King County [WA] Territorial and Superior Courts, 1864-1889 and 1906-1928*, 1 roll.

Naturalization records from the **Pierce County Superior Court** include declarations of intention, 1853-1908; records of citizenship, 1854-81; certificates of citizenship, 1889-1906; petitions, 1906-24; and an index to declarations,

1854-1911. An index to these records is included on M1238, *Indexes to Naturalization Records of the Pierce County [WA] Territorial and Superior Courts, 1853-1923,* 2 rolls.

Naturalization records from the **Snohomish County Territorial Court** include declarations of intention, 1876-90. Naturalization records from the **Snohomish County Superior Court** include declarations of intention, 1890-1973; depositions, 1896-1929; certificates of citizenship, 1890-1903; petitions, 1906-74; citizenship records, 1903-6; certificates of naturalization, 1907-26; citizenship petitions granted and denied, 1929-75; repatriation petitions, 1919-73; general index to naturalization, 1892-1974; and a card index to naturalization, 1950-74. Indexes to these records have been filmed on M1235, *Indexes to Naturalization Records of the Snohomish County [WA] Territorial and Superior Courts, 1876-1974,* 3 rolls.

Records from the **Thurston County Superior Court** include declarations of intention, 1849-1974; petitions, 1906-74; naturalization journals for adults, 1891-1907; naturalization journal for minors, 1903-6; stub books for certificates of naturalization, 1907-24; naturalization court orders, 1930-74; naturalization interrogatories, 1929-41; repatriation oaths, 1940-64; transferred petitions, 1952-74; other naturalization records, 1846-1907; and a card index to naturalizations, 1952-74. A filmed index to these records has been included on M1234, *Indexes to Naturalization Records of the Thurston County (WA) Territorial and Superior Courts, 1850-1974,* 2 rolls.

Some naturalization records from the four counties are reproduced on M1543, *Naturalization Records of the Superior Courts for King, Pierce, Thurston, and Snohomish Counties, Washington, 1850-1974,* 103 rolls.

West Virginia

NARA's Mid Atlantic Region (Center City Philadelphia) has records of the **U.S. District Court for the Northern and Southern Districts of West Virginia**. Records of the Northern District relating to naturalization include, for the Clarksburg Division, petitions for naturalization, 1908-50, and declarations of intention 1908-52; for the Elkins Division, petitions for naturalization, 1926-56 and 1970-80, and declarations of intention, 1908-52 and 1972-85; for the Fairmont Division, petitions for naturalization, 1944-74, and declarations of intention 1944-74; for the Phillipi Division, petitions for naturalization, 1910-25, and declarations of intention, 1920-29.

Records for the Wheeling Division include declarations of intention, 1912-89, and petitions for naturalization, 1844-75 and 1912-78, with a few petitions dated as early as 1844 and a few dated as late as 1875. The petitions are filmed as M1643, *Naturalization Petitions of the U.S. District Court for the Northern District of West Virginia, Wheeling, 1856-1867,* 2 rolls. Records of the **U.S. Circuit Court** for Wheeling include petitions for naturalization, 1910-11, and declarations of intention, 1907-11.

Records of the Southern District relating to naturalization include petitions for naturalization, 1906-29; declarations of intention 1906-52; and an index to petitions for naturalization, 1904-62. The records include military petitions for soldiers stationed at Nitro and Point Pleasant, WV, in 1918.

Wisconsin

NARA's Great Lakes Region in Chicago has records of the **U.S. District Court for the Western District of Wisconsin**. Naturalization records include, for the Madison Division, an index to declaration of intention, 1848-99; declarations of intention, 1876-1902; a naturalization docket book, 1876-1906; petitions, 1941-69; repatriation records, 1961; and petitions and duplicate certificates of naturalization for armed forces personnel serving overseas, 1941-56; for the LaCrosse Division, declarations of intention, 1870-1900, and a naturalization docket book, 1871-1900; for the Superior Division, a naturalization petition and record book, 1910-18; declarations of intention, 1902-21; and other small series of miscellaneous records; and for the Wausau Division, naturalization petitions, 1954-55.

Naturalization records of the **U.S. District Court for the Eastern District of Wisconsin**, Milwaukee, include naturalization petition and record books, 1848-1970; a card index to petitions, 1848-1990; declarations of intention, 1848-1971, and indexes, 1856-1906 and 1943-54. Also available are depositions, 1906-72, in support of petitioners who had moved to the Eastern District within the previous 5 years; transfer cases from other courts, 1952-82; court orders granting or denying citizenship, 1929-79; repatriation order books, 1940-61; and petitions of armed forces personnel serving overseas, 1943-56.

3.2 Naturalization Information in Other Federal Records

An alphabetically arranged index, 1918, containing the names of World War I soldiers naturalized pursuant to an act of May 9, 1918 (40 stat. 546), is located in RG 85, Records of the Immigration and Naturalization Service, in the National Archives Building. The act stated that any soldier serving honorably could be naturalized without proving that he had resided in the United States for the required time period. The index includes the name, date of naturalization, court and certificate number, and sometimes the American name adopted after naturalization.

Records of the Immigration and Naturalization Service held by three of NARA's regional facilities include records that are particularly relevant to this chapter.

The Great Lakes Region in Chicago has a Soundex index, 1840-1950, covering Federal and local naturalization records in northern Illinois (including Cook County and Chicago), southern and eastern Wisconsin, eastern Iowa, and northwest Indiana. References to Cook County and Chicago records do not begin until after the fire of 1871. An explanation of the Soundex system is given in 1.2.1.

Photocopies of naturalization records and indexes to the records for New York City and New England were prepared by a Work Projects Administration (WPA) project designed to centralize, photocopy, and index information in naturalization records scattered among Federal, state, and local courts. The WPA was terminated before the project was completed. The resulting photocopies and index to naturalization documents filed in the courts of New York City, 1792-1906, are in NARA's Northeast Region (New York City). The photocopies are arranged by court name and thereunder numerically by volume or bundle, number, and page or record number. The index is available as microfilm publication M1674, *Index (Soundex) to Naturalization Petitions Filed in Federal, State, and Local Courts in New York, New York, Including New York, Kings, Queens, and Richmond Counties, 1792-1906,* 294 rolls.

The photocopies of records and the index to naturalization documents filed in courts in Maine, Massachusetts, New Hampshire, Vermont, and Rhode Island, and an index only to naturalizations filed in Connecticut are in NARA's Northeast Region (Boston). The copies of the records are arranged by state, thereunder by court, and thereunder by date of naturalization. The index contains some cards for New York, but the records to which they refer are not among this series of photocopies.

The records in both the New York and New England sets of files from the WPA project consist of photographic copies of naturalization documents, usually two pages for each naturalization, containing some or all of the following information: petition for citizenship, oath of allegiance and previous citizenship, place and date of birth, occupation, place and date of arrival in the United States, place of residence at the time of application, and name and address of a witness to these statements. Earlier records contain less information than later ones.

The WPA indexes are arranged by the petitioner's surname converted to the Soundex system. The index cards are printed with spaces for the Soundex code, the individual's name, name and location of the court, date of naturalization, volume or bundle number, page or record number, address of the person naturalized, occupation, date of birth, former nationality, port of arrival in the United States, date of arrival, and names and addresses of witnesses. Spaces for personal and arrival information are left blank on many of the cards. Only in rare cases will the naturalization documents supply more information than the index card.

Other Federal records that provide naturalization information are **passport applications,** among the General Records of the Department of State, RG 59, and **homestead applications,** in the Records of the Bureau of Land Management, RG 49. If a naturalized citizen applied for a passport before 1906, record of their naturalization is usually in the passport application file. Homestead applicants had to present evidence that they were citizens or had applied for citizenship, so naturalization papers are often in a homestead applicant's file. For more information about passports, *see* 18.5.1; for more about homestead applications, 15.2.

Finally, a volume entitled *List of Naturalization Certificates Sent to the U.S. Attorney for Review, and Returned by Him to the Board of Civil Service Examiners of Persons Taking Civil Service Examinations, 1905-06,* is part of Records of the U.S. Civil Service Commission, RG 146. References to naturalization certificates for persons taking Federal civil service examinations in New York State are entered under the initial letter of the surname, thereunder chronologically by date the certificate was sent to the U.S. attorney. The list shows the name of the court that issued each naturalization certificate, the kind of civil service examination taken and where, and the date the certificate was returned by the attorney.

3.3 Naturalization Records Not in the National Archives

To obtain information about naturalization records that are not in the custody of the National Archives and Records Administration, the researcher should write to the appropriate court official—usually the clerk of the court that issued the certificate of naturalization. If the subject of research is a person who was naturalized after September 26, 1906, inquiries should be sent to the Immigration and Naturalization Service, 425 Eye Street NW, Washington, DC 20536.

bear the same file number and office designation.

The 95 volumes of **letters sent**, 1800–90, constitute the main or central series of letters sent by the Adjutant General's Office. The Appointment, Commission, and Personal Branch; Volunteer Service Branch; Colored Troops Division; Bounty and Claims Division; and the Military Prison Record Division maintained their own series of outgoing correspondence during their existence. Copies of some replies sent by various War Department offices and branches are filed with related letters in the letters received series described above. The volumes have been reproduced as M565, *Letters Sent by the Office of the Adjutant General (Main Series), 1800-1890,* 63 rolls. Most of the volumes have an index preceding the letters.

Muster rolls, 1791–October 31, 1912, are another kind of record useful for identifying individual officers and enlisted men. A muster roll is a list of all troops actually present on parade or otherwise accounted for on the day of muster or review of troops under arms. Muster rolls were made to account for the number of soldiers assigned to the unit and to examine their condition, including discipline, instruction, military appearance, arms, accoutrements, and clothing.

The muster roll from which the names were called also served as the voucher for issuance of pay. The several types include descriptive rolls and the regular muster-for-pay rolls for individuals, detachment companies, and regiments. Muster-for-pay rolls, the larger series, include the names of personnel of the organization, with names of commissioned officers and noncommissioned officers coming first, followed by names of privates in alphabetical order. Given are date and place of enlistment, by whom enrolled and for what period, date of muster into service, date and amount of last pay and for what period, and remarks that may include disposition of any absentees, notes of desertions, and deaths. Troops mustered for pay on the last day of February, April, June, August, October, and December. Muster and descriptive rolls give additional information about the individual, including place of birth, age at date of muster, previous occupation, color of hair, color of eyes, complexion, bounty paid and amounts due, clothing accounts, and remarks. Special musters of troops were taken at various times, and such records may include all or much of the information contained on the muster-for-pay rolls.

Beginning in 1821 the rolls include a "record of events" section, which can provide information relating to military activities such as battles and skirmishes in which the unit participated.

To use muster rolls, the researcher needs to know which units an individual was assigned to and the dates of service. Prior to 1861 the muster rolls are arranged by arm of service, thereunder numerically by regiment, and thereunder chronologically. Muster rolls for special units and detachments are filed at the end of the series. Beginning in 1861 muster rolls are arranged by arm of service, thereunder numerically by regiment, thereunder alphabetically by company or troop or other unit, and thereunder chronologically. As with the earlier series, rolls for special units are filed at the end of the series. Included with some of the earlier muster rolls are inspection returns, various papers relating to pay, bounty books, order books, and other material. Where they exist, similar records for the later period are filed separately in various other series.

Among other series of War Department records are additional records relating to officers and enlisted personnel who were prisoners of war, served in special capacities, were ill or wounded, received decorations or awards, or were court-martialed. For example, M1832, *Returns of Killed and Wounded in Battles or Engagements With Indians and British and Mexican Troops, 1790-1848 (Eaton's Compilation),* 1 roll, provides names of both Regular and Volunteer officers killed in such actions and the number of enlisted casualties.

Carded medical records, 1821–84 and 1894–1912, contain information relating to Regular Army personnel admitted to hospitals for treatment. Each card includes name, rank, organization, cause for admission, date admitted and discharged (or date deserted or died, if applicable), transfers, and remarks. The 1821–84 records are arranged by regiment number, thereunder by initial letter of patient's surname. The 1894–1912 records are arranged by arm of service, thereunder by number of regiment, and thereunder by initial letter of the individual's surname.

Many of the original medical records from which the carded abstracts were prepared exist, as do records that were not included in the abstracting project but that contain varying amounts of information relating to the treatment of individuals at specific hospitals. RG 94 has records relating to medical activities in specific wars for the period 1821–1912; Records of the Office of the Surgeon General (Army), RG 112, has them for later periods. Because of the volume, arrangement, and specialized topics of such records, researchers should consult NARA inventories and then seek the advice of the archivists familiar with such records for information relating to a specific person, unit, and period of service.

Records relating to officers and enlisted **medical personnel**, as well as those who served in civilian capacities, such as contract surgeons and dentists, are contained in both Record Groups 94 and 112. Records of interest in RG 112 that relate to medical personnel, 1775 to 1947, include records relating to Regular Army surgeons and assistant surgeons, dental surgeons, nurses, veterinarians, and hospital stewards and corpsman. Records relating to volunteer and reserve officers include records concerning volunteer medical officers, medical reserve officers, dental reserve officers, and National Guard medical and dental officers.

Records relating to civilian medical personnel, 1862–1939, are discussed in 14.2.6. For types and descriptions of the various records, researchers should consult *Preliminary Inventory of the Textual Records of the Office of the Surgeon General (Army), (Record Group 112),* compiled by Patricia Andrews and revised by Garry Ryan (Washington: National Archives and Records Service, 1964).

Of particular interest in RG 112 is the consolidated correspondence file, which contains information about medical officers and nurses. The correspondence was received after 1889, but the records contain some references to the period 1818–90.

The major series in RG 94 is personal papers of medical officers and physicians who served prior to 1912. These records include extracts of orders, appointment information, personal reports, information concerning duty stations, records of promotions, and, for contract medical officers, information relating to the contract terms and duty stations. The series is arranged alphabetically by name of medical officer. Files are included in this series for officers who served with volunteer units before 1903.

There are also papers relating to medical cadets in the Civil War. This series contains information relating to appointments, discharges, and the service of medical cadets. Information relating to pre-Civil War service is included in some files. The files are arranged alphabetically by surname of cadet.

A three-volume "Address Book" shows the name, rank, organization, post office address, and date of death of Civil War medical employees. One volume identifies surgeons and assistant surgeons serving in volunteer organizations; another, surgeons; and the third, surgeons and assistant surgeons serving with the U.S. Army. The entries, arranged alphabetically by surgeon's name, are dated from 1860 to 1894.

Papers relating to hospital stewards, 1862–93, consist of orders; correspondence concerning appointments, discharges, and service; and the personal reports of hospital stewards. The records are arranged alphabetically by name of steward.

Other records relating to officer and enlisted medical personnel are described in the inventory for RG 94.

The **court-martial records** in Records of the Office of the Judge Advocate General (Army), RG 153, are dated 1808–1939. Of greatest genealogical significance in these records is a large series of case files for general courts-martial, courts of inquiry, and military commissions. These files are arranged by case number. The **registers of court-martial cases**, 1809–90, which serve as an index to that portion of the series, is available on microfilm as M1105, *Registers of the Records of the Proceedings of the U.S. Army General Courts-Martial, 1809–1890*, 8 rolls. A carded name index for the period 1891–1917 gives name and rank of defendant, army unit, case number, and date. These records will be of greatest use to the researcher who knows when and where the subject of research was court-martialed.

Each case file generally includes a copy of the trial transcript. Related documents, such as correspondence or orders pertaining to the case, are sometimes included. The trial transcript usually indicates the charges and specifications, plea(s) and arraignment(s) of defendant(s), testimony of defendant(s) and witnesses, findings and sentencing of the court, and, upon occasion, reviewing authorities' reports and statements of action by the Secretary of War and the President. Case files also indicate names, ranks, and units of soldiers court-martialed, and, in some instances, their dates of birth and places of residence. Case files of Union soldiers executed during the Civil War are reproduced on M1523, *Proceedings of U.S. Army Courts-martial and Military Commissions of Union Soldiers Executed by U.S. Military Authorities, 1861–1866*, 8 rolls.

Records relating to wars are separate series of records relating to military activities during a given emergency. They are included in the records of the Adjutant General's Office, in records of the various War Department offices and bureaus, and in records relating to military units. Examples of such records are correspondence series with name and subject indexes; records of Regular Army units maintained by those units; and special correspondence series concerning particular situations or circumstances, such as records relating to persons gassed during World War I; individuals who served in civilian capacities during war and peacetime; and records relating to those who initially served in a military capacity and were subsequently discharged and hired as civilians in the same capacity. These series usually contain more information about officers than enlisted men. Many include indexes from about 1861.

The names and descriptions of specific records series relating to officers or enlisted men are given in NARA inventories of the records. For example, PI 17, *Records of the Adjutant General's Office, 1784–1947,* includes the indexed series of post-Revolutionary War manuscripts; War of 1812 "miscellaneous records"; Mexican War letters received; unindexed Civil War staff papers; generals' papers and books; and generals' reports of service. Some of these series are available on microfilm: M904, *War Department Collection of Post-Revolutionary War Manuscripts*, 4 rolls; M1747, *Index to Records Relating to War of 1812 Prisoners of War*, 3 rolls; M2019, *Records Relating to War of 1812 Prisoners of War*, 1 roll; and M1098, *U.S. Army Generals' Reports of Civil War Service, 1864–1887*, 8 rolls.

There are also **records relating to Regular Army military units** in Records of U.S. Regular Army Mobile Units, 1821–1942, RG 391; Records of U.S. Army Coast Artillery Districts and Defenses, 1901–1942, RG 392; Records of U.S. Army Commands, 1784–1821, RG 98; Records of U.S. Army Continental Commands, 1821–1920, RG 393; Records of U.S. Army Overseas Operations and Commands, 1898–1942, RG 395; and, to a limited extent, Records of the Headquarters of the Army, RG 108; and other record groups containing records incidental to military service.

Because the records relating to volunteers also contain information about Regular Army personnel, researchers may locate material about an ancestor who was a Regular Army officer in the **general correspondence of the Record and Pension Office** (R&P Office). The R&P Office was established by War Department orders of July 8 and 16, 1889, as the Record and Pension Division in the War Department; it was redesignated the Record and Pension Office by an act of Congress approved on May 9, 1892. The R&P Office was created to consolidate all records relating to volunteers; the Record and Pension Division of the Surgeon General's Office and 13 divisions of the Adjutant General's Office that dealt with muster rolls and other military records of volunteers were combined to form it. In addition to War Department records, certain other records from the Departments of the Interior, State, and the Treasury were brought into the Record and Pension Office. Most of them pertain to the Revolutionary War and are now part of RG 93, War Department Collection of Revolutionary War Records. There is a consolidated name index, 1889-1904, for the document file of the Record and Pension Office. *See* 4.3, 4.4, and 5.2.6 for additional series relating to the R&P Office.

4.3 Records of Officers

Researching an officer's military career during the period before 1917 is difficult because few histories of officers were kept, and the War Department did not begin the practice of creating and maintaining consolidated personnel files until 1863. Accordingly, the researcher should first consult published biographies and histories to identify the period of the officer's service, the units to which he was attached, and any other particulars of his service that can be gleaned from secondary sources. Among such publications are *Historical Register and Dictionary of the United States Army from Its Organization, September 29, 1789, to March 2, 1903,* by Francis B. Heitman, 2 vols. (Washington: Government Printing Office, 1903, Congressional serial 4535 and 4536; reprinted by the University of Illinois Press, Urbana, 1965); *Biographical Register of the Officers and Graduates of the U.S. Military Academy*, by George W. Cullum, 9 vols. (various publishers, 1850-91); *U.S. Army Register*, published biannually since 1815; and the various registers of volunteer officers mentioned in Tables 7, 10, 12, and 13 in Chapter 5.

Heitman's *Historical Register*, which is also available on microfilm as M1858, *Historical Register and Dictionary of the United States Army from its Organization, September 29, 1789, to March 2, 1903*, 1 roll, is a complete list of commissioned officers of the Army, including officers of the volunteer staff and brevet major or brigadier generals of volunteers. It gives their full names and shows their service as cadets, officers, or enlisted men, either in

the Regular Army or volunteer service. A separate list of Confederate officers who served in the U.S. Army is included.

The *U.S. Army Register*, a published list of Regular Army officers, begins with the year 1813. Early editions provide name, rank, military specialty, date of commission, staff appointments and brevets, and regiment and military district. *A Compilation of Registers of the Army of the United States from 1815 to 1837*, compiled by William A. Gordon (Washington: James C. Dunn, 1837), comprises most of the early registers in a single volume. Annual editions of the register were published in this same series until 1945. Complete army registers for the years 1813-38 can also be found in the *American State Papers, Class 5, Military Affairs*. For the years 1891-1943, an alphabetical *Army Directory* published by the Adjutant General's Office is also available. The following War Department *Annual Reports*, which can be found among the Congressional Serial Set, contain lists of officers with the name, rank, date of commission, brevets or commissions of prior date, number of months for which pay accounts were received, annual pay, rations, allowance for servants, cost of forage, fuel, and quarters:

1848 (Ser. 543-56)
1849 (Ser. 577-54)
1850 (Ser. 679-48)
1851 (Ser. 679-50)
1852 (Ser. 679-58)
1853 (Ser. 721-59)
1854 (Ser. 783-58)
1855 (Ser. 851-22)
1856 (Ser. 897-24)
1857 (Ser. 955-66)
1858 (Ser. 1006-58)
1859 (Ser. 1048-35)
1860 (Ser. 1100-54)

The most recent edition of the U.S. Army Register in RG 287, Publications of the U.S. Government, was issued in three volumes for 1976.

Basic evidence of an officer's service consists of documents relating to his appointment and to the termination of his service. This usually includes a letter of appointment, an oath of office, a letter of acceptance of the appointment, and records or documents relating to the termination of his service by resignation, dismissal, death, or retirement.

The most accessible sources of information about officers are in the records of the Adjutant General's Office and its subdivisions. The War Department fire of 1800 destroyed much of the documentation pertaining to officers who served in the Regular Army from 1784 to 1800. Compiled military service records do exist for officers who served in the few organizations that were predecessors of the Regular Army, principally the First American Regiment, First U.S. Regiment, Battalion of Artillery, and U.S. Levies.

Service in other organizations may be documented in muster rolls and returns. The most important series for information about Regular Army officers who served during the period 1800-62 are the correspondence files, muster and pay rolls, and returns in RG 94. Information about some officers who served during the period 1800-21 can be obtained from the registers of enlistments.

The Commission Branch was organized in the Office of the Adjutant General on January 1, 1863, to handle such matters as appointments, promotions, resignations, discharges, retirements, assignments, and details of commanding officers of the Regular Army, volunteer officers in staff corps, officers appointed by the President, officers in the District of Columbia Militia, veterinary surgeons, post traders, and noncommissioned staff officers up to 1882. On January 1, 1871, the branch was designated the Appointment, Commission, and Personal (ACP) Branch of the Adjutant General's Office and continued as such until 1894. Because the branch, in addition to creating records of it own, drew from the central files of the Adjutant General's Office's earlier papers dealing with appointments and commissions, its records are a good resource for documenting the service of officers.

A detailed description of the various record series of the branch is given in PI 17, mentioned above. Records of the branch include such material as letters sent and received, registers of letters received, indexes, and registers of applications for appointments or commissions. The letters received by the Commission Branch (CB Files) for the period 1863-70 have been microfilmed as M1064, *Letters Received by the Commission Branch of the Adjutant General's Office, 1863-70*, 527 rolls. An alphabetical card file index is available. Some of the letters received by the Appointment, Commission, and Personal Branch (ACP files) for the period 1871-94 have been microfiched as M1395, *Letters Received by the Appointment, Commission, and Personal Branch, Adjutant General's Office, 1871-94*, 1,693 fiche. The fiche in this publication are arranged alphabetically by surname of the officer. The carded index to the 1871-94 series is microfilmed as M1125, *Name and Subject Index to the Letters Received by the Appointment, Commission, and Personal Branch of the Adjutant General's Office*, 1871-94, 4 rolls.

Applications for appointment to positions in the U.S. Army and War Department, 1871-80, were made to the President, the Secretary of War, and others. The applications are arranged chronologically by year, thereunder numerically. Entries in two volumes of registers of applications identify the correspondent or applicant, position applied for, date received, by whom recommended, and action on the application. Indexes identify the correspondent or applicant and give the file number assigned to the consolidated ACP file.

The records of the ACP Branch include various series relating to army commissions, including original commissions that were never delivered, copies of commissions issued, and copies of letters of appointment and promotion. Original commissions, signed by the President but never delivered, are arranged chronologically, 1812-1902, and thereunder alphabetically by name of officer. Registers of commissions vary but usually show the name of the officer, rank, date of commission, date of acceptance, and remarks. Registers of appointment include name, residence, rank, organization, and date of appointment; some also include date and place of birth. The commission and appointment records are variously dated, and some relate to type of appointment.

Three **historical registers of commissioned officers of the line of the Army**, 1799-1915, show name, place of birth, military unit, date of commission, date of resignation, date of death, and sometimes other information and remarks. Volume 1 covers the period 1799-1860; volume 2, 1861-1900; and volume 3, 1901-15. Within each volume, arrangement is alphabetical by initial letter of surname of officer, thereunder chronological by year. (Similar registers are in the records of the Ordnance Department, Paymaster's Department, Quartermaster's Office, and the Signal Corps described below.)

In 1816 every officer made a personal **report of place of birth.** The records of these reports are arranged alphabetically by initial letter of surname of officer.

A one-volume **roster of officers**, 1783-1826, gives the officer's name, place of residence, date of acceptance of first commission, date and change of each rank held during the period indicated, and remarks, which consist of pertinent information relating to the individual's military service. Entries are arranged alphabetically by initial letter of the officer's surname.

Most of the U.S. Military Academy **cadet application papers**, 1805-66, are arranged by year and thereunder numerically by file number. The file designation consists of the year in which the application was received and the number assigned to the file; a few unnumbered applications at the end of each calendar year are arranged alphabetically by the candidate's name. No applications exist for the year 1811. An index to this series is arranged alphabetically by the initial letter of the surname of the applicant, thereunder by initial vowel sound of the surname, and thereunder chronologically by date of application. The index entries show the name of the applicant, year of application, state from which the candidate applied, and file number of the application papers. Some of these applications contain a considerable amount of information about the family background of applicants. Some incorrect spellings of names have been noted in the index, but no corrections have been made. A list of early applications, 1804-9, that were forwarded to the Record and Pension Office in 1896, appears at the beginning of the name index. Many of the papers to which the list refers are now filed among the records microfilmed as M221, *Letters Received by the Secretary of War, Registered Series, 1801-1870*, 317 rolls.

	TABLE 5	
	Microfilm Publications of Regular Army Returns	
M665	Returns from Regular Army Infantry Regiments, June 1821–December 1916	300 rolls
M690	Returns from Regular Army Engineer Battalions, September 1846–June 1916	10 rolls
M691	Returns from Regular Army Coast Artillery Corps Companies, February 1901–June 1916	81 rolls
M727	Returns from Regular Army Artillery Regiments, June 1821–January 1901	38 rolls
M728	Returns from Regular Army Field Artillery Batteries and Regiments, February 1901– December 1916	14 rolls
M744	Returns from Regular Army Cavalry Regiments, 1833–1916	117 rolls
M851	Returns of the Corps of Engineers, April 1832–December 1916	22 rolls
M852	Returns of the Corps of Topographical Engineers, November 1831–February 1863	2 rolls

The application papers have been reproduced as M688, *U.S. Military Academy Cadet Application Papers, 1805-1866,* 242 rolls. Roll 1 contains the index. In addition, a list of applicants for whom no papers have been found in this series has been prepared and is filmed after the microfilm publication introductory remarks.

RG 94 includes additional information relating to West Point and the cadets, and one should consult the finding aids to RG 94 for specific series. Two additional series relating to cadets have been microfilmed as M2037, *Register of Cadet Applicants, 1819-67,* 5 rolls, and M2061, *Military Academy Registers, 1867-94,* 3 rolls.

There is considerably more information about West Point cadets and the officers in charge at West Point in the Records of the U.S. Military Academy, RG 404, described in PI 185, *Records of the United States Military Academy*, compiled by Stanley P. Tozeski (Washington: National Archives and Records Service, 1976). The original records are in the U.S. Military Academy Archives, West Point, NY.

The Volunteer Service Branch was established in the Office of the Adjutant General in October 1861. It was charged with all matters pertaining to the authorization, recruitment, organization, service, and discharge of volunteer troops and organizations, together with the officers. The branch was transferred to the Record and Pension Office when that office was created in 1889.

Some Regular Army officers initially entered the military service as volunteers, resigned their regular commissions in favor of higher volunteer commissions during wartime, or were assigned to duty with volunteers. Evidence of this service is contained in the compiled military service

records of volunteers (*see* Chapter 5). Information about such officers can be found among the records of the Volunteer Service Branch, which consist primarily of letters sent, letters received, and alphabetical name indexes to letters sent and letters received. The indexes show the register numbers assigned to communications. The index volumes are arranged chronologically, and some indexes to letters received contain briefs of the communications. The compiled military service records contain cross-references to the appropriate Volunteer Service Branch records.

Every commander of a body of troops was required to furnish **returns** (or official reports) to the Adjutant General at specified intervals, usually monthly, on forms provided by that office. The station of troops, strength of each unit, and names of commissioned personnel and their whereabouts were thus kept currently available in the Adjutant General's Office. This body of records, used in conjunction with the muster rolls, constitutes a valuable source of historical information. Separate series of returns are available for departments, divisions, posts, and military organizations. The most useful returns for genealogical research are the post and military organization returns.

Post returns, early 1800s–December 1916, are monthly returns of most military posts, camps, and stations. Returns generally show units that were stationed at a particular post and their strength, the names and duties of officers, number of officers present and absent, a list of official communications received, and a record of events. These records have been reproduced as M617, *Returns from United States Military Posts, 1800-1916,* 1,550

THE UNITED STATES OF AMERICA.

OATH OF ENLISTMENT AND ALLEGIANCE.

STATE OF *Massachusette*
TOWN OF *Boston* }ss:

I, *William Low*, born in *Haverhill* in the State of *Massachusette*, and by occupation a *Laborer*, DO HEREBY ACKNOWLEDGE to have voluntarily enlisted this *fourteenth* day of *September*, 1871, as a **Soldier** in the Army of the United States of America, for the period of FIVE YEARS, unless sooner discharged by proper authority: And do also agree to accept from the United States such bounty, pay, rations, and clothing as are, or may be established by law. And I do solemnly swear, that I am *twenty one* years and *——* months of age, and know of no impediment to my serving honestly and faithfully as a Soldier for five years under this enlistment contract with the United States. And I, *William Low* do also solemnly swear, that I will bear true faith and allegiance to the **United States of America**, and that I will serve them honestly and faithfully against all their enemies or opposers whomsoever; and that I will observe and obey the orders of the President of the United States, and the orders of the officers appointed over me, according to the Rules and Articles of War.

William Low **L.S.**

Subscribed and duly sworn to before me, this *14* day of *Sept* A.D. 1871.

Joseph Bush
Capt 2nd Inft
Recruiting Officer. *U.S.A.*

I CERTIFY, ON HONOR, That I have carefully examined the above-named recruit, agreeably to the General Regulations of the Army, and that, in my opinion, he is free from all bodily defects and mental infirmity which would, in any way, disqualify him from performing the duties of a soldier.

A. K. McLaren
Surgeon, U.S.A.
Examining Officer.

I CERTIFY, ON HONOR, That I have minutely inspected the above-named recruit *William Low*, previously to his enlistment, and that he was entirely sober when enlisted; that, to the best of my judgment and belief, he is of lawful age; and that I have accepted and enlisted him into the service of the United States under this contract of enlistment as duly qualified to perform the duties of an able-bodied soldier, and, in doing so, I have strictly observed the Regulations which govern the Recruiting Service. This soldier has *gray* eyes, *dark* hair, *ruddy* complexion, is *five* feet *seven 1/4* inches high.

Joseph Bush
Capt 2nd Inft **L.S.**
Recruiting Officer, United States Army

[A. G. O. No. 73.]

DECLARATION OF RECRUIT.

I, *William Low*   , desiring to ENLIST in the Army of the United States, for the term of FIVE YEARS, **Do declare**, That I have neither wife nor child; that I have never been discharged from the United States Service on account of disability, or by sentence of a court martial, or by order before the expiration of the term of enlistment; and that I am of the legal age to enlist of my own accord, and believe myself to be physically qualified to perform the duties of an able-bodied soldier.

GIVEN at *Boston Mass* this *14* day of *Sept*, 1871.

WITNESS:
Chas F Clark
Lieu Sergt

William Low

No. *16*

William Low

Enlisted at *Boston Mass* on the *14* day of *Sept*, 1871, by *Capt Joseph Bush 22 Regiment of Infantry*

—— enlistment; last served in Company ( )

—— Reg't of ——

Discharged ——, 18:

DIRECTIONS.

Enlistments must, in all cases, be taken in triplicate. The recruiting officer will send one copy to the Adjutant General with his monthly accounts, a second to the superintendent with his monthly return, and a third to the depot at the time the recruits are sent there. In cases of soldiers re-enlisted in a regiment, or of regimental recruits, the third copy of the enlistment will be sent at its date to regimental headquarters for file.

Received A. G. O. ——

Assigned to the —— Regiment of *Infty Batty B.*, U. S. Army.

Received —— ——

CONSENT IN CASE OF MINOR.

I, _____, Do CERTIFY, That I am the _____ of _____; that the said _____ is _____ years of age; and I do hereby freely give my CONSENT to his enlisting as a SOLDIER in the ARMY OF THE UNITED STATES for the period of FIVE YEARS.

GIVEN at _____
the _____ day of _____

WITNESS: _____

rolls. They are arranged alphabetically by name of post, thereunder chronologically.

In connection with post returns, *Historical Information Relating to Military Posts and Other Installations, ca. 1700-1900,* M661, 8 rolls, may be useful. Reproduced on this microfilm is the 27-volume National Archives series **Outline Index of Military Forts and Stations.** The volumes also contain a few references to 16th, 17th, and 20th century sites. The purpose of **returns of military organizations** was to report unit strength in total numbers of men present, absent, sick, or on extra or daily duty, and to give a specific accounting of officers and enlisted men by name. Additional information was required on returns from time to time. These returns, for the period 1821-1916, are arranged by arm of service, thereunder numerically by regiment, and thereunder chronologically by date of return.

Station books of officers and organizations of the Regular Army, 1861-1915, show officer's name, company designation, station, whereabouts at last report, date of information, and remarks about such matters as special assignments and leaves. For cadets at the U.S. Military Academy, residence and date and place of birth are included. Place and date of marriage of officers are often mentioned, and addresses, occupations, and date of death of retired officers are given. The 188 volumes in this series are arranged generally chronologically by year and arm of service, thereunder by number of regiment, and thereunder by rank for the following groups for the periods indicated: infantry, 1862-1913 (61 vols.); infantry, 1861, and cavalry and artillery, 1861-1906 (51 vols.); cavalry, 1907-13 (6 vols.); artillery, 1907-13 (7 vols.); general staff officers, 1861-1913 (50 vols.); retired officers, 1891-1915 (10 vols.); unattached, 1870-71 and 1911 (2 vols.); and Signal Corps and hospital chaplains, 1864-67 (1 vol.).

Typewritten military histories of officers, 1903-4, contain information concerning officers who served from as early as 1861. This series, which includes indexes, is arranged roughly by arm of service, thereunder alphabetically. In addition to information about military service, the records contain extracts from officers' efficiency reports, summaries of Civil War volunteer service, and information about honors awarded. Military histories of some Regular Army and volunteer officers, chiefly those who served in the Civil War, were prepared between 1875 and 1890 and bound in three volumes. They contain citations to the consolidated files upon which they are based. Each volume contains an index.

In addition to Records of the Adjutant General's Office, several other record groups contain information about officers of the Regular Army. Records of the Office of the Chief of Engineers, RG 77, includes four volumes of military service **registers of officers of the Engineer Corps,** 1857-94. Among Records of the Office of the Quartermaster General, RG 92, are eight volumes of personal histories of regular officers in the Quartermaster's Department, 1846-1905.

Records of the Office of the Surgeon General (Army), RG 112, includes 11 volumes of **registers of military service of officers,** 1806-20 and 1849-1902, as well as a single volume of lists showing the **service and stations of medical officers,** 1829-33. Eight volumes of **military service histories of ordnance officers,** ca. 1815-1922, and a single volume of **military service histories of ordnance officers serving at field establishments,** 1838-82, are among Records of the Office of the Chief of Ordnance, RG 156. Records of the Office of the Paymaster General, RG 99, includes a **register of paymasters,** 1815-68, and nine volumes of **personal histories of paymasters,** 1848-1910. Organizational returns available on microfilm are listed in Table 5.

Records of the Office of the Chief Signal Officer, RG 111, includes one volume of **synopses of military histories of officers,** 1860-67, and two volumes of **military histories of officers,** 1861-65. A number of Regular Army regiments also maintained volumes of officers' histories; these can be found in RG 391. A few officers' histories are in RG 393; one collection of some interest consists of nine volumes of **military histories of officers in the Department of Texas,** 1869-99.

4.4 Records of Enlisted Men

Researching the career of an enlisted man is generally less complicated than researching the career of an officer but only because there are fewer records relating to enlisted personnel. As with officers' records, most material about enlisted men is in the records of the Adjutant General's Office, RG 94. Genealogists will find useful the information to be gleaned from the enlistment papers and registers of enlistment.

An **enlistment paper** was a contract required of every enlisted man who served in the Regular Army. The records are arranged in three series: 1784-1815; 1798-July 14, 1894; and July 15, 1894-October 31, 1912. The first series, which is part of the post-Revolutionary War papers, is arranged by the initial letter of the surname. The second and third series are arranged alphabetically by name of soldier, thereunder chronologically by date of enlistment. Enlistment papers for persons who served two or more enlistments have sometimes been consolidated.

Enlistment papers generally show the soldier's name, place of enlistment, date, by whom enlisted, age, occupation, personal description, regimental assignment, and certification of the examining surgeon and recruiting officer. Papers relating to enlistments after July 15, 1894, include descriptive and assignment cards, prior service cards, certificates of disability, final statements, inventories of effects, and records of death and interment, if applicable. The highest of the handwritten numbers on the front side of each enlistment paper, at the top center, identifies the enlistment register entry for that soldier.

Enlistment papers for Indian scouts are discussed in 11.2.

Registers of enlistment, 1798-1914, generally contain information relating to the enlistment and termination of service of enlisted personnel. Registers for the period 1798-June 30, 1821, volumes 1-35, also contain information about officers in service during that period. A register entry spans two pages and varies in content. To locate the enlistment register of a particular serviceman, a researcher should know approximately when he served. It is helpful to know the department or arm of service in which he served. The enlistment registers, except those for hospital stewards, quartermaster sergeants, and ordnance sergeants, have been reproduced as M233, *Registers of Enlistments in the U.S. Army, 1798-1914,* 81 rolls. The registers for 1798-June 30, 1821, are arranged in strict alphabetical order. The later registers are arranged by initial letter of the surname, thereunder chronologically by month and year of enlistment. Some volumes in later registers are arranged in groups of months for a period of several years during the Mexican War, July 1846-October 1850.

Register entries for the period 1798-June 30, 1821, contain soldier's name, military organization, physical description, date and place of birth, enlistment information, and remarks. Complete service information is not given for every soldier; in particular, the date or reason for termination of service may not be supplied. Entries in the remarks column contain cryptic references to the source record from which the information was obtained. A partial key to the references, generally a two-initial abbreviation of the title of the original record, appears in volume 1 of the enlistment registers. Source documents cannot always be identified.

Registers for the period July 1, 1821-1914 are uniform in content. A two-page entry contains the same information that appears on the enlistment paper, as well as information relating to termination of service. The termination information came from muster rolls and other records. The left-hand page gives the enlisted man's name, date and place of enlistment, by whom enlisted, period of enlistment, place of birth, age, civilian occupation at the time of enlistment, and personal description.

The right-hand page gives the unit number and arm of service, company, and information relating to separation from service. If the individual was discharged, the date, place, and reason for discharge are given, as well as rank at time of discharge. Additional information, such as notations concerning courts-martial or desertions, appears in the remarks column. For the period July 1, 1821-1914, the remarks column does not show the source of the information.

Separate registers are found for mounted rangers, 1832-33; Indian scouts, 1866-1914; post quartermasters, 1884-90; sergeants appointed under an act of July 5, 1884; ordnance sergeants, 1832-90; commissary sergeants, 1873-91; Philippine scouts, October 1901-13; Puerto Rican provisional infantry, 1901-14; and hospital stewards, 1887-99.

There are a few military histories of enlisted personnel. Resumes of retiring enlisted personnel and those of principal musicians and drum majors are generally found in the correspondence files of the Adjutant General's Office. Separate histories of quartermaster sergeants, 1884-93, are contained in RG 92; separate registers and lists of ordnance personnel, 1832-1917, are contained in RG 156; and separate registers, lists, and descriptive books, 1856-87, of hospital stewards are contained in RG 112.

RG 94 includes **personal papers**, 1861-1912, consisting of various types of papers, including descriptive lists, orders, assignment cards, reports of physical examinations, certificates of disability, discharges, final statement papers, medical papers, burial records, and other papers relating to the personnel of the Regular Army. An attempt was made at some point to arrange them according to subject but was only partially completed. (*See* certificates of disability and final statements described below.) It was the intention of those in charge of these records at the War Department to eventually file all personnel papers relating to an individual soldier in his enlistment jacket. The series is arranged in several subseries. The first is arranged by unit number, thereunder alphabetically by name of soldier. The second is arranged by arm of service, thereunder by unit number, and thereunder alphabetically. Following these two subseries are papers for personnel of field artillery, signal corps, hospital corps, Philippine scouts, National Guard, prisoners, Navy and Marines on army transports, and civilians. There are also several groups of "miscellaneous" papers.

Certificates of disability, 1812-99, are certificates issued by surgeons recommending discharges for soldiers. They contain statements about types of disabilities. Complete information relating to the individual is given, including name; rank; organization; when, where, and by whom enlisted; period of enlistment; age; place of birth; personal description; and duty station. The papers are arranged as follows: War of 1812, thereunder by unit, thereunder by initial letter of surname; Mexican War, thereunder by unit, thereunder by initial letter of surname; 1825-95, thereunder by arm of service (beginning with 7th U.S. Infantry), thereunder by unit number, and thereunder by initial letter of surname; and a miscellaneous series, 1825-99.

Final statements, 1862-99, are papers relating to the deaths of soldiers. Each contains a record of death and burial, an inventory of personal effects, and a final statement relating to the military service of the individual that includes personal description, cause and place of death, and an account of the soldier's financial affairs. The records are arranged generally by organization for various groups of years.

Descriptive Lists, 1901-14, are papers that provide descriptive and other information on enlisted personnel. Information on the lists includes name of soldier, rank, unit, name and address of next of kin, personal description and other information from the enlistment paper, information regarding the soldier's clothing and money accounts and allotments, and remarks. The lists are arranged for the most part alphabetically by name of soldier. A portion of the series is unarranged.

Reports of **medical examination of recruits**, 1884–1912, are in records relating to the sick and wounded in the medical records of the Record and Pension Office of the Adjutant General's Office. The reports show name, residence, date and place of birth, occupation, race, marital status, previous employment, father's nationality, citizenship status, previous military service, name and address of dependents, personal description and remarks, report of physical examination, date and place of acceptance, and enlistment or rejection. The records are arranged alphabetically by name of the recruit, thereunder by the date of enlistment.

Information about the service of enlisted men may also be found in the records of the Enlisted Branch of the Adjutant General's Office, which was created in December 1862 to handle recruitment, discharge, transfers, furloughs, and other matters regarding enlisted personnel. The office inherited the "Addison File" relating to the military service of enlisted men. The file was created or kept by a clerk in the War Department. The papers in the file are dated 1848–62. In 1889 the functions of the Enlisted Branch were transferred to the Record and Pension Office.

Correspondence files of the Enlisted Branch consist of letters sent, 1851–52, 1860–62, and 1863–89; registers of letters received, 1862–89; and letters received, 1848–62 and 1863–89. Letters sent, arranged chronologically by the date sent, are indexed for the period 1863–89. Letters received are generally arranged chronologically by year, thereunder by symbol assigned in the register of letters received. Name indexes, 1863–89, and subject indexes, 1863–81, serve to locate communications in the letters received series. References to communications contained in this and other series of records relating to Regular Army personnel are sometimes contained on the jackets of the enlistment papers, 1894–1912, and in the registers of enlistment.

Military records described in other sections of this volume also relate to officers and enlisted personnel of the Regular Army. *See* Chapter 7 for pension records, Chapter 8 for bounty land warrant records, and Chapter 9 for records of veterans' homes and soldiers' burials. Since these and other chapters also contain descriptions of records of genealogical value concerning military dependents, be sure to check the Index for additional references.

CHAPTER 5

Service Records of Volunteers

5.1 Introduction

Compiled Military Service Records

During periods of warfare or military disturbances, Regular Army units were supplemented by state and territory militia and volunteers units, the forerunners of today's National Guard. The individual service records of these **volunteer** units cover service during the Revolutionary War, 1775–83; the post-Revolutionary War period, 1784–1811; the War of 1812, 1812–15; Indian Wars, 1817–58; the Mexican War, 1846–48; the Civil War, 1861–65; and the Spanish-American War and the Philippine Insurrection, 1898–1903. Volunteers also served during Indian disturbances, civil disorders, and disputes with Canada and Mexico.

The military service records of volunteer soldiers were abstracted onto cards from muster and pay rolls, descriptive rolls, returns, hospital records, prison records, accounts for subsistence, and other material. The card abstracts for each individual soldier were placed into a jacket-envelope bearing the soldier's name, rank, and military unit. This jacket-envelope, containing one or more abstracts and, in some instances, including one or more original documents relating specifically to that soldier, is called a **compiled military service record.**

A compiled military service record is only as complete as the material about an individual soldier or their unit. A typical record shows the soldier's rank, military unit, dates of entry into service, and discharge or separation by desertion, death, or dismissal. It may also show age, place of birth, and residence at time of enlistment. Beginning with those for the Spanish-American War, the record may also include medical data or information on the soldier's next of kin.

Compiled military service records are arranged by war or period of service, thereunder by state or other designation, thereunder by military unit, and thereunder alphabetically by surname of the soldier. To consult the compilation for a particular soldier's record, the researcher must find out, either from an appropriate index or from family records, in which military unit or units (usually a regiment) the soldier served.

Compiled military service records were prepared under a War Department program begun some years after the Civil War in order to permit more rapid and efficient checking of military and medical records in connection with claims for pensions and other veterans' benefits. The abstracts were so carefully prepared that there is virtually no need to consult the original records from which they were made. Original records do not contain additional information about particular soldiers.

A researcher may fail to locate the record of an individual's volunteer military service for several reasons. The soldier may have served, for instance, in the Regular Army (*see* Chapter 4), in a unit from a state other than the one in which he lived, or in a unit that was not mustered into Federal service. He may have served under more than one name or used more than one spelling of his name. Proper records of his service may not have been made; or, if made, they may have been lost or destroyed in the confusion that often attended mobilization, military operations, and disbandment of troops. It is also possible that references to the soldier in the records may be so vague that his correct name or unit cannot be determined.

The name on the jacket-envelope was chosen from one of the abstracts contained in a soldier's compiled military service record. It is not necessarily the correct name of the soldier, nor is it necessarily the way his name was most frequently spelled in the original records. The rank shown at termination of a soldier's service may not be the highest rank he attained while in service, and it may not show any brevet (honorary) rank that may have been conferred after service. If a soldier served in more than one unit, there may be more than one service record for him, and his other service may not be cross-referenced in the record or on the jacket. Additional service by the same soldier rendered in a state militia unit that was never mustered into Federal service will not be documented in the records at the National Archives.

General indexes containing the names of all the soldiers for whom there are compiled military service records are available for each of the segments in which the compiled military service records are arranged; that is, for the Revolutionary War, post-Revolutionary War period, War of 1812, Mexican War, Indian wars, Confederate Army, and Spanish-American War and Philippine Insurrection, but not for the Union Army in the Civil War. These general indexes include cross-references to variants of soldiers' names.

The compiled military service records of soldiers serving in a unit bearing a state name as a part of its official unit designation (for example, 1st Virginia Militia) were also indexed in **state indexes**, except for records of the Mexican War and the Philippine Insurrection.

Each index card contains the soldier's name, rank, and military unit. Cross-references are made to the final unit designation if a unit was known by more than one name, and the various names are shown on one or more abstracts. In addition, cross-references are made to the appropriate unit designation if the records of the soldier's service in different units are consolidated into a single record.

A pension or bounty land warrant application file also contains evidence of the service of a veteran. These records are described in Chapters 7 and 8.

There may be information about a serviceman available in records other than his compiled military service record or pension application file, such as in documents relating to the service of his unit, his officers, or other military units participating in the same disturbance.

A rough chronology of the stations and movements of a military unit can be developed by using **record-of-events cards** that were compiled at the same time as the service records for individuals. The information on them was abstracted from the record-of-events section of muster rolls and returns. They are filed by military unit in jacket-envelopes along with the compiled military service records for the personnel of that military organization. There are record-of-events cards for units that served in the Mexican War and later wars, and for some units in Indian wars; there are none for organizations in the Revolutionary War, the post-Revolutionary War period, or the War of 1812. Record-of-events cards do not document the service of an individual.

The record-of-events cards for the Union Army are filmed as M594, *Compiled Records Showing Service of Military Units in Volunteer Union Organizations*, 225 rolls, while the cards for the Confederate Army are filmed as M861, *Compiled Records Showing Service of Military Units in Confederate Organizations*, 74 rolls. Additional information on these records can be found in Chapter 4 of this guide.

Records of U.S. Army Continental Commands, 1821–1920, RG 393, include series of correspondence, orders, returns, and other records relating to military operations and the personnel who conducted them. Searching the command records for information about specific individuals, however, is difficult. The records are fragmentary and poorly indexed. The command in which a soldier served must be established before any research at all is undertaken, and a considerable knowledge of military history is necessary to use these records.

Useful records may also exist in one of the many series of correspondence in Records of the Adjutant General's Office, 1780's–1917, RG 94, and the jacket of the compiled military service record may carry notations of or cross-references to them. The most important series and related indexes are described in Chapter 4, Records of the Regular Army. A more comprehensive description of the record group is in Preliminary Inventory (PI) 17, *Records of the Adjutant General's Office, 1784-1947*, compiled by Lucille H. Pendell and Elizabeth Bethel (Washington: National Archives and Records Service, 1949).

For information about wars and battles through the 19th century, *Alphabetical List of Battles, 1754-1900 …*, by Nelson A. Strait (Washington: 1905; reprinted Detroit, 1968) may be consulted.

Copies of compiled military service records can be ordered through the mail by using a National Archives Trust Fund form, which may be obtained from the Customer Service Center, National Archives and Records Administration, Room 406, 700 Pennsylvania Ave., NW, Washington, DC 20408-0001. Copies of the form can also be requested through email at *inquire@nara.gov*.

5.2 Volunteer Service Records by War

5.2.1. Revolutionary War

Compiled military service records for men who fought in the Revolutionary War were abstracted from records in the War Department Collection of Revolutionary War Records, Record Group (RG) 93. This record group resulted from the War Department's attempts to find substitutes for records that were destroyed by fires in 1800 and 1814. The department purchased several private collections, such as the papers of Timothy Pickering, who served George Washington as adjutant general and quartermaster general during the Revolutionary War and who held various cabinet posts under Presidents Washington and John Adams. In this record group are also military records of the Revolutionary War that were transferred to the War Department from other executive departments in the latter parts of the 19th century.

Descriptions of the various records series included in the collection are contained in PI 144, *War Department Collection of Revolutionary War Records,* compiled by Mable E. Deutrich and Howard H. Wehmann (Washington: National Archives and Records Service, 1970). Entry 13 in this preliminary inventory refers to a "Catalog of State and Continental Organizations, Revolutionary War," which names each organization and its commanding officer.

Records for individual soldiers are available on microfilm as M881, *Compiled Service Records of Soldiers Who Served in the American Army During the Revolutionary War,* 1,097 rolls. Some of the Revolutionary War compiled service records for persons other than soldiers appear on microfilm as M880, *Compiled Service Records of American Naval Personnel and Members of the Departments of the Quartermaster General and the Commissary General of Military Stores Who Served During the Revolutionary War,* 4 rolls.

The compiled service records are arranged under the designation "Continental Troops" or under a state name, thereunder by organization, and thereunder alphabetically by soldier's surname. Military organizations designated "Continental Troops" were generally state units adopted by the Continental Congress in the first years of the Revolutionary War or units raised in more than one state. Regular units of the Continental Army raised in only one state are generally listed with that state's military organizations.

The most comprehensive name index is the *General Index to Compiled Military Service Records of Revolutionary War Soldiers* [Sailors, and Members of Army Staff Departments], M860, 58 rolls. This index may refer the user to more than one jacket-envelope if a soldier served in more than one unit. In addition to the general index, the following state indexes are available: *Index to Compiled Service Records of Volunteer Soldiers Who Served During the Revolutionary War in Organizations from the State of North Carolina*, M257, 2 rolls; *Index to Compiled Service Records of Revolutionary War Soldiers Who*

TABLE 6
Selected Genealogical Research Aids: Revolutionary War

MANY PUBLICATIONS CONTAIN INFORMATION THAT IDENTIFIES REVOLUTIONARY WAR SOLDIERS AND SHOWS THEIR SERVICE. SOME OF THESE PUBLICATIONS SHOW THE NAME AND MILITARY ORGANIZATION FOR EACH SOLDIER LISTED AND ARE BASED IN WHOLE OR IN PART ON STATE SERVICE RECORDS OR STATE AND NATIONAL SERVICE RECORDS. THEY OFTEN SUPPLY INFORMATION THAT WILL MAKE POSSIBLE EFFECTIVE SEARCHES IN THE RECORDS AT THE NATIONAL ARCHIVES OR SUPPLEMENT THE INCOMPLETE RECORDS.

General

Heitman, Francis B. *Historical Register of Officers of the Continental Army During the War of the Revolution, April 1775-December 1783.* Revised edition. Washington: Rare Book Shop Publishing Co., 1914.

Saffell, William T.R. *Records of the Revolutionary War: Containing Military and Financial Correspondence of Distinguished Officers.* New York: Pudney and Russell, 1858.

Peterson, Clarence Stewart. *Known Military Dead During the American Revolutionary War, 1775-1783.* Baltimore, 1959; reprinted by the Genealogical Publishing Co., Baltimore, 1967.

Brown, Margie G., comp. *Genealogical Abstracts. Revolutionary War Veterans. Script Act of 1852.* Lovettsville, VA: Willow Bend Books, 1997.

Revolutionary War Pensions

Index of Revolutionary War Pension Applications in the National Archives ("Hoyt's Index"). Revised edition. National Genealogical Society (NGS) Special Publication 40. Washington: NGS, 1976; reprinted 1977, 1979, and 1987.

Ainsworth, Mary Govier, comp. "Recently Discovered Records Relating to Revolutionary War Veterans Who Applied for Pensions Under the Act of 1792," *National Genealogical Society Quarterly* 46 (1958): 8-13, 73-78.

War Department. *Letter From the Secretary of War, Communicating a Transcript of the Pension List of the United States* .... Washington: A.&G. Way, 1813. Reprinted in *Collections of the Minnesota Historical Society* 6 (1894):502-539, and by the Genealogical Publishing Co., Baltimore, 1959.

War Department. *... Report of the Names, Rank, and Line, of Every Person Placed on the Pension List [Acts of 1818 and 1820],* 16th Cong., 1st sess., H. Exec. Doc 55, serial 34; reprinted by the Southern Book Co., Baltimore, 1955.

War Department. *Report From the Secretary of War ... in Relation to the Pension Establishment of the United States,* [1835], 23rd Cong., 1st sess., S. Exec. Doc. 514, serials 249-251; reprinted in 4 volumes by the Genealogical Publishing Co., Baltimore, 1968.

State Department. *A Census of Pensioners for Revolutionary or Military Services; With Their Names, Ages, Places of Residence* .... Washington: State Department, 1841. Available on roll 3 of microfilm publication T498, *Publications of the Bureau of the Census: 1790 Census, Printed Schedules,* and also reprinted by the Southern Book Co., Baltimore, 1954, and the Genealogical Publishing Co., Baltimore, 1967.

Genealogical Society. *A General Index to a Census of Pensioners ... 1840.* Baltimore: Genealogical Publishing Co., 1965.

Pension Bureau. *List of Pensioners on the Rolls January 1, 1883, ...* 47th Cong., 2nd sess., S. Exec. Doc. 84, serials 2078-2082; reprinted by the Genealogical Publishing Co., Baltimore, 1970.

Report of the Secretary of the Interior, With a Statement of Rejected or Suspended Applications for Pensions, 32nd Cong., 1st sess., S. Exec. Doc. 37, serial 618; reprinted with index by the Genealogical Publishing Co., Baltimore, 1969.

Scott, Craig R., comp. *The "Lost" Pensions. Settled Accounts of the Act of 6 April 1838.* Lovettsville, VA: Willow Bend Books, 1996.

American State Papers, Claims. Washington: Gales and Seaton, 1834.

Alabama

Owen, Thomas McAdory. *Revolutionary Soldiers in Alabama.* Montgomery: Alabama Department of Archives and History, 1911; reprinted by the Genealogical Publishing Co., Baltimore, 1967.

Pierce, Alycon Trubey, comp. *Alabama Revolutionary War Records. Selected Final Pension Payment Vouchers, 1818-1864. Alabama: Decatur-Huntsville-Mobile-Tuscaloosa.* Lovettsville, VA: Willow Bend Books, 1997.

Connecticut

Smith, Stephen R. et al. *Record of Service of Connecticut Men in the 1.—War of the Revolution. 11.—War of 1812. 111.—Mexican War.* Hartford: Connecticut Adjutant General's Office, 1889.

"Lists and Returns of Connecticut Men in the Revolution, 1775-1783." In *Collections of the Connecticut Historical Society* 8 (1901) and 12 (1909).

Delaware

Delaware Archives. *Military and Naval. Vols. 1-3, Revolutionary War.* Wilmington: Delaware Public Archives Commission, 1911-19; reprinted by AMS Press, New York, 1974.

Whiteley, William G. *The Revolutionary Soldiers of Delaware.* Wilmington: Historical Society of Delaware, 1896.

Florida

Fritot, Jessie Robinson, comp. *Pension Records of Soldiers of the Revolution Who Removed to Florida.* Jacksonville: Jacksonville Chapter, Daughters of the American Revolution, 1946.

TABLE 6
Selected Genealogical Research Aids: Revolutionary War

Georgia

Knight, Lucian Lamar, comp. *Georgia's Roster of the Revolution*. Atlanta: Georgia Department of Archives and History, 1920.

Candler, Allen D. *The Revolutionary Records of the State of Georgia ... 1769-1782*. Atlanta: Georgia Legislature, 1908.

Illinois

Meyer, Virginia M. (Mrs. Harold S.). *Roster of Revolutionary War Soldiers and Widows Who Lived in Illinois Counties*. Chicago: Illinois Daughters of the American Revolution, 1962.

Maryland

Archives of Maryland, Vol. 18, Muster Rolls and Other Records of Service of Maryland Troops in the American Revolution, 1775-1783. Baltimore: Maryland Historical Society, 1900; reprinted by the Genealogical Publishing Co., Baltimore, 1972.

Pierce, Alycon Trubey, comp. *Selected Final Pension Payment Vouchers, 1818-1864. Maryland: Baltimore*. Lovettsville, VA: Willow Bend Books, 1997.

Massachusetts

Massachusetts Soldiers and Sailors of the Revolutionary War. 17 vols. Boston: Secretary of the Commonwealth, 1896-1908. This publication is incomplete; more names are on file at the Massachusetts State Archives. However, the volumes do cover Maine.

New Hampshire

Hammons, Isaac W., ed. *State and Provincial Papers, Vols. 14-17, Rolls and Documents Relating to Soldiers in the Revolutionary War*. Concord: New Hampshire Legislature, 1885-89. *Vol. 30, Miscellaneous Revolutionary Documents*. Manchester, 1910.

New Jersey

Stryker, William S., comp. *Official Register of the Officers and Men of New Jersey in the Revolutionary War*. Trenton: New Jersey Adjutant General's Office, 1872. The *Index* for this register was prepared and published by the New Jersey Historical Records Survey, Newark, 1941; reprinted by the Genealogical Publishing Co., Baltimore, 1965.

New York

Fernow, Berthold, ed. *Documents Relating to the Colonial History of the State of New York*. 15 vols. Albany: New York State University, 1853-87.

Mather, Frederick G. *The Refugees of 1776 From Long Island to Connecticut*. New York: J.B. Lyon Co., 1913; reprinted by the Genealogical Publishing Co., Baltimore, 1972.

New York State Comptroller's Office. *New York in the Revolution as Colony and State*. 2 vols. Albany: J.B. Lyon Co., 1901-4. Earlier editions of volume 1 were compiled by James A. Roberts. Volume 2 has as cover title *New York in the Revolution*. Supplement.

North Carolina

Clark, Walter, ed. *The Colonial and State Records of North Carolina*. Vol. 16, 1782-83. Goldsboro: Nash Brothers, 1899. *Index*, edited by Stephen B. Weeks. 4 vols. 1909-14.

Roster of Soldiers from North Carolina in the American Revolution. Durham: North Carolina Daughters of the American Revolution, 1932; reprinted by the Genealogical Publishing Co., Baltimore, 1967.

Ohio

Henderson, Frank D., John R. Rea, and Jane Dowd (Mrs. Orville D.) Dailey, comps. *The Official Roster of the Soldiers of the American Revolution Buried in the State of Ohio*. Columbus: F.J. Heer Printing Co., 1929.

Dailey, Jane Dowd, comp. *Soldiers of the American Revolution Who Lived in the State of Ohio*. Greenfield: Ohio Daughters of the American Revolution, 1938.

Pennsylvania

Pennsylvania Archives. 2nd series, vols. 10-11, *Pennsylvania in the War of the Revolution, Battalions and Line, 1775- 1783*. Edited by John B. Linn and William H. Egle. Harrisburg: Secretary of the Commonwealth, 1895-96. Vols. 13-14, *Pennsylvania in the War of the Revolution, Associated Battalions and Militia, 1775-1783*. Edited by William H. Egle, 1895-96. Vol. 15, *Journals and Diaries of the War of the Revolution with Lists of Officers and Soldiers, 1775-1783*. Edited by William H. Egle, 1892. 3rd series, vol. 23, *Muster Rolls of the Navy and Line, Militia and Rangers, 1775-1783*. Edited by William H. Egle, 1898. 5th series, vols. 2-8, and 6th series, vols. 1-2, [Muster rolls and lists of Pennsylvania Associators, Militia, and Continental Troops, 1743 to 1787]. Edited by Thomas L. Montgomery, 1906. There are general indexes within the series, especially 1st series, vol. 14; 3d series, vol. 27; and 6th series, vol. 15. See also *Guide to the Published Archives of Pennsylvania . . . .* Compiled by Henry Howard Eddy. Harrisburg: Pennsylvania Historical and Museum Commission, 1949.

South Carolina

Salley, A.S., Jr., ed. *Documents Relating to the History of South Carolina During the Revolutionary War*. Columbia: Historical Commission of South Carolina, 1908.

DeSaussure, Wilmot G., comp. *. . . .Officers Who Served in the South Carolina Regiments . . . .* Charleston, 1894.

TABLE 6
Selected Genealogical Research Aids: Revolutionary War

Boddie, William Willis. *Marion's Men—A List of Twenty-five Hundred.* Charleston: Heisser Printing Co., 1938

Revill, Janie. *Copy of the Original Index Book Showing the Revolutionary Claims Filed in South Carolina Between August 20, 1773–August 31, 1776.* Columbia, 1941; reprinted by the Genealogical Publishing Co., Baltimore, 1969.

South Carolina Treasury. *Stub Entries to Indents Issued in Payment of Claims Against South Carolina Growing Out of the Revolution.* Edited by A.S. Salley, Jr. 11 vols. Columbia: Historical Commission of South Carolina, 1910–57.

Pruitt, Jayne Conway Garlington. *Revolutionary War Pension Applicants Who Served From South Carolina.* Fairfax County, VA, 1946.

Tennessee

Allen, Penelope Johnson. *Tennessee Soldiers in the Revolution.* Bristol: Tennessee Daughters of the American Revolution, 1935; reprinted by the Genealogical Publishing Co., Baltimore, 1975.

Vermont

Goodrich, John E., ed. *Rolls of the Soldiers in the Revolutionary War, 1775 to 1783.* Rutland: Tuttle Co., 1904.

Virginia

Pay Rolls of Militia Entitled to Land Bounty—Virginia. Richmond: Virginia Auditor of Public Accounts, 1851.

McAllister, Joseph Thompson. *Virginia Militia in the Revolutionary War.* Hot Springs, VA: McAllister Publishing Co., 1913.

Gwathmey, John H. *Historical Register of Virginians in the Revolution, Soldiers, Sailors, Marines, 1775–1783.* Richmond: Dietz Press, 1938; reprinted by the Genealogical Publishing Co., Baltimore, 1973.

Burgess, Louis A., ed. *Virginia Soldiers of 1776.* Richmond: Richmond Press, 1927; reprinted by the Reprint Co., Spartanburg, SC.

Eckenrode, H.J., comp. *List of Revolutionary Soldiers of Virginia. Special Report of the Department of Archives and History.* 2 vols. Richmond: Virginia State Library, 1912–13.

Brumbaugh, Gaius Marcus. *Revolutionary War Records: Virginia.* Washington, DC, and Lancaster, PA: Lancaster Press, 1936; reprinted by the Genealogical Publishing Co., Baltimore, 1967.

Wilson, Samuel Mackay, comp. *Catalog of Revolutionary Soldiers and Sailors of the Commonwealth of Virginia to Whom Land Bounty Warrants Were Granted by Virginia for Military Services in the War of Independence.* Lexington: Kentucky Sons of the Revolution, 1913. Reprinted by the Southern Book Co., Baltimore, 1953, and by the Genealogical Publishing Co., Baltimore, 1967.

A List of Claims for Bounty-Land for Revolutionary Service. Governor of Virginia, Document 35. Richmond, 1835.

West Virginia

Johnston, Ross B., ed. *West Virginians in the American Revolution.* West Virginia Historical Society Publication 1. Parkersburg, WV: West Augusta Historical and Genealogical Society, 1959.

Special Categories

Duncan, Louis Caspar. *Medical Men in the American Revolution, 1775–1783.* Army Medical Bulletin 25. Carlisle Barracks, PA: Medical Field Service School, 1931.

Dandridge, Danske. *American Prisoners of the Revolution.* Baltimore: Genealogical Publishing Co., 1967.

Dickore, Maria, comp. and trans. *Hessian Soldiers in the American Revolution—Records of Their Marriages, and Baptisms of Their Children in America Performed by the Rev. G.C. Coster, 1776–1783, Chaplain of Two Hessian Regiments.* Cincinnati: C.J. Krehbiel Co., 1959.

Mercenaries From Hessen-Hanau Who Remained in Canada and the United States After the American Revolution. German-American Genealogical Research Monograph No. 5. Dekalb, IL: Westland Publications, 1976.

Muster Rolls and Prisoner-of-War Lists in American Archival Collections Pertaining to the German Mercenary Troops Who Served with the British Forces During the American Revolution. German-American Genealogial Research Monograph No. 3. Dekalb, IL: Westland Publications, 1974.

Ford, W.C., comp. *British Officers Serving in the American Revolution, 1774–1783.* Brooklyn: Historical Printing Club, 1897.

O'Brien, Michael J. *A Hidden Phase of American History: Ireland's Part in America's Struggle for Liberty.* New York: Dodd, Mead and Co., 1919.

Les Combattants Français de la Guerre Americaine, 1778–1783, 58th Cong., 2nd sess., S. Doc. 77, serial 4595. This is an incomplete list, relating chiefly to men who returned to France, based on French records and published by the Ministère des affaires étrangères. The 1905 Senate document was indexed. Reprinted by the Genealogical Publishing Co., Baltimore, 1969.

Left Card

Burlew, Thomas

1 New Jersey Regiment.

(Revolutionary War.)

Private		*Private*

CARD NUMBERS.

1	3 5 3 5 2 3 5 5	26
2	4 3 8 6	27
3	2 4 6 0	28
4	4 4 6 9	29
5	2 5 0 0	30
6	4 5 2 9	31
7	2 5 9 5	32
8	4 6 2 0	33
9	2 6 6 2	34
10	4 6 8 5	35
11	2 7 7 9	36
12	4 7 7 9	37
13	3 7 1 7 5 5 7 6	38
14		39
15		40
16		41
17		42
18		43
19		44
20		45
21		46
22		47
23		48
24		49
25		50

Number of personal papers herein _____

Book Mark: R. P. 436.786.

See also _____

Right Card

B | I | N. J.

Thomas Burlew

Longstreets Co.,

1st New Jersey Reg't, commanded by the Rt. Honble. Wm. Earl Sterling.

(Revolutionary War.)

Appears in a book *

Copied from Rolls

of the organization named above.

Date of appointment } *May 23*, 17*78*.
or enlistment

Term enlisted for *9 Mo*

Casualties *dead Nov. 15, 78*

Remarks : _____

_____

_____

_____

_____

_____

*This book appears to have been copied (from original rolls) in the Office of Army Accounts under the Paymaster General, U. S. A., who was authorized by Congress, July 4, 1783, to settle and finally adjust all accounts whatsoever between the United States and the officers and soldiers of the American army. (Journal American Congress, Vol. 4, page 237.)—R. & P., 436,786.

Vol. *4*, page *14*

Wise

(575)   Copyist.

Revolutionary War compiled military service record. War Department Collection of Revolutionary War Records, RG 93. National Archives Microfilm Publication M881.

Thos Burlew

Pvt., { Capt. Elias Longstreet's Co., 1st
New Jersey Regiment, commanded
by Col. Matthias Ogden.*

Appears on (**Revolutionary War.**)

Company Pay Roll

of the organization named above for the month

of .... *June*, 17 78.

Commencement of time............, 17 .

Commencement of pay *June 1*, 17 .

To what time paid............, 17 .

Pay per month *6 ⅔ dolls*

Time of service .... *1 mo.*

Whole time of service ....

Subsistence............

Amount *of pay £ 2 - 10 s*

Amt. of pay and subsistence............

Pay due to sick, absent............

Casualties............

Remarks: ....

*This company was designated at various times as Captain Elias Longstreet's, Capt. Peter V. Voorhies', Capt. Jacob Piatt's, Capt William Piatt's and 7th Company.

T. Jones

(545) Copyist.

Thomas Burlew

pvt., { Capt. Elias Longstreet's Co., 1st New
Jersey Regiment, commanded by
Col. Matthias Ogden.*

(**Revolutionary War.**)

Appears on

Company Muster Roll

of the organization named above for the month

of .... *June*, 1778.

Roll dated *Elizabeth Town July 14*, 17 78.

Appointed ...., 17 .

Commissioned............, 17 .

Enlisted ...., 17 .

Term of enlistment *9 mos.*

Time since last muster or enlistment ....

Alterations since last muster ....

Casualties............

Remarks: ....

*This company was designated at various times as Captain Elias Longstreet's, Capt. Peter V. Voorhies', Capt. Jacob Piatt's, Capt William Piatt's and 7th Company.

Howell

(543) Copyist.

133

Served With the American Army in Connecticut Military Organizations, M920, 25 rolls; and *Index to Compiled Service Records of Revolutionary War Soldiers Who Served With the American Army in Georgia Military Organizations,* M1051, 1 roll. Additional indexes, which are not microfilmed, are available for soldiers serving in organizations from the states of Delaware, Maryland, Massachusetts, New Hampshire, New Jersey, New York, Pennsylvania, Rhode Island, South Carolina, Vermont, and Virginia.

The original records and copies of records from which the Revolutionary War compiled service records were made are available on microfilm: M246, *Revolutionary War Rolls, 1775-1783,* 138 rolls, and M853, *Numbered Record Books Concerning Military Operations and Service, Pay and Settlement of Accounts, and Supplies in the War Department Collection of Revolutionary War Records,* 41 rolls. Notations in the lower left corner of the card abstracts frequently indicate the volume number of the original record copied.

Miscellaneous Numbered Records (The Manuscript File) in the War Department Collection of Revolutionary War Records, 1775-1790's, M859, 125 rolls, also contains information about civilians who are included in the compiled service records because they performed some service, furnished supplies, or were mentioned in correspondence files for other reasons. Records relating to civilians were not compiled; they include information about paymasters, chaplains, medical personnel, judges, quartermasters, wagon masters, teamsters, and others. The miscellaneous numbered records, approximately 35,500 items, generally contain originals and copies pertaining to Revolutionary War military operations, service of individuals, pay, and settlement of accounts and supplies, 1775-1790s. However, they include some 19th century documents relating to the settlement of accounts and pension matters.

In this varied collection there are lists of persons on various pension rolls; records removed from pension files and transferred to the War Department; copies of commissions, resignations, enlistment papers, orders, and accounts; and correspondence that includes various lists of individuals. The records relating primarily to military service have been examined, copied, and included in the compiled military service records. A name index to persons mentioned has been microfilmed as M847, *Special Index to Numbered Records in the War Department Collection of Revolutionary War Records, 1775-1783,* 39 rolls.

RG 93 contains photostat copies of records that are in the custody of public and private institutions and individuals in Virginia, North Carolina, and Massachusetts; the copies were made in accordance with an act of 1913 (37 Stat. 723). They include correspondence of the State Boards of War, minutes of the boards, and, for Virginia, county court records. For identification of the records copied, including the names of the Virginia counties from which records were copied, *see* H.C. Clark's "Report on Publication of Revolutionary Military Records," *Annual Report of*

the American Historical Association for the Year 1915, pp. 193-199. Photostats for Virginia and some of those for Massachusetts are numbered and are included in the index microfilmed as M847. A separate card index to the Virginia photostats is more nearly complete but is not on microfilm.

Related records include muster rolls, strength returns, payrolls, military lists of various sorts, journals, correspondence, and other records in Records of the Continental and Confederation Congresses and the Constitutional Convention, RG 360. These records have been microfilmed as M247, *Papers of the Continental Congress, 1774-1789,* 204 rolls, and M332, *Miscellaneous Papers of the Continental Congress, 1774-1789,* 10 rolls. A comprehensive personal name and major subject **index** to documents in RG 360 is *Index to the Papers of the Continental Congress,* 5 vols., compiled by John P. Butler (Washington: National Archives and Records Service, 1978).

Central Treasury Records of the Continental and Confederation Governments Relating to Military Affairs, 1775-1789, M1015, 7 rolls, includes military pay records that could be used as evidence of service. Records in this publication are from Records of the Bureau of Accounts (Treasury), RG 39; Records of the Bureau of Public Debt, RG 53; and Records of the Accounting Officers of the Department of the Treasury, RG 217. For example, the company record of the 1st Pennsylvania Regiment, dated March 1779-August 1780, is filmed on roll 4. Payrolls and muster rolls are arranged by type of record, thereunder chronologically. The records are not indexed, but they consist of about 50 pages that can easily be scanned for particular names. The similar account book of James Johnston, Paymaster of the 2nd Pennsylvania Regiment, 17 March 1777-11 August 1779, is also filmed on roll 4. This volume is part of RG 217.

The company book of Capt. Aaron Ogden, 1st New Jersey Regiment, dated February 1782-March 1783, is also on roll 4. It includes copies of size rolls, muster rolls, and returns. A size roll shows the name; age; personal description; trade; town, county, and state of birth; place of residence; and date of enlistment of each soldier. For information about particular soldiers, the researcher must search the whole volume, which is not indexed. This volume is part of RG 53.

Annotated copies of the printed *Register of the Certificates Issued by John Pierce, Esquire, Paymaster General, and Commissioner of the Army Accounts, for the United States* (New York: Francis Childs, 1786) are also part of RG 53, filmed on roll 6. The *Register* names officers and men of the Continental Army (except South Carolinians) to whom certificates of indebtedness were issued between 1783 and 1787 under the Continental Congress resolution of July 4, 1783, empowering the paymaster "to settle and finally adjust all accounts whatsoever, between the United States and the officers and soldiers of the American army." An alphabetical index to the *Register,* showing the number of each certificate, to whom issued, and the amount, was published in the Daughters of the American Revolution's *Seventeenth Report,* 1913–14, pp. 149–712 (63d Cong., 3d sess., S. Doc. 988, serial 6777). This index was filmed on roll 5; it was also reprinted by the Genealogical Publishing Co., Baltimore, 1973.

5.2.2 Post-Revolutionary War Period

RG 94 contains military service records of soldiers who served in the various Indian campaigns, insurrections, and disturbances that occurred in the post-Revolutionary period. These are available as M905, *Compiled Service Records of Volunteer Soldiers Who Served From 1704 to 1811,* 32 rolls. M1832, *Returns of Killed and Wounded in Battles or Engagements With Indians, British, and Mexican Troops, 1790–1848, Compiled by Lt. Col. J.H. Eaton (Eaton's Compilation),* 1 roll, provides names of both regular and volunteer officers killed in such actions and the number of enlisted casualties.

The compiled service records are arranged by U.S. organization, including the 1st and 2nd Regiments of U.S. Levies, by state organizations alphabetically, and by territorial organizations alphabetically. The records are further arranged according to military unit, thereunder alphabetically by surname of soldier. Researchers who do not know the unit in which the subject of their research served may find the *Index to Compiled Service Records of Volunteer Soldiers Who Served From 1784 to 1811,* M694, 9 rolls, helpful. Each index card gives the soldier's name, rank, unit, and the general dates served. Cross-references exist for names that appear in the records under more than one spelling and for service in more than one unit or organization.

Also in RG 94 are indexes for soldiers who served in units supplied by a single state or territory. Each of these indexes, composed of cards that duplicate the ones contained in the general index, is arranged alphabetically by name of soldier. In addition, correspondence, records of accounts, and other records created by the early military establishment pertain to the mustering, equipping, provisioning, and paying of the volunteer forces.

The *War Department Collection of Post-Revolutionary War Manuscripts,* M904, 4 rolls, is also from RG 94. Dated 1784–1811, the documents consist of miscellaneous muster rolls, accounts, and related materials, with a name index on cards. Some documents show such information as the name, rank, and military organization of a soldier; most are dated.

In addition to records in RG 94, several numbered record books in RG 93 include material relating to military affairs after the Revolutionary War. They are available on M853, described above.

5.2.3 War of 1812

When the United States declared war against Great Britain in 1812, Congress authorized the President to increase the size of the regular military establishment, accept and organize volunteers, raise units of Rangers and Sea Fencibles, and create a Flotilla Service. The Ranger units were raised for the protection of the frontier along the Mississippi River and in the adjacent states. The Sea Fencibles was the first organization of the U.S. Army charged exclusively with coastal defense; with the Flotilla Service, it protected ports, harbors, and the coast.

Some confusion arose as to whether service in the Rangers, Sea Fencibles, and some volunteer units had been rendered in the regular establishment or in the volunteers. The War Department, while abstracting and compiling these military service records decided that the unit of Rangers, Sea Fencibles, Flotillas, and some volunteer units that include the name "United States" or the initial "U.S." as part of their official designation were volunteer units and not units of the regular establishment. As a result of the confusion, records about members of these units are found in records of the Regular Army (and Navy and Marine Corps for the Sea Fencibles and Flotilla Service), as well as in compiled military service records.

Regulars, volunteers, and militia units were also fighting Indians during the period 1812–15. Records of service in the Florida or Seminole War of 1812, the Peoria (Illinois) Indian War of 1813, and the Creek Indian War of 1813–14 are found in the War of 1812 segment of the compiled military service records in RG 94. Records relating to service in the Regular Army, except as mentioned above, are described in Chapter 4.

Many of the War of 1812 volunteer units were mustered into service for short periods of time (30, 60, 90, and 120 days; 6, 9, and 12 months). Consequently, many persons served more than one enlistment in the same unit or in different units. There may be two or more compilations relating to the service of the same soldier. Generally, records in the War of 1812 segment of the compiled military service records do not refer to service in other units or to earlier or later service in the same unit.

Members of volunteer units in the War of 1812 may also have served in Federal units before and after that war, either in volunteer units or the regular military or naval establishments. Some veterans whose records are in this segment served in the Revolutionary War and the War of 1812, and a few served in the Civil War as well as the War of 1812. Most War of 1812 soldiers, however, performed their other service in the 1784–1811 period or in the Indian wars after the War of 1812.

The majority of the compiled military service records for the War of 1812 are arranged by state or territory, thereunder by unit. Others are for units whose complements were not limited to a single state or territory, or whose designation did not include the name of a state, such as the U.S. Volunteers; U.S. Rangers; Sea Fencibles; Cherokee, Chickasaw, Choctaw, and Creek Indian regiments; 1st Battalion U.S. Volunteers (Louisiana); 1st Regiment U.S. Volunteers (Mississippi Territory); 2nd Regiment

Artillery (New York); and Captain Booker's Company, U.S. Volunteers (Virginia). Under the name of each unit, the compiled military service records are arranged alphabetically by surname of soldier.

Records of Mississippi soldiers are available as M678, *Compiled Service Records of Volunteer Soldiers Who Served During the War of 1812 in Organizations From the Territory of Mississippi,* 22 rolls.

Records of two Indian regiments are also available as M1829, *Compiled Military Service Records of Maj. Uriah Blue's Detachment of Chickasaw Indians in the War of 1812,* 1 roll, and M1830, *Compiled Military Service Records of Maj. McIntosh's Company of Creek Indians in the War of 1812,* 1 roll.

The consolidated name index has been reproduced as M602, *Index to Compiled Service Records of Volunteer Soldiers Who Served During the War of 1812,* 234 rolls. In addition to the general index, there are separate indexes for persons who served in units from particular states and territories, and indexes for persons who served in miscellaneous units not attributed to a state or territory. The indexes for Louisiana, North Carolina, and South Carolina have been microfilmed as M229, *Index to Compiled Service Records of Volunteer Soldiers Who Served During the War of 1812 in Organizations from the State of Louisiana,* 3 rolls; M250, *Index to Compiled Service Records of Volunteer Soldiers Who Served During the War of 1812 in Organizations from the State of North Carolina,* 5 rolls; and M652, *Index to Compiled Service Records of Volunteer Soldiers Who Served During the War of 1812 in Organizations from the State of South Carolina,* 7 rolls.

The indexes, compiled service records, and original records from which the compiled records were abstracted are in RG 94. Related records that were not abstracted during the compilation project include numerous rolls known as **receipts for payroll**. They are filed with the muster rolls for War of 1812 volunteer units. Because of their fragile condition, these rolls cannot be used without permission of an archivist.

A series of miscellaneous records or **"manuscripts" of the War of 1812**, mostly dated 1812-15, describe events or transactions that occurred during the war. Many of the files relate to state militia organizations and to claims of persons who served in them. Other files pertain to civilians who rendered services, such as transporting troops and supplies or laboring on fortifications, or who furnished various goods for army use, including forage, foodstuffs, tents, carts, and horses. Few of the documents provide any detailed information about particular individuals, but some may indicate names and residences of civilians and names, ranks, and military organizations of soldiers. The manuscripts are arranged numerically in jacketed files; an extensive card index to names is available.

RG 94 includes three series of **prisoner-of-war records**, 1812-15, relating to both British and American prisoners: miscellaneous correspondence arranged in numbered bundles, each with a separate card index; correspondence and lists of prisoners sent from the Treasury Department to the Adjutant General's Office, arranged numerically with separate card indexes; and unarranged and unindexed lists of prisoners sent from the Navy Department to the Adjutant General's Office. The index to the first two series have been microfilmed as M1747, *Index to Records Relating to War of 1812 Prisoners of War,* 3 rolls. The second series is available as M2019, *Records Relating to War of 1812 Prisoners of War,* 1 roll.

Numerous records relating to American and British prisoners of war can be found in Naval Records Collection of the Office of Naval Records and Library, RG 45. Most are filed in the **subject files** and arranged alphabetically by name of the prison where they were held, by name of the vessel on which they served or by the vessel which captured them, or by name of the vessel on which they were returned.

Table 7 lists published works concerning military service in the War 1812.

5.2.4 Indian Wars

In the decades after the War of 1812, volunteer units often served during Indian hostilities, either assisting units of the Regular Army or acting independently. The compiled military service records, 1815-58, reflect volunteer service in the Seminole or Florida Wars, 1817-18, 1835-42, and 1855-58; Winnebago War, 1827; Sac and Fox War, 1831; Black Hawk War, 1832; Creek War, 1836-37; Indian wars in Texas, 1849-51; the Indian removal, 1835-41; and various other hostilities.

The War Department did not recognize some Indian campaigns as "wars," even though the Treasury Department under various legislative acts reimbursed the states and territories for the services of volunteer units, and the men who served in such units, or their heirs, received bounty land and sometimes pensions. Notable examples are the Osage War, 1832; Patriot and Aroostock War, 1838-39; Heatherly War, 1836; and Cayuse War, 1848.

Among the individuals who served in American forces during this period were some Native Americans, especially those of the Choctaw, Creek and Friendly Creek (Apalachicola), Menominee, Potawatomi, Delaware, Shawnee, and Winnebago tribes. *See* 11.2 for records concerning military service by Indians.

The designations of volunteer units generally include the name of the state or territory from which they served, although it should be noted that area boundaries have changed. For example, service records of volunteers in militia units mustered from Green Bay, WI, in the Black Hawk War are found under Michigan Territory, not under Wisconsin.

Compiled military service records of volunteer soldiers serving in the various Indian campaigns usually do not contain personal papers for officers or enlisted men. Records for Indian units are generally separate.

TABLE 7
Selected Genealogical Research Aids: War of 1812

General

Pension Bureau. *List of Pensioners on the Roll January 1, 1883 ...,* 47th Cong., 2nd sess., S. Exec. Doc. 84, serials 2078-2082; reprinted by the Genealogical Publishing Co., Baltimore, 1970.

White, Virgil D., ed. *Index to U.S. Military Pension Applications of Remarried Widows for Service between 1812 and 1911.* Waynesboro, TN: The National Historical Publishing Company, 1997.

Connecticut

Smith, Stephen R., et al. *Record of Service of Connecticut Men in the I.—War of the Revolution. II.—War of 1812. III.—Mexican War.* Hartford: Connecticut Adjutant General's Office, 1889.

Delaware

Delaware Archives, Military and Naval. Vols. 4-5, War of 1812. Wilmington: Delaware Public Archives Commission, 1916; reprinted by AMS Press, New York, 1974.

Maryland

Dielman, Louis Henry, ed. "Maryland Roster, War of 1812." In William Matthew Marine, *The British Invasion of Maryland 1812-1815,* pp. 195-495. Baltimore: Society of the War of 1812 in Maryland, 1913. Reprinted by Tradition Press, Hatboro, Pa., 1965, and by the Genealogical Publishing Co., Baltimore, 1977.

Maine

See Massachusetts.

Massachusetts

Baker, John, comp. *Records of the Massachusetts Volunteer Militia ... War of 1812-14.* Boston: Massachusetts Adjutant General's Office, 1913. This volume also covers Maine.

New Jersey

Records of Officers and Men of New Jersey in Wars, 1791-1815. Trenton: New Jersey Adjutant General's Office, 1909; reprinted by the Genealogical Publishing Co., Baltimore, 1970.

Pennsylvania

Pennsylvania Archives. 2nd series, vol. 12, *Muster Rolls of the Pennsylvania Volunteers in the War of 1812-14.* Edited by John B. Linn and William H. Egle. Harrisburg: Secretary of the Commonwealth, 1896. 6th series, vols. 7-9, *War of 1812-14.* Edited by Thomas L. Montgomery, 1907.

Vermont

Johnson, Herbert T., comp. *Roster of Soldiers in the War of 1812-14.* St. Albans: Vermont Adjutant and Inspector General's Office, 1933.

Only two groups of service records for these Indian wars have been microfilmed: *Compiled Military Service Records of Michigan and Illinois Volunteers Who Served During the Winnebago Indian Disturbances of 1827,* M1505, 3 rolls; and *Compiled Service Records of Volunteer Soldiers Who Served in Organizations From the State of Florida During the Florida Indian Wars, 1835-58,* M1086, 63 rolls

Index to Compiled Service Records of Volunteer Soldiers Who Served During Indian Wars and Disturbances, 1815-58, M629, 42 rolls, contains a card for each person who served during the period for whom a compiled military service record was prepared. The cards, which show name, rank, regiment, and war, are especially useful to the researcher who does not know the campaign or unit in which the subject being researched served. In addition to the general index, there are indexes for persons who served in units from various states and territories, although separate indexes are not available for each state or territory for each disturbance. Some entries for several states or territories have been combined into a single index; for example, the index for Illinois troops in the Black Hawk War includes the names of persons who served from Michigan and those who served in Potawatomi Indian units. Nevertheless, knowing the state in which the subject of research served and the name of the disturbance will help the researcher determine the unit designation from one of these smaller indexes. Some of them have been microfilmed, as shown in Table 8.

RG 393 includes series of correspondence, orders, returns, and other records relating to the various Indian wars, disturbances, and removals, and the military activities and personnel connected with them. Because many of the records are fragmentary and poorly indexed, however, research in them is difficult. The researcher must know the command in which the subject of research served before any search can be undertaken. A considerable knowledge of military history is necessary to make use of these records. One series of note that has been microfilmed is M1475, *Correspondence of the Eastern Division Pertaining to Cherokee Removal, April–December 1838,* 2 rolls.

5.2.5. Mexican War

War with Mexico was declared on May 13, 1846, less than 6 months after Texas was admitted to the Union. During the congressional debates concerning admission of the new state, the United States, in anticipation of war with Mexico, ordered units of volunteers into service. One unit came from Louisiana, and five from Texas. The Texas units commenced service in the fall of 1845, and some served until the end of the war. Such service was not continuous, but many of the units were mustered out at the end of one enlistment and mustered in again a day or so later.

The act of Congress by which war was declared specified the service of the regular military and naval establishment and the use of volunteers and the militia. Militia

TABLE 8
Microfilmed Indexes to Compiled Military Service Records of Volunteers During the Indian Wars

STATE	DISTURBANCE AND DATE	MICROFILM PUBLICATION	NUMBER OF ROLLS
Alabama	Creek War, 1836–37	M244	2
Alabama	Cherokee Removal, 1838	M243	1
Alabama	Florida War, 1836–38	M245	1
Georgia	Cherokee Disturbances and Removal, 1836–38	M907	1
Louisiana	Florida War, 1836	M239	1
Louisiana	War of 1837–38	M241	1
Michigan	Patriot War, 1838–39	M630	1
New York	Patriot War, 1838	M631	1
North Carolina	Cherokee Disturbances and Removal, 1837–38	M256	1
Tennessee	Cherokee Disturbances and Removal, and Field and Staff of the Army of The Cherokee Nation	M908	2

service was limited to no more than 6 months of continuous service, while volunteers could be mustered for 12 months or until the end of the war. Volunteer units came from 24 states, the territory of California, and the District of Columbia. One unit was composed of Indians, and a separate battalion, formed of members of the Church of Jesus Christ of Latter-Day Saints, was known as the Mormon Battalion. An additional unit, called the Santa Fe Battalion, Missouri Mounted Volunteers, was organized in New Mexico.

Some of the volunteers who served in the Mexican War were also in the earlier Indian wars or would later serve in the Civil War. Some Texas Volunteers were retained in service after the Mexican war to protect the frontier areas of Texas from Indian attack. The service of these units is documented in records relating to the Indian wars, 1815–58.

Evidence of Federal service of volunteer and militia units, 1846–48, is in the compiled military service records, which are arranged alphabetically by state or territory, followed by compilations for soldiers who served in Mormon organizations. The records are further broken down by organization, ending with the regiment, independent battalion, or company. Under each unit, service records are arranged alphabetically by surname of soldier. The compiled service records of volunteer soldiers who served in various organizations have been microfilmed as follows: *Compiled Service Records of Volunteer Soldiers Who Served During the Mexican War in Organizations from the State of Mississippi*, M863, 9 rolls; . . . *Pennsylvania*, M1028, 13 rolls; . . . *Tennessee*, M638, 15 rolls; . . . *Texas*, M278, 19 rolls; and *Compiled Service Records of Volunteer Soldiers Who Served During the Mexican War in*

Mormon Organizations, M351, 3 rolls. The name index has been reproduced as *Index to Compiled Service Records of Volunteer Soldiers Who Served During the Mexican War*, M616, 41 rolls.

For an alphabetical list of volunteer officers in the Mexican War, showing rank and organization, see *Historical Register and Dictionary of the United States Army, from Its Organization, September 29, 1789, to March 2, 1903*, by Francis B. Heitman (Washington: Government Printing Office, 1903), 2:43–73. This publication is also available on microfilm as M1858.

5.2.6 Civil War—Union

President Lincoln's proclamation of April 15, 1861, called for 75,000 militiamen from the loyal states and territories to suppress the rebellion in the southern states. Subsequent proclamations and acts of Congress provided for additional increases in the size of the Regular Army and Navy and called for additional volunteers and militiamen. States and territories met the requirements by activating the militia, calling for voluntary enlistments, and instituting the draft. The Federal draft system, created by Congress in 1863, superseded the state and territorial draft systems; draft records are described later in this section.

During the first 2 years of the war, many units were mustered for short periods (30, 60, and 90 days; 6, 9, and 12 months), but normal enlistments were for 1 to 3 years. Most soldiers served in units formed within their neighborhoods, states, or territories of residence. Some enlisted in the Regular Army or were assigned to Regular Army units. Others joined units formed at their place of birth or previous residence. Some soldiers were assigned to units composed of persons from a different state or territory, or to units composed of individuals from several states or territories. Others were detailed or transferred to special units created to serve a particular need or to units created for persons having special talents, such as the U.S. Sharpshooters, Mississippi Gunboat Flotilla, Mississippi Ram Fleet, Pontoon Brigade, Engineers, Signal Corps, Marines (Army), U.S. Colored Troops, Indian Home Guards, or Balloon Corps. A reenlisting soldier was not necessarily assigned to the same unit in which he had previously served or even to the same branch or arm of service. By orders of the War Department, blacks and Indians were prohibited from serving in separate units before 1863, but individuals did serve in various units throughout the war. U.S. Colored Troops and Indian regiments are discussed in later chapters devoted to records about blacks and Native Americans, respectively.

Some units included civilian personnel as part of their complements. Soldiers serving in the Signal Corps as telegraphers were discharged and rehired as civilians in 1863. Soldiers serving in the Mississippi Ram Fleet were transferred to the U.S. Navy in 1862.

Disabled soldiers still capable of performing a service were assigned to the Veteran Reserve Corps. Before 1863 a Confederate soldier who was taken prisoner could ask to serve in the Union Army, in which case he might be assigned to a Regular Army or volunteer unit. After 1863 such prisoners of war would be assigned to one of the six numbered regiments of U.S. Volunteers raised specifically to fight Indians in the western part of the United States.

Upon organization many units adopted or used a unique name, generally the name by which they had been known as militia units. When mustered into the Union Army, the unit name was changed to conform to army regulations. A unit designation generally consisted of a number, the state or territory name, and the arm of service; for example, 1st Iowa Cavalry. Some unit designations included the name of the officer who formed the company, or its commanding officer. While units were in service, their designations were changed for a variety of reasons, sometimes several times. Some units had two or more successive designations; for example, 1st Pennsylvania Cavalry and 44th Pennsylvania Volunteers. State and territory names were not used for units composed of soldiers from several states or territories or for special units. Records are generally filed under the unit's final designation. A compilation of the various names for units, *List of Synonyms of Organizations in the Volunteer Service of the United States During the Years 1861, '62, '63, '64, and '65*, compiled by John T. Fallon (Washington: Adjutant General's Office, 1885), permits identification of the final unit designation.

Compiled military service records exist for nearly all soldiers who were accepted for service in the Union Army as militiamen or volunteers, 1861–65, whether or not they actually served. Records relating to soldiers who participated in actions that occurred between 1861 and 1865 are included in the records of the Civil War, even if the actions were unrelated to the war, such as Indian warfare.

Records of enlisted men sometimes include information about age, residence, occupation at the time of enlistment, and physical description. Personal papers occasionally give additional information about residence, family, or business of officers and enlisted men. Information about heirs is sometimes found in records concerning hospitalization or death in service.

The records generally refer to Federal service in other units during, before, and after the Civil War. They may also refer to related files among various correspondence series of the records of the Adjutant General's Office described in Chapter 4. Genealogical researchers should look for cross-references when using the compiled military service records. Although they are nominally found on the lower part of the file jackets, with unit references appearing in the "See Also" section and file references in the "Book Mark" section, similar cross-references may appear elsewhere on the jacket.

Table 9 gives microfilm publication numbers for compiled service records of those states and territories whose records have been microfilmed. Filming of these records is continuing so researchers should consult the reference staff for latest availability. For information about purchasing microfilm publications, call 1-800-234-8861, or fax 1-301-713-6169.

In addition to the compiled military service records in jacket-envelopes, separate series of card abstracts and personal papers exist that are not in jacket-envelopes. These series were accumulated by the War Department but were not interfiled with the regular compilations for various reasons, often because the information was insufficient or contained discrepancies and could not be positively identified with any soldier for whom there was a compiled service record. Sometimes no compiled service record had been created on the basis of other records, and the item did not provide enough evidence to justify establishing one. Unjacketed card abstracts are arranged alphabetically or in the same general regimental order as the jacket-envelopes. The unfiled personal papers are arranged alphabetically.

To locate the compiled service record of a Union Army soldier, the researcher must determine the name of the unit in which he served. No general comprehensive name index to the compiled service records for Union Army Volunteers exists. Separate indexes are available for each state and territory except South Carolina, which furnished no white troops to the Union Army. Separate indexes are also available for the compiled service records of soldiers who served in units with troops from several states and territories, such as the Veteran Reserve Corps, U.S. Colored Troops, U.S. Volunteers (including former Confederate prisoners of war), U.S. Veteran Volunteer Engineer and Infantry units, U.S. Sharpshooters, Indian Home Guards, Mississippi Marine Brigade, Prisoners of War (partial index to Confederate prisoners who enlisted in the Union Army),

TABLE 9
Microfilmed Indexes and Compiled Military Service Records for Union Army Volunteers

| STATE | INDEX | | COMPILED MILITARY SERVICE RECORDS | |
	MICROFILM PUBLICATION	NUMBER OF ROLLS	MICROFILM PUBLICATION	NUMBER OF ROLLS
Alabama	M263	1	M276	10
Arizona Territory	M532	1		
Arkansas	M383	4	M399	60
California	M533	7		
Colorado Territory	M534	3		
Connecticut	M535	17		
Dakota Territory	M536	1	M1960	3
Delaware	M537	4	M1961	117
District of Columbia	M538	3		
Florida	M264	1	M400	11
Georgia	M385	1	M403	1
Idaho Territory (*See* Washington Territory)				
Illinois	M539	101		
Indiana	M540	86		
Iowa	M541	29		
Kansas	M542	10		
Kentucky	M386	30	M397	515
Louisiana	M387	4	M396	50
Maine	M543	23		
Maryland	M388	13	M384	238
Massachusetts	M544	44		
Michigan	M545	48		
Minnesota	M546	10		
Mississippi	M389	1	M404	4
Missouri	M390	54	M405	854
Montana (*See* Washington Territory)				
Nebraska Territory	M547	2	M1787	43
Nevada	M548	1	M1789	16
New Hampshire	M549	13		
New Jersey	M550	26		
New Mexico Territory	M242	4	M427	46
New York	M551	159		
North Carolina	M391	2	M401	25
Ohio	M552	122		
Oklahoma (Indian Territory) (*See* Arkansas, Colorado Territory, Kansas, Missouri, New Mexico, and Texas)				
Oregon	M553	1	M1816	34
Pennsylvania	M554	136		
Rhode Island	M555	7		
South Carolina	None			
Tennessee	M392	16	M395	220
Texas	M393	2	M402	13
Utah Territory	M556	1	M692	1
Vermont	M557	14		
Virginia	M394	1	M398	7
Washington Territory	M558	1		
West Virginia	M507	13	M508	261
Wisconsin	M559	33		
Wyoming (*See* Washington Territory)				
U.S. Colored Troops	M589	98		
Cavalry Regiments (All)			M1817	107
Artillery Regiments (All)			M1818	299
1st Infantry Regiment			M1819	18
2nd thru 7th Infantry Regiments			M1820	116
54th Massachusetts Colored Infantry			M1898	20
55th Massachusetts Colored Infantry			M1801	16
Union Volunteers Not Raised by States or Territories (Except VRC and USCT)	M1290	36		
U.S. Volunteers (former Confederate soldiers, 1st and 6th Regiments only)			M1017	65
Veteran Reserve Corps	M636	44		

Pioneer Brigade, U.S. Signal Corps, Captain Turner's Company Volunteer Pioneers, Brigade and Post Bands, Departmental Corps, and Varner's Battalion of Infantry. Table 9 gives microfilm publication numbers for indexes that have been filmed. No separate index cards exist for those soldiers mentioned in unjacketed abstracts or unfiled personal papers.

To locate the record of service of a particular soldier, the researcher may need to consult several indexes. A soldier may have enlisted in or been assigned to a unit from a different state or territory than the researcher expects or to a special unit composed of persons from several different areas. For example, the index for regiments of U.S. Colored Troops may contain entries for the service records of white officers.

Most officers who served in Union Army volunteer units are listed in the *Official Army Register of the Volunteer Force of the United States Army for the Years 1861, '62, '63, '64, '65* (Washington: Adjutant General's Office, 1865-67). A list of the field officers of volunteers and militia in the service of the United States during the Civil War appear in Heitman's *Historical Register and Dictionary of the United States Army, from Its Organization, September 29, 1789, to March 2, 1903*, mentioned above, which is also available on microfilm as M1858, and in the numerous published registers of Union Army troops compiled by the adjutants general of the various states and territories. These publications are listed in Table 10.

Carded medical records were prepared from records relating to soldiers treated at field, camp, post, and general hospitals. (A few cards relate to treatment during the Mexican War and the Spanish-American War.) Particulars of the length of stay at a hospital and the reason for confinement are generally mentioned in the carded abstracts. Cards are arranged alphabetically by state or territory, thereunder by unit number, and thereunder in rough alphabetical order by surname of soldier. A miscellaneous series following the cards for the state or territory contains abstracts for persons who served in units that did not have a number as part of their official designation and for persons whose full unit designation could not be identified. In some instances the abstracts relating to a particular soldier have been interfiled with their compiled military service record.

Records relating to volunteer general officers and officers serving in staff capacities not attached to a particular unit are usually not found with the compilation for a state or territory but are in a separate series of abstracts.

Additional information about some Union Army officers and soldiers is in a number of series of correspondence files among the records of the Adjutant General's Office. Correspondence relating to officers is generally found among the records of the Volunteer Service Division, 1861-89; Record and Pension Office, 1889-1904; and letters received series, 1800-1917. Correspondence relating to enlisted personnel is usually found among records of

the Enlisted Branch, 1848-89; Record and Pension Office, 1889-1904; and correspondence series, 1800-1917. Correspondence relating to officers and enlisted personnel of the U.S. Colored Troops is contained in records of the Colored Troops Division, 1863-89; Record and Pension Office, 1889-1904; and correspondence series, 1800-1917. In nearly every instance, proper cross references to additional files have been noted on the compiled service record.

At the same time that service records of individual Union soldiers were compiled, the War Department compiled **record-of-events cards** similar to those discussed in the introduction to this chapter and in Chapter 4. Those for units that served in the Civil War have been microfilmed as M594, *Compiled Records Showing Service of Military Units in Volunteer Union Organizations*, 225 rolls.

Other records of various War Department offices and bureaus may contain information about specific soldiers and Civil War activities in general. RG 393 includes correspondence, reports, orders, and returns relating to Civil War military operations and the personnel who conducted them. For some commands there may also be such personnel-related records as registers or lists of furloughs, leaves of absence, and discharges; troop rosters and station books or lists; and registers of officers. These records are rarely rewarding in genealogical research; most are not arranged by name, and indexes are few and incomplete. Furthermore, information about specific soldiers may be duplicated in the compiled military service records.

A comprehensive description of the various records available is given in *Guide to Federal Records Relating to the Civil War*, compiled by Kenneth W. Munden and Henry P. Beers (Washington: National Archives and Records Service, 1962; reprinted 1998). Some information also appears in *War of the Rebellion: A Compilation of the Official Records of the Union and Confederate Armies*, 128 vols. (Washington: War Department, 1880-1901). This publication is available on microfilm as M262, *Official Records of the Union and Confederate Armies, 1861-1865*, 128 rolls, and was also reprinted by the National Historical Society, Gettysburg, PA, 1971-72 and again in 1985. Libraries may shelve it among Federal Government documents under SuDocs. No. W45.5.130 or in Serial Set 4209-558. The name index may enable researchers to discover actions in which their ancestors participated. The National Archives produced two research aids to this compilation. The researcher may wish to consult M1036, *Military Operations of the Civil War: A Guide Index to the Official Records of the Union and Confederate Armies, 1861-1865, Volume 1, Conspectus*, 1 roll, and M1815, *Military Operations of the Civil War: A Guide-Index to the Official Records of the Union and Confederate Armies, Volumes II-V*, 18 fiche.

As the Civil War entered its third year, it became increasingly apparent that recruiting systems for the Union

TABLE 10
Selected Genealogical Research Aids: Civil War—Union

General

Official Army Register of the Volunteer Force of the United States Army for the Years 1861, '62, '63, '64, '65. 8 vols. Washington: Adjutant General's Office, 1865.

Van Sickles, Ron R., comp. *General Index to Official Army Register of the Volunteer Forces of the United States, 1861-1865.* Gaithersburg, MD: Ron R. Van Sickles Military Books, 1987.

Dyer, Frederick H. *A Compendium of the War of the Rebellion.* Des Moines: Dyer Publishing Company, 1908; New York: T. Yoseloff, 1959; and Dayton, OH: The Press of Morningside Bookshop, 1978 .

Henry, Guy Vernor. *Military Record of Civilian Appointments in the United States Army.* Vol. 1, New York: Carleton, 1870. Vol. 2, New York: D. Van Nostrand, 1873.

Heitman, Francis B. *Historical Register and Dictionary of the United States Army, from Its Organization, September 29, 1789, to March 2, 1903.* 2 vols. Washington, 1903. Published as 57th Cong., 2nd sess., H. Doc. 446, serial 4536; reprinted by the University of Illinois Press, Urbana, 1965. This work is also available on microfilm as M1858, 1 roll.

Strait, Newton A. and J.W. Wells, comps. *Alphabetical List of Battles of the War of the Rebellion With Dates . . . and a roster of All Regimental Surgeons.* Washington: N.A. Strait, 1882.

War College Division, U.S. General Staff. *Bibliography of State Participation in the Civil War, 1861-1866.* 3rd edition. Washington: War Department, 1913.

Dornbusch, Charles E. *Military Bibliography of the Civil War.* 3 vols. New York, 1961-72.

California

Orton, Richard H., comp. *Records of California Men in the War of the Rebellion, 1861-1867.* Sacramento: California Adjutant General's Office, 1890.

List of Electors, Resident of California, in the Military Service . . . . Sacramento: California Adjutant General's Office, 1865.

Connecticut

Smith, Stephen R., comp. *Record of Service of Connecticut Men in the Army and Navy of the United States During the War of the Rebellion.* Hartford: Connecticut Adjutant General's Office, 1889.

Morse, Horace I., comp. *Catalog of Connecticut Volunteer Organizations, With Additional Enlistments and Casualties to July 1, 1864.* Hartford: Connecticut Adjutant General's Office, 1864.

Ingersoll, C.M., comp. *Catalog of Connecticut Volunteer Organizations (Infantry, Cavalry, and Artillery) in the Service of the United States, 1861-1865 . . . .* Hartford: Connecticut Adjutant General's Office, 1869.

Illinois

Reece, J.N., comp. *Report of the Adjutant General of the State of Illinois.* 9 vols. Revised edition. Springfield: Illinois Military and Naval Department, 1900-1902.

Indiana

Terrell, W.H.H., comp. *Report of the Adjutant General of the State of Indiana.* 8 vols. Indianapolis: Indiana Adjutant General's Office, 1869.

Iowa

Alexander, William L., comp. *List of Ex-Soldiers, Sailors, and Marines Living in Iowa.* Des Moines: Iowa Adjutant General's Office, 1886.

Baker, N.B., comp. *Report of the Adjutant General and Acting Quartermaster General of the State of Iowa, January 1, 1865, to January 1, 1866.* Des Moines: Iowa Adjutant General's Office, 1866.

Thrift, William H. and Guy E. Logan, comps. *Roster and Record of Iowa Soldiers in the War of the Rebellion.* 6 vols. Des Moines: Iowa Adjutant General's Office, 1908-11.

Kansas

Noble, P.S., comp. *Report of the Adjutant General of the State of Kansas . . . 1861-1865.* 2 vols. Leavenworth: Kansas Adjutant General's Office, 1867-70. Volume 1 was reprinted by the Kansas State Printing Co., Topeka, 1896.

Louisiana

Burt, W.G., comp. *Annual Report of the Adjutant General of the State of Louisiana for the Year Ending December 31st, 1889.* New Orleans: Louisiana Adjutant General's Office, 1890.

Maine

Hodsdon, John L., comp. *Annual Report of the Adjutant General of the State of Maine, for the Year Ending December 31, 1863.* Augusta: Maine Adjutant General's Office, 1863.

Annual Report, 1861-66. 7 vols. Augusta: Maine Adjutant General's Office, 1862-67, with supplement, *Alphabetical Index of Maine Volunteers, Etc., Mustered Into the Service of the United States During the War of 1861.*

Hodsdon, John L., comp. *Returns of Desertions, Discharges, and Deaths in Maine Regiments . . . .* Augusta: Maine Adjutant General's Office, 1864.

Maryland

Williams, L. Allison, J.H. Jarrett, and George W.F. Vernon. *History and Roster of Maryland Volunteers, War of 1861-65.* Baltimore: Commission on the Publication of the Histories of the Maryland Volunteers During the Civil War, 1898-99.

TABLE 10
Selected Genealogical Research Aids: Civil War—Union

Massachusetts

Record of the Massachusetts Volunteers, 1861-65. Boston: Massachusetts Adjutant General's Office, 1868-70.

Massachusetts Soldiers, Sailors, and Marines in the Civil War . . . . 8 vols. Norwood and Brookline: Massachusetts Adjutant General's Office, 1931-35. A ninth volume, subtitled *Index to Army Records* and published in Boston in 1937, pertains to vols. 1-6 and part of vol. 7.

Michigan

Brown, Ida C. *Michigan Men in the Civil War.* Michigan Historical Collections Bulletin 9. Ann Arbor: University of Michigan, 1959.

Robertson, John, comp. *Michigan in the War.* Revised edition. Lansing: Michigan Adjutant General's Department, 1882.

Turner, George H., comp. *Record of Service of Michigan Volunteers in the Civil War, 1861-1865.* 46 vols. Kalamazoo: Michigan Adjutant General's Department, 1905.

Robertson, John. *Annual Report of the Adjutant General of the State of Michigan for the Year 1864.* Lansing: Michigan Adjutant General's Department, 1865. . . . *For the Years 1865-66.* Lansing, 1866.

Michigan Adjutant General's Department. *Alphabetical General Index to Public Library Sets of 85,271 Names of Michigan Soldiers and Sailors Individual Records.* Lansing: Michigan Secretary of State, 1915.

Minnesota

Minnesota in the Civil and Indian War, 1861-65. 2 vols. St. Paul: Minnesota Board of Commissioners on Publication of History of Minnesota in Civil and Indian Wars, 1890-93.

Warming, Irene B., comp. *Minnesotans in the Civil and Indian Wars: An Index to the Rosters in Minnesota in the Civil and Indian Wars, 1861-1865.* St. Paul: Minnesota Historical Society, 1936.

Missouri

Simpson, Samuel P. *Annual Report of the Adjutant General of Missouri . . . 1865.* Jefferson City: Missouri Adjutant General's Office, 1866.

Nebraska

Roster of Soldiers, Sailors, and Marines of the War of 1812, the Mexican War, and the War of the Rebellion Residing in Nebraska June 1, 1893. Lincoln: Nebraska Secretary of State, 1891; reprinted by Nebraska State Genealogical Society, Lincoln, 1984.

Patrick, John R. *Report of the Adjutant General of the State of Nebraska.* Lincoln: Nebraska Adjutant General, 1871; reprint by Mills & Co., Des Moines, IA.

New Hampshire

Ayling, Augustus D., comp. *Revised Register of the Soldiers and Sailors of New Hampshire in the War of the Rebellion, 1861-66.* Concord: New Hampshire Adjutant General's Office, 1895.

New Jersey

Stryker, William S., comp. *Record of Officers and Men of New Jersey in the Civil War, 1861-1865.* 2 vols. Trenton: New Jersey Adjutant General's Office, 1876.

New York

Irvine, William, comp. *A Record of the Commissioned and Non-commissioned Officers and Privates of the Regiments Organized in the State of New York* . . . . 8 vols. Albany: New York Adjutant General's Office, 1864-68.

Phisterer, Frederick, comp. *New York in the War of the Rebellion, 1861 to 1865.* 6 vols. 3rd edition. Albany, 1912.

Ohio

Reid, Whitelaw. *Ohio in the War.* Cincinnati and New York: Moore, Wilstach, and Baldwin, 1868; reprinted by the Eclectic Publishing Co., Columbus, OH, 1893.

Official Roster of the Soldiers of the State of Ohio in the War of the Rebellion, 1861-66. 12 vols. Akron: Ohio Roster Commission, 1886-95.

Pennsylvania

Bates, Samuel P. *History of Pennsylvania Volunteers, 1861-65.* 5 vols. Harrisburg: Pennsylvania State Legislature, 1869-71.

Russell, A.L. *Annual Report of the Adjutant General of Pennsylvania, 1863.* Harrisburg: Pennsylvania Adjutant General's Office, 1864.

Rhode Island

Dyer, Elisha. *Annual Report of the Adjutant General of Rhode Island and Providence Plantations for the Year 1865.* 2 vols. Revised edition. Providence: Rhode Island Adjutant General's Office, 1893-95.

Vermont

Peck, Theodore S., comp. *Revised Roster of Vermont Volunteers and Lists of Vermonters Who Served in the Army and Navy of the United States During the War of the Rebellion, 1861-66.* Montpelier: Vermont Adjutant and Inspector General's Office, 1892.

Wisconsin

Chapman, Chandler P., comp. *Roster of Wisconsin Volunteers, War of the Rebellion, 1861-65.* 2 vols. Madison: Wisconsin Adjutant General's Office, 1886.

Wisconsin Volunteers, War of the Rebellion, 1861-65, Arranged Alphabetically. Madison: Wisconsin Adjutant General's Office, 1914.

forces were inadequate. To remedy this, Congress passed the First Conscription Act on March 3, 1863 (12 Stat. 731). It made all men aged 20 to 45 subject to military service, although service could be avoided by payment of $300 or procuring a substitute to enlist for 3 years. State quotas that were proportionate to total population were also established under the act.

Civil War **draft records** include consolidated lists and descriptive rolls of enrollment districts in Records of the Provost Marshal General's Bureau (Civil War), RG 110, and case files on drafted aliens in the General Records of the Department of State, RG 59.

The **consolidated lists** are the principal records of the Washington office of the Provost Marshal General's Bureau that relate to individual men. Most are in bound volumes arranged by state, thereunder by enrollment or congressional district, and thereunder by class. The three classes established by the draft acts were Class I: men between the ages of 20 and 35 subject to military duty and unmarried men above 35 and under 45 subject to military duty; Class II: married men above 35 and under 45; and Class III: veterans or those currently in the service. Entries in each class are arranged in rough alphabetical order by initial letter of surname. Each entry shows name; place of residence; age on July 1, 1863; occupation; marital status; state, territory, or country of birth; and, if Class III, the military organization.

Descriptive rolls or lists are the principal records of the enrollment districts that relate to individual men. They are arranged by state, thereunder by number of enrollment or congressional district. The rolls are chiefly in bound volumes. Arrangement of the entries varies considerably from district to district. Some are not indexed; some are indexed by initial letter of surname; and some are indexed by place of residence.

An entry often shows, in addition to information in the corresponding consolidated list, the physical description, place of birth, and whether accepted or rejected for military service. Entries in many volumes, however, are not complete.

It is difficult to find a particular serviceman in either the consolidated lists or the descriptive rolls unless the congressional district in which he lived is known. If the researcher knows the county in which the serviceman lived in 1863, the number of the congressional district can be ascertained from the *Congressional Directory for the Second Session of the Thirty-Eighth Congress of the United States of America* (Washington: U.S. House of Representatives, 1865).

Under terms of the Conscription Act, the President on May 8, 1863, issued a proclamation announcing that aliens who had declared their intention to become citizens and were in the United States 65 days after that date would not be allowed to avoid the draft on the plea of alienage. The State Department became involved in the release from military service of aliens who were drafted from 1862 onward. The records of this activity in RG 59 include an alphabetical case file containing draft notice depositions of aliens regarding their foreign citizenship and correspondence. Other correspondence of the Secretary of State regarding the release of aliens is in separate letter books (indexed) and in files of loose papers. An alphabetical list of draft cases shows the states and counties from which the aliens were drafted.

5.2.7 Civil War—Confederate

As the Confederate Government evacuated Richmond in April 1865, the central military records of the Confederate Army were taken to Charlotte, NC, by the Adjutant and Inspector Generals, who then transferred them to a Union officer. The records were taken to Washington, where along with other Confederate records captured by the Union Army, they were preserved by the U.S. War Department. In 1903 the Secretary of War persuaded governors of most southern states to lend to the War Department for copying the Confederate military personnel records, which were in the possession of the states. These records are part of the War Department Collection of Confederate Records, RG 109.

The **compiled military service records of Confederate officers, noncommissioned officers, and enlisted men** consist of cards on which the War Department, between 1903 and 1927, recorded information abstracted from Union prison and parole records and from captured and other surviving Confederate records. They are similar to those for Union Volunteers. In addition to the usual information found on compiled military service records, some of these show facts about a soldier's imprisonment. If he was captured, they may show the date of his release and parole, or if he died in prison, the date of his death. References to the original records are included on the cards. Researchers should note, however, that original records rarely contain any additional information. Table 11 gives the microfilm publication number for the compiled service records for each state.

Two other series of service records are listed in Table 11. One consists of jacket-envelopes for men who served in military units raised directly by the Confederate Government (such as the 1st Confederate Infantry, Morgan's Cavalry, and the Cherokee Mounted Rifles), arranged by organization, thereunder alphabetically by name. These records have been reproduced as M258, *Compiled Service Records of Confederate Soldiers Who Served in Organizations Raised Directly by the Confederate Government*, 123 rolls.

The other series consists of jacket-envelopes known as the general and staff officers' papers, which include records not only for officers occupying staff positions, but for noncommissioned officers and enlisted men performing staff services. These records are arranged alphabetically by name. They have been reproduced as M331, *Compiled Service Records of Confederate Generals and Staff Officers and Nonregimental Enlisted Men*, 275 rolls.

TABLE 11
Microfilmed Indexes and Compiled Military Service Records for Confederate Army Volunteers

STATE	INDEX MICROFILM PUBLICATION	NUMBER OF ROLLS	COMPILED MILITARY SERVICE RECORDS MICROFILM PUBLICATION	NUMBER OF ROLLS
Alabama	M374	49	M311	508
Arizona Territory	M375	1	M318	1
Arkansas	M376	26	M317	256
Florida	M225	9	M251	104
Georgia	M226	67	M266	607
Kentucky	M377	14	M319	136
Louisiana	M378	31	M320	414
Maryland	M379	2	M321	22
Mississippi	M232	45	M269	427
Missouri	M380	16	M322	193
North Carolina	M230	43	M270	580
South Carolina	M381	35	M267	392
Tennessee	M231	48	M268	359
Texas	M227	41	M323	445
Virginia	M382	62	M324	1,075
Organizations Raised Directly by the Confederate Government	M818	26	M258	123
General and Staff Officers	M818	26	M331	275
Consolidated Index	M253	535		

Card indexes, arranged alphabetically by name of soldier can be used to locate the name of a unit in which a soldier served. M253, *Consolidated Index to Compiled Service Records of Confederate Soldiers,* 535 rolls, refers to records for the individual states and records in the two other series. Each card gives a soldier's name, rank, and unit. A statement concerning the origin or background of the unit is often included. In addition to the consolidated index, there is a separate index to the records for each state. Table 11 gives the microfilm publication numbers of these indexes.

Cross-reference cards in the compiled service records will sometime refer the researcher to a numbered **manuscript file**. This series consists of a miscellaneous collection of manuscripts, mainly Confederate but including some Union, apparently brought together by the Adjutant General's Office for the purpose of placing on cards the references to military personnel. Included in the series are correspondence concerning prisoners, deserters, and bushwackers; lists of prisoners and deserters; election returns of Confederate organizations; lists of employees in Confederate Government departments; payrolls, vouchers, quarterly reports of expenditures, and other reports for a variety of offices and departments (hired men, extra-duty men, nitre and mining service, iron works, arsenals, and the like); proceedings of boards of inquiry, surveys, and courts-martial; and burial lists. The series is arranged numerically by number assigned by the Adjutant General's Office when the records were accumulated and arranged

by that office. There is a separate index to the series, but it is arranged alphabetically by name of place or organization, not by name of individual. Access to these records for genealogical purposes is provided by a carded reference in the compiled service record.

"Unfiled Papers and Slips Belonging in Confederate Compiled Service Records" were accumulated by the War Department to be interfiled with the compilations, but they never were. Items most commonly included are card abstracts and personal papers similar to those found in compiled service records of Union soldiers. Card abstracts contain entries taken from sources like those used to create the compiled military service records. Letters, vouchers, requisitions, paroles, oaths of allegiance, and references to original records are included.

Papers were placed in the unfiled paper series when their proper filing was uncertain or there was no other place to file them, usually because the information was insufficient or contained discrepancies and could not be positively identified with any soldier for whom there was a compiled service record. Sometimes no compiled service record had been created on the basis of regular service records, and the item did not provide enough evidence to justify establishing one. In certain cases a soldier may have served in a home guard unit or state organization never called into the service of the Confederate States. It is sometimes difficult to tell whether an item refers to a soldier, civilian employee, or private individual.

Papers concerning Confederate civilians are similar to

many of the documents in the Confederate papers relating to citizens or business firms described in 14.4, but the identity of each person was not always clearly indicated. Civilian records include employment information about hospital attendants, clerks and other employees. Also included are some papers relating to Confederate sympathizers, some of whom are the same individuals whose names appear in the Union provost marshals' files described in 10.4.2.

The records are arranged alphabetically by surname with cross-references to spelling variations, and guide cards show how similar-sounding names are placed together. Researchers should be aware that it may be necessary to search for a name under a number of different spellings. The records included in this series generally are not covered by any of the indexes relating to Confederate compiled service records or to any other records relating to Confederate service or civilians. The series is available as M347, *Unfiled Papers and Slips Belonging in Confederate Compiled Service Records,* 442 rolls.

Included in the series are some cross-references to records or documents contained in other series of Confederate records, some of which have not been microfilmed, and to compiled service records. Certain correspondence originally filed in other series has been included in this series.

Compiled military service records that give histories of Confederate military units consist of jacket-envelopes bearing the names of the units and the title "Captions and Record of Events." These jacket-envelopes typically contain cards showing captions that were copied from original muster rolls and certificates of the mustering officer verifying the accuracy of the rolls. They also contain record-of-events cards like those for Union military units described earlier. The amount of information varies from card to card. Some cards give only date and name of station. Others give detailed accounts of a unit's operation and activities.

Because some records of the Confederate Army were lost or destroyed during the war and at its close, compiled military histories of most units are incomplete. There are no record-of-events cards for a few state units that were mustered into Confederate service or for militia units that were never mustered into service.

The service records of Confederate military units and the service records of Confederate soldiers were compiled at the same time. Abstracts were made from documents in the War Department's collection and from documents borrowed mostly from southern states by the War Department in an effort to obtain as complete military histories of units as possible. The original muster rolls and returns were the principal sources of information abstracted on the caption cards, but rosters, payrolls, hospital registers, casualty lists, Union prison registers and rolls, parole rolls, and inspection reports were also examined. Abstracts were verified by separate comparison, and every precaution was taken to ensure their accuracy. The carded

abstracts have been reproduced as M861, *Compiled Records Showing Service of Military Units in Confederate Organizations,* 74 rolls.

Most of the compiled records are arranged alphabetically by state and thereunder by type of unit: cavalry, artillery, and infantry, followed by reserve, militia, local defense, conscript, prison guard, instruction, or other organizations. Other names by which units were known are shown on the records. The arrangement of compiled records for units raised directly or otherwise formed by the Confederate Government is similar, except that they are not arranged by state.

Confederate casualty records are available on microfilm as M836, *Confederate States Army Casualties: Lists and Narrative Reports, 1861–1865,* 7 rolls. These records are arranged in three groups: Lists and Reports of Casualties in Individual States; Lists and Reports of Casualties by a Single Unit in More Than One State; and Lists and Reports of Casualties in Indian Territory. The lists for individual states are further arranged alphabetically by name of state, thereunder alphabetically by engagement, and thereunder by type and number of unit. The second group of records is arranged chronologically. The lists for Indian Territory are arranged by name of engagment. The descriptive pamphlet for M836 includes a list of all the casualty lists appearing on the film.

Lists of **Confederate soldiers and civilians who died in Federal prisons** were compiled in compliance with a statute of 1906 (34 Stat. 56) that provided "for the appropriate marking of the graves of the soldiers and sailors of the Confederate Army and Navy who died in Northern prisons and were buried near the prisons where they died." The burial lists, located in Records of the Office of the Quartermaster General, RG 92, are generally arranged alphabetically by name of the prison camp or other location where the deaths occurred. Each list is alphabetical by name of deceased and usually gives the name, rank, company, regiment, date of death, and number and location of grave for each person interred. Some of the lists include private citizens. Available on microfilm is M918, *Register of Confederate Soldiers, Sailors, and Citizens Who Died in Federal Prisons and Military Hospitals in the North, 1861–65,* 1 roll. There are also records of cemeteries in RG 92 that contain burial registers and lists.

Located in RG 109 are other registers of Confederates who died in Union prisons, which have been reproduced as part of *Selected Records of the War Department Relating to Confederate Prisoners of War, 1861–1865,* M598, 145 rolls. Particularly useful is a two-volume series of registers of prisoner deaths compiled by the U.S. Office of the Commissary General of Prisoners (rolls 5 and 6) and a five-volume series of registers of prisoner deaths compiled by the U.S. Surgeon General's Office (rolls 11–12).

Among the records of the Confederate Secretary of War and Adjutant and Inspector General's Offices in RG 109 are a number of **records of appointments** and subsequent

TABLE 12
Selected Genealogical Research Aids: Civil War—Confederate

General

Wright, Marcus G. *General Officers of the Confederate Army....* New York: Neale Publishing Co., 1911.

Estes, Claude. *List of Field Officers, Regiments, and Battalions in the Confederate States Army, 1861-65.* Macon, GA: J.W. Burke Co., 1912.

List of Staff Officers of the Confederate States Army, 1861-1865. Washington: Government Printing Office, 1891.

Sifakis, Stewart. *Compendium of the Confederate Armies: Alabama.* New York: Facts On File, Inc., 1992.

Sifakis, Stewart. *Compendium of the Confederate Armies: Florida and Arkansas.* New York: Facts On File, Inc., 1992.

Sifakis, Stewart. *Compendium of the Confederate Armies: Kentucky, Maryland, Missouri, The Confederate Units and The Indian Units.* New York: Facts On File, Inc., 1995.

Sifakis, Stewart. *Compendium of the Confederate Armies: Louisiana.* New York: Facts On File, Inc., 1995.

Sifakis, Stewart. *Compendium of the Confederate Armies: North Carolina.* New York: Facts On File, Inc., 1992.

Sifakis, Stewart. *Compendium of the Confederate Armies: Tennessee.* New York: Facts On File, Inc., 1992.

Sifakis, Stewart. *Compendium of the Confederate Armies:Virginia.* New York: Facts On File Inc., 1992.

Alabama

McMorries, Edward Young. *History of the First Regiment Alabama Infantry, Volunteer Infantry, C.S.A.* Montgomery: Brown Printing Co., 1904.

Georgia

Candler, Allen D., ed. *The Confederate Records of the State of Georgia.* 5 vols. Atlanta: Georgia Legislature, 1909-11.

Henderson, Lillian. *Roster of the Confederate Soldiers of Georgia, 1861-65.* 6 vols. Hapeville, GA.: Longino and Porter, 1959-64.

Kansas

Fox, S.M., comp. "Roll of the Officers and Enlisted Men of the Third, Fourth, Eighteenth and Nineteenth Kansas Volunteers, 1861," *13th Biennial Report of the Adjutant General of the State of Kansas, 1901-2,* appendix. Topeka: Kansas Adjutant General's Office, 1902.

Kentucky

Harris, Abner, comp. *Reports of the Adjutant General of the State of Kentucky—Confederate Kentucky Volunteers, War 1861-1865.* 2 vols. Frankfort: Kentucky Adjutant General's Office, 1915-18.

Lindsey, D.W., comp. *Report of the Adjutant General of the State of Kentucky, 1861-1866.* 2 vols. Frankfort: Kentucky Adjutant General's Office, 1866-67.

Louisiana

Booth, Andrew B. *Records of Louisiana Confederate Soldiers and Louisiana Confederate Commands.* New Orleans: Military Record Commission, 1920.

North Carolina

Moore, John W. *Roster of North Carolina Troops in the War Between the States.* Raleigh: Ashe and Gatling, 1882.

Jordan, Weymouth T., Jr., and Louis H. Manarian. *North Carolina Troops, 1861-1865: A Roster.* Raleigh: North Carolina Department of Archives and History, 1966.

Tennessee

Tennesseans in the Civil War. 2 vols. Nashville: Tennessee Civil War Centennial Commission, 1964.

Wright, Marcus J. *Tennessee in the War, 1861-65.* New York: Ambrose Lee Publishing Co., 1908.

Virginia

Wallace, Lee A., Jr. *A Guide to Virginia Military Organizations, 1861-1865.* Richmond: Virginia Civil War Commission, 1964.

careers of military personnel. Many of the volumes consist of registers of applications and recommendations for appointments, registers and lists of appointments, and registers of applications and recommendations for promotions. Volumes are variously arranged: chronologically by date of appointment or application, alphabetically by surname of appointee, or by type of appointment. Some of the books include indexes, but there is also a master alphabetical card index to appointments of officers, which was prepared by the U.S. Adjutant General's Office. The card index covers entries in many of the significant volumes. Appointment registers give such information as name; rank; dates of appointment, rank, confirmation, and acceptance; arm of service; state; to whom the officer or appointee reported; and subsequent personnel actions. Rosters of commissioned officers of regiments and battalions contain information similar to that found in the appointment registers. Other records of military personnel include registers of resignations, discharges, and deaths, which show name, rank, organization, and dates and places of resignation, discharge, or death. However, much of this information, at least for individual officers, may already be available in more convenient form in the compiled military service records.

Information about Confederate officers and other soldiers is also interspersed among the various correspondence series of the Confederate War Department. These are available as M437, *Letters Received by the Confederate Secretary of War, 1861–1865,* 151 rolls; M474, *Letters Received by the Confederate Adjutant and Inspector General, 1861–1865,* 164 rolls; and M469, *Letters Received by the Confederate Quartermaster General, 1861–1865,* 14 rolls. Alphabetical card indexes to names of correspondents and persons mentioned in the letters are available as M409, *Index to the Letters Received by the Confederate Secretary of War, 1861–1865,* 34 rolls, and M410, *Index to the Letters Received by the Confederate Adjutant and Inspector General and by the Confederate Quartermaster General, 1861–1865,* 41 rolls.

Information about the confirmation of appointment of Confederate officers is given in *Journal of the Congress of Confederate States of America, 1861–65* (58th Cong., 2nd sess., S. Doc. 234, serials 4610–4616). A general index is included in the last volume.

Some Confederate soldiers are named in *War of the Rebellion: A Compilation of the Official Records of the Union and Confederate Armies,* listed above in 5.2.6. The last volume is a general index. As indicated earlier, this publication, including the index, has been microfilmed as M262, *Official Records of the Union and Confederate Armies, 1861–1865,* and has also been printed by the National Historical Society, Gettysburg, PA.

5.2.8 Spanish-American War

During the Spanish-American War in 1898, volunteers served in existing state militia units accepted into Federal service, additional units raised in states and territories, and units raised directly by the Federal Government. Because methods of enlistment varied, compiled military service records for these soldiers are arranged in four subseries: records of state units arranged alphabetically by state; records of volunteers from the continental territories; records of volunteers raised directly by the Federal Government; and records of volunteers from Puerto Rico. The compiled service records are further arranged by organizational breakdown ending with the regiment or independent battalion or company. Under each unit service records are arranged alphabetically by surname of the soldier.

A general comprehensive index identifies the compiled service records of volunteers regardless of their military units. It has been reproduced as M871, *General Index to Compiled Service Records of Volunteer Soldiers Who Served During the War with Spain,* 126 rolls. Each index card gives name, rank, and unit in which the soldier served. Cross-references are included to names that appeared in the records under more than one spelling.

Some index cards refer to "miscellaneous personal paper," but there are no compiled service records for individuals whose index cards contain this entry. The papers themselves follow the jacket-envelopes for most units. The War Department apparently accumulated these papers to be interfiled with the regular series of compiled service records but never did so.

Separate indexes exist for each state and unit of U.S. Volunteers. The index for Louisiana is available as M240, *Index to Compiled Service Records of Volunteer Soldiers Who Served During the War with Spain in Organizations from the State of Louisiana,* 1 roll, and for North Carolina as M413, *. . . North Carolina,* 2 rolls. The only microfilm publication of compiled military service records for the Spanish-American War is M1087, *Compiled Service Records of Volunteer Soldiers Who Served in the Florida Infantry During the War with Spain,* 13 rolls.

Information about volunteers during the Spanish-American War is found in the general correspondence of the Adjutant General's Office. An extensive name and subject index is available on microfilm as M698, *Index to General Correspondence of the Adjutant General's Office, 1890–1917,* 1,269 rolls. Operational records for the Army and its subcommands are in Records of U.S. Army Overseas Operations and Commands, 1898–1942, RG 395. Published research aids are listed in Table 13.

5.2.9. Philippine Insurrection

The acts of Congress authorizing the raising of troops to fight in the Philippine Insurrection, 1899–1902, allowed for the recruitment of volunteers from all the continental states and territories and from the Philippines. Some units were composed of persons from a single place, but many were made up of men from more than one place. Accordingly, units of volunteers accepted into Federal service for

TABLE 13
Selected Genealogical Research Aids: Spanish-American War and Philippine Insurrection

General

Heitman, Francis B. *Historical Register and Dictionary of the United States Army* . . . . Washington: Government Printing Office, 1903, 2:185-272. A separate list of acting assistant or contract surgeons, U.S. Army, in service at any time between April 17, 1898, and January 1, 1903, appears on pages 273-279. This publication is also available on microfilm as M1858.

Official Register of Officers and Volunteers in the Service of the United States . . . March 2, 1899, . . . June 1, 1900. Washington: Adjutant General's Office, 1900.

Peterson, Clarence Stewart. *Known Military Dead During the Spanish-American War and the Philippine Insurrection, 1898-1901.* Baltimore, 1958.

Mawson, Harry P. and J.W. Buel, comps. *Leslie's Official History of the Spanish-American War.* Washington, 1899.

Correspondence Relating to the War with Spain . . . With an Appendix Giving . . . a Brief History of the Volunteer Organizations. . . . . Washington: Adjutant General's Office, 1902.

Connecticut

Connecticut Volunteers Who Served in the Spanish-American War, 1898-1899. Hartford: Connecticut Adjutant General's Office, 1899.

Illinois

Reece, Jasper N. *Report of the Adjutant General of the State of Illinois. . . .* Springfield: Illinois Adjutant General's Office, 1900-1902.

Indiana

Gore, James K. *Record of Indiana Volunteers in the Spanish American War, 1898-1899.* Indianapolis: Indiana Adjutant General's Office, 1900.

Kansas

Fox, S.M. *13th Biennial Report of the Adjutant General of the State of Kansas, 1901-2.* Topeka: Kansas Adjutant General's Office, 1902.

Minnesota

Eleventh Biennial Report . . . Including Military Operations Up to November 30, 1900. St. Paul: Minnesota Adjutant General's Department, 1901.

Nebraska

Pool, Charles H. *Roster of Veterans of the Mexican, Civil, and Spanish-American Wars, Residing in Nebraska, 1915.* Lincoln: Nebraska Secretary of State, 1915.

New Jersey

Report of the Adjutant General of New Jersey. Somerville: New Jersey Adjutant General's Office, 1899.

New York

New York Adjutant General's Office. *New York in the Spanish-American War, 1898.* 3 vols. Revised edition. Albany: J.B. Lyon, 1902. Chauncey W. Herrick, comp. *Index.* 1914.

North Carolina

Roster of the North Carolina Volunteers in the Spanish-American War. Raleigh: North Carolina Adjutant General, 1900.

Ohio

Hough, Benson W. et al., comps. *Official Roster of Ohio Soldiers in the War With Spain, 1898-1899.* Columbus: Ohio Adjutant General's Department. 1916.

Oregon

Gantenbein, C.U., comp. *The Official Records of the Oregon Volunteers in the Spanish War and Philippine Insurrection.* 2nd edition. Salem: Oregon Adjutant General's Office, 1903.

Pennsylvania

Stewart, Thomas J., comp. *Record of Pennsylvania Volunteers in the Spanish-American War, 1898.* 2nd edition. Harrisburg: Pennsylvania Adjutant General's Office, 1901.

West Virginia

Biennial Report of the Adjutant General of West Virginia, 1899-1900. Charleston: West Virginia Adjutant General's Office, 1900.

the Philippine Insurrection did not include the name of the state or territory as part of their official designations, as had been customary in previous wars. Designations, therefore, do not provide a clue as to the state or territory of residence of persons serving in the unit, even if the unit was formed in a single state.

The compiled military service records are arranged by regiment number and name, thereunder jacket-envelopes are arranged alphabetically by surname of soldier. Only Americans who served in regiments formed in the United States and in the Philippines are represented. No records relating to Filipinos are included. Records relating to the Puerto Rican Regiment, U.S. Volunteers, which was organized for service in the Philippines but remained in Puerto Rico, are filed and indexed with the compiled service records of the Spanish-American War.

A general comprehensive index was published as M872, *Index to Compiled Service Records of Volunteer Soldiers Who Served During the Philippine Insurrection*, 24 rolls. There is no compiled service record for a soldier whose index card contains a cross-reference to the miscellaneous papers. This is a separate series of personal papers following the compiled service records. As indicated earlier, these were apparently accumulated by the War Department for an interfiling that never took place.

The index in M698, mentioned above, may lead to other information about volunteers and enlisted men. Operational records for the Army and its subcommands are among the records in RG 395.

Historical sketches of volunteer organizations were prepared in response to the Adjutant General's instructions of October 19, 1900, which were distributed in Circular No. 23 of December 23, 1900, Headquarters, Division of the Philippines. The histories are arranged by arm of service, thereunder numerically by regiment. Histories for all the regiments that participated in the war are not in this file, but the typescripts comprise detailed unit histories of the 26th–49th U.S. Volunteer Infantry Regiments. No history was found for the 11th U.S. Volunteer Cavalry, and miscellaneous units of volunteers are arranged by unit number.

5.3 Records of Military Service in the 20th Century

5.3.1 World War I: Draft Records

NARA's Southeast Region in Atlanta has World War I draft records, which are part of Records of the Selective Service System (World War I), RG 163.

Draft registration cards (Series 1 PMGO Form 1) contain information supplied by each registrant, including name, address, date of birth, age, race, citizenship status, birthplace, occupation and employer, dependent relative, marital status, father's birthplace, and name and address of nearest relative. They are arranged alphabetically by state, thereunder by local (county) board, and thereunder by

individual registrant. The cards have been filmed as M1509, *World War I Selective Service System Draft Registration Cards*, 4,277 rolls.

Docket books (Series 2 PMGO Form 178) and **classification lists** (Series 3 PMGO Form 1000) show for each registrant the dates of each step in the induction process through acceptance or rejection at mobilization camps.

List of Men Ordered to Report for Induction, 1917 (PMGO Form 164A) and **All Men from a Local Board Actually Inducted**, 1918 (PMGO Form 1029) are arranged by state and local board coded index number, thereunder chronologically by reporting date. Each list includes the name of the mobilization camp the men were sent to, dates they were to report, name of each inductee ordered to report, and whether the men actually reported and were inducted or rejected at the mobilization camp. The Form 1029 is a revision and replacement of the Form 164A.

Appeals to the President from district boards include decisions affirmed and returns of record on appeal. They detail the reasons for appeal (such as dependents) and physical, marital, and draft status of members of the family. An index is available.

5.3.2. World War II: Draft Records

NARA's Great Lakes Region in Chicago has draft registration cards for the "Fourth Registration" for men born on or between April 28, 1877, and February 16, 1897, who lived in Illinois, Indiana, Michigan, Ohio, and Wisconsin. The cards contain information supplied by each registrant, including name, address, date and place of birth, age, name and address of employer, and physical description. The cards are arranged alphabetically by state, thereunder alphabetically by name of registrant.

5.3.3 Other Records

Records relating to the following groups of military personnel are at the National Personnel Records Center in St. Louis, MO: **U.S. Army** officers separated after June 30, 1917, and enlisted personnel separated after October 31, 1912; **U.S. Air Force** officers and enlisted separated after August 1947; **U.S. Marine Corps** officers and enlisted separated after 1904; **U.S. Navy** officers separated after 1902 and enlisted separated after 1885; and **U.S. Coast Guard** officers and enlisted separated after 1897. *See* I.7 in the introduction to this volume for more information about obtaining access to material about veterans at the National Personnel Records Center (NPRC), Military Records Facility, 9700 Page Ave., St. Louis, MO 63132-5100.

6.1 Introduction

Responsibility for naval matters was vested in the Secretary of War until an act of 1798 (1 Stat. 553) established the Department of the Navy. The act empowered the Secretary of the Navy "to take possession of all the records, books and documents, and all other matters and things appertaining to this department. . . ." Most of the records of officers and enlisted men are in two record groups, Records of the Bureau of Naval Personnel, Record Group (RG) 24, and Naval Records Collection of the Office of Naval Records and Library, RG 45. Established originally to collect and prepare for publication manuscripts dealing with naval affairs in the Civil War, the Naval Records and Library Office became for a time the de facto archival unit of the Office of the Secretary of the Navy.

The U.S. Marine Corps was also established in 1798 (1 Stat. 594), but until 1834 no one knew whether the corps was more akin to the Navy or to the Army, because the 1798 act placed the Marines under the Navy when afloat, and under the Army when ashore. An act of 1834 (4 Stat. 712) adopted the concept that the Marine Corps should be part of the Navy Department.

6.2 U.S. Navy Records

6.2.1 Revolutionary War

The naval and marine service records of the Revolutionary War are fragmentary. In addition to those in RG 24 and RG 45, relevant records are in War Department Collection of Revolutionary War Records, RG 93, and in Records of the Continental and Confederation Congresses and the Constitutional Convention, RG 360.

The **record books** assembled by the Navy Department include the payroll of the Continental Ship *Confederacy*, 1780-81, 1 vol.; a photostatic copy of the rosters of officers and men of the *Bonhomme Richard, Pallas,* and *Vengeance*, 1779, 1 vol.; and a photostatic copy of the log of the Continental Ship *Ranger*, 1778-80, 1 vol. A separate typewritten index is available for each volume. Information varies from volume to volume but generally shown are the names of individuals and the vessels on which they served. Sometimes other service or payment data is included.

Some of the **unbound papers** assembled by the Navy Department form part of a large series called the **area file** because the papers therein are arranged by geographical regions or areas. These papers vary widely in form and content. Documents that contain references to naval men of the Revolutionary War, along with other early parts of the area file, are covered by a card index. Some records may show such information as the name and rank of a naval man of the Revolutionary War, the vessel on which he served, and a service date.

The area file includes photostatic copies of letters and other documents from the period of the American Revolution that were copied from originals in manuscript collections of the states of Massachusetts, Virginia, and North Carolina. The documents are microfilmed on M625, *Area File of the Naval Records Collection, 1775-1910,* 414 rolls. An alphabetical card index to names of vessels, American and foreign naval officers and privateersmen, and other individuals mentioned in the documents is available but not microfilmed.

Three lists identify captured American naval personnel and other prisoners and individuals entitled to prize money for service under John Paul Jones. Each list is an alphabetically arranged set of printed cards captioned "War of the Revolution, Navy and Privateer Records," containing information derived from several sources. The first subseries of cards pertains to persons taken to Forton Prison in England: officers and men of captured American vessels (including Continental warships, privateers, and prizes) and a few passengers. The cards show the name of the individual and often state of residence, date committed to prison, rank, name of the vessel on which captured and port from which it sailed, date of capture, name of the vessel making the capture, and whether the prisoner escaped or died in prison.

The second subseries of cards pertains to prize money due to the "heirs" of John Paul Jones. The entries were taken from Senate Executive Document 11, 37th Congress, 2nd sess. Each card shows the name of an individual, rank, vessel on which he served (*Bonhomme Richard* or *Alliance*), amount of prize money due, and sometimes nationality (French or American).

The third subseries of cards relates to persons sent to Mill Prison in England. The cards are similar in content to those in the first list. Some also show city or town of residence of prisoners, if exchanged, and if joined the British Navy. The information was taken from "A List of the Americans Committed to Old Mill Prison Since the American War," *New England Historical and Genealogical Register* 19 (1865): 74-75, 136-141, and 209-213, and *A Relic of the Revolution,* by Charles Herbert (Boston: C.H. Pierce, 1847), which was reprinted by the *New York Times*, New York, 1968.

A card index prepared by the Office of Naval Records and Library cites names mentioned in documents of RG 45 relating to the Revolutionary War. The index is incomplete, but it is more comprehensive than the index to the area file. The index consists mainly of names of American naval officers and enlisted men, but it also includes names of Marine Corps officers and men, officers and men of the Virginia State Navy, officers and men of privateers, French volunteers, and American military officers.

The War Department collected only a few naval records of the Revolutionary War and transferred most of them to the Navy Department in 1906. Before that time, however, **compiled service records** for naval personnel were created. This series of card abstracts is available on rolls 3 and 4 of M880, *Compiled Service Records of American*

Naval Personnel and Members of the Departments of the Quartermaster General and the Commissary General of Military Stores Who Served During the Revolutionary War, 4 rolls. The most comprehensive name index to the Revolutionary War compiled service records is M860, *General Index to Compiled Service Records of Revolutionary War Soldiers,* 58 rolls. A separate index to names of naval personnel is M879, *Index to Compiled Service Records of American Naval Personnel Who Served During the Revolutionary War,* 1 roll. The names appearing in M879 are generally duplicated in M860.

Information on the cards in the compiled service records was carefully transcribed from lists of American sailors and vessels, pay rolls, portage bills, and assignments of pay relating to ships of the Continental Navy and state navies, the frigate *Alliance,* brigantines *Dartmouth* and *Polly,* sloops *Independence* and *Montgomery,* schooner *Putnam,* and ship *Raleigh;* lists of American prisoners taken by the British ships *Gibraltar, Hunter,* and *Felicity;* lists of vessels arriving and departing from Tribel's Landing in October 1781; and entries in volume 175 of the numbered record books, which includes the names of many sailors from the states of New York and Virginia.

A five-volume published name and subject index to the *Papers of the Continental Congress* makes it easy to determine whether a reference to the individual being researched exists in that part of RG 360.

6.2.2 Records of Commissioned Officers

Several series in RG 45 relate to commissioned officers of the Regular Navy and acting or volunteer officers who served during the Civil War and the Spanish-American War.

Among the earliest records in RG 45 is a **register of officers** of the Navy, May 1815 to June 1821. The register is alphabetical by first letter of surname, thereunder chronological. Each entry gives the officer's name, rank, date of appointment to the rank, age, and remarks of their superior concerning promotion potential.

Also for this early period are two series of **statements of place of birth** of officers. Those for 1816 are largely records for individuals whose names began with the letters "C" and "D." The records also give the officer's age. Similar statements for 1826 are on printed forms, arranged alphabetically. Those relating to chaplains and pursers are in a separate volume. Each record shows the name of the officer and the name of the state or territory in which he was born, from which he was appointed, and of which he was a citizen.

A record of **officers serving in 1829** is in one indexed volume. Each entry shows the name of the officer and gives the service record from date of appointment to 1829.

Acceptances are letters from those accepting appointments as officers, often with oaths of allegiance enclosed. Commissioned and warrant officers' acceptances, 1804-64, are arranged chronologically and thereunder alphabetically; those for volunteer officers, 1861-71, are arranged chronologically in subseries according to rank. Dates of coverage vary within each rank. Many of the letters or accompanying oaths of allegiance contain statements of birthplace or residence. Some subseries are indexed. Also available is a series of acceptances for acting engineers, 1862-65, with oaths of allegiance enclosed.

Statements of service of officers are found in several record series. In RG 45 one series consists of two volumes, indexed by name, containing statements of service submitted by officers, 1842-44, in response to a navy questionnaire. Another series, also indexed by name, contains tabular summaries of these statements. These 1842-44 statements give name, date of entry into service, and dates and descriptions of subsequent orders and service, including the names of vessels to which the officer was assigned. A separate series in RG 24 contains similar statements of service submitted by officers in 1865-66. These are also indexed by name and give name, place (and sometimes date) of birth, state from which appointed, state of residence, date of entry into the service, date of present commission, naval battles in which engaged, and other details of service.

The **age certificates** of naval and marine officers were prepared as a result of the retirement provisions of an Act of 1861 (12 Stat. 329). The certificates are in four volumes, two for 1862 and two for 1863. The entries in each series are arranged alphabetically by surname of officer and are indexed. Each certificate is signed by the officer and shows name, rank, and date of birth. These volumes are in RG 24.

Abstracts of service of officers, 1798-1924, in RG 24, are arranged in three subseries. The first consists of 21 lettered and numbered volumes. They relate to most naval and Marine Corps officers, volunteer officers of the Civil War, some noncommissioned officers, and a few professors and teachers at the U.S. Naval Academy. The abstracts in the lettered series refer to letters sent conveying appointments, orders and letters accepting resignations, and applications for appointment as midshipmen or cadets, 1798-1893. A list of the lettered volumes, with the inclusive dates covered by each, follows. Because the abstracts are filed chronologically, a particular officer can only be located if the approximate date of their commission is known.

A	1798-1801	I	1840-45
B	1801-3	J	1846-58
C	1804-8	K	1859-63
D	1809-13	L	1864-71
E	1813-17	M	1872-78
F	1818-25	N	1879-88
G	1825-31	O	1889-93
H	1832-40		

Each of the volumes J-O is bound in two separate parts. Part 1 relates to officers above the rank of master; Part 2, to officers of the rank of master or below. Some volumes are indexed; in others, the entries are arranged alphabetically. An entry shows name of officer, date of appointment, date and nature of changes in rank, and, where pertinent, date and nature of termination of service. These records are reproduced as M330, *Abstracts of Service of Naval Officers ("Records of Officers"), 1798-1893*, 19 rolls.

The second subseries is a single, indexed volume, covering the period 1799-1829, that summarizes service records of officers of certain ranks. The entries are arranged by rank, thereunder chronologically by date of commission.

The third subseries, 38 numbered volumes covering the period 1829-1924, is reproduced as M1328, *Abstracts of Service Records of Naval Officers ("Records of Officers"), 1829-1924*, 18 rolls. The records often show such information as the name of the officer, date and place of birth, date of entrance on duty, ranks held, names of stations to which assigned, place of residence, date and place of death, and, if serving in 1908 or later, names and addresses of beneficiaries. The volumes contain indexes arranged alphabetically by initial letter of surname, but separate indexes are also available.

Several series of miscellaneous records concern volunteer officers in the Civil War and later. These records are variously arranged, usually alphabetically by surname or chronologically in volumes with name indexes. Correspondence concerning volunteer officers, 1861-67, contains letters of application, recommendation, and appointment, together with many lists of officers. Letters sent transmitting appointments and orders, 1861-79, also include notifications of promotion and approvals of requests for leave. A register of volunteer officers, 1861-87, gives date of original entry into service, name, state of birth, state of which a resident, and duty station. The entries in this register are arranged by rank, thereunder alphabetically by initial letter of surname. Registers of volunteer officers honorably discharged, 1861-70, include the officer's permanent address at the time of discharge. A list of volunteer officers dismissed from service, 1861-65, whose surnames began with A or B, gives the officer's name, rank, and date of dismissal.

A **register of engineer officers**, 1843-99, in one indexed volume in RG 45, relates to the officers who served in the Engineer Corps of the Navy until the corps was abolished in 1899 (30 Stat. 1004). Each entry shows the name of the officer, date and place of birth, date of appointment to the Engineer Corps, a detailed service record, and date and place of death or date of retirement.

Also in RG 45 is an incomplete three-volume compilation of biographical data for some officers who served in the War of 1812, the Mexican War, and the Civil War. Name indexes to the series are available. Included are date of birth, date of appointment, and information concerning war service.

Personnel record cards of officers of the Naval Auxiliary Service, chiefly 1907-17, in RG 24 are arranged alphabetically by name of officer. Each card shows the name of the officer, place of residence, place and date of birth, name and address of next of kin, and service record summary.

6.2.3 Records of Midshipmen and Cadets

Records relating to midshipmen or cadets concern chiefly those who served from the time of the establishment of the U.S. Naval Academy at Annapolis, MD, in 1845. They include registers of admissions and records of appointees. Information about the relatively few midshipmen in the Navy during the years 1798-1848 is meager; however, some information concerning midshipmen can be found in letters received from officers by the Secretary of the Navy and in the navy "Subject File" in RG 45. Other facts may be garnered from the abstracts of service records of naval officers in the lettered volumes, described in 6.2.2, and from Navy Department general correspondence files.

Records of the U.S. Naval Academy, RG 405, contain **registers of candidates for admission** to the academy, 1849-1930, with some gaps, arranged chronologically according to date of appointment. Most entries show candidate's name, residence, date and place of birth, and signature, as well as name, residence, and occupation or profession of their parent or guardian. Names of parents or guardians are also included in the data about each cadet in a **list of cadets**, 1864-68, and in a **register of names and addresses of parents and guardians of cadets**, 1871-76. The records reproduced in M991, *U.S. Naval Academy Registers of Delinquencies, 1846-1850 and 1853-1882, and Academic and Conduct Records of Cadets, 1881-1908*, 45 rolls, provide further personal information about cadets enrolled in the academy at those dates. These series and others are described in *Records of the U.S. Naval Academy*, Inventory 11, compiled by Geraldine N. Phillips and Aloha South (Washington: National Archives and Records Service, 1975).

In RG 24 are **letters of appointment, naval cadets**, 1894-1940, 12 volumes. The letters show name of appointee, date of issuance and effective date of appointment, and congressional district from which the cadet was appointed.

The Bureau of Naval Personnel, Washington, DC, 20370, retains the index for this series, but the file numbers of the jackets of midshipmen or cadets for the period 1862-93 can be obtained from the records of officers in the lettered volumes of abstracts of service described previously. The archives of the Naval Academy in Annapolis, MD, has microfilm copies of the jackets of midshipmen who entered the academy after 1906, but they are largely restricted under privacy considerations.

6.2.4 Records of Enlisted Men

Records about navy enlisted men are dated 1798-1956. Muster and pay rolls of ships and shore establishments through 1859 are in RG 45. Records for the years

1860-1900 are in RG 24 and are described in *Records of the Bureau of Naval Personnel,* Preliminary Inventory 123, compiled by Virgil E. Baugh (Washington: National Archives and Records Service, 1960).

Several series of bound volumes of **muster rolls and pay rolls** of ships and stations are available. Muster rolls generally show the name of the enlisted individual, ship or station on which they served, dates of service, and, in some cases, ship or station from which they were transferred. Payrolls generally show name of enlisted person, station or rank, date of commencement of service, and terms of service. To use muster rolls and pay rolls, researchers should know where the subject of research was stationed during the time pertinent to the research.

Muster and pay rolls of vessels, 1798-1859, are arranged alphabetically by name of ship, thereunder chronologically. A typewritten name index is available for each of the first three volumes of records of the frigate *Constitution,* 1798-1815. Muster and pay rolls of shore establishments, 1805-49 and 1859-69, are also arranged alphabetically by name of station, thereunder chronologically.

Muster rolls of vessels, 1860-1900, make up 366 volumes arranged chronologically in three separate series, thereunder alphabetically by name of vessel. The volumes contain, for each person aboard, information concerning enlistment, whether entitled to an honorable discharge, personal description, date received on board, and applicable data concerning transfer, discharge, desertion, or death. Eleven volumes of muster rolls, 1861 and 1863, cover ships that captured prize vessels during the Civil War. These rolls were probably used as a basis for awarding prize money. They show the name, rank, and pay for each officer and member of the crew.

Muster rolls of ships and stations, 1891-1900, make up 154 volumes arranged in two groups: rolls of naval vessels and rolls of naval stations, torpedo boats, and vessels of the U.S. Coast and Geodetic Survey. The first group is arranged alphabetically by name of ship, thereunder alphabetically by initial letter of the individual's last name. The second group is unarranged. Information contained in these volumes includes, when applicable, name of individual, time of enlistment, period of service on the vessel or station, and applicable data on transfer, discharge, desertion, or death.

Muster rolls of ships and shore establishments, 1898-1939, make up 3,539 volumes arranged in chronological periods, thereunder alphabetically by name of vessel or shore establishment. The rolls contain the names of individuals assigned to a vessel or shore establishment, period of service, and information regarding transfer, discharge, desertion, or death.

Muster rolls for ships, stations, and other naval activities, 1939-56, are microfilmed on 21,120 rolls. They are arranged alphabetically by name of vessel or symbol of unit, thereunder chronologically. The rolls for the period 1941-56 are indexed by name of vessel or unit. The microfilmed rolls contain copies of several documents: the quarterly roll, an alphabetical list of enlisted personnel attached to a ship, station, or other naval unit; report of changes, an alphabetical list of enlisted personnel showing changes relating to rating and transfers; a list of any passengers on board submitted at the time of sailing; and the recapitulation sheet, a summary of all changes in the status of personnel aboard ship or in a naval unit.

Registers of enlistments provide the chief source of information about enlisted men for the years 1845-54. The registers are in three volumes (two volumes for 1845-53 and one volume for 1854) with entries that have been copied in part from records later destroyed. Each entry shows the name of individual, date and place of enlistment, place of birth, and age. In some entries a column for remarks is filled out with such information as the name of ship or duty station assigned to or the date of discharge. Entries are arranged alphabetically by initial letter of surname. The records were indexed, and the index was incorporated into T1098, *Index to Rendezvous Repents, Before and After the Civil War, 1846-1861 and 1865-1884,* 32 rolls.

Weekly returns of enlistments at naval rendezvous (or recruiting stations), 1855-91, provide the chief source of information about enlisted men for the years 1855-65 and are an important source for the years 1866-85. Returns are arranged in volumes chronologically by week, thereunder by name of naval rendezvous, and thereunder by date of enlistment. Returns for each year are numbered consecutively. Most entries in the weekly returns of enlistments show, under the name of the naval rendezvous, the name of the enlisted individual, date and term of enlistment, rating, a reference to any previous naval service, place of birth, age, occupation, and personal description. Some entries show place of residence. The records for the period 1855-84 were indexed, and the index entries were incorporated into either T1098 or T1099, *Index to Rendezvous Reports, Civil War, 1861-1865,* 31 rolls. For 1885 a key to enlistment returns contains entries arranged alphabetically by initial letter of surname.

Also on microfilm are T1100, *Index to Rendezvous Reports, Naval Auxiliary Service, 1917-1918,* 1 roll, and T1101, *Index to Rendezvous Reports, Armed Guard Personnel, 1917-1920,* 3 rolls.

Quarterly returns of enlistments of vessels, 1866-91, are also an important source for data about enlisted personnel, 1866-84. Returns are in 43 volumes, which are arranged by year; within each volume, returns are arranged by number, thereunder by quarter, thereunder by name of vessel, and thereunder by date of enlistment. Most entries show, under the name of the vessel, the name of the enlisted individual, date and term of enlistment, rating, a reference to any previous naval service, place of birth, age, occupation, and personal description. Some entries show place of residence. Returns for the years 1866-84 were indexed, and the index entries were incorporated into T1098, mentioned above.

Jackets for enlisted men relate to service between 1842 and 1885. The jackets, which are arranged alphabetically, were prepared between 1885 and 1941 and contain documents assembled or created in connection with pension claims, requests for service records, and requests for copies of honorable discharge. A jacket usually shows the name, full service record, and place of residence after service.

Continuous service certificates, 1865-99, are arranged alphabetically by surname. Given for each individual are name, date of entry for pay, vessels on which service was performed, rating, professional qualifications, dates of transfer to and discharge from vessels, character of discharge, age, description, health record, and dates of reenlistment.

Personnel record cards for enlisted of the Naval Auxiliary Service in RG 24 are dated chiefly 1901-17 and are arranged alphabetically by name. The cards show name, rating, name of vessel on which served, year and place of birth, occupation, personal description, name of next of kin, date and nature of separation from service, and place of residence.

Also in RG 24 are **card abstracts of World War I service records**, which cover the period 1917-19. They are arranged alphabetically by name of state, thereunder alphabetically by surname. The cards show name, serial number, date and place of enrollment or enlistment, age and rating, home address, dates and places of service, and date and place of discharge.

Three series of records relate to **naval apprentices**. The naval apprentice system was established under authority of an act of March 2, 1837 (5 Stat. 153), to supply the Navy with disciplined and well-trained seamen. The first real training program for apprentices was set up in 1864, but after the Civil War, the crews of naval vessels had more foreign-born seamen than Americans. Another apprentice system, therefore, was established in 1875 for boys between the ages of 16 and 18 to serve until they were 21. By the close of the Spanish-American War, the apprentice system had reduced the number of foreign seamen in the U.S. Navy to a small percentage of the enlisted personnel.

Certificates of consent, 1838-40, in RG 24, which are arranged chronologically and not indexed, reflect the first use of the system. A certificate shows the name of the apprentice, date of birth, and name of parent or guardian.

Apprenticeship papers, 1864-89, are in individual folders arranged alphabetically by the first two letters of surname. They consist of forms filled out by parents or guardians and, for the years 1864-69, testimonials of character. Each apprenticeship paper shows the name of the apprentice, place of service, date of entrance into service, place and date of birth, and name, residence, and relationship of parent or guardian.

A register of naval apprentices, 1864-75, concerns service aboard the training ships *Sabine, Portsmouth,* and *Saratoga.* An entry shows the name of the apprentice, date and place of birth, date and place of enlistment, name of parent or guardian, and date of detachment from the service. The single volume is indexed by initial letter of surname.

6.2.5 Records of Officers and Enlisted Men

Court-martial and other personnel records in Records of the Office of the Judge Advocate General (Navy), RG 125, are dated 1799-1943. They include name indexes and registers to some of the court-martial records, transcripts of proceedings of general courts-martial and courts of inquiry, records for summary courts-martial and deck courts, records of proceedings of boards of investigation and inquest, proceedings and registers of examining and retiring boards, personnel reports of commanding officers, and correspondence relating to desertions and discharges. These series are usually arranged in numerical order. To find information about a particular court-martial, the researcher must know the approximate date; in some cases, it may be necessary to know the type of offense as well.

Information given in the records includes, when applicable: name of the sailor charged; rating, ship or station, and other service information; the alleged offense; place and date of trial; and sentence. Medical information used in evaluating a sailor's fitness for duty is in the records of examining and retiring boards. Reports of commanding officers include punishment lists and lists of men who were in naval prisons. Correspondence relating to desertions pertains to the efforts of individuals to have their discharge status changed from dishonorable to honorable.

Early records are available on M273, *Records of General Courts-Martial and Courts of Inquiry of the Navy Department, 1799-1867,* 198 rolls.

Claims files for special naval awards relate chiefly to claims for prize money. Although naval personnel were in some instances entitled to bounty land warrants, a principal benefit in addition to their pay was prize money awarded on the basis of prizes captured on the high seas during a time of war. These claims files are interfiled with Treasury Department payment records, in the large "Miscellaneous Account" file. For a description of the part of the files that relates to prize money, *see* Edward H. West's "Applications for Prize Money," *National Genealogical Society Quarterly* 32 (1944): 65-68.

Files for claims for half pay of Virginia naval officers of the Revolutionary War are described with pension records in 7.2.1.

A **casualty list** for World War I is printed in *Officers and Enlisted Men of the United States Navy Who Lost Their Lives During the World War From April 6, 1917, to November 11, 1918* (Washington: Government Printing Office, 1920). This volume is subdivided into three parts: Officers, Regular and Reserve; Enlisted Men; and Navy Enlisted Men Not in Active Service. Each entry includes name and rank of deceased; date, place, and cause of death; and name and address of next of kin.

The combined list of Navy, Marine Corps, and Coast Guard casualties in World War II, *State Summary of War Casualties* (Washington: Navy Department, 1946), consists of separate booklets for individual states and lists those persons on active duty with the U.S. Navy, Marine Corps, and Coast Guard whose deaths resulted directly from enemy action or from operational activities against the enemy in war zones from December 7, 1941, to the end of the war. Casualties that occurred in the United States or as a result of disease, homicide, or suicide anywhere are not included. Entries in the list include the name and rank of the decedent, and the name, address, and relationship of next of kin.

The National Archives and Records Administration (NARA) holds a few electronic records series of potential interest to genealogists. These include records of casualties and prisoners of war resulting from the conflicts in Korea and Vietnam among Records of the Veterans Administration, RG 15; Records of the Army Staff, RG 319; Records of the Office of the Secretary of Defense, RG 330; and Records of the Adjutant General's Office, 1917-, RG 407. Records of World War II prisoners of war are in Records of the Office of the Provost Marshal General, 1941-, RG 389. For information about additional electronic records of possible genealogical value, consult the electronic records section of the NARA web site at *www.nara.gov.*

For further information about records concerning casualties, prisoners of war, and persons missing in action, please consult the following National Archives reference information papers (RIP):

RIP 80, *Records Relating to Personal Participation in World War II: American Prisoners of War and Civilian Internees*, compiled by Benjamin L. DeWhitt and Jennifer Davis Heaps;

RIP 82, *Records Relating to Personal Participation in World War II: American Military Casualties and Burials*, compiled by Benjamin L. DeWhitt;

RIP 90, *Records Relating to American Prisoners of War and Missing in Action From Vietnam War Era, 1960-1994*, compiled by Charles E. Schamel;

RIP 102, *Records Relating to American Prisoners of War and Missing in Action from the Korean Conflict and Cold War Era*, compiled by Tim Wehrkamp; and

RIP 104, *Presidential Libraries Holdings Relating to Prisoners of War and Missing in Action*, compiled by Dale C. Mayer.

6.2.6 Related Records

Biographical information about enlisted personnel is found in conduct reports and shipping articles in RG 24. Scattered documentation is found in records relating to medical officers and patients in Records of the Bureau of Medicine and Surgery, RG 52; inmates of the Naval Asylum (later U.S. Naval Home) in RG 24; officers and apprentices

in Records of the Bureau of Yards and Docks, RG 71; and personnel assigned to navy yards in Records of Naval Districts and Shore Establishments, RG 181. Published research aids are listed in Table 14.

Registers of French and American prisoners of war held by the British at Halifax, Barbados, and Jamaica, 1805-15, and at Quebec, 1813-15, are in RG 45. Entries include name and number of each prisoner, ship that captured them, date and location of capture, name and type of vessel on which served before capture, and dates and conditions of the beginning and end of imprisonment.

In certain cases, special funds were put aside to satisfy claims by heirs of personnel lost at sea. Some of these claims can be found in Records of the Veterans Administration, RG 15.

6.3 Records of the U.S. Marine Corps

6.3.1 Introduction

The U.S. Marine Corps was created in 1798 (1 Stat. 594). In 1834 the corps was made a part of the U.S. Navy (4 Stat. 712), but in 1952 the Marine Corps was made a distinct service, with its commandant enjoying coequal status with other members of the Joint Chiefs of Staff (66 Stat. 282). The National Archives has service records relating to officers and enlisted of the Marine Corps, chiefly for the years 1798-1904, with a few as early as 1776 and some as late as 1945. Most records relating to U.S. Marine Corps personnel after 1904 are at the National Personnel Records Center. *See* I.7 in the introduction to this volume for more information about obtaining access to material about veterans at the National Personnel Records Center (NPRC), Military Records Facility, 9700 Page Ave., St. Louis, MO 63132-5100.

Many of the records described in this section are part of Records of the U.S. Marine Corps, RG 127. If the subject of research was a Marine, the navy sections of this guide may be useful; some records relating to Marines are part of the navy series, and some of the published research aids listed in Table 14 apply to both services. Although some records described in this section are part of Records of the Bureau of Naval Personnel, RG 24, and of Naval Records Collection of the Office of Naval Records and Library, RG 45, unless otherwise indicated in the descriptions, the records are in RG 127. The most useful finding aid for Marine Corps records, regardless of location, is *Records of the United States Marine Corps*, Inventory 2, compiled by Maizie Johnson (Washington: National Archives and Records Service, 1970).

6.3.2 Records of Officers

The records of appointments and military service of Marine Corps officers are widely scattered throughout many small, chronologically arranged series in RGs 127, 24, and 45. They cannot be used to ascertain whether a particular person was a commissioned officer or when he served. Edward Callahan's *List of Officers of the Navy of the United States and of the Marine Corps, From 1775 to 1900* (New York: L.R. Hamersly, 1901) or other sources will provide dates of appointment and service. With this knowledge, a researcher can seek documentation in the records for a person's commission or an abstract of their service. In some cases records show place of birth.

In RG 45 are letters of acceptance of appointments, 1805-12; letters of resignation, 1804-20; confirmations of appointments, 1814-42; a register of some Marine Corps and civilian personnel, 1799-1854; lists of officers at shore establishments, 1855-97; and records of promotions, 1909-20.

In RG 24 are confirmations of appointments, 1843-1909; lists of officers at shore establishments, 1878-1909; copies of commissions, 1844-1918; abstracts of marine officers' service, 1798-1802 and 1809-13 in volumes A and D described in 6.2.2 and microfilmed on M330; and letters of resignation, 1878-86.

Series in RG 127 are the best sources of documentation of the **military service** of Marine Corps officers. A one-volume register shows the name, rank, and state of birth of commissioned officers of the Marine Corps for each year, 1819-48. A similar register for each year, 1849-58 (contained in the front part of the first of two volumes of abstracts of military service of Marine Corps officers), shows the same information and date of entry into service, state from which appointed, and state of residence. The remainder of the first volume pertains to officers serving during the period 1869-73, and the second volume, to officers serving during the period 1899-1904. Entries are arranged by rank, but name indexes are included in the volumes. The entries give information about promotions, appointments to boards, assignments and transfers, and retirement. The second volume also shows for each officer their date and place of birth, state from which appointed, state of residence, and date of commission. Another series of two volumes contains press copies of military histories and statements of service of officers that were prepared by the Marine Corps during the 1904-11 period in response to inquiries from military officials. The records are arranged chronologically, but there are name indexes. Certificate books of officers and enlisted men (*see* 6.3.4) contain similar information.

For an officer of the Marine Corps who served during the Civil War, there may be information in the **age certificates** of navy and marine officers in RG 24. These certificates were prepared as a result of the retirement provisions of an act of 1861 (12 Stat. 329) and are in four volumes, two for 1862 and two for 1863. The entries in each series are arranged alphabetically by surname. Each certificate is signed by the officer and shows name, rank, and date of birth. Similar records in RG 45—statements of place of birth of officers in 1816 and 1826—are described in 6.2.2.

For a marine officer who served during the Spanish-American War, information may be found in the **register of living and retired officers**, 1899-1904, in RG 127. It lists each officer serving in 1899 and each officer commissioned during the years 1899-1904. An entry shows the name of the officer, date and place of birth, state from which appointed, and service record, 1899-1905.

An **alphabetical card list** of officers shows only name, and "reserve" if applicable, for persons who served before 1900 and for persons who served thereafter, date of entry into service, and serial number.

6.3.3 Records of Enlisted Men

Enlisted personnel of the Marine Corps, 1798-1941, are identified by an alphabetical **card list**. Each card gives name and date and place of enlistment or last reenlistment. Date of enlistment is a useful date for researchers examining any military service records, making this series a good starting point for research.

Enlisted service records are dated 1798-1904. They are arranged chronologically for the period 1789-1895, by year of enlistment or latest reenlistment, thereunder alphabetically by initial letter of surname, and thereunder chronologically by date of enlistment or reenlistment. For 1896-1904 they are arranged alphabetically by surname. A service record may contain one or more of the following: conduct record, descriptive list, enlistment papers, notice of discharge, report of medical survey, service report, and military history.

Size rolls, 1798-1901, contain the name, rank, age, place of birth, date and place of enlistment, personal appearance, and occupation of enlisted personnel. **Descriptive lists**, 1879-1906, contain the same information as well as family and service history. These series are variously arranged; to use them, the researcher must know at least the approximate date the subject of research enlisted.

Five different series relate to **discharges**, 1829-1927. These registers, certificates, and lists generally give name, rank, date of enlistment, and date and place of discharge. These series are variously arranged; to use the records, the researcher must know approximately when a particular Marine was discharged.

Entries in a one-volume **list of retired enlisted men**, 1885-1906, give date of last enlistment, location when retired, and date and place of death if the Marine died before July 1906. The entries are arranged chronologically by date of retirement.

Death registers of enlisted men consist of five volumes with overlapping dates, 1838-1942. Entries are arranged by time period, thereunder by initial letter of surname, and thereunder generally chronologically by date of death. To use the records, the researcher must know the approximate date of death of the subject being researched. Each entry shows name of Marine, rank, serial number (if any), date of enlistment or last reenlistment, and occasionally, regiment, and date, place, and cause of death.

6.3.4 Records of Officers and Enlisted Men

Muster rolls, 1798-1958, are arranged chronologically by month, and thereunder by post, station, ship detachment or other unit, except for periods during World War I and World War II, when they are arranged in two subseries: (1) posts and stations, and (2) mobile units. The volumes include indexes to the names of ships and stations. A muster roll generally shows name of ship or station and, for personnel, gives name, rank, date of enlistment or reenlistment, and if applicable, date of desertion or apprehension, sentence of court-martial (and the offense), injuries sustained or illness and type of treatment, and date of death or discharge. Depending on the date, the researcher must know the vessel on which the subject served, unit in which they served, or station.

The USMC muster rolls for 1798-1892 have been filmed on T1118, *Muster Rolls of the United States Marine Corps, 1798-1892*, 123 rolls. Some roll numbers are duplicated. Most volumes are indexed by the name of the vessel or station. The USMC muster rolls for 1893-1940 have been filmed on T977, *Muster Rolls of Officers and Enlisted Men of the U.S. Marine Corps, 1893-1940*, 461 rolls.

Certificate books of officers and enlisted contain certified statements of military service, showing such information as dates of service, appointments, enlistments and reenlistments, promotions, transfers, duty assignments, wounds, debts, troops commanded, desertions, discharges, and physical characteristics. The information was abstracted from other records of the Marine Corps about persons who served in the general period 1837-1911. Research in this series is laborious. It consists of 15 volumes of statements, and most of them are press copies. The statements are arranged chronologically by date of certification, and only a few of the volumes have name indexes.

Information about officers or enlisted personnel who were wounded or died in service with the U.S. Marine Corps, can be found in the **card list of casualties**. Each card generally shows name, rank, and military organization of a Marine; injury sustained or date and place of death; and often such additional information as date of birth and name and address of next of kin. Most of the lists consist of more than one part; that is, duplicate sets of cards are arranged more than one way. The most common arrangement is alphabetical by surname of Marine, but some sets are arranged by date of casualty, type of casualty (for example, killed in action, died of wounds, or died of disease), place of casualty, state of residence, and regiment. The subarrangement is often alphabetical in parts of lists where the primary arrangement is by type of casualty, geography, and name of Marine.

There are about twenty lists. The most comprehensive are of officers who died in service, 1776-1930, and enlisted who died in service, 1776-1930. Other lists are of casualties in the War of 1812; casualties in the Civil War; casualties in the Spanish-American War; casualties in the Philippine Islands, Samoa, and Puerto Rico, 1899-1901;

casualties in overseas expeditions, 1900-31, including the Boxer Rebellion and in Nicaragua, Veracruz, Haiti, and the Dominican Republic; overseas burials, 1898-1918; aviation casualties, 1918-33; casualties from explosions and earthquakes, 1924-37; and casualties from miscellaneous causes, 1889-1945.

Several of the lists relate to Marine Corps casualties during World War I. They include lists of officers wounded in France, enlisted personnel wounded in Europe, enlisted who died in Europe, Marine Corps personnel who died in the United States, and enlisted who suffered from shellshock.

An additional **register of deaths** in World War I consists of a single volume in two parts, one part for officers and one for enlisted. Entries in each part are arranged alphabetically by surname. Each entry gives the Marine's name, rank, company, regiment, cause of death, date and place of death, and name and address of next of kin.

Two Marine Corps mimeographed casualty lists for World War I in RG 127, Records of the U.S. Marine Corps, show names of officers and names of enlisted. Each part is arranged alphabetically by name of deceased. Entries include name, rank, and unit of deceased; date, place, and cause of death; and name, address, and relationship of next of kin. These two listings are preceded by statistical summaries of the number of officers and enlisted from each state who died overseas. Because a portion of the page of this summary is missing, there are no figures for enlisted casualties from Alabama through Louisiana.

For marine casualties, prisoners of war, and Marines missing in action for World War II and the Korean and Vietnam conflicts, *see* 6.2.5.

Information about **courts-martial** is found in four series in RG 127. Proceedings of general courts-martial for officers and enlisted personnel of the Marine Corps are dated 1816-52 and are arranged chronologically. Charges and specifications prepared by the Navy Department and the commandant of the Marine Corps against officers and enlisted of the Marine Corps are dated 1823-55 and are arranged chronologically. Orders for courts-martial and most sentences are found in orders issued and received, 1798-1866, and in orders and circulars issued by the commandant, 1805-60; both series are arranged chronologically. Therefore, the researcher must know the date of a particular court-martial to locate the records.

Court-martial records in Records of the Office of the Judge Advocate General (Navy), RG 125, relate also to officers and enlisted of the Marine Corps. The records include transcripts of proceedings of general courts-martial. A name index identifies the case file of a particular person and the records relating to a court of inquiry. Each dossier, when complete, contains the precept appointing the court; letters detailing or detaching its several members; a letter dissolving the court; charges and specifications; minutes of the court, consisting chiefly of a verbatim transcript of testimony; plea of the defendant (often printed);

TABLE 14
Selected Genealogical Research Aids: U.S. Navy and U.S. Marine Corps

Callahan, Edward W., ed. *List of Officers of the Navy of the United States and of the Marine Corps, From 1775 to 1900.* New York: L.R. Hamersly & Co., 1901. An alphabetical list of the names of officers of the Regular Navy and Marine Corps and of the acting or volunteer officers of the Civil War, with dates of appointment. Reprinted by Haskell House, 1969.

Bureau of Naval Personnel. *Register of Commissioned and Warrant Officers of the United States Navy and Marine Corps.* Washington: Government Printing Office. The best source of information about officers who served after 1900. This register has varied in title and frequency since it first appeared in 1798.

Smith, Charles R. *Marines in the Revolution.* Washington: History and Museum Division, Headquarters U.S. Marine Corps, 1975. Reproduces selected muster, pay, and prize rolls and contains brief biographies of Continental marine officers.

Office of Naval Records and Library. *Register of Officer Personnel, United States Navy and Marine Corps and Ships' Data, 1801-1807.* Washington: Navy Department, 1945. Gives the name and brief service record for each commissioned, warrant, and acting officer in the Navy and Marine Corps during the years of the Barbary Wars. Supplements Office of Naval Records and Library, *Naval Documents Related to the United States Wars With the Barbary Powers.* Washington: Navy Department. 1939-44.

Official Records of the Union and Confederate Navies in the War of the Rebellion: General Index. Washington: Navy Department, 1927. Consists in part of a personal name index to 30 volumes of transcripts of

official records. It was also published as 69th Cong., 1st sess., H. Doc. 113, serial 8603, and on roll 31 of NARA microfilm publication M275, *Official Records of the Union and Confederate Navies, 1861-1865,* 31 rolls.

Office of Naval Records and Library. *Register of Officers of the Confederate States Navy, 1861-65.* Washington: Navy Department, 1931. Identifies Confederate naval officers alphabetically by surname.

Register of Alumni, Graduates and Former Naval Cadets and Midshipmen. Annapolis: United States Naval Academy Alumni Association, 1995. Published since 1886 by the Alumni Association. Gives for each graduate the name, date of graduation, state of birth, highest rank at time of publication, and, where appropriate, date of retirement or death.

Hamersly, Lewis R. *The Records of Living Officers of the United States Navy and Marine Corps.* 7 editions. Philadelphia: J.B. Lippincott & Co., 1870, 1878, 1884, 1890, 1894, 1898, 1902.

Bureau of Navigation. *Navy Directory: Officers of the United States Navy and Marine Corps.* Washington: Navy Department, 1908-42.

Drury, Clifford Merrill, comp. *The History of the Chaplain Corps, United States Navy.* Vols. 3, 4, and 5. Washington: Bureau of Naval Personnel, 1949-60. Biographical sketches and service-record data about navy chaplains.

Medal of Honor, 1861-1949, The Navy. Washington: Bureau of Naval Personnel, 1950. Officers and enlisted men who received the Medal of Honor.

copies of correspondence introduced as part of the minutes; finding of the court, the sentence in case of a finding of guilty; endorsements of the Judge Advocate General (beginning in 1880), the Secretary of the Navy, and the President; and documents introduced in evidence and collected in an appendix, often designated by numbers or letters by which they are referred to in the minutes. Early Marine records are also reproduced on M273, *Records of General Courts-Martial and Courts of Inquiry of the Navy Department, 1799-1867*, mentioned in 6.2.5.

6.4 Confederate Navy and Marine Corps Records

Records of service in the Confederate Navy and Marine Corps consist of carded service records and carded hospital and prison records in the War Department Collection of Confederate Records, RG 109, and a few shipping articles, muster rolls, pay rolls, and subject files in the Naval Records Collection of the Office of Naval Records and Library, RG 45.

Naval and Marine Corps **service records**, which are known to be incomplete, consist of cards prepared by the U.S. War Department, probably in the late 19th century, referring to vessel papers, pay rolls, muster rolls, and other documents relating to service in the Confederate Navy and Marine Corps. Sometimes original documents relating solely to particular persons are filed with them. The records are in two series—one for naval personnel and one for Marines—and they are arranged alphabetically by surname in each series. The records show the name and rank of the sailor or Marine and sometimes lead to other information about their service. The records are available as M260, *Records Relating to Confederate Naval and Marine Personnel*, 7 rolls.

Hospital and prison records consist of cards on which the War Department, when it was compiling the military service records, abstracted information about naval and marine personnel from such sources as Union and Confederate hospital registers and prescription books, and from Union prison and parole rolls. Filed with these are original papers, primarily from prison records, that relate to individuals. Records are arranged alphabetically by name of sailor or Marine, with appropriate cross-references to other series. The records are also available on M260. The cards and papers show the name of the person and their ship or station, and such other information as date and place of capture, release, or parole; place of confinement; date, place, and cause of admission to a hospital; and date of discharge. References to the original records are included on the cards.

The few **shipping articles** for enlisted personnel in the Confederate Navy, 1861-65, are bound in one volume, which contains a typed index. A typical article shows the name, rating, signature, and date of enlistment.

The National Archives has some **muster rolls and pay rolls** of ships and shore establishments of the Confederate Navy. They are unindexed, but NARA staff members have prepared lists of vessels and shore establishments to facilitate their use. To use the records, the researcher must know where the subject of research was stationed. An entry in the rolls shows the name and rank of the naval serviceman or Marine.

Related muster rolls and pay rolls, as well as papers on such personnel-related topics as battle and accident casualties, admissions to medical facilities, courts-martial, heroic acts, commendations, and memorials, are found in the **Confederate Navy subject file**. These records are arranged according to a subject classification scheme, thereunder chronologically. It has been reproduced as M1091, *Subject File of the Confederate States Navy, 1861-1865*, 61 rolls.

6.5 Records of the U.S. Coast Guard

The U.S. Coast Guard (USCG), which operates on the high seas and navigable waters of the United States and its territorial possessions, functions as part of the Navy in time of war or when the President directs. The USCG was established in the Department of the Treasury in 1915 (38 Stat. 800), and was formed by merging the Revenue Cutter Service and the Life Saving Service. Functions of the Bureau of Lighthouses were added in 1939 when it was abolished. Records of the U.S. Coast Guard and of these three agencies make up RG 26, Records of the U.S. Coast Guard. The most valuable records for genealogical research in this record group are the **service records of the officers and crews**, which the USCG inherited from the three agencies. Unfortunately, the abundance of records overlapping in date makes searching for the record of a particular individual difficult.

Lighthouse keepers were nominated by Collectors of Customs until 1895 and thereafter by inspectors designated by the **Lighthouse Board**. They were placed under Civil Service in 1896. Correspondence concerning keepers and their assistants, 1821-1902, contains nominations of these officials, testimonials in their behalf, notifications of appointment, oaths of office, resignations, and other personnel records. The series is indexed. Another series of records about lighthouse keepers, 1853-1907, gives the name of the keeper, title, residence, and dates of employment. These records are difficult to search unless the researcher knows the district and light where a person was stationed.

Also available are lists, records of service, and notices of appointments for lighthouse keepers and other employees of the Lighthouse Bureau, such as the crews of vessels and tenders. When the Lighthouse Bureau was placed under the U.S. Coast Guard, a record was prepared of the proceedings for induction, 1939-40, giving detailed information about each employee of the Lighthouse Bureau at that time. The records list age, marital status, qualifications, and previous service.

Registers of Lighthouse Keepers, 1845-1912, were compiled chronologically. These 19 volumes have been reproduced on M1373, *Registers of Lighthouse Keepers, 1845-1912*, 6 rolls. The registers are filmed in geographic order by five regions: New England, New York through Virginia, North Carolina through Texas, Great Lakes, and West Coast, Alaska, and Hawaii. Indexes to each of the volumes are alphabetical by surname of keeper and/or name of lighthouse and were filmed in their entirety each time a volume or part of a volume was filmed. The registers cover keepers and assistant keepers. Register entries typically consist of the person's name; district and name of the light; date of appointment; date of resignation, discharge, or death; and sometimes annual salary.

Correspondence concerning keepers and assistant keepers, 1821-1902, is arranged alphabetically by surname. These letters may contain nominations of keepers and assistant keepers, with testimonials; lists of examination questions; notifications of appointments; oaths of office; requests for transfer; recommendations for promotion; complaints; petitions; reports of inspectors; and letters of resignation.

The **Revenue Cutter Service** (RCS) originated under an act of August 4, 1790 (1 Stat. 175). It was intended to enforce laws governing the collection of customs and tonnage duties. Records in RG 26 relating to officers of the RCS include **records of officer personnel**, 1791-1919, in 15 volumes arranged alphabetically by name of officer. Entries provide dates of service, citations to pertinent correspondence, and charges. Copies of commissions, 1791-1910, are in two series. One, for 1791-1848, is arranged chronologically as commissions were issued; the other, for 1815-1910, is arranged chronologically, thereunder alphabetically by surname of officer. The latter series, and a small volume covering the period 1850-60, also include applications for commissions.

Applications for appointment as cadet engineer, 1861-65, and other positions in the RCS, 1844-80, are also available. Ships' rosters, 1819-1904, provide names of officers on board the cutters; they are arranged alphabetically by name of vessel and thereunder chronologically.

Records relating to **enlisted crew members** of the RCS include muster rolls, payrolls, and shipping articles. In one series of muster rolls are unbound monthly reports, 1848-1910, arranged by name of vessel, thereunder chronologically. These are not indexed, so they can be searched only by name of vessel and the individual's approximate date of service. Muster rolls and pay rolls show the name and, when appropriate, signature or mark of each crew member. Entries in 160 volumes of **muster rolls,** 1833-1932, compiled for Revenue Cutter Service Headquarters, give for each crew member the name, rating, date and place of enlistment, place of birth, age, occupation, personal description, and number of days served during the reported month, along with notes if the individual was detached, transferred, or discharged or if they deserted or died

during the report period. The records are arranged alphabetically by name of vessel.

Shipping articles, 1863-1915, are bound in 32 volumes arranged alphabetically by name of vessel; the volumes are not indexed. Use of these records requires knowledge of the name of the ship and the approximate date of crewman's service. Information includes crew member's name, rating, wages, date and place of enlistment, place of birth, age, occupation, personal description, and signature or mark. Some dated 1907 and later give the name and address of the nearest relative or beneficiary.

The Life Saving Service was set up as a bureau of the Treasury Department in 1878 (20 Stat. 163), although cruisers and lifesaving stations to aid the shipwrecked had been previously authorized for several ports along the northeastern Atlantic coast. Employees of the service were station keepers and surfmen. The service was organized into 12 districts, expanded to 13 by 1915 when it was made a part of the U.S. Coast Guard.

Relevant records of the Life Saving Service include registers, service record cards, and disability correspondence. **Registers of station masters and surfmen**, 1878-1913, usually show name of employee, post office address, previous occupation, year of birth, year when employee would reach age 55, present age, any military service, state from which appointed, date of appointment, compensation, date discharged, and reason for leaving. The registers are bound volumes arranged by district and station. Two volumes are name indexes.

Service record cards, 1900-14, show name of employee, legal residence, place of birth, place and status of employment, changes of status, and salary. The cards are arranged alphabetically.

Records of Life Saving Service employees who were injured on the job are documented in the **disability correspondence**, 1878-1910, which is arranged by district, thereunder alphabetically by name of employee.

Articles of engagement for surfmen, 1878-1914, are arranged chronologically, thereunder by district. The article shows a list of surfmen, terms of engagement, and compensation. They may include reports of changes in crew, along with the reason for the change, and biographical information on new crew members. Medical inspection reports providing physical descriptions of the surfmen examined are frequently included.

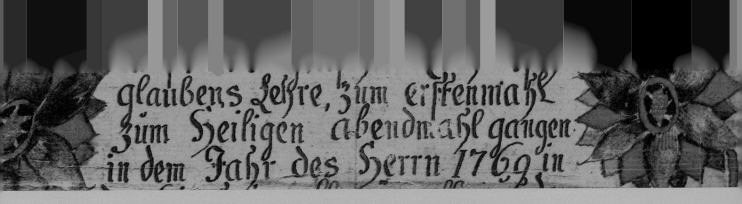

CHAPTER 7   *Pension Records*

7.1   *Introduction*

7.2   *Pension Application Files*

7.2.1   *Revolutionary War*

7.2.2   *Old Wars*

7.2.3   *War of 1812*

7.2.4   *Indian Wars*

7.2.5   *Mexican War*

7.2.6   *Civil War and Later*

7.3   *Other Records*

CHAPTER 7

Pension Records

7.1 Introduction

For more than a century before the Revolutionary War, British colonies in North America provided pensions for disabled soldiers and sailors. During and after the Revolutionary War, the U.S. Government continued this practice and expanded it to include other kinds of pensions. Because the applications for pensions by veterans and their dependents often contain personal and family information, the pension records have long been a primary source for genealogical research.

The National Archives has pension applications and records of pension payments for veterans, their widows, and other heirs. They are based on service in the armed forces of the United States between 1775 and 1916, but not duty in the service of the Confederate States of America, 1861–65. In a few cases, the Federal Government assumed responsibility for pensions based on service in state militia and other state military organizations, and records of these pensions are also in the National Archives. Most pension records are in Records of the Veterans Administration, Record Group (RG) 15.

Three principal types of pensions were provided to servicemen and their dependents by the Federal Government. Disability or invalid pensions were awarded to servicemen for physical disabilities incurred in the line of duty; service pensions were awarded to veterans who served for specified periods of time; and widows' pensions were awarded to women and children whose husbands or fathers had served in war for specified periods of time or had been killed.

Applications for pensions were made under numerous public and private acts of Congress. Public acts, under which the majority of pensions were authorized, encompassed large classes of veterans or their dependents who met common eligibility requirements. Private acts concerned specific individuals whose special services or circumstances merited consideration but who could not be awarded pensions under existing public acts.

Application procedures followed by would-be pensioners varied according to the act under which benefits were sought. Generally, the process required applicants to appear before a court of record in the state of their residence to describe under oath the service for which a pension was claimed. Widows of veterans were required to provide information concerning the date and place of their marriage. The application statement, or declaration, as it was usually called, with such supporting papers as property schedules, marriage records, and affidavits of witnesses, was certified by the court and forwarded to the official, usually the Secretary of War or the Commissioner of Pensions, responsible for administering the specific act under which the claim was being made. Names of applicants who were eligible were placed on the pension list. Payments were usually made semiannually through pension agents of the Federal Government in the states. Applicants who were rejected under the terms of an early pension act often reapplied for benefits under later, more liberal laws.

7.2 Pension Application Files

Initially, documents relating to an individual claim for a pension were folded and placed in an annotated jacket. Later these documents were flattened and filed with the jackets in large envelopes. The jacket, now obsolete as a container, was kept because of the annotations on it. The envelopes with their contents are called pension application files.

The number and nature of documents in a file vary considerably. A single claim file consists of the application of the claimant, supporting documents of identity and service, and evidence of the action taken by the Government on the claim. When two or more claims relate to the service of the same veteran in the same war, the claims are filed together. For example, a veteran might apply for a pension, citing his military service; after his death, his widow might apply for a pension on the basis of the same service. A file with a widow's application normally contains more genealogical information than a veteran's file.

Pension applications submitted by widows of veterans are filed under the name of the veteran on whose service the application is based. If the widow remarried, there are "former widow" and "remarried widow" cross-reference cards showing the state or organization in which her deceased first husband served, his name, and the surname his widow acquired upon remarriage. These cards are interfiled according to the widow's latest surname, but the papers will be found under the name of the veteran. Cross-reference cards account for variations in spelling of a veteran's name.

The pension files in the National Archives number many millions. They are divided into the following major series: Revolutionary War, Old Wars, War of 1812, Indian wars, Mexican War, and Civil War and later. The records in each series are arranged alphabetically by name of veteran, except those in the Civil War and later series, which are arranged numerically by application, certificate, or file number. All series of pension application files have alphabetical name indexes.

The information below is typical of what may be found in applications for pensions or bounty land based on a veteran's service at any period:

A. Veteran's application

1. Name
2. Rank
3. Military unit
4. Period of service
5. Residence
6. Birthplace
7. Date of birth or age
8. Property (when claims were made on basis of need)

B. Widow's application

1. Most of the above
2. Her name
3. Her age
4. Residence
5. Maiden name
6. Marriage date and place
7. Husband's death, date and place

C. Children's or heirs' applications

1. All of the above
2. Heirs' names
3. Dates and places of their births
4. Residence
5. Date of their mother's death

Application files often include supporting documents such as discharge papers, affidavits and depositions of witnesses, narratives of events during service (to prove that the veteran had served at a particular time even though he might not have documentary evidence), marriage certificates, birth records, death certificates, pages from family Bibles, and other papers.

In addition to information about individual applicants, historical information pertaining to the organization of military units, movement of troops, details of battles and campaigns, and activities of individuals may also be obtained from application statements of veterans, from affidavits of witnesses, and from the muster rolls, diaries, orders, or orderly books that were occasionally submitted as proofs of service, if they had not been sent by the Bureau of Pensions to other Government departments. Naval and privateer operations are documented by applications, affidavits, and in some files, orders based on service at sea. A few files contain letters written to or by soldiers and sailors during the Revolutionary War that give firsthand accounts of land and sea engagements and civil events and conditions. Furloughs, passes, pay receipts, enlistment papers, commissions, warrants, and other original records of the period from 1775 to 1783 are also in some of the files.

The rest of this chapter contains descriptions of pension application records for the veterans and widows of particular wars and other periods of military service. *Only exceptions to the typical list will be noted.*

Copies of pension application files can be ordered through the mail by using a National Archives Trust Fund form, which may be obtained from the Customer Service Center, National Archives and Records Administration, Room 406, 700 Pennsylvania Ave., NW, Washington, DC 20408-0001. Copies of this form can also be requested by email at *inquire@nara.gov.*

7.2.1 Revolutionary War

During the Revolutionary War, Congress used pension legislation and the promise of free land to encourage enlistment and the acceptance of commissions. After the war, such legislation constituted a reward for service already

rendered. As years passed and the number of Revolutionary War veterans, widows, and their heirs decreased, pensions became increasingly generous, and qualifications for pensions increasingly less stringent. Most Revolutionary War pension application files are in envelopes containing applications and other records pertaining to claims for pensions or bounty land warrants. They may also appear in the form of summary cards with information about claimants for whom no original application papers exist or cross-reference cards to envelopes and summary cards.

A file can therefore be a single card or an envelope containing many pages of records. Each file pertains to one or more claims by one or more persons for pensions or bounty land warrants, based on the participation of one individual in the Revolution, along with an occasional file relating to claims based on later service.

The records are arranged in alphabetical order by surname of the veteran. When two or more veterans have the same surname and given name, the further arrangement of the files based on their service is generally alphabetical by state or organization in which a veteran served, or by the word "Continental," "Navy," or some other designation placed in the heading of some files above or before the name of a state. Within each file the records are unarranged.

All of the contents of all of the files are reproduced on M804, *Revolutionary War Pension and Bounty-Land-Warrant Application Files*, 2,670 rolls, a publication cited several times in this chapter. An introduction to this microfilm publication is reproduced on each roll and is also printed in the accompanying descriptive pamphlet. This introduction contains an excellent explanation of the eligibility requirements of the various resolutions and acts of Congress, 1776–1878, establishing pensions for Revolutionary War service. Also explained are the symbols and numbers on the envelopes. Understanding the symbols is not essential to use the records, however, because the files are now arranged in alphabetical order.

A second microfilm publication, M805, Selected Records From Revolutionary War Pension and Bounty-Land-Warrant Application Files, 898 rolls, reproduces all records from envelope files containing up to 10 pages of records, but only significant genealogical documents from larger files are included.

A fire in the War Department in 1800 destroyed Revolutionary War pension applications and related papers submitted before that date. Consequently, if a veteran applied for a disability or invalid pension before 1800, the envelope of his file will show his name, the state or organization in which he served, and a file symbol. In place of the missing papers, most of the files contain one or more small cards giving such information as rank, unit, date of enlistment, nature of disability, residence, and amount of pension. The information was transcribed by the Bureau of Pensions from *American State Papers, Claims* (Washington: Gales and Seaton, 1834). This volume contains transcriptions of the eight War Department

Baptismal fraktur of Henry Muskenug, submitted as documentation as part of a pension application. Revolutionary War Pension and Bounty Land Warrant Application Files. Records of the Veterans Administration, RG 15. National Archives Microfilm Publication M804.

pension reports based on original applications and submitted to Congress during the period 1792–95. The volume is indexed. The reports themselves are in Records of the U.S. House of Representatives, RG 233, and Records of the U.S. Senate, RG 46. The 1792 report is in the second volume of a House publication entitled "Reports War Department 1st Cong. 3rd Sess., to 2nd Cong. 2nd Sess." The seven reports for 1794 and 1795 are in a Senate volume entitled *War Office Returns of Claims to Invalid Pensions.* Each report identifies many applicants for invalid pensions. Entries are arranged by date of report, thereunder by state, and thereunder by name of applicant.

Similar reports, 1794–96, were retained by the War Department and are now among the Records of the Office of the Secretary of War, RG 107. They constitute pages 526–612 of a War Department record book, identified on the backstrip as "War Office Letter Book 1791–97." The entries duplicate many entries in the reports submitted to Congress, but some entries are unique. The reports are reproduced as part of M1062, *Correspondence of the War Department Relating to Indian Affairs, Military Pensions, and Fortifications, 1791–1797,* 1 roll.

The 1796 reports were transcribed and printed in "Recently Discovered Records Relating to Revolutionary War Veterans Who Applied for Pensions Under the Act of 1792," *National Genealogical Society Quarterly* 46 (March 1958): 8–13 and (June 1958): 73–78.

Most pension rolls published by the Federal Government before the Civil War were printed only in the Congressional Serial Set. In 1817 the War Department published a list of approximately 1,000 invalid pensions, providing name, state, rank, and annual allowance of each pensioner. The same volume of the Congressional Serial Set includes a list of 300 half-pay pensions derived from land relinquishments showing the number of the pension certificate, names of the guardians of heirs of deceased soldiers, names of original claimants, rank, annual allowance, and state (serial 6-documents 34, 35). In 1818 a list of 7,300 invalid pensioners was issued with similar information (serial 3-170). In 1820 the War Department issued an extensive list of over 15,000 American Revolutionary pensioners, showing name, rank and line (serial 34-55). Other pension lists printed before the Civil War in the Congressional Serial Set are as follows:

1823 (74-43)
1828 (171-24 and 185-68)
1831 (208-86 and 219-120)
1835 (249, 250, 251-514)
1849 (579-74)
1857 (959-119)

The 1835 report was issued to replace papers and applications for invalid pensions submitted after 1800 that were destroyed in another War Department fire in 1814. The transcribing was not systematic but was apparently done only to answer inquiries about specific veterans. The report, however, does contain names appearing on annual lists of invalid pensioners prepared by the states in response to a 1785 resolution of the Congress of the Confederation. The volumes are not indexed.

Information from the files and from other sources about the Virginia military and naval forces has been published in Gaius Marcus Brumbaugh's *Revolutionary War Records: Virginia* (Washington, DC, and Lancaster, PA: Lancaster Press, 1936); reprinted by the Genealogical Publishing Co., Baltimore, 1967.

In addition, cross-reference slips in the files published on M804 describe those diaries, account books, muster rolls, returns, and other records of historical value that were transferred to the Library of Congress and other bureaus of the War Department between 1894 and 1913.

While the U.S. Congress was enacting laws granting increasingly generous pensions to Revolutionary War soldiers and veterans, the states were also passing legislation to encourage or reward military service. In May 1779 the Virginia General Assembly authorized the payment of half pay for life to the state's naval officers and militia officer who would serve for the rest of the war in state units within the state's borders or in the Continental Army. After the cessation of hostilities, Virginia was unable to satisfy all claims brought and sought to have the U.S. Government assume the obligation, stating that the cession to the United States of large tracts of Virginia land northwest of the Ohio River had reduced the state's expected revenues. A Federal act of 1832 directed the Secretary of the Treasury to reimburse the state of Virginia for half pay pension payment made to officers of the Virginia State Navy and certain designated units of the Virginia Line. The secretary was further to assume any additional pension payments due officers in these units.

The pension records reproduced on M804 include cross-references to these **Virginia half pay files.** The files themselves have been reproduced on M910, Virginia Half Pay and Other Related Revolutionary War Pension Application Files, 18 rolls.

Final payment vouchers in the Records of the Accounting Officers of the Department of the Treasury, RG 217, are another source of genealogical data about Revolutionary War pensioners. A final payment voucher is the record of the payment made to the heirs after the pensioner's death. If the heirs did not file for the money that was due the pensioner from the time of the last payment until the time of death, there is no final payment, only a last payment. Vouchers for both last and final payments were filed among the pension agents' accounts where they were difficult to find, so the National Archives staff removed some 55,000 of them from the pension agents accounts and arranged them by state, thereunder alphabetically by the surname of pensioner. An alphabetical index was also prepared.

Vouchers for Delaware and Georgia have been microfilmed as M2079, *Final Revolutionary War Pension*

Payment Vouchers: Delaware, 1 roll, and M1746, *Final Revolutionary War Pension Payment Vouchers: Georgia,* 6 rolls.

The name of every Revolutionary War veteran listed in the registers of payments to U.S. pensioners, available on microfilm as T718, *Ledgers of Payments, 1818-1872, to U.S. Pensioners Under Acts of 1818 Through 1858, From Records of the Office of the Third Auditor of the Treasury,* 23 rolls, was placed on a card along with location of the pension agent's office, act authorizing payment, date of pensioner's death, and date of either the last or final payment. Cards for veterans whose vouchers were located were annotated with an asterisk. The same procedure was followed for widows and invalid pensioners, if the ledgers indicated that a final payment had been made after their deaths.

These cards and vouchers are not available to researchers. The National Archives staff will search the index cards and the segregated vouchers. If the voucher requested by a researcher (in person or by letter) is not among these files, no further search will be made unless the researcher has examined microfilm publication T718 and found evidence that a final payment was made. In this case, the researcher must furnish the name of the pensioner, the act under which the pension was paid, date of death, and date of final payment. Final payment vouchers of pensioners paid by agencies in Alabama, Arkansas, California, and some of those paid by Connecticut agencies were consolidated with the related Revolutionary War pension application files.

An alphabetical name index to the Revolutionary War pension application files has been published as *Index Revolutionary War Pension Applications in the National Archives,* revised edition, NGS Special Publication 40 (Washington: National Genealogical Society, 1976). The index shows the name of the veteran; state from which they served, except for service in the naval forces; name of the widow, if appropriate; and pension application file number and bounty land warrant, if appropriate. Other published works dealing with Revolutionary War pensions are listed in Table 6 (*see* Chapter 5).

Using available pension records of veterans of the Revolutionary War, interviews, and an early camera, Reverend E.B. Hilliard produced a book, *The Last Men of the Revolution* (Hartford, CT: N.A. and R.A. Moore, 1864), containing a brief biography and a photograph of each surviving veteran; reprinted by Barre (MA) Publishers in 1968.

7.2.2 Old Wars

The "Old Wars" series of pension application files relates chiefly to claims based on death or disability incurred in service in the regular forces between the end of the Revolutionary War in 1783 and the outbreak of the Civil War in 1861. The claims concern service in the Regular Army, Navy, or Marine Corps during the War of 1812, Mexican War, Indian wars, and in some cases the Civil War. A few

Old Wars pension application files have been consolidated with the files in the separate series for the War of 1812, Mexican War, Indian wars, and Civil War.

The files in the Old Wars series are arranged alphabetically by name of veteran. The alphabetical *Old War Index to Pension Files, 1815-1926,* T316, 7 rolls, shows the name of the veteran; name and class of dependent, if any; service unit; application, file, and certificate number; and state from which the claim was made. Cross-references to files in other series are included when appropriate.

Related records, the YI series, once a part of the records of the Navy Department, pertain to naval and marine personnel. This alphabetical file contains papers maintained by pension agents in the field, 1815-37, and correspondence between the Navy Department and the Bureau of Pensions concerning pension claims, 1880-91.

7.2.3 War of 1812

The War of 1812 series of pension application records relates to claims based on service performed between 1812 and 1815. The records chiefly concern pensions granted by acts of 1871 (16 Stat. 411) and 1878 (20 Stat. 27). The former provided pensions to veterans who had been cited by Congress for specific service if they did not later support the Confederate cause during the Civil War, and to many widows of such veterans if the marriage had taken place before the treaty of peace in 1815. The 1878 act provided for pensions to veterans who had served 14 days in any engagement and to widows of such veterans.

Interfiled or consolidated with the files in the series are some War of 1812 pension application files that previously formed a part of the Old Wars pension series. Likewise interfiled or consolidated with the files in this series are some War of 1812 bounty land warrant application files from the post-Revolutionary War series described in 8.2.2.

A file includes such documents as a veteran's or widow's application or declaration for pension, a report from the Third Auditor of the Treasury Department containing a summary of the veteran's service record, and a statement showing action on the claim.

The files in the War of 1812 series are arranged alphabetically by name of veteran. The alphabetical name index is available as M313, *Index to War of 1812 Pension Application Files,* 102 rolls. Each frame shows the face side of a jacket-envelope containing relevant documents. Given are the name of a veteran; name of the widow, if any; service data; pension application and certificate numbers; and/or a bounty land warrant application number, if any. Certain pension application files in the War of 1812 series can be located through the use of the Remarried Widows Index, which is available on microfilm as M1784, *Index to Pension Application Files of Remarried Widows Based on Service in the War of 1812, Indian Wars, Mexican War, and Regular Army Before 1861,* 1 roll.

7.2.4 Indian Wars

The Indian wars series of pension application records relates to service performed in the Indian campaigns between 1817 and 1898. Consolidated with this series are some Indian wars pension application files that were formerly filed in the Old Wars series.

In addition to the usual types of records found in pension applications, the Indian wars records contain a family questionnaire and, for the veteran, a personal history questionnaire. The family questionnaire shows the maiden name of the wife; date and place of the marriage of the couple and the name of the person who performed the ceremony; name of a former wife, if any, and date and place of her death or divorce; and names and dates of birth of living children.

The files are arranged alphabetically by name of veteran. An alphabetical name index is reproduced on T318, *Index to Indian Wars Pension Files, 1892-1926*, 12 rolls. Entries in this index show name of the veteran; name and class of dependent, if any; service data; and application number and, for an approved claim, pension certificate number and state from which the claim was made.

For pension application files concerning men who were disabled or killed in Indian wars and in whose behalf no service claims were made, *see* the records in the Old Wars series. For pension applications relating to persons who served in an Indian campaign during the War of 1812, Mexican War, or Civil War, *see* the pension indexes relating to claims based on service in that war.

7.2.5 Mexican War

The Mexican War series of pension application records relates to claims based on service performed in 1846-48. An act of Congress approved January 29, 1887 (24 Stat. 371), provided pensions for veterans who had served 60 days or for their unremarried widows.

Consolidated with this series are some pension application files, formerly filed in the Old Wars series, that relate to men who were disabled or killed in the Mexican War. Like pension applications for veterans of the Indian wars, the Mexican War pension files contain a family questionnaire.

The files are arranged alphabetically by name of veteran. An alphabetical name index is on T317, *Index to Mexican War Pension Files, 1887-1926*, 14 rolls. Entries in this index show name of the veteran; name and class of dependent, if any; service data; and application number and, for an approved claim, pension certificate number and state from which the claim was made. Certain pension application files in the Mexican War series can be located through the Remarried Widows Index on M1784, mentioned above.

Pension records for members of the Mormon Battalion have been reproduced on T1196, *Selected Pension Application Files Relating to the Mormon Battalion, Mexican War, 1846-1848*, 21 rolls.

For pension application files concerning men who were disabled or killed in the Mexican War and in whose behalf no service claims were made, *see* the records in the Old Wars series.

7.2.6 Civil War and Later

The Civil War and later series of pension application file relates chiefly to army, navy, and marine service performed between 1861 and 1916. Excluded, however, are records of service in Confederate forces, certain records relating to service in the Indian wars, and records of pensioners still on the rolls in 1934, the date of termination of claims in this series. Most of the records relate to Civil War service; some relate to earlier service by a Civil War veteran; and others relate to service in the Spanish-American War, the Philippine Insurrection, the Boxer Rebellion, and the regular establishment. A few files relating to naval service of men who were killed or disabled during the Civil War are interfiled with the Old Wars series of pension application files. For information about Confederate pensions, write the appropriate archival depository of the state for which service was rendered or in which the veteran lived after the war.

Five acts passed during the period 1862-1907 provided pensions based on Civil War service, each extending benefits on more liberal terms. The information in the files varies depending on the act under which the pension was applied for, the number of years the veteran survived after the war, and whether or not they were survived by a widow or other dependent.

The number and type of documents in the Civil War and later series vary greatly from file to file. Documents of the greatest genealogical interest include the declaration of the veteran, declaration of the widow, statement of service from the War or Navy Department, personal history questionnaire, family questionnaire, and documents relating to the termination of pensions.

The records are arranged numerically by application, certificate, or file number. Index cards, arranged alphabetically by surname of veteran, have been microfilmed as T288, *General Index to Pension Files, 1861-1934*, 544 rolls. A card shows the name of the veteran, name and class of dependent, if any; service data; application number or file number; and, for an approved claim, certificate number or file number and state from which the claim was filed. Also available on microfilm is M1785, *Index to Pension Application Files of Remarried Widows Based on Service in the Civil War and Later Wars and in the Regular Army After the Civil War*, 7 rolls.

Because the alphabetical index often shows several veterans with the same name, it may be difficult to identify the file desired without time-consuming research. This difficulty can be resolved if the researcher knows the military or naval unit the veteran served in or the given name of the veteran's widow. It is also helpful to know, in addition, the residence or date of birth of the veteran. Such

DECLARATION FOR WIDOW'S PENSION
ACT OF APRIL 19, 1908—AMENDED BY ACT OF SEPTEMBER 8, 1916, AND ACT OF MAY 1, 1920

State of _Minnesota_, County of _Otter Tail_, ss:

On this _3_ day of _June_, 19_22_, personally appeared before me, a _Notary Public_ within and for the County and State aforesaid, _Luella E._ Shaw who, being duly sworn by me according to law, declares that she is _66_ years of age and that she was born _Sept 10_, 1855, at _New York State_.

That she is the widow of _Darius N. Shaw_, who enlisted _Oct 12_, 1861, at _Lansing, Minn_, under the name of _Darius N. Shaw_, as a _Privat_ (Rank) in Company _"E" 4th Regiment, Minnesota_.

(Here state company and regiment, if in the Army; or vessels, if in the Navy.)

and was honorably discharged _Oct 15_, 1862, having served ninety days or more or was discharged for or died in service of a disability incurred in the service and in the line of duty during the Civil War.

That he also served _as Privat in Company "B" 2nd Regiment of Minnesota Calvalry and was honorbly discharged on_

(Here give a complete statement of all other military, naval, or coast guard service, if any, at whatever time rendered.)

Dec 7, 1865. That she was married to said soldier (or sailor) _August 4_, 1891, under the name of _Luella E. Taylor_, at _Grant Forks, N. Dak._, by _Alex McGregor, Past. M. E. Chur_ that she had _____ been previously married; that he had _____ been previously married, _to Milton W. Taylor, + was divorced   and Darius N. Shaw had previous married Sylvia Wood and that she died Jan 7, 1891_

(Here state all prior marriages of either, and give the names and dates and places of death or divorce of all former consorts.)

and that neither she nor said soldier (or sailor) was ever married otherwise than as stated above.

(If any former husband rendered military or naval service, here describe same and give number of any pension claim based thereon.)

That said soldier (or sailor) died _May 2d_, 19_22_, at _Ottertail Minn_; that she was _not_ divorced from him; and that she has _not_ remarried since his death.

That the following are the ONLY children of the soldier (or sailor) under sixteen years of age NOW living, namely:

None, born _____, 1___, at _None_
_____, born _____, 1___, at _____
_____, born _____, 1___, at _____
_____, born _____, 1___, at _____
_____, born _____, 1___, at _____

That the above-named child_____ of the soldier (or sailor) {is} {are} _____ now receiving a pension, and that such child _____ {is a} {are} member_____ of her family and _____ cared for by her.

That she has _Not_ heretofore applied for pension, the number of her former claim being _____; that said soldier (or sailor) was _____ a pensioner, the number of his pension certificate being _289563_

That she makes this declaration for the purpose of being placed on the pension roll of the United States under the provisions of the ACT OF APRIL 19, 1908, as amended by the ACT OF SEPT. 8, 1916, and ACT OF MAY 1, 1920.

She hereby appoints M. Elliott Waggaman & Co. (De Lapointe Rice and M. Elliott Waggaman), Washington, D. C., her true and lawful attorneys.

(1) _G. B. Schult_ (Signature of first witness.)
Ottertail, Minn (Address of first witness.)
(2) _N. G. Schulz_ (Signature of second witness.)
Ottertail, Minn (Address of second witness.)

Luella E. Shaw (Claimant's signature in full.)
Ottertail (Claimant's address in full.)
Minn

Subscribed and sworn to before me this _3_ day of _June_, 19_22_, and I hereby certify that the contents of the above declaration were fully made known and explained to the applicant before swearing, including the words _____ erased, and the words _____ added; and that I have no interest, direct or indirect, in the prosecution of this claim.

H. H. Dudley (Signature)

(SEAL.) Notary Public, Ottertail Co. Minn.
My Commission Expires Jan. 24, 1925.
(Official character.)

information appears on the award cards described below in 7.3.

Approximately 20,000 approved pension applications of widows and other dependents of U.S. Navy veterans who served between 1861 and 1910 are reproduced on microfiche publication M1279, *Case Files of Approved Pension Applications of Widows and Other Dependents of Civil War and Later Navy Veterans ("Navy Widows' Certificates"), 1861-1910*, ca. 40,000 microfiche.

About 7,000 rejected applications make up a separate publication, M1274, *Case Files of Disapproved Pension Applications of Widows and Other Dependents of Civil War and Later Navy Veterans ("Navy Widows' Originals"), 1861-1910*, ca. 8,500 microfiche. Also available is M1391, *Lists of Navy Veterans for Whom There are Navy Widows' and Other Dependents' Disapproved Pension Files ("Navy Widows' Originals"), 1861-1910*, 15 microfiche.

Other index cards known as the **organization index** have been microfilmed as T289, *Organization Index to Pension Files of Veterans Who Served Between 1861 and 1900*, 765 rolls. These index cards contain entries for men in army organizations in service chiefly between 1861 and 1917. The cards are arranged alphabetically by state, thereunder by arm of service (infantry, cavalry, artillery), thereunder numerically by regiment, thereunder alphabetically by company, and thereunder alphabetically by the veteran's surname. The informational content and format of the organization index cards is virtually the same as that of the alphabetical index described above.

7.3 Other Records

In addition to pension application files, certain other related records contain material for genealogical research. Documentation of pension payments appears in two record groups. In Records of the Veterans Administration, RG 15, are Pension Office record books of **payments to invalid pensioners**, 1801-15, and to other Revolutionary War pensioners; **field record books**, 1805-1912; and **award cards**, 1907-33. In the Records of the Accounting Officers of the Department of the Treasury, RG 217, are **Treasury Department pension payment vouchers** for pensioners, including naval and privateer pensioners. The segregated **last and final payment vouchers** of Revolutionary War pensions were discussed above in 7.2.1.

Because they are not arranged by name of pensioner, pension payment records are difficult to use and in most cases are consulted only as a last resort, when other series have not yielded the information sought.

Pension Office record books include one volume for payments to invalid pensioners labeled "Revolutionary War and Acts of Military Establishment, Invalid Pensioners Payments, March 1801 through September 1815," microfilmed as M1786, *Record of Invalid Pension Payments to Veterans of the Revolutionary War and the Regular Army and Navy, March 1801-September 1815*, 1 roll.

Many of the pensioners were Revolutionary War veterans whose papers were presumably destroyed in the War Department fires of 1800 and 1814. The entries, which record semiannual payments, are arranged by state, thereunder alphabetically by initial letter of surname. An entry shows name and rank of pensioner, state in which payment was made, and amount paid in March and September of each year. If the pensioner died or moved to another state during the period of the records, the fact is indicated, and in some cases the date of death is shown.

Pension Office records of payments to other Revolutionary War pensioners pursuant to acts of Congress approved between 1818 and 1853 are in unnumbered volumes. They cover pensioners in states or territories as follows: Maine; New York (acts of 1818-32); New York (acts of 1836-53); Rhode Island, New Jersey, Delaware, District of Columbia, and Nebraska; Virginia and Tennessee; Kentucky, Missouri, and Mississippi; Massachusetts (part); Massachusetts (part), and Ohio; Pennsylvania, Maryland, and Illinois; New Hampshire and Indiana; Connecticut, Vermont, and Georgia; North Carolina, South Carolina, Louisiana, Alabama, and Michigan; and Arkansas, Florida, Wisconsin, Iowa, Texas, California, Minnesota, and Oregon.

Searches should be made in the volume for the state or territory where the veteran or widow lived while receiving the pension. Entries are arranged by state or territory of residence of the pensioner, thereunder by date of the act under which the pension was paid, and thereunder alphabetically by initial letter of the surname of the pensioner. An entry shows name of the agency through which payment was made, name of pensioner, and amount of pension. Many entries also show the date of pensioner's death.

Pension Office **field record books** document the periodic payment of pensions, 1805-1912. The volumes are arranged alphabetically by name of the city in which the last pension agency having jurisdiction over a specific area was located.

Entries show for each pensioner the date of the payments made; sometimes name of county of residence or post office address of the pensioner; date the pension was discontinued, if appropriate; and sometimes the date of death or of remarriage of the widow. To use these records, it is necessary to obtain from the related pension application file the certificate number and name of the agency through which payment was last made.

A card index to these volumes is arranged alphabetically by name of the city in which the pension agency was located, thereunder by class of pensioner. The cards show city, class of pensioner, and volume designation. Sometimes the date of the act under which the pension payment was made also appears on the card. The researcher must know the city where the pension agency served the veteran.

Pension Office **award cards** record payments to pensioners on the rolls, 1907-33, except for World War I pensioners. Arranged alphabetically by surname of pensioner, the cards were microfilmed as M850, *Veterans Administration Pension Payment Cards, 1907-1933*, 2,539 rolls. Each card shows name of pensioner, military unit, date of the act and certificate or file number under which payment was made, and date the pension began. Some cards show place of residence and date of death of a pensioner, names of the pension agencies from which or to which jurisdiction was transferred, and name of widow or other recipient of death benefits. The cards are sometimes useful in identifying Civil War or other pension application files that cannot be identified from the microfilmed indexes.

Treasury Department **pension payment volumes** record semiannual payments from 1819 to 1871. As mentioned earlier in this chapter, these volumes have been microfilmed on the 23 rolls of T718, *Ledgers of Payments, 1818-1872, to U.S. Pensioners Under Acts of 1818 Through 1858, From Records of the Office of the Third Auditor of the Treasury*. The entries are arranged by act of Congress under which payment was made, thereunder by name of pension agency. Pensioners' names appear in rough alphabetical order by initial letter of surname. Following each name is a record of payments made to the pensioner. Each volume contains a record of payments made for a specific time period. Succeeding payments are in the next volume. Some entries terminate abruptly in 1820, because a number of pensioners who applied for pensions under the 1818 act were dropped from the rolls. Other entries terminate because pensioners died or failed to claim payments.

An entry shows name of pensioner, name of veteran (if different), name of pension agency through which payment was made, and quarter and year of last payment to the pensioner. When an heir or legal representative claimed an unpaid balance due the pensioner at the time of death, the dates of the pensioner's death and of the final payment made to the family or heirs are given.

To locate an entry, the following information should be obtained from the pensioner's pension application file: name of the veteran and, if the pensioner was the widow, name of the widow; date of the latest act of Congress under which payment was authorized; name of last pension agency through which payment was made; and amount of the periodic pension payment. A typescript "Key to the Pension Payment Volumes Relating to Revolutionary War Pensioners," available at the National Archives Building, identifies the volumes and pages containing entries relating to payments made by a specific pension agency under the appropriate act.

Most vouchers for last and final payments for Revolutionary War pensions have been placed in the separate series described in 7.2.1, but, as stated earlier, some vouchers for last and final payments to veterans of other wars remain interfiled in large series of vouchers arranged alphabetically by name of state, thereunder by name of pension agency, thereunder by quarter year of payment,

thereunder by date of act under which payment was made, and thereunder numerically or alphabetically by surname.

Final payment vouchers show the date and place of death of the pensioner and names of the heirs. These vouchers usually exist only if the date of death of the pensioner appears in one of the pension payment volumes described above. Last payment records indicate the date the pensioner was last paid. Other Treasury Department **records of payment to naval pensioners** concern men who were disabled as a result of service with the Navy or Marine Corps or as privateers, chiefly between 1798 and 1865, and the widows of men who died in such service. Related pension application files are, for the most part, in the Old Wars series or the Civil War and later series of the pension application files.

Three pension payment volumes cover the periods 1815-38, 1838-63, and 1846-73 (primarily 1848-66). Entries in the volumes are arranged by state, thereunder in rough alphabetical order by initial letter of the pensioner's surname. An entry shows name of pensioner, rank of veteran, date the pension began, amount of the monthly allowance and the quarterly or semiannual dates of payment, and, in some instances, name of the vessel on which the veteran was injured or the date of death.

Finally, the Federal Government has published several **lists of pensioners**. A five-volume list of persons on the pension roll in 1883, giving name of pensioner, reason for pension, post office address, rate of pension per month, and date of original allowance, is available in both the departmental set of Pension Bureau publications (I24.6:883) and the Serial Set (serials 2078-2082). All of this information is arranged by state, thereunder alphabetically by county and post office. Names and addresses of U.S. pensioners in Canada (I24.6:899/1) and other foreign countries in 1899 (I24:6:899/2), along with their class, service, rate of allowance, type of disability, and number of certificate, can also be found in the departmental publications. John G. Ames provided a list of approximately 2,300 names of pensioners in the *Index to Publications of the U.S. Government 1881-1893*, vol. 2: 1036-59 (serial 4746).

8.1 Introduction

A bounty land warrant provided the right to free land on the public domain. In 1776, during the Revolutionary War, the Continental Congress promised free land to soldiers as an inducement to enter and remain in military service. For that conflict and later wars in which the United States was involved, the Federal Government issued bounty land warrants during the period 1788–1855. These were given to veterans as compensation for military service, or to their heirs or assignees. However, most veteran recipients of these warrants did not use them to settle on the public domain; instead they assigned or sold their warrants.

Congress greatly increased bounty land benefits through the acts of 1847 (9 Stat. 125), 1850 (9 Stat. 520), 1852 (10 Stat. 4), and 1855 (10 Stat. 701). These acts provided for bounty land or additional bounty land for veterans and heirs of veterans from the Revolutionary War through 1855. As a result, veterans and other persons such as wagon masters who served as few as 14 days during wartime were entitled to bounty land. The benefits were increasingly generous. The 1855 act, for instance, provided that any veteran who had received less than 160 acres under previous acts was entitled to a warrant for additional acres to total 160 acres. The acts of 1850, 1852, and 1855 differ from the earlier acts in that the warrants were granted as a reward for past service rather than as an inducement to serve. Nearly all these warrants were assigned and the assignees used the warrants as payment or partial payment for tracts of land on the public domain.

Depending on the period in which a claim was made, claimants for bounty land warrants sent applications to the Secretary of War, the Commissioner of Pensions, or the Secretary of the Interior. Affidavits of witnesses, marriage records, and other forms of evidence of identity and service were also sometimes forwarded. A claimant whose application was approved was issued a warrant for a specified number of acres. The veteran, their heir, or their assignee could then "locate" the warrant; that is, they could select part of the public domain in exchange for the warrant. The Treasury Department and, after 1849, the Interior Department accepted the warrants and issued patents which gave title to the land.

This process produced two types of especially valuable genealogical records: bounty land warrant application files in Records of the Veterans Administration, Record Group (RG) 15, and surrendered bounty land warrant files in Records of the Bureau of Land Management, RG 49.

8.2 Bounty Land Warrant Applications

A **bounty land warrant application file** contains the documents relating to claims for bounty land: an application for a warrant by the veteran or his widow, records submitted as evidence of the veteran's service, and a file jacket showing whether the claim was approved or disapproved.

A file containing an approved bounty land warrant application is identified by a number made up as follows: the abbreviation B.L. Wt., number of the warrant, number of acres granted, and year (often represented by the last two digits) of the act under which the claim was submitted. In the example B.L. Wt. 79615-160-55, 79615 is the number of the warrant, 160 the number of acres, and 55 stands for the Act of 1855. This information—warrant number, number of acres, and year of the act—is sufficient to identify the surrendered bounty land warrant filed with the land entry papers discussed in Chapter 15. Because most bounty land warrant claimants assigned their warrants, surrendered bounty land warrant files seldom provide much information about the veteran or their family. When the recipient of the warrant died before locating or assigning it, the surrendered bounty land warrant file may reveal the names of heirs and some information about them.

The envelope containing a disapproved bounty land warrant application is identified by the abbreviation B.L. Reg, or Rej., the register number assigned to the application, and the year or last two digits of the year of the act under which the claim was submitted. Rejected applications are similar in content to those that were approved.

An application file usually contains the name, age, residence, military unit, and period of service of the veteran. If the applicant was an heir, the file should also show the name, age, and place of residence of the widow or other claimant, and the date of the veteran's death. If the application was approved, the file shows the warrant number, number of acres granted, year of the act, and, where appropriate, name of the assignee. Two or more claims, under different acts, may be filed together if they relate to the service of the same veteran.

Copies of bounty land warrant application files can be ordered through the mail by using a National Archives Trust Fund form, which may be obtained from the Customer Service Center, National Archives and Records Administration, Room 406, 700 Pennsylvania Ave., NW, Washington, DC 20408-0001. Copies of this form can also be requested by email at *inquire@nara.gov.*

8.2.1 Revolutionary War Applications

The **bounty land warrant application files** for Revolutionary War veterans in RG 15 are arranged alphabetically and are interfiled with the pension application files described in 7.2.1. These files have been microfilmed as *Revolutionary War Pension and Bounty-Land Warrant Application Files*, M804, 2,670 rolls. The alphabetical name index to the Revolutionary War pension files described in 7.2.1 also contains entries for veterans who applied for bounty land warrants.

Fire destroyed the application files relating to more than 14,000 numbered warrants issued between 1789 and 1800. However, basic information about each file had been transcribed on a record card. This card shows the name of the veteran, rank, military unit, warrant number, number of acres granted, date issued, and, where appropriate, name of heir or assignee. The record cards are interfiled alphabetically with the pension and bounty land warrant application files and are included on M804.

8.2.2 Post-Revolutionary War Applications

Congress passed numerous acts during the period 1812–55, providing bounty land benefits for veterans who served after the Revolutionary War, or their heirs or assignees. The last and most liberal act, approved March 3, 1855 (10 Stat. 701), authorized the issuance of bounty land warrants if the veteran had served 14 days or participated in a battle. These benefits were also extended to wagon masters and teamsters who were employed in time of war in the transportation of military stores and supplies.

The post-Revolutionary War bounty land warrant applications relate to claims based on service from 1790 to 1855, mostly in the War of 1812, Indian wars, and Mexican War. Congress did not authorize bounty land warrants for service after 1855, so no bounty land warrants exist for veterans of the Union Army in the Civil War. However, Union veterans were given special consideration when they applied for lands under the Homestead Act of 1862.

The application files are arranged alphabetically by name of veteran. Each file consists of the application of the veteran or widow, records submitted as evidence of service, and a file jacket which shows whether the claim was approved or disapproved. No index to the post-Revolutionary War bounty land warrant application files is available.

Bounty land warrant application files for the War of 1812 were consolidated with the pension application files for the War of 1812, which are described in 7.2.3.

8.3 Surrendered Bounty Land Warrants

In addition to bounty land warrant application files, the National Archives also holds records relating to the warrants that were surrendered to the Federal Government for tracts of land in the public domain. These include records relating to Revolutionary War warrants surrendered for land in the U.S. Military District of Ohio; records relating to Virginia military warrants surrendered for land in the Virginia Military District of Ohio; records relating to warrants issued for service in the War of 1812; and records relating to warrants issued for unspecified land. Except for some warrants issued for service in the War of 1812, warrants were assignable, so, as stated above, most veterans assigned or sold them and did not themselves settle on public land. All these surrendered bounty land warrant records are in Records of the Bureau of Land Management, RG 49.

Most Revolutionary War warrants issued under acts before 1855 were entered on tracts of land in the U.S. Military District of Ohio. Early warrants for service in the War of 1812 limited the location of the warrants to public land in Arkansas, Illinois, and Missouri. Later acts, however,

enabled warrant owners to exchange warrants for script that could be used to file for land elsewhere on the public domain. Warrants surrendered after 1841 could be located anywhere on the public domain.

8.3.1 Revolutionary War Warrants

The first warrants surrendered for land in the U.S. Military District of Ohio were issued under an ordinance of 1788 (*Journals of the Continental Congress*, vol. 34: 397–398) and an act of 1803 (2 Stat. 36), as extended in 1806 (2 Stat. 378). Under an act of 1796 (1 Stat. 490), as amended, the U.S. Military District of Ohio was reserved for holders of these warrants.

The 1796 act specified that the public land was to be distributed in minimum quantities of quarter townships or 4,000 acres. Thus it was necessary for persons possessing warrants totaling less than that amount to entrust their warrants to an agent who located the land and received a patent. The land was then distributed by the agent among the original warrant holders, and a deed was issued to each one by the agent. The act of 1796 also provided that the Secretary of the Treasury should give public notice in the states and territories and then register warrants for 9 months. At the end of this period, a lottery was held to determine the priority in which registered warrant holders could select the specific quarter township they desired. Those persons who had failed to register during the 9-month period could make their selections from any land still available after lottery participants had made their choice. Originally, the lands in the U.S. Military District of Ohio were to be distributed by January 1, 1800; but in 1803, 1806, and later years, Congress extended the time limit for registering and locating the warrants.

Surrendered bounty land warrant files usually include the warrant and related records. Two registers with indexes are available. The surrendered bounty land warrant files are arranged by date of act, thereunder by warrant number.

The first series includes U.S. bounty land warrants issued under the ordinance of 1788; they are numbered 1–14220. A warrant normally shows date of issuance, name and rank of veteran, state from which enlisted, and, where applicable, name of heir or assignee. If the warrant was assigned by the veteran or inherited by heirs, notes on the reverse of the warrant usually indicate subsequent transfers of ownership.

However, most of the warrants numbered 1–6912 in this first series were destroyed by fires in the War Department. Generally, the only surviving documents from this early part of the series are copies of patents granted for land claims. Beginning with warrant 6913, most of the actual warrants are intact. Those that are missing are presumed lost or not surrendered by the veteran, heir, or assignee. In the few instances where a warrant was exchanged for script, a cross-reference sheet indicates the script application number and the appropriate act under which it was filed.

BOUNTY LAND CLAIM.

FORM OF DECLARATION FOR SURVIVING OFFICER OR SOLDIER.

State of Illinois,
County of Coles.

On this _2 6_ day of _March_ A. D. one thousand eight hundred and _fifty five_ personally appeared before me _W Bush_ a _Justice of the peace_, duly authorized to administer oaths within and for the _County_ and State aforesaid, _David Dryden_ aged _61_ years, a resident of _Coles County_ in the State of _Illinois_ who being duly sworn according to law, declares that he is the identical _David Dryden_ who was a _private_ in the Company commanded by Captain _Wily Jones_ in the _5_ Regiment of _Va Militia_ commanded by _Col Preston_ in the war _1812_ that he _Volunteered_ at _Abington Va_ on or about the _15 day_ of _October_ A. D. _1893_ for the term of _six months_ and continued in actual service in said war for the term of _Six months_ and was honorably discharged at _Norfolk Va_ on the _15 day_ of _March_ A. _1814_ on account of _expiration of term of service_ as will appear by the muster rolls of said Company.

He makes this declaration for the purpose of obtaining the bounty land to which he may be entitled under the "act granting additional bounty land to certain officers and soldiers who have been engaged in the military service of the United States," approved March 3, 1855. And refers to his former declaration made under act of _1852_ upon which he obtained a Land Warrant No. _____ for _80_ acres, which he having legally transferred and disposed of, is not within his power now to return

He further declares that he has not received a warrant for bounty land under any other act of Congress, nor made any application therefor, than the one above referred to, under act of _1850_ upon which he obtained the said Land Warrant, No. _____ for _80_ acres, and the one now presented.

David Dryden

Sworn to and subscribed before me the day and year above written; and I hereby certify that I believe the said _David Dryden_ who signed and executed the above declaration, and is now present, to be the identical man who served as aforesaid, and that he is of the age above stated, and that I have no interest in said claim.

W Bush .... J. P.

State of Illinois,
County of Coles.

Personally appeared _Byrd Monroe_ and _George B. Balch_ citizens of the said County and State aforesaid, who being duly sworn, depose and say that they are personally acquainted with _David Dryden_ and that he is the person now present who signs and executes the within declaration.

Byrd Monroe

....

George B Balch ....

Sworn to and subscribed before me this _26_ day of _March_ A. D., 185_5_; and I certify that the said _Byrd Monroe_ and _George B. Balch_ are credible and respectable citizens.

W Bush .... J. P.

Two finding aids to these warrants are the "Index to the Register of Army Land Warrants" and the "Register of Army Land Warrants per Acts of 1796 and 1799." The index contains entries arranged alphabetically by initial letter of the surname of the warrant holder who registered and located the warrant on public land in the U.S. Military District of Ohio between 1799 and 1805. An entry also shows warrant number, number of acres, and page number in the register where the name of the veteran or the warrant holder is cited. The register contains entries arranged chronologically by date of warrant registration from April 11, 1799, to March 20, 1805. Each entry gives the registration date, name of patentee, and name and rank of the warrantee. Warrants are registered in 4,000-acre groupings, and a legal description (section, township, range) is provided only for each allocated quarter township. Additional information for each quarter township includes the lottery numbers drawn and the number of land certificates surrendered for the 4,000 acres.

The second series consists of surrendered bounty land warrant files issued under the acts of 1803 and 1806. The warrants are numbered 1–272 under the act of 1803, and 273–2119 under the act of 1806. Eighteen warrants issued under later acts are also included. A warrant in this series shows date of issuance, name and rank of veteran, state of enlistment, and name of heir or assignee. Most of the individual warrants are available, along with a certificate of location that indicates where the bounty land was located in the U.S. Military District of Ohio.

Occasionally, the files contain documents showing transfer of warrant ownership. When there is no certificate of location, a legal description is usually provided on the front or reverse of the warrant by a series of numbers indicating lot, section, township, and range in the U.S. Military District of Ohio

Finding aids for these warrants include an index prepared by the staff of the National Archives and the "Register of Military Land Warrants Presented at the Treasury for Locating and Patenting, 1804–35." The index was prepared from the warrant files and from the register. An entry usually indicates name of the veteran, warrant number, and act under which the warrant was issued; it may contain a cross-reference to the script application number. For those entries extracted from the register, the number of the page containing the information is given.

Entries in the register are arranged chronologically by date of warrant registration, 1804–35. Each entry provides date of registration; name of person registering the warrant; warrant number; service rank of the warrantee; number of acres shown on the warrant; location of the land selected by lot, section, township, and range in the U.S. Military District of Ohio; date of patent; and name of person to whom the patent was delivered. There are also entries for warrants registered in exchange for script.

Both series of surrendered bounty land warrant files and the registers and indexes have been reproduced as

M829, *U.S. Revolutionary War Bounty Land Warrants Used in the U.S. Military District of Ohio and Related Papers (Acts of 1788, 1803, 1806)*, 16 rolls. For a detailed calendar of these warrants, *see* vol. 2, *Federal Bounty-Land Warrants of the American Revolution, 1799–1835* of *Federal Land Series* by Clifford Neal Smith (Chicago: American Library Association, 1973).

8.3.2 Virginia Military District Warrants

The National Archives also has surrendered Revolutionary War bounty land warrants issued by the Commonwealth of Virginia for Federal land in the Virginia Military District of Ohio. Application files for these Virginia warrants are in the Virginia State Library, Richmond, VA 23219.

Revolutionary War veterans from Virginia, and their heirs and assignees, were eligible for Virginia bounty land warrants. The warrants were originally issued for land located in the present state of Kentucky, but when Virginia agreed to cede its western lands to the United States, Congress approved an act in 1794 (1 Stat. 394) enabling holders of the Virginia warrants to enter land in Ohio. This Ohio area, located between the Scioto and Little Miami Rivers, became known as the Virginia Military District of Ohio. Unused warrants could be exchanged for script in 1830 or later.

The Virginia bounty land warrant records include the surrendered Virginia bounty land warrant files, 1782–1892, and related documents. A file generally consists of a surrendered warrant, a survey, assignments, and, where appropriate, related documents concerning heirs of the veteran. The file may also show date and place of death of the warrantee, names of assignees and heirs, and places of residence. Often an assignee who had several warrants assigned to them requested that one large tract be surveyed to satisfy the warrants; in such cases, a file will contain more than one warrant. Sometimes one warrant was used to acquire more than one tract of land. In such cases, the surrendered warrant will be in one file, but other files based on the warrant will contain a copy of the warrant.

The volume and page number of the record copy of patent, which is maintained by the Eastern States Office of the Bureau of Land Management, is usually found in the file. This is important because the surrendered Virginia bounty land warrant files are arranged by these volume and page numbers.

Finding aids are available to assist in locating surrendered Virginia bounty land warrant case files. Entries in the index to names of warrantees are arranged alphabetically by initial letter of surname. Those in a register entitled "Virginia Military Warrants—Numerical—Continental and State Lines," are arranged by warrant number with the survey number; entries in a register entitled "Surveys for Land in Virginia Military District, Ohio," are arranged by survey number and give the volume and page number that identifies the case file. If only the name of the warrantee is known, it is necessary to use all three finding aids in succession to identify the surrendered bounty land warrant case file.

Related records are in the custody of the Virginia State Library, Richmond, VA 23219. In addition to the application files, these include military certificates, which were issued after veterans presented proof of Revolutionary War service; a "Register of Military Certificates Located in Ohio and Kentucky"; record copies of warrants 1–9969, with gaps; and registers of military warrants.

The names of warrantees with warrant numbers have been published in *Revolutionary War Records: Virginia* by Gaius Marcus Brumbaugh (Washington, DC, and Lancaster, PA: Lancaster Press, 1936); reprinted by the Genealogical Publishing Co., Baltimore, 1967. For information about the Virginia Revolutionary War warrants used to patent land in Kentucky, 1782–93, see *Old Kentucky Entries and Deeds* by Willard Rouse Jillison (Louisville: Standard Printing Company, 1926); reprinted by the Genealogical Publishing Co., Baltimore, 1969. For a detailed calendar of these warrants, *see* vol. 4, part 1, *Grants in the Virginia Military District of Ohio* of *Federal Land Series* by Clifford Neal Smith (Chicago: American Library Association, 1982).

8.4 War of 1812 Warrants

War of 1812 bounty land warrants derive mainly from an act of May 6, 1812 (2 Stat. 729), with subsequent amendments. A noncommissioned officer or soldier who served in the Regular Army for the duration of the war was entitled to bounty land in one of three bounty land districts, totaling about 6 million acres, located in Arkansas, Illinois, and Missouri. After 1842 the warrants could be used to enter land anywhere in the public domain and, after 1852, warrants could be assigned to anyone. Each veteran was entitled to 160 acres, with a few veterans entitled to 320 acres, or double bounty, in accordance with an act of 1814 (3 Stat. 147).

Unlike most of the warrants issued under bounty land acts, these warrants were not delivered to the veterans, but were retained by the General Land Office. The veteran received a notification that a warrant had been issued in his name. Most of the warrants are in bound volumes in two series, one for 160-acre warrants and the other for 320-acre warrants.

The warrants provide the following information: name of veteran and rank when discharged from military service; company, regiment, and branch of service; date the warrant was issued; and, usually, date the land was located and number of the page on which the location was recorded in abstracts maintained by the General Land Office. The abstracts are chronological lists of locations for which patents—documents conveying title to land—were granted on the basis of bounty land warrants. Issue dates extend from August 19, 1815, to June 2, 1858, for the 160-acre warrants, and from August 23, 1815, to April 1, 1839, for the 320-acre warrants.

Warrants 1–2519 of the 160-acre series and 1–79 of the 320-acre series were detached from the volumes and are now included with the notifications. For these warrants, stubs remaining in the volumes provide warrant number; name of veteran, rank, and regiment; and, in many cases, date of location and citation from the abstracts. Warrants 27116–28085 under the act of 1814 and warrants 1077–1101 under the act of 1812 are missing from the records of the General Land Office, but copies of them are in Records of the Veterans Administration, RG 15.

Indexes identify patentees in Arkansas, Illinois, and Missouri, and patentees under the act of 1842, which permitted the warrants to be used anywhere on the public domain. Warrant numbers are more easily identified, however, in the bounty land warrant application files.

Warrants, stubs, and indexes are available on M848, *War of 1812 Military Bounty Land Warrants, 1815–1858*, 14 rolls. The index for Illinois is incomplete.

8.5 Warrants, 1847–55

Warrants issued for unspecified land under acts of 1847, 1850, 1852, and 1855 are dated mostly 1847–59, with some as late as 1915. A surrendered bounty land warrant file for these acts usually contains a warrant or a certificate that a warrant would be filed in the General Land Office; assignments, where applicable; affidavit required of a preemption claimant who had purchased the warrant; and certificate of location specifying the location of the land to be entered. The files are arranged by date of the act under which the warrants were issued, thereunder by number of acres awarded (usually 40, 80, 120, or 160), and thereunder by warrant number.

The alphabetically arranged bounty land warrant application files serve as keys to identify the warrantees, or persons who received the warrants, named in the files. If a warrant was surrendered on the basis of an application made under one of these acts, the related bounty land warrant application file provides the information (year of act, number of acres, and warrant number) necessary to locate a surrendered bounty land warrant file. Names of the patentees are not indexed.

Most surrendered bounty land warrant files relating to these acts contain little information of genealogical interest about the warrantee because most individuals assigned their warrants and didn't use them personally to file a claim. In the infrequent cases where the warrantee died possessing the warrant, the surrendered file normally contains the names and places of residence of the warrantee's heirs.

These files identify the patentee by name. They show where the land acquired by the warrant was located and when it was acquired. In the numerous instances where a patentee acquired a warrant to be applied against a tract for which they held a preemption claim, the file shows where the patentee settled on the land, size of the household, and nature of improvements on the land.

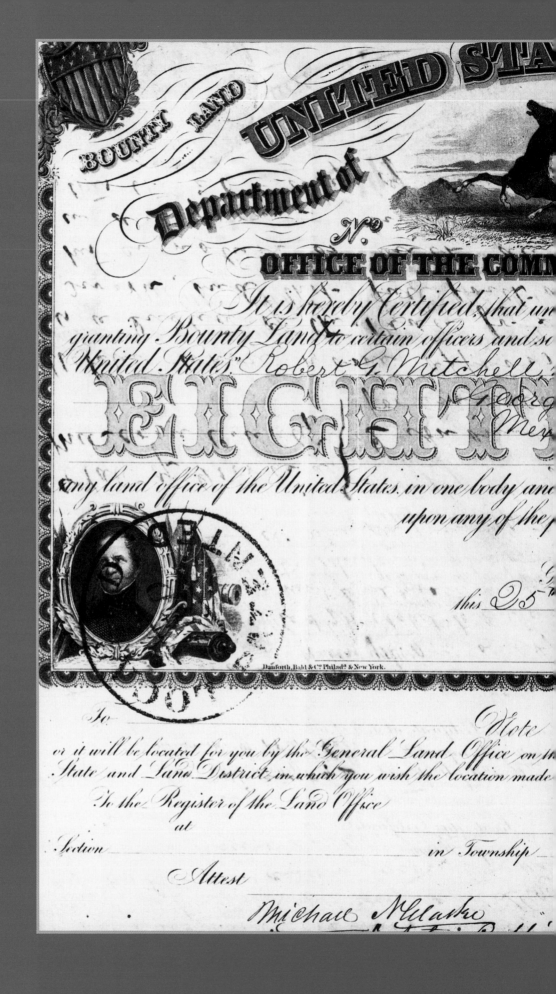

Military Bounty Land Warrant No. 8816-80-50, based on service in the Mexican War.
Records of the Bureau of Land Management, RG 49.

9.1 Introduction

The National Homes for Disabled Volunteer Soldiers were established by Congress in 1866 (14 Stat. 10) to provide residences for needy veterans. Honorably discharged officers, sailors, soldiers, or Marines who served in regular, volunteer, or other forces of the United States (or in the organized militia or the National Guard called into Federal service) were eligible if they were disabled by disease or wounds, without adequate means of support, and incapable of earning a living. Women who had served as nurses or in other capacities were admitted to the homes under later laws. Branches of the homes, their locations, and the years of their creation are shown in Table 15. After 1930, when the homes were consolidated with other agencies to form the Veterans Administration, the branches became known as Veterans Administration Homes.

9.1.1 Records of Soldiers' Homes

Records of the homes are dated 1866-1938 and are part of Records of the Veterans Administration, Record Group (RG) 15. The records of greatest genealogical value generally consist of historical registers of residents (called "members") of the homes and, for some homes, hospital and death records. The National Archives has no records for the Biloxi, St. Petersburg, or Tuskegee homes.

A record of veterans admitted to the homes was kept in the **historical registers** maintained at the various branches. A home number was assigned to each individual upon admission. The member retained this number even if they were discharged and later readmitted to the branch. Each page of the register is divided into four sections: military history, domestic history, home history, and general remarks. The veteran's military history gives the time and place of each enlistment, rank, company and regiment, time and place of discharge, reason for discharge, and nature of disabilities when admitted to the home. The domestic history gives birthplace, age, height, various physical features, religion, occupation, residence, marital status, and name and address of nearest relative. The home history gives the rate of pension, date of admission, conditions of readmission, date of discharge, cause of discharge, date and cause of death, and place of burial. Under general remarks is information about papers relating to the veteran, such as admission paperwork, army discharge certificate, and pension certificate. Information also was entered about money and personal effects if the member died while in residence at the branch.

The only **registers of deaths** in existence pertain to the former New York State Home at Bath, 1879-1937, and to the former Oregon State Home at Roseburg, 1894-1937. Entries show name, service rendered in the armed forces, place of birth, age, date and place of death, and place of burial. If the place of burial was in the home cemetery, the grave number is given. An entry may include the name and address of the relative notified of the veteran's death. Entries are arranged chronologically, but each of the three New York volumes has a rough alphabetical index by surname.

Also of interest to genealogists are **funeral records** at the Bath Home, 1918-21, and reports relating to the value of personal belongings of deceased members of the Danville Home, 1923-29. **Burial registers** are available for the Togus Home, 1892-1932 and 1935-38. Each entry in these registers includes the decedent's name, regiment and company, date of death, and section of row of the home cemetery where buried or remarks if buried elsewhere. Entries in **hospital registers** for the Togus Home, 1873-83, contain the veteran's name, military organization, nature of disability when admitted to the home, age, physical description, occupation, marital status, number of children, place of birth, amount of veteran's pension, and remarks. Remarks generally include date of discharge from the hospital or date of death.

The U.S. Soldiers' and Airmen's Home, originally named the United States Military Asylum, was created by Congress in 1851 (9 Stat. 595). Under that act, three temporary homes were established: East Pascagoula Asylum (also called Greenwood's Island), East Pascagoula, MS; New Orleans Asylum, New Orleans, LA; and the Washington Asylum, Washington, DC. Under a different act, a fourth home called the Western Military Asylum was established in 1853 at Harrodsburg, KY. The New Orleans Asylum was in operation about one year; the East Pascagoula Asylum operated until 1855, when its members were transferred to the Western Military Asylum, which was closed in 1858. The Washington Asylum was renamed the U.S. Soldiers' Home in 1859, and the name was subsequently changed to the U.S. Soldiers' and Airmen's Home in 1972. It began admitting disabled and retired members of the U.S. Air Force in 1942.

Records of greatest genealogical value in Records of the Armed Forces Retirement Home, RG 231, consist of general and monthly registers of members, hospital records, and death records. To use the records, the researcher must know which home the subject of research lived in and the approximate date of admission, hospital treatment, or death. For the East Pascagoula Asylum, records consist of lists of veterans admitted, June 1853 and March-August 1855. Only the names of members are given. Lists are arranged chronologically. For the Western Military Asylum, monthly reports exist for members and civilian employees, June 1853-September 1858. Only the names of members and employees are given, and the records are arranged chronologically. One volume of monthly registers lists members admitted to the Western Military Asylum and the Washington Asylum, 1853-58. Entries are arranged chronologically, thereunder alphabetically by member's surname. An entry usually shows the name of the resident, name of the home, date of admission, military history, physical description, date and place of birth, occupation at the time of admission, marital status, size of family, and remarks. Additional members' registers, dated 1852-1941, which

TABLE 15
Branches of the National Homes for Disabled Volunteer Soldiers

LOCATIONS AND DATES FOUNDED

Eastern Branch, Togus, ME, 1866	Mountain Branch, near Johnson City, TN, 1903
Central Branch, Dayton, OH, 1867	Battle Mountain Sanitarium, Hot Springs, SD, 1907
Northwestern Branch, Wood, WI, 1867	Bath Branch, Bath, NY, 1929, successor to the New York State Home at Bath
Southern Branch, Kecoughtan, VA, 1870	
Western Branch, Leavenworth, KS, 1885	St. Petersburg Home, St. Petersburg, FL, 1930
Pacific Branch, Sawtelle, CA, 1888	Biloxi Home, Biloxi, MS, 1930
Marion Branch, Marion, IN, 1888	Tuskegee Home (formerly a hospital), Tuskegee, AL, 1933
Roseburg Branch, Roseburg, OR, 1894, successor to the Oregon State Home at Roseburg Danville Branch, Danville, IL, 1898	

show the same information, are available for the Washington Asylum/U.S. Soldiers' Home.

For the Soldiers' Home, there are also muster rolls and returns that in part duplicate the information in the members' registers. They show names of veterans assigned to the home and their status—whether present, sick in the hospital, in prison, on furlough, discharged, or dead. The muster rolls, dated February 1870–November 1879, are arranged chronologically by month, thereunder generally alphabetically by surname of member. The returns, January 1879–December 1908, are arranged chronologically; a name index exists for June 1904–8. Additional lists, 1886–87 and 1898–1912, which show members admitted, suspended, readmitted, and dismissed, are arranged chronologically by type of list.

Hospital records for the U.S. Soldiers' Home consist of registers of persons admitted to the hospital, 1872–1943. They give the member's name; age; date and place of birth; military unit; diagnosis; date of admission, discharge, or death; and remarks. In addition, there are registers of members reporting to the hospital, registers of the sick, and the daily registers of patients admitted and discharged. Records are generally arranged by type, thereunder chronologically.

NARA's Rocky Mountain Region in Denver has **case files** for veterans treated at the Battle Mountain Sanitarium, Hot Springs, SD. The Great Lakes Region in Chicago has sampled case files and other records from the following facilities: Central Branch, Dayton, OH, 1867–1935; Danville Branch, Danville, IL, 1898–1934; Marion Branch, Marion, IN, 1890–1931; and the Northwestern Branch, Milwaukee, WI, 1867–1934.

Death records for the Soldiers' Home include registers and certificates of death. The registers, 1852–1942, show the number assigned to the entry, date, name of the deceased member, age, place of birth, and cause of death. Certificates of death, 1876–89 and 1913–29, are copies of the official record of death prepared by the District of Columbia Health Department; they vary in content according to the date of death. Generally they include the name of the deceased; date, place, and cause of death; date and place of birth; marital status; and name of the person reporting the death. The registers and certificates are arranged chronologically.

Other records relating to members of the U.S. Soldiers' Home, 1880–1942, consist of **case files for deceased members** of the home. Included in a case file is the member's military and home history; date, place, and cause of death; and date and place of burial. These records are alphabetically arranged by surname of the member. Records of residents since 1942 are in the custody of the home. Information about such members and access to the records may be requested by writing to the Superintendent, U.S. Soldiers' and Airmen's Home, 3700 North Capital St., NW, Washington, DC 20317.

9.2 Soldiers' Burial Records

The National Archives does not have a record of the burial of every soldier who died in service. It does have registers and lists of burials at national cemeteries and post cemeteries of military installations in the United States, Cuba, the Philippines, Puerto Rico, and China. It also has a few burial registers for private cemeteries, but in most cases, if a soldier was buried in a private cemetery, no record of the burial was kept by the Federal Government. Burials recorded in the registers were generally those of soldiers on active duty, as well as those of family members and civilian dependents who were buried in cemeteries at frontier army posts. Most soldiers burial records are in Records of the Office of the Quartermaster General, RG 92. They are dated chiefly 1861-1914, with some as early as 1807 and a few as late as 1939.

NARA has approximately 200 **burial registers for national cemeteries and post cemeteries**. One register has been microfilmed as M918, *Register of Confederate Soldiers, Sailors, and Citizens Who Died in Federal Prisons and Military Hospitals in the North, 1861-1865*, 1 roll. Microfilm publication M2014 has *Burial Registers for Military Posts, Camps, and Stations, 1768-1921*, 1 roll.

The arrangement, inclusive dates, and contents of the burial registers vary considerably. At a minimum, they show each soldier's name, military organization, and date and place of burial. The most detailed registers are four volumes for the U.S. Soldiers' Home Cemetery; the first two volumes are dated 1861-63, and the second two, 1864-68. Each volume is indexed by initial letter of the surname of the interred soldier. Entries in these volumes also show rank; place of residence before enlistment; name and residence of widow or other relative; age; cause, place, and date of death; and date of burial.

In addition, there are compiled **lists of Union soldiers buried at the U.S. Soldiers' Home**, 1861-1918. Entries are arranged alphabetically by surname. A separate set of lists is arranged by state from which the soldiers served. Entries usually show the name of the soldier, military organization, date of death, and place of burial. Additional records of deaths at the U.S. Soldiers' Home are described in 9.1.1.

Other lists were compiled of **Union soldiers buried at national cemeteries**. These lists relate chiefly to burials during the years 1861-65, but some are as late as 1886. They are arranged alphabetically by state of burial. For each state, there are three kinds of lists: on one the names are arranged by cemetery, on another by military organization, and on another alphabetically by initial letter of surname of the soldier. Lists arranged by surname, however, exist only for Connecticut, Delaware, District of Columbia, Iowa, Maine, Maryland, Massachusetts, Michigan, New Hampshire, New Jersey, Pennsylvania, Rhode Island, Vermont, and Wisconsin. An entry usually shows the name of the soldier, military organization, date of death, and place of burial.

Lists of Union soldiers who were buried in public and private cemeteries during the Civil War are published in *Roll of Honor...*, 27 vols. (Washington: U.S. Quartermaster Department, 1865-71). Entries are arranged by name of cemetery, thereunder alphabetically by name of soldier; they show the date of death. An accompanying *Alphabetical Index to Places of Interment of Deceased Union Soldiers* (Washington: U.S. Quartermaster Department, 1868) pertains to volumes 1-13. The National Archives has an unpublished place index to all 27 volumes.

Also in RG 92 are letters received relating to buried soldiers, 1864-90, and quartermaster's notifications, 1863-66, which alerted post or station quartermasters to make preparations for the interment of remains in post or station cemeteries. Reports of the sexton of Arlington National Cemetery, 1864-67, pertain to burials and reinterments mainly in that cemetery but also in other federally owned cemeteries.

The Cemetery Service, National Cemetery System, Veterans Administration, 810 Vermont Ave. NW, Washington, DC 20420, has alphabetically arranged carded records identifying practically all **soldiers who were buried in national cemeteries** and other cemeteries under Federal jurisdiction from 1861 to the present.

9.3 Headstone Applications

Applications for headstones, 1879-1964 and 1965-85, relate only to servicemen who were buried in private cemeteries and whose heirs applied for a government-furnished headstone. Under terms of an act of 1879 (20 Stat. 281), headstones were to be erected at the unmarked graves of Union servicemen, Revolutionary War soldiers, and servicemen from other wars in which the United States was engaged.

Applications for headstones were made by relatives of the deceased veteran, veterans associations, local or state governments, or civic groups. Each application shows the name and address of the applicant for the headstone, name of veteran, military organization, rank, years of service, place and date of burial, and sometimes date and cause of death.

Applications are in several series, with most arranged by state of burial, thereunder by county, and thereunder by cemetery. Applications for headstones for the graves of soldiers, sailors, and Marines buried outside the United States, 1911-24, are arranged alphabetically by country of burial, thereunder by surname of deceased. A few of the applications that relate to servicemen who were buried at branches of the National Home for Disabled Volunteer Soldiers are arranged by name of the home, thereunder by date of application.

Alphabetically arranged cards document the applications dated 1879-1903. Each card shows the soldier's name, military organization, name and location of cemetery where buried, date and place of death, and date of application. These cards have been microfilmed as M1845, *Card Records of Headstones Provided for Deceased Union Civil War Veterans, ca. 1879-ca. 1903*, 22 rolls.

Applications for headstones for Confederate veterans are included in the records. Many applications or copies of applications are interfiled with the following case files.

9.4 Other Records

Case files, 1915-39, consist of correspondence and completed forms in folders, each folder relating to a soldier's existing or proposed burial place. Folders are arranged alphabetically. Although most folders relate to service personnel who died during the period covered by the files, some relate to those who died before 1915, and some relate to individuals living when the documents were dated. Files include many types of documents concerning burial, including copies of applications for headstones. Each file shows information such as name, military organization, place of residence, date of death, and place of burial.

Records of **World War I soldiers who died overseas**, 1917-22, are on cards in several series arranged alphabetically by name of soldier or name of cemetery. Most cards are **grave registrations**, each showing name of the soldier, military organization, cause and date of death, date and place of burial, and name and address of nearest kin or guardian. Some of the cards record American names listed in European chapels. These cards usually show name of the soldier, military organization, date of death, a statement of death in action, name and address of nearest kin or guardian, and name of the chapel.

In Records of the American Battle Monuments Commission, RG 117, are **lists of soldiers missing in action**, 1923-60, compiled from missing-in-action lists supplied by the various branches of the armed services. Lists include names of missing soldiers, units with which they served, and dates on which they disappeared. These missing soldiers are memorialized at war monuments and cemeteries maintained by the Commission.

War crimes investigation records of World War II in Records of the Office of the Judge Advocate General (Army), RG 153, 1942-54, consist of card indexes, case files and trial records, and reports of interviews with U.S. soldiers and airmen who were **prisoners of war**.

The indexes are alphabetically arranged cards that refer to all individuals connected—as alleged perpetrators, victims, or witnesses—with war crimes in Europe and the Far East. Each card shows the name of the individual and the number that refers to the case files and trial records. Sometimes a brief description of the incident is given.

Case files are arranged numerically. Use the indexes to locate pertinent records. The testimony of victims or witnesses to German and Japanese atrocities in the case files and trial records contains information about the experiences of individuals in concentration camps.

Interviews contain information about name, rank, military unit, hometown, marital status, education, and employment of former prisoners of war. Some of the same information, as well as date and place of death, if known, was recorded for U.S. soldiers who died in action while being captured or while prisoners of war. Some interviews are arranged alphabetically by name, some are arranged by area, and some are unarranged.

NARA holds a few electronic records series of potential interest to genealogists. These include records of casualties and prisoners of war resulting from the conflicts in Korea and Vietnam, which are among Records of the Veterans Administration, RG 15; Records of the Army Staff, RG 319; Records of the Office of the Secretary of Defense, RG 330; and Records of the Adjutant General's Office, 1917-, RG 407. Records of World War II prisoners of war are in Records of the Provost Marshal General, 1941-, RG 389. For information about additional electronic records of possible genealogical value, consult the electronic records section of the NARA web site at *www.nara.gov.*

Medal of Honor Recipients, 1863-1973, is available from the Government Printing Office as "Committee Print Number 15 of the Committee on Veterans' Affairs, U.S. Senate, 93d Congress, 1st Session." It lists the names of all those awarded the Medal of Honor from the time that this medal was created in the Civil War to 1973. The publication provides the rank and organization of each of the approximately 3,400 medal winners, as well as an account of the act of heroism for which the medal was awarded (Y4.V64/4: M46/3/863-973).

SECTION C

Records Relating to Particular Groups

10.1 Introduction

Genealogists may be most familiar with the records of ancestors who served in U.S. military forces during the Revolutionary War, the Civil War, and other American conflicts, but records in the National Archives may also document the activities of civilian ancestors during wartime. Among the records described in this chapter are fiscal records of the Revolutionary War; several series relating to aliens during the War of 1812; several series relating to Confederate civilians during the Civil War, including amnesty records; and several series relating to persons of Japanese ancestry in the United States during World War II.

10.2 Revolutionary War

The National Archives has several series of fiscal records relating to the Revolutionary War that may be used for genealogical research, including records of Continental loan offices in Records of the Bureau of the Public Debt, Record Group (RG) 53.

Continental loan offices were authorized by a resolution of the Congress of October 3, 1776, to receive subscriptions for loans to help finance the Revolutionary War and to issue interest-bearing certificates to the subscribers. The National Archives has Continental loan office records for Connecticut, Delaware, Maryland, New Hampshire, New Jersey, New York, Pennsylvania, Rhode Island, and Virginia. They show the creation of a part of the U.S. domestic public debt generated during the Revolutionary War.

The records consist mainly of registers of loan office certificates and liquidated debt certificates. The loan certificate represents an early effort to fund the war and circulate the currency; the liquidated debt certificate was an instrument used to consolidate the public debt by settling the claims of individual citizens. In the absence of a circulating medium, certificates of interest (or "indents") were issued on these obligations. Other types of records include registers of interest certificates, indexes, journals, ledgers, and accounts current.

Many of these records have been microfilmed: M925, *Records of the Massachusetts Continental Loan Office, 1777-1791*, 4 rolls; M1005, *Records of the Connecticut, New Hampshire, and Rhode Island Continental Loan Offices, 1777-1789*, 2 rolls; M1006, *Records of the New Jersey and New York Continental Loan Offices, 1777-1790*, 2 rolls; M1007, *Records of the Pennsylvania Continental Loan Office, 1776-1788*, 3 rolls; and M1008, *Records of the Delaware and Maryland Continental Loan Offices, 1777-1790*, 1 roll. Records of the Virginia Continental Loan Office have not been filmed, and there are no records for North Carolina, South Carolina, or Georgia.

Efficient research in these records requires knowledge of the state where the subject of research lived when the debt was collected, although the microfilm publications for all the states could be consulted. Loan certificate registers typically consist of entries under specific denomination, arranged chronologically by date of issue, and giving the name of the subscriber and serial number of the note. This arrangement makes a search for a particular name tedious, but the process merely involves reading down the name column. Some registers of interest certificates show the signatures of subscribers, but the records seldom show their addresses or other identifying information. Certificates were transferred freely from one person to the next and, to a limited extent, passed in trade.

Two other National Archives publications related to this record group may also be useful: M521, *Card Index to "Old Loan" Ledgers of the Bureau of the Public Debt, 1790-1836*, 15 rolls, and Preliminary Inventory (PI) 52, *"Old Loans" Records of the Bureau of the Public Debt*, compiled by Philip D. Lagerquist, Archie L. Abney, and Lyle J. Holverstott (Washington: National Archives and Records Service, 1953). Both publications, however, also concern the U.S. public debt for many years after the Revolutionary War.

Some of the miscellaneous numbered records described in 5.2.1 pertain to civilians hired by the military during the Revolutionary War.

10.3 War of 1812

"An Act respecting Alien Enemies" of July 6, 1798 (1 Stat. 577), one of the Alien and Sedition Acts, was the basis for restrictions on aliens during the War of 1812. That law defined all male citizens of a nation formally at war with the United States, who were age 14 or older, as alien enemies; it was extended to apply to the War of 1812 by an act of 1812 (2 Stat. 781). Under provisions of these laws, on July 7, 1812, the Department of State issued a public notice requiring all British subjects to report the following information to U.S. marshals in their state or territory: name, age, length of residence in the United States, names of members of their families, place of residence, occupation, and whether they had applied for naturalization. The marshals were instructed to make returns of these reports to the Department.

The National Archives has these **U.S. marshals' returns**, 1812-15, and letters from marshals, 1812-14, relating to enemy aliens. Included with the returns are some lists of prisoners of war who were delivered to marshals from U.S. ships. The marshals' returns are arranged for the most part by marshal's district, thereunder chronologically, so that to use them the researcher must know the place of residence of the subject of research during the War of 1812. The letters are arranged for the most part chronologically; prisoner-of-war lists are arranged chronologically. Some of the letters and returns are in General Records of the Department of State, RG 59, and these have been microfilmed on rolls 1-4 of M588, *"War of 1812 Papers" of the Department of State, 1789-1815*, 7 rolls. Other letters and returns are in the Naval Records Collection of the Office of Naval Records and Library, RG 45.

The returns list male aliens only and usually give name, age, occupation, length and places of residence in the United States, names of dependent family members, and date of application for naturalization.

Letters contain evidence, pleas, and recommendations for the exemption of certain aliens from the regulations applicable to them. Prisoner lists show name, age, years in the United States, names of dependent family members, residence, and occupation.

Also in RG 59 are **lists of persons authorized to sail** from the United States during the war, generated primarily at the port of Philadelphia. The lists are arranged chronologically, so that searching for particular names involves a document-by-document inspection. They list only adults and provide each person's name, nationality, and, in some cases, occupation, age, date of arrival in the United States, and physical characteristics.

In RG 45 is a **register of alien enemies** reported by the U.S. marshal at New York City and of alien enemies removed from New York City, March–July 1813. This register consists of two parts. In the first part, entries are arranged alphabetically by initial letter of surname and thereunder chronologically; in the last part, entries are arranged chronologically. Recorded in the first part of the register are the permit number issued to the alien; name; height; age; color of skin, eyes, and hair; place of residence and occupation; a date, presumably the one on which the permit was issued; and the name of the person who recommended the alien for surveillance. The last part of the register provides the following information for each alien removed: name; height and age; color of skin, eyes, and hair; place to which transferred after removal from New York City; and date of removal.

Under the July 1812 order, 380 aliens reported to the marshal of New York; the number who reported under a February 1813 order was about 272. Even though the year is not stated in the register, it seems probable that the entries were made in 1813. This volume may originally have been part of the "War of 1812 Papers" of the Department of State.

A **register of persons removed** from the Atlantic coast during the War of 1812, May–September 1813, is also in RG 45. Entries are arranged alphabetically by initial letter of surname, thereunder chronologically by date of the order for removal. A note on the front cover of the register states that the volume contains the names of persons "whose requests for indulgence" (permission to remain) were granted or rejected. They were not suspects but persons who were removed from the coast because of their "nativity, etc." Officers responsible for issuing the removal orders and for preparing this register are not identified. Information about each alien includes name and residence, whether or not indulgence was granted, place of relocation, date of the order for removal, and remarks, which usually include reason for removal or for indulgence. The "volume of letters sent" referred to in the remarks column

is unidentified. The register may originally have been part of the "War of 1812 Papers" of the Department of State.

The miscellaneous records, or "manuscripts," of the War of 1812 material described in 5.2.3 pertain to some civilian as well as military matters.

10.4 Civil War

Because the Civil War was fought almost entirely in the South, many more records relate to Confederate civilians than to those in the North.

10.4.1 Civilians in the North

The Internal Revenue Act of July 1862 (12 Stat. 432) was supposed "to provide Internal Revenue to support the Government and to pay Interest on the Public Debt." Monthly, annual, and special taxes were levied on personal property such as yachts and carriages, and on the receipts of certain businesses; licenses were required for all trades and occupations. The assessment lists prepared for every state and territory are in the Records of the Internal Revenue Service, RG 58. Many of the lists have been microfilmed; *see* Table 24 in Chapter 18.

General Records of the Department of State, RG 59, has case files that relate to **aliens drafted** into the U.S. Army and released, 1862–64. Included are draft notices, depositions, and correspondence relating to releases. These files are arranged alphabetically by surname of alien, and the National Archives staff will search for the file of a particular alien. Each file contains the alien's name, district from which drafted, country of citizenship and, occasionally, date of release. Some files also give age, length of time in the United States, and physical description of the alien.

10.4.2 Civilians in the South

Much information about the effect of the war on the southern population can be found in the records of the provost marshals of the Union Army who were assigned as military police to the various territorial commands, armies, and corps. The records of their activities are in the **Union provost marshals' files**. Their duties included enforcing law and order among the civilian population, maintaining Union Army prisons, and, to a certain extent, settling disputes caused by the war itself. They sought out and arrested deserters from the Union Army, some Confederate deserters, Confederate spies, and civilians suspected of disloyalty; investigated theft of Government property; controlled the passage of civilians in military zones and those using Government transportation; confined prisoners; and maintained records of paroles and oaths of allegiance. Provost courts were established in some territorial commands to try civilian violators of military orders and the laws of war or to handle other offenses arising under the military jurisdiction. They also tried military personnel accused of civil crimes.

Because many of these records deal with Confederate citizens, they have been placed in the War Department

Collection of Confederate Records, RG 109. They are arranged in two series: papers relating to one named person, and papers relating to two or more named persons. Papers in the first series vary from a single document to a complete dossier on an individual. Papers in the second series consist of documents, lists, and papers generally numbered or chronologically arranged. While the records for the most part concern civilians, some information in them relates to Confederate servicemen, foreigners, and soldiers in the Union Army who conducted the activities of the provost marshal's various bureaus. Although the records may relate to some of the same individuals for whom papers are found in the "Unfiled Papers and Slips Belonging in Confederate Compiled Service Records" (*see* 5.2.7) and in Confederate papers relating to citizens and business firms, the material is generally not similar in content. In some instances there may be compiled service records for Confederate soldiers mentioned in this series.

The Union provost marshals' files relating to individual civilians consists of correspondence, provost court papers, orders, passes, parole records, oaths of allegiance, transportation permits, and claims for compensation for property used or destroyed by military forces. Information in the records concerns Confederate sympathizers, deserters, guerrillas, civilian and Confederate military prisoners, persons accused of violations of military and civil law, citizens residing in areas occupied by Union forces who wished to travel across Union lines to visit relatives or friends in prison or in other areas, persons taking the oath of allegiance to the Union, merchants and others wishing to transport merchandise, and persons living in Union states who were considered to be involved in treasonable activities.

The records are arranged alphabetically by name of the civilian or soldier concerned. They are available on M345, *Union Provost Marshals' File of Papers Relating to Individual Civilians,* 300 rolls. Cross-reference slips in the series identify some of the persons for whom documents also appear in the Union provost marshals' file of papers relating to two or more civilians or in other series in RG 109.

The second series of Union provost marshals files, relating to two or more civilians, is similar in content to the papers relating to individuals, and documents are generally located through cross-references in the first series. The second series is composed of several parts: an incomplete place and subject index; documents numbered 1 to 22737, which are also chronologically arranged, March 1861–December 1866; unnumbered documents arranged chronologically, January–October 1867; lists of civilian and some military prisoners confined at various military prisons, arranged by name of the prison, thereunder chronologically, which include information about status (received, released, transferred, or died); and documents relating to the confiscation and destruction of property. The records are available as M416, *Union Provost Marshals' File of*

Papers Relating to Two or More Civilians, 94 rolls.

Information about Confederate civilians is also interspersed throughout the various **War Department correspondence** series in RG 109. It is available on microfilm as M437, *Letters Received by the Confederate Secretary of War, 1861–1865,* 151 rolls; M474, *Letters Received by the Confederate Adjutant and Inspector General, 1861–1865,* 164 rolls; and M469, *Letters Received by the Confederate Quartermaster General, 1861–1865,* 14 rolls. Alphabetical card indexes to names of correspondents and persons mentioned in the bodies of the letters are available as M409, *Index to the Letters Received by the Confederate Secretary of War, 1861–1865,* 34 rolls, and M410, *Index to the Letters Received by the Confederate Adjutant and Inspector General and by the Confederate Quartermaster General, 1861–1865,* 41 rolls. Correspondence and other documents, as well as card abstracts relating to Confederate citizens and civilian employees, are included on M346, *Confederate Papers Relating to Citizens or Business Firms,* 1,158 rolls, and M347, *Unfiled Papers and Slips Belonging in Confederate Compiled Service Records,* 442 rolls, described in 5.2.7.

Records of the **Confederate Bureau of Conscription** mostly for the state of Virginia, are in RG 109. Included are registers of individuals exempted from military service and registers of persons detailed to agricultural and other jobs. Entries in several registers of free African Americans detailed to jobs in Virginia show names of individuals, occupations, dates exempted or detailed, and, in some instances, physical descriptions and places of residence. Registers are alphabetically or chronologically arranged and generally unindexed. Locating information about a particular individual may entail reading all the entries.

Records of civilian employees of the Confederate Government are described in 14.4. Records of African Americans on payrolls of civilian personnel at Confederate shore establishments are described in 12.3.3.

In NARA's Southeast Region in Atlanta are records in RG 109 relating to the sequestration of **alien enemy property** in South Carolina. These include a minute book of proceedings, account books, writs of garnishment, and a docket of cases. These bound records contain information about individuals whose property was affected, and a number are indexed by name. Sequestration case files, 1861–62, are arranged alphabetically by name of individual, company, or other organization, and contain numerous cross-reference cards prepared by the U.S. War Department.

Headquarters records of the Land Division in Records of the Bureau of Refugees, Freedmen, and Abandoned Lands, RG 105, include reports of abandoned or confiscated land. Files from Records of District Courts of the United States, RG 21, are available on microfilm as M435, *Case Papers of the U.S. District Court for the Eastern District of Virginia, 1863–1865, Relating to the Confiscation of Property,* 1 roll, and M436, *Confederate Papers of the U.S. District Court for the Eastern District of North Carolina,*

1861–1865, 1 roll. Maps relating to property abandoned by its owners and captured by Federal forces during the Civil War are described in 19.5.

Several small series of records relating to the sale and destruction of cotton, 1862–65, document transactions between individual cotton sellers and the Confederate States of America. These records are part of the Treasury Department Collection of Confederate Records, RG 365, and they are described in *Treasury Department Collection of Confederate Records*, PI 169, compiled by Carmelita S. Ryan (Washington: National Archives and Records Service, 1967).

Some information in the records is transcribed in *Cotton Sold to the Confederate States* (62nd Cong., 3rd sess., S. Doc. 987, serial 6348). Entries are arranged by name of seller in two alphabetical sequences, one for sellers in Alabama, Arkansas, Florida, Georgia, Louisiana, Mississippi, and South Carolina, and one for sellers who sold through the Texas Cotton Bureau at Houston.

10.4.3 Amnesty and Pardon Records

Early in the Civil War, Congress authorized the President to extend pardon and amnesty to participants in the rebellion (12 Stat. 592). Presidential proclamations of December 8, 1863; May 29, 1865; and September 7, 1867, granted pardon and amnesty to increasingly larger groups of individuals on the condition that they take an oath of allegiance. President Andrew Johnson's proclamation of July 4, 1868, granted pardon and amnesty to virtually all remaining participants without the requirement of an oath. Amnesty and pardon records in the National Archives are in RG 59 and are described in *Inventory of the General Records of the Department of State*, 1789–1949, Inventory 15, Microfiche Edition (Washington: National Archives and Records Administration, 1992).

Several series of **amnesty oaths**, 1863–66, relate to the vast number of southerners who wished to gain or regain U.S. citizenship. Usually a single document, the oath is all that relates to one person. Filed with the oaths, in appropriate instances, are acknowledgments of warrants of Presidential pardons and agreements to accept the conditions of pardon. One series consists of documents relating to one person arranged by name of state, thereunder usually alphabetically by the first two letters of the surname. To use the records, the researcher must know the state where the subject of research took the oath of allegiance. Another series of documents that relate to more than one person is arranged numerically, usually under the name of a state. In the series of documents relating to one person are cross-references to the names on documents in the series of papers relating to more than one person.

An oath shows the name of the person; place the oath was taken, which was often the place of residence; date the oath was taken; and usually the signature of the person taking the oath. Sometimes an oath gives the age and a description of the person taking the oath and, in appropriate instances, their Confederate military organization.

Several of the oaths show specific places of residence, and for many persons, the places of residence were the same in 1860 and 1870. An effective search of the amnesty oaths may provide a county name, which in turn can lead to the population census schedules.

The series of **amnesty papers** in Records of the Adjutant General's Office, 1780's–1917, RG 94, are dated chiefly 1865–67. President Andrew Johnson's 1865 proclamation of amnesty excluded most people who had held high civilian or military rank under the Confederacy, as well as all southerners with taxable property exceeding $20,000 in value. These persons were required to petition the President directly for special pardons. The application files of 14,000 such individuals are in this series. The files, which include oaths of allegiance and other supporting documents, are arranged by state, thereunder alphabetically by name of applicant. A general name index to the entire collection has been prepared by National Archives staff members. An application file gives the name, age, occupation, and place of residence of the applicant, together with biographic data. The files and index are available as M1003, *Case Files of Applications from Former Confederates for Presidential Pardons ("Amnesty Papers"), 1865–1867*, 73 rolls.

The series of **pardons** in RG 59 consists of copies of Presidential pardons for Confederates, 1865–66, arranged chronologically. Also available are lists of persons accepting amnesty pardons, 1865–67. There is a consolidated name index to the pardons, as well as indexes in the separate volumes.

Copies of pardons show the name and address of the person pardoned and the date of the pardon. Lists of acceptances include name and, in some cases, addresses. The consolidated index entries give the name and county for each person pardoned.

Lists of the names of most of individuals who receive pardons in the years 1865–67 were published in various congressional documents:

Message of the President . . . . [May 4, 1866] (39th Cong., 1st sess., H. Doc. 99, serial 1263)

Message of the President . . . . [Jan. 8, 1867] (39th Cong., 2nd sess., H. Doc. 31, serial 1289)

Message of the President . . . . [Mar. 2, 1867] (39th Cong., 2nd sess., H. Doc. 116, serial 1293)

Message of the President . . . . [July 8, 1867] (40th Cong., 1st sess., H. Ex. Doc. 32, serial 1311)

Impeachment of the President [Nov. 25, 1867] (40th Cong., 1st sess., H. Rept. 7, serial 1314)

Final Report of the Names of Persons Engaged in Rebellion Who Have Been Pardoned by the President [Dec. 4, 1867] (40th Cong., 2nd sess., H. Ex. Doc. 16, serial 1330).

The first message includes lists showing the names of persons with property worth more than $20,000 who were pardoned and others listing the amount of property seized and returned. The messages of January 8, March 2, and July 8, 1867, responded to a House resolution of December 10,

United States of America.

GEORGIA,

Cass County.

I do solemnly swear, or affirm, in the presence of Almighty God, that I will henceforth faithfully SUPPORT, PROTECT, AND DEFEND the Constitution of the United States and the union of the States thereunder, and that I will, in like manner, ABIDE BY AND FAITHFULLY SUPPORT ALL LAWS AND PROCLAMATIONS which have been made during the existing rebellion with reference to the emancipation of slaves—SO HELP ME GOD.

Sworn to and subscribed before me at
this 24th day of August 1865.

John C. Pankey
Cartersville Georgia
S A Howard
Ordinary

Atlanta Intelligencer Print.

Amnesty oath of John C. Pankey, 1865, Amnesty Oaths, 1864–66. Civil War Amnesty and Pardon Records. General Records of the Department of State, RG 59.

1866, which requested the names of all persons engaged in the late rebellion who had been pardoned from April 15, 1865, to that date [December 10]. House Report 7, by the House Judiciary Committee, includes a reprint of the list of March 2, 1867. The message of December 4, 1867, was the final report on persons pardoned.

10.4.4 Claims Arising from the Civil War

Another source of genealogical information about civilians in the Civil War period is the series of **case files of the Southern Claims Commission**. The commission was established under an act of Congress approved March 3, 1871, to examine and recommend action on claims for property seized for use by the Union Army from citizens in southern states who remained loyal to the Union. An act approved May 11, 1872, extended the commission's jurisdiction to include property used by the Union Navy. The commission received 22,298 claims, but only 7,092 satisfied the rigid tests of sworn statements and cross-examinations in proving both the sustained Union loyalty of the claimant throughout the war and the validity of the claim. The commission was terminated effective March 10, 1880. Excluding the case files, records of the Southern Claims Commission are part of the General Records of the Department of the Treasury, RG 56. They have been reproduced on M87, *Records of the Commissioners of Claims (Southern Claims Commission), 1871-1880*, 14 rolls. Summary reports on claims are on roll 9, a geographical list of claims on roll 13, and a consolidated index on roll 14.

Most of the case files for the claims approved in whole or in part are among the settled accounts and claims of the Third Auditor of the Treasury in the Records of the Accounting Officers of the Department of the Treasury, RG 217. Files are arranged alphabetically by state, thereunder alphabetically by county, and thereunder alphabetically by name of claimant. A typical Civil War claim file includes the petition of the claimant, formal report of the commission, testimony of the claimant and of other persons supporting or opposing the granting of the claim, and sometimes additional documents submitted in evidence, such as proof of title to the property, proof of relationship to the owner, or proof of other legal interest in the property. The claims files for Georgia and Alabama have been reproduced as M1658, *Southern Claims Commission Approved Claims, 1871-1880: Georgia*, 761 microfiche, and M2062, *Southern Claims Commission Approved Claims, 1871-1880: Alabama*, 36 rolls.

The *Consolidated Index of Claims Reported by the Commissioners of Claims to the House of Representatives from 1871-1880* (Washington: U.S. House of Representatives, 1892) facilitates the use of these records. It gives an alphabetical listing of claimants who appeared before the Southern Claims Commission and for each claimant provides the state of residence, claim number, and action taken.

Claims that were barred and disallowed by the Southern Claims Commission are among the Records of the U.S.

House of Representatives, RG 233, and the Records of the U.S. Court of Claims, RG 123. These, as well as similar claims brought before the quartermaster general by loyal citizens in loyal states, are discussed in Chapter 16.

10.5 World War I: Aliens

Three series of records of the U.S. Marshal for the District of Kansas in NARA's regional archives in Kansas City relate to the registration of German aliens during World War I under provisions of Regulation 4 of the President's Proclamation of April 6, 1917. These series, part of the Records of the U.S. Marshals Service, RG 527, consist of alien permit applications, 1917-18, two typescript lists of permits issued, ca. 1918, and alien registration affidavits, 1918. The permit applications list the applicant's name, residence, date of birth, years of residence in the United States, and employment since July 1, 1914. They include a physical description and photograph of the applicant. Alien registration affidavits list the registrant's name; present and previous residences since January 1, 1914; date and place of birth; employment since January 1, 1914; date and port of arrival in the United States; name and residence of spouse; names and dates of birth of minor children; names and relationships of male relatives in military service; draft status; previous military, naval, and Government service; and naturalization status. The affidavits include a physical description with a photograph and fingerprints of the registrant.

10.6 World War II: Evacuees

During World War II, about 110,000 persons of Japanese ancestry were evacuated from parts of California, Oregon, Washington, Arizona, Alaska, and Hawaii that were designated as military areas. At first evacuation was voluntary, and all persons of Japanese descent were advised to move outside the military zone. During this voluntary phase of the evacuation, approximately 9,000 Japanese Americans moved inland. Shortly thereafter, however, a new order established assembly centers under the Wartime Civil Control Administration (WCCA), and the War Relocation Authority (WRA) was set up to carry out the removal, relocation, maintenance, and supervision of persons excluded from military areas. The Japanese Americans were eventually transferred to 10 inland centers administered by the WRA. As early as July 1942, evacuees were permitted to leave the relocation centers to resettle in nonrestricted areas of the country. On December 17, 1944, the West Coast general exclusion order was revoked, and by 1946 all the relocation centers had been closed.

Files compiled by the WRA and WCCA that contain much personal information about the evacuees are now in Records of the War Relocation Authority, RG 210.

One roll of accessioned microfilm contains **change of residence cards** submitted by persons of Japanese descent who moved from their former residence during the

Japanese Americans, grandfather and grandchildren, awaiting transportation to a relocation camp. Hayward, CA, May 8, 1942. Photograph No. 210-G-C160 by Dorothea Lange. Records of the War Relocation Authority, RG 210.

voluntary migration phase of the evacuation program. The cards contain the following information for each individual: name, previous address, new address or destination, sex, age, race, citizenship, and alien registration number.

Two **social data registration forms** were used by the WCCA for initial registration of evacuees. These forms were microfilmed and contain the following information for each evacuee family: address at the time of evacuation, number of persons in the family moving and therefore registering together, and family number. The forms give the following information for each individual evacuee: name, relationship to head of family, sex, age, place of birth, education, occupation, alien registration number, and physical condition. Arrangement is in two sets: by civilian exclusion number, 1–108, thereunder by family number; and by family number.

WCCA and WRA evacuee transfer lists are photostatic copies of lists of evacuees transferred from assembly centers to war relocation centers. Each list contains the names of the assembly and relocation centers involved; the name, age, sex, and, occasionally, family number or assembly center number for each evacuee; and a memorandum of transmittal.

An accessioned microfilm copy of the **WCCA master card index of evacuees** is available. The following information is given for each evacuee: name, age, sex, place of birth, family number, alien registration number, occupation, name of nearest relative, previous address, and assembly center address.

Evacuee case files contain interview records, basic family fact sheets, health records, property records, leave records, and school records. The information given for each individual includes name, individual and family numbers, birthplace, birth date, religion, marital status, educational level, linguistic ability, employment history, military service record, previous addresses (including any abroad), dates of entrance into assembly and relocation centers, parents and relatives' names and countries of origin, illness and treatments during residence in the relocation center, stored personal property, real property, relocation center employment earnings, and leave.

IBM punched **summary data cards** exist for all evacuees at relocation centers. Given for each individual evacuee are (a) name, individual number, last permanent address, date of entrance into relocation center, relocation center address, and miscellaneous notations; and (b) place and date of birth, sex, marital status, religion, highest school grade attained, language schools attended, languages spoken, occupations, assembly center address, residence in Japan (if any), extent of education in Japan (if any), parents' birthplaces, and father's occupation. The (a) items are typed or written; the (b) items are punched in code. A guide to the code is available.

Cards for institutionalized evacuees were made for persons who, under WRA jurisdiction, were confined to such institutions as general hospitals, mental hospitals, tuberculosis sanitariums, and orphanages. Some of these persons had entered these institutions from a relocation center; others had been admitted before evacuation occurred. A typical card contains the following information regarding an individual: name, family number, alien registration number, date of birth, age, marital status, citizenship, pre-evacuation address, name and type of institution, dates of admission and release, type of release, and destination after release.

A typical **basic family card** contains the following information for each family: name of head of family, family number, names of family members and others in the household, their relationship to the family head, their birthdates and birthplaces, their occupations or other status at the center, address of the family at the center, and record of the family earnings and compensation there. The cards are arranged alphabetically by center, thereunder alphabetically by name of family head. There are no cards for the Jerome Center.

Final accountability rosters list all evacuees at each relocation center. A typical entry contains the following information for each evacuee: name, family number, sex, date of birth, marital status, citizenship status, alien registration number, method of entry into relocation center (from an assembly center, other institutions, Hawaii, another relocation center, or birth), date of entry, pre-evacuation address, center address, type of final departure (indefinite leave, internment, repatriation, segregation, relocation, or death), date of departure, and final destination. Included in each roster are summary figures for evacuees at each center and total admissions and departures.

Vital statistics records are microfilm copies of photostats of birth, stillbirth, and death certificates for persons of Japanese descent. The certificates originated in public health departments in California, Oregon, Washington, and Arizona.

Records relating to persons, other than those of Japanese ancestry, who were excluded from sensitive, domestic military areas during World War II are in Records of the Office of the Judge Advocate General (Army), RG 153. The records, dated 1941–48, include individual **exclusion case files,** which document the relocation of German and Italian aliens and U.S. citizens of German and Italian extraction from militarily sensitive areas to other parts of the country. Records show name of the person excluded, date and place of birth, marital status, education, employment record, military service, date of order of exclusion, and information about proceedings and appeals. Most are arranged alphabetically by name of person excluded.

CHAPTER 11

Records of Native Americans

11.1 Introduction

The emphasis in this chapter is on textual records generated or compiled by the Bureau of Indian Affairs, but the records of many other executive, legislative, and judicial agencies of the Federal Government include information about specific tribes and individual Indians, just as they do about non-Indians. Service records of volunteer and Regular Army units, bounty land warrant applications, pension applications, claims, and census schedules described in other chapters in this guide may include information of interest to researchers engaged in Indian genealogy. It is important to remember, however, that many persons of Native American ancestry belonged to tribes that had no official relationship with the Federal Government, while others dropped their tribal associations and became citizens of the United States. In such cases, they may be mentioned in some of the records referred to above, but they may not be specifically identified as Indians. Consequently, it may not be possible to document them as Native Americans. Such individuals should be researched following the same procedures used to research other members of the general population.

Jurisdiction of the Bureau of Indian Affairs (BIA), in existence since 1824, extends to those tribes officially recognized by the Federal Government, usually tribes involved in a treaty or guardianship relationship with the Government. Consequently, the National Archives has few holdings concerning eastern tribes, many of whom were nearly extinct by the time the Federal Government was established. Those tribes that survived, particularly in the East, often were under state rather than Federal authority. Although some tribes that had all but disappeared as political entities have been able to gain Federal recognition in recent years, it will be some 30 years before the National Archives receives records relating to them.

Information about individual members of tribes that did come under the jurisdiction of the Bureau of Indian Affairs is difficult to locate before Congress passed an act in 1884 (23 Stat. 98), requiring Indian agents to submit an annual census of all Indians in their charge. Some earlier census rolls and other enumerations exist, but most of them only list heads of families. Beginning in 1885, however, chances are good that some information about individual members of federally recognized tribes will be found in census or other records maintained by the Bureau of Indian Affairs. The records described below, primarily in Records of the Bureau of Indian Affairs, Record Group (RG) 75, deal specifically with Native Americans. This discussion of the census and other types of general BIA records held by the National Archives and Records Administration (NARA) in Washington, DC, and its regional archives facilities is followed by Table 16, which identifies the BIA jurisdictions whose records are held by NARA.

General descriptions of BIA records held by NARA in the National Archives Building and the regional facilities are given in *Guide to Federal Records in the National*

Archives of the United States (Washington: National Archives and Records Administration, 1995). More specific descriptions of relevant records created by the Bureau and other Government agencies are found in *Guide to Records in the National Archives Relating to American Indians,* compiled by Edward E. Hill (Washington: National Archives and Records Service, 1982). This publication is useful for understanding the administrative structure of the Bureau of Indian Affairs and its relationship to other Government agencies. It contains considerable information of value to persons doing extensive genealogical research in Indian records. Most of the microfilm publications cited throughout this chapter are listed in *American Indians: A Select Catalog of National Archives Microfilm Publications* (Washington: National Archives and Records Administration, revised 1998), cited hereafter as *American Indians*. For costs and more information about purchasing the volumes or the microfilm publications, call 1-800-234-8861, or fax 1-301-713-6169.

Available in the research rooms is *Preliminary Inventory of the Records of the Bureau of Indian Affairs*, Preliminary Inventory (PI) 163, 2 vols., also compiled by Edward E. Hill (Washington: National Archives and Records Service, 1965), which contains detailed descriptions of the records that were in the National Archives on March 31, 1965. Like Hill's *Guide*, cited above, it provides much information about records valuable for genealogical research.

11.2 Records Relating to Military Service

Over the years some Native Americans went to war as members of regular military or volunteer units that were composed largely of non-Indians. Documentation regarding the service of such individuals should be looked for in the records of the units in which they served (see *Section B, Military Records*, in this volume for additional information). Several record groups, however, include records relating specifically to Native Americans who performed military service during the period 1812–1945; those records are discussed below.

Service records for Native Americans who served in the War of 1812 are found in Records of the Adjutant General's Office, 1780's–1917, RG 94. These records are available on microfilm as M1829, *Compiled Military Service Records of Maj. Uriah Blue's Detachment of Chickasaw Indians in the War of 1812*, 1 roll, and M1830, *Compiled Military Service Records of Maj. McIntosh's Company of Creek Indians in the War of 1812*, 1 roll. Indians serving in these units were eligible for benefits provided by the act of Congress of March 3, 1855 (10 Stat. 701) extending the bounty land laws to Indians. Thus, Native Americans who were in the military prior to 1855 were rewarded for their service with bounty land warrants entitling them to free land in the public domain (*see* Chapter 8). Applications submitted by Indians claiming entitlement on the basis of their own military service and by persons claiming to be heirs of qualified Indians are recorded in an **abstract list of Indian applicants for military bounty lands**, 1855-82, found in the Land Division records in RG 75. Abstract entries give name of applicant, age, tribe, war in which service was claimed, name of commanding officer, information regarding the processing of the application, and, when applicable, the bounty land warrant. Entries are arranged in rough chronological order. A separate alphabetical **index to the abstract** covers applications received during the years 1855-75 (chiefly those in the 1855-58 period). Arranged by surname of applicant, the index entries identify the applicants and their tribe and show whether a warrant was issued. The **case files of bounty land warrant applications of Indians based on service between 1812 and 1855**, showing name of Indian, military organization, and dates of service, are among the bounty land warrant application files in Records of the Veteran's Administration, RG 15. The files are arranged alphabetically by initial letter of the first name, usually a phonetically spelled Indian name.

Native Americans fought for both the Confederacy and the Union in the Civil War, and their **service records** are found in War Department Collection of Confederate Records, RG 109, and Records of the Adjutant General's Office, 1780's-1917, RG 94, respectively. Records usually consist of a jacket-envelope for each soldier, labeled with name, rank, and name of the unit or special corps in which they served. The envelope typically contains card abstracts of entries relating to the soldier as found in original muster rolls, returns, rosters, pay rolls, appointment books, hospital registers, prison registers and rolls, parole lists, and inspection reports; and the originals of any papers relating solely to the particular soldier. Cross-references for soldiers' names that appeared in the records under more than one spelling are included.

Most of the compiled service records reproduced in microfilm publications cited below are arranged according to an organizational breakdown, ending with the regiment or the independent battalion or company. Under each unit service records are arranged alphabetically by soldiers' surnames. Records of military units composed of members of Indian tribes located in Indian Territory and Arkansas have been reproduced on rolls 77-91 of M258, *Compiled Service Records of Confederate Soldiers Who Served in Organizations Raised Directly by the Confederate Government*, 123 rolls. Included are files for Cherokee, Choctaw, Chickasaw, Creek, Osage, and Seminole units. The various Indian units covered by the service records are listed on pages 136-137 of *American Indians*. Researchers who do not know the organizational unit can identify individual service records by using the master index, which is available on M253, *Consolidated Index to Compiled Service Records of Confederate Soldiers*, 535 rolls. Entries give name of soldier, rank, and unit. Histories of the Indian units are reproduced on roll 74 of M861, *Compiled Records Showing Service of*

Military Units in Confederate Organizations, 74 rolls.

Some Native Americans loyal to the Union cause fought in home guard units organized in Kansas and Missouri, and their records are in RG 94. Service records for these soldiers are reproduced on roll 225 of M594, *Compiled Records Showing Service of Military Units in Volunteer Union Organizations*, 225 rolls. Members of the Omaha and Pawnee tribes in Nebraska Territory served as scouts; their records, arranged by tribe and thereunder alphabetically by name on rolls 41-43 of M1787, *Compiled Service Records of Volunteer Union Soldiers Who Served in Organizations from the Territory of Nebraska*, 43 rolls.

RG 94 also includes a separate series of **enlistment papers for Indian scouts** who served in the Regular Army during the period 1866-1914. It is arranged in two parts: enlistment papers, and jackets containing consolidated "personal papers" for each scout. Files in both parts are arranged by initial letter of surname, thereunder by enlistment number. The papers are indexed by four volumes identified as New Mexico, 1866-74; Indian Territory and Oklahoma, undated; Northern, 1874-1914; and Arizona, 1866-1914. Index entries give name of scout and enlistment number.

Enlistment papers for individual scouts can also be accessed by using a series of five bound registers reproduced on rolls 70-71 of M233, *Registers of Enlistments in the U.S. Army, 1798-1914*, 81 rolls. Register entries show the names of enlisted men, when, where, and by whom enlisted, period of enlistment, place of birth, age, civilian occupation, personal description, organization assignment, and enlistment number, with pertinent remarks.

Some records concerning Indian scouts were also maintained by the Bureau of Indian Affairs. Filed with the records of the Finance Division in RG 75 is an 1892 **list of Sioux scouts and soldiers and heirs**, which identifies members of the Sisseton, Wahpeton, Mdewakanton, and Wahpekute Sioux who served as scouts and soldiers during the Civil War or the Sioux uprising in Minnesota in 1862. Also shown are names and relationships of the heirs of those who were deceased. Persons listed were those considered to be eligible to participate in a payment authorized by an act of March 3, 1891. Names of persons actually paid are among the Bureau's annuity payment rolls, which are discussed in 11.4.1 below.

Records of the Bureau's Land Division include several series concerning claims arising from military service of Indians during the Civil War. Bound **lists of claimants**, 1865-72, identify persons filing claims for bounties, for arrears of pay, and for pensions. Entries give name of claimant, name of soldier on whose service the claim was based, organization of soldier, and other information. Entries are arranged in part by date the claim was filed, in part by type of claim, and in part by geographical location. A **register of claims for bounties and back pay**, 1869-90, gives name of claimant, rank and organization, name of claimant's agent and information concerning the nature of the claim, evidence submitted, and action taken. Entries are arranged alphabetically by initial surname of claimant, thereunder chronologically by date of filing of claim or other action. Entries in a **register of pension claims**, 1873-75, arising from deaths or injuries that resulted from service during the Civil War, give name of claimant (the soldier or, more frequently, the heirs), name of soldier and rank and organization, name of responsible Indian agent, tribe of soldier, date of entering service, date of discharge, date of filing claim, and other information concerning the claim and action taken. These entries are arranged alphabetically by initial letter of surname of claimant, thereunder chronologically by filing date of claim. A **register of admitted pension claims**, 1866-69, lists claims of heirs of Indians killed in service during the Civil War and claims of invalid Indians. Each entry gives name, rank, and organization of soldier; name of heir, if applicable; address of heir or invalid; relation of heir to soldier; date of certificate of approval of claim; and other pertinent information of an administrative nature. The entries are arranged alphabetically by surname of soldier, thereunder chronologically by date of certificate.

The Bureau's documentation of Native American participation in World War I and World War II includes an extensive **card index**, identifying members of federally recognized tribes who served in World War I. Separate sections of the index identify decorated individuals, officers, and women nurses. The index entries give name, tribe, reservation, and military unit. In 1920 the Office of Indian Affairs, as the BIA was then called, distributed **questionnaires** designed to secure information concerning activities of individual Indians in the war. The questions cover name, tribe, age, post office address, whether drafted or enlisted, branch of service, rank, medical status (wounded, gassed), whether cited for bravery, or decorated. Completed questionnaires, about one linear foot, make up the bulk of a series called "records relating to Indians in World War I and World War II." The few files relating to World War II contain lists of servicemen who were wounded, missing in action, prisoners of war, or recipients of awards for valor. Lists are usually arranged by state. Entries give name, rank, tribe, agency, war zone, and source of information.

General information concerning Native American participation in the world wars can be found under the "General Service" heading in the Bureau's central classified correspondence, 1907-69 (classification no. 125). The jurisdictional (agency) segments of the central classified correspondence may also include pertinent records under that classification number.

11.3 Indian Census Records

NARA does not have enrollment records for all tribes even though such records may exist. Since 1934 **tribal enrollments** have been entirely governed by the tribes themselves. As an outcome of the Indian Reorganization Act, Indian tribes have the right to determine their own membership. Most tribes have adopted constitutions that specify conditions for enrollment. Even though persons may ultimately be of Indian heritage, they are not necessarily entitled to membership in a tribe or to tribal benefits.

The Indian census records considered in this chapter are found in four record groups. The Federal decennial census rolls and related enrollments are in Records of the Bureau of the Census, RG 29, and some rolls are found in Records of the U.S. Court of Claims, RG 123, and Records of the Office of the Secretary of the Interior, RG 48. Most enrollments, however, are part of the central office records of the Bureau of Indian Affairs in RG 75. Some of the more prominent series are discussed below, but researchers should bear in mind that information of a genealogical nature is widely dispersed throughout the Bureau's records, depending upon the nature of the actions involved. For example, the comprehensive series of census rolls, 1885–1940, comes from the records of the Bureau's Statistics Division, while other tribal rolls are found in removal records, records of the Land and Finance Divisions, and some correspondence series. Unless stated otherwise, all of the enrollment records discussed below are in the National Archives Building in Washington, DC.

11.3.1 Federal Decennial Census Records and Related Enrollments

The Federal census population schedules described in Chapter 1 often include the names of Native Americans who were paying taxes and were living away from reservations, but before 1870 there is seldom a way to identify such individuals in the census. Sometimes the abbreviations "In." or "Ind." appear under the heading "race." An exception is the **1860 census** for Arkansas, which includes entries for Indians living in Indian Territory on roll 52 of M653, *Eighth Census of the United States, 1860*, 1,438 rolls. The **1870** and **1880** censuses both list Indians living on reservations under the states and counties where the reservation were located. For example, entries for the Sisseton and Wahpeton Sioux on the 1880 rolls for Dakota Territory are on roll 115 of T9, *Tenth Census of the United States*, 1,454 rolls. The schedules of a **special 1880 enumeration** of select groups of Indians living in Washington and Dakota Territories and in California have been microfilmed as M1791, *Schedules of a Special Census of Indians, 1880*, 5 rolls. Additional information about this census and others is provided in "A Note About Native Americans" in 1.1 of this guide. Not until **1890** did the Federal Government make an all out effort to enumerate all Native Americans. Unfortunately, the individual returns have been lost, but the aggregate data is still available as a Census Bureau publication printed in the Congressional Serial Set as 52nd Cong., 1st sess., H.Rept. 340, Pt. 15, serial 3016, *Report on Indians Taxed and Indians Not Taxed in the United States (excluding Alaska) at Eleventh Census, 1890* (Washington: Government Printing Office, 1894).

The volume is also available on roll 34, item 70, of NARA microfilm publication T825, *Publications of the Bureau of the Census, 1790-1916*, 42 rolls. Although the *Report* does not include names of individual tribal members, it does provide considerable background information on the various tribes that researchers interested in Indian ancestry will find of value.

A two-part **census of Shawnee Indians in Kansas Territory** follows the 1857 census of Kansas Territory reproduced on roll 1 of M1813, *Kansas Territorial Censuses, 1855-1859*, 2 rolls. Part 1 of the census covers those members of the tribe who had selected 200 acres of land under terms of a treaty of May 10, 1854; part 2 covers those tribal members who elected to hold their land in common. Both parts of the census are indexed in rough alphabetical order by first letter of surname. Entries in the first part of the census include name, legal description of the land selected (range, township, and section number), and number of acres. The index to part 1 includes remarks for some persons on such matters as relationships to other enumerated Shawnees, physical disabilities, deaths since the taking of the census, and place of residence. The 1858 and 1859 censuses include information about Shawnee Indians living in Shawnee Township. The original census rolls are held by the Kansas State Historical Society, 6425 SW Sixth Ave., Topeka, KS 66615-1099.

In response to a Presidential directive, a census was taken of the populations of Indian Territory and the Territory of Oklahoma prior to their admittance to the Union as the State of Oklahoma. Only the **schedules for Seminole County**, in what was then Indian Territory, have survived. They have been reproduced as M1814, *1907 Census of Seminole County, Oklahoma*, 1 roll.

11.3.2 Annual Census and Enumeration Rolls

The **census rolls and supplements, 1885–1940**, submitted yearly by Indian agents and superintendents pursuant to the 1884 act and subsequently filed in the Statistics Division, constitute the most extensive and comprehensive enrollment series in RG 75. Because of its scope and continuity of coverage, this series is the most useful single source for Indian genealogy, although it does not include census rolls for the Five Civilized Tribes in Oklahoma. It does, however, include rolls for the Cherokee of North Carolina for most years, 1898-1939, and for the Choctaw in Mississippi, 1926-39.

The census rolls are arranged alphabetically by name of Indian agency, thereunder by name of tribe, and thereunder by year. Names of individual Indians on the rolls before 1916 are seldom arranged alphabetically and locating a particular name may require scanning all entries for the tribe. After 1916 most entries are alphabetized by names of heads of families. Data on the rolls vary to some extent, but usually given are the English and/or Indian name of the person, roll number, age or date of birth, sex,

and relationship to head of family. Beginning in 1930 the rolls also show the degree of Indian blood, marital status, ward status, place of residence, and sometimes other information. For certain years—including 1935, 1936, 1938, and 1939—only supplemental rolls of additions and deletions were compiled.

The series is available on microfilm as M595, *Indian Census Rolls, 1885-1940*, 692 rolls. Segments of this publication, based on the geographic locations of the tribes, have been placed in NARA's regional archives facilities. Copies of the publication may also be available at historical and genealogical societies. Over the years tribes often came under the jurisdiction of several Indian agencies, so it is important to know which agency had jurisdiction for a particular tribe at any given time. *American Indians* includes a list of tribes and jurisdictions compiled to help identify rolls of microfilm on which census rolls for each tribe are reproduced, pp. 52-56. It is followed by a complete roll list for M595, pp. 56-72.

Additional supplements, chiefly birth and death rolls, are for the period 1938-55, and were still held by the Bureau of Indian Affairs when M595 was produced. They have since been accessioned into the National Archives of the United States and are now available for research at the National Archives Building.

Because most census rolls were compiled by agents and superintendents in the field, the records of Indian agencies and other Bureau jurisdictions held by many of NARA's regional archives facilities include copies of census rolls submitted to the Washington office of the Bureau. Some may be earlier than 1885 and others later than 1940 but, for the most part, regional census records largely duplicate those reproduced on M595. An exception is NARA's Southwest Region in Fort Worth, TX, which holds the bulk of the Bureau's records relating to the enrollment of the Five Civilized Tribes by the Dawes Commission, named for its chairman, Senator Henry Dawes.

11.3.3 Censuses and Other Enumerations of the Five Civilized Tribes

In 1893 the Dawes Commission was charged with securing agreements with the Cherokee, Chickasaw, Choctaw, Creek, and Seminole Indians to extinguish tribal title to all their lands in Indian Territory and to allot their lands in severalty. When the Commission began its compilation of a complete Indian census that could be used as the basis for the distribution of tribal lands to individual Indians, the Five Tribes exercised sole jurisdiction over tribal citizenship. Congress confirmed the existing citizenship rolls of the several tribes by the Indian appropriation act of June 10, 1886 (29 Stat. 339), but it also directed the Commission to hear and "determine the applications of all persons who may apply to them for citizenship and....determine the right of such applicant to be admitted and enrolled." The application and appeal process had been underway for two years when Congress passed the Curtis Act on

1420	Ong Cokala	Without a Rump	Father	M	62
1421	Hunkhapaya	Hunkpapa	Wife	F	60
1422	Tasunke Topa	Four Horses	Daughter	F	21
1423	Cetan ska win	White Hawk	Daughter	F	19
1424	Wasicun	White Man	Son	M	12
1425	Heraka-Ota	Plenty Elks	Son	M	37
1426	Suta win	Red woman	Sister	F	27
1427	Ehake Hinape	Last to Appear	Mother	F	55
1428	Ta anpetu Suta	Red Day	Niece	F	1
1429	Sunka-Mani	Walking Dog	Brother	M	24
1430	Cehupa	Jaw	Brother	M	29
1431	Winican	Pretty Woman	Sister	F	15
1432	Pe-zan	Sore Head	Brother	M	11
1433	Istinela	Sleeping	Father	M	57
1434	Ta-anpetu waste	Pretty Day	Wife	F	38
1435	Oye Wanbli	Eagle Track	Daughter	F	5
1436	Sinte Sna	Rattling Tail	Daughter	F	1
1437	Wasicun Wakan	Holy White Man	Father	M	34
1438	Nahoton win	Tramp Noise	Wife	F	27
1439	Blotanhunka	Leader of War Party	Daughter	F	1
1440	Ktela	Kill	Brother In Law	M	17
1441	Tatanka Iyotake "Chief"	Sitting Bull	Father	M	51
1442	Oyate wanyakapi	Seen by the Nation	Wife	F	46

217

June 28, 1898 (30 Stat. 495), authorizing the Commission to prepare for each tribe new citizenship rolls incorporating names of successful applicants. These "Final Rolls" were to be the only rolls used for allotment purposes. Applications received by the Commission under the 1896 act and related indexes have been microfilmed as M1650, *Applications from the Bureau of Indian Affairs, Muskogee Area Office, Relating to Enrollment in the Five Civilized Tribes Under the Act of 1896*, 54 rolls. The publication reproduces the applications for enrollment of Cherokees, Chickasaws, Choctaws, and Creeks, as well as those of former slaves (freedmen) of the Chickasaw and Choctaw tribes. No Seminole applications have been located. Applicants included Indians by blood; spouses of Indians, although the spouses themselves were not Indians by blood; and freedmen who had formerly belonged to members of the Five Civilized Tribes.

The final rolls of the Five Civilized Tribes in Indian Territory prepared by the Commission and approved by the Secretary of the Interior list the names of both those persons who were approved as eligible to receive land and those who were disapproved. Most rolls give name, age, sex, degree of Indian blood, and the roll and census card number for each individual. Rolls are arranged by name of tribe, thereunder by separate categories for citizens by blood, citizens by marriage, and freedmen. Also included are final rolls for the Mississippi Choctaw and the Delaware Cherokee and separate rolls for minor children and newborn babies for some groups. Names on the final rolls are arranged numerically in the order in which they were recorded, and locating information about a particular Indian requires scanning the entire roll(s) for the appropriate tribe. Original rolls are part of the Records of the Office of the Secretary of the Interior, RG 48, in the National Archives at College Park, MD, but applications received under the 1896 and later acts and related records are at Fort Worth. Some Federal records relating to the Five Civilized Tribes are in the Oklahoma Historical Society, 2100 N. Lincoln Blvd., Oklahoma City, OK 73105, one of NARA's affiliated archives.

Original rolls received by the Secretary of the Interior from the Dawes Commission are reproduced as T529, *Final Rolls of Citizens and Freedmen of the Five Civilized Tribes in Indian Territory (as Approved by the Secretary of the Interior on or Before Mar. 4, 1907, With Supplements Dated Sept. 25, 1914)*, 3 rolls. Choctaw and Chickasaw rolls are reproduced on roll 1, Cherokee rolls on roll 2, and Creek and Seminole rolls on roll 3. The Commission printed the approved rolls as *Final Rolls of Citizens and Freedmen of the Five Civilized Tribes in Indian Territory* (1 vol.), and the index (1 roll). Much of the index is available on the National Archives Information Locator (NAIL). The electronic form is searchable by individual names. For more information about NAIL, *see* I.2 in the Introduction to this volume.

The **index and final rolls** are also reproduced on roll 1 of M1186, *Enrollment Cards of the Five Civilized Tribes,*

1898-1914, 93 rolls. Sometimes referred to as a "census card," the enrollment card records information taken from individual applications submitted by members of the same family group or household and includes remarks on actions taken. Each enrollment card contains references to earlier tribal rolls, parents' names and places of residence, and decisions by the Secretary of the Interior. Each card also includes the names of related enrollees—husband, wife, children, and sometimes grandchildren and wards— and the individual's application number, which is necessary to locate their application. Cards are arranged by tribe, thereunder by category, and thereunder by the "census card" number, shown as part of the individual's entry on the final roll. Similar **enrollment cards** originating with the Realty Branch of the Bureau of Indian Affairs in Muskogee, OK, are available as reference microfilm CC (74 rolls) at NARA's Central Plains Region in Kansas City, MO.

The actual **application forms** submitted to the Dawes Commission contain information not abstracted to the enrollment (census) cards. The forms are arranged by tribe, thereunder by category, and thereunder numerically by the application number shown on the enrollment card. They are reproduced as M1301, *Applications for Enrollment of the Commission to the Five Civilized Tribes, 1898-1914*, 468 rolls. Original enrollment cards prepared by the Commission and the applications are held by NARA's Southwest Region in Fort Worth. Paper copies of the applications or census cards can be obtained for a fee by contacting that region at the address shown in Table 1.

Cherokee Enumerations

On May 18, 1905, the Court of Claims settled three suits in favor of the Cherokee Nation, and in 1906 Congress appropriated more than $1 million to compensate the Cherokee for funds owed them under treaties of 1835, 1836, and 1845 with the United States. The Secretary of the Interior appointed Guion Miller to compile a roll of all Eastern and Western Cherokee Indians who were alive on May 28, 1906, and could prove either that they were members of the Eastern Cherokee tribe at the time of the treaties or were descended from members who had not been subsequently affiliated with any other tribe. Miller submitted his report and roll on May 28, 1909, and a report on exceptions and two supplementary rolls on January 5, 1910. **Guion Miller's roll of Eastern Cherokee**, his reports, an index to findings on individual applications (10 vols.), and related testimony (10 vols.) taken by Miller and his staff, 1908-9, have been reproduced as M685, *Records Relating to Enrollment of Eastern Cherokees by Guion Miller, 1908-1910*, 12 rolls. Miller stated that 45,847 separate applications had been filed, representing a total of about 90,000 individual claimants, 30,254 of whom were entitled to share in the fund. Indexes and copies of early census rolls of Eastern Cherokee Indians used in determining the eligibility of the Cherokee are reproduced on roll 12 of M685. Commonly known as the

Chapman, Drennen, and Old Settler rolls, 1851–52, and the **Hester roll, 1884**, these censuses generally were made to determine eligibility for payments due under the provisions of the 1835 removal treaty. The Chapman roll is a receipt roll for payments actually made. For further details on these rolls and what they contain, *see* Gaston Litton's "Enrollment Records of the Eastern Band of Cherokee Indians," in *North Carolina Historical Review*, 17 (July 1940): 199–231. It should be noted that there are no applications or other associated records containing information about the individuals listed on these earlier enrollments.

Guion Miller's census roll and the general index to Eastern Cherokee applications (2 vols.), reproduced as part of M685, are also on roll 1 of M1104, *Eastern Cherokee Applications of the U.S. Court of Claims, 1906-1909*, 348 rolls. This publication reproduces the **applications** filed by individuals who wished to participate in the Court of Claims award. These documents are a particularly rich source of genealogical information because each applicant was asked to furnish full English and Indian name, residence, age, place of birth, name of husband or wife, names of children, place of birth and date of death of parents and grandparents, names and ages of brothers and sisters, and names of uncles and aunts. Most of the related records reproduced on M685 are in RG 75, but the applications themselves are in Records of the U.S. Court of Claims, RG 123. They are arranged by application number; the appropriate number can be found in the two-volume index on roll 1 of M1104. Complete roll listings of both M685 and M1104 are provided in *American Indians*, pp. 51 and 82–86. A reproduction of the index of all applications whether accepted or rejected can be accessed online through the NARA web page at *www.nara.gov*. More detailed information about the applications, Miller's reports and rolls, and the copies and indexes of earlier special rolls appears in *Preliminary Inventory to the Records of the United States Court of Claims*, PI 58, compiled by Gaiselle Kerner (Washington: National Archives and Records Service, 1953).

At the same time Guion Miller was preparing his roll of Eastern Cherokees, Frank C. Churchill was compiling a roll of persons who were recognized as members of the Eastern Band of Cherokee of North Carolina. Churchill submitted his report and the roll to the Secretary of the Interior in 1908. Because of objections raised by the tribe, the roll had still not been approved by the Secretary when Congress passed an act on June 4, 1924 (43 Stat. 376), providing for the final disposition of the affairs of the Cherokee Indians in North Carolina. An Eastern Cherokee Enrolling Commission was established to prepare the required census roll, but in 1928 Commission member Fred A. Baker assumed sole responsibility for the roll. He submitted his report and two rolls to the Secretary of the Interior on December 1, 1928. They were approved in 1931.

Records documenting the enrollment efforts are among those of the Land Division of the Bureau of Indian Affairs.

They include a 1907 roll of persons recommended for enrollment by the tribal council of the Eastern Band known as the **Harris, Blythe, and French Roll**, an index to the roll, and two versions of the 1908 **Churchill roll**. One roll lists rejected as well as accepted applicants; the other revised roll lists only the accepted applicants. Entries on all three rolls give Indian name, English name, position in family, sex, age, degree of Indian blood, roll numbers of parents, and residence. Family groups are enrolled together. Also included are copies of Guion Miller's roll of Eastern Cherokee, his report, and the census rolls and other exhibits mentioned above. **Baker's rolls, applications, transcripts of testimony, and related indexes** are among the records of the Eastern Cherokee Enrolling Commission. Individual entries on the rolls give name, position in family, sex, age in 1926 (age in 1912 on the roll of deceased annuitants), date of birth, degree of Cherokee blood, several numbers from other rolls, and other information.

During the period 1889-97 several commissioners investigated the status of many ex-slaves of the Cherokee of Indian Territory, as well as some Shawnee and Delaware Indians whose claims of Cherokee citizenship were disputed by the Cherokee. Records relating to Cherokee citizenship include several sets of affidavits submitted to the commissioners over the years. The most complete set, submitted to Commissioner John W. Wallace during the period 1889-90, is divided into the following groups: Admitted Shawnee, Rejected Shawnee, Deceased Shawnee, Admitted Delaware, Rejected Delaware, Free Negroes (free at the beginning of the Civil War), Admitted Cherokee Freedmen, Authenticated Cherokee Freedmen, and Rejected Cherokee Freedmen. Admitted Freedmen were persons who had not previously been recognized as Cherokee citizens but who were now so recognized. Authenticated Freedmen had been recognized previously and most of their affidavits were intended to secure the enrollment of young children or to establish their identity as persons who were recognized as citizens. Wallace submitted his rolls and some drafts in 1890. The rolls cover the groups represented in the affidavits as well as some special groups, mainly children and deceased persons. Individual entries give name, age, sex, residence, and other pertinent information. After revisions were made by the Bureau, the final versions of **Wallace's rolls covered the Authenticated and Admitted Freedmen, and the Shawnee and the Delaware Indians**. Included with the rolls is a copy of an **1896 roll of the Shawnee Cherokees** compiled by Special Agent James G. Dickson. The records also include Dickson's original roll and a roll of Shawnees admitted to Cherokee citizenship before June 10, 1871, which he submitted with his roll. These rolls and accompanying indexes are on available as M1833, *Revisions to the Wallace Rolls of Cherokee Freedmen and Delaware and Shawnee Cherokees, ca. 1890-96*, 1 roll. Also among the records is a roll of Cherokee Freedmen compiled by Commissioners William Clifton, William Thompson, and Robert H. Kern,

1896–97, covering authenticated and admitted freedmen and their descendants. Indexes for most rolls are available.

An **1897 Cherokee freedmen roll** identifying persons who were entitled to participate in an award by the Court of Claims is filed with the records of the BIA's Finance Division. Entries give name, age, sex, amount of money due, and sometimes other information. Some persons were paid and their signatures appear on the roll. A supplemental payment roll lists those freedmen whose payments were not recorded on the original roll. An index and accompanying affidavits are available for each roll. Also among the Finance Division records is an **1895 "Old Settler" Cherokee census roll**, listing persons who were eligible to participate in a payment to the members of the tribe who moved to Indian Territory prior to general removal in the 1830s. Entries give name, age, sex, address, and sometimes other information. The records include an index to the payment roll, but the roll itself has not been located among the Bureau's records. Entries in the index are in two parts: names of those who were alive at the time of payment, and names of those who were dead and whose heirs were paid. The roll and the index are available on microfilm as T985, *Old Settler Cherokee Census Roll, 1895, and Index to Payment Roll, 1896,* 2 rolls.

Following the Louisiana Purchase in 1803, the Federal Government officially encouraged Indians living east of the Mississippi River to move to lands located west of it. Indian removal became an explicit policy during Andrew Jackson's administration. Treaties were negotiated with the Five Civilized Tribes and others whereby the tribes agreed to give up their lands in the East and move west. Individual Indians who wished to stay in the East could accept a reservation of land in fee simple and remain as citizens. Certain problems arose concerning reservations granted to Indians in the East and compensation for losses suffered by those Indians who moved west. Consequently, records stemming from the removal of the Five Civilized Tribes and others consist of nearly 100 series. In addition to removal censuses and muster rolls, many records relating to land reserves and claims contain information of interest to genealogists, but for reasons of space, only a few such series are discussed in this chapter.

It should be noted that the genealogical value of the census and muster rolls varies. Most census rolls show only the names of the heads of families, making it difficult to relate these names to later generations. Others show, in addition, the number of persons, by age group and sex, in each family, and the original place of residence of each head of family. Muster rolls are arranged chronologically by date of emigration and are, for the most part, not indexed. Unless the date on which a particular Indian emigrated is known, it is extremely difficult to find an individual's name on a muster roll. Since relatively few musters rolls are available on microfilm, research on these records must be conducted at the National Archives Building. All of the removal records are described in some detail in Edward Hill's *Preliminary Inventory of the Records of the Bureau of Indian Affairs*, mentioned previously.

The earliest enrollment is a **register of Cherokees who wished to remain in the East** as citizens and to receive a 640-acre reservation under provisions of the treaty of July 8, 1817. The register, which is indexed, is reproduced as part of M208, *Records of the Cherokee Indian Agency in Tennessee, 1801-1835,* 14 rolls. A separate register accompanies **applications for reservations**, 1819, submitted by Cherokee Indians who wished to remain in the East under terms of the treaties of 1817 and 1819. The Cherokee removal treaty was negotiated in 1835, and **the Henderson roll**, the customary roll made before removal, lists heads of families and gives information concerning the family and its property. The roll and its index are available on film as T496, *Census Roll of the Cherokee Indians East of the Mississippi and Index to the Roll, 1835,* 1 roll. Filed with the Henderson roll in the removal records are several rolls made to determine eligibility for payments due under provisions of the 1835 treaty. Two of these, the Chapman and Hester rolls, were used by Guion Miller and, as stated previously, are reproduced on roll 12 of M685. The others are commonly known as: **Mullay Roll**, 1848; **Siler Roll**, 1851; **Powell Roll**, 1867 (no index); and **Swetland Rolls**, 1869 (one roll not indexed). Most of the rolls are arranged by geographical location of residence.

Emigration rolls, 1817–38, include lists of Cherokee Indians who wished to emigrate, rolls of actual emigrants, muster rolls of conducted parties, and lists of Indians able to emigrate by themselves. Some rolls are signed by the Indians and constitute relinquishments of their lands in the East. Usually only heads of families are listed, but often there is some information concerning the other members of the family. Alphabetical indexes are available for some rolls.

Chickasaw and Choctaw Enumerations and Related Records

Relatively few records document the Chickasaw removal. They do include a **census** listing members of the tribe, which was prepared in 1839, and some **muster rolls** of Indians emigrating in 1837. The census and the muster rolls are bound together in one volume.

Records concerning the Choctaw removal are more voluminous, largely due to claims filed under articles of the removal treaty of 1830. An 1831 census roll, known as the **Armstrong Roll**, lists individual Indians owning farms. Entries give name, number of acres cultivated, number in family, number of males over 16, number of males and females under 10, location of farm, probable value, and other information. The entries are arranged by Choctaw district; included for each district is a list of Indians entitled to additional land under provisions of the treaty. An alphabetical name index for each district is included with an unbound copy of the roll. A separate alphabetical **list of Choctaw reserves** can also be used as an index. **Emigration lists**, 1831–57, identify tribal members who were about to emigrate or who had already emigrated, either under Government supervision or by themselves. Some of the lists are indexed. An **1856 census roll**, compiled by Agent Douglas H. Cooper, lists Choctaw Indians who still remained east of the Mississippi. Given are the names of heads of families as well as the number of men, women, and children in the family and the place of residence. A typed alphabetical name index is filed with the roll. Many of the records relating to the Choctaw claims also include enumerations.

The enrollment records in the Land Division include **rolls of Choctaw freedmen, 1885**, submitted to the Bureau by the National Secretary of the Choctaw Nation. They consist primarily of rolls of freedmen who were admitted to citizenship, but included are lists of those whose status was considered doubtful and also some unbound lists of those who had elected to leave the Choctaw Nation. Entries give name, position in family, nationality of parents, name of former master, acreage of cultivated land, amount of livestock, and other pertinent information. Family groups are entered together, but there is no apparent pattern to the order in which they are listed. A separate set of rolls exists for each of the Choctaw districts. Listings for the First and Second Districts are numbered in order.

Also in the Land Division is an extensive collection of **records relating to applications for identification as Mississippi Choctaw, 1901–7**, received by the Bureau from the Dawes Commission. Records include applications, petitions, affidavits and other evidence, transcripts of testimony, copies of correspondence of the Commission (including notifications of decisions), and other kinds of records. Almost all of the original applications received by the Commission as well as later applications for review were rejected. Related applications were consolidated into a single case, and the cases are arranged in dossiers. Included with each dossier is an index to the records within it. Until recently these records were unindexed, but a comprehensive index, prepared by a NARA staff member, is now available.

Creek Census Rolls and Related Records

The **removal census, 1833**, compiled by Benjamin S. Parsons and Thomas J. Abbott in accordance with article 2 of the treaty of March 24, 1832, is available on T275, *Census of Creek Indians Taken by Parsons and Abbott in 1832*, 1 roll. Entries give the names of heads of families and the number of males, females, and slaves in each family. The census is in two parts: information for the families living in Upper Towns and Lower Towns, respectively. Each part is arranged by name of town, thereunder by name of head of family. The roll is indexed by name of town. An **index to Creek reserves**, which is an alphabetical list of the Creek Indians whose names are on location registers prepared by John J. Abert and James Bright, can be used to find the town in which a particular Indian is listed. Land location registers give the name of each reservee and a

description of the land. **Emigration lists**, 1836–38, consist of muster rolls of Creek Indians about to emigrate and those who had emigrated. Included are lists of Indians entitled to subsistence.

Two enrollments are filed with the records of the Finance Division. A **roll of Creek orphans and list of payments to be made**, 1870, gives the names of orphans and their heirs who were entitled to benefits of the treaty of 1832 and lists the payments to be made on the basis of the census. A 1904 **roll of self-emigrant Creek Indians** lists members of the tribe and their heirs who were entitled to participate in a payment authorized by Congress in an act of May 27, 1902 (32 Stat. 250), for those persons who had moved west of the Mississippi River and had subsisted themselves for one year in accordance with article 12 of the treaty of March 24, 1832. For original claimants, entries give the name and amount of claim; for heirs, entries give the name, age, sex, relationship to original claimant, address, amount due, and other information.

11.3.4 Records of the Commissary General of Subsistence

In 1830 the War Department's Office of the Commissary General of Subsistence was assigned the task of conducting the removal of the Indians to the West. It was responsible for their transportation and for their subsistence for one year after they reached their new homes. In November 1836 the Secretary of War transferred the Office's functions concerning Indian emigration to the BIA. Thereafter, army officers in charge of the removal performed their duties under direction of the Commissioner of Indian Affairs. Some muster rolls are found among the letters received by the Office, which are filed under the following headings: Cherokee, Chicago, Choctaw, Creek, Florida, Kickapoo, Miscellaneous, Ohio, Ottawa, Potawatomi, Quapaw, St. Louis Superintendency, Seminole, Western Superintendency, and Winnebago.

11.3.5 Miscellaneous Muster Rolls.

Miscellaneous muster rolls include enumerations of Seminole Indians and slaves from the Apalachicola towns, 1833, and other Seminole Indians and slaves, 1836, 1837; Kickapoo and Potawatomi Indians, 1833; New York Indians at the Osage Subagency, 1846; Ottawa Indians from Miami, OH, 1837; Potawatomi Indians of Chicago, 1836, 1837; Quapaw Indians from Arkansas, 1834–35; and Wyandot Indians from Ohio, Michigan, and Canada, 1843. These rolls, which are arranged alphabetically by name of tribe or state, are available on microfilm as: M1831, *Miscellaneous Indian Removal Rolls, 1832–1846*, 1 roll.

11.3.6 Other Enrollment Records

General Enrollments

Several tribes are covered by a series consisting of 11 bound **registers of Indian families**, 1884–1909, that were compiled by allotting agents. The format of the volumes varies but, in general, entries give information concerning heads of families, their grandparents, parents, uncles, aunts, brothers, sisters, and children. Information about age, marital status, tribal affiliation, and land allotment is sometimes recorded. Volumes cover Indians of the Turtle Mountain (Chippewa), Colville (Spokane), Klamath, Makah, Nez Perce, Coeur d'Alene, Wittenburg, Omaha, and Winnebago agencies or reservations. Alphabetical name indexes are included in the volumes. The **index to the Nez Perce register** is a separate volume.

The surveying and allotting records of the Bureau's Land Division include three versions of a **roll of Yankton and Santee Sioux, Omaha, Oto, and Iowa claimants to allotments on the Nemaha Half-Breed Reserve**, ca. 1857–59. Entries for individuals give roll number, name, family status, sex, age, degree of blood, band, information concerning guardian (if applicable), residence, decision on rejection or acceptance, and other pertinent information. The series consists of the original roll, a revised version, and a third version listing only accepted claimants. An alphabetical index to names of persons claiming rights is available. Also available is a **schedule of Santee and Yankton Sioux, Oto, Omaha, and Iowa mixed-bloods entitled to participate in the distribution of funds** arising from the sale of a tract excluded from the Nemaha Half-Breed Reserve by a survey of 1837–38. Entries give name, age, sex, band, and, if applicable, date of payment and name of person making the payment. Entries are arranged alphabetically by initial letter of surname.

A series called "**applications and other records relating to registrations under the Indian Reorganization Act of 1934**" includes application forms and affidavits, 1935–42, submitted by persons of at least one-half Indian blood who were not enrolled as members of any tribe but who were eligible for loans for education and for preference in employment with the Indian Service.

Under provisions of the Reorganization Act, funds were made available for purchasing lands for groups or individuals. Records are arranged alphabetically by name of state—California, Montana, Nevada, North Carolina, and North Dakota—and thereunder by Indian groups. The miscellaneous group consists of applications relating to applications for other locations. Records relating to applications for each tribal group are usually arranged alphabetically by name of applicant or numerically by application number.

Apache Indians

In 1914 a roll was prepared assigning **permanent English names to the Apache Indians at the Fort Apache Reservation**, formerly part of the White Mountain Reservation. Entries on the roll give the old Indian and English names, new English surnames and first names, English translation of former Indian names, relationships, sex, date of birth, and remarks. Entries are arranged by family groups, according to previously assigned numbers.

This roll is part of Special Series A (box 106), a collection of oversized items maintained by the Bureau apart from related correspondence.

Blackfeet Indians

A **schedule for enrollment of Blackfeet children** born since December 30, 1919, was prepared under provisions of an act of Congress of March 3, 1931 (46 Stat. 1495). Entries give name, age, date of birth, degree of Indian blood, place of birth, names of father and mother, and allotment number or race. The entries are arranged alphabetically by child's surname.

Brothertown Indians in Wisconsin

An act of March 3, 1839 (5 Stat. 349), provided for the partition of lands of the Brothertown Reserve in Wisconsin Territory among the individual tribal members. Indian Reserve files in Records of the Bureau of Land Management, RG 49, include a **list of the 378 heads of families who received land** and a legal description of their allotments.

Chippewa Indians

Records relating to Chippewa and Munsee Lands in Kansas Territory include census rolls of the United Tribes of Chippewa of Swan Creek and Black River and the Munsee or Christian Indians that were compiled in 1859. The entries, names only, are by family group. In some cases annotations in the allotment schedules and tract books that are also part of the series show relationships and give names of heirs. For Chippewa of Michigan, *see* "Ottawa"; for Munsee of Wisconsin, *see* "Stockbridge".

An **1890 census of the Turtle Mountain Band of Chippewa Indians** on the Turtle Mountain Reservation in North Dakota includes rolls for mixed-bloods living on and outside of the reservation. The entries, which give names, sex, ages, and relationships, are listed by family groups and arranged alphabetically by initial of surname. This census is item 88 in the "Irregularly Shaped Papers" series maintained by the Bureau.

Filed with the Bureau's oversize documents in Special Series A is a proposed official **roll of the Chippewa Indians on the White Earth Reservation**, compiled in 1910 (box 106). The roll is in five parts: full-blood Indians who had received allotments (927 persons); allottees less than full blood (2532); deceased allottees (1529); Mille Lac Indians, who were entitled to allotments as residents of the reservation (26 full bloods, 20 less than full blood); and Mille Lac Indians who had not yet moved to the reservation (100 full bloods and 25 less than full blood). Entries give Indian name, English name, sex, and blood degree.

California Indians

An act of Congress of May 18, 1928 (45 Stat. 602), authorized the Attorney General of California to bring suit in the U.S. Court of Claims on behalf of the Indians of California for benefits they would have received under 18 treaties that had not been ratified by the Senate. The act stipulated that any judgment resulting from the suit should be used to establish a trust fund "for educational, health, industrial, and other purposes" benefitting the California Indians. It authorized the creation of two census rolls. One was to include all California Indians, defined as those living in the state on June 1, 1852, and their descendants, who were residing in the state on May 18, 1928. Individuals listed on that roll were eligible to share as beneficiaries in any favorable judgment recovered in the U.S. Court of Claims. The second roll, apparently intended for informative purposes, listed non-California Indians who were living in California on May 18, 1928.

Fred A. Baker, having completed his work on the 1928 roll of Eastern Cherokee, assumed responsibility for compiling the rolls. Records in the Land Division consist of a **numerical list of applications**, 1928–32, **"indexes" to rejected applications**, 1928–32, and the **applications**. Forms completed by the applicants for themselves and minor children give for each person their name, position in family, age, sex, birth date, and degree of Indian blood claimed. Additional information provided concerns residence, marital status, land allotments, ancestry, and other subjects. Some of the applications—usually rejected ones—include letters, depositions, transcripts of testimony, and notifications of rejections. The applications are arranged numerically by application number. Application numbers can be determined from entries on the final roll, which, for the most part, are arranged alphabetically by surname. Entries give the final roll number, application number, allotment number, census number as of June 30, 1928, English name, Indian name, relationship in family, sex, age in 1928, date of birth, degree of Indian blood, name of tribe or band, where enrolled and allotted, post office, amount and kind of property owned, and remarks. The Bureau completed and certified the roll in 1932 and certified a supplement in 1933. Final rolls deposited with the central office of the Bureau are part of the annuity rolls filed in the Finance Division.

Copies of the rolls were maintained by the Sacramento Indian Agency and its successors, and annotations were made through 1964. The agency's set of rolls is reproduced as M1853, *Indians of California Census Rolls Authorized under the Act of May 18, 1928 (45 Stat. 602) as Amended, Approved May 16-17, 1933,* 1 roll. Rolls and reference microfilm copies (33 rolls) of the applications described above are among the records of the Sacramento Indian Agency held by NARA's Pacific Region (San Francisco). Microfilm copies of the rolls and applications are also available at NARA's Pacific Region (Laguna Niguel).

The roll was reopened in 1948 (completed in 1955) and again in 1968 (completed in 1972). Each time the roll was opened, a series of application files and a final roll was created by the Sacramento Agency or Sacramento Area Office of the Bureau of Indian Affairs. Records for these enrollments are also held by NARA's Pacific Region (San Francisco). Those for the 1948–55 enrollment consist of the final roll and original application files, which are subject to privacy restrictions. The records typically contain less genealogical information than the 1928–33 records. The 1948 enrollment applications are primarily arranged in two parts, new enrollees and 1928 enrollees who reapplied for enrollment. New enrollee files can be searched by the name of the 1928 enrollee through whom the 1948 individual claimed enrollment. Applications of the 1928 enrollees can be searched by the individual's 1928 roll number. Also subject to privacy restrictions are the original application files for the 1968–72 enrollment. These applications are arranged by folder number. In order to locate an individual's file, the folder number must be obtained from the Bureau of Indian Affairs, Sacramento Area Office, 2800 Cottage Way, Sacramento, CA 95825.

Fox Indians

Entries in an **1884 census of the Fox Indians at Tama, IA**, are arranged in family groups and show name, sex, age, and family relationships. Notes give "the pedigree and residence of these Indians." The census includes an index. This census is item 135 in the "Irregularly Shaped Papers."

Flathead (Confederated Tribes)

In 1905 Special Agent Thomas Downs compiled a new **roll of the Indians of the Flathead Agency in Montana (Flathead, Kutenai, Pend d'Oreille, Kalispel, and Spokane Indians)**. The records consist of correspondence and evidence, 1904–5; the 1905 census roll and 1908 supplements; and copies of a 1903 roll and supplement. Rolls are in the form of registers similar to those discussed above under General Enrollments. Individual entries for enrollees give Indian name, English name, age, degree of blood or nationality, tribal affiliation, position in family, marital status, and (if applicable) information concerning marriage, name of father, name of mother, and other pertinent information. Family groups are enrolled together but in no discernable order. The rolls, applications, and other related records are available on M1350, *Selected Records of the Bureau of Indian Affairs Relating to the Enrollment of Indians on the Flathead Reservation, 1903-8,* 3 rolls. Contents of the publication are shown in *American Indians*, pp. 80–81.

Kansa Indians

Records relating to the Kansas Trust Lands and Diminished Reserve in Kansas include an 1862 **census roll of the Kansa Indians**, indicating the land allotment of each Indian and an appraisal of improvements by white settlers on the Kansas Diminished Reserve. Entries on the census roll are arranged by family.

New York Indians

In 1898 the Court of Claims ruled that individual New York Indians were entitled to the proceeds from the sale of lands in Kansas allocated to the New York Indians but never occupied by them. Applications filed by persons wishing to participate in the award and several related series are among the records of the Bureau's Finance Division. The **applications, 1901–4**, are arranged by tribe—Onondaga, St. Regis, Seneca (and Cayuga), Stockbridge and Munsee, Tuscarora, Brothertown, and Oneida—and thereunder by claim number. Filed with the application forms are affidavits, copies of letters sent to applicants, and other documents concerning individual claims. Records are arranged alphabetically by name of tribe, thereunder by claim number, which was assigned in rough chronological order by date of receipt of application. Most of the claims were filed in 1901. Two **indexes** give the names of claimants and claim numbers. One includes penciled notations showing names of tribes and decisions. Entries in both indexes are arranged in alphabetical sections by surname of applicant. Related records removed from the general incoming correspondence and brought together by subject for easier reference constitute Special Cases 29 and 42.

Special Agent Guion Miller investigated the claims and compiled rolls of the names of persons he considered to be eligible. Rolls were revised under orders of the Court of Claims in 1905 and 1906. Final rolls showing the names of persons who were actually paid are among the annuity payment rolls. Guion Miller's reports include a copy of an **1859 report by Special Agent A.S. Stevens**, who heard testimony from persons concerning their rights to participate in the allotment of lands in Kansas. A separate index giving the names of the persons who testified is available.

Ottawa Indians (Kansas and Michigan)

A **census roll and list of allotments of Ottawa Indians of Kansas, 1863–64**, compiled by Agent Clinton C. Hutchinson and Special Commissioner Edward Wolcott gives names of individuals, sex, age, and location and acreage of land allotted under the provisions of the treaty of June 24, 1862. Family groups are listed together, and both names of individuals and names of families are numbered in order. The records are filed with those of the Bureau's Land Division.

The **"Durant Roll"** and its supplement were compiled by Horace B. Durant to determine those members of the Sault St. Marie, Mackinac, Little Traverse, Grand Traverse, and Grand River bands of Ottawa and Chippewa Indians of Michigan who were eligible to receive monies due the tribes under terms of the treaties of May 27, 1836, and July 31, 1855. The supplemental roll contains the names of children born between March 4, 1907, and August 1, 1908. Information included on the census is a follows: 1870 roll number (this number indexes Durant's field notes, which contain genealogical information), the Durant roll number, Indian name, English name, relationship to head of household, age, sex, tribal band, residence, and remarks. The rolls, field notes, and related records are reproduced on M2039, *Correspondence, Field Notes, and the Census*

Roll of All Members or Descendants of Members Who Were on the Roll of the Ottawa and the Chippewa Tribes of Michigan in 1870 and Living on March 4, 1907 (Durant Roll), 4 rolls. A roll list and explanation of the arrangement of the records appears in *American Indians*, p. 80. These materials are part of the Special Agent files in the records of the Bureau's Inspection Division.

Sioux Indians

During the period 1903–10, the Bureau established permanent family names for the Indians of several agencies in North Dakota, South Dakota, and Montana. Entries in the **rolls for revisions of names of Indians** give permanent name, position in family, Indian name, previous English name, sex, age, names of relatives, and sometimes other information. Rolls are available for the Cheyenne River, Devil's Lake, Lower Brulé, Fort Peck, Pine Ridge, Rosebud, Sisseton, and Standing Rock agencies. Names of family groups are entered together. Most of the roll entries are arranged alphabetically by initial letter of permanent surname, but some are arranged by previous English surname.

An **1886 census of Sioux Indians living on the Lake Traverse Reservation** in North and South Dakota provides information regarding the property of each head of family. The entries, arranged by family groups in rough alphabetical order by surname, give Indian and English names, sex, age, and relationship to other family members and show the number of acres under cultivation, acreage being used for various crops, and the number of horses and cattle owned. The census is filed as item 46 in the Bureau's "Irregularly Shaped Papers."

Stockbridge and Munsee Indians of Wisconsin

This **1894 roll**, from the records of the Bureau's Land Division, was compiled by Special Agent C.C. Painter, as provided for by an act of Congress of March 3, 1893 (27 Stat. 744), and was revised in the Bureau. Entries for individuals give name, sex, position in family, age, and sometimes other information. Family groups are listed together. Entries are arranged alphabetically by initial letter of surname of head of family.

Washington Indians (Various Tribes)

In 1916 Special Agent Charles E. Roblin was instructed to enumerate and enroll Indians living in western Washington who were neither affiliated with nor allotted at any Indian agency. Roblin's report, and the roll he compiled, part of the file "1167-19-053 Taholah" in the Bureau's central classified files, have been combined with supporting **applications** from the Land Division and microfilmed as M1343, *Applications for Enrollment and Allotment of Washington Indians, 1911–19*, 6 rolls. Tribal groupings on Roblin's roll are not arranged in any discernable order, although names of the families belonging to each tribe usually are arranged in a rough alphabetical order by surname. Applications and evidence are grouped together by tribe and arranged in strict alphabetical order by the tribe's name. Under each tribal grouping, records relating to families are arranged in strict alphabetical order by name of the family head. Within each family grouping, records relating to members are arranged alphabetically by surname of the individual, which sometimes differs from that of the head of the family. At the end of some tribal groupings are applications received from persons who already were enrolled at another Indian agency, although they might not have been allotted at that agency.

Special Agent Roblin was also responsible for investigating the validity of **applications for adoption submitted to the Quinaielt tribal council** after an act of Congress of March 4, 1911 (36 Stat. 1345), authorized the allotment of the Quinaielt reservation lands. Roblin grouped together records of persons who claimed a common ancestry and consolidated records of all family members under the name of the head of the family or the name of the persons whom they claimed as their common ancestor, numbering the cases from 1 to 125. Records vary considerably in completeness and legibility. Documentation relating to some families is exhaustive while that of other families is meager and confusing. The records are not indexed. Roblin's report and the cases files, arranged numerically, are reproduced as M1344, *Records Concerning Applications for Adoption by the Quinaielt Indians, 1910-19*, 5 rolls.

Roll lists and more detailed discussions of the records reproduced on M1343 and M1344 are available in *American Indians*, pp. 81-82.

11.4 Other Central Office Records of the Bureau of Indian Affairs

11.4.1 Records Relating to Treaties

The negotiation of formal treaties with the Indians by the Government of the United States followed a custom established by Great Britain and the colonial governments. Ratified Indian treaties are one of the basic sources of documentation of the Government's policy toward Indians and the legal status of the tribes. Treaty provisions concern many subjects. For the genealogist the most important are those relating to the extinguishment of Indian titles to land. Typically the Indians agreed to reduce their land holdings or to move to an area less desired for white settlement. Often they were compensated for their land and property by lump sum or annuity payments of money or by payments in services or commodities. Some treaties provided for the allotment of land to individual Indians and for the dissolution of tribes. Most of the enrollments mentioned above are related to provisions found in Indian treaties.

The treaties were negotiated by special commissioners acting for the President under the supervision of the Secretary of War and, after 1849, the Secretary of the Interior. They were signed by the commissioners, representatives of the Indian tribes, and other witnesses. Original Indian treaties are in General Records of the U.S. Government, RG 11. They have been microfilmed as M668, *Ratified Indian Treaties, 1722-1869*, 16 rolls. The texts of treaties, including names of the officials and Indians who signed them, are published in Charles J. Kappler's compilation, *Indian Affairs, Laws and Treaties*, vol. 2, *Treaties*, (Washington: Government Printing Office, 1904). This volume may be consulted at many large libraries. It is also available as part of the Congressional Serial Set (58th Cong., 2nd sess., S. Doc. 319, serial 4624). Individual treaties are also printed in *Statutes at Large*.

Many of the treaties contained provisions calling for the allotment of land to specifically named individuals. Records of the Bureau's Land Division relating to claims include **Reserve Files, A, B, C, and D**, which consist of correspondence, reports, legal documents, maps, plats, and other material concerning land reserved for individual Indians mentioned in the treaties. Reserve File C concerns reserves for individual Indians specified in the 1830 Choctaw Treaty of Dancing Rabbit Creek. The records in each set of files are arranged by case numbers, which can be determined from indexes filed with the records. Each "case" consists of records resulting from a reserve claim of an individual Indian. Although some records relate to the establishment and location of the claim, most are about later actions concerning the reserve, often the transfer of it to another person or the solution of problems arising through inheritance.

Many treaties or acts of Congress required the Federal Government to make annual payments to tribal members for stated periods of time. In such cases, **annuity payment rolls** 1848-1940, were prepared by the agent to record the payments to individual Indians and ensure that each person received the appropriate sum. For the early to mid-1800s, an entry in an annuity payment roll may well be the only record of a particular person as a member of a federally recognized and administered tribe. The rolls, which are among the records of the Bureau's Finance Division, are usually in bound volumes arranged by name of tribe, thereunder chronologically. They are sometimes very difficult to read and may not have much identifying information other than the names of heads of households. It was not until late in the 1800s that the names of other family members were recorded. To locate a particular name, it may be necessary to scan the entire roll for each appropriate year. As a minimum the payment roll entries show the name of each head of family; but later rolls usually show the name, age, sex, amount of payment, and signature or mark of recipients. Since the payment rolls are not microfilmed, they must be viewed in the research room in the National Archives Building in Washington, DC. After 1885 annual census rolls are more useful than annuity payment rolls for genealogical research. Most of NARA's regional archival facilities also have sets of annuity payment rolls, and many of them are duplicated in the central office records.

Land allotment records were created when, under the terms of various treaties and acts of Congress, the Federal Government extinguished title to reservations and allotted land to individual members of tribes. An incomplete set of **allotment schedules** is arranged in rough alphabetical order by name of tribe, reservation, or geographic location. Entries in the individual volumes usually give name of allottee, some personal information such as age, sex, and position in family, and location and acreage of the allotment. Related records exist for some tribes, although the quantity and kinds of related records vary greatly from tribe to tribe. They may include applications for allotment, plat maps designating allotted land, registers of names of allottees and descriptions of their allotments, and information about contested allotments and improvements made to the land before selection. For some tribes, records containing information about sales and leases of allotted land may be available. Applications for allotment sometimes include information about an individual's place of residence and enrolled relatives.

The Bureau's cartographic records are filed apart from the textual records. **Maps of Indian reservations** are described in 19.5.

11.4.2 General Correspondence Files

Records of the BIA in the National Archives Building in Washington, DC, are those of the central office of the Bureau, which has been primarily responsible for administration. Bureau field officials maintain actual contact with Native Americans and carry out functional operations. Records of their work in the field are held by the National Archives regional archives facilities (*see* Table 16 below). During the 19th century, field operations were conducted by two principal types of BIA officials: superintendents, who had general responsibility for a particular geographical area and the agencies within that area; and agents, who were immediately responsible for relations with one or more tribes living within the jurisdiction of their agency. Correspondence with these employees forms a large portion of the general correspondence files of the Central Office, which fall into three chronological periods: 1824–80; 1881–1907; and 1907–ca. 1969.

1824-80

Most of the incoming letters for this period are microfilmed as M234, *Letters Received by the Office of Indian Affairs, 1824–1881*, 962 rolls. The **letters received** are arranged alphabetically by name of agency or superintendency, with general subjects such as "Annuity Goods," "Miscellaneous Emigration," and "Schools" interspersed. Many of the emigration related letters from agencies located in the East are filed under separate headings, such as "Ohio Agency Emigration." The letters are a rich source of information about tribes and sometimes about particular

individuals. As explained previously, in the course of conducting its business, the Bureau of Indian Affairs often prepared enumerations of Indian tribes. Nearly all of these enumeration rolls were originally received by the Bureau as enclosures to incoming letters. While some of the rolls were filed separately, others can still be found filed with their transmittal letters. The rolls with the letters were compiled for a specific purpose and most list only the heads of families. No comprehensive list of these rolls exists, but a few that have been located by the reference staff are identified in an informal list of enrollments and related records that is available for use in the research room at the National Archives Building. Because the Bureau did not index these letters, searching them can be time-consuming unless the researcher has an event or date in mind. Nevertheless, genealogists who are seeking information about individuals, particularly heads of family, who lived during this period may find a search of these letters worthwhile. Copies of M234 are available for use in most NARA regional facilities, and a complete list of the rolls in M234 is provided in *American Indians*, pp. 8–17.

1880-1907

Information about individuals can be located more easily during this period because the Bureau began indexing incoming letters in 1880. Indexes and registers, which provide a synopsis of the contents of all but the most routine letters received, have been microfilmed and can be used in the main microfilm reading room of the National Archives Building. The **indexes** (reference microfilm P2187) are grouped into five time blocks: 1881–86, 1887–92, 1893–99, 1900–6, and 1907. Within each group, index entries are arranged by subject in rough alphabetical order. Entries cover persons, firms, Govern-ment agencies, and many other subjects, in addition to the field jurisdictions of the Bureau (chiefly agencies and schools). Entries relating to agencies and schools and some of the other entries are subdivided into subjects arranged in alphabetical order. The **registers** (reference microfilm P2186) are arranged by year and by file number. After locating a file number and year from the indexes, the corresponding register entry should be checked to determine the letter's content. The actual letters, which have not been microfilmed, may then be requested from the reference staff for examination in the research room.

1907-ca. 1969

In 1907 the BIA adopted a new filing system that returned to the pre-1880 method of filing by agency. The **central classified files** contain all correspondence, both letters received and copies of letters sent, between the headquarters and the tribe and/or agency. Records are grouped as follows: those relating to the central office of the Bureau ("Indian Office"); general administrative records ("General Service"); and records relating to individual field units of the Bureau, with a few subject designations, arranged alphabetically by name of jurisdiction or subject. Records are arranged according to the jurisdictions and decimal classifications listed in both Edward Hill's *Guide to Records of American Indians in the National Archives* and his *Inventory to the Records of the Bureau of Indian Affairs (see* 11.1). The advantage of this system for the researcher is that individual segments of the file can be requested merely by specifying the name of the agency, the years, and the subject classification number. As noted above in 11.2, information about military service can be found under classification number 125. Correspondence concerning an individual's attempts to enroll in a particular tribe may be under classification number 053 (enrollment, citizenship, degrees of Indian blood), while heirship information may be found in files under the classification number 350 (estates, heirship cases). Information about allotments is under number 313 (allotments and homestead entries). The means of locating individual letters remained essentially unchanged, a detailed index and register system using index cards instead of volumes. This index is not presently in a form available to the researcher, and requests for file citations must be processed by a reference archivist.

Correspondence Filed Separately for Easier Reference

Several series of records consist of materials Bureau staff members removed from the larger correspondence files because they expected them to be used frequently during the course of business or because they were oversized. **Special files**, 1807-1904, consists of correspondence, reports, accounts, affidavits and other records relating principally to investigations and claims, including those of Indians and non-Indians for losses from depredations, of Indians for losses resulting from their removal from the East, and of persons seeking shares in tribal benefits. The approximately 300 special files are reproduced on M574, *Special Files of the Office of Indian Affairs, 1807-1904*, 85 rolls. A complete list of the special files is provided in *American Indians*, pp. 18-25. The second series, **special cases**, 1821-1907, chiefly concerns land disputes, and genealogists may find cases relating to such matters as allotments, leases, and sales to be of interest. An index and a list of the 203 Special Cases are available, but the cases have not been microfilmed. The two remaining series have already been referred to in connection with the enrollment records cited in 11.3.6. **Special series A**, ca. 1859-1934, relates to land matters, heirship cases, claims, and enrollments, as well as many other subjects. These records are not available on microfilm. The records filed separately because of unusual size or bulk are "**Irregularly Shaped Papers**," 1849-1907. They relate to such matters as enrollment of Indians and appraisals and allotments of land, and include census rolls, schedules, land patent applications, journals, and testimony. A list of the papers is available for use, but the records have not been microfilmed.

11.4.3 Employment records

Among the records of the central office are numerous bound **rosters of employees**, 1853-1909, generally arranged by type of position (field employees, superintendents and agents, agency employees, school employees, and Indian police), thereunder chronologically by agency or jurisdiction. Information concerning individual employees varies, but entries usually include name, position, salary for that year, name of tribe for whom appointed, dates of service, age, sex, race, marital status, birthplace, reason for termination of employment, and sometimes legal residence or state from which appointed. Most of the volumes contain indexes. Information about employees of the Bureau can also be found in the biennial register of employees of the Federal Government, 1816-1921. This publication, commonly known as the "Official Register" or the "Blue Book," is discussed in 14.1. The "Official Register" can usually be located in the Government documents section of large reference libraries.

11.4.4 School Records

Information about Indian schools and students can be found in all segments of the Bureau's correspondence files, but it was not until the early 20th century that periodic reports listing the names of Indian students and the dates they attended school were maintained as separate series. **Quarterly School Reports**, submitted for both Government and private contract schools, cover the time period 1910 to 1939. Entries for individual students usually give name, age, sex, tribe and degree of Indian blood, date of entry in school, grade, type of training, number of days in attendance, distance of home from a public school, and other pertinent information. Beginning in 1936 information concerning individual pupils was gradually eliminated. The reports are arranged by fiscal year, thereunder alphabetically by name of agency or other jurisdiction, thereunder by name of school, and thereunder chronologically. A list of the schools is available for researcher use. The number of quarterly reports submitted was greatly reduced when **semiannual school reports**, 1925-37, came into general use. Information provided on these reports is substantially the same as that found in the quarterly reports, and the records are arranged in a similar fashion. No list of schools is available for this series. None of the quarterly or semiannual reports are available on microfilm. Annual school reports, 1933-37, and quarterly school reports, 1937-40, for schools in Alaska are filed with records of the Bureau's Alaska Division.

Records of the Carlisle Indian Industrial School are maintained separately. They include student records, 1879-1918, related indexes, and student record cards. Student folders include correspondence, cards designated as "Descriptive and Historical Record of Student," applications for enrollment, form reports concerning post-school careers, clippings, photographs, and other documents. The quantity and type of records for individual students vary; there are, in general, more records for the later years than the earlier ones. Folders are arranged numerically by numbers found in the indexes.

As mentioned above, information about schools can be found in the Bureau's correspondence files. Relevant letters received for the 1824-80 period were filed under the general category "Schools," 1824-73 (rolls 772-799 in M234), or with the letters relating to the agency having jurisdiction over the school. Whole sections of the indexes for the 1881-1907 period contain references to letters relating to individual schools. From 1907 forward, letters relating to school matters were filed under the 800 classification numbers (800-855); they concern education, schools, and pupils. Records are arranged alphabetically under the name of the agency or, in some cases, the school. Schools having their own headings in the 1907-39 central classified files include: Carlisle, Carter Boarding School, Carter Seminary, Chemawa, Cherokee Orphan Training School, Cherokee School, Chilocco, Genoa, Hampton Institute, Haskell, Hayward, Mount Pleasant, Pueblo Day School, Salem, Sequoyah Orphan Training Institute, Sherman Institute, Springfield, Theodore Roosevelt School, and Wittenburg. These records are not filmed, but the name of a person can be looked up in the index to the central classified files. If the person was the subject of correspondence, their name will be in the index, and the correspondence may be accessed and copied.

11.5 Bureau of Indian Affairs Field Office Records

Besides the records of the central office of the Bureau Indian Affairs, there are records created by field offices of the BIA, chiefly agencies and schools. Most of the field office records that are part of the National Archives of the United States are in selected NARA regional archives facilities. The kinds of records maintained by the field offices did not vary much from one agency to another or from one school to another. The fact that officials in the field report their activities to and receive direction from the Bureau's central office in Washington, DC, has resulted in considerable duplication between the records of the central office and those of field offices. To avoid repetition, the **types of field office records** that are particularly helpful for genealogical research are described below. Table 16 lists the principal Indian agencies and the location of their records.

Census rolls are described in 11.3.

Allotment records similar to those described in 11.4.1.

Annuity payment rolls are described in 11.4.1.

Agency employee records often relate to Indian judges and Indian police, as well as to Indian and non-Indian teachers in both boarding and day schools and to other employees who may have been either Indian or white.

Records are usually arranged by date of employment, necessitating a search of the entire list for a particular name if no index is available. Some of the information that may appear in employee rosters are name, position, salary, date and place of employment, sex, race, age, marital status, birthplace, legal residence, previous occupation, and date and cause of termination.

Individual student history cards usually show name, tribe, sex, birth date, and names and census or allotment numbers of parents, brothers, sisters, uncles, and aunts.

Marriage cards usually give Indian and English name; sex; tribe; census or allotment number; how married (by tribal custom or U.S. law); name of spouse; if divorced, when, where, and how; and names, sex, and birth and death dates of children born of the marriage.

Marriage registers may include names of principals, age, nationality, tribe, father's and mother's names, and previous marriages. Occasionally a divorce decree has been entered.

Individual Indian index cards, prepared pursuant to the Indian Office Circular 652, June 29, 1912, show for males, name; address; allotment number, if any; and tribe affiliation.

Vital statistics records of births and deaths are arranged chronologically. Birth records may include parents' names, child's name, sex, degree of Indian blood, tribe, and residence. Death registers often consist of name of deceased; age; sex; degree of Indian blood; tribe; place, date, and cause of death; and residence.

Sanitary records concerning the sick and injured usually show name, age, and sex of patient; disease; date taken sick; and when recovered or deceased. Separate lists of births and deaths are often associated with sanitary records. Entries are usually arranged chronologically.

Heirship records often include correspondence with inheritance examiners and listings of heirs to allotments. Heirship ledgers may show name of land allottee, date of allotment, date of allottee's death, and names of approved heirs.

Registers of Indian families include Indian name, English name, age, blood or nationality, tribe or allegiance, marital status, date of marriage, how married, and parents' names and register numbers.

Indian School Records

Records for most reservation schools are among the field records of the various Indian agencies listed in Table 16. They usually contain school reports, individual pupil records, and school censuses in which students are listed by name. Also available are records for nonreservation boarding schools identified in Table 16.

School census records in the early 20th century were the means of determining the amount of Federal payment to the school, which was based on a certain amount per student per day of attendance. The record for each student usually shows name, sex, age, percent of Indian blood, names of parents, and name of school.

CARLISLE INDIAN INDUSTRIAL SCHOOL
DESCRIPTIVE AND HISTORICAL RECORD OF STUDENT

NUMBER 4187	ENGLISH NAME		AGENCY		NATION
5587	Sylvester Long		Robison Co. Agy		Cherokee
BAND	INDIAN NAME		HOME ADDRESS		
			Jos. Long		
			Kinston, N.C.		

PARENTS LIVING OR DEAD	Both Liv.	BLOOD	AGE	HEIGHT	WEIGHT	FORCED INSP.	FORCED EPXR.	SEX.
	Sallie M. Long	½	18	5' 8"	148¾	33	36²	M
FATHER, L	MOTHER, L							

ARRIVED AT SCHOOL	FOR WHAT PERIOD	DATE DISCHARGED	CAUSE OF DISCHARGE
Aug. 28, 1909	Three Years	Oct. 10. 1913	Term expired

TO COUNTRY	PATRONS NAME AND ADDRESS	FROM COUNTRY
6-23-11	On leave	7-4-
6-6-12	J. A. Beamer, Tyrone, Pa.	10-16-
5-31-10	J. A. Beamer, Tyrone, Pa.	

Months in school before Carlisle, 48 6th Gr.
Pub. Sch. 1897-1904 7th Gr.
Geneva Parochial 1908 6th Gr.
Grade entered at Carlisle, 7

Grade at date of Discharge,

Trade or Industry,

Church, Meth.

Mother claims descendency of Croton Tribe.
Boy left sch. to travel with Childs Street Show.
Given address, Salem, N.C.
Enlisted to sch. 2

Individual history card for student at Carlisle Indian Industrial School, PA. The student later became the show business celebrity "Chief Buffalo Long Lance." Records of the Bureau of Indian Affairs, RG 75.

School reports may report attendance, pupil examination and promotion, and records of supervisory visits to homes of adult students. Quarterly school reports often describe each student by name, age, tribe, degree of Indian blood, name of home agency, date entered, grade, subjects of study, and attendance. Monthly reports are usually only statistical summaries.

Public school contracts and reports contain much the same information for comparable time periods.

Group of Indian boys in cadet uniforms, Carlisle Indian Industrial School, PA. Photograph No. 75-IP-1-9 by J.N. Choate, ca. 1880. Records of the Bureau of Indian Affairs, RG 75.

TABLE 16
Bureau of Indian Affairs Field Office Records

THIS ALPHABETICAL LISTING SHOWS THE INDIAN AGENCIES, SCHOOLS, AND OTHER FIELD JURISDICTIONS OF THE BUREAU OF INDIAN AFFAIRS AND THE LOCATION OF THE NARA REGIONAL ARCHIVES FACILITIES HOLDING THEIR RECORDS. FREQUENT REORGANIZATIONS OF THE BIA, AS WELL AS MANY TRANSFERS OF TRIBES FROM ONE AGENCY AND LOCATION TO ANOTHER, MAKE IT IMPOSSIBLE TO DESIGNATE ONE AGENCY AS HOLDING THE RECORDS OF A PARTICULAR TRIBE. THE RESEARCHER SHOULD CONSULT EDWARD E. HILL'S *GUIDE TO RECORDS IN THE NATIONAL ARCHIVES RELATING TO AMERICAN INDIANS*, PP. 117–194, FOR A DETAILED ACCOUNT OF EACH FIELD OFFICE AND THE INDIANS UNDER ITS JURISDICTION AT VARIOUS TIMES. NAMES IN PARENTHESES IN THIS TABLE IDENTIFY THE AGENCY OR SCHOOL HEADING UNDER WHICH RECORDS FOR THE LISTED AGENCY ARE DISCUSSED IN HILL'S BOOK.

IN TABLE 16 "WASHINGTON, DC" REFERS TO RECORDS AT THE NATIONAL ARCHIVES BUILDING IN WASHINGTON. A SPECIFIC CITY REFERS TO THE NATIONAL ARCHIVES REGIONAL FACILITY HOLDING THE RECORDS; E.G., FORT WORTH REFERS TO NARA'S SOUTHWEST REGION. SEE TABLE 1 IN THE INTRODUCTION TO THIS VOLUME FOR THE LOCATIONS OF NARA'S REGIONAL ARCHIVES FACILITIES.

JURISDICTION	LOCATION	JURISDICTION	LOCATION
Aberdeen Area Office	Denver and Kansas City	Cheyenne River Agency	Kansas City
Abiquiu and Cimarron Agencies	Denver	Chicago Field Employment	
Albuquerque Area Office	Denver	Assistance Office	Chicago
Albuquerque Indian School	Denver	Chickasaw Agency, East	Washington, DC
Anadarko Area Office	Fort Worth	Chilocco Indian School	Fort Worth
Arapaho, *see* Cheyenne and Arapaho		Chinle Subagency	
Agency (Concho Agency)	Fort Worth	(Navajo Agencies)	Laguna Niguel, CA
Bad River Agency	Chicago	Chippewa Commission	Chicago
Bannock, *see* Shoshone and Bannock		Choctaw Agency, East	Washington, DC
Agency (Wind River Agency)	Denver	Cimarron Agency	
and (Fort Hall Agency)	Seattle	(Abiquiu Agency)	Denver
Billings Area Office	Denver	Cleveland Field Employment	
Birch Cooley School (Pipestone		Assistance Office	Chicago
Indian School)	Kansas City	Coeur d'Alene Agency	
Bismarck Indian School	Kansas City	(Colville Agency)	Seattle
Blackfeet Agency	Denver	Colorado River Indian Agency	Laguna Niguel, CA
California Agency (Sacramento		Colville Agency	Seattle
Area Office)	San Francisco	Concho Agency	Fort Worth
California Agency (Riverside		Consolidated Chippewa Agency	Kansas City and Chicago
Area Field Office)	Laguna Niguel, CA	Choctaw and Chickasaw Agency	
California Mission Indians	Laguna Niguel, CA	(Muskogee Area Office)	Washington, DC
Campo Superintendency		Creek Agency, East	Washington, DC
(California Mission Indians)	Laguna Niguel, CA	Crow Agency	Denver
Canton Asylum for Insane Indians		Crow Creek Agency	Kansas City
(Pipestone Indian School)	Kansas City	Cushman School	
Cantonment Agency		(Puyallup Agency)	Seattle
(Concho Agency)	Fort Worth	Denver Field Employment	
Carlisle Indian Industrial School	Washington, DC	Assistance Office	Denver
Carson School and Agency	San Francisco	Devil's Lake Agency	
Carter and Laona Agencies	Chicago	(Fort Totten Agency)	Kansas City
Charles G. Burke Indian School	Denver	Digger Agency	San Francisco
Chamberlain Indian School	Washington, DC	Eastern Navajo Agency	Laguna Niguel, CA
Chermawa Indian School	Seattle	Fallon School and Agency	San Francisco
Cherokee Agency, East	Washington, DC	Fifth Irrigation District	Denver
Cherokee Agency, North Carolina	Atlanta	Five Civilized Tribes Agency	
Cherokee Agency, West	Washington, DC	(Muskogee Area Office)	Fort Worth
Cheyenne and Arapaho Agency		Flandreau School and Agency	Kansas City
(Concho Agency)	Fort Worth	Flathead Agency	Denver

TABLE 16
Bureau of Indian Affairs Field Office Records

JURISDICTION	LOCATION	JURISDICTION	LOCATION
Flathead Irrigation Project	Denver	Juneau Area Office	Seattle
Fond du Lac Agency		Kansas Agency	
(Red Lake Agency)	Kansas City and Chicago	(Potawatomi Agency)	Kansas City
Fort Apache Indian Agency	Laguna Niguel, CA	Kaw Agency (Pawnee Agency)	Fort Worth
Fort Belknap Agency	Denver	Keshena Agency	
Fort Berthold Agency	Kansas City	(Menominee Agency)	Chicago
Fort Bidwell School and Agency	San Francisco	Kickapoo Agency	
Fort Bridger Agency		(Potawatomi Agency)	Kansas City
(Wind River Agency)	Denver	Kiowa Agency	
Fort Defiance Subagency		(Anadarko Area Office)	Forth Worth
(Navajo Agencies)	Laguna Niguel, CA	Klamath Agency	Seattle
Fort Hall Agency	Seattle	Lac du Flambeau Agency	
Fort Lapwai Agency		and School	Chicago
(Northern Idaho Agency)	Seattle	Laguna Sanatorium	Denver
Fort Lewis Indian School	Denver	Laona Agency (Great Lakes	
Fort Peck Agency	Denver	Consolidated Agency)	Chicago
Fort McDermitt Agency		LaPointe Agency (Hayward	
(Reno Agency)	San Francisco	Indian School and	
Fort Mohave Subagency		Lac du Flambeau Agency)	Chicago
and School	Laguna Niguel, CA	Leech Lake Agency	Chicago and Kansas City
Fort Shaw Indian School	Denver	Lemhi Agency (Fort Hall Agency)	Seattle
Fort Totten Agency	Kansas City	Leupp Training School	
Fort Yuma Agency	Laguna Niguel, CA	(Navajo Agencies)	Denver
Fox Day School		Los Angeles Field Office	
(Sac and Fox Agency)	Chicago	(California Mission Indians)	Laguna Niguel, CA
Gallup Area Office	Denver	Lovelocks School (Fallon School)	San Francisco
Gila River Agency		Lower Brulé Agency	Kansas City
(Pima Agency)	Laguna Niguel, CA	Mackinac Agency	Chicago
Grand Portage School (Consolidated		Malheur Agency	Washington, DC
Chippewa Agency)	Washington, DC	Malki Superintendency	
Grand Rapids Agency	Chicago	(California Indian Missions)	Laguna Niguel, CA
Grand River Agency		Menominee Agencies,	
(Standing Rock Agency)	Kansas City	Minneapolis Area Office	Kansas City
Grand Ronde-Siletz Agency	Seattle	Menominee Agencies in	
Great Lakes Consolidated Agency	Chicago	Wisconsin	Chicago
Great Nemaha Agency		Mescalero Agency	Denver
(Potawatomi Agency)	Kansas City	Mesquakie Day School	
Green Bay Agency		(Sac and Fox Agency)	Chicago
(Menominee Agencies)	Chicago	Miami Agency	Fort Worth
Greenville School and Agency	San Francisco	Michigan Agency	Chicago
Haskell Institute	Kansas City	Milk River Agency	
Hayward Indian School	Chicago	(Fort Peck Agency)	Denver
Hoopa Valley Agency	San Francisco	Minneapolis Area Office	Chicago and Kansas City
Hope School (Springfield School)	Washington, DC	Minnesota Agency	Kansas City
Hopi Indian Agency	Laguna Niguel, CA	Mission Agency	
Horton Agency		(California Mission Indians)	Laguna Niguel, CA
(Potawatomi Agency)	Kansas City	Moqui Pueblo Agency	
Ignacio Boarding School	Denver	(Navajo Agencies)	Washington, DC
Intermountain Indian School	Denver	Morongo	
Jicarilla Agency	Denver	(California Mission Indians)	Laguna Niguel, CA

TABLE 16
Bureau of Indian Affairs Field Office Records

JURISDICTION	LOCATION	JURISDICTION	LOCATION
Mount Pleasant Indian School	Chicago	Portland Area Office	Seattle
Muskogee Area Office	Fort Worth and Washington, DC	Potawatomi Agency	Kansas City
		Prairie du Chien Agency	
Navajo Agencies	Denver and Laguna Niguel, CA	(Winnebago Agency)	Kansas City
		Pueblo and Pueblo and	
Navajo Area Office	Laguna Niguel, CA	Jicarilla Agencies	Denver
Navajo Springs Agency	Denver	Pueblo Day Schools at	
Neah Bay Agency		Albuquerque and Santa Fe	Denver
(Taholah Agency)	Seattle	Pueblo Indian Agency and	
Neosha Agency (Miami Agency)	Fort Worth	Pueblo Day Schools	Denver
Nett Lake Agency	Chicago and Kansas City	Puget Sound District Agency	Seattle
Nevada Agency	San Francisco	Puyallup Agency and	
New York Agency	Washington, DC	Cushman School	Seattle
Nez Perce Agency		Quapaw Agency (Miami Agency)	Fort Worth
(Northern Idaho Agency)	Seattle	Quinaielt Agency	
Nisqually and Skokomish Agency		(Puyallup Agency)	Seattle
(Puyallup Agency)	Seattle	Rapid City Indian School	Kansas City
Northern Cheyenne Agency	Denver	Red Cliff School and Agency	Chicago
Northern Idaho Agency	Seattle	Red Cloud Agency	
Northern Navajo Agency	Laguna Niguel, CA	(Pine Ridge Agency)	Kansas City
Northern Pueblos Agency	Denver	Red Lake Agency	Kansas City
Oakland Agency		Red Moon Agency	
(Pawnee Agency)	Fort Worth	(Concho Agency)	Fort Worth
Omaha Agency		Reno Agency	San Francisco
(Winnebago Agency)	Kansas City	Riggs Institute (Flandreau School)	Kansas City
Oneida School and Agency	Chicago	Rincon Superintendency	
Osage Agency	Fort Worth	(California Mission Indians)	Laguna Niguel, CA
Otoe Agency (Pawnee Agency)	Fort Worth	Riverside Area Field Office	
Ouray Agency		(California Mission Indians)	Laguna Niguel, CA
(Uintah and Ouray Agency)	Denver	Rosebud Agency	Kansas City
Pala Agency and Subagency		Roseburg Agency	San Francisco
(California Mission Indians)	Laguna Niguel, CA	Round Valley Agency	San Francisco
Palm Springs Subagency		Sac and Fox Agency	
(California Mission Indians)	Laguna Niguel, CA	and Sanatorium	Chicago
Papago Indian Agency	Laguna Niguel, CA	Sacramento Agency and	
Paiute Agency (Uintah and		Area Office	San Francisco
Ouray Agency)	Denver	Salem (Chemawa) School	
Pawnee Agency	Fort Worth	(Grand Ronde-Siletz Agency)	Seattle
Pechanga Superintendency		San Carlos Apache Agency	Laguna Niguel, CA
(California Mission Indians)	Laguna Niguel, CA	San Jacinto Agency	
Phoenix Area Office	Laguna Niguel, CA and Denver	(Tule River Agency)	San Francisco
		Santa Fe Indian School	Denver
Phoenix Indian Agency	Laguna Niguel, CA	Santee Agency	
Pierre Agency	Kansas City	(Flandreau Agency)	Kansas City
Pierre Indian School	Kansas City	Seger Agency (Concho Agency)	Fort Worth
Pima Indian Agency	Laguna Niguel, CA	Seminole Agency, Florida	Atlanta
Pine Ridge Agency	Kansas City	Seneca School (Miami Agency)	Fort Worth
Pipestone Indian School	Kansas City	Shawnee Agency in Oklahoma	Fort Worth
Ponca Agency (Pawnee Agency)	Fort Worth	Sherman Institute	Laguna Niguel, CA
and (Winnebago Agency)	Kansas City		

TABLE 16
Bureau of Indian Affairs Field Office Records

JURISDICTION	LOCATION	JURISDICTION	LOCATION
Shiprock Boarding School		Tule River Agency	San Francisco
(Navajo Agencies)	Denver	Turtle Mountain Agency	Kansas City
Shoshone and Bannock Agency		Uintah and Ouray Agency	Denver
(Wind River Agency)	Denver	Umatilla Agency	Seattle
Siletz Agency		United Pueblos Agency	Denver
(Grand Ronde-Siletz Agency)	Seattle	Union Agency	
and (Roseburg Agency)	San Francisco	(Muskogee Area Office)	Washington, DC
Sioux Sanatorium	Kansas City	Upper Arkansas Agency	
Sisseton Agency	Kansas City	(Concho Agency)	Fort Worth
Six Nations Agency		Upper Missouri Agency	
(New York Agency)	Washington, DC	(Crow Creek Agency)	Kansas City
Skokomish Agency		Upper Platte Agency	
(Tulalip Agency)	Seattle	(Rosebud Agency)	Kansas City
Soboba		Utah Agency (Abiquiu Agency)	Denver
(California Mission Indians)	Laguna Niguel, CA	Vermillion Lake Agency	Chicago
Southern Apache Agency	Washington, DC	Vermillion Lake School	
Southern Mission Agency		(Nett Lake Agency)	Washington, DC
(Pale Subagency)	Laguna Niguel, CA	Volcan Superintendency	
Southern Paiute Field Station	Denver	(California Mission Indians)	Laguna Niguel, CA
Southern Pueblos Agency	Denver	Wahpeton Indian School	Kansas City
Southern Ute and		Walker River Agency	San Francisco
Consolidated Ute Agencies	Denver	Warm Springs Agency	Seattle
Southwestern Indian		Western Navajo Agency	Laguna Niguel, CA
Polytechnic Institute	Denver	Western Shoshone Agency	San Francisco
Spokane Agency	Seattle	Western Washington Agency	
Spotted Tail Agency		(Taholah and Tulalip Agencies)	Seattle
(Rosebud Agency)	Kansas City	Whetstone Agency	
Springfield (Hope)		(Rosebud Agency)	Kansas City
Indian School	Washington, DC	White Earth Agency	
Standing Rock Agency	Kansas City	(Lower Brulé Agency)	Chicago and Kansas City
Taholah Agency	Seattle	White River Agency	Kansas City
Toadlena Day School	Denver	Wichita Agency	
Tomah Indian School		(Anadarko Area Office)	Fort Worth
and Agency	Chicago	Window Rock Area Office	
Tongue River Agency		(Navajo Agencies)	Denver and Laguna
(Northern Cheyenne Agency)	Seattle	Niguel, CA	
Torres-Martinez Subagency		Wind River Agency	Denver
(California Mission Indians)	Laguna Niguel, CA	Winnebago Agency	Kansas City
Truxton Canyon Agency	Laguna Niguel, CA	Wittenberg Indian School	Chicago
Tuba City Subagency		Yakima Agency	Seattle
(Navajo Agencies)	Laguna Niguel, CA	Yankton Agency	Kansas City
Tulalip Agency	Seattle	Zuni Agency	Denver

CHAPTER 12

Records of African Americans

12.1 Introduction

For the most part, records in the National Archives relating to African Americans are not found as separate entities but are interspersed among various record series. In many records, the race of individuals is indicated, but in most it is not. Generally, however, from the close of the Civil War to the present, genealogy for Black Americans follows the same research paths as does genealogy for others. Researchers of African American genealogy should first gather the information available from living relatives, in family records, and in cemeteries. (*See* I.2.) The same county, state, and Federal sources, libraries, historical and genealogical societies, and other records usually consulted in genealogical research are useful to researchers in the genealogy of African Americans.

Federal records generally useful for genealogical research are thus also useful for African American genealogy. The most helpful series in the census, military, and Freedmen's Bureau records are described in this chapter. Other series contain information relating to African Americans but are not generally useful for genealogy because of their arrangement, the lack of indexes, or the fact that they relate only to a few people, a specific geographical area, or a particular occupation or class. Among such records are the peonage case records of the Justice Department, relating to people enslaved after the Civil War; records of the Bureau of Customs and other Federal agencies that administered programs for free blacks and former slaves before the Freedmen's Bureau was established; records relating to the suppression of the slave trade; records relating to labor and the employment of African Americans before, during, and after the Civil War; and records relating to Federal employment in general. A distinction has also been made between records documenting the history of African Americans as a group (African American history) and those providing information about individuals (genealogy).

The series of records that are described in the following paragraphs either include racial descriptions or comprise separate series of records that relate specifically to African Americans. Records described in the various chapters and sections of this guide relating to military service, bounty land, pensions, land records, Native Americans, court records, civilian personnel records, and passenger lists are all pertinent to African American research; consequently, the entire guide should be studied by researchers of African American genealogy. For supplemental reading, see *Who Do You Think You Are, Digging for Your Family Roots?*, by Suzanne Hilton (Philadelphia: Westminster Press, 1976); *Black Genealogy: How To Begin*, by James D. Walker (Athens: University of Georgia Center for Continuing Education, 1977); *Family Pride: The Complete Guide to Tracing African-American Genealogy*, by Donna Beasley (New York: Macmillan, 1997); *How to Trace your African-American Roots*, by Barbara Thompson Howell (New Jersey: Carol Publishing Group, 1999); *Black History: A Guide to Civilian Records in the National Archives*, compiled by Debra L. Newman (Washington: National Archives Trust Fund Board, 1984); and *Guide to Federal Archives Relating to Africa*, by Aloha South (Honolulu: Crossroads Press, 1977.)

12.2 Census Records

The first listing of all African Americans by name in a Federal census was made in 1870, in the first Federal census taken after the Civil War. In 1850 and 1860, slave statistics were gathered, but the census schedules did not list slaves by name; they were tallied unnamed in age and sex categories. These slave schedules are useful, however, as circumstantial evidence that a slave of a certain age and sex was the property of a particular owner in 1850 or 1860.

Free blacks who were heads of households were enumerated by name in the censuses from 1790 to 1840, and the names of all free household members were included in the censuses of 1850 and 1860. Slaves, however, were listed in total numbers or recorded in age and sex categories, 1790–1840. *List of Free Black Heads of Families in the First Census of the United States, 1790*, Special List 34, compiled by Debra L. Newman (Washington: National Archives and Records Service, 1974), lists roughly 4,000 free blacks recorded as heads of families. Chapter 1 in this guide describes in detail the contents of the various census schedules, including what is available regarding slaves and free blacks.

12.3 Military Service and Related Records

12.3.1 Revolutionary War and After

African Americans have served in all the wars of the United States, sometimes in all-black units. Records of their service and of their applications for veterans' benefits are contained in the series of military records fully described in Chapters 4–9.

Some African Americans who served in the Revolutionary War are noted in *List of Black Servicemen Compiled From the War Department Collection of Revolutionary War Records*, Special List 36, compiled by Debra L. Newman (Washington: National Archives and Records Service, 1974). Additional information about servicemen in the Revolutionary War can be obtained from the pension application files available as M804, *Revolutionary War Pension and Bounty-Land Warrant Application Files*, 2,670 rolls. Selections from the files are available on M805, *Selected Records from Revolutionary War Pension and Bounty-Land Warrant Application Files*, 898 rolls.

Another part of the experience of African Americans during the Revolutionary War is documented in Records of the Continental and Confederation Congresses and the Constitutional Convention, Record Group (RG) 360. When the British evacuated New York in 1783, they took with them many former slaves. Lists of those who left with the British, called **inspection rolls**, were created so that

SCHEDULE 2.—Slave Inhabitants in *The Eleventh District* in the County of *Carroll* State of *Georgia*, enumerated by me, on the *15* day of *Sep*, 1850. *T S Martin* Ass't Marshal

NAMES OF SLAVE OWNERS.	Number of Slaves.	Age.	Sex.	Colour.	Fugitives from the State.	Number manumitted.	Deaf & dumb, blind, insane, or idiotic.
1	2	3	4	5	6	7	8
L S Chapman	10	8	M	B			
	11	7	M	B			
	12	6	F	B			
	13	4	M	B			
	14	3	M	B			
✓	15	1	F	B			
A H Harrison	1	60	F	B			
	2	28	M	B			
	3	26	F	B			
	4	26	M	B			
	5	19	F	B			
	6	6	M	B			
	7	4	M	B			
	8	11	M	B			
	9	11	M	B			
	10	9	F	B			
✓	11	6	F	B			
Wm H Robards ✓	1	32	M	M			
I H Cartright ✓	1	11	F	B			
Anst McMullin	1	18	M	M			
✓	2	15	F	B			
F W Richards ✓	1	25	F	B			
E W Holland	1	22	F	M			
	2	4	M	B			
	3	3	F	B			
	4	1	F	M			
	5	34	F	M			
	6	7	F	M			
	7	13	F	M			
	8	12	M	M			
	9	19	M	M			
	10	25	M	B			
	11	17	M	B			
	12	19	M	B			
	13	18	M	B			
	14	18	M	B			
	15	18	M	B			
	16	18	M	B			
	17	25	M	B			
	18	12	M	M			
	19	10	M	B			
	20	10	M	B			

NAMES OF SLAVE OWNERS.	Number of Slaves.	Age.	Sex.	Colour.	Fugitives from the State.	Number manumitted.	Deaf & dumb, blind, insane, or idiotic.
1	2	3	4	5	6	7	8
	21	9	M	B			
	22	9	M	B			
	23	12	F	B			
	24	9	M	B			
	25	18	M	M			
	26	4	F	M			
	27	18	F	B			
✓	28	15	M	B			
Wm Bailey	1	53	F	B			
	2	27	M	B			
	3	21	F	B			
	4	2	F	B			
✓	5	1	F	B			
A H Green	1	30	F	B			
	2	12	M	B			
	3	10	M	B			
✓	4	10	F	M			
G L Little	1	8	M	B			
Wm Awbry	1	35	M	B			
	2	32	M	B			
	3	28	M	B			
✓	4	10	F	B			
Quincy McCorkle	1	30	M	B			
	2	20	F	B			
	3	4	F	M			
✓	4	2	F	M			
A M Robinson	1	22	M	B			
Ephraim Jackson	1	70	M	B			
Jno Aldridge	1	35	F	B			
	2	29	M	B			
	3	15	M	B			
	4	8	F	B			
	5	2	F	B			
Geo H Portmore	1	23	M	B			
	2	23	M	B			
	3	18	F	B			
Wyatt Moore ✓	1	20	M	B			
Thos W Burton	1	45	F	B			
	2	30	F	M			
	3	26	F	B			
	4	17	M	B			
	5	11	M	B			

Card 1 (left):

Reed, Jeremiah ⌐32⌐

Co E , **102** U.S. Col'd Inf

Private | Private

CARD NUMBERS.

1	6887083	26	
2	6887151	27	
3	6893800	28	
4	6893905	29	
5	6893946	30	
6	9217494	31	
7		32	
8		33	
9		34	
10		35	
11		36	
12		37	
13		38	
14		39	
15		40	
16		41	
17		42	
18		43	
19		44	
20		45	
21		46	
22		47	
23		48	
24		49	
25		50	

Book Mark :

See also

Card 2 (center):

R | 102 | U.S.C.T

Jeremiah Reed

, Co E , 102 Reg't U. S. Col'd Inf

Appears on

Company Descriptive Book

of the organization named above.

DESCRIPTION.

Age 28 years; height 6 feet 1 inches

Complexion Blk

Eyes Blk ; hair Blk

Where born Canada

Occupation Farmer

ENLISTMENT.

When Jan. 30 , 1865

Where Grand Rpds

By whom Capt. Bailey ; term 1 y'rs

Remarks Capt. Bailey,

Feb. 2, '65.

US bounty, $33⁴

Sabine

Card 3 (right):

K | 102 | U.S.C.T.

Jeremiah Reed

Appears with rank of Prvt. on

Muster and Descriptive Roll of a Detachment of U. S. Vols. forwarded

for the 102 Reg't U. S. Col'd Inf. Roll dated

Jackson, Mich., Mch. 1, 1865.

Where born Canada

Age 28 y'rs; occupation Farmer

When enlisted Jan. 30 , 1865.

Where enlisted Gr. Rapids

For what period enlisted 1 years.

Eyes Hzl. ; hair Blk

Complexion Col'd ; height 6 ft. 1 in.

When mustered in Feb. 2 , 1865.

Where mustered in Grd. Rapids

Bounty paid $ 33⅓/100 ; due $ /100

Where credited Fair Plains, Montcalm 4 Cong. Dist.

Company to which assigned

Remarks :

Book mark :

Sam'l J Armstrong Copyist

(389)

Three cards from a compiled military service record of a volunteer soldier, U.S. Colored Troops. Records of the Adjutant General's Office, 1780's–1917, RG 94.

reparations could be made to former owners under terms of the Treaty of Paris in 1783. Consequently, accurate information was carefully recorded for each evacuee. Given are the name, sex, sometimes age, and brief physical description for each individual; name and residence of former owner; and additional information in a "remarks" column. The lists are available on roll 7 of M332, *Miscellaneous Papers of the Continental Congress, 1774-1789*, 10 rolls, and roll 66 of M247, *Papers of the Continental Congress, 1774-1789*, 204 rolls.

African Americans served as enlisted men and occasionally as officers during wars of the late 19th and early 20th centuries. At various times there were African Americans in the Regular Army, Volunteers, Navy, Marine Corps, and Coast Guard. Although race is not always noted in the records, physical descriptions are sometimes given. It may be helpful to consult *Data Relating to Negro Military Personnel in the 19th Century*, Reference Information Paper 63, by Aloha South (Washington: National Archives and Records Service, 1973).

12.3.2 Civil War

During the Civil War, African American soldiers served with Union forces in regiments of **U.S. Colored Troops (U.S.C.T.)** and also in the Navy and Marine Corps. As with other compiled military service records of the Civil War, the records are among Records of the Adjutant General's Office, 1780's-1917, RG 94. They are arranged according to military organization, with an alphabetical index that is available on M589, *Index to Compiled Service Records of Volunteer Union Soldiers Who Served with the United States Colored Troops*, 98 rolls. All of the U.S.C.T. cavalry units (1-6) have been reproduced as M1817, *Compiled Service Records of Volunteer Union Soldiers Who Served with the United States Colored Troops: 1st Through 5th United States Colored Cavalry, 5th Massachusetts Cavalry (Colored), 6th United States Colored Cavalry*, 107 rolls; artillery units have been reproduced as M1818, *Compiled Military Service Records of Volunteer Union Soldiers Who Served with the United States Colored Troops: Artillery Organizations*, 299 rolls. Also reproduced on microfilm are M1659, *Records of the Fifty-Fourth Massachusetts Infantry Regiment (Colored), 1863-1865*, 7 rolls; M1898, *Compiled Military Service Records of Volunteer Union Soldiers Who Served with the United States Colored Troops: 54th Massachusetts Infantry Regiment (Colored)*, 20 rolls; M1801, *Compiled Military Service Records of Volunteer Union Soldiers Who Served with the United States Colored Troops: 55th Massachusetts Infantry (Colored)*, 16 rolls; M1819, *Compiled Military Service Records of Volunteer Union Soldiers Who Served with the United States Colored Troops: 1st United States Colored Infantry, 1st South Carolina Volunteers (Colored), Company A, 1st United States Colored Infantry (1 Year)*, 19 rolls; and M1820, *Compiled Military Service Records of Volunteer Union Soldiers Who Served with the United*

States Colored Troops: 2d Through 7th Colored Infantry, Including 3d Tennessee Volunteers (African Descent), 6th Louisiana Infantry (African Descent), 7th Louisiana Infantry (African Descent), 116 rolls. Historical information about volunteer organizations is available on rolls 204-217 of M594, *Compiled Records Showing Service of Military Units in Volunteer Union Organizations*, 225 rolls. Regimental records, including correspondence, orders, descriptive books, and morning reports, are described in *Tabular Analysis of the Records of the U.S. Colored Troops and Their Predecessor Units in the National Archives of the United States*, Special List 33, compiled by Joseph B. Ross (Washington: National Archives and Records Service, 1973). The Colored Troops Division of the Adjutant General's Office was responsible for recruiting and other matters relating to African American soldiers; records of the division are dated 1863-89 and are part of RG 94. Letters received, 1863-88, contain consolidated files pertaining to individual African American soldiers. In most instances a reference to the correspondence file is on the jacket of the compiled military service record of the particular soldier. Colored Troops Division records also include 54 volumes of descriptive lists of colored volunteers who enlisted in Missouri, 1864, arranged chronologically, with name indexes. The lists give name, age, eye and hair color, complexion, height, place of birth, occupation, and date of enlistment. In the case of former slaves, former owners' names may be entered. Information about various colored troop regiments, including lists of officers, combats, and casualties, can be found in the following publications: Volume 8 of *Official Army Register of the Volunteer Force of the United States Army for the Years 1861, '62, '63, '64, '65* (Washington: Adjutant General's Office, 1865-67); *A Compendium of the War of the Rebellion*, by Frederick H. Dyer (Des Moines: Dyer Publishing Co., 1908; New York: T. Yoseloff, 1959; and Dayton OH: The Press of Morningside Bookshop, 1978); *War of the Rebellion, A Compilation of the Official Records of the Union and Confederate Armies*, 128 volumes (Washington: War Department, 1880-1902), which has been microfilmed as M262, *Official Records of the Union and Confederate Armies, 1861-1865*, 128 rolls, and reprinted by the National Historical Society, Gettysburg, PA, 1972; and *Official Records of the Union and Confederate Navies in the War of the Rebellion*, 31 volumes (Washington: Navy Department, 1894-1927), microfilmed as M275, *Official Records of the Union and Confederate Navies, 1861-1865*, 31 rolls.

African Americans were usually conscripted to provide labor for the **Confederate States military forces**. However, all members of the Regiment of Native Guards mustered for the defense of New Orleans were African Americans. Identification of these men as African Americans must generally be made from sources outside the National Archives, as military records do not usually show race.

Following the Civil War, some African Americans applied for (and in a few instances were granted) admission to the

U.S. Military Academy. Records relating to these applications are available on M1002, *Selected Documents Relating to Blacks Nominated for Appointment to the U.S. Military Academy During the 19th Century, 1870-1887,* 21 rolls.

Records relating to African Americans granted the **Medal of Honor** during the late 19th century are available on M929, *Documents Relating to the Military and Naval Service of Blacks Awarded the Congressional Medal of Honor from the Civil War to the Spanish-American War,* 4 rolls.

Regimental histories and other information concerning African American troops in the Spanish-American War and the Philippine Insurrection can be found in volume 1 of *Correspondence Relating to the War with Spain . . .* (Washington: War Department, 1902), and also in unpublished historical accounts in RG 94.

After the Civil War, African Americans served in the Regular Army during war and peace. The 9th and 10th Cavalry and 38th, 39th, 40th, and 41st Infantry Regiments were organized as all-black units in July 1866. In 1869 the four infantry units were consolidated to form the 24th and 25th Regiments. Published works on this subject are *The Buffalo Soldiers: A Narrative of the Negro Cavalry in the West,* by William Leckie (Norman: University of Oklahoma Press, 1967); *Black Infantry in the West, 1869-1891,* by Arlen L. Fowler (Westport, CT: Greenwood Publishing Corp., 1971); *The Black Soldier and Officer in the United States Army, 1891-1917,* by Marvin Fletcher (Columbia: University of Missouri Press, 1974); *Under Fire With the Tenth U.S. Cavalry,* by Hershel V. Cashin (New York: Arno Press, 1969); *The Colored Regulars in the United States Army . . . .* Theophilus G. Steward (Philadelphia: A.M.E. Book Concern, 1904; reprinted by Arno Press, New York, 1969).

In Records of the Accounting Officers of the Department of the Treasury, RG 217, are **disallowed military claims** of persons who served in the U.S. Colored Troops (U.S.C.T.), including cavalry (U.S.C.C.) and artillery (U.S.C.A.) units, 1864-93. Records of the Office of the Second Auditor of the Treasury Department document claims filed by such soldiers or their heirs for bounty or other pay allowances due. Typically, a claim file consists of a petition, affidavits, and correspondence directly relating to the claim, but some files include discharge papers and proof of origin or identity. These records are arranged by unit number—there are some for the 15th and 21st U.S.C.T.; 22nd to 138th U.S.C.T.; 1st to 6th U.S.C.C.; 1st to 14th U.S.C.A.; 5th, 10th, and 55th Massachusetts Volunteers; 29th Connecticut Volunteers; and files for persons in miscellaneous units—and thereunder alphabetically by surname of soldier. These records appear to be related to records of the Colored Troops Division of the Adjutant General's Office, 1863-89, in RG 94, and many letters passed between the offices in attempts to decide claims. Allowed claims of this type were not segregated by unit but were filed with the large, comprehensive series of Second Auditor's accounts, which were destroyed with congressional approval in the 1950s.

12.3.3 Naval Records

Records of the U.S. Navy include information about African Americans who enlisted in this service. The pre-1840 records are indexed, but, in general, all of the records are difficult to search. **Ships' muster rolls** in Records of the Bureau of Naval Personnel, RG 24, for example, may indicate race, beginning with the Civil War, or contain a description of the enlisted man ("Negro" or "mulatto") in addition to name, rating, date and place of enlistment, and state of birth. However, in this instance, to locate information about a particular black seaman, the researcher must know the date and place of enlistment or the name of the vessel on which they served.

Fragmentary records relating to African slaves and African Americans who were prisoners of war, declared contraband or refugees, or wartime civilian laborers may be found in Naval Records Collection of the Office of Naval Records and Library, RG 45. Some of the more significant series are noted below.

African Americans are among the persons mentioned in a register of American and French **prisoners of war** held by the British at Halifax, Barbados, and Jamaica, 1805-15, and at Quebec, 1813-15. Register entries show name, rank, and number of each prisoner; ship that captured them; date and location of capture (usually at sea); name and type of vessel (man of war, privateer, merchant) on which they served before capture; vessel that delivered them to Halifax, Barbados, or Jamaica and date of delivery; and dated notations about exchange, discharge, death, or escape.

The register for prisoners held at Quebec also shows prisoner's place of birth; age; height; weight; color of hair, skin, and eyes; distinguishing marks or wounds; and supplies and clothing furnished.

African Americans are identified on the **payrolls of civilian personnel at Confederate shore establishments**, May 1861-December 1864. Among the pay rolls is a pay and receipt roll of personnel, including slaves, employed at Fluvanna County, VA, July 1863-March 1864; pay and receipt rolls of slaves at Moseley's Farm, Powhatan County, VA, August-September 1862, at Keswick, Powhatan County, VA, July-August 1862, and in Powhatan County, VA, November 1862-December 1863; a pay roll of slaves employed at Richmond, VA, July 1862-December 1863; and a pay roll of slaves employed on board the C.S.S. *Cotton* at Shreveport, LA, January-February 1864.

Lists and a **register of slaves** used by the Engineer Office at Charleston and Georgetown Harbors, SC, to work on the fortifications for the city of Charleston, August 1862-September 1863, show dates on which the slaves were received, districts from which they were received, names of slaveholders, first names of the slaves, and total number of slaves received from each slaveholder. Also included in the register are notes concerning slaves who ran away from the fortifications and a small number of entries for slaves who were hired to work on the fortifications during January through June 1864.

African American enlisted men who served in the Union or Regular Navy are mentioned in the letters received concerning Union and Confederate **naval prisoners of war**, May 1862–March 1865, including the place where Union naval prisoners were held and arrangements made for their exchange. The letters are frequently accompanied by lists of Union naval prisoners paroled by the Confederates, announced as exchanged, or still held in the South. Also included are other lists of Union naval prisoners held in the South during the years 1863-65, extracts of declarations of exchange of prisoners, and general orders announcing exchanges, 1862-65.

In the journal kept by Capt. George Emmons while commanding the U.S.S. *Lackawanna* is a list of African American refugees and others given passports to enter or depart from Galveston, TX, 1864-65. Letters received by the commandants of the Boston and Washington navy yards for 1862 contain reports of arrivals of "contrabands" (free Negroes or slaves) at those yards; similar reports are included in the letters received by the commandant of the Portsmouth Navy Yard in 1864. Usually names of the vessels or names of the army officers who delivered the contrabands are given.

12.4 Freedmen's Bureau and Related Records

After the Civil War, Congress created the Freedmen's Bureau (officially designated the Bureau of Refugees, Freedmen, and Abandoned Lands) by an act of 1865 (13 Stat. 507). The Bureau was a part of the War Department and was assigned responsibilities that included "the control of all subjects relating to refugees and freedmen from rebel States, or from any district . . . within the territory embraced in the operations of the Army." The Bureau helped former slaves make the transition to citizenship.

The period of the Bureau's greatest activity extended from June 1865 to December 1868. These activities included aiding in legalizing marriages consummated during slavery, witnessing labor contracts, issuing rations and clothing to destitute freedmen and refugees, leasing land, operating hospitals and freedmen's camps, and providing transportation to refugees and freedmen returning to their homes or relocating them to other parts of the country. Included are records relating to freedmen and white citizens, military employees, teachers, and agents of civic and religious organizations. As Congress increased the responsibilities of the Bureau, it became involved in helping former Union servicemen to file and collect claims for bounties, pay arrears, and pensions. Congress later authorized additional funds, and the Bureau began issuing and distributing food and supplies to destitute people in the South. Much of the work of the Bureau ended in early

1869, and it was abolished in 1872 (17 Stat. 366). The unfinished business of the Bureau—claims, arrears, pension and bounty actions—was turned over to the Freedmen's Branch, Office of the Adjutant General. Records contain information useful to researchers of African American genealogy, including, in some instances, names of persons, residences, occupations, and dates. In general, however, nature and arrangement of the records and lack of name indexing precludes easy access to specific genealogical data. The records commonly are administrative or statistical in nature; many of them consist of official communications or issuances. The researcher should, therefore, bring as much knowledge as possible to their research effort and be prepared to make a substantial item-by-item search in correspondence files using the indexes and registers.

Records of the Bureau of Refugees, Freedmen, and Abandoned Lands, RG 105, is subdivided into two major groups, the first consisting of records of the Washington, DC, headquarters, 1865-72. These records are described in *Records of the Bureau of Refugees, Freedmen, and Abandoned Lands, Washington Headquarters*, Preliminary Inventory 174, compiled by Elaine Everly (Washington: National Archives and Records Service, 1973), and some of them are microfilmed on M742, *Selected Series of Records Issued by the Commissioner of the Bureau of Refugees, Freedmen, and Abandoned Lands, 1865-1872*, 7 rolls, consisting of letters and endorsements sent and circulars and special orders; M752, *Registers and Letters Received by the Commissioner of the Bureau of Refugees, Freedmen, and Abandoned Lands, 1865-1872*, 74 rolls; and M803, *Records of the Education Division of the Bureau of Refugees, Freedmen, and Abandoned Lands, 1865-1871*, 35 rolls.

The second major group contains records of the various district or field offices in the southern states, which include for each district records of the assistant commissioner in charge. Field office records are incomplete, but for most districts there are also records of the superintendents of education and other staff officers, as well as those of subordinate officers and agents serving in the subdistricts. Table 17 shows the availability of these records as microfilm publications. Bureau headquarters and field office records are discussed below, with primary emphasis on the series having more genealogical significance.

Records of Bureau headquarters. Records of the Washington, DC, headquarters include freedmen's marriage certificates, 1861-69. The series also includes marriage licenses, monthly reports of marriages from bureau offices, and other proofs of marriage. Documents are arranged alphabetically by state in which the marriage was performed, thereunder in general alphabetical order by surname of the bridegroom. Most of the records are dated 1865-68 but included are some reports of marriages performed before the war and some performed at contraband

TABLE 17

Microfilmed Freedmen's Bureau Field Office Records

STATE	ASSISTANT COMMISSIONER		SUPERINTENDENT OF EDUCATION	
	MICROFILM PUBLICATION	NUMBER OF ROLLS	MICROFILM PUBLICATION	NUMBER OF ROLLS
Alabama	M809	23	M810	8
Arkansas	M979	52	M980	5
District of Columbia	M1055	21	M1056	24
Georgia	M798	36	M799	28
Louisiana	M1027	36	M1026	12
New Orleans (Field Office)	M1483	10		
Mississippi	M826	50		
North Carolina	M843	38	M844	16
South Carolina	M869	44		
Tennessee	M999	34	M1000	9
Tennessee (Field Office)	T142	73		
Texas	M821	32	M822	18
Virginia	M1048	67	M1053	20

camps during the war. The researcher must know where the particular marriage was performed.

The collection is fragmentary; the number of certificates for each state varies from several hundred each for Louisiana, Mississippi, and Tennessee to one for Alabama and none for other states. Certificates frequently include such information as names and residences of brides and grooms, dates and places of marriages, and names of persons who performed the ceremonies. Certificates may also indicate ages and complexions of brides and grooms, complexions of parents, periods of time brides and grooms lived with previous spouses and causes for separation, and numbers of children by present and previous unions.

Records of district or field offices contain fragmentary records of marriages. Most of these records consist of marriage registers maintained by local superintendents and agents. Knowledge of the place and date of a particular marriage is necessary to locate it in the records. Registers generally give the names of couples and the dates marriages were registered. Many registers also provide information about previous marriages, numbers of children, and names of ministers or others who performed the ceremonies. Entries in the registers may be arranged chronologically or alphabetically by surname. Most of the records are for the states of Arkansas, Kentucky, Louisiana, and Mississippi, with a few scattered items for several other states. A series of consolidated registers for the state of Mississippi is available on roll 42 of M826, *Records of the Assistant Commissioner for the State of Mississippi, Bureau of Refugees, Freedmen, and Abandoned Lands, 1865–1869*, 50 rolls. Additional records relating to marriages performed by Freedmen's Bureau personnel are among records maintained by the counties in which the marriages were performed.

Other field office records of possible genealogical significance include scattered census returns, fairly extensive series of labor contracts and registers, hospital and transportation records, records of complaints registered by freedmen, and records relating to the administration of relief. Labor contract records exist at both the state and local levels and provide information such as dates of contracts, periods of service, names of contracting parties and/or family members, types of work performed, and rates of wages. Included among records of the Assistant Commissioner for the District of Columbia are descriptive lists of freed people for whom transportation was requested by employment agents, 1867–68, showing names, heights, complexions, names of former owners, and former and present residences. Scattered applications and certificates for relief, 1866–68, list heads of families who received relief. They also give race; number of men, women, and children in the family; signatures of heads of families and witnesses; and, in some instances, age, sex, and cause of destitution.

In 1865 Congress incorporated the **Freedman's Savings and Trust Company** (also known as Freedman's Bank) primarily for the benefit of former slaves. Although established as a private corporation, the Freedman's Bank often shared offices rent-free with the Freedmen's Bureau. Many Freedmen's Bureau officials also served as trustees and cashiers of the Freedman's Bank. Because of the close association with the Freedmen's Bureau, researchers often confuse Freedman Bank records with those of the Bureau, which is a separate body of records.

The main office of the Freedman's Bank was in Washington, DC, but branches were located in a number of cities in New York, Pennsylvania, Mississippi, Louisiana, Arkansas, Tennessee, Florida, and Texas. The bank branches

Date.	Name of Male.	Place of Residence.	Name of Female.	Place of Residence.	Age-Years.	
1864.						
June 25	John Davis	F, 50th U.S.C.I.	Martha Jane Williams	Natchez, Miss.	23	M
" 28	Robert Davinis	66th "	Elizabeth Paine	Hines Co., "	26	Bl
July 8	Samuel de Lane	Vicksburg, Miss.	Theodosia Gibson	Vicksburg, Miss.	48	
" 20	Samuel Davis	Hinds Co. "	Katie Bankson	Hinds Co. "	23	
" 30	Edward Dabney	A, 49th U.S.C.I.	Sarah Jane Talbot	Goodrich Ldg	48	
August 4	Richard Dowring	Vicksburg, Miss.	Melinda Holmes	Vicksburg, Miss.	34	
" 7	Reuben Dempsey	"	Mary Dempsey	"	58	
July 17	Johnson Daniels	Bolivar, Miss.	Rosella	Bolivar, Miss.	40	
August 18	Andrew Dent	Vicksburg, "	Sarah Johnson	Vicksburg, "	32	M
" 18	Richard Dimitt	47 U S C I.	Eliza Sherka	Greenwood "	41	
June 4	William Davis	49" " "	Alice Williams	Vicksbg Miss	21	
Sept 1	Edward Dodson	66 " " "	Eliza Dodson	" "	45	
" 4	Humphry Deason	47th U.S.C.I.	Mary McPherson	Lake Providence La	37	M
" 8	Edmond Douglas	E 49th U.S.C.I	Hannah Williams	Vicksburg Miss	37	Bl
" 10	Raphael Devers	I., 52nd U.S.C.I.	Mary Wild	Isaquena Co "	36	

Do. of Mother.	Lived with another Woman. Years.	Separated by.	No. of Children by Previous Connection.	Age-Years.	Color.	Do. of Father.	Do. of Mother.	Lived with another Man. Years.	Separated by.	No. of Children by Previous Connection.	No. of Children Unitedly.	Name of Officiating Minister. and Witness.
Mixed				21	Blk	Blk	Blk					James Peet / John A. Davis
Blk				24	"	"	"					Walter C. Yancy / S. C. Feemster
"	4	Force	2	16	"	"	"					Joseph Warren / L. B. Eaton
"				21	"	"	"					R. L. Howard / Adin Mann
"	11	Death		27	"	"	"	7	Death	1	1	Joseph Warren / Patsy Monson
"				23	Mixed	Mixed	Mixed					Page Tyler / Robert McCary
"	1			57	Blk	Blk	Blk	6	Force	6		Joseph Warren / S. A. Dickey
"	5	"		39	Mixed	Mixed	Mixed	18	death			G. N. Carruthers / John Edmonson
Mxd	2	Her desertion		18	Blk	Blk	Blk					Joseph Warren / Adam Bowie
"				35	Mxd	"	Mxd					C. W. Buckley / Luther P Fitch
Blk				18	Brown	"	Brown					G. G. Edwards / P Yancey
"				35	Blk	"	Blk	8	Force	4		J A Hawley / Morrison King
"	1	force	1	30	Mxd	Mxd	"				4	C. W. Buckley / Luther P. Fitch
"	11	death	1	25	Blk	Blk	"	1	death			James A. Hawley / Louisa Woodin
"	2	"	2	30	"	"	"	5	desertion	4		Joseph Warren

Register of marriages of freedmen. Records of the Assistant Commissioner for the State of Mississippi, v. 43, pp. 124–125. Records of the Bureau of Refugees, Freedmen, and Abandoned Lands, RG 105. National Archives Microfilm Publication M826.

maintained **registers of depositors**, most of whom were African Americans, in which they recorded some personal and family information. Not all branches asked for the same information, and not all forms were completed. However, information in the registers includes account number; name; age; complexion; place of birth; place raised; name of former master and mistress; residence; occupation; names of parents, spouse, children, brothers, and sisters; remarks; and signature. Registers are arranged alphabetically by name of state; entries in the registers are arranged alphabetically by name of city where the bank was located, thereunder chronologically by date the account was opened, and thereunder numerically by account number. Registers are in Records of the Office of the Comptroller of the Currency, RG 101, and have been reproduced on M816, *Registers of Signature of Depositors in Branches of the Freedman's Savings and Trust Company, 1865-1874*, 27 rolls. Also in RG 101 are 46 volumes of indexes to the deposit ledgers that provide the names of depositors in 26 branch offices of the Freedman's Bank. The indexes are arranged alphabetically by name of state, thereunder by city where the branch was located. Names in the indexes are arranged, for the most part, alphabetically by the first letter of the surname. The indexes have been reproduced on M817, *Indexes to Deposit Ledgers in Branches of the Freedman's Savings and Trust Company, 1865-1874*, 5 rolls.

To use records of the Freedman's Savings and Trust Company, the researcher must first determine the city where the subject of research had an account. Because index entries included account numbers, researchers can use them as a rough finding aid to the registers of signatures. Researchers, however, should proceed with caution when using the indexes. More than one index exists for certain bank offices, and some indexes are not arranged in strict alphabetical order. It is therefore necessary to examine every name under the letter of the alphabet beginning the surname. Some indexes do not list all depositors whose surnames appear in the registers of signatures; many account numbers are missing; and in some instances account numbers assigned to depositors in the indexes are different from those in the signature records. In such cases, it is necessary to search entire rolls of signature cards for bank offices where the subject of the research resided. If there were no bank offices in the state and city where the subject lived, researchers should search for information about the subject in the records of branch offices in neighboring states and cities.

The Treasury Department established **special agencies** in 1861 to trade in insurgent areas of the South controlled by the U.S. military and in adjacent areas of loyal states. In addition to other functions, the agencies were responsible for the employment and welfare of freed men until the establishment of the Bureau of Refugees, Freedmen, and Abandoned Lands. The records are similar to those of the Freedmen's Bureau. Included in Records of Civil War Special Agencies of the Treasury Department, RG 366, are reports relating to labor contracts and to food and other supplies furnished to individuals and families, as well as some material concerning the disposition of confiscated and abandoned property. For the period 1861-66, records are arranged by agency, thereunder by subject, and generally thereunder chronologically. Because the boundaries and duties of the special agencies often changed, the researcher must have a good knowledge of the administrative history of the agencies. Some of this background information is given in *Guide to Federal Archives Relating to the Civil War*, compiled by Kenneth W. Munden and Henry P. Beers (Washington: National Archives and Records Service, reprinted 1998): 233-240.

Because some of the programs for African Americans later administered by the Freedmen's Bureau were initially carried out by army commands headquartered in various southern states, records relating to African Americans exist in Records of U.S. Army Continental Commands, 1821-1920, RG 393. Army involvement continued, although to a somewhat lesser extent, into the Reconstruction period. Army command records relating to African Americans are few, fragmentary, and generally unindexed. Information relating to specific individuals can be obtained from general records series only through painstaking research performed with the assistance of experienced archivists. Like the Freedmen's Bureau, army commands supervised employment of African Americans as agricultural laborers on farms and plantations. Records of the Department of the Gulf and Louisiana, for example, include pay rolls of laborers employed on plantations, 1864-67, and a small collection of descriptive lists ("registers") of laborers employed on plantations, 1864. The latter indicates age, sex, type of labor, former owner, and former residence. Military commands were also concerned, like the Bureau, with abuses perpetrated by whites upon freedmen. Records of the Departments of the South and South Carolina and the Second Military District include several series of reports of such "outrages," 1865-68, with registers, 1867-68. Provost marshals in various commands occasionally took censuses of African Americans and white inhabitants in their respective areas. Fragmentary censuses for 1864 are among records of the Department of the Gulf, mostly for Plaquemines Parish, LA, indicating name, age, sex, occupation, place of birth, and number of children. Records of the Department of the South have similar 1864 censuses for Florida, including the Jacksonville and St. Augustine areas. Entries indicate name; height; eye, skin, and hair color; age; last residence; former owner; and date individual entered the military department.

Confederate records relating to black civilian laborers, 1861-65, in the War Department Collection of Confederate Records, RG 109, are described in 14.4. For a general monograph, see *The Confederate Negro, Virginia's Craftsmen and Military Laborers, 1861-1865*, by James H. Brewer (Durham, NC: Duke University Press, 1969).

12.5 Records of the Commissioners of Claims

The Commissioners of Claims, commonly known as the Southern Claims Commission, was established by an act of Congress on March 3, 1871 (16 Stat. 524), to review and make recommendations regarding the claims of Southern Loyalists who had "furnished stores and supplies for the use of the U.S. Army" during the Civil War. Congress, by an act of May 11, 1872 (17 Stat. 97), extended this to include property taken by or furnished to the U.S. Navy. Persons who filed claims before the Commission had to be U.S. citizens, show proof of loss of property, and provide evidence of their loyalty to the Federal Government throughout the war. A small but impressive number of African Americans (former slaves and free blacks) submitted claims before the Commission. African Americans were also among the 220,00 witnesses who testified on behalf of African American and white claimants.

Southern Claims files are found among the records of several Federal agencies in the National Archives. The **approved case files** are with the settled accounts and claims of the Third Auditor of the Treasury in RG 217. Files are arranged by state, thereunder by county, and then alphabetically by surname of the claimant. The approved case file for the state of Georgia, 1871-1880, has been reproduced as M1658, *Southern Claims Commission Approved Claims, 1871-1880: Georgia*, 761 microfiche.

The **disallowed and barred case files** of the Commission are part of Records of the U.S. House of Representatives, RG 233. Disallowed files are arranged by office and report number; barred files are arranged alphabetically by surname of claimant. Because very little or no evidence was collected for barred claims, researchers will find them less informative for genealogical purposes. Files generally contain the claimants petition and little else. Both the barred and disallowed case files have been reproduced as M1407, *Barred and Disallowed Case Files of the Southern Claims Commission, 1871-1880*, 4,829 microfiche.

Congress published **summaries of the disallowed claims** in four volumes entitled *U.S. Commissioners of Claims Summary Reports in All Cases Reported to Congress as Disallowed Under the Act of March 3, 1871* (Washington: Government Printing Office, 1876). In each volume African American claimants are identified as "former slaves," "colored," "negro," "free born color," and "Mulatto." In addition, summaries provide an itemized list of and the amount of compensation sought for goods furnished or seized by Federal troops. They also give information concerning the evidence submitted regarding a claimant's loyalty and ownership of property; state, county, and town where the claim was filed; office and report number; claim number; and commissioners' reasons for disallowing the claim. In some instances, summary reports may be the only records that exist for an individual claim. The volumes have been reproduced on microfilm as P2257, *Records of the U.S. House of Representatives; A: Consolidated Order of Claims; B: Summary Reports of the Commissions, 1871-1880*, 1 roll. This microfilm publication is available for purchase through the National Archives Center for Legislative Archives.

Under provisions of the Bowman Act of 1883 and the Tucker Act of 1887, any claim that had been previously disallowed or barred by the Commission could be reconsidered by Congress and submitted to the U.S. Court of Claims for a "finding of fact." As a result, many of the original disallowed and barred Southern Claims case files are among the Records of the U.S. Court of Claims, RG 123. Claims that were sent to the Court of Claims are usually identified by a notation in the file. To access these files, researchers will need to obtain the Court of Claims case file number. Congressional case file numbers for the U.S. Court of Claims have been reproduced as M2007, *U.S. Court of Claims Docket Cards for Congressional Case Files, 1884-1943*, 5 rolls. Docket cards are arranged alphabetically by surname of the claimant.

To determine whether an ancestor filed a claim before the commission, researchers should first consult the *Consolidated Index of Claims Reported by the Commissioner of Claims to the House of Representatives, 1871 to 1880*. For the most part, the index provides an alphabetical list of all persons who filed claims before the Commission; researchers should be aware of spelling variations when using the index. For the African American genealogist, however, usefulness of the index is limited because it does not identify claimants by race. It is also less helpful to those researchers interested in conducting a search by individual counties. It does include information necessary to locate an individual file, such as the state of residence; commission number; office and report number; year of report; amount claimed; whether the claim was allowed, disallowed, barred, withdrawn, or dismissed; and the nature of the claim. The consolidated index has been reproduced on P2257; the first four microfiche of M1407; and M87, *Records of the Commissioners of Claims (Southern Claims Commission), 1871-1880*, 14 rolls. Researchers who want to do general research by county or determine the county from which a claim was filed should consult *Southern Loyalists in the Civil War: The Southern Claims Commission* by Gary Mills (Baltimore: Genealogical Publishing Co., Inc., 1994).

Additional records relating to the Southern Claims Commission can be found in General Records of the Department of the Treasury, RG 56. These records have been reproduced as part of M87 and include the journal of the commissioners; miscellaneous letters received by the commissioners; miscellaneous papers, consisting chiefly of memorandum copies of bills for goods; 57 summary reports; letters received by the commissioners from and about special agents; and a printed but unpublished geographical list of claims.

This Indenture made this twenty sixth day of July in the year eighteen hundred & fifty nine by & between Henry C Matthews of Washington County in the District of Columbia, Sole Executor & residuary legatee in the last will & testament of Alexander Matthews late of Charles County in the State of Maryland, deceased, of the first part. and Negro woman Rebecca now residing in the District of Columbia, a Slave of the said Alexander Matthews at the time of his death, & since then, & by virtue of the laws of Maryland in relation to the manumission of Slaves, the property of the said Henry C Matthews of the Second part - Witnesseth, that the said Henry C Matthews for divers good causes him thereto Moving, & in Consideration of the Sum of One Dollar to him paid by the said Negro Woman Rebecca, at the ensealing & delivery of these presents the receipt of which is hereby acknowledged, hath liberated set free manumitted & discharged from Slavery & from every species of Servitude to him, either in his private right, or as Executor aforesaid the said Negro Woman Rebecca. She being of the Age of Twenty two years, in good health & Capable of maintaining herself by labour - and doth hereby declare & pronounce the said Negro Woman Rebecca to be from henceforth a free Woman

250

In testimony whereof the said Henry C Matthews hath hereunto set his hand & seal, the day & year first aforesaid —

Signed sealed & delivered 　　　H. C. Matthews 　　(seal) in our presence —

Smith Hyde

W D Matthews

Washington County District of Columbia —

On this twenty Seventh day of July 　in the year Eighteen hundred & fifty Nine , Personally appeared before the Subscriber a Justice of the Peace in & for the County aforesaid, Henry C Matthews, party of the first part, named in the aforegoing instrument of writing, & acknowledged the same to be his act and deed ; Witness my hand and Seal.

Smith Hyde
JP 　(seal)

Manumission record, Henry C. Matthews, for "Negro Woman Rebecca," July 9, 1859. Records of District Courts of the United States, RG 21.

12.6 Records of Slaves in the District of Columbia

Several series of records exist that relate to slaves and the emancipation of slaves in the District of Columbia. If the subject of research was a resident of the District, *see also* Chapter 17.

Persons alleged to be fugitive slaves are the subject of most of M434, *Habeas Corpus Case Records, 1820-1863, of the United States Circuit Court for the District of Columbia,* 2 rolls. This series consists of writs of habeas corpus (orders to produce a prisoner and show cause for his capture and detention) and related documents filed in habeas corpus proceedings. Records are arranged chronologically; to use them, the researcher must know the year of the case, although both rolls of film can be searched. Similar records are among those of other U.S. district courts.

Other papers, 1851-63, relating to claims under the 1850 law to recover fugitive slaves then living in the District of Columbia are available on M433, *Records of the United States District Court for the District of Columbia Relating to Slaves, 1851-1863,* 3 rolls. Many cases contain only a warrant for the Negro's arrest; others contain documents and papers related to proof of ownership. Records are arranged chronologically.

Before 1821 deeds of manumission and certificates of freedom were recorded in the District deed books in Records of the Government of the District of Columbia, RG 351. Deed books also contain bills of sale for slaves and certificates of slave ownership submitted to local authorities when slaves were brought into the District of Columbia.

Six volumes of unmicrofilmed manumission and emancipation records, 1821-62, are in District of Columbia court records in Records of District Courts of the United States, RG 21. Volumes are arranged chronologically, and at the beginning of each, names of owners, trustees, or administrators are indexed in rough alphabetical order. These volumes also include registers of freedom that contain proofs submitted by free blacks to receive registers of freedom proving their free status.

An act of April 16, 1862 (12 Stat. 376), abolished slavery in the District of Columbia. Slave owners were required to free their slaves in exchange for compensation. By an act of July 12, 1862 (12 Stat. 538), slaves whose owners refused or neglected to free them could petition for their freedom. Also on M433 are **emancipation papers**, 1862-63, that, pursuant to these acts, consist of claims for compensation filed by former owners and claims for manumission from former slaves. Schedules show when the court issued certificates of freedom to former slaves; the certificates are arranged chronologically. **Manumission papers**, 1857-63, also filmed on M433, consist of similar schedules but relate only to masters' voluntary freeing of slaves. These are arranged chronologically.

A board of commissioners was appointed to receive petitions for compensation under the 1862 act. This board's records consist of a volume of minutes, April 28, 1862-January 14, 1863, with a name and subject index in the front of the volume. Unbound records contain a record of filed petitions. Petitions, which include the petition number, name of the petitioner, and names of the slaves and their value, are arranged chronologically, with an index by surname of the petitioner at the front of the volume. A printed version of the records of the petition is in H. Exec. Doc. 42, 38th Congress, 1st sess., serial 1189. This final report of the Board of Commissioners contains an alphabetical index to the names of the petitioners. The board's records also include various other material relating to administration of the 1862 acts; a series of 900 petitions filed under the act of April 16; and other petitions filed under the act of July 12.

These records have been reproduced on M520, *Records of the Board of Commissioners for the Emancipation of Slaves in the District of Columbia, 1862-1863,* 6 rolls. They are part of RG 217, which also contains records relating to this subject among Miscellaneous Treasury Accounts.

12.7 Other Records

12.7.1 Cherokee Freedmen

A few records relating to African Americans are among the Records of the Bureau of Indian Affairs, RG 75.

Cherokee citizenship for many ex-slaves who had belonged to Cherokees in Indian Territory was disputed by the Cherokee. Establishment of their status was important in determining the right of the ex-slaves to live on Cherokee land and share in certain annuity and other payments.

A series of investigations was conducted in order to compile rolls of Cherokee freedmen and other claimants to Cherokee citizenship. The investigations were begun in 1889-90 by Commissioner John W. Wallace, and though the resulting rolls were frequently revised in later years, they were called the **Wallace Rolls**. Claimants presented affidavits which were divided into "Free Negroes," who had been free at the beginning of the Civil War; "Admitted Cherokee Freedmen," who had not previously been recognized as Cherokee citizens; "Authenticated Cherokee Freedmen," who had been recognized previously; and "Rejected Cherokee Freedmen," with similar designations for other claimants. Among the records are letters received, supplements and revisions, and an index to revised copies of the Wallace Rolls of Cherokee Freedmen. Records relating to the Wallace Rolls are reproduced on M1833, *Revisions to the Wallace Rolls of Cherokee Freedmen and Delaware and Shawnee Cherokees, ca. 1890-96,* 1 roll. The last revision of the "Roll of Cherokee Freedmen" was completed in 1896-97; it lists family groups and their descendants under authenticated and admitted freedmen.

Also in RG 75 are reports on appraisals of improvements

by persons considered by the Cherokee to be intruders, including some freedmen, on Cherokee lands.

RG 217 has annuity payment rolls, often duplicating those in RG 75.

Among the Records of the Office of the Secretary of the Interior, RG 48, are rolls created by the Indian Territory Division that contain the names of some persons identified as freedmen. These rolls are available on T529, *Final Rolls of Citizens and Freedmen of the Five Civilized Tribes in Indian Territory (As Approved by the Secretary of the Interior on or Before Mar. 4, 1907, With Supplements Dated Sept. 25, 1914)*, 3 rolls. These records are more fully described in Chapter 11 about Native Americans. The original enrollment cards are held by NARA's Southwest Region at Fort Worth, TX.

12.7.2 Records Relating to the Slave Trade and African Colonization

Africans liberated from slave vessels bound for the United States were frequently transported to reception centers at Sherbro Island, Cape Mesurado, and Liberia, West Africa. M205, *Correspondence of the Secretary of the Navy Relating to African Colonization, 1819-1844,* 2 rolls, provides much information concerning this transport. Also discussed in these letters are arrangements made by U.S. district attorneys and other Federal officials for the temporary placement of some Africans in the southern states. Letters received by the Secretary of the Navy from commanding officers of the African Squadron, 1843-61, are reproduced as rolls 101-112 of M89, *Letters Received by the Secretary of the Navy From Commanding Officers of Squadrons ("Squadron Letters"), 1841-1886,* 300 rolls. *Letter Books of Commodore Matthew C. Perry, 1843-1845,* filmed as M206, 1 roll, and letter books of Commodore William C. Bolton, 1847-49, both commanding officers of the African Squadron, are also available. All these series are in Naval Records Collection of the Office of Naval Records and Library, RG 45.

Diplomatic correspondence pertaining to the slave trade is scattered through *Despatches from U.S. Ministers to Great Britain, 1791-1906,* M30, 200 rolls; . . . *Brazil, 1809-1906,* M121, 74 rolls; . . . *Liberia, 1863-1906,* M170, 14 rolls; and *Despatches from U.S. Consuls in Monrovia, Liberia, 1852-1906,* M169, 7 rolls. M40, *Domestic Letters of the Department of State, 1784-1906,* 171 rolls, and M179, *Miscellaneous Letters of the Department of State, 1789-1906,* M179, 1,310 rolls, include scattered correspondence with various colonization societies. These series are in General Records of the Department of State, RG 59.

The records in each series are arranged chronologically. These records are of marginal value for genealogical research, but they are useful to help place African American family history in the context of the 19th century.

M160, *Records of the Office of the Secretary of the Interior Relating to the Suppression of the African Slave Trade and Negro Colonization, 1854-1872,* 10 rolls, consists of three bound volumes and a quantity of unbound records relating to the suppression of the African slave trade and the colonization of recaptured and free blacks. These records, dated between August 10, 1854, and February 3, 1872, are part of RG 48.

Certain correspondence pertaining to the suppression of the slave trade and to colonization projects has been published: *Liberated Africans* . . . . (37th Cong., 3rd sess., H. Ex. Doc. 28, serial 1161); . . . *Transportation, Settlement and Colonization of Persons of the African Race* (39th Cong., 1st sess., S. Ex. Doc. 55, serial 1238); and . . . *Operations of the United States Squadron on the West Coast of Africa, the Condition of the American Colonies There.* . . . (28th Cong., 2nd sess., S. Doc. 150, serial 458), which includes "Roll of Emigrants That Have Been Sent to the Colony of Liberia, Western Africa, by the American Colonization Society and Its Auxiliaries, to September, 1843," pp. 152-307, and "Census of the Colony of Liberia, September 1843," pp. 308-393.

In RG 21 are case files concerning admiralty and criminal matters pertaining to the slave trade. Admiralty cases in district courts were largely proceedings in rem (against the ship, her cargo, and tackle); they are related to the seizure, condemnation, and sale of ships engaged in the slave trade. Criminal cases in district and circuit courts concerning the slave trade pertain to charges of outfitting slave ships and to the service of masters and crews. To locate the records of a specific case, the researcher must know the court, date, and name of the defendant. The records of RG 21 are in the custody of the various regional archives facilities. *See* Table 1 in the Introduction to this volume for the location of NARA's regional archives.

General Records of the Department of Justice, RG 60, contains scattered correspondence concerning the slave trade; Records of the Foreign Service Posts of the Department of State, RG 84, includes material supplementing that in RG 59. Records of United States Attorneys, RG 118, held by NARA's Southeast Region in Atlanta contains scattered correspondence of the U.S. Attorney for the Southern District of Alabama, 1830-60, that deals with laws prohibiting the further importation of slaves.

Slave manifests in Records of the U.S. Customs Service, RG 36, are of marginal value in genealogical research about African American families. Masters of ships bringing cargoes into the United States from abroad had to submit a manifest or list of all of the goods they were importing. The National Archives has manifests for a few of the ships that brought in slaves between 1789 and 1808, before foreign slave trade became illegal. Manifests give the number of slaves, African port or area from which the ship sailed, U.S. port it entered, shipper, and name and address of the recipient of the cargo. Because no names appear on the lists, these manifests are useful only for circumstantial evidence.

Masters of ships carrying slave cargoes between domestic ports were required to submit a manifest of their human cargoes. These manifests generally include the slave's name (almost always a given name, not a surname), sex, age, and height. They also contain the name of the shipper and the person or firm to whom the slaves were shipped. Inward and outward manifests that exist for several ports, including Savannah, Mobile, and New Orleans, are arranged by port, thereunder chronologically. To locate information about a particular slave, a researcher must know where, when, and by whom the slave was sold.

CHAPTER 13 *Records of Merchant Seamen*

13.1 *Introduction*

13.2 *Impressed American Seamen*

13.3 *Seamen's Protection Certificates*

13.4 *Crew Lists*

Table 18 *Abstracts of Seamen's Protection Certificates*

Table 19 *Crew Lists on Microfilm*

13.5 *Shipping Articles*

13.6 *Logbooks*

13.7 *Other Records*

Chapter 13

Records of Merchant Seamen

13.1 Introduction

Records held by the National Archives and Records Administration (NARA) pertaining to merchant seamen include series relating to impressed America seamen and to seamen's protection certificates, as well as to crew lists, shipping articles, and logbooks of merchant vessels.

13.2 Impressed American Seamen

Unbound **letters received by the State Department relating to American seamen impressed by Great Britain** before the War of 1812 or imprisoned during the war, 1794-1815, are arranged alphabetically by name of seaman. They include letters from collectors of customs, impressed seamen and their relatives and friends, and U.S. agents in such cities as London and Liverpool. Some letters report cases of impressment; others transmit requests for the release of individual seaman, for seamen's certificates, and for affidavits of U.S. citizenship.

Bound **registers of applications** for the release of impressed seamen, 1793-1802, are arranged chronologically, but they are indexed by the first letter of the seaman's surname. Each entry in the registers shows the name of the seaman and such related information as date of capture, date of application for release, name of vessel from which taken, name of vessel on which impressed or place of imprisonment, and, occasionally, the number of the seaman's protection certificate and the name of the port where it was issued. Similar registers for 1804-17 were maintained by the U.S. consulate in London; these are also arranged chronologically, but there is a separate name index.

Letters and bound applications for release of impressed seaman are in General Records of the Department of State, Record Group (RG) 59. In the same record group is a list of impressed seamen prepared by the State Department in October 1805. It was indexed by Elizabeth Pearson White in "Impressed American Seamen," *National Genealogical Society Quarterly* 60 (1912): 125-131, 188-193. The registers maintained by American diplomats in London are in Records of the Foreign Service Posts of the Department of State, RG 84.

Several lists of impressed seamen were published in *American State Papers: Foreign Relations*, 6 vols. (Washington: Gales and Seaton, 1832-59). The first set of lists (vol. 2, doc. 197, pp. 777-793) includes over 900 names of seamen impressed between September 1, 1804, and September 26, 1805, generally giving for each seaman the date of impressment, the ship of war into which they were impressed, and remarks relating to proof of citizenship. The second set consists of 12 lists submitted to Congress on March 2, 1808 (vol. 3, doc. 212, pp. 36-79). In 1816 Secretary of State James Monroe provided Congress with three final lists of impressed American seamen (vol. 4, doc. 282, pp. 56-95). List A shows the names of 1,421 seamen impressed into the service of British public ships, and later transferred to and confined in English prisons as prisoners of war. The information was taken from official lists furnished by the British authorities to the American agent for prisoners in London. List B shows the names of 158 American seamen impressed and finally transferred to prisons in the West Indies or Nova Scotia. Both lists provide the names of seamen impressed, their rank, name of the British man-of-war that impressed them, place confined, date of release, the vessel in which they returned to the United States, and date of arrival. List C identifies 219 American seamen impressed on board British public ships and discharged in England after the end of the War of 1812.

13.3 Seamen's Protection Certificates

Attempts to protect American seamen from impressment by Great Britain and other powers during the 18th and early 19th centuries led to the creation of records now useful to genealogists. The famous case of the *Lydia*, from which five American seamen were impressed on the high seas in February 1796, caused great outrage in the country and the Congress. As a result, an act of 1796 (1 Stat. 477) required each district collector of customs to keep a register of those seamen who applied for seamen's protection certificates and presented evidence of citizenship, such as a birth certificate, passport, old seaman's protection certificate issued in another port, or an oath taken before a notary public, alderman, or other official. Collectors or deputy collectors of customs received applications, issued certificates to the seamen, kept proofs of citizenship on file in the districts, and regularly sent lists of registered seamen to the Secretary of State.

The National Archives holds **registers of seamen who received certificates** for the ports of Bath, ME, 1828-40; Fairfield district, CT, 1845-66; Frenchman's Bay, ME, 1865-66; and Portsmouth, NH, 1796-98; and registers of seamen protection certificates issued at Baltimore, MD, 1808-67; Bath, 1804-40; Bristol and Warren, RI, 1828-40, 1855-73; Fairfield, 1801-39; Middletown, CT, 1842-67; and New London, CT, 1796-1828. Registers of seamen are also available at NARA's Northeast Region in Boston for the districts of Fall River, MA, 1837-69; Gloucester, MA, 1796-1860; Marblehead, MA, 1790-1866; New Haven, CT, 1793-1801, 1803-41; New London, 1796-1827, 1833-78; Newport, RI, 1812-77; and Salem, MA, 1796-1832. Because the certificates were used for identification, registers include the following information about individual seamen: name; certificate number and date of issue; age; place of birth; how citizenship was obtained (birth or naturalization); and physical description including height, weight, complexion, color of hair and eyes, and, in some cases, identifying marks such as scars, limps, or deformed limbs. Names are arranged in rough alphabetical order by the initial letter of the surname, thereunder chronologically.

The certificates themselves were carried by the seamen; certificates did not become Federal records except in those infrequent cases when a seaman turned in an old, worn

American Consulate Falmouth

These are to certify that during the Ship
Ann Charles Bradford Master being at
this port loading, John Monday and
Thomas Beal two of the Crew of said Ship
have been taken out of said Ship by
an Officer in the British Service, who
would not give them up on application
being made for that purpose. —

Given under hand & Consular Seal at
Falmouth this 14 day of Novem.ʳ 1806 —

Thoˢ. W. Fox

Consular Agent of
the United States of
America

Certificate of impressment of two American merchant seamen, 1806, Letters Received Regarding Impressed Seamen. Records of Impressed Seamen. General Records of the Department of State, RG 59.

Philadelphia City ſſ.

On the *twenty ſeventh* day of *October* one thouſand eight hundred and *one* Perſonally came before Alexander Tod, Eſq. one of the Aldermen of the City aforeſaid, *Thomas Liney* *five* feet *1¾* inches high, *fair* complection, *dark* hair, *18* years of age, marked *a large* mark *on left arm above his elbow, cut above his left eye, a few marks if the small pox on his face* being legally ſworn, ſays, that according to the beſt of his knowledge, he was born *in the City of New York* At the ſame time appeared *John Schanlan* who being alſo ſworn, ſays, that he has known and been well acquainted with ſaid *Thomas Liney for many* years, and that according to the beſt of his knowledge and belief, he the ſaid *Thomas Liney* was born at the place aforeſaid. Witneſs my hand and ſeal, the day and year firſt written.

Sworn before
Alexr Tod
Alderman

Thomas Liney
his
John X Schanlan
mark

Seaman's protection certificate, issued to merchant seamen in attempt to thwart British press gangs. Records of the U.S. Customs Service, RG 36. Few of these certificates are in the National Archives.

certificate and applied for another.

An application shows the name, age, physical description, place of birth, and signature or mark of each seaman and the signature or mark of witnesses, who sometimes were relatives. However, relatively few applications and supporting proofs of citizenship are held by NARA. Original applications and proofs of citizenship, with gaps, are available for the following ports or districts: Alexandria, VA, 1802-38; Bath, ME, 1833, 1836, 1841, and 1845-68; Middletown, CT, 1796-1801, 1805-61; Mobile, AL, 1819-59; New Bedford, MA, 1801-26; New Haven, 1801-43; New London, 1799-1894; New Orleans, LA, 1804-21, 1851-57; Newport, RI, 1813-17; Philadelphia, PA, 1796-1861; Portsmouth, NH, 1857; Rockland, including Thomaston, South Thomaston, ME (protection oaths), 1855-61; and Salem/Beverly, MA, 1798, 1811, and 1813. Indexes to these records are available.

Records for Bath, Portsmouth, and New Orleans are available on M1825, *Proofs of Citizenship Used to Apply for Seamen's Protection Certificates at the Ports of Bath, Maine, 1833, 1836, 1839-50, 1853-65, 1867-68; and at Portsmouth, New Hampshire, 1857-58*, 3 rolls, and M1826, *Proofs of Citizenship Used to Apply for Seamen's Protection Certificates for the Port of New Orleans, Louisiana, 1800, 1802, 1804-7, 1809-12, 1814-16, 1818-19, 1821, 1850-51, 1855-57*, 12 rolls. Applications for Philadelphia for the war period 1812-15, were thoroughly analyzed by Ira Dye, and the results are available as M972, *Computer-Processed Tabulations of Data From Seamen's Protective Certificate Applications to the Collector of Customs for the Port of Philadelphia, 1812-1815*, 1 roll. Information from the records is arranged in several different ways, including alphabetically by name of seaman.

Some additional documentation regarding the citizenship of seamen can be found among records of the custom houses and districts. For example, certificates of citizenship, 1796-1897, and proofs or oaths of citizenship, 1796-1806, are filed with the records of the Salem and Beverly, MA, custom house, while records of the Fairfield and Bridgeport district, CT, include proofs for seamen's citizenship, 1797-1801. A close examination of the National Archives publication "Preliminary Inventory of the Records of the Bureau of Customs," NC 154 (1968), compiled by Forrest R. Holdcamper, and its microfiche supplement, may identify similar documents for other ports.

The most fruitful source for genealogical information research is the **abstract of applications**, which shows the name, age, physical description, and place of birth of each seaman. These abstracts are found for most ports. Access is provided by two card indexes, one relating to New York City and the second to most other ports. Indexes are arranged alphabetically by surname of seaman. Abstracts for the port of Baltimore, 1808-67, and the district of Fairfield, CT, 1801-80, are bound. Other abstracts date from 1815 to 1869. Table 18 lists the ports and the overall dates of the available abstracts.

To use the records effectively, the genealogist needs to know when and where the seaman went to sea. In general, applications and proofs are less rewarding for research than the abstracts, because they pertain to fewer places and require more information to search. Their value as documentary evidence is, however, greater than the abstracts, because they bring the researcher one step closer to the life of the seaman.

All of the records described thus far in this section are in Records of the U.S. Customs Service, RG 36. Several small series of related records, including seamen's certificates and protests, 1817-20, are among the State Department records in RG 59. Records of some consular posts such as those in Vancouver and Victoria, British Columbia, in RG 84, include registers of seamen and related records.

Applications for **seamen's protection certificates for the years 1916–40** are in Records of the Bureau of Marine Inspection and Navigation, RG 41. They are arranged by port, thereunder usually chronologically. Those for San Francisco, however, are arranged alphabetically, and those for New Orleans are in rough alphabetical order. Applications for Boston, New York, and Philadelphia are indexed. These later applications show name of seaman, age or date of birth, often place of birth, photograph or personal description, signature or mark, and, if naturalized, date of naturalization and name of court that granted it. Fingerprints are often included in both the application files and copies of the certificates.

13.4 Crew Lists

An act of 1803 (2 Stat. 203) "for the further protection of American seamen" required masters of American vessels leaving U.S. ports for foreign voyages or arriving at U.S. ports from foreign voyages to file crew lists with collectors of customs. This law did not apply to foreign vessels or to American vessels on coastal voyages. A crew list shows the name, place of birth and residence, and description of each member of the crew.

RG 36 includes crew lists for New York, 1803-1919; New Orleans, 1803-1902; Philadelphia, 1803-99; and San Francisco, 1851-99. San Francisco crew lists for 1900-30 are in NARA's Pacific Region (San Francisco). Crew lists exist for some other ports but mostly for shorter periods in the 19th century. Lists are arranged by port, thereunder chronologically, and thereunder by ship. To use crew lists, the researcher must know which ports a particular crew sailed from and the approximate dates. Vessel arrival and clearance registers are available for many of the ports, but they do not necessarily cover the same years as the crew lists. The registers may help to establish the exact date of arrival or departure of a particular ship and will also supply the name of the master.

Information about New Orleans crew lists, 1803-25, also available in RG 36, consists of 15 volumes of typescripts of records. Lists show name of the seaman, rank, state or

TABLE 18
Abstracts of Seamen's Protection Certificates

ENTRIES SHOW PORTS AND DATE SPANS OF AVAILABLE CERTIFICATES. MOST OF THE DATE SPANS INCLUDE GAPS.

Port	Dates	Port	Dates
Alexandria, VA	1815–61	New Bedford, MA	1813–69
Annapolis, MD	1841, 1849	New Bern, NC	1841–46, 1860–61
Appalachicola, FL	1847–66	New Haven, CT	1813–15, 1821–34, 1837–44, 1861–69
Baltimore, MD	1819–60		
Barnstable, MA	1812–62	New London, CT	1813–31, 1837–47, 1860–62
Bath, ME	1814–69		
Belfast (District of), ME	1825–60	New Orleans, LA	1812–60
Boston and Charlestown, MA	1813–68, 1873	New York City, NY	1814–69
Bristol and Warren, RI	1812–69	Newark, NJ	1843, 1847–50, 1856–60
Camden (District of), NC	1860–61	Newburyport, MA	1824–69
Castine, ME	1866, 1868	Norfolk and Portsmouth, VA	1807, 1813–69
Charleston, SC	1826–27, 1836–37, 1858–60	Passamaquoddy, ME	1852–67
		Penobscot, ME	1813–66
Cherrystone, VA	1857	Pensacola, FL	1823–24, 1829–45
Darien, GA	1821–35	Perth Amboy, NJ	1830, 1832
Dighton-Fall River, MA		Petersburg, VA	1815–16, 1819, 1821–22
Dighton	1815–16, 1819–36	Philadelphia, PA	1813–72
Fall River	1834–66	Plymouth, MA	1813–16, 1820–66
Dumfries, VA	1814, 1819–20	Plymouth, NC	1812–61
East River, VA	1813, 1819–31	Portland-Falmouth, ME	1812–61
Edenton, NC	1812, 1815–16 1825, 1859–62	Portsmouth, NH	1814–68
		Providence, RI	1813–68
Edgartown, MS	1830–69, 1874	Richmond, VA	1819–60
Fairfield, CT	1815–27	Rockland, ME	1857–64
Fernandina, FL	1866	Saco, ME	1813–64
Folly Landing, VA	1820–23, 1837, 1840–41	Sag Harbor, NY	1830–45, 1860
Frenchman's Bay, ME	1812–64	St. Augustine, FL	1844
Galveston, TX	1850–52, 1860	St. Marks, FL	1847, 1860
Georgetown, DC	1819–27, 1843–48	Salem-Beverly, MA	1813, 1823, 1826, 1836–69
Gloucester, MA	1812–68	Savannah, GA	1812–15, 1843–60
Ipswich, MA	1830, 1840–44	Stonington, CT	1843–50
Kennebunkport, ME	1814–67	Waldoboro, ME	1813–31, 1834–53, 1860–61
Key West, FL	1832–64		
Machias, ME	1842–66	Washington, NC	1815–16, 1820–45, 1860
Marblehead, MA	1813–69	Wilmington, DE	1819–30, 1842–49
Milwaukee, WI	1861	Wilmington, NC	1815–16
Mobile, AL	1837–40, 1851–60	Wiscasset, ME	1813, 1821–29, 1860–63
Nantucket, MA	1813–69	York, ME	1815, 1821–31, 1834

country of birth, and country of citizenship. Each of the 15 volumes contains a composite alphabetical index to names of the seamen, names of masters, and names of ships mentioned in the lists in that volume. The indexes and typescript format of these records make the New Orleans lists for these two decades easier to use than other crew lists.

Two other volumes in this series of typescripts are valuable to researchers interested in merchant seamen working in or out of New Orleans. "Flatboats on the Mississippi in 1807" contains typescripts of manifests of vessels for the month of May; they show the name of the master, name of vessel, names of crew members, and cargo. "Returns of Seamen for Marine Hospital Tax" shows names of vessels, masters, and crew members and the length of time crew members were employed. Typescripts of these returns are arranged chronologically and cover the years 1805–33. They pertain to coastal as well as foreign voyages.

Microfilm copies of some 20th-century crew lists are in Records of the Immigration and Naturalization Service (INS), RG 85. The originals were microfilmed and then later destroyed by INS, so the microfilm copies are now

DISTRICT AND PORT OF SAN FRANCISCO.

LIST OF ~ PERSONS

Composing the Crew of the _Bark Laura_ of _Plymouth Mass_

whereof _R S Easton_ is Master, bound for _Valparaiso_

NAMES.	PLACES OF BIRTH.	PLACES OF RESIDENCE.	OF WHAT COUNTRY CITIZENS, OR SUBJECTS.	AGED.	DESCRIPTION OF THEIR PERSONS.		
					HEIGHT. FEET | INCHES.	COMPLEXION.	HAIR.
S R Easton	"	Massachusetts	United States				
Willm F Tripp	"	Massachusetts	United States				
Phineas A Leach	"	do	do				
Charles Monro	"	London	Great Britain	Not on board			
W Thompson	"	New York	United States				
Marion Louis	"	Bordeaux	France				
Francis Mari	"	do	do				
Simion Horton	"	New York	United States				
Edwin Read	"	do	do				
George Herbert	"	London	Great Britain				
William Dunbar	"	Philadelphia	United States				

6

DISTRICT AND PORT OF SAN FRANCISCO.

I _R S Easton_ Master or Commander of the _Bark_ called the _Laura_ of _Plymouth Mass_ now about clearing for _the Port of Valparaiso_, do solemnly and sincerely swear that the above list contains a true and correct statement of the names of all the Officers and Crew of the said _Bark Laura_, together with the places of their birth and residence, so far as I have been able to ascertain the same.

Rueben S Easton

Sworn to this 25th day of _November_ 1851, before me,

G W Hopkins

Deputy Collector.

DISTRICT AND PORT OF SAN FRANCISCO.

I _R S Easton_ Master or Commander of the _Bark_ called the _Laura_ of _Plymouth Mass_, now about clearing for _the Port of Valparaiso_, do solemnly and sincerely swear that I have been unable to obtain two-thirds American seamen for the said _Bark Laura_ for her now intended voyage.

Rueben S Easton

Sworn to this 25th day of _November_ 1851, before me,

G W Hopkins

Deputy Collector.

Crew list of vessel departing from San Francisco, 1851.
Records of the U.S. Customs Service, RG 36

TABLE 19
Crew Lists on Microfilm

LISTS WITHOUT MICROFILM PUBLICATION NUMBERS ARE ONLY AVAILABLE FOR USE IN THE MICROFILM READING ROOM AT THE NATIONAL ARCHIVES BUILDING IN WASHINGTON, DC.

PORT	PERIOD COVERED	MICROFILM PUBLICATION	NUMBER OF ROLLS
Ashland, WI	Aug. 1922–Oct. 1954	M2005	2
Baton Rouge, LA	Jan. 1, 1919–Mar. 31, 1924		1
Boston, MA	1916–43	T938	269
Brunswick, GA	Jan. 1, 1904–Dec. 31, 1938		2
Charleston, SC	Jan. 1, 1910–Dec. 31, 1945		28
Fort Lauderdale, FL	Dec. 1, 1939–Dec. 1945		11
Gloucester, MA	1918–43	T941	13
Gulfport, MS	Oct. 19, 1904–Mar. 30, 1945		7
Gulfport, MS (alien changes)	1919–45		5
Hartford, CT	Feb. 1929–Dec. 1943		4
Jacksonville, FL	1906–45		39
Key West, FL	Aug. 1, 1914–Dec. 31, 1945		19
Lake Charles, LA	Oct. 1, 1940–Dec. 31, 1945		1
Miami, FL	1920–45		123
Mobile, AL	Aug. 1, 1903–Dec. 31, 1945		59
Mobile, AL (Form 689: aliens)	Jan. 1, 1925–Dec. 31, 1931		4
New Bedford, MA	1917–43	T942	2
New Orleans, LA	1910–45	T939	311
New York, NY	June 16, 1897–Dec. 31, 1942	T715	8,892*
Pascagoula, MS	Jan. 1, 1907–Sept. 5, 1928		3
Pascagoula, MS (aliens)	July 1903–May 1935	M2027	1
Pensacola, FL	1905–45		11
Pensacola, FL (Form 689: aliens)	Jan. 1, 1907–Dec. 31, 1939		5
Philadelphia, PA	May 1917–Dec. 31, 1945		220
Philadelphia, PA (alien changes)	1918		1
Portland, ME	May 1, 1917–Jan. 1944		37
Providence, RI	Aug. 1918–Dec. 31, 1943		22
San Francisco, CA	1905–54	M1416	174
San Francisco, CA (aliens)	1896–1921	M1436	8
Savannah, GA	1910–Dec. 31, 1945		32
Seattle, WA	1903–17	M1399	15
Tampa, FL	Jan. 1, 1904–Dec. 31, 1945		72
West Palm Beach, FL	Sept. 21, 1925–Dec. 31, 1945		12

* Includes passenger lists

the only record. Table 19 shows the ports for which there are crew lists, dates of lists, and numbers of rolls. Also shown are ports for which there are records of aliens employed as members of the crews. Microfilm publication numbers are included for INS film that has been converted to National Archives microfilm publications. Those without numbers are only available for use in the microfilm reading room at the National Archives Building in Washington, DC.

13.5 Shipping Articles

Shipping articles are another useful series of records for genealogical information about merchant seamen. Shipping articles are legal contracts between the seamen and the owners of vessels specifying wages and some working conditions. Shipping articles were required as early as 1790 (1 Stat. 131), but they were not regularly filed with collectors of customs at ports of engagement or discharge until

DISTRICT OF SAN FRANCISCO.

STATE OF CALIFORNIA.   UNITED STATES OF AMERICA.

It is Agreed, between the Master and Seamen, or Mariners of the *Bark Laura* of *Plymouth, Mass.* whereof *R. S. Easton* is at present Master, or whoever shall go for Master, now bound from the Port of San Francisco to *The Port of Valparaiso or Port or Ports in the Pacific*

THAT, In consideration of the monthly or other wages against each respective Seaman or Mariner's name, hereunder set, they severally shall and will perform the above-mentioned voyage: And the said Master doth hereby agree with, or hire the said Seamen and Mariners for the said voyage, at such monthly wages or prices, to be paid pursuant to this agreement, and the laws of the Congress of the United States. And they, the said Seamen or Mariners, do severally hereby promise and oblige themselves to do their duty, and obey the lawful commands of their officers on board the said vessel or the boats thereunto belonging, as become good and faithful seamen or mariners; and at all places where the said vessel shall put in, or anchor at, during the said voyage, to do their best endeavors for the preservation of the said vessel and cargo, and not to neglect or refuse doing their duty by day or night, nor shall he go out of the said vessel on board any other vessel, or be on shore, under any pretense whatsoever, until the above said voyage be ended, and the said vessel be discharged of her loading, without leave first obtained of the Captain or commanding officer on board; and in default thereof, he or they shall be liable to all the penalties and forfeitures mentioned in the Marine Law, enacted for the government and regulation of Seamen in the Merchant's service, in which it is enacted, "That if any Seaman or Mariner shall absent himself from on board the ship or vessel, without leave of the master or officer commanding on board, and the mate, or other officer having charge of the log-book, shall make an entry therein of the name of such seaman or mariner, on the day on which he shall so absent himself; and if such seaman or mariner shall return to his duty within forty-eight hours, such seaman or mariner shall forfeit three days pay for every day which he shall so absent himself, to be deducted out of his wages; but if any seaman or mariner shall absent himself for more than forty-eight hours at one time, he shall forfeit all the wages due to him, and all his goods and chattels, which were on board the said ship or vessel, or in any store where they may have been lodged at the time of his desertion, to the use of the owner or owners of the said ship or vessel, and moreover shall be liable to pay him or them all damages which he or they may sustain by being obliged to hire other seamen or mariners in his or their

place." And it is further agreed, that in case of desertion, death, or impressment, the wages are to cease. And it is further agreed by both parties, that each and every lawful command which the said master or other officer shall think necessary hereafter to issue for the effectual government of the said vessel, suppressing immorality and vice of all kinds, to be strictly complied with, under the penalty of the person or persons disobeying, forfeiting his or their whole wages or hire, together with everything belonging to him or them on board said vessel. And it is further agreed on, that no officer or seaman belonging to the said vessel shall demand or be entitled to his wages, or any part thereof, until the arrival of the said vessel at the last above-mentioned port of discharge, and her cargo delivered. And it is hereby further agreed, between the master, officers and seamen of the said vessel, that whatever apparel, furniture and stores each of them may receive into their charge, belonging to the said vessel, shall be accounted for on her return; and in case anything shall be lost or damaged, through their carelessness or insufficiency, it shall be made good by such officer or seaman, by whose means it may happen, to the master and owners of the said vessel. And whereas, it is customary for the officers and seamen, while the vessel is in port, or whilst the cargo is delivering, to go on shore at night to sleep, greatly to the prejudice of such vessel and freighters—be it further agreed by the said parties, that neither officer nor seaman shall, on any pretence whatever, be entitled to such indulgence, but shall do their duty by day in discharging of the cargo, and keep watch by night as the master shall think necessary to order relative to said vessel or cargo; and whereas, it frequently happens that the owner or captain incurs expenses while in a foreign port, relative to the imprisonment of one or more of his officers or crew; or in the attendance of nurses, or in the payment of board on shore, for the benefit of such person or persons: Now, it is understood and agreed by the parties hereunto, that all such expenditures as may be incurred by reason of the foregoing premises, shall be charged to and deducted out of the wages of any officer, or each one of the crew, by whose means or for whose benefit the same shall have been paid. And whereas, it often happens that part of the cargo is embezzled, after being safely delivered

into lighters, and as such losses are made good by the owners of the vessel, be it therefore agreed by these presents, that whatever officer or seaman the master shall think proper to appoint, shall take charge of her cargo in the lighters, and go with it to the lawful quay, and there deliver his charge to the vessel's husband, or his representative, to see the same safely landed : That each seaman or mariner, who shall well and truly perform the above-mentioned voyage, (provided always that there be no desertion, plunderage, embezzlement, or other unlawful acts committed on the said vessel's cargo or stores,) shall be entitled to the payment of the wages or hire that may become due to him, pursuant to this agreement, as to their name is severally affixed and set forth. Provided, nevertheless, that if any of the said crew disobey the orders of the said master, or other officer of the said vessel, or absent himself at any time without liberty, his wages due at the time of such disobedience or absence, shall be forfeited ; and in case such person or persons so forfeiting wages shall be reinstated or permitted to do farther duty, it shall not do away such forfeiture. It being understood and agreed by the said parties, that parol proof of the misconduct, absence, or desertion of any officer, or any of the crew of said vessel, may be given in evidence at any trial between the parties to this contract, any act, law or usage to the contrary thereof notwithstanding. That for the due performance of each and every of the above-mentioned articles and agreements, and acknowledgment of their being voluntary, and without compulsion, or any other clandestine means being used, agreed to, and signed by us.

In Testimony Whereof, We have, each and every of us, hereunto affixed our hands, the month and day against our names, as hereunder written. And it is hereby understood, and mutually agreed by and between the parties aforesaid, that they will render themselves on board the said vessel on or before the ____ day of ____ at ____ o'clock in the ____ noon.

We, who have subscribed our names in this column, do promise that the man who has engaged for this present voyage, and signed his name in the third column of the same line, shall proceed on the said voyage, agreeably to the Shipping Papers, or refund the Advance Money with like amount, according to Act of Congress, to ____ on demand.

DATE OF ENTRY.	NAMES.	PLACES OF RESIDENCE.	STATIONS.	WITNESS TO SIGNING.	MONTHLY WAGES.	ADVANCE WAGES.	WAGES BY THE RUN.	TIME OF DISCHARGE.	TIME OF SERVICE. MONTHS.	DAYS.	WHOLE AMOUNT OF WAGES.	ADVANCED ABROAD.	HOSPITAL MONEY.	WAGES DUE.
1851	Reuben S Easton	Massachusetts	Master	S. R. Beals										
	William F. Nyyro	Massachusetts	1st Officer	Geo Guerara	$40	$60								
	Phineas A Leach	Massachusetts	2nd Officer	S. R. Beals	$38	$50								
Nov. 24	Charles Monro	London	Carpenter &c	Geo Guerara	$60	$60								
Nov. 24	Jon Ruyero	Portugal	Seaman	Geo Guerara	$45	$45								
" 24	William Tongum	New York	Seaman	Geo Guerara	$45	$45								
" 24	Marion Louis	Bordeaux	Seaman	Geo Guerara	$45	$45								
" 24	Lewis	Bordeaux	Seaman	Geo Guerara	$45	$45								
" 24	John X Copeland	Boston	Seaman	S. R. Beals	$45	$45								
" 24	Mark X Ridgeway	Boston	Seaman	S. R. Beals	$45	$45								
" 24	Simeon X Horton	New York	Seaman	Geo Guerara	$45	$45								
" 24	Edwin Read	New York	Seaman	Geo Guerara	$45	$45								
" 24	George X Herbert	London	Seaman	Geo Guerara	$45	$45								
" 25	William X Dunbar	Philadelphia	Cook & Steward	Geo Guerara	$60	$60								

Custom House, San Francisco, Nov. 25 1851

I do hereby certify that these Shipping Articles are the Original this day produced to me in conformity with the Act of Congress approved July 20th A. D. 1840

Given under my hand & seal of Office this Twenty-fifth day of Nov. A. D. 1851

W. O. Rh. Dud

R. W. Hopkins D. Collector

1840 (5 Stat. 394).An act of 1872 (17 Stat. 262) made shipping commissioners in certain ports responsible for superintending the shipping and discharge of seamen, and these officials largely took over from the collectors of customs the function of filing the articles. In general, shipping articles through 1872 are in RG 36 and articles from later years in RG 41, but the dividing date varies from port to port.

Shipping articles show for each seaman their name, signature or mark, state or country of birth, age, personal description, shipboard occupation, monthly wages, date and place the articles were signed, date and place the seaman was paid (on the "paid-off," copy of the articles only), and, sometimes, name and address of next of kin or other designated person.

Shipping articles exist for many ports for varying parts of the overall period 1840-1938. They are arranged by port, thereunder chronologically, with some variations. To use them, the researcher must know where and when the subject of research was hired as a merchant seaman. Shipping articles after 1872 for New York, Philadelphia, Boston, Baltimore, and San Francisco are indexed by ship or arranged in rough alphabetical order.

Shipping articles and crew lists for the port of San Francisco in the periods 1854-56, 1861-62, 1883-86, and 1900-50 are at NARA's Pacific Region (San Francisco). They are arranged chronologically, thereunder alphabetically by name of ship. That regional facility also has a register of discharges, 1883-84, that lists in chronological order discharges of seamen at the completion of voyages.

Crew bonds were required of each master of vessels as an assurance that, at the time of the vessel's return to a U.S. port, he would account for all persons named on a verified list that had been delivered to the collector of customs when the vessel departed from the United States. NARA's Pacific Region (San Francisco) has bonds for San Francisco for 1896, arranged chronologically.

13.6 Logbooks

Official logbooks of U.S. flag vessels, primarily ships engaged in foreign trade from the late 19th century through the 1960's, are in RG 41. The logbooks contain names, occupations, and ratings of the performance or ability of the crew members, and slop accounts, or expenditures of crew members for personal items while on board.

Also required by law to be entered in logbooks were records of offenses committed by crew members; inquiries, illnesses, deaths, and births that occurred during a voyage; changes in crew; and deductions from seamen's wages or sale of their effects.

Typically, logbooks are arranged by port of voyage termination, thereunder sometimes by date of deposit and sometimes alphabetically by name of vessel. To use the logbooks, researchers should know the ship's name and port and approximate date of arrival. Access to logbooks may be restricted because of privacy concerns.

NARA's Pacific Alaska Region (Seattle) has official logbooks and shipping articles for the Puget Sound District at Port Townsend, 1890-1911, and official logbooks for voyages paying off in Seattle, WA, and Portland, OR, 1942-ca. 1965. Earlier logbooks are on M1633, *U.S. Customs, Puget Sound District Log Books and Shipping Articles, ca. 1890-1937,* 68 rolls.

13.7 Other Records

Records of the U.S. Coast Guard, RG 26, held by NARA's Central Plains Region in Kansas City relate to the enrollment of vessels and licensing of crews at several inland lake and river ports. Vessel documentation may sometimes be useful in establishing the name and residence of the owner, master, or captain of the vessel at the time of enrollment. Casualty reports or investigations may also contain some personal information. Masters' oaths, sworn on assuming command of a vessel, provide information on the citizenship status of the master; if naturalized, the state, court, and date of naturalization are given.

Records include masters' oaths for renewal, 1901-40, for Duluth, MN; operators' license stubs, 1870-1910, for Galena, IL; masters' oaths for renewal, 1870-1948, for St. Louis, MO; and operators' license stubs, 1879-95, for St. Paul, MN. Records for the port of Dubuque, IA, are more varied. They include indexes, 1870-1910, to various types of individual licenses; individual license files, 1917-55, arranged alphabetically; and stubs, 1905-59, from licenses of engineers, masters, pilots, mates, and operators.

NARA's Southeast Region in Atlanta has masters' oaths, masters' oaths on renewal, oaths of new masters, and oaths on renewals for the ports of Mobile, AL; Apalachicola, Fernandina, Jacksonville, Miami, and Tampa, FL; Savannah, GA; and Wilmington, NC.

NARA's Pacific Alaska Region (Seattle) has new masters' oaths from the Puget Sound District, 1872-1904, and the Washington District, 1930-51. Oaths from 1885-1904 have been alphabetized by master's surname.

Records similar to those mentioned above are part of Records of the Bureau of Marine Inspection and Navigation, RG 41, held by NARA's Pacific Region (Laguna Niguel). Included for several southern California ports are masters' oaths for licenses, arranged chronologically, showing the residence and citizenship of the master. For masters who were naturalized, oaths give the court, state, and date of naturalization. Also included are enrollments and registry documents for vessels, 1877-1953.

Reports of persons hired for ships of the Quartermaster Department and the U.S. Army Transport Service are described in 14.2.6. Records from the Office of the U.S. Shipping Commissioner at San Francisco include shipping articles for U.S. Army transports for 1898-1920. These are in RG 41.

14.1 Introduction

The National Archives and Records Administration (NARA) has many records relating to civilian employees of the executive and judicial branches of the Federal Government. Personnel records are in several record groups, often in the record group set up for the general headquarters records of an executive department, such as General Records of the Department of State, Record Group (RG) 59. No consolidated civilian personnel files are among the records in the National Archives.

Types and dates of records vary from agency to agency. They include letters of application, recommendation or endorsement, and acceptance; registers of appointments; oaths of office; surety bonds for bonded officials; commissions; and letters of resignation. Most are dated from the time of establishment of the agency to about 1910.

For many years the Federal Government issued an annual or biennial list of its employees, civilian and military, at first including every person on Federal payrolls to the lowest paid laborer or charwoman. The earliest issue of this *Official Register*, or Blue Book, was entitled *Register of Officials and Agents* and was published in 1816 by the State Department. In 1816 and then every other year from 1817 to 1907, this official register was issued under varying titles but in the same form. It showed officials and employees by departments and divisions in tabular arrangement, with a name index, and often listed such information as office, place of birth, place of appointment, place employed, and financial compensation. The number of names listed increased steadily from 6,327 in 1816 to 349,000 in 1907. In 1921 the Bureau of the Census issued the last comprehensive edition of the *Official Register* that listed all employees in the civil service (C3.10:921). After 1921 it listed only those civil servants in administrative positions, and in 1959 the publication was discontinued altogether. (SI. 11, 11.25; C3.10; CSI.31).

The National Personnel Records Center (NPRC), Civilian Records Facility, 111 Winnebago St., St. Louis, MO 63118-4119, maintains most personnel folders for Federal employees whose employment ended after about 1910. Records less than 75 years old are closed to public examination. A researcher requesting a record from NCPC should provide the full name of the employee, date of birth, social security number if known, name of the agency where last employed, and place and approximate date of employment.

Most records relating to civilian employees give full name, position held, agency, and place and terminal dates of employment. Some also show state, territory, or country of birth; age; place from which appointed; and salary. Letters of application and letters of recommendation may include considerable biographical information, such as the name of a relative of the applicant and the nature of the applicant's previous employment and political activity. The amount of material in a file varies considerably and sometimes is voluminous if the position sought was an important one.

Arrangement of civilian personnel records is usually complex. Surety bonds, other than those relating to postmasters, are filed together. Record cards for bonds dated 1789-1910 and for those dated 1911-15 are arranged alphabetically by name of bonded official. A few agencies filed letters of application with letters of recommendation or other personnel records in separate name files. In other cases, letters of application and recommendation are interfiled in large correspondence series that may be inadequately indexed. Many other records relating to employment with a government agency are arranged by type of record, thereunder chronologically; they generally are not indexed. Even in the best research circumstances, where good indexes or finding aids exist, the researcher must know which department or agency employed the subject of research and the approximate dates of service.

Described in this chapter are the following: letters of application and recommendation of the State and Treasury Departments; appointment files and other records of the Justice Department; appointment records of postmasters; Interior Department appointment papers; Internal Revenue Service rosters; records of applicants and civilian employees of the War Department; records of medical personnel who served the War Department; reports of persons and articles hired and other records of the Quartermaster Department; records of civilian employees of the Navy; and records of employees of the Confederate Government. Records of employees of the government of the District of Columbia are described in Chapter 17. Records of employees of some Indian agencies are in the custody of the various regional archives; these records are described in Chapter 11.

Citations in parentheses following a sentence are references to a Superintendent of Documents publication number.

14.2 U.S. Government Employees

14.2.1 Department of State

State Department **letters of application and recommendation** relate to appointments under the jurisdiction of the Department, 1797-1901, and to Foreign Service officers, 1901-24. Letters also are related to positions in other executive departments in the early years of the Federal Government. Letters are arranged by Presidential administration, thereunder alphabetically by applicant's name; those from 1901 to 1924 are arranged alphabetically. All are part of RG 59.

Applications and recommendations for office during the Presidency of George Washington are in the custody of the Manuscript Division of the Library of Congress. State Department application and recommendation files for the administrations of John Adams through Ulysses S. Grant are available on the microfilm publications shown in Table 20. A descriptive pamphlet that accompanies

TABLE 20
Microfilmed State Department Letters of Application and Recommendation

PRESIDENTIAL ADMINISTRATION	DATES	MICROFILM PUBLICATION	NUMBER OF ROLLS
John Adams	1797–1801	M406	3
Thomas Jefferson	1801–9	M418	12
James Madison	1809–17	M438	8
James Monroe	1817–25	M439	19
John Quincy Adams	1825–29	M531	8
Andrew Jackson	1829–37	M639	27
Martin Van Buren, William Henry Harrison, and John Tyler	1837–45	M687	35
James Polk, Zachary Taylor, and Millard Fillmore	1845–53	M873	98
James Buchanan and Franklin Pierce	1853–61	M967	50
Abraham Lincoln and Andrew Johnson	1861–69	M650	52
Ulysses S. Grant	1869–77	M968	69

each microfilm publication lists the name of each person for whom there is a file and cites the roll where the file is located.

A useful publication issued by the Department of State is the list of Foreign Service personnel. Beginning in 1898 this list, called the *Diplomatic and Consular Service of the United States*, gives for each member their name, rank, residence, place of birth, place appointed from, date of commission, annual compensation, and to what country accredited. Each issue of this publication contains an index of places and an index of names. After 1929 the title of this publication was changed to the *Foreign Service List*. The list provides information on assignments of Foreign Service and other U.S. personnel in the field. It includes chiefs of missions, Foreign Service officers, and consular agents, as well as staff members of other organizations, such as the Agency for International Development, Peace Corps, and U.S. Information Agency (S1.7). The *Register of the Department of State* (S1.6) can also be consulted.

14.2.2 Department of the Treasury

Letters of application and recommendation for positions in the Treasury Department date from about 1833 to 1910. Files for bureau heads and other headquarters staff are arranged alphabetically by personal name. Field staff files are arranged by name of bureau or title of position (such as Bureau of Internal Revenue or Collector of Customs), thereunder by state, thereunder by district or city, and thereunder alphabetically by surname of applicant or employee. To use them, you must first know the name and location of the position for which the subject of your research applied. Both series are part of General

Records of the Department of the Treasury, RG 56.

In Records of the Internal Revenue Service, RG 58, at NARA's Great Lakes Region in Chicago, is a roster of officers and employees of the 1st District of Michigan (Detroit). The roster gives the name, rank, post office address, compensation, date of appointment, date and cause of termination of service, birthplace and date, military service, and names of relatives employed by the government and where employed.

NARA's Central Plains Region in Kansas City has similar records for officers and employees of the 6th Collection District of Missouri (Kansas City), 1881–1921.

14.2.3 Department of Justice

Two series of appointment files in General Records of the Department of Justice, RG 60, contain information about applicants for positions in the Justice Department. **Appointments of Federal judges, marshals, and attorneys**, 1853–1901, are primarily applications and endorsements for positions in judicial districts. They are arranged by state or territory, thereunder chronologically by Presidential administration, and then alphabetically by surname. To use them, the researcher must know where and when the subject of research sought a position. Parts of this series are available on the following microfilm publications: *Records Relating to the Appointment of Federal Judges, Attorneys, and Marshals for the Territory and State of Idaho, 1861–1899*, M681, 9 rolls; . . . *Oregon, 1853–1903*, M224, 3 rolls; . . . *Utah, 1853–1901*, M680, 14 rolls; and . . . *Washington, 1853–1902*, M198, 17 rolls. The pamphlet that accompanies each microfilm publication contains an alphabetical list of persons for whom files exist.

In a similar series, **applications and endorsements**, 1901-33, are files about Federal judges, marshals, attorneys, and other field staff, arranged by judicial district, thereunder by office, and alphabetically by surname. To locate a particular name, the researcher must know the position the person applied for, its location, and the date of application.

Two microfilm publications are useful to the genealogist searching for records relating to U.S. marshals and deputy marshals. T577, *Index to Names of United States Marshals, 1789-1960,* 1 roll, is an alphabetical list giving dates and places of service, information required for the use of most of the other pertinent series in RG 60. M701, *Letters Sent by the Department of Justice: Instructions to U.S. Attorneys and Marshals, 1867-1904,* 212 rolls, is also available.

Correspondence of U.S. marshals occasionally includes lists of deputies, oaths of office, and other reference to deputies. Other than the *Annual Reports of the Attorney General,* which from 1897 to 1921 contain lists of office and field deputies, and the *Registers of the Department of Justice,* which frequently list office deputies, there is no general name index for deputy marshals. The one major Department of Justice series relating to deputies is **correspondence concerning deputy marshals**, 1896-1937. These records are arranged by judicial district, thereunder chronologically. The researcher must be able to supply the dates and place of the subject's service as a deputy marshal.

Although the majority of letters described in the following five series pertain to substantive issues and cases, there is also considerable information about individual marshal and deputies, including oaths of office, resignations, and requests for leave.

Attorney general's papers, 1789-1870, are letters received by the Attorney General, most dating after 1818. They are arranged by source of correspondence, such as the President, Senate and House of Representatives, various executive offices, and judicial district officials, including U.S. marshals. Chronological registers of letters received can be searched to locate references to particular letters. A few of the registers are indexed.

Source chronological files, 1871-84, are letters received by the Department of Justice, arranged by source of correspondence. Registers of letters received are available. Parts of this series have been microfilmed: *Letters Received by the Department of Justice from the State of Alabama, 1871-1884,* M1356, 7 rolls; . . . *Arkansas, 1871-1884,* M1418, 5 rolls; . . . *Territory of Dakota, 1871-1884,* M1535, 3 rolls; . . . *Florida, 1871-1884,* M1327, 2 rolls; . . . *Georgia, 1871-1884,* M996, 5 rolls; . . . *Kentucky, 1871-1884,* M1362, 2 rolls; . . . *Louisiana, 1871-1884,* M940, 6 rolls; . . . *Maryland, 1871-1884,* M1352, 2 rolls; . . . *Mississippi, 1871-1884,* M970, 4 rolls; . . . *North Carolina, 1871-1884,* M1345, 3 rolls; . . . *South Carolina, 1871-1884,* M947, 9 rolls; . . . *Tennessee, 1871-1884,* M1471, 4 rolls; . . . *Texas, 1871-1884,* M1449, 7 rolls; and . . . *Virginia, 1871-1884,* M1250, 4 rolls.

Year files, 1884-1903, are letters received by the Department of Justice, primarily from judicial district officials. They are arranged numerically by subject or case file number with registers and indexes available.

Numerical files, 1904-37, are letters received and copies of letters sent by the Department of Justice. The series overlaps the classified subject files, described next. Most of the correspondence is from judicial district officials. Letters are arranged numerically by subject or case file number. Finding aids include volume indexes to 1908; a card index to letters received and sent, 1908-10; a card index for persons, concerns, and subjects, 1910-20; a card index for persons, 1917-33; and record slips of correspondence, 1910-46, arranged by source.

Classified subject files, 1914-41 and 1945-49, are letters received and sent; the series overlaps the numerical files, 1904-37. Letters are arranged numerically by class number; for example, class 5 relates to tax violations and class 60 to antitrust violations. Finding aids for numerical files are also used for this series, along with the general index, 1928-51.

The Register of the Department of Justice and the Judicial Officers of the United States; Including Instructions to Marshals, District Attorneys, and Clerks of the United States Courts (1885-1970) was compiled by authority of the Attorney General. The 46 volumes in this series in the Publications of the U.S. Government, RG 287, list the name, office, place of birth, place appointed from, where employed, annual compensation, and date of appointment for virtually all civil servants in the Justice Department for the given year.

14.2.4 Post Office Department

In Records of the Post Office Department, RG 28, are appointments of postmasters for the years 1789-1832, documented in a **record of the first returns** (quarterly account statements) received from postmasters by the Postmaster General, 1789-1818, and in **registers of the appointment of postmasters**, 1815-32. These first returns and registers of appointments of postmasters are reproduced on M1131, *Record of Appointment of Postmasters, October 1789-1832,* 4 rolls. Roll 1 of this microfilm publication includes the first returns of postmasters, 1789-1818; Roll 2 reproduces appointments of postmasters, 1815-23; Roll 3 covers appointments of postmasters, 1824-28; and Roll 4 has appointment of postmasters, 1828-32. Entries in the volumes on Rolls 2-4 are arranged alphabetically by post office on a national, not a state, basis. Information given for each post office includes the name and date of appointment of each postmaster, any changes in the name of the post office, and date of discontinuance. Registers do not include genealogical information about each postmaster.

The National Archives staff has prepared a typed list of postmasters for the 1789-1832 period, based on the first returns and registers of appointments of postmasters, in addition to the **letters sent by the Postmaster General**, 1789-1832, and **ledgers of the General Post Office**, 1782-1803. The typed list, called the Hecht List, is arranged alphabetically by state, thereunder alphabetically by name of post office. The list is available in the National Archives Building at Washington, DC. The first returns (entry 67), registers of appointments (entry 69), letters (entry 2), and ledgers (entry 168) are described in *Records of the Post Office Department*, Preliminary Inventory (PI) 168, compiled by Arthur Hecht, Frank J. Nivert, Fred W. Warriner, Jr., and Charlotte M. Ashby (Washington: National Archives and Records Service, 1967).

The 98 volumes of **registers of appointments of postmasters for the period 1832–1971** have been filmed alphabetically by state, thereunder by county, on M841, *Record of Appointment of Postmasters, 1832- September 30, 1971*, 145 rolls. Entries in the registers include names of postmasters for each post office and dates of their appointments, as well as dates of discontinuance, reestablishment, and name changes of post offices. Registers don't include genealogical information about postmasters or their families, nor does RG 28 have personnel files of postal employees. Personnel files of postal employees separated from service after 1909 are in the custody of the National Personnel Records Center. *See* 14.1 for address.

Information about the appointment of postmasters after September 30, 1971, may be obtained from the Office of the Historian, United States Postal Service, 475 L'Enfant Plaza SW, Washington, DC 20260-0012.

The earliest listing of postmasters can be found in the *Official Register* for 1816. (*See* 14.1 for information about the *Official Register*.) The 1817 *Official Register* lists postmasters, postal clerks, and mail contractors. Postal employees are listed in the *Official Register* through the 1911 volume.

On January 18, 1820, Postmaster General R.J. Meigs presented to the House of Representatives a list of 21 clerks employed in the post office at salaries from $800 to $1,700, as well as a list of contracts for carrying the mail, drawn up by the Postmaster General in the year 1819. This second list shows the names of 312 contractors for carrying mail, indicates their state, the sums paid to them, and the locality and numbers of their routes. This list is found in the Congressional Serial Set Volume 33. General Post Office entries in the *Official Register* for 1831 and thereafter consistently list names of postmasters, clerks, and contractors. Some of the volumes of the *Official Register* can be found printed in the Congressional Serial Set. Serial set volume numbers can be obtained from the published index to the Congressional Serial Set.

From 1877 to 1905, volumes of the *Official Register* include name indexes. These indexes are useful in identifying the position and geographic location of individual employees of the Post Office Department. Entries in the

volumes of the *Official Register* for 1907-11 are arranged by state, thereunder alphabetically by city, so it is necessary to know the place where an individual worked before searching the volumes of the *Official Register*. The volumes can be used to verify employment. Biographical or genealogical information in the volumes consists of date and place of employment.

Index and registers of substitute mail carriers in first- and second-class post offices, 1885-1903, have been microfilmed on the one roll of M2076. These records are designated as Entries 87 and 88 in PI 168, *Records of the Post Office Department*. The index, which covers the years 1891-96, is arranged alphabetically by the first two letters of the carrier's surname and gives the date of appointment, city, and remarks. Entries in the registers are arranged roughly alphabetically by name of post office, thereunder chronologically by date of appointment. Reproduced on M2075, *Record of Appointment of Substitute Clerks in First- and Second-Class Post Offices, 1899-1905*, 1 roll, is a two-volume record of appointment of substitute clerks in 1,294 first- and second-class post offices, 1899-1905, designated as Entry 79 in PI 168. Entries in the volumes are listed in rough alphabetical order by name of post office, volume one covering the letters A-M, volume two, N-Z. Each page has two main columns, "Males" and "Females," subdivided into three columns each: Date Appointed, Name, and Appointed Regular. Due to lack of space, entries for large city post offices may include names of males in the females column.

M2077, *Indexes to Rosters of Railway Postal Clerks, ca. 1883-ca. 1902*, 1 roll, reproduces records designated as Entry 118 in PI 168. Indexes are arranged roughly alphabetically by the first one or two letters of the clerk's name. For each clerk, a volume letter (A–F) and a page number are indicated. The volumes A–F referred to by this index are part of the records designated in PI 168 as Entry 119, Rosters of Special, Route, and Local Blank and Stamp Agents and Rosters of Railway Postal Clerks, 1855-97, 24 volumes.

Records of the Post Office Department also include a series entitled **record cards of carriers separated from the Postal Service**, 1863-99. These cards include name of carrier, date of appointment, reason for separation, and, after 1873, date of separation. This series, which may soon be available as a National Archives microfilm publication, is arranged alphabetically by state, thereunder alphabetically by name of post office, and thereunder alphabetically by surname of carrier.

Personnel files of pilots, supervisors, and other Air Mail Service employees, 1918-27, include substantive records relating to operations of the Air Mail Service, with correspondence, reports, applications, and other documents concerning activities of pilots and other employees. These records are arranged alphabetically by the individual's surname.

14.2.5 Department of the Interior

Appointment papers of the Interior Department date from 1849 to 1907. These files are part of Records of the Office of the Secretary of the Interior, RG 48, and are arranged by name of state or territory, thereunder by name of bureau, thereunder by name of place, and thereunder by personal name. Some indexes exist. Interior Department appointment papers for some states are available as microfilm publications, as shown in Table 21.

14.2.6 War Department

Records of the Office of the Secretary of War, RG 107, includes a number of series relating to applications for civilian jobs in the War Department, appointments to positions, and careers of employees. Arrangement of the different series varies considerably; many are not indexed. To use them, a researcher needs to know approximately when and where the subject of research worked for the War Department and sometimes the subject's legal state of residence.

Registers of applications and application papers are dated 1820-1903. Entries in the registers generally show the applicant's name and place of birth, position desired, names of persons submitting letters of recommendation on behalf of the applicant, and whether the application papers were filed in the Office of the Secretary of War or forwarded to another War Department bureau.

Application files themselves vary greatly in size and in the quantity of genealogical information they contain. Some simply consist of a single letter from the applicant requesting a civilian position in the War Department or a commission in the Army. Other more extensive files may contain letters of recommendation, oaths of allegiance, letters of appointment, and copies of replies the War Department sent to the applicant or to individuals recommending them. Such files might show the applicant's name, place of birth, current residence, and information concerning education, former military service, general character, profession, political ties, health, previous job experience, and the military service or political affiliation of relatives.

Series containing applications for civilian appointments in the War Department include the following: applications for War Department appointments, 1820-46; applications for commissions and civilian appointments, 1847-70 and 1872-82; applications for civilian positions in the War Department, 1898-1902; and applications for positions as laborers and charwomen, 1901-3. Files are generally arranged alphabetically by surname of applicant and pertain to requests for such positions as Indian agents, cutlers, watchmen, pension agents, clerks, messengers, copyists, librarians, scouts, guides, surveyors, stenographers, bookkeepers, and typists.

Entries in **registers and lists of appointments and employees**, 1863-1913, may show the employee's name, state from which appointed, date of appointment, position, office to which appointed, and remarks that indicate dates of promotions, transfers, details, reductions in salary, resignation, discharge, or death. The series include registers of civilian War Department employees stationed in Washington, DC, 1863-94 and 1898-1908; registers of civilian War Department employees, 1885-94 and 1898-1913; printed annual registers of civilian War Department

TABLE 21
Microfilmed Interior Department Appointment Papers

STATE OR TERRITORY	DATES	MICROFILM PUBLICATION	NUMBER OF ROLLS
Alaska	1871-1907	M1245	6
Arizona	1857-1907	M576	22
California	1849-1907	M732	29
Colorado	1857-1907	M808	13
Florida	1849-1907	M1119	6
Idaho	1862-1907	M693	17
Mississippi	1849-1907	M849	4
Missouri	1849-1907	M1058	9
Nevada	1860-1907	M1033	3
New Mexico	1850-1907	M750	18
New York	1849-1906	M1022	5
North Carolina	1849-92	M950	1
Oregon	1849-1907	M814	10
Wisconsin	1849-1907	M831	9
Wyoming	1869-1907	M830	6

employees in Washington, DC, 1885-1909; registers of appointments and changes in the status of civilian War Department employees, 1894-1901, 1903-9, and 1911-13; lists of civilian War Department appointments in Cuba, Puerto Rico, and the Philippine Islands, 1898-1900; and registers of appointments and changes in the status of temporary employees in the War Department, 1902-5.

Lists and registers of applications and appointments for civilian employees similar to those described for RG 107 are also found among records of the various War Department bureaus, including the following: Records of the Office of the Chief of Engineers, RG 77; Records of the Office of the Quartermaster General, RG 92; Records of the Adjutant General's Office, 1780's-1917, RG 94; Records of the Office of the Paymaster General, RG 99; Records of the Bureau of Refugees, Freedmen, and Abandoned Lands, RG 105; Records of the Provost Marshal General's Bureau (Civil War), RG 110; Records of the Office of the Surgeon General (Army), RG 112; and Records of the Office of the Chief of Ordnance, RG 156.

Some of the **records of the Appointment, Commission, and Personal Branch** in RG 94 relate to civilian employees of the Army and the War Department. These include applications for appointments, 1871-80; 12 volumes of registers of these applications; and a 2-volume name index to the registers and applications. Most of these records concern applications for military commissions, but there are also applications for some civilian positions, such as post trader and military cemetery superintendent. The index will identify appropriate entries in the registers of applications. A register entry gives the name of the applicant, rank or residence, date of the application, position applied for, who recommended the applicant, and the action taken. Actual applications are arranged by year, thereunder numerically; file numbers are given in the registers of applications.

Other records of civilian employment include personal histories of civilian War Department employees stationed in Washington, DC, 1882-94. These histories are on standard forms and include name, birthplace, and legal voting residence (state, county, and congressional district) of employee; past military service; disabilities; merit; status; number of dependents; date of original appointment in the War Department; names of persons submitting letters of recommendation; age and occupation when appointed; current position title and grade; home address in Washington, DC; War Department bureau and building where assigned; and names and places of relatives employed in government service. Because the records are arranged by state, thereunder by name, a researcher must know the state of legal residence to locate the history for a specific employee.

Information about civilians and civilian employees is also interspersed among the Secretary of War's letters received and general correspondence, some of which is available on microfilm as M221, *Letters Received by the Secretary of War, Registered Series, 1801-1870,* 317 rolls, and M222, *Letters Received by the Secretary of War, Unregistered Series, 1789-1861,* 3 rolls. Corresponding registers of letters received, containing abstracts of the letters, are available on M22, *Registers of Letters Received by the Office of the Secretary War, Main Series, 1800-1870,* 134 rolls. Book indexes are reproduced as M495, *Indexes to Letters Received by the Secretary of War, 1861-1870,* 14 rolls. Also available but not on microfilm is a card index to the general correspondence for the period 1890-1913.

Additional records relating to civilian employees are scattered throughout the letters received and general correspondence of the Adjutant General's Office in RG 94. To make a thorough search of these files, however, it is generally necessary to know where and for whom the subject of research worked and their period of employment. The letters received have been microfilmed and are available as M566, *Letters Received by the Office of the Adjutant General, 1805-1821,* 144 rolls; M567, *Letters Received by the Office of the Adjutant General (Main Series), 1822-1860,* 636 rolls; . . . *1861-1870,* M619, 828 rolls; . . . *1871-1880,* M666, 593 rolls; and . . . *1881-1889,* M689, 740 rolls. Available indexes and other finding aids for the letters received include M711, *Registers of Letters Received by the Office of the Adjutant General (Main Series), 1812-1889,* 85 rolls, and M725, *Indexes to Letters Received by the Office of the Adjutant General (Main Series), 1846, 1861-1889,* 9 rolls. An extensive name and subject index to the general correspondence has been reproduced as M698, *Index to General Correspondence of the Adjutant General's Office, 1890-1917,* 1,269 rolls.

RG 94 includes several series relating to **civilian medical personnel**. In the 19th and early 20th centuries, the U.S. Army frequently relied on the services of civilian physicians and surgeons to supplement the small number of Regular Army medical officers. The **personal papers** of these contract medical officers and surgeons, ca. 1820-1917, is a large series that constitutes an important genealogical resource. Arranged in individual jackets alphabetically by surname of physician, the files include copies of contracts signed by the physicians, which show date, salary, assignment, and contracting parties; personal reports giving duty station and responsibility by months; correspondence relating to applications for appointment, for renewal of contract, or for termination of employment (annulment of contract); and miscellaneous biographical information, such as post-employment residences and date of death. The volume and value of documentation vary considerably among the jackets, the majority of which are for physicians who served during the Civil War, 1861-65.

Several smaller series can be used to search for a physician whose approximate dates of service are known. These deal with contract surgeons, including 7 volumes of chronologically arranged copies of contracts, 1839-49 and 1861-65; alphabetically arranged pay accounts, ca. 1820-94, but primarily 1861-65; 11 numerically arranged volumes pertaining to contracts, with 2 accompanying name index volumes, 1847-92; station cards of acting assistant surgeons, 1862-68 and 1898-1901, arranged alphabetically by name of physician, which provide information on dates of contract and service and duty stations; a 1-volume record of Civil War contract surgeons arranged by hospital, which provides name of surgeon, dates of contract and service, and post office address; and a 1-volume record of accounts, 1865, arranged chronologically. One volume in a three-volume series of alphabetically arranged address books, 1860-94, pertains to contract surgeons.

The researcher who knows the name of the command in which a contract surgeon served, as well as the approximate dates of service, can use three series of monthly returns of medical officers: 64 volumes, 1859-86, arranged by command, thereunder chronologically; 25 feet of unbound records, 1861-65, arranged by state or command, thereunder chronologically; and 17 feet of unbound records, 1898-1909, arranged by command, thereunder chronologically. These records give the surgeon's name, date of contract, post or station, and organization of troops with which they served—information that may only make previous knowledge more exact.

Records relating to contract surgeons, 1862-1915, are also in RG 112.

A series of cards in RG 112 contains service records of **hospital attendants, matrons, and nurses**, 1861-65. Cards are arranged by initial letter of surname and include information on dates of employment, capacity in which hired, salary, and place of employment. Female personnel are represented by returns of hospital matrons, 1876-87, which are arranged by post, department, or division, thereunder chronologically. These provide names of individual matrons and, for posts only, dates of appointment. Other records relating to contract nurses during the Spanish-American War and to matrons, cooks, and laundresses during the Civil War and during the period 1893-1904 are also found in RG 112.

Quartermaster officers throughout the United States were required to submit to the Quartermaster General in Washington monthly reports, listing by name all persons employed by them and all articles hired. These **reports of persons and articles hired** in RG 92 cover the period 1818-1913 and are perhaps the single most important source of information in the National Archives about Quartermaster Department civilian employees. Report forms were originally drawn by hand, but printed blanks were introduced in 1856 and by 1861 had entirely superseded the handwritten forms. Format and content of the reports were remarkably uniform throughout the entire period, generally providing in columns the following information about each employee: full name, inclusive dates of monthly service, number of days employed, rate of compensation, date of contract, amount paid or due, and occupation. The rate of compensation was normally based on a uniform time segment (day, month, or year), but occasionally used a different basis, such as the number of trips made or packages carried by dispatch riders. Various occupations are listed, but most fall under a few broad categories, such as office employees (clerks); construction workers (carpenters, joiners, masons, laborers); blacksmiths, farriers, hostlers, and other occupations related to the care of horses and draft animals; transport workers (teamsters, wagonmasters, draymen); and certain specialized occupations (scouts, guides, interpreters, telegraph operators).

The main series of persons and articles hired consists of more than 1,500 feet of records dated 1818-1905, arranged chronologically by year, thereunder alphabetically by surname of the reporting officer, 1818-60, or numerically, 1861-1905. Genealogical research in this series is difficult because to use it the researcher must know the name of the employing quartermaster. A researcher who knows the post or station at which the subject of research was hired and the approximate dates of employment, however, may find that several finding aids, though incomplete, can help identify the quartermaster: a one-volume register of reports, 1834-60, arranged by year, thereunder alphabetically by name of reporting officer to 1849, then alphabetically by station; a seven-volume reporting officer index for the period 1861-94, arranged by time period, thereunder alphabetically; an incomplete two-volume index to stations, 1861-67, arranged by station (but not alphabetically), thereunder chronologically; and a card index to names of reporting officers, ca. 1898-1905, arranged by station in two subseries (Philippine Islands and non-Philippines), thereunder chronologically.

Direct access by name of employee is possible for a few brief time periods through specialized finding aids, which are also incomplete. For the years 1898-1902, there is an alphabetical card index to employees entered in the reports, and there is an alphabetical card index to names of those employed as scouts and in related occupations. An alphabetical card index exists for individuals employed in the Mississippi Marine Brigade and Ram Fleet, July–September 1863, and a similar one-volume list for the period May–July 1864. Index entries give the names of reporting officers. For 1861 only, the Quartermaster Department compiled individual employment service cards (similar to compiled military service records) for the civilian employees listed in the reports of persons and articles hired. These **"Record of Personal Services" cards** are arranged alphabetically by name of employee.

Additional reports of persons and articles hired are found among the quartermaster records of the Mexican War, 1846-48, arranged by name of reporting officer, and among the surviving records of individual quartermaster officers, 1837-97, generally arranged chronologically. Again, the researcher must know the name of the quartermaster and dates. Additional reports, arranged chronologically, are sometimes found among the quartermaster records of the geographical departments into which the post-Civil War army was divided; for example, the Department of Dakota, 1872-1900, and the Department of the Platte, 1866-96. To use them, the researcher must know which army command hired the subject of research.

Reports of persons and articles hired for the ships of the **Army Transport Service**, 1898-1913, were removed by the Quartermaster Department from the main series and are now maintained separately with other related records. These are arranged in three subseries by type of vessel (mine planters, short-term transports, major transports), thereunder alphabetically by name of vessel, and thereunder chronologically by date of report. To find information about an individual serving aboard ship, the researcher must know the type and name of the vessel and the approximate period of employment.

Two finding aids are available for the quartermaster ships mentioned in the reports. For the Civil War period, 1861-65, there is a one-volume alphabetical index to names of vessels, while for the period 1898-1901, there is a similar alphabetical card index. Both finding aids were prepared before the segregation of the Army Transport Service reports and, therefore, refer to file numbers in the main series. However, cross-references in the main series direct researchers to the Army Transport Service reports of persons and articles hired.

Other records of the U.S. Army Transport Service relate to individuals, such as a vessel card index to correspondence relating to crews of the service, which refers to the general correspondence (or "Document File") of the Office of the Quartermaster General, 1890-1914. Also available are a list of crews and "Persons and Articles Transferred on or Between Army Transports, 1906-9," on which entries are arranged alphabetically by name of vessel; lists of vessels and crews, 1898-1913, arranged alphabetically by name of vessel; unarranged records entitled "Name of Ships Officers and Time of Entering Service 1898-1899"; lists of officers, engineers, masters, and stevedores employed in the U.S. Army Transport Service, 1899-1900, unarranged; a list of applications for positions on U.S. Army transports and notes on former employees ineligible to be rehired, 1900-1901, arranged chronologically; a record of employees discharged from the U.S. Army Transport Service, 1907-13, arranged alphabetically by name of discharged employee; shipping articles or articles of agreement between masters and seamen in the Merchant Service of the United States, 1898-1906, arranged alphabetically by U.S. Army Transport Service vessel, and thereunder chronologically; and crew lists of the U.S. Army Transport Service and correspondence relating to them, 1899-1901, unarranged. Among the records of the U.S. Shipping Commissioner at San Francisco are shipping articles for U.S. Army transports for 1898-1920. These are in Records of the Bureau of Marine Inspection and Navigation, RG 41.

Another large series of records of the Office of the Quartermaster General, the **consolidated correspon-**dence file, 1784-1890, also contains information about regular employees of the Quartermaster Department, as well as records about many other diverse subjects. Using the series is easier because it is arranged alphabetically by name and subject. If a file exists about the research subject, it might contain such records as applications for employment; requests for promotion, transfer, and reinstatement; reports of disciplinary action and investigation; oaths of appointment providing age, date of birth, marriage status, or residence; and receipts for wages.

The period 1891-1914 has a **general correspondence file relating to personnel**. Record cards to that correspondence provide summaries or full texts of the letters or documents pertaining to an individual. These series are arranged chronologically under one or more file numbers. You will find information similar to that in the earlier consolidated correspondence file, 1794-1890. However, because arrangement is numerical rather than alphabetical, the researcher must first consult the alphabetical name and subject card index to the general correspondence to obtain file designations for the correspondence or record cards relating to the subject of research.

14.2.7 Department of the Navy

Many series in Naval Records Collection of the Office of Naval Records and Library, RG 45, and General Records of the Department of the Navy, 1798-1947, RG 80, contain records of civilian employees of the Navy Department. These series are variously arranged, but some contain name indexes. To use the records, the researcher must know approximately when the subject of research applied for or held a position.

Records of applicants usually show name of applicant, date of application, and type of position applied for. Registers of applications for civilian positions, 1834-71, also show the applicant's state of residence and contain name indexes, except for the period January 1854-May 1864. Letters of application and recommendation for civilian positions at navy yards, 1839-42, are arranged by date of application. There are lists for 1849 and abstracts and information for 1853 concerning applicants for civilian positions, with an incomplete name index. In a register pertaining to clerkships, 1872-74, entries are arranged according to type (applications received, candidates eligible for examination, and candidates examined). Additional information in an entry in this register includes the applicant's age and state of residence.

Records of appointment and discharge contain letters of appointment sent to civilian employees, 1825-55; lists of appointments of acting assistant paymasters, 1861-65; press copies of letters sent appointing and discharging civilian employees, 1882-86; and notices of appointment sent by the chief clerk to the auditor for the Navy, 1904-11. Name indexes exist for the letters of appointment, except for letters for the period 1882-86, which are arranged chronologically. Records contain names of employees and types of positions to which they were appointed or from which they were discharged.

Registers of employees consist of a register of Marine Corps and civilian personnel, 1799-1854, and a register of pay stewards and clerks for captains, commanders, and paymasters, 1844-71. Both registers contain name indexes. An entry in the first series shows the name of employee, state of residence, and dates of appointment, promotion, resignation, orders, and leaves of absence. An entry in the later series shows name of clerk, vessel on which served, and dates of service.

Returns of civilian employees in shore establishments, 1887-1910, are arranged by shore establishment, and service records of civilian employees, 1917-23, are arranged by place of employment, thereunder by name. To use these records, the researcher must know where the subject of research worked. Other records of civilian employees, 1900-51, are at the National Personnel Records Center in St. Louis. *See* 14.1 for address.

14.3 Members of Congress

For information about senators and representatives in Congress, the most readily available source is the *Biographical Directory of the American Congress, 1774-1989: Bicentennial Edition* (100th Congress, 2nd sess., S. Doc. 100-34). The directory provides reliable biographical information on more than 11,000 members of Congress. This volume—Serial 13849—is the 15th in a series. It incorporates numerous added features not found in earlier editions. The information, with still more updates, is now available in electronic format at *bioguide.congress.gov.*

14.4 Records of the Confederate Government

The War Department Collection of Confederate Records, RG 109, includes some records pertaining to civilian workers of the Confederate Government; however, much of the documentation is for War Department employees, most of whom were hired on a temporary basis. One of the largest and most significant series in RG 109 is among records of the Quartermaster General's Office and consists of unbound **pay rolls** for hired civilian workers, 1861-65. The rolls are arranged numerically (1-16239) and include some other types of records, principally reports of persons and articles hired. Most of the rolls were prepared by local quartermaster or commissary officers in the field, but a number were also submitted by engineer, medical, and ordnance officers and superintendents of niter and mining districts. Types of workers hired included arms fabricators and finishers, blacksmiths, carpenters, cartridge makers, clerks, clothing cutters, couriers, forage masters, hospital matrons and stewards, laborers on military defenses, nurses, packers, plumbers, seamstresses, shoemakers, teamsters, wagoners, and wagon masters. Pay rolls

or reports of persons and articles hired generally show names of employing officers, places of employment, periods of service, rates of pay, and signatures of payees and witnesses. A smaller series of unbound slave pay rolls is also arranged numerically (1-5889). It pertains largely to slaves employed on military defenses but also includes ordnance establishments, quartermaster depots, and elsewhere. In addition to the information appearing on the other pay rolls, slave pay rolls often show names of owners and names and occupations of slaves. Both unbound series of pay rolls are covered by a single alphabetical card index prepared by the U.S. War Department.

For more detailed information about the employment of slaves by the Confederate Government, *see* 12.3.3.

Records of civilian employees are also found among those for various offices of the Confederate Government. Records of some Confederate hospitals, for example, contain lists of both black and white workers, including stewards, matrons, and cooks. Arsenal or ordnance establishment records include time books and lists of those hired. These records, however, are widely scattered and often unindexed. In addition, they generally contain minimal information, perhaps only the names of persons employed. In a few instances, information may be available about the nature of duties performed and dates of work.

One of the most useful and readily accessible sources of information for all types of civilian government personnel is a large file of Confederate papers relating to citizens or business firms, more commonly known as the **Citizens File**. Available as M346, *Confederate Papers Relating to Citizens or Business Firms*, 1,158 rolls, the series consists of some 650,000 vouchers and other related documents filed in more than 350,000 alphabetically arranged jackets. The file, artificially assembled from original Confederate records by U.S. War Department employees during the late 19th century, relates mostly to domestic business or commercial transactions between individuals, companies, or industries and the Confederate Government. Some material pertains to individuals who furnished forage, food, slaves for labor, horses, wagons, building supplies, and various types of equipment, or to those who rendered services, such as hauling supplies or provisions, transporting prisoners, building or repairing equipment, and grazing livestock. Other records pertain to civilian government employees and officials and include those for detectives, hospital matrons, clerks, depot laborers, messengers, and purchasing agents. These jackets will normally consist of vouchers, bills, or receipts relating to pay or work expenses. Material for government officials may also include copies or drafts of letters, endorsements or memorandums, letters of application or recommendation, copies of regulations, copies of printed government documents, and worksheets. Files for individuals often indicate the dates of transactions, and some may contain information about the person's place of residence. In addition to original documents, a number of files include information recorded by the U.S. War Department, particularly in the form of cross-references to related materials among other Confederate records.

Other records relate to civil servants in the Confederate Government. These, however, pertain to a relatively limited number of people. Available records are also rather sparse and often unindexed. Records of the Office of the Secretary of War in RG 109 include monthly lists of War Department employees and their salaries, March 1861–March 1865, arranged chronologically. Lists are found in a volume of War Department requisitions on the Treasury Department for funds to pay salaries of civilian officers and employees; this volume is identified as Chapter IX, vol. 98. Also available is a volume of pay rolls of War Department civilian officers and employees, July 1862–March 1865 (Chapter IX, vol. 88) and a quarterly pay roll of the same, January–March 1865 (Chapter IX, vol. 87). These bound pay rolls are generally arranged chronologically by month, thereunder by War Department office. Records relating to civilian appointments in the Confederate War Department include a register of applications and recommendations for military and civil appointments (Chapter IX, vol. 90), arranged chronologically. Entries give the names of prospective employees, nature of position sought, and names of persons making recommendations. Among the records of the Adjutant and Inspector General's Office is a one-volume listing of civil and military officers, 1861–64 (Chapter I, vol. 121). Unarranged entries show names of appointees and dates of appointments and resignations. There are three registers of applications for clerkships and other positions in the Treasury Department, 1861–65 (Chapter X, vols. 156, 156½, and 157). Entries are arranged alphabetically in two of the volumes and numerically in the other; the numerically arranged volume contains a name index. Entries show names and residences of applicants, dates of applications, positions applied for, and sometimes names of references.

Other records of civilian employment include pay rolls of civilian navy personnel at Confederate shore establishments, 1861–64, which are in RG 45. These records are unindexed, but lists prepared by the National Archives staff indicate shore establishments for which there are such records. Pay rolls for slave laborers are noted for some establishments; these are listed in 12.3.3.

CHAPTER 15
Land Records

15.1 Introduction

Much of the land in the present United States was once part of the **public domain**, that is, land owned by the Federal Government and subject to sale or transfer of ownership under laws passed by Congress. States that were formed from the public domain are called **public land states**; they are listed in Table 22. Land records held by the National Archives and Records Administration (NARA) that are most valuable for genealogical research consist principally of documents relating to the transfer of land in the public domain states. Dated chiefly 1800–1973, land entry records normally consist of documents generated at a district land office and then submitted to the General Land Office (GLO), or its successor, the Bureau of Land Management (BLM), in Washington, DC, before patents were issued by the Federal Government.

Unless otherwise indicated, the textual records described in this chapter are from Records of the Bureau of Land Management, Record Group (RG) 49. Cartographic records, such as township survey plats, private land claim plats, and U.S. land district maps, are described in Chapter 19.

A good general survey of public land policy is *History of Public Land Law Development,* by Paul W. Gates (Washington: Government Printing Office, 1968). For information about the records of land transfer, consult Robert W. Harrison's "Public Land Records of the Federal Government," *Mississippi Valley Historical Review* 41 (Sept. 1954): 277–288. Valuable information about property research can be gotten from *Land & Property Research in the United States*, by E. Wade Hone (Salt Lake City: Ancestry, 1997).

The records of transactions whereby the Government transferred land to individuals, either by sale or by grant, are **land entry papers**, and the document that guarantees title to such land is a **patent**. Some early settlers in the public domain exercised the right of **preemption**, by which they occupied and made improvements on public land, without permission, and were allowed to purchase such land when the surrounding land was put up for public sale.

The United States has used the public domain for several purposes. The military bounty land has been discussed in Chapter 8. Before the Civil War, the Government gave land in Arkansas, Florida, Oregon, and Washington to persons who would settle on the land because settlement was a means of confirming the Federal claim to territory where ownership was being disputed by another nation. Because the Government donated this land free to individuals, these grants were known as **donation entries**. For additional information about these entries, *see* 15.2. Other types of land grants, such as grants to railroad companies, were made to encourage economic development.

Until the Homestead Act was passed in 1862, most land entry papers contain very little genealogical information. Normally, the pre-1862 land entry files contain only name of the "entryman" (term applied to any individual or

organization filing for land) and place of residence at the time of purchase or entry. Donation entry files and preemption cash files are more likely to provide additional information about the patentee, the individual who got the patent for the land.

Private land claims files may contain substantial genealogical information. Most of these claims arose because the United States acquired inhabited territory from another country. For example, when California was acquired from Mexico at the end of the Mexican War, settlers who had been granted land by the Mexican Government were required to prove to the U.S. Government the legality of their Mexican titles. Because some of the owners of these lands were probably descendants of the original grantees, files of these private land claims may contain useful genealogical information. Such claims are described in detail in 15.4.

TABLE 22 *Public Land States*	
Alabama	Missouri
Alaska	Montana
Arizona	Nebraska
Arkansas	Nevada
California	New Mexico
Florida	North Dakota
Idaho	Ohio
Illinois	Oklahoma
Indiana	South Dakota
Iowa	Utah
Kansas	Washington
Louisiana	Wisconsin
Michigan	Wyoming
Minnesota	

Title to a tract of land could normally be obtained only after it had been surveyed. Under the provisions of the land ordinance of 1785 (*Journals of the Continental Congress* 28: 375–381), land in the public domain was to be sold by the Government through the loan offices of the Board of Treasury. The first such land, located in present-day Ohio, was surveyed and sold in 1787. With the exceptions of surveys of certain parts of Ohio, the surveys followed a uniform pattern, providing standard **land descriptions**—section, township, range.

The surveys depend upon east-west base lines and north-south meridians. Parallel to the meridians are ranges of townships. Each township is 6 miles square and usually consists of 36 numbered sections. A section consists of 640 acres and is divided into quarter sections of 160 acres each. A tract is normally described in terms of fractional section, section, township, and range: for example, "northeast quarter of section 15, township 2 north, range 8 east."

METHOD OF NUMBERING TOWNSHIPS.

North and South from Base Line and East and West from Meridian.

R. 3 W.	R. 2 W.	R. 1 W.	R. 1 E.	R. 2 E.	R. 3 E.
			T. 3 N.		
			T. 2 N.		
	TOWNSHIP LINE		T. 1 N.		
	BASE		LINE		
			T. 1 S.		
		RANGE LINE	T. 2 S.	TOWNSHIP LINE	
			T. 3 S.		

RANGE LINE — MERIDIAN

I. V. S.

Townships 6 miles square were numbered according to their position relative to a meridian (running vertically, north and south) and a base line (running horizontally, east and west). In the diagram above, the townships immediately south of the base line and east of the meridian would be numbered "Township 1 South, Range 1 East" or T.1 S., R.1 E.

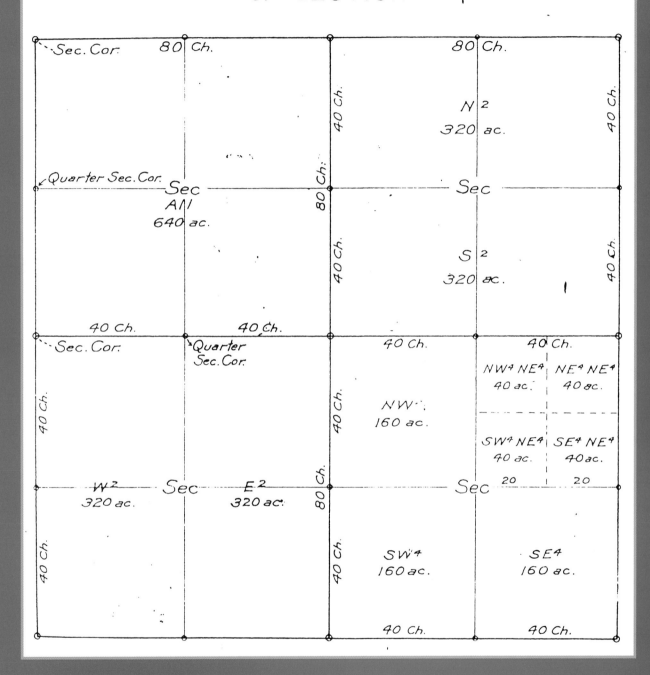

LEGAL SUBDIVISIONS
OF SECTION

Each 6-square-mile township was divided into 36 sections of 640 acres each, 4 of which are represented in the diagram above. In the upper left is one complete section, undivided. The upper right section has been divided into half sections, designated "half section north" (N 1/2) and "half section south" (S 1/2). A section could also be split vertically, creating "half section east" (E 1/2) and "west" (W 1/2) shown in the lower left portion of the diagram. Quarter sections, shown in the lower right section, were designated "quarter section northwest" (NW 1/4), "quarter section southwest" (SW 1/4), "southeast" (SE 1/4) or "northeast" (NE 1/4). When a quarter section was divided into 40-acre lots, the descriptions indicated both the quarter section and the position of the lot in the quarter section. Thus "NW1/4 NE1/4" means the northwest quarter lot in the northeast quarter section.

THE UNITED STATES OF AMERICA,

To all to whom these presents shall come, greeting:

CERTIFICATE No. 35487. } *Whereas,* Lewis S. Green of Shelby County, Alabama

has deposited in the GENERAL LAND OFFICE of the UNITED STATES, a CERTIFICATE of the Register of the Land Office at Tuscaloosa, wh

it appears that FULL PAYMENT has been made by the said Lewis S. Green, acco

to the provisions of the Act of Congress of the 24th of April, 1820, entitled "An act making further provision for the sale of the public lands," for the West half of the North

quarter of Section eleven, in Township twenty three, of Range fourteen, East, in the District of lands only

to sale at Tuscaloosa, Alabama, containing seventy nine acres and seventy seven hundredths of an acre,

according to the OFFICIAL PLAT of the Survey of the said Lands, returned to the GENERAL LAND OFFICE by the Surveyor General, which said Tract has been purchased by the

Lewis S. Green.

Now know ye, That the *UNITED STATES OF AMERICA,* in consideration of the premises, and in conformity with the several Acts of Congress in such case mad

provided, HAVE GIVEN AND GRANTED, and by these presents Do GIVE AND GRANT, unto the said Lewis S. Green,

and to his heirs, the said Tract above described; TO HAVE AND TO HOLD the same, together with all the rights, privileges, immunities, and appurtenances, of whatsoever na

thereunto belonging, unto the said Lewis S. Green and to his heirs and assigns fo

In testimony whereof, I, James Buchanan PRESIDENT OF THE UNITED STATES OF AMER

have caused these letters to be made Patent, and the Seal of the GENERAL LAND OFFICE to be hereunto affixed.

Given under my hand, at the CITY OF WASHINGTON, the first day of June in the year of OUR LOR

thousand eight hundred and fifty eight and of the Independence of the United States the eighty second

BY THE PRESIDENT: James Buchanan

By _____ J. J. Albright Sec

_____ Recorder of the General Land Offi

RECORDED, Vol. 69 Page 36. E

A land description is often needed to locate records relating to a land transaction.

For information about the system of identifying individual tracts, *see* plate 87 in the *Atlas of American History*, edited by James T. Adams and Roy V. Coleman (New York: Scribner, 1943).

A record of the disposition of each tract of land was kept in a **tractbook**. These volumes, arranged by state, usually include the following information: land description, type of entry, number of acres, date of sale or transfer, name of land entryman, and entry or patent number. Other information of a varied nature, such as the name of the land office, may appear in the tractbooks, especially preceding section 1 of each township and range.

The master set of tractbooks was maintained in the headquarters office of the GLO/BLM in Washington, DC. Each district land office usually maintained a set of local office tractbooks. The local office tractbooks remained with the district land offices as long as those offices existed. Afterwards, many of the local office tractbooks were turned over to successor field offices, such as the BLM state and area offices; some of the volumes were turned over to state and local historical societies or state archives; and others are now found in the National Archives Building (NAB) in Washington, DC, or in NARA's regional archives facilities. (*See* Table 1 in the Introduction to this volume for the locations of NARA's regional archives.)

The headquarters set of tractbooks is presently divided between the NAB and the Eastern States Office (ESO) of the BLM. The Eastern States Office of the Bureau of Land Management (ESO/BLM) is located at 7450 Boston Blvd., Springfield, VA 22153. The ESO holds the tractbooks for the public land states east of the Mississippi River and the first tier of states west of the Mississippi (Minnesota, Iowa, Missouri, Arkansas, and Louisiana); NARA has the volumes for the public domain states further west. A microfilm copy (1,340 rolls) of all headquarters tractbooks is available for use at the ESO and at the BLM state offices, and can be purchased from these offices. The National Archives does not have a copy of this extensive microfilm set.

The ESO has indexes to Ohio tractbooks for the years 1800–20, the credit period when land could be purchased for installment payments (*see* 15.2), with a few entries for transactions of later dates. These indexes cover the Canton, Chillicothe, Cincinnati, Marietta, Steubenville, Wooster, and Zanesville district land offices. Entries in the indexes are arranged alphabetically by first letter of surname of entryman, the individual (or organization) who applied for the land. From the descriptions of the tracts in the Ohio tractbooks, it is possible to identify the land entry file number and then locate the land entry file in the National Archives.

Most record copies of **land patents** issued to persons who acquired land through June 30, 1908, are in volumes arranged by state, thereunder by land office. The "copy of patent" volumes are divided between the ESO and the National Archives in the same way as the headquarters tractbooks. Copies of patents not arranged by state, such as those issued for military bounty land warrants, are maintained by the ESO. Copies of patents issued from July 1, 1908, are also held by the ESO. Patents normally provide name of patentee, land description, name of land office, patent number, and date of patent.

The township and range number for any given tract can be determined from most commercial atlases. Details about the land transfer can be determined from entries in the tractbook covering the area concerned. If the date of entry, type of entry, and approximate location of the land are known, the chronologically arranged entries in one of the land office abstract volumes held by the National Archives can be searched for the patent number. Abstract volumes were assembled in the GLO from the monthly reports prepared in the district land offices and submitted by the local register and receiver to the GLO in Washington, DC. They contain information similar to that found in the tractbooks, but the abstract volumes are more difficult to use because of their arrangement and their chronological format.

NARA has abstract volumes from all the public land states, although some monthly abstracts from certain land offices are missing. Also in the National Archives is a four-volume "Index List of [Land] Offices," which identifies the land office with responsibility for a specific township and range at any given date.

Genealogical use of land entry papers is complex. Requirements for a search vary depending upon the nature of the facts available. For example, if a person applied for land between 1800 and June 30, 1908, and the land was located in Alabama, Alaska, Arizona, Florida, Louisiana, Nevada, or Utah, there is a card index (the "Seven States Index") to those land entry files in the National Archives; if a person applied for land after June 30, 1908, there is a card index to land entries in all public domain states (*see* 15.3); if a person entered land in Ohio between 1800 and 1820, there should be an entry in the book index relating to Ohio land offices in the ESO; and if a person received land in the Virginia Military District of Ohio, the U.S. Military District of Ohio, or one of the War of 1812 bounty land districts, there should be an entry in the indexes pertaining to those respective areas described in Chapter 8.

Once a researcher has an accurate description of the land in terms of section, township, and range, the related land entry file number can be ascertained by using the tractbooks in the National Archives and the ESO. If the researcher does not have the legal description of the land, it is often possible to obtain the legal description from the office of the county recorder of deeds in the county where the land is located.

15.2 Public Land Records, 1800–1908

Pursuant to an act of 1800 (2 Stat. 73), four district land offices were established in the part of the Northwest

Territory that became Ohio. Gradually, other district land offices were set up throughout the public domain to process requests for land. Documents pertaining to a request for land were normally transmitted from the district land offices to the GLO in Washington, DC, after the entry had been completed or the land abandoned. The GLO generally arranged records of land purchases or of land distributed under special conditions of settlement by state, name of land office, type of file, and file number. A list of land offices before 1908, together with the principal series of records for each land office, is given in *Land-Entry Papers of the General Land Office*, Preliminary Inventory (PI) 22, compiled by Harry P. Yoshpe and Philip P. Bower (Washington: National Archives, 1949).

Credit Files

Nearly all of the land sold by the Federal Government between 1800 and June 30, 1820, was sold on credit at no less than $2.00 per acre. Records of these transactions are the **credit entry files**. Sale of land on credit was discontinued after June 30, 1820, but purchasers who had not completed payment were able to obtain title to their land through those relief acts after 1820 that allowed them to extend their payments.

Credit final certificates, 1800–35, and a few of later date, were issued to the land entryman when the credit installments were completed. A certificate states that the purchaser has met all requirements to purchase the land and is entitled to a patent. The certificates are filed among the papers of each appropriate land office in two numerical series: certificates issued for purchases before July 1, 1820, in **credit prior certificate files**; and certificates issued for purchases finalized after June 30, 1820, in **credit under certificate files**.

Receipts for purchases (documents stating that a person has paid an amount of money) are not normally filed with the related certificate files but are in a separate receipt series. Other types of documents relating to land sales are occasionally found in the credit certificate files.

A final certificate normally shows name and place of residence of the entryman as given at the time of purchase, date of purchase, number of acres purchased, land description, summary of credit payments, and volume and page number of the copy of patent in the ESO.

Cash Files

Nearly all of the land sold by the Federal Government to purchasers after June 30, 1820, was sold for cash at no less than $1.25 per acre, pursuant to the Act of April 24, 1820 (3 Stat. 566). The **cash entry files**, dated from July 1, 1820, to June 30, 1908, are arranged by name of land office. A cash file includes a receipt for money paid and a final certificate authorizing issuance of a patent. If the tract was claimed on the basis of preemption, the file may include a preemption proof or similar document; if the tract was entered as a homestead or related entry and the entry had been commuted to cash, the cash file will include those documents normally found in the homestead or related file.

Each cash final certificate shows name of entryman, place of residence at time of purchase, land description, number of acres, date of patent, and volume and page number of the copy of patent in NARA or the ESO. Testimony of the purchaser in a preemption proof may, in addition, include age, citizenship, date of entry on the land, number and relationship of members of the household, and nature of improvements to the land.

Entries in the Seven States Index, mentioned previously, are alphabetically arranged by name of entryman and cover credit, cash, homestead, timber culture, and desert land entry files, both for patented lands and for rejected, canceled, and relinquished lands. It does not include entries for military bounty lands, private land claims, and mineral lands. An index card shows name of entryman, date of entry, state and land office, land description, type of entry, and certificate number.

The ESO/BLM has placed a database on their web site, *www.glorecords.blm.gov*, that provides access to information about the 1820–1908 land patents, including the military bounty land warrant patents, for each of the eastern public domain states (Alabama, Arkansas, Florida, Illinois, Indiana, Louisiana, Michigan, Minnesota, Mississippi, Missouri, Ohio, and Wisconsin) except Iowa. This database does not include information about credit entries, 1800–20, or any pre-1908 rejected, canceled, or relinquished homestead, timber culture, or desert land files. Each entry in the database shows name of entryman, name of land office, type of file, file number, date of patent, and legal description. Entries are searchable by name of entryman, file number, and legal description. As of this time, the database serves as an index to all of the pre-1908 patented land entry files of the eastern public domain states held by NARA, except those for Iowa.

Donation Files

Donation files concern land given away by the Federal Government in return for certain conditions of settlement. They include files for Arkansas, Florida, Oregon, and Washington.

Under terms of the Florida Armed Occupation Act of 1842 (5 Stat. 502), as amended, men able to bear arms were entitled to apply for 160 acres of land in certain unsettled areas of East Florida and were given patents to the land upon fulfilling the condition of 5 years settlement. The **Florida donation files**, mainly 1842–50, for each appropriate Florida land office are arranged numerically. Documents in each file vary depending upon the extent to which title was perfected. A complete file includes permit to settle, application for patent, report by the land agent, and final certificate authorizing a patent. The Seven States Index, described above, covers the patented Florida donation files but not the unpatented files.

A permit to settle shows name of applicant, marital status, month and year the applicant became a resident of Florida, and land description. An application for patent shows name of applicant, land description, name of settler (the person actually living on the land), and period of settlement. A final certificate shows the name of applicant, land description, date of patent, and volume and page number of copy of patent in the ESO.

Under terms of an act of 1850 (9 Stat. 496), certain white settlers and Indians of mixed blood in the Oregon Territory (which then included Washington) and certain settlers arriving there between December 1850 and December 1853 were entitled to land in Oregon Territory. The number of acres granted varied from 160 to 640 acres depending on the marital status of the settler and date of settlement. Settlers were required to live on the land and cultivate it for 4 years. The **Oregon and Washington donation files** for each appropriate land office are arranged numerically in two series. One series relates to patented entries, the other to incomplete or canceled entries. Both series have been reproduced on M815, *Oregon and Washington Donation Land Files, 1851–1903*, 108 rolls.

Abstracts with indexes for both the Oregon and the Washington donation entries are also available on M145, *Abstracts of Oregon Donation Land Claims, 1852–1903*, 6 rolls, and M203, *Abstracts of Washington Donation Land Claims, 1855–1902*, 1 roll. The abstracts fully identify each claim by name, land office, and patent number, and can be used to locate files on M815.

An alphabetical index to the Oregon donation entries is also available on a roll of microfilm prepared by the Oregon State Library and published by the Genealogical Forum of Portland, OR, under the title *Index to Oregon Donation Land Claims*. Each index entry gives name of entryman, name of land office, certificate number, number of acres, and land description of each approved claim. On another roll of microfilm, this information is arranged by land description.

Documents in a donation file include notification of settlement, which described the land either by legal description or by natural features (metes and bounds), sometimes accompanied by a plat; affidavit of settlement, which shows the settler's date and place of birth and, if applicable, of marriage; proofs of cultivation; oath that the land has been used for cultivation only; for naturalized citizens, proof of citizenship (not filmed on M815); and donation certificate, which shows name of entryman, place of residence, land description, date of patent, and volume and page number of copy of patent in the National Archives.

Homestead Files

Under the Homestead Act of 1862 (12 Stat. 392), as amended, citizens and persons who had filed their intention to become citizens were given 160 acres of land in the public domain if they fulfilled certain conditions. In general, an applicant had to build a home on the land, reside there for 5 years, and cultivate the land. Some later acts modified or waived certain of these conditions. An act of 1872 (17 Stat. 333), for instance, provided special benefits for Union veterans and their widows and orphans.

Homestead entry files, dated January 1, 1863–June 30, 1908, are arranged by state, thereunder by name of land office. There are generally two types of homestead files for each land office, one for patented homestead entries, the other for unpatented or canceled homestead entries. A patented homestead file usually contains a homestead application; certificate of publication of intention to enter land; testimony of the applicant and two witnesses; final certificate authorizing patent; and, where appropriate, copy of naturalization proceedings or copy of a Union veteran's discharge certificate.

A **homestead application** shows name of entryman, place of residence at time of application, land description, and number of acres. Testimony of the applicant on a **homestead proof** includes land description; name, age, and address of applicant; description of the house and date when residence was established; number and relationship of members of the family; nature of crops; and number of acres under cultivation. A **final certificate** shows name and address of applicant, land description, date of patent, and volume and page number of copy of patent in NARA and the ESO. Naturalization proceedings normally show name of the immigrant, name of court, date of proceedings, and country of previous allegiance; they do not usually include the town of birth or previous residence, name of ship on which the immigrant arrived in the United States, or date and port of arrival.

Individuals who applied for homestead land but later wanted to obtain title to it before expiration of the 5-year period required by law usually purchased the land for cash at the established price instead of fulfilling the homestead conditions. In such cases, the various homestead documents are filed in cash files for the same land office or its successor land office.

15.3 Public Land Records, 1908–73

Land entry documents based on patents that were issued between July 1, 1908, and May 16, 1973, are in the **serial patent files.** Arranged in numerical order by patent number, these files contain records of cash, homestead, timber culture, desert land, Indian allotment, and other types of entries completed within this period. A card index lists the names of the applicants alphabetically with the corresponding land office and serial application number. This index covers all applications, those that went to patent and those that were rejected, canceled, or relinquished. A second card index, arranged by state, thereunder by land office, and thereunder by serial application number, provides serial patent numbers for those entries that went to patent.

Homestead proof, testimony of claiman[t] and of a witness, Guthrie, OK, Homest[ead] FC 4480. Records of the Bureau of Land Management, RG 49.

HOMESTEAD PROOF---TESTIMONY OF WITNESS.

Louis West being called as a witness in support of homestead

entry of *Albert Smith* for *S.E. ¼ Sec. 4 Tp. 14ᵗʰ Range 3 E 2 M.* testifies as follows:

Ques. 1.   What is your name, age, and postoffice address?

Ans. *Louis West age 27 years, P.O. Wellston Okla.*

Ques. 2.   Are you acquainted with the claimant in this case and the land embraced in this claim?

Ans. *Yes*

Ques. 3.   Is the said tract within the limits of an incorporated town, or selected site of a city or town, or used in any way for trade or business?

Ans. *No No.*

Ques. 4.   State specifically the character of this land—whether it is timber, prairie, grazing, farming, coal or mineral land?

Ans. *Timber-farming land*

Ques. 5.   When did claimant settle upon the homestead, and at what date did he establish actual residence thereon?

Ans. *Claimant settled and established actual residence upon homestead March 1ˢᵗ 1892*

Ques. 6.   Have claimant and family resided continuously on the homestead since first establishing residence thereon?   (If settler is unmarried, state the fact.)

Ans. *Yes*

Ques. 7.   For what period or periods has the settler been absent from the land since making settlement, and for what purpose; and if temporarily absent, did claimant's family reside upon and cultivate the land during the absence?

Ans. *None*

Ques. 8.   How much of the homestead has the settler cultivated, and how many seasons did he raise crops thereon?

Ans. *Cultivated about 75 acres, raised crops thereon for nine seasons including present*

Ques. 9.   What improvements are on the land, and what is their value?

Ans. *2 log dwelling houses, hog lots, stable, shed out houses, 45 acres fenced into pasture, 75 acres in cultivation, 2½ acres orchard, value $1000 ᵒᵒ*

Ques. 10.   Are there any indications of coal, salines, or minerals of any kind on the homestead?   (If so, describe what they are, and state whether the land is more valuable for agricultural than for mineral purposes.)

Ans. *No.*

Ques. 11.   Has the claimant mortgaged, sold, or contracted to sell, any portion of said homestead?

Ans. *No.*

Ques. 12.   Are you interested in this claim; and do you think the settler has acted in entire good faith in perfecting this entry?

Ans. *I am not interested in claim. I think the settler has acted in entire good faith in perfecting this entry*

(Sign plainly with full Christian name.)   *Louis West*

I hereby certify that the foregoing testimony was read to the witness before being subscribed to and sworn to before me at Chandler, Lincoln county, Oklahoma, this *23* day of *October* 190*0*

(See note on 4th page.)

John Finley U. S. Commissioner.
Probate Judge

(The testimony of witnesses must be taken at the same time and place and before the same officers as claimant's final affidavit.   The answers must be full and complete to each and every question asked; officers taking testimony will be expected to make no mistakes in dates, description of land, or otherwise.)

HOMESTEAD PROOF—TESTIMONY OF CLAIMANT.

Albert Smith being called as a witness in his own behalf in support of homestead

entry No. _____ for _S.E 1/4 Sec 4 Tp 14 N R 8 E_ testifies as follows:

Ques. 1.   What is your name, age, and postoffice address?

Ans. _Albert Smith, age 44 years, P.O. Warwick, Okla._

Ques. 2.   *Are you a native born citizen of the United States, and, if so, in what state or territory were you born?

Ans. _Yes, born in Missippi_

Ques. 3.   Are you the identical person who made homestead entry No. _____ at the _Guthrie_

Okla. land office on the _9th_ day of _November_ 1891 and what

is the true description of the land now claimed by you?

Ans. _Yes. S.E. 1/4 Sec. 4 Township 14 N of Range_
_8 E I. M._

Ques. 4.   When was your house built on the land, and when did you establish actual residence therein? (Describe said house and other improvements which you have placed on the land, giving the total value thereof.

Ans. _Log dwelling house 14 x 16 ft, built January 1892_
Established actual residence therein March 1st
_1892_
Other improvements, 2 log houses, 45 pasture fenced with
wire, 75 acres in cultivation, 2 1/2 acres orchard
out houses, hog lots all of the value of $1500

Ques. 5.   Of whom does your family consist; and have you and your family resided continuously on the land since first establishing residence thereon?   (If unmarried, state the fact.)

Ans. _Myself, wife and six children, and we have_
resided continuously on land since first establishing
residence thereon

Ques. 6.   For what period or periods have you been absent from the homestead since making settlement, and for what purpose; and if temporarily absent, did your family reside upon and cultivate the land during such absence?

Ans. _None_

Ques. 7.   How much land have you cultivated each season, and for how many seasons have you raised crops thereon?

Ans. _Cultivated 20 acres 1892, 40 acres 1893, 90 acres 1898, 90 acres in 1899,_
90 acres crops 1898, 1899 1900 and
have raised crops there nine seasons including present

Ques. 8.   Is your present claim within the limits of an incorporated town, or selected site of a city or town, or used in any way for trade or business?

Ans. _No_

Ques. 9.   What is the character of the land? Is it timber, mountainous, prairie, grazing, or ordinary agricultural land?
State its kind and quality, and for what purpose it is most valuable

Ans. _Timber, ordinary agricultural land, most valuable_
for valuable for farming

Ques. 10.   Are there any indications of coal, salines, or minerals of any kind on the land? (If so, describe what they are, and state whether the land is more valuable for agricultural than for mineral purposes.)

Ans. _No._

Ques. 11.   Have you ever made any other homestead entry? (If so, describe the same.)

Ans. _No_

Ques. 12.   Have you sold, conveyed, or mortgaged any portion of the land, and if so, to whom and for what purpose?

Ans. _No_

Ques. 13.   Have you any personal property of any kind elsewhere than on this claim?   (If so, describe the same, and state where the same is kept.)

Ans. _No_

Ques. 14. Describe the legal subdivisions, or by number, kind of entry, and office where made, any other entry or filing (not mineral), made by you since August 30, 1890.

Ans. _Made None_

(Sign plainly with full Christian name.)   _Albert Smith_

I hereby certify that the foregoing testimony was read to the witness before being subscribed to and was

sworn to before me at Chandler, Lincoln county, Oklahoma, this _23_ day of _October_ 19 _00_

John Embry
Probate Judge   U. S. Commissioner.

THIS PAGE TOP: *"Bankers and Railroad Men's Party on Blue Grass Lawn at Calexico." The California Development Company hoped that this campout would persuade the men to invest in Imperial Valley schemes, ca. 1904. Photograph No. 48-RST-7-17.*

THIS PAGE BOTTOM: *Turn-of-the-Century Land Booms "Holding Down a Lot in Guthrie." Photograph No. 48-RST-7B-6 by C.P. Rich, ca. 1889. Both photographs, Records of the Office of the Secretary of the Interior, RG 48.*

OPPOSITE PAGE TOP: *"In line at the Land Office, Perry, Sept. 23, 1893. 9 o'clock AM. waiting to file." Photograph No. 49-AR-32.*

OPPOSITE PAGE BOTTOM: *"First train [and wagons] leaving the line north of Orlembo [Orlando] for Perry [Oklahoma Territory], Sept. 16, 1893." Photograph No. 49-AR-7. Both photographs, Records of the Bureau of Land Management, RG 49.*

In Line At The Land Office Perry, Oklahoma 1893 7 Oclock A.M. Waiting To File

Each serial patent file shows name of patentee, place of residence, land description, date of patent, and patent number. Type of land entry determines the nature of additional information in the file. All copies of patents for the period after June 30, 1908, are in the ESO. Most serial patent files are held by NARA; many of the Indian allotment serial patent files, however, are not in the National Archives. Rejected, canceled, or relinquished serial application files for the eastern states, July 1, 1908-1933, arranged by state, thereunder by land office, and thereunder by serial application number, are also in the National Archives. Those for the western states are mostly in NARA's regional archives facilities (see 15.5).

15.4 Private Land Claims

Private land claims, 1789-June 30, 1908, are claims based on grants, purchases, or settlements of land that took place before the United States acquired sovereignty over the land. The term "private land claim" is also sometimes used to apply to land claims based on special considerations. For example, French emigrants claimed land at Gallipolis, OH, on the basis of a special act of Congress. Although such claims are not described separately, they are occasionally included or referred to among the private land claims. A series entitled "Records of Special Acts" contains information on some private land claims.

Private land claims were usually made by persons who claimed to have grants from foreign sovereigns, by descendants of such persons, by citizens of the United States who settled these lands with the permission of the foreign government, and by U.S. citizens who bought up rights to lands acquired under foreign sovereignty and presented them to the Federal Government for the purpose of acquiring title.

Much of the land in what is now the United States was granted, purchased, or settled between 1685 and 1853, while it was under the rule of France, Great Britain, Spain, or Mexico. The land was often described by the indiscriminate method of surveying by natural features in terms of metes and bounds; it was usually confirmed in these same terms, rather than in terms of section, township, and range.

Whenever the United States acquired land from a foreign government, it established a board of commissioners or other agency to adjudicate private land claims. The agencies thus established rarely completed their work, and the unfinished business was often referred to others, such as the district land offices, U.S. district courts, Court of Claims, Supreme Court, GLO, and the Court of Private Land Claims.

NARA holds records concerning private land claims in the following states: Alabama, Arizona, Arkansas, California, Colorado, Florida, Illinois, Indiana, Iowa, Louisiana, Michigan, Mississippi, Missouri, New Mexico, and Wisconsin. Each of these states was originally in one of the following

areas: the Northwest Territory (Illinois, Indiana, Michigan, and Wisconsin); Mississippi Territory (Alabama and Mississippi); Louisiana Purchase (Louisiana, Arkansas, Iowa, and Missouri); Florida Cession (Florida); and Mexican Cession (Arizona, California, Colorado, and New Mexico).

Records relating to individual claims presented before boards of commissioners or other Federal agencies, 1790-1837, were sent to Congress and transcribed and indexed in *American State Papers: Public Lands*, 8 vols. (Washington: Gales and Seaton, 1832-61). Claims from 1790-1809 are in volume 1; 1809-15 in vol. 2; 1815-24 in vol. 3; 1824-28 in vol. 4; 1827-29 in vol. 5; 1829-34 in vol. 6; 1834-35 in vol. 7; and 1835-37 in vol. 8. Each volume is indexed. A consolidated index has been published under the title *Grassroots of America*, edited by Phillip W. McMullin (Salt Lake City: Gendex, 1972). Most of the reports published in the Gales and Seaton edition were also published in the less complete edition of *American State Papers* issued by Duff Green in 1834.

Originals of the congressional committee reports on private land claims are among the Records of the U.S. Senate, RG 46, and the Records of the U.S. House of Representatives, RG 233. They are filed by session of Congress, thereunder by name of committee, and thereunder chronologically.

Committee reports on individual land claims considered from 1826 to 1876 by the two congressional committees on private land claims are collected and published in *Reports of the Committees on Private Land Claims of the Senate and House of Representatives*, 2 vols. (45th Cong., 3rd sess., Misc. Doc. 81, serial 1836). Each volume is indexed by name of claimant or subject, but many names were omitted. Also available is an "Index to Reports of Committee on Private Land Claims, House of Representatives" on pages 5-20 of *House Index to Committee Reports* by T.H. McKee (Y1.3:C73/2). The Congressional Serial Set provides digested summaries and alphabetical lists of private claims presented to the U.S. Congress from the 1st to the 60th Congress (1789-1909). *See* Table 23.

Those **private land claim case files** in RG 49 where title to the land has been approved are arranged by state or other geographic area, thereunder by docket number, with indexes for most states or geographic areas. Case files include correspondence, reports, maps and plats, petitions, affidavits, transcripts of court decisions, and deeds and abstracts of title. Because proof of title was required, wills, deeds, marriage certificates, and assignments may be found among these records. For the most part, the case files contain copies of original documents. Many of these records were created during the adjudication of claims by agencies of the United States. These case files do not include the original grant or other documents of the original land transfer, except perhaps some copies in translation. For California, however, there are records, for the most part in Spanish, concerning land claims based on grants made by the Mexican Government, 1822-46.

Diseño No. 398. Map submitted in support of a private land claim in California, 1854. Records of the Bureau of Land Management, RG 49.

The following microfilm publications reproduce some of the records and indexes to private land claims in California: T1207, *Private Land Grant Case Files in the Circuit Court of the Northern District of California, 1852-1910*, 28 rolls; T1214, *Index to Private Land Grant Cases, U.S. District Court, Northern District of California, 1853-1910*, 1 roll; T1216, *Index by County to Private Land Grant Cases, U.S. District Court, Northern and Southern Districts of California*, 1 roll; and T1215, *Index to Private Land Grant Cases, U.S. District Court, Southern District of California*, 1 roll.

Genealogical information in the private land claims case files varies from file to file. Some case files mention only the name of the claimant and the location of the land; others show additional information about the claimant such as place of residence at the time the claim was made and the names of relatives, both living and dead. There is often more information about the heirs or assignees of the claimant than about the original claimant.

15.5 Land Records at National Archives Regional Facilities

Some of the records of the GLO/BLM are held by NARA's regional archives. They are listed in this section by state. Arrangement of the records within a state is usually by district land office. Not all district land offices are represented in regional records, and most land entry case files are found at the National Archives Building in Washington, DC.

Alabama

NARA's Southeast Region in Atlanta, GA, holds GLO records of the Cahaba, Huntsville, Mobile, and St. Stephens district land offices. These records include local office registers, tractbooks, and correspondence, 1805-54.

Alaska

NARA's Pacific Alaska Region in Anchorage, AK, holds GLO/BLM records of the Alaska state office and the Anchorage, Circle City, Fairbanks, Juneau, Nukalo, Rampart, Sitka, St. Michael, and Weare district land offices. These records include local office registers, tractbooks, and correspondence, 1885-1977; and rejected, canceled, and relinquished serial application case files, 1908-69.

Arizona

NARA's Pacific Region in Laguna Niguel, CA, holds GLO/BLM records of the Arizona state office and the Florence, Phoenix, Prescott, and Tucson district land offices. These records include registers, tractbooks, and correspondence, 1870-1970; serial patent case files, 1970; and rejected, canceled, and relinquished serial application case files, 1908-55.

Arkansas

NARA's Southwest Region in Fort Worth, TX, holds GLO records of the Champagnolle, Clarksville, Dardanelle, and Little Rock district land offices. These records include local office registers, tractbooks, and correspondence, 1857-61 and 1877-79.

California

NARA's Pacific Region in Laguna Niguel, CA, holds GLO/BLM records of the Bakersfield, Los Angeles, and Riverside district land offices. These include local office registers, tractbooks, and correspondence, 1853-1972; serial patent case files, 1961-70; and rejected, canceled, and relinquished serial application case files, 1908-61.

NARA's Pacific Region in San Francisco, CA, holds GLO/BLM records of the California state office and the Aurora (Nevada), Bodie, Eureka, Humboldt, Independence, Marysville, Oakland, Redding, Sacramento, San Francisco, Shasta, Stockton, Susanville, Ukiah, and Visalia district land offices. These records include local office registers, tractbooks, and correspondence, 1858-1981; serial patent case files, 1963-74; and rejected, canceled, and relinquished serial application case files, 1908-74.

Colorado

NARA's Rocky Mountain Region in Denver, CO, holds GLO/BLM records of the Colorado state office and the Akron, Central City, Del Norte, Denver, Durango, Fair Play, Glenwood Springs, Golden City, Gunnison, Hugo, Lake City, Lamar, Leadville, Montrose, Pueblo, and Sterling district land offices. These include local office registers, tractbooks, and correspondence, 1863-1977; and rejected, canceled, and relinquished serial application case files, 1908-25.

Florida

NARA's Southeast Region in Atlanta, GA, holds GLO/BLM records of the Gainesville district land office. These include local office lists and correspondence, 1879 and 1932-33.

Idaho

NARA's Pacific Alaska Region in Seattle, WA, holds GLO/BLM records of the Idaho state office and the Blackfoot, Boise, Burley, Coeur d'Alene, Hailey, Idaho Falls, Lewiston, Oxford, and Shoshone district land offices. These include local office registers, tractbooks, and correspondence, 1869-1973; and rejected, canceled, and relinquished serial application case files, 1908-66.

Illinois

NARA's Great Lakes Region in Chicago, IL, holds GLO records of the Chicago, Danville, Dixon, Edwardsville, Galena, Kaskaskia, Palestine, Quincy, Shawneetown, Springfield, and Vandalia district land offices. These include local office registers, tractbooks, and correspondence, 1814-76.

Indiana

NARA's Great Lakes Region in Chicago, IL, holds GLO records of the Brookville, Crawfordsville, Fort Wayne, Indianapolis, Jeffersonville, La Porte, Terre Haute, Vincennes, and Winnamac district land offices. These include

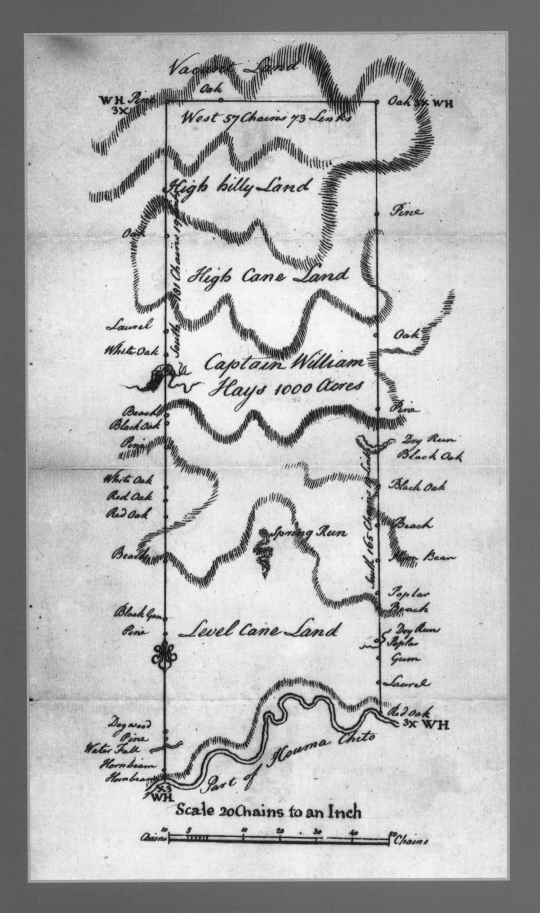

Survey plat of a 1773 British Florida land grant in support of a private land claim in Florida. Records of the Bureau of Land Management, RG 49.

local office registers, tractbooks, and correspondence, 1807-17 and 1820-76.

Iowa

NARA's Central Plains Region in Kansas City, MO, holds GLO records of the Burlington, Chariton, Council Bluffs, Dacorrah, Des Moines, Dubuque, Fairfield, Fort Dodge, Iowa City, Kanesville, Marion, Osage, and Sioux City district land offices. These include local office registers, tractbooks, and correspondence, 1836-1909.

Kansas

NARA's Central Plains Region in Kansas City, MO, holds GLO records of the Augusta, Cawker City, Colby, Concordia, Dodge City, Fort Scott, Garden City, Hays City, Humboldt, Independence, Junction City, Kirwin, Larned, Lecompton, Mapleton, Neodesha, Oberlin, Ogden, Salina, Topeka, Wakeeney, and Wichita district land offices. These include local office registers, tractbooks, and correspondence, 1854-1919.

Louisiana

NARA's Southwest Region in Fort Worth, TX, holds GLO records of the Baton Rouge, Greensburg, and Monroe district land offices. These include local office registers, tractbooks, and correspondence, 1832-1907.

Minnesota

NARA's Great Lakes Region in Chicago, IL, holds GLO records of the Benson, Forest City, Greenleaf, Litchfield, and Minneapolis district land offices, 1855-82.

Mississippi

NARA's Southeast Region in Atlanta, GA, holds GLO records of the Augusta, Chocchuma, Columbus, Grenada, Jackson, Pontotoc, and Washington district land offices. These include local office registers, tractbooks, and correspondence, 1807-1917.

Montana

NARA's Rocky Mountain Region in Denver, CO, holds GLO/BLM records of the Montana state office and the Billings, Bozeman, Glasgow, Great Falls, Havre, Helena, Kalispell, Lewistown, Miles City, and Missoula district land offices. These include local office registers, tractbooks, and correspondence, 1867-1969; serial patent case files, 1963-68; and rejected, canceled, and relinquished serial application case files, 1908-55.

Nebraska

NARA's Central Plains Region in Kansas City, MO, holds GLO records of the Alliance, Broken Bow, Chadron, Lincoln, McCook, North Platte, O'Neill, Sydney, and Valentine district land offices. These include local office registers, tractbooks, and correspondence, 1875-1934.

Nevada

NARA's Pacific Regions in San Francisco and Laguna Niguel, CA, hold GLO/BLM records of the Nevada state office and the Aurora, Austin, Battle Mountain, Belmont, Carson City, Elko, Ely, Eureka, Las Vegas, Pioche, Reno, and Winnemucca district land offices. These include local office registers, tractbooks, and correspondence, 1862-1977; serial patent case files, 1964-71; and rejected, canceled, and relinquished serial application case files, 1908-74.

New Mexico

NARA's Rocky Mountain Region in Denver, CO, and NARA's Southwest Region in Fort Worth, TX, hold GLO/BLM records of the New Mexico state office and the Clayton, Folsom, Fort Sumner, La Mesilla, Las Cruces, Roswell, Santa Fe, and Tucumcari district land offices. These include local office registers, tractbooks, and correspondence, 1858-1958; and rejected, canceled, and relinquished serial application case files, 1908-50.

Housed at the New Mexico State Records Center and Archives, 404 Montezuma, Santa Fe, NM 87503, are Spanish and Mexican land grants and related records, 1685-1846, and case files of the Court of Private Land Claims in New Mexico, 1892-1912.

North Dakota

NARA's Rocky Mountain Region in Denver, CO, holds GLO/BLM records of the Bismark, Creelsburg, Devils Lake, Dickinson, Fargo, Grand Forks, Minot, and Williston district land offices. These include local office registers, tractbooks, and correspondence, 1864-1950; and rejected, canceled, and relinquished serial application case files, 1908-50.

Ohio

NARA's Great Lakes Region in Chicago, IL, holds GLO records of the Canton, Chillicothe, Cincinnati, Steubenville, Wooster, and Zanesville district land offices. These include local office registers, tractbooks, and correspondence, 1801-28.

Oregon

NARA's Pacific Alaska Region in Seattle, WA, holds GLO/BLM records of the Oregon state office and the Burns, Coos Bay, Eugene, La Grande, Lakeview, Medford, Portland, Oregon City, Roseburg, Salem, The Dalles, Tillamook, Vale, and Winchester district land offices. These include local office registers, tractbooks, and correspondence, 1853-1972; and rejected, canceled, and relinquished serial application case files, 1908-78.

South Dakota

NARA's Rocky Mountain Region in Denver, CO, holds GLO records of the Aberdeen, Belle Fourche, Chamberlain, Deadwood, Gregory, Huron, Lemmon, Mitchell, Pierre, Rapid City, Sioux Falls, Springfield, Timber Lake, Vermillion, Watertown, and Yankton district land offices. These include local office registers, tractbooks, and correspondence, 1862-1940.

Utah

NARA's Rocky Mountain Region in Denver, CO, holds GLO/BLM records of the Utah state office and the Cedar City, Moab, Richfield, Salt Lake City, and Vernal district land offices. These include local office registers, tractbooks, and correspondence, 1869-1970; and rejected, canceled, and relinquished serial application case files, 1908-25.

Washington

NARA's Pacific Alaska Region in Seattle, WA, holds GLO/BLM records of the Colfax, New Olympia, North Yakima, Seattle, Spokane, Vancouver, Walla Walla, Waterville, and Yakima district land offices. These include local office registers, tractbooks, and correspondence, 1861-1972; and rejected, canceled, and relinquished serial application case files, 1908-78.

Wisconsin

NARA's Great Lakes Region in Chicago, IL, holds GLO records of the Wassau district land office, 1888 and 1905.

Wyoming

NARA's Rocky Mountain Region in Denver, CO, holds GLO/BLM records of the Wyoming state office and the Buffalo, Cheyenne, Douglas, Evanston, Lander, and Sundance district land offices. These include local office registers, tractbooks, and correspondence, 1870-1968; and rejected, canceled, and relinquished serial application case files, 1908-42.

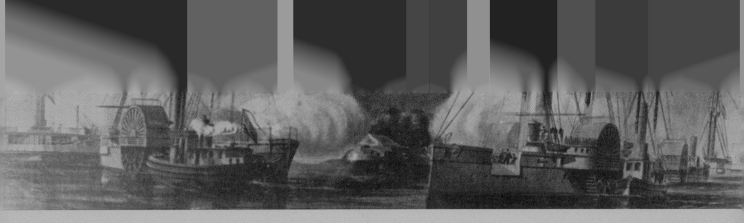

CHAPTER 16   *Claims Records*

16.1   *Introduction*

16.2   *Claims Brought Before Congress*

Table 23   *Lists of Private Claims Brought Before Congress*

16.3.   *U.S. Court of Claims*

16.3.1   *General Jurisdiction Cases*

16.3.2   *Congressional Jurisdiction Cases*

16.3.3   *Departmental Jurisdiction Cases*

16.3.4   *District of Columbia Jurisdiction Cases*

16.3.5   *Special Jurisdiction Cases*

16.4   *Quartermaster Claims*

16.5   Alabama *Claims*

CHAPTER 16
Claims Records

16.1 Introduction

For most of the 19th century, many claims against the U.S. Government were settled by the Treasury Department. If a claim was rejected by the Treasury Department, the claimant's only recourse was to appeal directly to Congress. Petitions to that body for relief had become so numerous by mid-century that Congress was finding it impossible to make the proper and necessary investigations required for action on the claims. Although the U.S. Court of Claims was established in 1855, it was not until the late 1880s that Congress ceased entirely to serve in an appellate capacity on private claims. Claims relating to services, supplies, or transportation requisitioned for or furnished to the Army were heard by the quartermaster general.

Papers relating to an individual claim are often in a single folder or jacket and usually consist of a filled-out form, correspondence, and supporting documents. Records concerning an individual claim vary considerably in the information they contain, depending on the nature of the claim. Almost any claim record, however, shows the name of the claimant, age, and place of residence at the date of filing; some also contain the names of parents, grandparents, or other family members and other personal information.

Discussed in this chapter are claims adjudicated by the Treasury Department and appealed to Congress, claims settled by the U.S. Court of Claims, claims against the U.S. Army settled by the quartermaster general, and claims known as the "*Alabama* Claims."

16.2 Claims Brought Before Congress

Congressional claims records often contain information about local political, social, and economic affairs. Private claims brought before Congress consist of petitions and memorials, sometimes with related papers, presenting claims against the Government for military service; for confirmation of land grants; for damages to persons or property committed by agents of the Government, by foreign governments, or by Native American tribes; and for other forms of private relief, such as the removal of political disabilities imposed on certain former Confederates by section 3 of the 14th Amendment.

A list of one group of claims brought before Congress was published as Document 216, "Claims Barred by the Statute of Limitations," in *American State Papers, Class IX: Claims* (Washington: Gales and Seaton, 1834): 386–407. On December 13, 1810, Secretary of the Treasury Albert Gallatin sent to the Senate a statement of all the claims that had been adjusted and allowed at the Treasury Department and for which certificates of registered debt were issued under an act passed March 27, 1792 (1 Stat. 245). This act provided for the settlement of claims of persons under particular circumstances barred by limitations heretofore established. The statement provides the names

of nearly 1,500 individuals who served during the Revolutionary War and gives for each the date of certificate, number of statement, type of service performed, date on which interest commenced, and amount of money allowed.

Lists of private claims brought before the Senate, 1815–1909, and the House of Representatives, 1789–1891, were printed as congressional documents. Each list is arranged alphabetically by name of claimant and includes the nature or object of the claim, Congress and session before which it was brought, nature and number or date of the committee report, and additional information. Table 23 shows the coverage of each list and cites the congressional document. Lists were compiled from entries in the journals of the Senate and the House. They do not accurately reflect the actual content of the claims files because individual files were often forwarded by Congress to the

Table 23
Lists of Private Claims Brought Before Congress

Congress	Dates	Congressional document containing list
Senate		
14th–46th	1815–81	46th Cong., 3rd sess., S. Misc. Doc. 14, serials 1945–46
47th–51st	1881–91	53rd Cong., 2nd sess., S. Misc. Doc. 266, serial 3175
52nd–55th	1891–99	56th Cong., 1st sess., S. Doc. 449, serial 3881
56th and 57th	1899–1903	57th Cong., 2nd sess., S. Doc. 221, serial 4433
58th	1903–5	59th Cong., 1st sess., S. Doc. 3, serial 4917
59th and 60th	1905–9	60th Cong., 2nd sess., S. Doc. 646, serial 6165
House of Representatives		
1st–31st	1789–1851	32nd Cong., 1st sess., H. Misc. Doc. (unnumbered), serials 653–655
32nd–41st	1851–71	42nd Cong., 3rd sess., H. Misc. Doc. 109, serial 1574
42nd–46th	1871–81	47th Cong., 1st sess., H. Misc. Doc. 53, serial 2036
47th–51st	1881–91	53rd Cong., 2nd sess., H. Misc. Doc. 213, serial 3268

various executive agencies for implementation or returned to the petitioners or their congressional representatives. Also, a petition submitted to an earlier Congress may have been transferred to the files of a later Congress when the claim was raised anew.

Claims brought before the Senate are in Records of the U.S. Senate, Record Group (RG) 46; those brought before the House are in Records of the U.S. House of Representatives, RG 233. Under rules of access established by the Senate and the House, most Senate records are open for research when they are 20 years old and most House records are open when they are 30 years old.

Although most of the claims files submitted to Congress are dispersed throughout the records of the Senate and the House of Representatives, the **barred and disallowed case files of the Southern Claims Commission** referred to the House are maintained as a separate collection among the records of the Committee on War Claims. The Southern Claims Commission was established by an act of March 3, 1871 (16 Stat. 524), to receive, examine, and consider claims submitted by Southern Unionist citizens seeking compensation for supplies that had been confiscated by or furnished to the Union Army. An act approved May 11, 1872 (17 Stat. 97), extended the Commission's purview to include property used by the U.S. Navy. The commissioners had no final jurisdiction in the cases they considered but were required to report their decisions, sending along the completed case files in annual increments to Congress for appropriate action. Congress retained the barred and disallowed claims, appropriated the funds to pay those allowed, and sent the allowed case files to the Treasury Department for settlement and custody. The Commission was terminated effective March 10, 1880, having approved about one-third of the more than 22,000 claims it received. Under provisions of the Bowman and Tucker acts (see 16.3), Congress reconsidered many of the barred and disallowed claims and in some instances referred cases to the U.S. Court of Claims for review and recommendation.

The case files contain valuable genealogical information and are among the most heavily researched of all House records. A typical case file contains the following types of records: a form petition, an application to have testimony taken by a special commissioner, a deposition or testimony of the claimant or a witness, summary report of the Commissioners of Claims, and miscellaneous papers such as oaths, memorandums, and evidential documents. Files give information regarding the claimant, circumstances of the purchase or seizure of goods, and value of each item. The claims files have been reproduced as M1407, *Barred and Disallowed Case Files of the Southern Claims Commission, 1871–1880*, 4,829 fiche. On the first four microfiche is the *Consolidated Index of Claims Reported by the Commissioner of Claims to the House of Representatives from 1871 to 1880* (Washington: Government Printing Office, 1892). This volume is the only record in which the names of all claimants appear in a single alphabetical list. It provides basic information on each claim and should be consulted by anyone doing research in records of the Southern Claims Commission. Information about records of the Commission and the approved claims is found in 10.4.4; information about the barred and disallowed claims referred to the U.S. Court of Claims is found below.

16.3 U.S. Court of Claims

The U.S. Court of Claims was established by an act of February 24, 1855 (10 Stat. 612), to hear claims against the United States based on any law of the Congress, regulation of an executive department, or contract with the Government, express or implied, including all claims referred to the court by the Congress. It was abolished in 1982 when its trial jurisdiction was transferred to the newly established U.S. Claims Court and its appellate jurisdiction was transferred to the U.S. Court of Appeals for the Federal Circuit.

Before establishment of the court, no procedure existed by which claims arising against the U.S. Government could be enforced by suit. All claims by or against the Government were considered by the Treasury Department. If that Department rejected the claim, the claimant's only recourse was to appeal directly to Congress (see 16.2). By the middle of the 19th century, Congress had received so many petitions for relief that it was impossible to make the proper and necessary investigations required for action on the claims. The Court of Claims was intended to relieve Congress of the pressure of investigating the claims, give persons having designated types of claims against the Government the opportunity for litigation, and protect the Government by regular investigation. It was soon apparent that the court's limited jurisdiction kept it from accomplishing its purpose; instead, it served primarily as a fact-finding agency whose conclusions were submitted to Congress for approval and the granting of awards. Not until the 1855 act was amended on March 3, 1863, was the situation remedied in any great measure.

The 1863 amendatory act (12 Stat. 765) increased the number of judges from three to five; broadened the court's jurisdiction to include all setoffs, counterclaims, claims for damages, or other demands on the part of the Government against any person making claims against it; and authorized the court to render final judgments against the United States. The act also permitted appeal by either party to the Supreme Court of the United States, but the Supreme Court initially refused to consider such appeals because it objected to a provision of the act that called for the Secretary of the Treasury to review all Court of Claims decisions involving funds. After that particular provision of the 1863 act was repealed in 1866, the Supreme Court accepted appeals from the Court of Claims until 1925 when a new law abolished the appeals and substituted writs of certiorari.

In the early 1880s further steps were taken to increase the effectiveness of the Court of Claims. The Bowman Act, approved March 3, 1883 (22 Stat. 485), provided that numerous claims still pending in Congress be sent to the Court of Claims for findings of facts that would be submitted to Congress for determination of final action. The Tucker Act, approved on March 3, 1887 (24 Stat. 505), gathered together the provisions in earlier acts that outlined the court's jurisdiction and enlarged that jurisdiction to include all claims founded upon the Constitution of the United States. This act also provided that district courts should have concurrent jurisdiction with the Court of Claims in certain cases.

Until 1925 the five judges handled all the business of the court. Their only assistance came from commissioners who merely took testimony and were without authority to exclude anything. After World War I petitions before the court so increased in volume that it was impossible for the court to keep up with the docket. On February 24, 1925, Congress passed an act (43 Stat. 964) granting the court the right to appoint seven commissioners with authority to hear evidence in cases assigned to them and report findings of fact to the court. These commissioners were authorized to take depositions of witnesses, generally near the residences of the witnesses, for presentation to the court. The Chief Judge and the judges could also, when duty permitted, take testimony in various parts of the United States. Cases were argued orally by attorneys, but no oral testimony of witnesses was offered and the court tried the cases without a jury.

Geographically the jurisdiction of the Court of Claims extended throughout the continental United States, its territories, and its possessions. Petitioners had the burden of proving that their cause of action was within the jurisdiction of the court, and a case could be disposed of on the ground of lack of jurisdiction at any stage of the proceedings. No limit was set on the fiscal amount involved in a claim. Vast sums could be at stake, or only a few dollars. Suits were instituted not only by citizens of the United States, corporations, or other business entities but also by citizens or subjects of any foreign government that accords to citizens of the United States the right to prosecute claims against it in its courts.

Litigation before the Court of Claims arose under legislation that conferred either permanent or temporary jurisdiction. The court had permanent jurisdiction in general jurisdiction cases, which concern claims brought directly by claimants under general provisions of law, and in congressional and departmental jurisdiction cases, which concern cases referred by Congress or by executive departments. It had temporary jurisdiction in Indian depredation cases, which are claims for property of U.S. citizens that was taken or destroyed by Native Americans in amity with the United States (*see* 16.3.5), and in District of Columbia cases (*see* 16.3.4) and French spoliation cases (*see* 16.3.5). An act of August 13, 1946 (60 Stat. 1049), gave Indian tribes and other identifiable groups of Native Americans the right to sue in the Court of Claims on claims accruing after the date the act was approved and arising under the Constitution, laws and treaties of the United States, and Executive orders of the President, or on claims that would be cognizable if the claimant were not an Indian tribe. Before passage of this act tribes could not sue the Government except under special jurisdictional acts.

The Court of Claims did not have jurisdiction over any claim for which a suit is pending in another court, over any claim for pensions, or over any claim growing out of any treaty with foreign nations.

The records, which are part of Records of the U.S. Court of Claims, RG 123, consist mainly of case files and are arranged by type of jurisdiction as follows: general, congressional, departmental, District of Columbia, French spoliation, and Indian depredation. They are described in *Records of the United States Court of Claims*, Preliminary Inventory (PI) 58, compiled by Gaiselle Kerner (Washington: National Archives and Records Service, 1953). Case papers filed under the court's concurrent jurisdiction are among the records of the district courts.

The General and Congressional Jurisdiction case files are the most numerous; Departmental Jurisdiction case records are the least. Records of District of Columbia jurisdiction cases are also comparatively few. French spoliation and Indian depredation case records probably are of more use than are records of the other types of cases. Since case files are arranged by case number, those researchers who begin their research already knowing the case number and appropriate jurisdiction should have little difficulty. Researchers who do not have this information must obtain it before attempting to use the records. When the case files were transferred to the National Archives, the Court of Claims retained the name indexes. Indexes for the Congressional Jurisdiction case files, 1884–1943 are available on microfilm as M2007, *U.S. Court of Claims Docket Cards for Congressional Case Files, ca. 1884–1943*, 5 rolls; individuals wishing to use the other jurisdictional case files should contact the Clerk of Court, U.S. Court of Federal Claims, Washington, DC 20005, and request that the indexes be searched to determine the appropriate case number.

Decisions of the Court of Claims are reported in various congressional documents and in *Cases Decided in the Court of Claims of the United States 1863* (Washington: Government Printing Office, 1867). Related records are found in Records of the Court of Claims Section (Justice), RG 205, and are described in *Records of the Court of Claims Section of the Department of Justice*, PI 47, compiled by Gaiselle Kerner and Ira N. Kellogg, Jr. (Washington: National Archives and Records Service, 1952). The Court of Claims Section prepared the cases for the Government lawyers, and dockets and indexes among the section's records are useful in locating material among the records of the Court of Claims. Some records relating to the Indian depredation cases are also in Records of the Bureau of Indian Affairs, RG 75.

16.3.1 General Jurisdiction Cases

General jurisdiction cases are those in which the claimants sue directly in the Court of Claims and in which the court's judgments, unless appeals are made to the Supreme Court, are final. Such cases are the most numerous on the court's dockets and relate to a wide variety of subjects. The case files generally cover the period May 23, 1855, through 1960. However, some of the early cases in this series contain evidentiary materials dated in the early 1800s and some of the later cases have material dated as late as 1966. Cases concern violations of contracts entered into by all Government departments, such as contracts for erecting public buildings; constructing bridges, aqueducts, battleships, cruisers, dry docks, dams, and sea walls; dredging and improving rivers and harbors; carrying mail; furnishing supplies and services to the Government; and operating and maintaining irrigation projects. A considerable amount of litigation has arisen because of violations of Indian treaties, infringement of patents, unlawful imprisonment, losses of funds by disbursing officers without their negligence, overassessment of taxes and other tax claims, the construing of statutes affecting the pay of Army, Navy, and civilian employees of the Government, and property taken under article V of the Constitution. Early cases involved turnpikes, the Cumberland Road, canals, and stagecoach companies carrying the mails. Later cases involve riparian rights, claims on the Chinese Indemnity fund for losses sustained because of the Boxer Rebellion in China in 1900, abrogation of the gold standard in 1933, and rescission of contracts with air mail lines in 1934.

Many cases have resulted from each war in which the United States has been engaged. Some of these concern property abandoned or captured during the Civil War, seizures of property at the termination of the Civil War, pay and allowances of officers and enlisted men serving in certain capacities during the Civil and Spanish-American Wars, import duties on shipments from Puerto Rico and the Philippines at the close of the Spanish-American War, and claims, arising at the end of World War I, concerning contracts for cotton litters.

A large number of claims are known as class cases and are filed under one docket number for each type of case, with the petition of each claimant being filed under a separate subnumber. These class cases include claims concerning the reimbursement of railway postal clerks for travel expenses, overtime pay for Government employees under the 8-hour law, and pay and allowances for certain officers and enlisted men serving in the Civil War and the war with Spain. Other such cases involve land-entry overcharges, deficits in sugar bounty appropriations, and rebates on internal revenue duties on alcohol used for art and medicinal compounds.

Case files are arranged by case number, 1 through 34758, A-1 through M-441, 41818 through 50491, and 1-52 through 554-59. Beginning with FY 1952, files are arranged by fiscal year, thereunder numerically by case number. Each case file may include some or all of the following: original, amended, and supplemental petitions, answers, and other pleadings; motions, briefs, powers of attorney, depositions, affidavits, interrogatories, transcripts of testimony, orders, findings of facts, and conclusions of law; and opinions, petitions for certiorari, orders of the Supreme Court granting certiorari, other mandates and opinions of the Supreme Court, and counter claims filed by the Government. The case file may also include evidentiary material, often furnished by Government departments, entered as exhibits by both claimant and defendant. This material includes correspondence, contracts, construction permits, patents, abandoned applications for patents with attached petitions and oaths, blueprints, composite drawings, graphic charts, last wills and testaments, titles to real estate, land certificates, certificates of insurance, tax-sale certificates, indictments with convictions and judgments, General Accounting Office certificates of settlement, vouchers, invoices, ordnance procurement orders, daily bulletins of contracting corporations, articles of incorporation, production reports, tabulations of surplus on hand, market reports, reports of chemical tests, and bound volumes of technical and scientific works. As stated above (16.3), the index to these files is still in the custody of the court. Individuals wishing to use these records must contact the Clerk of Court, U.S. Court of Federal Claims, Washington, DC 20005, to request a search of the index.

Part of the general jurisdiction case records, known as the **Guion Miller enrollment records**, concern the preparation of rolls for payments of awards to the Eastern Cherokee Indians (*see* 11.3.3). Under the act of July 1, 1902 (32 Stat. 726), the Court of Claims acquired jurisdiction over claims arising under treaty stipulations with the Cherokee tribe. Three suits were brought against the United States under the Treaty of New Echota (May 23, 1836) and the Treaty of Washington (Aug. 6, 1846). The court ruled in favor of the Eastern Cherokees on May 18, 1905, and directed the Secretary of the Interior to identify those persons eligible to share a special congressional claims compensation appropriation of June 30, 1906. Guion Miller, first as a special agent of the Department of the Interior, and after April 29, 1907, as a special commissioner of the Court of Claims, compiled a roll of eligible persons, which he submitted with a report to the court on May 28, 1909. On January 5, 1910, Miller submitted a supplemental roll and report that contained additional names. The rolls were approved by the court and payment authorized on March 15, 1910.

In compiling his lists, Miller utilized earlier rolls, including those prepared by Interior Department special agents Alfred Chapman, Eastern Cherokees, 1851; John Drennen,

Western Cherokees, 1851; and Joseph G. Hester, Eastern Cherokees, 1884. Copies of these rolls and related indexes are filed with the Miller material, which includes his reports, 1909 and 1920; his 1909 and 1910 enrollments; the Miller rolls, 1909 and 1910; the Eastern Cherokee applications, 1906-9, with index; transcripts of testimony, 1908-9; and correspondence, 1906-11. The Miller rolls, related indexes, and applications have been filmed as M1104, *Eastern Cherokee Applications of the U.S. Court of Claims, 1906-1909,* 348 rolls. Related records found in RG 75 are available as M685, *Records Relating to Enrollment of Eastern Cherokees by Guion Miller, 1908-1910,* 12 rolls. This publication, in addition to the Miller rolls, includes copies of Miller's 1909 report, transcripts of testimony, and the earlier census rolls and indexes Miller used to certify eligibility.

For a discussion of other records related to Cherokee and other tribal claims found in RG 75, *see* Chapter 11.

16.3.2 Congressional Jurisdiction Cases

Congressional Jurisdiction Case Files, dated January 10, 1884, to May 19, 1943, are arranged by case number, 1-17845. Some of the court papers filed in these cases extend through 1946. Each case file may contain some or all of the following: letters of reference from congressional committees to the Court of Claims transmitting petitions for investigation and determination of facts, with accompanying copies of congressional bills and resolutions memorials, and other pertinent papers; orders referring claims to the commissioners; and petitions, answers, and other pleadings, motions, briefs (a great many on loyalty), depositions, affidavits, interrogatories, orders (including those remanding cases), findings on loyalty, findings of facts and opinions of the court, and summary reports of commissioners. Also included is evidentiary material, much of which was furnished by Government departments to both claimant and defendant, including correspondence, contracts, muster rolls, certificates of burial, oaths of allegiance, inventories of captured subsistence stores, detailed statements of military service, records of proceedings under courts martial, records from Confederate archives relating to questions of loyalty and disloyalty, and offers to furnish stores to assist in defense work. Some of the evidentiary documents predate the filing of the petitions by several decades. A partial index to these files, covering the period 1884 to 1943, is available on microfilm as National Archives microfilm publication M2007, mentioned earlier.

Although they are not specifically identified as such, many of these cases appear to be for claims rejected by the Southern Claims Commission and referred by Congress to the Court of Claims for review and recommendation (*see* 16.2).

16.3.3 Departmental Jurisdiction Cases

The **Departmental Jurisdiction Case Files,** dated April 10, 1883-January 14, 1943, are arranged by case number,

1-176. Each case file contains some or all of the following: letters from Government departments to the court transmitting claims on which the court was to report its findings and opinions; orders referring cases to the claims commissioners; petitions, answers, and other pleadings; motions, briefs, depositions, interrogatories, findings of facts, and opinions of the court; summary reports of the commissioners; and orders remanding cases for argument. Evidentiary material, much of which was furnished by Government departments to both claimant and defendant, include blueprint plans of U.S. transports, contracts, deeds, orders of the Postmaster General changing service and pay on certain mail routes, directives of the Treasury Department to withhold payments, decisions of the Secretary of the Interior confirming actions of the General Land Office, approval by the General Land Office of maps showing locations of railroad lines, recommendations of the Justice Department's Solicitor as to claims of individuals, letters of auditors concerning payments, lists of swamp lands on which indemnity was allowed by the Secretary of the Interior, reports on sales of property, schedules of Government buildings sold at public auction, statements of money advanced as bounty to U.S. recruits, and War Department reports on the number of recruits mustered and delivered in conformity with arrangements made by the Provost Marshal with the Government. Papers filed in evidence may predate the filing of the petitions by several decades.

Naval-bounty Case Files, January 24, 1899-May 20, 1903, which are part of this series, are arranged by case number, 1-11 and 51-3990. The files for cases 1-11, inclusive, relate to claims made by or for all individuals on every vessel participating in a particular engagement. They contain letters from the Secretary of the Navy transmitting the claims to the court, with attached papers setting forth the names of the vessels, places and dates of the engagements, names of officers and crew present during the action, and other pertinent data; occasional individual petitions, answers, motions, briefs, and stipulations; and requests to various departments for information in support of the claims, replies thereto, and documents that were attached. These latter documents include copies of the following: lists of men serving on board vessels during engagements, together with statements of their ranks and salaries; the kind and quantity of supplies making up the ships' cargoes and weights of projectiles used in certain guns, both on vessels and in the harbor; statements concerning the tonnage and horsepower of the ships and the number and caliber of guns; statistics and statements by recognized authorities on ordnance; extracts from logs of ships; official notes taken on board ships; reports fixing positions of ships; and reports of commanding officers showing movements of vessels. These case files also include depositions, affidavits, interrogatories, findings of facts and conclusions of law, and opinions and decrees of the court fixing amounts of bounty to be awarded. Case numbers between

11 and 51 were not assigned. Case 51 is the petition of Commodore George Dewey and includes a motion to appeal to the Supreme Court, together with a mandate of that court. Cases 52–3990 consist only of petitions and powers of attorney filed by individual claimants who took part in the naval engagements covered by the first 11 cases.

16.3.4 District of Columbia Jurisdiction Cases

District of Columbia Jurisdiction Case Files, June 30, 1880–February 25, 1887, are arranged by case number, 1–398, and contain petitions, answers, and other pleadings; motions; briefs; powers of attorney; letters of administration; and calls on the District Commissioners for documents, their replies, and the documents attached to be used as evidence in support of claims. These latter documents include copies of contracts, extensions of contracts, specifications, statements of work done under contract, statements of accounts under contract, final measurements for contracts, reports of the Board of Public Works on improvements of streets, vouchers from the auditor of the Board of Public Works, unaudited engineers' vouchers, bills for work under contract with the Board of Public Works, maps, and diagrams and plats for streets, squares, and alleys. The series also includes counterclaims of the defendants, replications of claimants to pleas to setoffs, depositions, orders, findings of fact and opinions of the court, applications for permission to appeal to the Supreme Court, and mandates of the Supreme Court. Papers filed in evidence may predate the filing of petitions by several decades; mandates of the Supreme Court are dated as late as 1905.

16.3.5 Special Jurisdiction Cases

The **French spoliation case files**, arranged by case numbers 1–5574, are legal and evidentiary documents relating to claims arising from depredations committed by French warships and privateers on American commerce during the period 1793–1801. Included are shipping records and other documents dated as early as 1783. Appendix I of PI 58, mentioned earlier, provides a list of oversized documents submitted as evidence in individual cases. These claims contain genealogical information because the long period between the time an American merchant or shipowner suffered the loss and the time when the act of January 20, 1885, enabled his heirs to file claims made it necessary for claimants under the1885 act to prove descent from the original claimants.

Indexes to the files are in RG 205, Records of the Court of Claims Section (Justice). Included is the publication *French Spoliation Awards by the Court of Claims of the United States Under the Act of January 20, 1885* (Washington: U.S. Court of Claims, 1934), which gives the name of each original claimant, vessel, master, and case file number. The work is arranged alphabetically by name of original claimant. The "French Spoliation Cases: List of Vessels, With the Docket Number of Cases, Filed in the Court of Claims Under the Act of 20 January 1885," an alphabetical list of vessels that shows names of masters and case numbers of all pertinent cases, can be consulted at the National Archives Building in Washington, DC. Additional information on French spoliation claims can be found in Records of Boundary and Claims Commissions and Arbitrations, RG 76.

Indian depredation case files contain legal documents and correspondence relating to claims for property taken or destroyed by Indians of tribes at peace with the United States. Incidents on which the claims were based took place in the period from roughly 1814 through the Sioux uprising of 1890–91, although most occurred during the hostilities of the 1860s and 1870s. Documents used as evidence in the cases often present colorful pictures of frontier life, which could add an interesting note to the genealogy of a descendant of one of the claimants. Appendix II to PI 58 provides a list of Indian nations, tribes, and bands against which suits were filed.

Closely related material can also be found in RG 205. Perhaps the most useful record in this record group is a one-volume index to names of claimants and claimants' representatives and to the names of Indian tribes committing the depredations. Alphabetical index entries refer to appropriate case numbers.

16.4 Quartermaster Claims

Records relating to claims against the U.S. Army by civilians and settled by the Quartermaster General's Office covering the years 1839–1914, but principally 1861–90, are in Records of the Office of the Quartermaster General, RG 92. They normally consist of claims registers, correspondence, and other loose papers relating to individual claims, arranged by type of service rendered, and thereunder by the number assigned to each claim by the Third Auditor of the Treasury. Most of the individual registers include name indexes, and some separate name indexes that cover several registers are also available. Of particular importance is a two-volume **alphabetical name index** that covers most of the Civil War claims and other claims, 1861–94, discussed below. This index only provides the name of the claimant and claim number. It is necessary to then check the appropriate claims register to determine the identity of the person filing the claim, subject matter, and date. In many instances, unbound documents pertaining to an individual claim were removed from the quartermaster files and transferred to the Third Auditor's office as part of the settlement process; these documents may no longer exist. The researcher may need to search the appropriate series in Records of the Accounting Officers of the Department of the Treasury, RG 217, for claims filed among records of the Third Auditor.

For the pre–Civil War period, 1839–60, four registers are available. The volumes cover the following: claims examined in the Quartermaster General's Office, 1839-42, one vol., entries arranged numerically; claims received that relate chiefly to the Mexican War, 1847-58, one vol., entries arranged, for the most part, chronologically; and claims received from civilians (mostly Mexican War teamsters) for services performed, 1848-60, two vols., entries in one volume arranged alphabetically by initial letter of surname of claimant; entries in the other arranged chronologically by date of receipt of claim. All four volumes include name indexes.

Claims arising from the Civil War and settled in the following decades constitute the bulk of the quartermaster claims records. An act of July 4, 1864 (13 Stat. 381), made the quartermaster general responsible for investigating and recommending settlement of "all claims of loyal citizens in states not in rebellion, for quartermaster's stores" furnished to or seized by the Union Army, whether or not receipts had been issued for them. For the period 1861-70, these **"Fourth of July claims"** for horses and mules, forage and fuel, barracks and quarters, building materials, rent, personal services, mileage, postage, extra duty, damages, and supplies are registered by auditor's number in 68 volumes of claims registers. Also entered in these registers are rejected claims pertaining to services, horses, and property, 1866-86, and to horses and forage, 1864-90. Correspondence and related papers constituting the claims files are arranged by register volume, thereunder by auditor's number. Name indexes are included in each register volume.

For the period 1871-89, claims relating to rent, forage, and fuel and other Fourth of July claims are registered by year, thereunder by auditor's number in 29 volumes, 5 of which include a partial name index. The claims files parallel arrangement of the registers. Cross-references in the registers identify Fourth of July claims considered and rejected by the quartermaster general. **Rejected claims files**, 1871-90, are arranged according to the numbers of the boxes, thereunder the packages in which they were originally stored. An incomplete two-volume register, 1878-90, of these rejected claims is available, with entries arranged by box and package number.

Registers and claims files for these Fourth of July claims are a good resource for genealogists, because they pertain to a large number of individuals and the information is generally interesting. Using the series, however, is difficult and the search may not be worthwhile unless there is good reason to think the subject of research did in fact file a claim. The claimant must have been a loyal citizen of a loyal state. It may also be necessary to know approximately when the claim was filed and the type of goods or service involved. For most of the claims covering the period 1861-94, one should first consult the two-volume name index discussed above. For rejected claims, all entries in the two-volume register must be searched, even though this register is also incomplete.

Several single volume registers provide information

about **other Civil War claims**. The register covering claims received relating to transportation, 1861-62, and to personal services by persons later deceased, 1864-68, includes a name index to the entries, which are arranged by type of claim, thereunder numerically. Entries in a register of claims received relating to horses and mules, March-December 1864, are arranged chronologically, thereunder numerically. Entries in a register of claims received relating to national cemeteries, 1869-70, are arranged by auditor's number and indexed by name. Claims received concerning mileage, extra-duty pay, final pay, arrears, and bounty, January 1867-October 1870, are registered alphabetically by initial letter of surname of claimant.

Two series of claims files, one relating to property damage by Union troops, 1861-65, and the other to claims for public animals submitted to the Cavalry Bureau in 1864, are arranged numerically. To use the records, researchers must first search the registers of letters received by the quartermaster general, 1818-70 (142 vols.).

Claims for remuneration for extra duty, mileage, quarters and fuel, and services, 1871-78, are represented by seven volumes of registers and by claims files arranged by year, thereunder by auditor's number. Two volumes of registers and two volumes of name indexes cover claims received relating to supplies originating after the Civil War and to rents originating during and after the war, 1875-78. Claims files themselves are arranged by volume and auditor's number.

Eleven volumes of registers, 1879-90, with separate name indexes for some volumes, cover claims received for personal services and allowances (miscellaneous). The register entries and the related claims files are arranged by year, thereunder by auditor's number. Four volumes of registers, 1879-94, and four volumes of related name indexes cover claims received for regular supplies. Corresponding claims files, 1879-90 only, are arranged by time period, thereunder by auditor's number.

Transportation claims, 1861-87, are covered by 131 separately maintained registers arranged by type of claim. Fifteen of these relate to ocean and lake transportation claims and to claims for services and vessels, 1861-70, with vessel indexes; three volumes deal with claims relating to transportation, value and services of vessels on western rivers, ferriages, tolls, and services on military railroads, 1861-70, with name and vessel indexes included; and 113 volumes concern railroad transportation accounts, 1861-87.

By an act of 1902 (32 Stat 43), Congress authorized the quartermaster general to spend $50,000 to reimburse paroled Confederate soldiers of the Army of Northern Virginia for horses, sidearms, and baggage seized by Union soldiers who had acted under orders that violated the terms of surrender. Documentation generated in support of these **"Confederate horse claims"** includes registers of claims paid, 1901-10, 12 notepads arranged by time period, with name indexes, 1901-6; claims files, 1902-14, arranged by file numbers from the 1890-1914 correspondence of the quartermaster general; a few record cards for rejected claims, arranged by name of claimant; and unarranged press copies of lists of claims submitted to the Secretary of War, 1902-10.

Disallowed claims of U.S. Colored Troops who served in the Civil War are discussed in 12.3.2.

16.5 *Alabama* Claims

During the Civil War the Confederate Navy was strengthened by ships built in Great Britain, and Confederate vessels were allowed to use certain ports in the British Empire to take on armaments, supplies, and fuel. Two of the ships built in England, the *Alabama* and the *Florida*, and other Confederate cruisers caused extensive damage to the Union merchant and whaling fleets. The United States accused Great Britain of failing to act as a neutral during the conflict, even though she had professed her neutrality. The United States claimed that Great Britain was responsible for prolonging the war, transferring much of the American merchant fleet to the British flag, and causing the decline in trade and increased insurance rates. The United States also held Great Britain liable for the many claims resulting from the actions of the Confederate cruisers.

Differences between the United States and Great Britain that grew out of the Civil War, as well as other long standing disagreements, made it difficult for the two countries to carry on friendly diplomatic relations. Relations steadily deteriorated until 1871 when they agreed that a Joint High Commission should be established to negotiate a treaty that would provide the means for settling their chief differences. The Commission, composed of five representatives from each country, convened on February 27, 1871, in Washington. Negotiations were completed on May 6, and two days later the Treaty of Washington was signed.

Articles 1 to 11 of the Treaty of Washington provided that claims of U.S. citizens against Great Britain resulting from the actions of Confederate cruisers should be arbitrated at Geneva. This group of claims is generally known as the *Alabama* **claims**. The United States presented the claims to the Geneva Tribunal of Arbitration on December 15, 1871, and the tribunal granted the United States an award on September 14, 1872. The United States then established a domestic claims commission to examine the validity of each claim in order to divide the award equitably among the individual claimants. The Geneva award was distributed by two domestic Courts of Commissioners of *Alabama* Claims, which functioned in 1874-76 and 1882-85, respectively.

Records relating to the *Alabama* claims are part of Records of Boundary and Claims Commissions and Arbitrations, RG 76, and are described in *Records Relating to*

Civil War Claims: United States and Great Britain, PI 135, compiled by George S. Ulibarri and Daniel T. Goggin (Washington: National Archives and Records Service, 1962). They consist of 40 feet of case files submitted as evidence to the 1874-76 commissioners and 180 feet of case files submitted to the 1882-85 commissioners. An "Index to Dockets" serves as the index to the first group of claims. An "Alphabetical List of Claims" serves as the index to the second group. Additional records relating to these claims are listed in the Introduction to PI 135.

In 1872 the *Alabama* **claims** were described in a Department of State publication called *Revised List of Claims Filed with the Department of State Growing Out of the Acts Committed by the Several Vessels, which have Given Rise to the Claims Generically Known As the Alabama Claims* (S3.13/ 1:C52/2). The list provides information on losses to Confederate privateers, such as the *Alabama, Shenandoah, Florida*, and *Tallahassee*, and an index of the names of ships and individuals involved. A facsimile of the manuscript of the index to the *Alabama* claims was issued some time after 1872 under the title *List of the Documents and Correspondence in the Cases of the United States and of Great Britain* (S3.13/1:D65).

CHAPTER 17   *Records of the District of Columbia*

17.1   *Introduction*

17.2   *Court Records*

17.3   *Records of District of Columbia Government Employees*

17.4   *Records of the Board of Children's Guardians*

17.5   *Land and Property Records*

17.1 Introduction

The District of Columbia was created by acts of July 16, 1790 (1 Stat. 130), and March 3, 1791 (1 Stat. 214), from lands ceded to the Federal Government by Maryland and Virginia. Originally, the District included the town and county of Alexandria, VA, and the city of Georgetown, MD. The area ceded by Virginia was retroceded in 1846, and in 1878 Georgetown was annexed, giving the city its present limits and making the city of Washington coextensive with the District of Columbia. Until 1879 the area within the District but outside both Georgetown and Washington City was known as Washington County.

In Records of District Courts of the United States, Record Group (RG) 21, are Federal court records relating to the District of Columbia (except for the area returned to Virginia). They include equity case files, transcripts of wills, administration papers relating to estates of decedents, guardianship papers, and indentures of apprenticeship. Emancipation papers are described in 12.6; naturalization records are described in 3.1.2. For records of civilian employees of the Federal Government, many of whom were District residents, *see* Chapter 14.

In Records of the Government of the District of Columbia, RG 351, are several series relating to applications for and appointments to positions within the D.C. Government, and also series relating to children who were placed in temporary custody or in special facilities. In addition, there are assessment and taxation records and deeds pertaining to ownership of real property in the cities of Washington and Georgetown and the county of Washington.

17.2 Court Records

Chancery Case Files

From 1801 to 1863, chancery jurisdiction in the District of Columbia was exercised by the Circuit Court for the District of Columbia. The chancery case files contain information about divorces (starting in 1860), disputes over estates, disputes over guardianships, and the payment of debts or bills. These case files are arranged by docket or rules number, thereunder by case number. An index to the case files can be found in "Index to Chancery Case Files, 1801-63," volumes 1 through 7.

Equity/Civil Case Files

Chancery jurisdiction of the Circuit Court for the District of Columbia was abolished by an act of Congress in 1863 (12 Stat. 762), and the title of chancery was changed to equity. In 1936 the title of equity was changed to civil. Since the chancery docket books ended at volume 7, equity docket books start at volume 8.

Equity case files are arranged by case number. In addition to lunacy cases, equity jurisdiction included divorces, disputes over estates, disputes over guardianships, and the payment of debts or bills. Indexes to the equity case files, 1836-1938, are arranged alphabetically by names of the appellant and appellee.

While the National Archives and Records Administration (NARA) has custody of the indexes and docket books, equity case files dated after 1899 are in the custody of the District Court for the District of Columbia, 3rd Street and Constitution Ave., NW, Washington, DC 20001.

Transcripts of wills probated in the District of Columbia, 1801-88, are arranged chronologically in 25 volumes available at NARA. Each will normally shows the name and address of the maker, dates of the will and its probate, name of the executor, and often the names of children or other family members. A second series of transcripts, 1801-1919, is with the Register of Wills and Clerk of the Probate Court, U.S. Courthouse, Washington, DC 20001. A one-volume "General Index to Recorded Will," arranged by surname of the decedent, gives the volume and page numbers to both series. A two-volume index labeled "Probate Index to Wills Filed and Wills Recorded" gives the volume and page numbers for the second series only. Both the "General Index" and the "Probate Index" are in the custody of the National Archives.

Original wills dated 1801 through 1994 have been transferred to the District of Columbia Archives, 1300 Naylor Court, NW, Washington, DC 20001-4225. Wills probated after 1994 are at the office of the Register of Wills at the DC Courthouse.

Material relating to the estates of decedents is in **administration records**, 1801-78. These records include bound administration dockets, of which those between 1837 and 1853 are missing, and unbound administration case files. A "Probate Index" volume indexes both the dockets and the case files by surname of decedent.

A docket shows the name of the administrator, or if the deceased had made a will, the name of the executor; name and residence of the decedent; names of sureties (those who were legally liable for the debt, default, or failure in duty of another); and date letters of administration were granted. A case file usually contains an inventory of the estate, account or periodical accounts of the administrators or executors, related vouchers, and sometimes a petition for administration and related correspondence. It normally shows the name of the decedent, nature and value of the estate, and amount distributed to each named heir. It sometimes includes the date of death of the decedent and the names of heirs at law.

Records relating to estates inherited by wards of the court, chiefly minors, are in **guardian records**, 1801-18. They include bound guardian dockets and the unbound case files of guardian papers. Two sets of volumes entitled "Probate Index No. 1 & 2" and "General Index of Guardianships" index both the dockets and case files alphabetically by surname of ward.

A docket shows names of the guardian and the sureties; name and residence of the decedent; names of wards, and if they were minors, usually their ages or dates of births;

and value of the estate. A case file normally contains an account or periodical accounts by the guardian, related vouchers, and often related correspondence. The file also usually shows the name of the guardian and the amounts distributed periodically to each ward.

Indentures of apprenticeship, 1801-74, are arranged chronologically. Originals are unbound, but copies, which exist for 1801-11 only, are bound in one volume. This bound volume has been microfilmed as M2011, *Indentures of Apprenticeship Recorded in the Orphans Court, Washington County, District of Columbia, 1801-11*, 1 roll. Both the unbound originals and the bound copies are indexed. An indenture of apprenticeship is a single document that shows the name and usually the age of the apprentice, name of one parent, name and trade of the master, and terms of the apprenticeship.

17.3 Records of District of Columbia Government Employees

Entries in **registers of appointments** in the District of Columbia Government, 1871-80, relate to appointments as commissioners, trustees of the public schools, physicians to the poor, members of the Metropolitan Police Force, justices of the peace, commissioners of the Washington Asylum, and holders of the offices of collector, treasurer, assessor, and engineer. The material primarily concerns appointments made during the period 1871-80 but does include some appointments to the Metropolitan Police Force as early as 1861. Entries usually show the name of the appointee, position, salary, amount of bond, date of removal or resignation, and remarks. Most entries are arranged by office, thereunder chronologically by date of appointment.

A **roster of employees** in local government offices, 1876-78, includes employee's name, position, salary, and remarks concerning dismissal, resignation, salary changes, appointment, and other data. The roster is arranged alphabetically by name of office.

Applications for employment in the Bureau of Streets, Avenues, and Alleys are dated 1871-74. Entries include file number, name of applicant, residence, date of application, position desired, by whom recommended, and notations on action taken. They are arranged by file number and indexed in the front of the volume by surname of the applicant.

Several series cover individuals employed by the police force. A **register of appointments to the Metropolitan Police Force**, 1861-1930, includes those appointed between 1861 and 1906 and documents their careers on the force through 1930. Entries show name; date and place of birth; date and place of naturalization, if applicable; former occupation; marital status and number in the family; home address; dates of appointment, resignation, or dismissal; pensions; and remarks concerning promotion or reasons for dismissal. Many are closed with date of death. Entries

are arranged in rough alphabetical order by initial letter of the surname.

Metropolitan police service records, 1861-1930, cover individuals appointed between 1861 and 1917. Each record shows name and date, position, and summary of service, including promotions, resignation, discharge, suspensions, fines, and other official personnel actions. The records are arranged in rough alphabetical order by initial letter of the surname.

Metropolitan Police Force personnel case files, 1861-1930, are alphabetically arranged records of men appointed between 1861 and 1900, with a few as late as 1926. Contents of the files vary. A typical file may include application for appointment, recommendations, physical and medical information, summary of assignments, and records relating to complaints, disciplinary actions, and final board actions. Documents in these files are restricted.

Registers of oaths administered to members of the Metropolitan Police Force, 1862-65 and 1868-78, include name of officer, date, and signature of appointee as a patrolman, an additional patrolman, or a special patrolman. This series covers only temporary appointments and is arranged in rough chronological order.

17.4 Records of the Board of Children's Guardians

Several series relating to neglected, abused, abandoned, or destitute children committed to the board by the police or criminal courts and by the Board of Trustees of the Reform School for Boys or the Reform School for Girls are in the **Board of Children's Guardians records**, ca. 1884-1912. This board was given the responsibility to assign these children to homes, apprentice them, place them in special facilities, or offer them for adoption. Several related volumes provide background information about the children placed under the board's jurisdiction.

Lists of children placed in the custody of the board and information relating to the child and their parents are in the **Record of Children Received**, July 4, 1893-January 5, 1912. This volume is arranged chronologically and numbered 1-3042.

The **children's history** records, 1893, 1897-1906, and 1909-13, provide a detailed background of the child, including vital statistics; name and last known address of parents; remarks on physical, mental, and moral condition; and information concerning the circumstances that led to commitment. There is also a record of visits to the child during the period of custody, with remarks concerning progress, as well as a record of the various homes and institutions in which the child was placed. These records are arranged chronologically by date of commitment. An alphabetical index to names in the volumes exists for the periods July 23, 1909-September 27, 1911, and October 2, 1911-May 5, 1913. Volumes covering the period September 27, 1893-May 26, 1897, and January 1, 1907-July 23, 1909, are missing.

Directory of Placed-Out Children, July 7, 1893–July 31, 1908, provides a list of placed-out children, their background, and a history of the families where they were placed, as well as the terms of placement. This volume is arranged chronologically.

The three-volume **Record of Children in Temporary Custody**, November 9, 1987–July 19, 1909, gives a listing for each child, personal characteristics, cause of placement, where temporarily placed, and final disposition of the case. These records are arranged chronologically, and the front of each volume contains an alphabetical index to surnames of the children listed in that volume.

History of Committed Feebleminded Children, 1884–1907, gives personal and family backgrounds of children who were placed in the Pennsylvania Training School for Feebleminded Children in Elwyn, PA, and the Virginia Home and Training School for Feebleminded Children in Falls Church, VA. Each volume is arranged chronologically.

Histories of Children Committed to the Industrial Home School for White Children, 1896–1917, provides background, progress reports, and date discharged and to whom. These two volumes are numbered 729–2215, and the contents are arranged chronologically by date the child was received. The volume covering February 17, 1896–May 9, 1902, contains an index to the names of children in that volume.

17.5 Land and Property Records

Records relating to land and property in the District of Columbia include **deed books**, 1792–1869, that consist of handwritten copies of deeds that record the transfer of titles to real property. Also recorded are other legal documents, such as bills of sale, mortgages, deeds of manumission of slaves, and certificates of freedom establishing the free status of blacks during the antebellum period. Indexes to the records are maintained at the Office of the District of Columbia Recorder of Deeds.

DC building permits, 1877–1949, consist of applications for permits and permits issued for such things as private construction, repairs to existing structures, erection of fences and signs, razing of buildings, and installation of equipment. The completed application forms include name of owner, location of construction, names and addresses of the architect and builder, purpose of construction, cost estimates, and details concerning the nature of the work and materials utilized. Sometimes plans and sketches were included, but they have been systematically removed from these files and placed with the cartographic and architectural records in the National Archives. The building permits are arranged chronologically and numbered sequentially. They are currently being microfilmed as M1116, *DC Building Permits, 1877–1949*, 854 rolls. This publication includes a card index, 1877–1958, arranged by number of square (block), name of street, or name of subdivision. The District of Columbia

Government has custody of all building permits dated after September 7, 1949.

There are also **maps**, **plans**, **and atlases**, 1792–1915. These records consist primarily of manuscript and annotated maps but also include plats and survey descriptions for various dates. Plat books, 1793–96, 1809, and 1853–83, show subdivisions of squares. Also included is the "Brewer Collection," which consists of plats, surveys, and related material pertaining primarily to Georgetown, 1809–91.

Assessment books, city of Washington, 1814–1940, consist of periodic compilations by assessors of valuations of real property in the city of Washington. Lists for 1902–40 include data for the city of Georgetown. Entries vary, but usually they show square and lot number, square footage, rate of taxation, value of land, and name of owner. Some volumes, especially later ones, show the assessed value of improvements. The volumes are arranged mainly by year, thereunder by square number.

The records also contain **Cards Relating to Changes in Assessments**, 1906–76, which complement the index to building permits. These cards reflect changes in assessment of individual structures during the period. Most cards contain city location identifiers (square, lot, and parcel numbers), date of entry, house address, permit number, description of premises (including size of building and number of stories), estimated cost/value of property, and brief comments relating to the assessment. Cards are arranged by square number, thereunder by lot.

Tax books for the city of Washington are dated 1824–79. These are annual records of tax payments on real property in the city. A typical entry shows name of the property owner, square and lot number, and assessed value of land and improvements. Some volumes include information about assessed value of personal property. Arrangement is mainly in rough alphabetical order by surname of owner.

There are also records relating to land and property in Georgetown. Entries in **General assessment books for Georgetown**, 1800–19, 1835–83, and 1892–93, provide lists of assessments on real property improvements. Content varies but typical entries give information on the name of landholder, location of property, assessed value of the land, and, frequently, assessed value of improvements. Arrangement varies from volume to volume. Most of the earlier volumes contain entries in no discernible order but include a name index to property owners. Beginning in 1871, entries are in rough alphabetical order. Volumes dated 1880–83 are arranged by block or square number. Volumes covering the period 1800–19 and 1865–79 have been microfilmed as M605, *Records of the City of Georgetown (D.C.), 1800–79*, 49 rolls.

General assessment books for the county of Washington, 1855–64 and 1868–79, are lists of assessments of real property. Entries usually show name of the owner, location of property, number of acres, and value of land and improvements. Lists for 1855 and 1868 include

Members of Police Force.	Date of Birth.			Place of Birth.	Where Naturalized.	Time Naturalized.			Age.	Former Occupation.
	Month.	Day.	Year.			Month.	Day.	Year.		
Cook Samuel S.	Aug	23	1854	Virginia	Patrol Driver				38	Farmer
Cleveland Elijah	Mch	4	1859	Va	Patrol Driver				33	Patrol Driver
Clark Thomas E	Sept	26	1869	Va.					23	Farmer
Carter Robert			1864	Va.	Patrol Driver				28	Waiter
Carson William P	Dec	17	1869	Md.	Patrol Driver				23	Laborer
Carrington William W	Sept	22	1865	Md					27	Conductor
Cannon Walter S	May	16	1865	Ind	Police Surgeon				28	Physician
Campbell James W	Oct	28	1863	S Car					30	Policeman
Cooke Joseph	May	4	1824	England	Brooklyn N.Y				69	Teacher
Connor Daniel	Sept	11	1862	Va.					34	Soldier
Coffin Oliver H	Dec	31	1869	Ind					25	Collector
Clements James H	Apl	16	1867	S.C					27	Bookbinder
Case Francis H	Apl	17	1848	Ohio	Patrol Driver				46	Clerk
Cox Adelbert W	July	9	1872	Mass					23	Steward
Curry Edward	Aug	24	1868	Ireland	Washn D.C	July	3	1891	27	Gripman
Colbert Michael F	Dec	20	1867	Ireland	" "	Jany	30	1892	28	Tinner
Cochran James P	Oct	27	1862	Va.					33	Fireman
Cooper Singleton L	Nov	4	1867	Va.					28	Conductor
Corbey Richard A	Aug	3	1871	Md					24	Fireman
Cox Walter C	Sept	19	1866	Tenn					29	Cabt Maker
Copeland James W	Apl	21	1868	Ohio					28	Marine
Carroll Robert L	Aug	23	1869	S.C					27	Physician
Cornwell George S	Mar	20	1871	W Va.					25	Carpenter
Carlin Lewis A	Nov	11	1873	S.C					23	Bricklayer
Charlton Luther W	Aug	19	1864	Va.					32	Clerk
Catts George S	Oct	27	1872	Va					24	Conductor
Catts John E	Dec	25	1869	Va					27	Motorman
Coughlin Joseph	Mar	26	1869	Ireland	Springfield Ill	Nov	30	1892	26	Watchman
Carr Wm P	May	10	1858	Va	Police Surgeon				38	Physician
Cornwell Frederick W	Sept	23	1868	Va.					29	Fireman
Close Charles F	Mar	25	1870	S.C					27	Clerk
Clark Noble M	Aug	3	1845	Ala	Messenger				52	Ironworker
Chrisman John F	May	3	1862	Va					35	Watchman
Clark Robert H	Mar	25	1868	Va					29	Dairyman
Chriscaden Burt	Apr	6	1876	Mich	Driver				21	Fireman
Case Francis H	Apl	17	1848	Ohio	Station Keeper				49	Driver
Cleveland Philip S	Dec	26	1862	Va.	Driver				36	Laborer
Coleman Hand J	Jan	2	1854	Va.	Driver				45	Carpenter
Clements Claude L	Oct	26	1876	N.C					23	Motorman
Collins Ezra P	Mar	15	1867	N.C					32	Druggist
Cullinane Dennis J	Nov	15	1874	Ireland	Washington D.C	Aug	5	1895	25	Bartender
Combs David J	Feb	10	1868	Va					31	Conductor
Cox Isaiah	Feby	26	1874	S Car					26	Compositor
Over

RESIDENCE OF FAMILY.	DATE OF APPOINTMENT.			DATE OF RESIGNATION.			DATE OF DISMISSAL.			CAUSE OF DISMISSAL.	NUMBER OF ARRESTS MADE.	SPECIAL MERITORIOUS SERVICES.
	Month.	Day.	Year.	Month.	Day.	Year.	Month.	Day.	Year.			
102 M st S.W.	Mch	11	1892	Feb	28	1909				Salary increased to $1420 July 1, 1907		
209 I st. N.E.	Mch	18	1892				Apl	19	1898			
3236 M st N.W.	Mch	18	1892				Dec	31	1893			
520 20th st. N.W.	July	21	1892							Appt'd Laborer, Met. Police, D.C. July 2, 1900		
336 Pa. Av. N.W.	Aug	10	1892				Sept	30	1892			
1531 Ne. 1st st	Sept	1	1892							Hon. discharged Aug 31, 1900 Pensioned Sept 1, 1900		
	Aug	1	1893							Expiration of term July 31, '96.		
	Dec	16	1893	Died	Feby 4, 1894							
307 C st. N.W.	Dec	18	1893							Died June 4, '97		Station Keeper
1642 Valley st.	Apl	2	1894				Jan	14	1909	Promoted to Prt. Cl. 2, July 1, 1905 to Prt. Cl. 3 July 1, 1906 Conduct unbecoming an officer		
213 C st.	June	1	1894	Died			Apr	10	1919	Promoted to Prt. Cl. 2 Feb 7, 1900		
615 K st.	June	1	1894				Aug	16	1894	Conduct Unbecoming An Officer		
156 A st. N.E.	Sept	27	1894							Promoted to Station Keeper Dec 25, '97		
427 1st st N.E.	Jany	2	1895	Sept	30	1899				Appt'd Driver House of Detention		
901 F st.	May	13	1895							Promoted to Prt. Cl. 2, July 1, 1903		
2312 H st. N.W.	July	1	1895				Feby	29	1896	Honorably discharged July 31, 1924 Pensioned Aug 1, 1924		
2008 14th st. N.W.	July	1	1895	Oct	16	1899						
2143 G st.	July	19	1895							Promoted to Prt. Cl. 2 July 1, 1904 to Prt. Cl. 3 July 1, 1906		
231 C st. N.E.	Aug	17	1895							Hon. discharged Mar 31, 1919 Pensioned Apr 1, 1919 Committed suicide May 8, '98		
45 L st. N.E.	Nov	16	1895	Dec	2	1895						
Navy Yard	May	8	1896	Mar	31	1899				Promoted to Prt. Cl. 2 Feb 1, 1905 to Prt. Cl. 3, July 1, 1906		
948 R st N.W.	July	3	1896							Promoted to Prt. Cl. 2 Apr 18, 1905 to Prt. Cl. 3 July 1, 1916		
3310 Prospect Av.	July	3	1896	Died	Jood 14	1924						
315 12th st. S.	July	3	1896							Promoted to Prt. Cl. 2 May 4, 1905 to Prt. Cl. 3 July 1, 1906		
508 3d st. N.E.	July	4	1896							Promoted to Prt. Cl. 2 July 1, 1905 to Prt. Cl. 3 July 1, 1916		
419 12th st S.W.	July	4	1896							Honorably discharged Mar 31, 1922 Pensioned Apr 1, 1922		
417 12th st.	July	4	1896							Promoted to Prt. Cl. 2 July 12, 1905 to Prt. Cl. 3 July 1, 1916		
Washn Asylum	July	8	1896							Salary increased to $720 July 1, 1907		Patrol Driver
1319 13th st N.W.	Aug	1	1896	Aug	15	1897						
2311 H st.	Jan	15	1897							Promoted to Detective Sgt. July 1, 1903 to Prt. Cl. 3, July 1, 1906		
1809 5th st.	Jan	17	1897							Hon. discharged Dec 31, '98 Pensioned Jan 1, '99		
318 Ind. av.	June	7	1897	See from Book No. 2			Aug	1	1919	Promoted to Minger @ $700 Sept 10, '98		
432 10th st. N.W.	July	1	1897							Promoted to Prt. Cl. 3 July 1, 1906		
209 13th st. S.W.	July	1	1897				Dec.	16	1897	Hon. discharged Feb 26, 1909 Pensioned Mar 1, 1909 Reappointed Aug 7, 1902, — see next page		
1506 34th st N.W.	Dec	25	1897	Mar	16	1903				Appt'd Driver House of Detention June 2, 1904, see next page Promoted to Asst Sgt. May 10, 1901.		
	Dec	25	1897							Died June 24, 1911.		
323 G st. N.E.	Dec	21	1898							Transf'd to Board of Charities, D.C. July 1, 1903		
139 Mass. av.	Mar	6	1899							Reduced to Driver, House of Detention Jan 1, 1903, — see next page		
2911 Olive Av. N.W.	July	1	1899				Sept	1	1900	Conduct unbecoming an officer		
1003 E Capl. st.	July	1	1899				May	26	1902	Neglect of duty, etc. Promoted to Prt. Cl. 3 July 1, 1906		
2505 I st. N.W.	Aug	1	1899							Promoted to Prt. Cl. 3 July 1, 1906		
415 7th st. S.W.	Aug	17	1899							Hon. discharged Nov 30, 1924 Pensioned Dec 1, 1924		
1246 N. J. av. N.W.	July	1	1900	Apr	30	1913				Promoted to Prt. Cl. 3 July 1, 1906 Promoted to Det. Sgt. Aug 15, 1907		

entries for assessments on personal property. There are gaps in the records and arrangement varies. Lists for 1855–64 and 1868 are in no discernible order, but the volume for 1855–64 contains an alphabetical index to names. Beginning with 1871, most of the volumes are arranged in rough alphabetical order by surname of owner.

Lists of payments of assessments on real property are in **taxbooks for Washington County**, 1871–79. Entries vary but usually give name of the person assessed, location of the property, number of acres, lot number, value of land and improvements, total value, and amount of tax due. The eleven volumes are arranged in rough alphabetical order by initial letter of property owner's surname.

t. S.W. Mch. 11" 1892	Feb. 28 1909			Salary increased to $1920
t. N.E. Mch 18" 1892		Apl. 19" 1898		
t. N.W. Mch 18" 1892		Dec 31 1893		
t. N.W. July 21" 1892				Appt'd Laborer, Met
N.W. Aug 10" 1892		Sept. 30 1892		
est Sept 1" 1892				Hon. discharged Aug. 31," 19
Aug 1" 1893				Expiration of tin
Dec 16" 1893	Died Feby 4, 1894			
t. N.W. Dec 18" 1893				Died June 4" '97
t. Apl 24" 1894		Jan 14 1909		Promoted to Pot. Ct. 2. J Conduct unbecoming an
t. June 1" 1894	Died Apr. 10, 1919			Promoted to Pot. Ct. 2 Feb. 7, Turkln. Sgt. Sept. 11, 1915. Relieved
June 1" 1894		Aug 16" 1894		Conduct Unbecom
N.E. Sept 27" 1894				Promoted to Station
t. N.E. Jany 2" 1895	Sept. 30" 1899			Appt'd Driver House of Promoted to Pot. Ct. 2, July
t. May 13" 1895.				Honorably discharged Jul
t. N.W. July 1" 1895		Feby 29" 1896		
t. N.W. July 1" 1895	Oct. 16" 1899			
t. July 19" 1895				Promot'd to Pot. Ct. 2 July Hon. discharged Mar 31,
t. N.E. Aug 1" 1895				Committed suicide
t. N.E. Nov 16" 1895	Dec. 2" 1895			
ard May 8" 1896		Mar 31" 1899		Promoted to Pot. Ct. 2 Fre
t. N.W. July 3" 1896				Promot'd to Pot. Ct. 2 Ap
ect Aor July 3" 1896	Died Jad. 14 1929			July 25, 1912 To Sgt. Dec. 1, 1910 Promot'd to Pot. Ct. 2 W
t. S.W. July 3" 1896.				Promot'd to Pot. Ct. 2 Ja
t. N.E. July 4" 1896				Honorably discharged
t. S.W. July 4" 1896				Promot'd to Pot. Ct. 2 Ja Hon. discharged Apr. 30, 19
July 4" 1896				Promot'd to Pot. Ct. 2 Ja To Sgt. Mar 14, 1909 Acty. Lt. Dec. 14, 1914

18.1 Introduction

This chapter discusses several miscellaneous groups of records. Documentation of births, marriages, and deaths (except for Native Americans) is relatively scarce among the holdings of the National Archives and Records Administration (NARA); however, some series pertaining to these vital statistics for civilians at army posts and for U.S. citizens abroad do exist and are described here. While Federal tax records do not contain information about family relationships, some tax assessment lists may lead to interesting information about a family's financial circumstances. Similarly, case files relating to pardons, extraditions, and counterfeiters may be of interest.

The chapter also contains descriptions of passport records, records of the government of American Samoa, Historical Records Survey publications, and *The Territorial Papers of the United States*.

18.2 Civilian Records from Army Posts

Births, marriages, and deaths of civilians at U.S. Army posts are recorded on cards dated 1884-1912. These cards consist of abstracts of reports sent by the posts to the Adjutant General's Office and are in Records of the Adjutant General's Office, 1780's-1917, Record Group (RG) 94. Cards recording each type of event are filed separately and arranged alphabetically by surname. Each birth card shows the name and sex of the baby; name, rank, and military organization of the father; maiden name of the mother; number of children by the marriage; and date and place of birth. Each marriage card shows the name and rank or occupation of the husband; name, age, and place of birth of the wife; and date and place of marriage. Each death card shows the name of the civilian who died; name, and where appropriate, rank and military organization of the husband or nearest relative; sex and age of the civilian who died; and date, place, and cause of death.

Other records supplement the carded files and provide information for earlier and later periods. RG 94 also includes hospital registers, monthly reports of sick and wounded, and medical histories of posts, where information about births and deaths may be recorded. Records containing this type of information are less frequently found in Records of U.S. Army Continental Commands, 1821-1920, RG 393. Birth and death certificates can also be found in some of the later army post records in Records of U.S. Army Continental Commands, 1920-1942, RG 394. Most of the records are arranged chronologically; there are no name indexes. Registers of burials at army posts are found in Records of the Office of the Quartermaster General, RG 92, and are described in 9.2.

In Records of the Office of the Chief of Chaplains, RG 247, are 29 volumes of chapel registers, 1902-23 and 1939-51. These are arranged alphabetically by name of military installation, thereunder by type of service (baptism, marriage, funeral). Each volume contains a name index.

From the late 19th century to 1917, chaplains' reports document baptisms, marriages, and funerals performed. The reports, however, do not form a separate series but instead are interspersed in the letters received and general correspondence of the Adjutant General's Office in RG 94. The correspondence is indexed by name and is further described in 4.2.

18.3 Records of Americans Abroad

One of the responsibilities of American consuls abroad is to keep records of registrations, births, deaths, and marriages of U.S. citizens residing or traveling in foreign countries. The most extensive are **death notices**, made in accordance with an act of 1792 (1 Stat. 255). *See* section 18.5.1 below for a discussion of **birth**, **registration**, and **marriage records**.

Many of the reports, especially death notices, are found in despatches from U.S. consular, and sometimes diplomatic, officials abroad, which are in General Records of the Department of State, RG 59. They are interfiled with reports on many other subjects in chronological series of despatches arranged by country or city from the 1790s to 1906. From 1906 to 1910, the records are randomly filed in the numerical file, but there is a name index. From 1910 to 1962, they are in the decimal file, arranged by time period, thereunder by country, and thereunder alphabetically by surname. For the period from 1963 to 1974, the reports are arranged by year, thereunder alphabetically. To use these records, the researcher usually must know the place and approximate date of death of the subject of research. Diplomatic and consular despatches dated through 1906 are available on a variety of microfilm publications, which are listed in *Microfilm Resources for Research: A Comprehensive Catalog* (Washington: National Archives and Records Administration, rev. 2000). For costs and more information about purchasing this volume or the microfilm publications it describes, call 1-800-234-8861, or fax 1-301-713-6169.

Another useful series in RG 59 is a set of bound volumes for the period 1857-1922 containing copies of death notices sent by the Department of State to newspaper publishers, informing them of the deaths of U.S. citizens in foreign countries and requesting that the notices be published. These volumes pertain only to deaths and are not available on microfilm, but most of the volumes are indexed so that researchers can use them if they know the date of death of the subject of research.

Copies of reports of births, deaths, marriages, and registrations of U.S. citizens temporarily residing in a foreign country, especially in the period before 1912, are sometimes found among the records of U.S. consular and diplomatic posts abroad in Records of the Foreign Service Posts of the Department of State, RG 84. The completeness of these records varies from post to post. The names of posts and dates of the records are given in *List of Foreign*

Service Post Records in the National Archives, Special List 9, Revised Edition, compiled by Mark G. Eckhoff and Alexander P. Marvo (Washington: National Archives and Records Service, 1967). To use these records, the researcher must know the place and date of the registration or death of the subject of research. For the period after 1912, foreign service post copies of these types of documents were usually filed in segments of the subject filing system that were destroyed.

18.4 Other Vital Statistics

NARA's Pacific Region in Laguna Niguel, CA, has one roll of microfilm containing baptismal records of Los Angeles County, 1771-1873, and the Thomas Workman Temple collection of records from the San Gabriel Mission and the Plaza Church, 1945. Those records came from the California State Society, Daughters of the American Revolution.

NARA's Pacific Alaska Region in Anchorage, AK, has among its holdings records of the Pribilof Islands program, 1872-1970. Part of the Records of the U.S. Fish and Wildlife Service, RG 22, they include censuses of the islanders; lists of Native earnings; school records; records relating to individuals relocated during World War II; records on fisheries agents, teachers, and other staff sent by the Government to the islands; and extensive personal data in logbooks.

Birth, marriage, and death records of Native Americans are described in Chapter 11. Marriage certificates among records of the Freedmen's Bureau are discussed in 12.4. Records of deaths and burials of soldiers and about residents of veterans homes are described in Chapter 9; information about marriages and deaths of veterans may appear in pension files, described in Chapter 7.

18.5 Passport and Visa Records

18.5.1 Passport Records

A passport is an official document issued by the government of a country to one of its citizens authorizing that person to travel to a foreign country. Except for a short time during the Civil War, a passport was not required of a U.S. citizen traveling abroad until World War I. Although they were not mandatory until 1917, passports were frequently obtained because of the added overseas protection they might afford. NARA has passport records, 1791-1959, including passport applications, 1795-1925. The records are mostly in RG 59, with some related records in RG 84.

Passport applications vary in content, information being ordinarily less detailed before the Civil War than afterward. For the period 1791-1905, they usually contain name of applicant, signature, place of residence, age, and personal description; names or number of persons in the family intending to travel; and date of travel. Applications sometimes contain date and place of birth of the appli-

cant; spouse and minor children, if any, accompanying the applicant; and, if the applicant was a naturalized citizen, the date and port of arrival in the United States, name of vessel on which the applicant arrived, and, where appropriate, the date and court of naturalization.

For the period 1906-25, the records usually contain name of applicant, signature, and date and place of birth; name, date, and place of birth of spouse or minor children, if any; residence and occupation at time of application; immediate travel plans; physical description; and photograph. The applications are sometimes accompanied by transmittal letters and letters from employers, relatives, and others attesting to the applicant's purpose for travel abroad.

The main body of passport applications is arranged chronologically, and for the period 1830-1925 is in bound volumes. Occasionally the indexes contain helpful genealogical information, as can be seen from the illustrated examples. The passport applications are available on M1372, *Passport Applications, 1795-1905,* 694 rolls; M1490, *Passport Applications, January 2, 1906-March 31, 1923,* 2,740 rolls; and M1834, *Emergency Passport Applications (Passports Issued Abroad), 1877-1907,* 56 rolls. Indexes to the passport applications are on M1371, *Registers and Indexes for Passport Applications, 1810-1906,* 13 rolls, and M1848, *Index to Passport Applications, 1850-52, 1860-80, 1881, 1906-23,* 61 rolls.

Emergency passport applications, 1877-1925, and miscellaneous emergency passport applications, 1907-25, are also in bound volumes. These applications for passports or renewals of passports were made at U.S. Foreign Service posts abroad. For the period 1877-1905, they are arranged by name of post or country, thereunder chronologically. An index for the period 1874-1905 is available. Emergency passport applications, 1906-25, and miscellaneous emergency passport applications, 1907-25, are arranged by name of country or post, thereunder in rough chronological order. An index for emergency passport applications, 1906-18, contains entries citing the name of the country or the Foreign Service post along with the other pertinent information. An index to passport extensions, 1917-20, is also available.

For the period 1829-97, there are separate **applications for U.S. Foreign Service officers, military attaches, secretaries of legations, and other Government officers.** Some of these applications are indexed. For the period 1906-25, there are separate applications for U.S. Foreign Service personnel, military personnel, civilian government employees, residents of U.S. territorial possessions, aliens who had applied for citizenship, persons who intended to visit China, and wives of members of the American Expeditionary Forces, as well as for those who applied at U.S. passport offices located outside the Washington, DC, area. Some of these applications are covered by the indexes for the main series.

Other series include registers for passport applications,

1810-17 and 1834-1906; letters requesting passports, 1791-1910; letters concerning issued passports, 1874-80; originals and copies of passports, 1794-1901; records of the New York Passport Office, 1861-62; and records of the Boston Passport Office, 1860-62. Relevant information in the **decimal files of the Department of State** includes passport correspondence (Cutter file, decimal 130), 1910-25, and decimal file (classes 131-138), 1910-49. Decimal 131 contains registrations of children born to American parents abroad, 1910-49, and decimal 133 covers certificates of the marriage of American citizens abroad, 1922-38. The decimal file entries are indexed in the card index to the decimal file.

In addition, the National Archives has passport records that were maintained by diplomatic and consul posts abroad. Those records before 1874 were not always duplicated in the Department's own files. For the most part, these passport records are scattered and contain relatively little information.

18.5.2 Visa Records

A visa is a permit allowing the bearer entry into or transit through the country granting the permit. Before World War I aliens did not need visaed passports to enter the United States, except for a brief time during the Civil War. In 1917 all aliens were required to obtain visas from U.S. consular officers abroad before entering this country. After passage of the Immigration Act of 1924, consular officials were responsible for denying visas to applicants inadmissible under the quota system. These records are mostly in RG 59, with some related records in RG 84.

Visa records, like passport records, have traditionally been maintained apart from the main body of the decimal file of the Department of State. They include decimals 150, 151, and 800-811. These records do not generally include applications for entry into the United States.

The **visa case files** (decimal 811.111 name files), 1914-40, includes correspondence of the Department of State with applicants for visas, their relatives and attorneys, Members of Congress, Foreign Service officers, and organizations and firms regarding the granting of visas to enter the United States. These name files document only those special instances where a visa policy, rule, or regulation is in question; they are representative of only a very small percentage of those applicants entering the country with a visa.

Visa case files are arranged in three chronological groupings, 1914-23, 1924-32, and 1933-40, thereunder alphabetically by name of alien. Most of the case files for 1914-23 and some of the ones for 1924-32 have been disposed of, except for precedent cases and for case files that contain policy material or relate to significant individuals.

Other series include correspondence regarding immigration (decimals 150-151), 1910-49; general visa correspondence (decimals 800-811), 1919-49; and procedural correspondence, 1814-31.

Name files and correspondence files are indexed in the card index to the decimal file. The card index to the decimal file also contains entries to 811.111 name files for the period after March 1940, which files were disposed of by the Department of State.

In addition, NARA holds visa records that were maintained by the diplomatic and consular posts abroad, especially in the period leading up to World War II. These records are not always duplicated in the Department's own files.

18.6 Tax Records

18.6.1 Direct Tax Lists for Pennsylvania

NARA has only a small part of the records created under the first Federal direct tax, a 1798 levy on real property and slaves. Records in the National Archives pertain only to Pennsylvania; they are in Records of the Internal Revenue Service, RG 58, and have been filmed as M372, *United States Direct Tax of 1798: Tax List for the State of Pennsylvania*, 24 rolls.

The records consist mainly of assessment and collection lists, with a few other kinds of lists that were made from them to comply with various aspects of these laws and subsequent ones. The lists are in more than 700 volumes arranged in a complicated geographical scheme by division, district, county, and township, thereunder by type of list. On roll 1 of M372, however, is an alphabetical list of place names that appear in the records and the number of the roll on which the information is filmed. To use the lists, the researcher must know where in Pennsylvania the subject of research lived as of October 1, 1798.

The lists most useful for genealogical research are Particular Lists A, B, and C. Particular List A relates to dwellings (with outbuildings) of more than $100 in value on lots not exceeding two acres. It shows, for most dwellings, the name of the occupant, name of owner, location and dimensions of the dwelling and outbuildings, building materials used, number of stories and windows, and value.

Particular List B relates to land, lots, wharves, and buildings, except for those described in A. Particular List B generally shows, for each occupant of such land, lot, wharf, or building, the name of occupant, name of owner, number and dimensions of dwelling and outbuildings, number and description of all other buildings and wharves, location and name of adjoining proprietors, acreage, and value.

Particular List C usually shows the name of the superintendent or owner of slaves, total number owned, number exempt from the tax, and number subject to the tax. Very few slave lists are in the Pennsylvania records.

Some records, of varying amounts and arrangements, of the 1798 tax in other states are in the custody of the following depositories: Connecticut Historical Society, Historical Society of Delaware, Maryland Historical Society (Maryland and District of Columbia), New England

Assd. May 20, 1872

Cincinnati, Ohio, *May 16th* 187*2*

To The Department of State,
UNITED STATES OF AMERICA.

The undersigned respectfully asks for a U. S. Passport.

Geo. Eger.

UNITED STATES OF AMERICA,
The State of Ohio,
HAMILTON COUNTY. } S. S.

I, *George Eger* do swear, that I was born in the *Kingdom* of *Wuerttemberg (Germany)* on or about the *27th* day of *August* A. D. 18*36*, that I am a Naturalized and Loyal Citizen of the United States, and about to travel abroad, *and further that I am the identical person described in the certificate of naturalization herewith presented.*

Sworn to before me this *16th* day of *May* 187*2* *Geo Eger*

Wendell Joachim,
Notary Public.

I, *William Dupuis* do swear, that I am acquainted with the above named *George Eger* and with the facts above stated by him, and that the same are true, to the best of my knowledge and belief.

William Dupuis

Sworn to before me, this *16th* day of *May* 187*2*

Wendell Joachim,
Notary Public.

Description of *George Eger.*

Age, *35 1/2 yrs.*
Stature, *5 ft. 9 1/2 in.* Engl.
Forehead, *rather high,*
Eyes, *hazel*
Nose, *well proportioned*
Mouth, *medium*
Chin *oval*
Hair, *dark brown*
Complexion, *fair and healthy*
Face, *oval.*

UNITED STATES OF AMERICA,
The State of Ohio,
HAMILTON COUNTY, } S. S.

I, *George Eger* of the County of *Hamilton* and State of *Ohio* do solemnly *swear* that I will support, protect and defend the Constitution and Government of the United States against all enemies, whether Domestic or Foreign, and that I will bear true Faith, Allegiance and Loyalty to the same, any Ordinance, Resolution or Law of any State, Convention, or Legislature to the contrary notwithstanding, and further, that I do this with a full determination, pledge, and purpose, without any mental reservation or evasion whatsoever, and further, that I will well and faithfully perform all the duties which may be required of me by law: So help me God!

Geo Eger

Sworn to and subscribed before me, this *16th* day of *May* 187*2.*

Wendell Joachim,
Notary Public.

Post Office Direction:
Mohawk Drug-store, 839 & 841 Central Avenue,

Eger, George

Place of birth: Würtemberg, Germany
Date of birth: Aug. 27, 1836

Place of naturalization: Court Common Pleas, Hamilton Co., Ohio
Date of naturalization: Mar. 30, 1864

No.: 20973   Date: May 20, 1872   Vol.: 395

THE NATIONAL ARCHIVES
Form I-3

DIVISION OF CATALOGING
GPO   16—7094

Passport application with the index card to it. Records of the Passport Division. General Records of the Department of State, RG 59.

Historic Genealogical Society (Maine, Massachusetts, and New Hampshire), Rhode Island Historical Society, Tennessee State Library and Archives, and Vermont Historical Society.

18.6.2 Tax Assessment Lists

The Office of the Fifth Auditor had responsibility for land taxes assessed by the Federal Government in southern states during the Civil War. An act of August 5, 1861 (12 Stat. 292), apportioned an annual direct tax of $20 million among all the states and territories and the District of Columbia. Only one such annual payment, however, was required because later acts suspended further collections. While most states assumed the obligation to pay the tax, the states of the Confederacy, plus Delaware and the Territory of Colorado, did not. The task of collecting the taxes in the states that refused to assume the obligation was assigned to the Office of Internal Revenue. Every parcel of land was valued and taxed in proportion to the amount of tax to be paid by each state. These records are available in Records of the Accounting Officers of the Department of the Treasury, RG 217. Only the list for Tennessee has been microfilmed and is available as T227, *Civil War Direct Tax Assessment Lists: Tennessee*, 6 rolls.

Extensive and detailed tax lists were made under the supervision of district assessors appointed in each state or territory under the provisions of an act of 1862 (12 Stat. 432). The law provided for specific monthly and annual taxes to be assessed on goods and services at the level of production and distribution, including taxes on licenses, income, and personal property. An act of 1872 (17 Stat. 401) abolished the offices of assessors as of July 1, 1873, and greatly reduced the number of taxes to be collected. Lists in the National Archives Building in Washington, DC, are dated 1862-73. Those in NARA's regional archives facilities include some records, dated as late as 1917, which were created under other tax laws (*see below*). Other lists, 1874-1910, were compiled by district collectors for taxes on alcohol and tobacco products. All of these lists are in RG 58.

Assistant assessors of divisions prepared the lists in alphabetical order on large sheets. Pages for each division within an assessment district were later bound into yearly books by the district assessor. The amount of territory assigned to each division varied, depending on the population, from part of a city or county to several counties in a state. A majority of the lists are monthly returns of specific or ad valorem taxes on products owned by individual manufacturing companies or vendors. The next largest category of tax lists are annual returns of income of more than $600, personal property, and license fees. Lists are not included for every division for every month, nor are there lists of annual taxes in a district or state for every year.

Alphabetical lists for each division show the names of persons, partnerships, firms, associations, or corporations; post office addresses; amounts of annual income, value of articles subject to the special tax or duty, or quantities of goods made or sold that were charged with a specific or ad valorem tax or duty; and amounts of duty or tax due.

Some assessment lists for the Civil War period, 1862-66, are available on microfilm. (The 1866 records are included because the annual taxes were collected for 1865.) To use the records, the researcher must search the lists for the place where the subject of research lived or owned property subject to the tax. Table 24 lists the dates and microfilm publication numbers for each state. The descriptive pamphlet for each microfilm publication shows the counties assigned to each assessment district or division.

NARA's Rocky Mountain Region in Denver, CO, has original monthly assessment lists for Colorado, 1873-1917; New Mexico, 1885-1917; and Wyoming, 1874-79.

NARA's Central Plains Region in Kansas City, MO, has original monthly assessment lists for Iowa, 1873-1917; Minnesota, 1866-1917; Nebraska, 1906-17; South Dakota, 1915-17; Kansas, 1909-17 (including entries for Oklahoma, 1909-13); Missouri, 1910-17; and North Dakota, 1915-17.

NARA's Great Lakes Region in Chicago, IL, also has assessment lists. The majority of the volumes contain corporation tax lists, but some lists for individuals, giving names, addresses, and amounts paid, are included. The records relate to Springfield, IL, 1908-17; Detroit, MI, 1870-1917; Columbus, OH, 1906-17; and Milwaukee, WI, 1876-1917.

NARA's Pacific Region in San Francisco, CA, holds individual tax assessments, 1914-17; corporation taxes (individuals, firms, and corporations), 1909-17; corporation joint stock companies and associations, 1911-12 and 1915-17; and U.S. and foreign corporation taxes, 1917.

NARA's Pacific Region in Laguna Niguel, CA, has assessment lists for individuals, 1914-17. These alphabetical listings show the amount owed, at that time 1 percent of an individual's gross income. The volumes originated in the 6th District of California (Los Angeles).

NARA's Southeast Region in Atlanta, GA, has original monthly assessment lists for Alabama, 1867-74; Florida, 1867-74 and 1917-18; Georgia, 1867-74 and 1917-18; Kentucky, 1865-74; Mississippi, 1867-74; North Carolina, 1867-73 and 1914-19; South Carolina, 1866-75 and 1915-18; and Tennessee, 1867-73 and 1916-18.

18.7 Pardon and Parole Records

Early pardon records are in RG 59. **Petitions for pardon**, 1789-1860, request pardons for persons convicted of Federal crimes. The records are arranged by Presidential administration, thereunder numerically if the pardon was granted and alphabetically if the pardon was not granted. The cover sheet for each case shows the case number, name of criminal, and location in the series of pardons and remissions where a copy of the pardon is bound.

Copies of **pardons and remissions**, 1793-1893, are arranged chronologically in 16 volumes; each volume is indexed. A **register of pardons**, 1793-1871, is arranged by Presidential administration, and thereunder by pardon number. The part covering the period 1844-71 also contains an alphabetical list. An entry shows name, case number, place where the case arose, nature of the crime, President who issued the pardon, and location of the pardon in the series of pardons and remissions. Name **indexes to pardons and remissions** are in one volume (incomplete) for 1847-48 and one volume for 1847-71. To use these records, the researcher must know the approximate date of the pardon. The case file number can be found in the register and used to locate the petition for pardon.

Other records relating to Federal prisoners who appealed to the President for pardon are in Records of the Office of the Pardon Attorney, RG 204.

Case files, 1853-1946, consist of applications, correspondence, and reports on the case or prisoner. The files are arranged by case number, which is made up of a number or a letter and the number of the page of the docket volume where the case is entered.

The **docket of pardon cases**, 1853-1958, records in 81 volumes the formal steps in the history of each case, from the time the petition was filed until final action was taken. Information shown for each case includes name of prisoner, judicial district where convicted, nature of the crime, sentence and date, place of incarceration, and action by the President and date. Each volume contains an alphabetical index.

Entries in an **index for pardon cases**, 1853-89, are arranged alphabetically by applicant for the case files and docket volumes. Shown is name, judicial district, case number, and action taken.

Pardon warrants, 1893-1936, are copies of warrants for pardons that were granted by the President. Warrants before 1929 show case numbers. They are arranged by date of pardon in 29 volumes. Each volume includes an index to persons pardoned.

Also in RG 204 are records of pardons denied; files on pardons of political prisoners of World War I, ca. 1918-33; correspondence about pardon matters; applications for executive clemency, 1945-55; letters of advice, 1956-65; and the Pardon Attorney cases for Robert Stroud (Birdman of Alcatraz), 1915-63, and Julius and Ethel Rosenberg, 1952-53. See *Records of the Office of the Pardon Attorney,* PI 87, compiled by Gaiselle Kerner (Washington: National Archives and Records Service, 1955).

Many of the records discussed above are covered by entries in the **card index to executive clemency case files**, 1943-77, which is arranged alphabetically by name of applicant who applied for and/or received executive clemency under various Presidential pardon proclamations. Each card gives the name of applicant, case file number, state from which the application for executive clemency was filed, a brief description of the offense committed, and the final decision rendered.

TABLE 24
Microfilmed Internal Revenue Assessment Lists for the Civil War Period

STATE OR TERRITORY	DATE	MICROFILM PUBLICATION	NUMBER OF ROLLS
Alabama	1865-66	M754	6
Arkansas	1865-66	M755	2
	1867-74	T1208	4
California	1862-66	M756	33
Colorado	1862-66	M757	3
Connecticut	1862-66	M758	23
Delaware	1862-66	M759	8
District of Columbia	1862-66	M760	8
Florida	1865-66	M761	1
Georgia	1865-66	M762	8
Idaho	1865-66	M763	1
	1867-74	T1209	1
Illinois	1862-66	M764	63
Indiana	1862-66	M765	42
Iowa	1862-66	M766	16
Kansas	1862-66	M767	3
Kentucky	1862-66	M768	24
Louisiana	1863-66	M769	10
Maine	1862-66	M770	15
Maryland	1862-66	M771	21
Michigan	1862-66	M773	15
Minnesota	1862-66	M774	3
Mississippi	1865-66	M775	3
Missouri	1862-65	M776	22
Montana	1864-72	M777	1
Nevada	1863-66	M779	2
New Hampshire	1862-66	M780	10
New Mexico	1862-70	M782	1
	1872-74		
New York and New Jersey	1862-66	M603	218
North Carolina	1864-66	M784	2
Oregon District	1867-73	M1631	2
Pennsylvania	1862-66	M787	107
Rhode Island	1862-66	M788	10
South Carolina	1864-66	M789	2
Texas	1865-66	M791	2
Vermont	1862-66	M792	7
Virginia	1862-66	M793	6
West Virginia	1862-66	M795	4

18.8 Extradition Records

The main series of extradition records is in RG 59 and consists of chronologically arranged case files, 1836-1906. Later case files are part of the central numerical, decimal, and subject-numeric files of the Department of State. Case files include U.S. applications to foreign governments for extradition of fugitives from U.S. justice, applications of foreign governments to the United States for extradition of fugitives from justice in those countries, and related court papers. Extradition case files include the name of the person to be extradited, the country involved, and the nature, place, and date of the crime for which the person sought is accused. Cases before 1877 contain references to related correspondence in other State Department records. The index to Presidential pardons for the years 1843-68 also shows cases involving extradition.

18.9 U.S. Secret Service Records

Records relating to criminals and suspects in Records of the U.S. Secret Service, RG 87, are dated 1863-1971. These are mainly case files for persons arrested for counterfeiting U.S. currency and registers of persons suspected of this crime. Information in the case files includes, when applicable, time, place, and reason for arrest; date of trial; sentence; and the physical appearance and personal history of the accused person. Photographs of the accused are usually included. The records are arranged in rough chronological order, but some volumes contain indexes.

18.10 Other Records

The second Bank of the United States, chartered in 1816, was the subject of a congressional investigation in 1818. Among the records of the U.S. House of Representatives, RG 233, is a bound volume containing the *Report of the Committee to Inspect the Bank of the United States,* which has alphabetical lists of approximately 6,400 **stockholders of the Bank of the United States** at the time of the first dividend in July 1818. The statement shows the number of shares owned by, and the place of residence of, each stockholder. Also included is a list of attorneys and their places of residence. The report was published by Congress in 1819 as 15th Congress, 2nd sess., H. Doc. 92, serial 21.

The following three groups of **records about American Samoa** may be useful to genealogical researchers in this specialized area. They are located at NARA's Pacific Region (San Francisco) and are part of the Records of the Government of American Samoa, RG 284.

Records of the High Court include **census returns** for 1900, 1903, 1908-9, 1912, 1916, 1920, 1922-1923, 1926, and 1945. These contain population figures for villages, lists of village residents, numbers of foreign residents, and births and deaths. They are arranged chronologically. Also available are **alien registration forms**, 1940-44, arranged by

serial number, and preliminary forms for **petitions of naturalization**, 1946.

Coded administrative files in the records of the Governor's office contain several files related to **Matai names**. Correspondence, 1920-40, is arranged alphabetically by Matai name and concerns Matai name claims and case decisions by the High Court. The Matai name registrations, 1935-57, are arranged in rough chronological order. These registration documents, which give name of the registrant, Matai title assigned, and village of residence, include petitions signed by family members over 14 years old and applications to the high or talking chief. The Matai name resignations, 1936-55, give the name of the resignee, title resigned, date of petition, and sometimes the recommendation of the resignee or High Court for the new titleholder. The Matai name removals, 1925-55, are arranged chronologically and give the name of the titleholder, title, and reason for removal given by the High Court. The Matai name lists, 1940-50, give the name of the titleholder, name of title held, and the district.

Records of the Attorney General's Office include **immigration and emigration records**, 1937-65. This series contains letters of identity, affidavits of birth and identity in support of those letters, passenger lists, and correspondence regarding visas and travel permits. The records are arranged chronologically. Also in the series is a bound register of letters of identity, 1955-57, and a bound record of arrivals in American Samoa, 1955-61.

An imaginative and potentially useful program under the Work Projects Administration (WPA) of the New Deal was the **Historical Records Survey**. Affording employment for many professionals in the social sciences and humanities and for clerical workers left idle by the Depression, its goal was to locate and describe records at the county level across the United States. It also did some work in church and municipal records. The onset of World War II, solving the unemployment problem by siphoning individuals off into defense work and the armed forces, meant that few of the projects were completed, and much of what was accomplished has since been lost or destroyed by local government officials with little appreciation of the usefulness of the inventories.

NARA has record copies of most of the printed publications of the Historical Records Survey, including some of genealogical interest, 1936-43. These records are in Records of the Work Projects Administration, RG 69. The National Archives does not have the microfilm publications or the unpublished project material of the Historical Records Survey.

Publications of the Historical Records Survey are listed in the Work Projects Administration *Bibliography Research Projects Reports, Check List of Historical Records Survey Publications*, Technical Series, Research and Records Bibliography 7 (Washington: Work Projects Administration, 1943; reprinted by the Genealogical Publishing Co., Baltimore, 1969). Names and addresses of the state depositories for the unpublished project material appear in an appendix to this bibliography. *The WPA Historical Records Survey: A Guide to the Unpublished Inventories, Indexes, and Transcripts,* compiled by Loretta Hefner (Chicago: Society of American Archivists, 1990), contains lists of the specific holdings of Survey materials in each repository where they have been located.

Other Historical Records Survey materials in the National Archives include mimeographed copies of inventories of many county archives in the United States. These inventories give a description, with total volume and terminal dates, of records such as wills, land records, birth and death certificates, marriage licenses, and naturalization records located in courthouses and other depositories within the county. Contents vary depending on the subject. The proportion of counties in a state for which inventories were completed varies from complete coverage for the counties of North Carolina to no inventories for any of the counties of Connecticut, Maine, or Rhode Island.

Also available are copies of inventories of Federal archives in the states; copies of inventories of state, municipal, town, and church archives; church directories; guides to vital statistics records; transcripts of records, including those relating to Spanish land grants in Florida; and other inventories and miscellaneous publications.

NARA's Pacific Region (Laguna Niguel) holds one roll of microfilm consisting of an Arizona WPA inventory of Federal archives in Tucson, 1939.

The Territorial Papers of the United States is a multivolume documentary historical publication containing transcribed archival materials selected from many record groups of the National Archives. The objective of the series is to document the administrative history of U.S. territories with texts that are annotated, exact, representative, and particularly significant. In addition to governmental operations, the records relate to genealogy, economic development, Indian affairs, geographical features, and partisan politics.

The volumes are highly selective, representing perhaps 5 percent of the total material about a territory. Microfilm supplements whose purpose is to reproduce substantially all textual and cartographic materials in the National Archives bearing on each territory have been created for some territories. Certain categories are excepted, such as some Indian and military records that are included in other microfilm publications and repetitive accounting and land records. The microfilmed records have not been annotated or indexed. Genealogists may wish to devote special attention to the memorials and petitions reproduced in the microfilm supplements. This form of documentation serves to fix the residence of many territorial settlers at the given date of the record, provides an image of their signatures, and gives the settlers' opinions on varied subjects. The microfilmed records are arranged first by governmental branch (legislative, executive, or judicial), thereunder by department and agency. This hierarchical arrangement brings together for the researcher, logically

and conveniently, much of the pertinent documentation for specific areas of territorial life and history.

Volumes in this series have been published for territories northwest of the Ohio River, territories south of the Ohio River, Mississippi, Indiana, New Orleans, Michigan, Louisiana-Missouri, Illinois, Alabama, Arkansas, and Florida. Some of these volumes are no longer available for purchase, but they have been microfilmed as M721, *The Territorial Papers of the United States*, 16 rolls.

In addition, two published volumes for the territory of Wisconsin, with a microfilm supplement, are on M236, *The Territorial Papers of the United States: The Territory of Wisconsin, 1836–1848,* 122 rolls. Other relevant microfilm publications are M325, *The Territorial Papers of the United States: The Territory of Iowa, 1838–1846,* 102 rolls; M1050, *The Territorial Papers of The United States: The Territory of Minnesota, 1849–1858,* 19 rolls; and M1049, *The Territorial Papers of the United States: The Territory of Oregon, 1848–1859,* 12 rolls.

Publication of the series concluded in 1975 with the second of the two Wisconsin volumes. The "Territorial Papers" project continues in modified form with the ongoing publication of *The Trans-Mississippi West, 1804–1912: A Guide to Federal Records for the Territorial Period.* This multivolume guide, instead of providing transcripts of selected documents, identifies and describes significant series of records relating to the contiguous states and territories carved out of the area west of the Mississippi River. To date five volumes of the guide have been published. They cover records of component agencies and offices of the Departments of State, Justice, Agriculture, and the Interior (2 vols.), and include information about many of the records discussed in this volume. To purchase any of these publications, write Fee Publications, National Archives Trust Fund (NWCC2), P.O. Box 100793, Atlanta, GA 30384-0793, or call 1-800-234-8861, or fax 1-301-713-6169.

CHAPTER 19   *Cartographic Records*

19.1   *Introduction*

19.2   *Census Records*

19.3   *General Land Office Records*

19.4   *Military Records*

19.5   *Other Cartographic Records*

Table 25   *Checklist of National Archives Publications Relating to Cartographic Records*

CHAPTER 19
Cartographic Records

19.1 Introduction

Maps and related cartographic records are often useful for genealogical research. They provide important information on place names and localities contemporary with creation of the maps; show changing political boundaries, as for counties and minor civil subdivisions; and sometimes include names of individual land owners or residents. The National Archives and Records Administration (NARA) has custody of almost 2 million maps. Those accessioned through 1966 are described in general terms in the *Guide to Cartographic Records in the National Archives* (Washington: National Archives and Records Service, 1971). A general discussion of their value for genealogists is included in Ralph E. Ehrenberg's "Cartographic Records of the National Archives," *National Genealogical Society Quarterly* 64 (June 1976): 83-111.

The following cartographic series have particular significance to genealogists and may be used in the Cartographic and Architectural Research Room of the National Archives in College Park, MD. Electrostatic and other types of reproductions of these records can be purchased.

19.2 Census Records

Census **enumeration district maps** were prepared by the Bureau of the Census decennially from 1880 to 1970. They consist of approximately 110,000 printed, photocopied, and manuscript maps of cities, counties, lesser political units, and unincorporated areas. Only three maps exist for 1880, but the number of available maps increases with each succeeding census. The maps, arranged alphabetically by name of state, and thereunder by name of county and locality, are in Records of the Bureau of the Census, Record Group (RG) 29. Genealogists using the later 19th- and early 20th-century censuses will find that knowing the enumeration district for a particular town or other political unit will make access to the population schedules easier.

These maps were annotated to show the boundaries and the numbers of enumeration districts. Wards, precincts, incorporated areas, urban unincorporated areas, townships, census supervisors' districts, and congressional districts may also appear on some maps. The content of enumeration district maps varies greatly between states and over time.

Occasionally, enumeration districts are annotated on maps that indicate the names of residents or landowners, primarily in rural areas. Enumeration districts in several Texas counties are added to base maps that show land grants to individuals in Texas during the 1820s and 1830s.

Enumeration district maps for 1880-1940 are listed in *Cartographic Records of the Bureau of the Census,* Preliminary Inventory (PI) 103, compiled by James B. Rhoads and Charlotte M. Ashby (Washington: National Archives and Records Service, 1958).

Enumeration district descriptions, 1850-1950, are also useful. From 1850 to 1870, the Bureau of the Census collected data according to two designated units, the district and the subdivision. The district usually corresponded to a state or part of a state, and the subdivision corresponded to a county or a part thereof. Beginning with 1880, the smallest unit was redesignated as the enumeration district, which corresponded frequently to a minor civil division. Written descriptions of districts and subdivisions, 1850-70, exist in three manuscript volumes. Similar descriptions of enumeration districts, 1880-1950, are found in four manuscript and 489 typescript volumes.

The enumeration district descriptions for 1880 are incomplete, pertaining only to the following states and territories: Dakota (part), Delaware (part), District of Columbia, Florida, Georgia, Idaho, Illinois, Indiana, Iowa, Kansas, Kentucky, Louisiana, Maine, Maryland, Massachusetts, Michigan, Minnesota, Mississippi, Missouri, Nebraska, Nevada, New Hampshire, New Jersey, New Mexico, New York, North Carolina, Rhode Island, South Carolina, Tennessee, Texas, Utah, Vermont, Virginia, Washington, West Virginia, and Wyoming.

These volumes are arranged by census, thereunder generally alphabetically by name of state. Within individual volumes, the descriptions are usually arranged numerically by supervisors' districts, thereunder by enumeration districts, usually conforming to an alphabetical arrangement of counties. To locate a description of a particular enumeration district, the researcher must know at least the name of the county. In these volumes, census enumeration district and subdivision boundaries are described in terms of counties, parts of counties, townships, wards, precincts, blocks, and streets. Also included for some censuses are the names and addresses of enumerators and special instructions to them.

Descriptions are available on microfilm as T1224, *Descriptions of Census Enumeration Districts, 1830-1890 and 1910-1950,* 146 rolls, and T1210, *Census Enumeration District Descriptive Volumes for 1900,* 10 rolls.

Civil division outline maps among the records of the Bureau of the Census are approximately 500 printed and annotated maps of the United States and individual states from 1920 to 1970. They show county or municipality and minor civil division boundaries and names and locations of incorporated places. They are arranged chronologically, thereunder alphabetically by state.

19.3 General Land Office Records

Among the Records of the Bureau of Land Management, RG 49, are several cartographic series of interest to genealogists. These holdings include approximately 20,000 headquarters office **township survey plats** retained by the General Land Office (GLO) in Washington, DC, and more than 22,000 local office plats used by the local land office having jurisdiction over specified townships.

Census enumeration district description, Michigan, 1850. Records of the Bureau of the Census, RG 29. National Archives Microfilm Publication T1224.

CENSUS of 1850. Subdivisions in the   **District of** *Michigan*

No. of Subdivision.	Name of Assistant.	District comprised in the Subdivision.	No. of Square Miles.	Post Office.
26	Cornelius Wickware	East half of the City of Detroit Being Wards Nos. 3, 4, 7 and that part of Ward 2 lying East of Woodward Avenue, containing	3	Detroit
27	Wm. Y. Rumney	West half of the City of Detroit being Wards Nos. 1, 5, 6, 8 and that part of Ward lying West of Woodward Avenue. Containing	4	Detroit
28	Samuel Trusdell	Part. Wayne County, being Townships Springwell, Ecorse, Monguagon, containing	72½	Detroit
29	Daniel Forbes	Part. Wayne County. Being Townships Van Buren, Sumpter, Romulus, & Taylor, containing	144	Flat Rock
30	John L. Near	Part. Wayne County, Being Townships Huron & Brownstown	90	Flat Rock
31	John H. Kaple	Part. Macomb County Being Townships Bruce, Washington, Shelby, Sterling, Warren, and Erin	216	Utica
32	George F. Lewis	Part. Macomb County Being Townships Armada, Ray, Macomb, Clinton, Harrison, Chesterfield, Lenox & Richmond	256	Mt. Clemens
33	True P. Tucker	Part St. Clair County, Being Townships Lynn, Brockway, Birkville, Mats, Riley & Berlin	480	
34	Benjamin Woodworth	Part St. Clair County, Being Townships Columbus, St. Clair, Cass, China, Ira, Cottrellville, & Clay.	245	St Clair
35	John J. Merrill	Part Oakland County Being Townships Holly, Groveland, Brandon, Oxford, Addison, Rose, Springfield, & Independence	288	Clarkston
36	Sherman Stevens	Part Oakland County Being Townships Orion, Oakland, Highland, White Lake, Waterford, Pontiac, Avon, West Bloomfield, East Bloomfield, & Troy.	360.	Pontiac

Among the holdings are manuscript headquarters plats for the states of Illinois, Indiana, Iowa, Kansas, Missouri, and parts of Ohio, including the "Old Seven Ranges." Local office plats are available for Alabama, Illinois, Indiana, Iowa, Kansas, Mississippi, Missouri, Wisconsin, and parts of Ohio, Oklahoma, Oregon, and Washington.

These plats, arranged by state, principal meridian, range, and township, have been consolidated into one series and are available on microfilm as T1234, *Township Plats of Selected States*, 67 rolls.

Headquarters office plats show section numbers and boundaries, physical features, and any cultural features that preceded Federal survey of the township, such as the improvements and fields of the presurvey settlers. Surnames of such settlers, who were few in number, are usually given. Names and addresses of early patentees, such as "Isaac Craig of Pittsburgh," are indicated on some of the plats of the "Old Seven Ranges." Private land claim boundaries and the names of claimants also appear in some areas. Local office plats may show the names of patentees, but more often they merely show land entry symbols and numbers. Typical symbols shown are "E" for entry, "HE" for homestead entry, "AP" for application pending, "P" for patent, "FP" for final proof, "FC" for final certificate, and "SL" for school land.

Private land claim records include manuscript and annotated lithographed plats covering the states and territories of Arizona, California, Colorado, Florida, Illinois, Louisiana, Michigan, Missouri, New Mexico, Ohio, and Wisconsin. Most of these plats were compiled from surveys made by the GLO after the claims were finally confirmed, but there are a significant number of plats for disapproved claims in California. Other maps and plats of private land claims in California, Florida, Illinois, Indiana, Louisiana, Michigan, New Mexico, and Wisconsin are found in the "Old Map File"; some claims are documented on township survey plats. The source and nature of private land claims is explained in 15.4.

Additional records relating to private land claims in California consist of approximately 820 *expedientes*, 1822–46; copies of 785 *expediente* maps or *diseños* made for the California Board of Commissioners, 1852–56; nearly 300 unbound maps relating to claims papers (dockets) of the GLO; and standard published GLO maps of some individual states, 1876–1944. The *expedientes* are case files consisting of petitions for land, reports, concessions, patents, *diseños* (sketch maps), and other papers relating to the land claim. Such records, which are usually in Spanish, document claims based on Spanish or Mexican grants and were used by the California Board of Commissioners to adjudicate claims. The names of claims or claimants are usually shown, either within the boundaries of the claims or in tabular lists coordinated with claim locations. Claim acreage and numbers, buildings, topography, names of surrounding property owners, and other cultural and physical features may also be indicated.

Private land claim records are arranged by state, thereunder by sequences unique to each series. Typewritten and photocopied indexes list private land claims by name of claim and correlate the various records pertaining to specific claims. *List of Cartographic Records of the General Land Office*, Special List (SL) 19, compiled by Laura E. Kelsay (Washington: National Archives and Records Service, 1964), is helpful. Also useful are J.N. Bowman's "Index of the Spanish-Mexican Private Land Grant Records and Cases of California" (typewritten, 1958), available in the research room at the National Archives in College Park, and the *Annual Report of the Commissioner of the General Land Office for the Fiscal Year Ending June 30, 1880* (Washington: General Land Office, 1881): 395–495.

U.S. land district maps consist of manuscript and published maps of states, territories, and individual land districts. Individual land district maps pertain primarily to Ohio, Indiana, and Illinois. A map of the Virginia Military Tract in Ohio is included. Most of the maps were compiled from official sources during the 19th century; they document the changing locations of land districts and land offices. Many are arranged alphabetically by state, with the subsequent arrangement being chronological. Those maps filed among the Records of the U.S. Senate, RG 46, are arranged by Congress and session numbers; they can be searched by date only.

Commonly shown on the state and territory maps are locations of land offices and boundaries of land districts, private land claims, counties, and Federal land reserves. Maps of individual land districts are more detailed; some show townships with the names of landowners in numbered sections or parts thereof. In addition to the name of each patentee, the map of the Virginia Military Tract also indicates an entry number and amount of acreage within the limits of each tract.

Many of the maps relating to land districts are described in SL 19 and in *List of Selected Maps of States and Territories*, SL 29, compiled by Janet T. Hargett (Washington: National Archives and Records Service, 1971).

19.4 Military Records

Manuscript, annotated, and printed maps, plans, and charts were compiled or collected by various military organizations, ca. 1770–1960. Of foremost importance are those among the Records of the Office of the Chief of Engineers, RG 77, the organization responsible for most of the military mapping pertaining to civil works, exploration, military campaigns, and fortifications in the United States during the 18th, 19th, and 20th centuries. Map coverage is most heavily concentrated in, but not limited to, areas of substantial Federal activity. Notable are detailed area and county maps of parts of Arkansas, Georgia, Louisiana, Maryland, Texas, and Virginia during the 1860s; maps of colonies, states, and territories; city plans; and maps of canals and roads. These records are usually

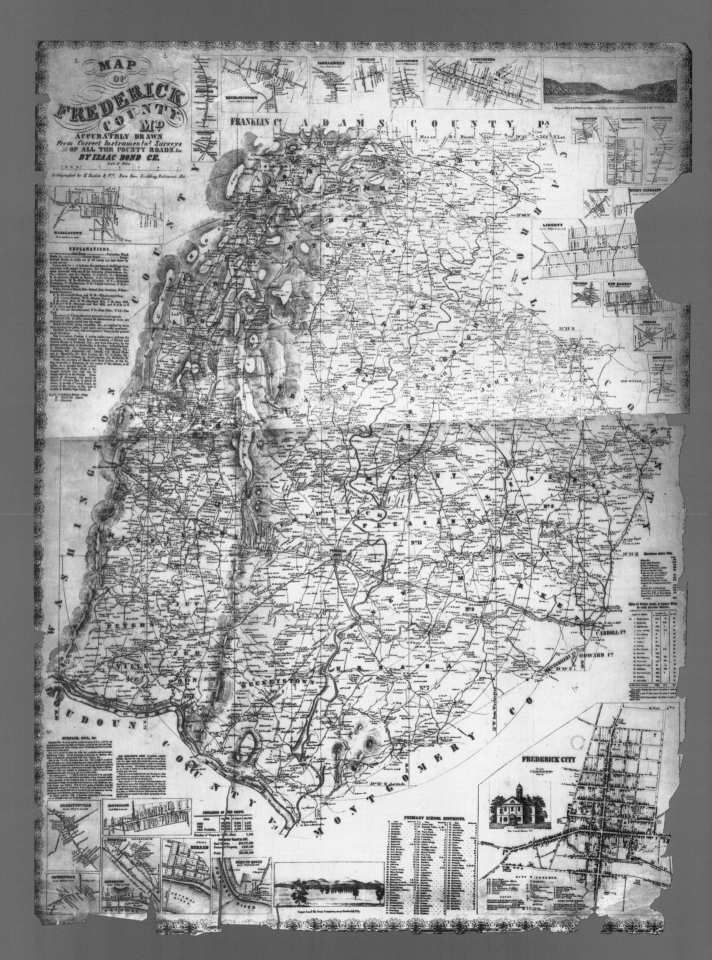

Map of Frederick County Md. Accurately Drawn From Correct Instrumental Surveys Of All The County Roads, &c. By Isaac Bond C.E.

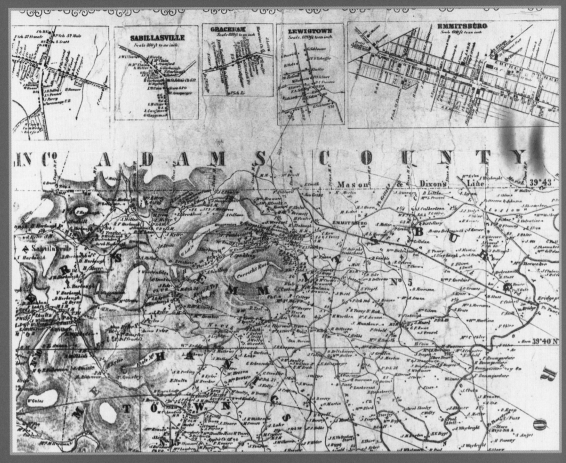

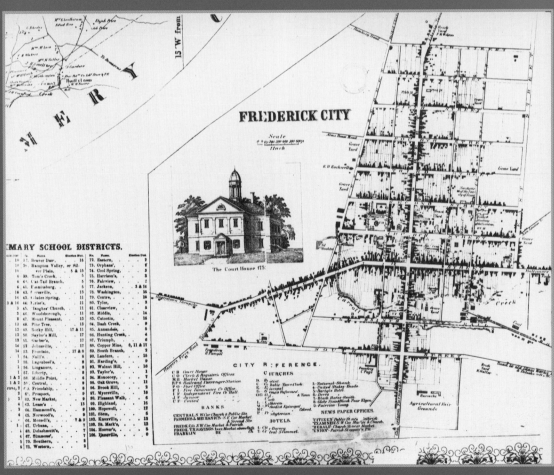

Outline map of the United States, 1840 (right half), showing county outlines. Records of the Office of the Secretary of Agriculture, RG 16.

arranged by state or region (by subject for canals and roads), thereunder primarily chronologically.

These records frequently indicate roads, canals, and waterways that could have been migration routes. They may include the names of residents, boundaries of civil divisions, inns, mills, churches, mountains, and other cultural and physical features.

Card catalogs, registers, and typed lists prepared by the Corps of Engineers and the National Archives staff constitute a comprehensive guide to these records. References and descriptions of many of the records are in the National Archives publications listed in Table 25.

Other records of particular interest to genealogists are those of the Army Graves Registration Service among the Records of the Office of the Quartermaster General, RG 92, and the Records of the American Battle Monuments Commission, RG 117. These maps, plans, diagrams, and tables provide the names and service numbers of some of the U.S. military personnel from both World War I and World War II who are buried overseas. The records are incomplete and unindexed for the purpose of locating individual names, but they do provide the locations of and plans for specific cemeteries. In addition, there are a limited number of similar records covering some Civil War cemeteries in the South for Union dead and a few Confederate soldiers. Only a few names of individuals are provided in these Civil War records.

19.5 Other Cartographic Records

The Department of Agriculture prepared and published **small scale civil division maps** of the United States decennially for the years 1840–1900. Similar maps are also available for 1909, 1915, 1920, 1931, 1935, and 1940. These maps indicate county boundaries and names as they then existed within all states and territories of the continental United States.

During the 1930s, approximately 2,200 civil division maps spanning the period 1789–1932 were prepared in conjunction with a Work Projects Administration (WPA) study known as the *Atlas of Congressional Roll Calls.* Small outline maps of states showing county boundaries and names during the various Congresses compose the bulk of this group of maps. A few maps show municipal ward boundaries and numbers in some major cities. Most of these civil division outline maps are found in two series of state maps designated "preliminary" and "approved," respectively. Many of the maps in the preliminary series are not professionally drawn; some are unfinished and may include inaccurate information. All states are not represented in this series. The approved series is more reliable but does not include maps for the entire period, 1789–1932. The preliminary series is arranged alphabetically by state, thereunder mostly chronologically; the approved series is arranged by Congress number (1st–53rd and 76th–77th). Much of the work of this WPA project

was synthesized and edited by Kenneth C. Martis as *The Historical Atlas of United States Congressional Districts, 1789–1983* (New York: The Free Press, 1982).

Regional and state **postal route maps** in the Records of the Post Office Department, RG 28, are dated 1839–1960. Rural delivery route maps cover the period 1900–37. State and regional postal route maps show county names and boundaries, post offices and delivery routes, and distances and frequency of service between post offices. Names of individuals are sometimes shown on rural delivery maps.

Postal route maps made before 1895 are listed in *Records and Policies of the Post Office Department Relating to Place Names,* Reference Information Paper (RIP) 72, compiled by Arthur Hecht and William J. Heynen (Washington: National Archives and Records Service, 1975), and *Transportation in Nineteenth-Century America: A Survey of the Cartographic Records in the National Archives of the United States,* RIP 65, compiled by Patrick D. McLaughlin (Washington: National Archives and Records Service, 1975). A card catalog lists rural delivery route maps. See also *Records of the Post Office Department,* PI 168, revised edition, compiled by Arthur Hecht et al. (Washington: National Archives and Records Service, 1967).

The Geological Survey records contain manuscript and published **topographical quadrangle maps,** 1888–present. They indicate extensive cultural and physical features, such as county and township names and boundaries, towns, roads, railroads, houses, schools, churches, cemeteries, mountains, valleys, streams, and lakes. Quadrangles are arranged by scale, then by state, and thereunder by name of map sheet. Current and historical graphic indexes are available for the Geological Survey quadrangle maps, and there is a card catalog for the manuscript maps among them. Geological Survey state gazetteers and dictionaries, 1894–1906, are among the textual material in Records of the Government Printing Office, RG 149.

The published **area and county soil maps** are dated from 1900 to about 1945. The information shown on some of them is similar to that found on the quadrangle maps. Certain soil maps surpass the quadrangle maps, however, in providing obscure and obsolete place names. Soil maps are arranged by state, thereunder by area or county, and the county soil maps are listed in a card catalog.

Because property taxes are assessed at local levels, very few **tax assessment maps** have become Federal records. One of the exceptions is a series of manuscript plats of St. Helena Parish, SC, 1865–66. These plats were compiled by the Direct Tax Commission in the District of South Carolina after that area came under Federal control during the Civil War. Tax sale certificate numbers and names of individuals appear on the plats.

Maps relating to captured and abandoned property during the Civil War are in the General Records of the Department of the Treasury, RG 56. Manuscript and printed maps compiled or used by Treasury agents pertain to land in parts of Desha and Chicot Counties, AR; (East) Carroll, Madison, and Tensas Parishes, LA; and Bolivar, Washington, Issaquena, Warren, Claiborne, Jefferson, Adams, and Wilkinson Counties, MS. The names of plantations, their boundaries, acreages, and names of owners are indicated.

Maps pertaining to American Indians include manuscript, annotated, printed, and photocopied maps of states and territories, counties, townships, towns, and Indian reservations, mostly in the western United States, ca. 1800–1944. Most items are arranged numerically by a Bureau of Indian Affairs assigned number. A substantial number of these maps show the names of individuals within the boundaries of the lands granted or allotted to them. Considerable place name information also appears on these maps. A card index provides access to these maps by state, thereunder by tribe or reservation; there is also a subject index and a shelf list. Summary descriptions of these maps appear in the *Cartographic Records of the Bureau of Indian Affairs,* SL 13, compiled by Laura E. Kelsay (Washington: National Archives and Records Service, 1977). Also useful is *Cartographic Records in the National Archives of the United States Relating to American Indians,* RIP 71, compiled by Laura E Kelsay (Washington: National Archives and Records Service, 1974).

The David Dale Owen map of southern Wisconsin was the result of a detailed 1839 geographical and geologic survey of the part of Wisconsin Territory between the Wisconsin River and the Illinois-Wisconsin boundary. The survey was conducted for the U.S. Treasury Department under the personal supervision of David Dale Owen to locate and research mineral lands. This large, detailed map is filed among the Records of the U.S. Senate, RG 46. Mines, mills, furnaces, smelters, and the names of the owners or operators are indicated on the map. Physical features, roads, settlements, and houses with the names of residents also appear. Overall, the names and locations (by township, range, and section numbers) of more than 50 individuals are documented on this map. *See* Herman R. Friis's "The David Dale Owen Map of Southwestern Wisconsin," *Prologue: The Journal of the National Archives* 1, No. 1 (Spring 1969): 9–28. Landowners appearing on this map are listed in Herman R. Friis's and Alison Wilson's "Individuals Identified by David Dale Owen as Living or Working in Southwestern Wisconsin, Autumn 1839," *National Genealogical Society Quarterly* 58 (Dec. 1970): 243–251.

TABLE 25

Checklist of National Archives Publications Relating to Cartographic Records

A Guide to Civil War Maps in the National Archives (1964 and 1987).

Guide to Cartographic Records in the National Archives (1971).

Hargett, Janet T., comp. *List of Selected Maps of States and Territories,* Special List 29 (1971).

Hecht, Arthur, and William J. Heynen, *Records and Policies of the Post Office Department Relating to Place Names,* Reference Information Paper 72 (1975).

Kelsay, Laura E., comp. *Cartographic Records in the National Archives of the United States Relating to American Indians,* Reference Information Paper 71 (1974).

Kelsay, Laura E., comp. *Cartographic Records of the Bureau of Indian Affairs,* Special List 13 (1977).

Kelsay, Laura E., and Frederick W. Pernell, comps. *Cartographic Records Relating to the Territory of Iowa, 1838–1846,* Special List 27 (1971).

Kelsay, Laura E., and Charlotte M. Ashby, comps. *Cartographic Records Relating to the Territory of Wisconsin, 1836–1848,* Special List 23 (1970).

Kelsay, Laura E., comp. *List of Cartographic Records of the General Land Office,* Special List 19 (1964).

McLaughlin, Patrick D., comp. *Pre-Federal Maps in the National Archives: An Annotated List,* Special List 26 (rev. 1975).

McLaughlin, Patrick D., comp. *Transportation in Nineteenth-Century America: A Survey of the Cartographic Records in the National Archives of the United States,* Reference Information Paper 65 (1975).

Rhoads, James B., and Charlotte M. Ashby, comps. *Cartographic Records of the Bureau of the Census,* Preliminary Inventory 103 (1958).

RG 11   General Records of the U.S. Government

RG 15   Records of the Veterans Administration

RG 16   Records of the Office of the Secretary of Agriculture

RG 21   Records of District Courts of the United States

RG 22   Records of the U.S. Fish and Wildlife Service

RG 24   Records of the Bureau of Naval Personnel

RG 26   Records of the U.S. Coast Guard

RG 28   Records of the Post Office Department

RG 29   Records of the Bureau of the Census

RG 32   Records of the U.S. Shipping Board

RG 36   Records of the U.S. Customs Service

RG 39   Records of the Bureau of Accounts (Treasury)

RG 41   Records of the Bureau of Marine Inspection and Navigation

RG 45   Naval Records Collection of the Office of Naval Records and Library

RG 46   Records of the U.S. Senate

RG 48   Records of the Office of the Secretary of the Interior

RG 49   Records of the Bureau of Land Management

RG 52   Records of the Bureau of Medicine and Surgery

RG 53   Records of the Bureau of the Public Debt

RG 56   General Records of the Department of the Treasury

RG 58   Records of the Internal Revenue Service

RG 59   General Records of the Department of State

RG 60   General Records of the Department of Justice

RG 69   Records of the Work Projects Administration

RG 71   Records of the Bureau of Yards and Docks

RG 75   Records of the Bureau of Indian Affairs

RG 76   Records of Boundary and Claims Commissions and Arbitrations

RG 77   Records of the Office of the Chief of Engineers

RG 80   General Records of the Department of the Navy, 1798-1947

RG 84   Records of the Foreign Service Posts of the Department of State

RG 85   Records of the Immigration and Naturalization Service

RG 87   Records of the U.S. Secret Service

RG 90   Records of the Public Health Service, 1912-1968

RG 92   Records of the Office of the Quartermaster General

RG 93   War Department Collection of Revolutionary War Records

RG 94   Records of the Adjutant General's Office, 1780's-1917

RG 98   Records of U.S. Army Commands, 1784-1821

RG 99   Records of the Office of the Paymaster General

RG 101 Records of the Office of the Comptroller of the Currency

RG 105 Records of the Bureau of Refugees, Freedmen, and Abandoned Lands

RG 107 Records of the Office of the Secretary of War

RG 108 Records of the Headquarters of the Army

RG 109 War Department Collection of Confederate Records

RG 110 Records of the Provost Marshal General's Bureau (Civil War)

RG 111 Records of the Office of the Chief Signal Officer

RG 112 Records of the Office of the Surgeon General (Army)

RG 117 Records of the American Battle Monuments Commission

RG 118 Records of United States Attorneys

RG 123 Records of the U.S. Court of Claims

RG 125   Records of the Office of the Judge Advocate General (Navy)

RG 127   Records of the U.S. Marine Corps

RG 146   Records of the U.S. Civil Service Commission

RG 149   Records of the Government Printing Office

RG 153   Records of the Office of the Judge Advocate General (Army)

RG 156   Records of the Office of the Chief of Ordnance

RG 163   Records of the Selective Service System (World War I)

RG 181   Records of Naval Districts and Shore Establishments

RG 204   Records of the Office of the Pardon Attorney

RG 205   Records of the Court of Claims Section (Justice)

RG 210   Records of the War Relocation Authority

RG 217   Records of the Accounting Officers of the Department of the Treasury

RG 231   Records of the Armed Forces Retirement Home

RG 233   Records of the U.S. House of Representatives

RG 247   Records of the Office of the Chief of Chaplains

RG 284   Records of the Government of American Samoa

RG 287   Publications of the U.S. Government

RG 319   Records of the Army Staff

RG 330   Records of the Office of the Secretary of Defense

RG 351   Records of the Government of the District of Columbia

RG 360   Records of the Continental and Confederation Congresses and the Constitutional Convention

RG 365   Treasury Department Collection of Confederate Records

RG 366   Records of Civil War Special Agencies of the Treasury Department

RG 389   Records of the Office of the Provost Marshal General, 1941–

RG 391   Records of U.S. Regular Army Mobile Units, 1821–1942

RG 392   Records of U.S. Army Coast Artillery Districts and Defenses, 1901–1942

RG 393   Records of U.S. Army Continental Commands, 1821–1920

RG 394   Records of U.S. Army Continental Commands, 1920–1942

RG 395   Records of U.S. Army Overseas Operations and Commands, 1898–1942

RG 404   Records of the U.S. Military Academy

RG 405   Records of the U.S. Naval Academy

RG 407   Records of the Adjutant General's Office, 1917–

RG 410   Records of the Office of the Chief of Support Services

RG 527   Records of the U.S. Marshals Service

Microfilm publications listed here without record group designations are copies of records that belong to no record group or are compilations from many. For an explanation of the "A," "M," "P," and "T" categories of National Archives microfilm publications, see I.5 in the introduction to this volume.

A1151   Passenger Lists of Vessels Arriving at Portland, Maine, November 29, 1893–March 1943. RG 85. 35 rolls.

A1154   Nonpopulation Census Schedules for Washington Territory, 1860–1880. RG 29. 8 rolls.

A3361   Register of Citizen (1943–1947) and Alien (1936–1949) Arrivals by Aircraft at San Francisco, California. RG 85. 1 roll.

A3363   Passenger and Crew Lists of Vessels Arriving at Ventura, California, May 1929–December 1956. RG 85. 1 roll.

M19   Fifth Census of the United States, 1830. RG 29. 201 rolls.

M22   Registers of Letters Received by the Office of the Secretary of War, Main Series, 1800–1870. RG 107. 134 rolls.

M30   Despatches from U.S. Ministers to Great Britain, 1791–1906. RG 59. 200 rolls.

M32   Second Census of the United States, 1800. RG 29. 52 rolls.

M33   Fourth Census of the United States, 1820. RG 29. 142 rolls.

M40   Domestic Letters of the Department of State, 1784–1906. RG 59. 171 rolls.

M87   Records of the Commissioners of Claims (Southern Claims Commission), 1871–1880. RG 56. 14 rolls.

M89   Letters Received by the Secretary of the Navy from Commanding Officers of Squadrons ("Squadron Letters"), 1841–1886. RG 45. 300 rolls.

M121   Despatches from U.S. Ministers to Brazil, 1809–1906. RG 59. 74 rolls.

M145   Abstracts of Oregon Donation Land Claims, 1852–1903. RG 49. 6 rolls.

M158   Schedules of the Colorado State Census of 1885. RG 29. 8 rolls.

M160   Records of the Office of the Secretary of the Interior Relating to the Suppression of the African Slave Trade and Negro Colonization, 1854–1872. RG 48. 10 rolls.

M169   Despatches from U.S. Consuls in Monrovia, Liberia, 1852–1906. RG 59. 7 rolls.

M170   Despatches from U.S. Ministers to Liberia, 1863–1906. RG 59. 14 rolls.

M179   Miscellaneous Letters of the Department of State, 1789–1906. RG 59. 1,310 rolls.

M198   Records Relating to the Appointment of Federal Judges, Attorneys, and Marshals for the Territory and State of Washington, 1853–1902. RG 60. 17 rolls.

M203   Abstracts of Washington Donation Land Claims, 1855–1902. RG 49. 1 roll.

M205   Correspondence of the Secretary of the Navy Relating to African Colonization, 1819–1844. RG 45. 2 rolls.

M206   Letter Books of Commodore Matthew C. Perry, 1843–1845. RG 45. 1 roll.

M208   Records of the Cherokee Indian Agency in Tennessee, 1801–1835. RG 75. 14 rolls.

M221   Letters Received by the Secretary of War, Registered Series, 1801–1870. RG 107. 317 rolls.

M222   Letters Received by the Secretary of War, Unregistered Series. RG 107. 3 rolls.

M224   Records Relating to the Appointment of Federal Judges, Attorneys, and Marshals for the Territory and State of Oregon, 1853–1903. RG 60. 3 rolls.

M225   Index to Compiled Service Records of Confederate Soldiers Who Served in Organizations from the State of Florida. RG 109. 9 rolls.

M226   Index to Compiled Service Records of Confederate Soldiers Who Served in Organizations from the State of Georgia. RG 109. 67 rolls.

M227   Index to Compiled Service Records of Confederate Soldiers Who Served in Organizations from the State of Texas. RG 109. 41 rolls.

M229   Index to Compiled Service Records of Volunteer Soldiers Who Served During the War of 1812 in Organizations from the State of Louisiana. RG 94. 3 rolls.

M230   Index to Compiled Service Records of Confederate Soldiers Who Served in Organizations from the State of North Carolina. RG 109. 43 rolls.

M231   Index to Compiled Service Records of Confederate Soldiers Who Served in Organizations from the State of Tennessee. RG 109. 48 rolls.

M232   Index to Compiled Service Records of Confederate Soldiers Who Served in Organizations from the State of Mississippi. RG 109. 45 rolls.

M233   Registers of Enlistments in the U.S. Army, 1798-1914. RG 94. 81 rolls.

M234   Letters Received by the Office of Indian Affairs, 1824-1880. RG 75. 962 rolls.

M236   The Territorial Papers of the United States: The Territory of Wisconsin, 1836-48. 122 rolls.

M237   Passenger Lists of Vessels Arriving at New York, New York, 1820-1897. RG 36. 675 rolls.

M239   Index to Compiled Service Records of Volunteer Soldiers Who Served During the Florida War in Organizations from the State of Louisiana. RG 94. 1 roll.

M240   Index to Compiled Service Records of Volunteer Soldiers Who Served During the War with Spain in Organizations from the State of Louisiana. RG 94. 1 roll.

M241   Index to Compiled Service Records of Volunteer Soldiers Who Served During the War of 1837-1838 in Organizations from the State of Louisiana. RG 94. 1 roll.

M242   Index to Compiled Service Records of Volunteer Union Soldiers Who Served in Organizations from the State of New Mexico. RG 94. 4 rolls.

M243   Index to Compiled Service Records of Volunteer Soldiers Who Served During the Cherokee Removal in Organizations from the State of Alabama. RG 94. 1 roll.

M244   Index to Compiled Service Records of Volunteer Soldiers Who Served During the Creek War in Organizations from the State of Alabama. RG 94. 2 rolls.

M245   Index to Compiled Service Records of Volunteer Soldiers Who Served During the Florida War in Organizations from the State of Alabama. RG 94. 1 roll.

M246   Revolutionary War Rolls, 1775-1783. RG 93. 138 rolls.

M247   Papers of the Continental Congress, 1774-1789. RG 360. 204 rolls.

M250   Index to Compiled Service Records of Volunteer Soldiers Who Served During the War of 1812 in Organizations from the State of North Carolina. RG 94. 5 rolls.

M251   Compiled Service Records of Confederate Soldiers Who Served in Organizations from the State of Florida. RG 109. 104 rolls.

M252   Third Census of the United States, 1810. RG 29. 71 rolls.

M253   Consolidated Index to Compiled Service Records of Confederate Soldiers. RG 109. 535 rolls.

M255   Passenger Lists of Vessels Arriving in Baltimore, 1820-1891. RG 36. 50 rolls.

M256   Index to Compiled Service Records of Volunteer Soldiers Who Served During the Cherokee Disturbances and Removal in Organizations from the State of North Carolina. RG 94. 1 roll.

M257   Index to Compiled Service Records of Volunteer Soldiers Who Served During the Revolutionary War in Organizations from the State of North Carolina. RG 93. 2 rolls.

M258   Compiled Service Records of Confederate Soldiers Who Served in Organizations Raised Directly by the Confederate Government. RG 109. 123 rolls.

M259   Passenger Lists of Vessels Arriving at New Orleans, Louisiana, 1820-1902. RG 36. 93 rolls.

M260   Records Relating to Confederate Naval and Marine Personnel. RG 109. 7 rolls.

M261   Index to Passenger Lists of Vessels Arriving at New York, 1820-1846. RG 36. 103 rolls.

M262   Official Records of the Union and Confederate Armies, 1861-1865. 128 rolls.

M263   Index to Compiled Service Records of Volunteer Union Soldiers Who Served in Organizations from the State of Alabama. RG 94. 1 roll.

M264   Index to Compiled Service Records of Volunteer Union Soldiers Who Served in Organizations from the State of Florida. RG 94. 1 roll.

M265   Index to Passenger Lists of Vessels Arriving at Boston, Massachusetts, 1848-1891. RG 36. 282 rolls.

M266   Compiled Service Records of Confederate Soldiers Who Served in Organizations from the State of Georgia. RG 109. 607 rolls.

M267   Compiled Service Records of Confederate Soldiers Who Served in Organizations from the State of South Carolina. RG 109. 392 rolls.

M268   Compiled Service Records of Confederate Soldiers Who Served in Organizations from the State of Tennessee. RG 109. 359 rolls.

M269   Compiled Service Records of Confederate Soldiers Who Served in Organizations from the State of Mississippi. RG 109. 427 rolls.

M270   Compiled Service Records of Confederate Soldiers Who Served in Organizations from the State of North Carolina. RG 109. 580 rolls.

M272   Quarterly Abstracts of Passenger Lists of Vessels Arriving at New Orleans, Louisiana, 1820-1875. RG 36. 17 rolls.

M273   Records of General Courts-Martial and Courts of Inquiry of the Navy Department, 1799-1867. RG 125. 198 rolls.

M275   Official Records of the Union and Confederate Navies, 1861-1865. 31 rolls.

M276   Compiled Service Records of Volunteer Union Soldiers Who Served in Organizations from the State of Alabama. RG 94. 10 rolls.

M277   Passenger Lists of Vessels Arriving at Boston, Massachusetts, 1820-1891. RG 36. 115 rolls.

M278   Compiled Service Records of Volunteer Soldiers Who Served During the Mexican War in Organizations from the State of Texas. RG 94. 19 rolls.

M311   Compiled Service Records of Confederate Soldiers Who Served in Organizations from the State of Alabama. RG 109. 508 rolls.

M313   Index to War of 1812 Pension Application Files. RG 15. 102 rolls.

M317   Compiled Service Records of Confederate Soldiers Who Served in Organizations from the State of Arkansas. RG 109. 256 rolls.

M318   Compiled Service Records of Confederate Soldiers Who Served in Organizations from the Territory of Arizona. RG 109. 1 roll.

M319   Compiled Service Records of Confederate Soldiers Who Served in Organizations from the State of Kentucky. RG 109. 136 rolls.

M320   Compiled Service Records of Confederate Soldiers Who Served in Organizations from the State of Louisiana. RG 109. 414 rolls.

M321   Compiled Service Records of Confederate Soldiers Who Served in Organizations from the State of Maryland. RG 109. 22 rolls.

M322   Compiled Service Records of Confederate Soldiers Who Served in Organizations from the State of Missouri. RG 109. 193 rolls.

M323   Compiled Service Records of Confederate Soldiers Who Served in Organizations from the State of Texas. RG 109. 445 rolls.

M324   Compiled Service Records of Confederate Soldiers Who Served in Organizations from the State of Virginia. RG 109. 1,075 rolls.

M325   The Territorial Papers of the United States: The Territory of Iowa, 1838-1846. 102 rolls.

M326   Index to Passenger Lists of Vessels Arriving at Baltimore, 1833-1866 (City Passenger Lists). RG 36. 11 rolls.

M327   Index to Passenger Lists of Vessels Arriving at Baltimore, 1820-1897 (Federal Passenger Lists). RG 36. 171 rolls.

M330   Abstracts of Service of Naval Officers ("Records of Officers"), 1798-1893. RG 24. 19 rolls.

M331   Compiled Service Records of Confederate Generals and Staff Officers and Nonregimental Enlisted men. RG 109. 275 rolls.

M332   Miscellaneous Papers of the Continental Congress, 1774-1789. RG 360. 10 rolls.

M334   Supplemental Index to Passenger Lists of Vessels Arriving at Atlantic and Gulf Coast Ports (Excluding New York), 1820-1874. RG 36. 188 rolls.

M345   Union Provost Marshals' File of Papers Relating to Individual Civilians. RG 109. 300 rolls.

M346   Confederate Papers Relating to Citizens or Business Firms. RG 109. 1,158 rolls.

M347   Unfiled Papers and Slips Belonging in Confederate Compiled Service Records. RG 109. 442 rolls.

M351   Compiled Service Records of Volunteer Soldiers Who Served During the Mexican War in Mormon Organizations. RG 94. 3 rolls.

M352   Schedules of the Nebraska State Census of 1885. RG 29. 56 rolls.

M360   Index to Passenger Lists of Vessels Arriving at Philadelphia, 1800–1906. RG 36. 151 rolls.

M372   United States Direct Tax of 1798: Tax List for the State of Pennsylvania. RG 58. 24 rolls.

M374   Index to Compiled Service Records of Confederate Soldiers Who Served in Organizations from the State of Alabama. RG 109. 49 rolls.

M375   Index to Compiled Service Records of Confederate Soldiers Who Served in Organizations from the Territory of Arizona. RG 109. 1 roll.

M376   Index to Compiled Service Records of Confederate Soldiers Who Served in Organizations from the State of Arkansas. RG 109. 26 rolls.

M377   Index to Compiled Service Records of Confederate Soldiers Who Served in Organizations from the State of Kentucky. RG 109. 14 rolls.

M378   Index to Compiled Service Records of Confederate Soldiers Who Served in Organizations from the State of Louisiana. RG 109. 31 rolls.

M379   Index to Compiled Service Records of Confederate Soldiers Who Served in Organizations from the State of Maryland. RG 109. 2 rolls.

M380   Index to Compiled Service Records of Confederate Soldiers Who Served in Organizations from the State of Missouri. RG 109. 16 rolls.

M381   Index to Compiled Service Records of Confederate Soldiers Who Served in Organizations from the State of South Carolina. RG 109. 35 rolls.

M382   Index to Compiled Service Records of Confederate Soldiers Who Served in Organizations from the State of Virginia. RG 109. 62 rolls.

M383   Index to Compiled Service Records of Volunteer Union Soldiers Who Served in Organizations from the State of Arkansas. RG 94. 4 rolls.

M384   Compiled Service Records of Volunteer Union Soldiers Who Served in Organizations from the State of Maryland. RG 94. 238 rolls.

M385   Index to Compiled Service Records of Volunteer Union Soldiers Who Served in Organizations from the State of Georgia. RG 94. 1 roll.

M386   Index to Compiled Service Records of Volunteer Union Soldiers Who Served in Organizations from the State of Kentucky. RG 94. 30 rolls.

M387   Index to Compiled Service Records of Volunteer Union Soldiers Who Served in Organizations from the State of Louisiana. RG 94. 4 rolls.

M388   Index to Compiled Service Records of Volunteer Union Soldiers Who Served in Organizations from the State of Maryland. RG 94. 13 rolls.

M389   Index to Compiled Service Records of Volunteer Union Soldiers Who Served in Organizations from the State of Mississippi. RG 94. 1 roll.

M390   Index to Compiled Service Records of Volunteer Union Soldiers Who Served in Organizations from the State of Missouri. RG 94. 54 rolls.

M391   Index to Compiled Service Records of Volunteer Union Soldiers Who Served in Organizations from the State of North Carolina. RG 94. 2 rolls.

M392   Index to Compiled Service Records of Volunteer Union Soldiers Who Served in Organizations from the State of Tennessee. RG 94. 16 rolls.

M393   Index to Compiled Service Records of Volunteer Union Soldiers Who Served in Organizations from the State of Texas. RG 94. 2 rolls.

M394   Index to Compiled Service Records of Volunteer Union Soldiers Who Served in Organizations from the State of Virginia. RG 94. 1 roll.

M395   Compiled Service Records of Volunteer Union Soldiers Who Served in Organizations from the State of Tennessee. RG 94. 220 rolls.

M396   Compiled Service Records of Volunteer Union Soldiers Who Served in Organizations from the State of Louisiana. RG 94. 50 rolls.

M397   Compiled Service Records of Volunteer Union Soldiers Who Served in Organizations from the State of Kentucky. RG 94. 515 rolls.

M398   Compiled Service Records of Volunteer Union Soldiers Who Served in Organizations from the State of Virginia. RG 94. 7 rolls.

M399   Compiled Service Records of Volunteer Union Soldiers Who Served in Organizations from the State of Arkansas. RG 94. 60 rolls.

M400   Compiled Service Records of Volunteer Union Soldiers Who Served in Organizations from the State of Florida. RG 94. 11 rolls.

M401   Compiled Service Records of Volunteer Union Soldiers Who Served in Organizations from the State of North Carolina. RG 94. 25 rolls.

M402   Compiled Service Records of Volunteer Union Soldiers Who Served in Organizations from the State of Texas. RG 94. 13 rolls.

M403   Compiled Service Records of Volunteer Union Soldiers Who Served in Organizations from the State of Georgia. RG 94. 1 roll.

M404   Compiled Service Records of Volunteer Union Soldiers Who Served in Organizations from the State of Mississippi. RG 94. 4 rolls.

M405   Compiled Service Records of Volunteer Union Soldiers Who Served in Organizations from the State of Missouri. RG 94. 854 rolls.

M406   Letters of Application and Recommendation During the Administration of John Adams, 1797-1801. RG 59. 3 rolls.

M407   Eleventh Census of the United States, 1890. RG 29. 3 rolls.

M409   Index to the Letters Received by the Confederate Secretary of War, 1861-1865. RG 109. 34 rolls.

M410   Index to the Letters Received by the Confederate Adjutant and Inspector General and by the Confederate Quartermaster General, 1861-1865. RG 109. 41 rolls.

M413   Index to Compiled Service Records of Volunteer Soldiers Who Served During the War with Spain in Organizations from the State of North Carolina. RG 94. 2 rolls.

M416   Union Provost Marshals' File of Papers Relating to Two or More Civilians. RG 109. 94 rolls.

M418   Letters of Application and Recommendation During the Administration of Thomas Jefferson, 1801-1809. RG 59. 12 rolls.

M425   Passenger Lists of Vessels Arriving in Philadelphia, 1800-1882. RG 36. 108 rolls.

M427   Compiled Service Records of Volunteer Union Soldiers Who Served in Organizations from the Territory of New Mexico. RG 94. 46 rolls.

M432   Seventh Census of the United States, 1850. RG 29. 1,009 rolls.

M433   Records of the United States District Court for the District of Columbia Relating to Slaves, 1851-1863. RG 21. 3 rolls.

M434   Habeas Corpus Case Records, 1820-1863, of the United States Circuit Court for the District of Columbia. RG 21. 2 rolls.

M435   Case Papers of the U.S. District Court for the Eastern District of Virginia, 1863-1865, Relating to the Confiscation of Property. RG 21. 1 roll.

M436   Confederate Papers of the U.S. District Court for the Eastern District of North Carolina, 1861-1865. RG 21. 1 roll.

M437   Letters Received by the Confederate Secretary of War, 1861-1865. RG 109. 151 rolls.

M438   Letters of Application and Recommendation During the Administration of James Madison, 1809-1817. RG 59. 8 rolls.

M439   Letters of Application and Recommendation During the Administration of James Monroe, 1817-1825. RG 59. 19 rolls.

M469   Letters Received by the Confederate Quartermaster General, 1861-1865. RG 109. 14 rolls

M474   Letters Received by the Confederate Adjutant and Inspector General, 1861-1865. RG 109. 164 rolls.

M495   Indexes to Letters Received by the Secretary of War, 1861-1870. RG 107. 14 rolls.

M496   Index to the Eleventh Census of the United States, 1890. RG 29. 2 rolls.

M507   Index to Compiled Service Records of Volunteer Union Soldiers Who Served in Organizations from the State of West Virginia. RG 94. 13 rolls.

M508   Compiled Service Records of Volunteer Union Soldiers Who Served in Organizations from the State of West Virginia. RG 94. 261 rolls.

M520 Records of the Board of Commissioners for the Emancipation of Slaves in the District of Columbia, 1862-1863. RG 217. 6 rolls.

M521 Card Index to "Old Loan" Ledgers of the Bureau of the Public Debt, 1790-1836. RG 53. 15 rolls.

M531 Letters of Application and Recommendation During the Administration of John Quincy Adams, 1825-1829. RG 59. 8 rolls.

M532 Index to Compiled Service Records of Volunteer Union Soldiers Who Served in Organizations from the Territory of Arizona. RG 94. 1 roll.

M533 Index to Compiled Service Records of Volunteer Union Soldiers Who Served in Organizations from the State of California. RG 94. 7 rolls.

M534 Index to Compiled Service Records of Volunteer Union Soldiers Who Served in Organizations from the Territory of Colorado. RG 94. 3 rolls.

M535 Index to Compiled Service Records of Volunteer Union Soldiers Who Served in Organizations from the State of Connecticut. RG 94. 17 rolls.

M536 Index to Compiled Service Records of Volunteer Union Soldiers Who Served in Organizations from the Territory of Dakota. RG 94. 1 roll.

M537 Index to Compiled Service Records of Volunteer Union Soldiers Who Served in Organizations from the State of Delaware. RG 94. 4 rolls.

M538 Index to Compiled Service Records of Volunteer Union Soldiers Who Served in Organizations from the District of Columbia. RG 94. 3 rolls.

M539 Index to Compiled Service Records of Volunteer Union Soldiers Who Served in Organizations from the State of Illinois. RG 94. 101 rolls.

M540 Index to Compiled Service Records of Volunteer Union Soldiers Who Served in Organizations from the State of Indiana. RG 94. 86 rolls.

M541 Index to Compiled Service Records of Volunteer Union Soldiers Who Served in Organizations from the State of Iowa. RG 94. 29 rolls.

M542 Index to Compiled Service Records of Volunteer Union Soldiers Who Served in Organizations from the State of Kansas. RG 94. 10 rolls.

M543 Index to Compiled Service Records of Volunteer Union Soldiers Who Served in Organizations from the State of Maine. RG 94. 23 rolls.

M544 Index to Compiled Service Records of Volunteer Union Soldiers Who Served in Organizations from the State of Massachusetts. RG 94. 44 rolls.

M545 Index to Compiled Service Records of Volunteer Union Soldiers Who Served in Organizations from the State of Michigan. RG 94. 48 rolls.

M546 Index to Compiled Service Records of Volunteer Union Soldiers Who Served in Organizations from the State of Minnesota. RG 94. 10 rolls.

M547 Index to Compiled Service Records of Volunteer Union Soldiers Who Served in Organizations from the Territory of Nebraska. RG 94. 2 rolls.

M548 Index to Compiled Service Records of Volunteer Union Soldiers Who Served in Organizations from the State of Nevada. RG 94. 1 roll.

M549 Index to Compiled Service Records of Volunteer Union Soldiers Who Served in Organizations from the State of New Hampshire. RG 94. 13 rolls.

M550 Index to Compiled Service Records of Volunteer Union Soldiers Who Served in Organizations from the State of New Jersey. RG 94. 26 rolls.

M551 Index to Compiled Service Records of Volunteer Union Soldiers Who Served in Organizations from the State of New York. RG 94. 157 rolls.

M552 Index to Compiled Service Records of Volunteer Union Soldiers Who Served in Organizations from the State of Ohio. RG 94. 122 rolls.

M553 Index to Compiled Service Records of Volunteer Union Soldiers Who Served in Organizations from the State of Oregon. RG 94. 1 roll.

M554   Index to Compiled Service Records of Volunteer Union Soldiers Who Served in Organizations from the State of Pennsylvania. RG 94. 136 rolls.

M555   Index to Compiled Service Records of Volunteer Union Soldiers Who Served in Organizations from the State of Rhode Island. RG 94. 7 rolls.

M556   Index to Compiled Service Records of Volunteer Union Soldiers Who Served in Organizations from the Territory of Utah. RG 94. 1 roll.

M557   Index to Compiled Service Records of Volunteer Union Soldiers Who Served in Organizations from the State of Vermont. RG 94. 14 rolls.

M558   Index to Compiled Service Records of Volunteer Union Soldiers Who Served in Organizations from the Territory of Washington. RG 94. 1 roll.

M559   Index to Compiled Service Records of Volunteer Union Soldiers Who Served in Organizations from the State of Wisconsin. RG 94. 33 rolls.

M565   Letters Sent by the Office of the Adjutant General (Main Series), 1800-1890. RG 94. 63 rolls.

M566   Letters Received by the Office of the Adjutant General, 1805-1821. RG 94. 144 rolls.

M567   Letters Received by the Office of the Adjutant General (Main Series), 1822-1860. RG 94. 636 rolls.

M574   Special Files of the Office of Indian Affairs, 1807-1904. RG 75. 85 rolls.

M575   Copies of Lists of Passengers Arriving at Miscellaneous Ports on the Atlantic and Gulf Coasts and at Ports on the Great Lakes, 1820-1873. RG 36. 16 rolls.

M576   Interior Department Appointment Papers: Territory of Arizona, 1857-1907. RG 48. 22 rolls.

M588   "War of 1812 Papers" of the Department of State, 1789-1815. RG 59. 7 rolls.

M589   Index to Compiled Service Records of Volunteer Union Soldiers Who Served with the United States Colored Troops. RG 94. 98 rolls.

M593   Ninth Census of the United States, 1870. RG 29. 1,748 rolls.

M594   Compiled Records Showing Service of Military Units in Volunteer Union Organizations. RG 94. 225 rolls.

M595   Indian Census Rolls, 1885-1940. RG 75. 692 rolls.

M596   Quarterly Abstracts of Passenger Lists of Vessels Arriving at Baltimore, Maryland, 1820-1869. RG 36. 6 rolls.

M597   Nonpopulation Census Schedules for Pennsylvania, 1850-1880: Social Statistics and Supplemental Schedules. RG 29. 23 rolls.

M598   Selected Records of the War Department Relating to Confederate Prisoners of War, 1861-1865. RG 109. 145 rolls.

M602   Index to Compiled Service Records of Volunteer Soldiers Who Served During the War of 1812. RG 94. 234 rolls.

M603   Internal Revenue Assessment Lists for New York and New Jersey, 1862-1866. RG 58. 218 rolls.

M605   Records of the City of Georgetown, DC, 1800-79. RG 351. 49 rolls.

M616   Index to Compiled Service Records of Volunteer Soldiers Who Served During the Mexican War. RG 94. 41 rolls.

M617   Returns from United States Military Posts, 1800-1916. RG 94. 1,550 rolls.

M619   Letters Received by the Office of the Adjutant General (Main Series), 1861-1870. RG 94. 828 rolls.

M625   Area File of the Naval Records Collection, 1775-1910. RG 45. 414 rolls.

M629   Index to Compiled Service Records of Volunteer Soldiers Who Served During Indian Wars and Disturbances, 1815-58. RG 94. 42 rolls.

M630   Index to Compiled Service Records of Volunteer Soldiers Who Served from the State of Michigan During the Patriot War, 1838-1839. RG 94. 1 roll.

M631   Index to Compiled Service Records of Volunteer Soldiers Who Served from the State of New York During the Patriot War, 1838. RG 94. 1 roll.

M636   Index to Compiled Service Records of Volunteer Union Soldiers Who Served in the Veteran Reserve Corps. RG 94. 44 rolls.

M637 First Census of the United States, 1790. RG 29. 12 rolls.

M638 Compiled Service Records of Volunteer Soldiers Who Served During the Mexican War in Organizations from the State of Tennessee. RG 94. 15 rolls.

M639 Letters of Application and Recommendation During the Administration of Andrew Jackson, 1829-1837. RG 59. 27 rolls.

M650 Letters of Application and Recommendation During the Administrations of Abraham Lincoln and Andrew Johnson, 1861-1869. RG 59. 52 rolls.

M652 Index to Compiled Service Records of Volunteer Soldiers Who Served During the War of 1812 in Organizations from the State of South Carolina. RG 94. 7 rolls.

M653 Eighth Census of the United States, 1860. RG 29. 1,438 rolls.

M661 Historical Information Relating to Military Posts and Other Installations, ca. 1700-1900. RG 94. 8 rolls.

M665 Returns from Regular Army Infantry Regiments, June 1821-December 1916. RG 94. 300 rolls.

M666 Letters Received by the Office of the Adjutant General (Main Series), 1871-1880. RG 94. 593 rolls.

M668 Ratified Indian Treaties, 1722-1869. RG 11. 16 rolls.

M678 Compiled Service Records of Volunteer Soldiers Who Served During the War of 1812 in Organizations From the Territory of Mississippi. RG 94. 22 rolls.

M680 Records Relating to the Appointment of Federal Judges, Attorneys, and Marshals for the Territory and State of Utah, 1853-1901. RG 60. 14 rolls.

M681 Records Relating to the Appointment of Federal Judges, Attorneys, and Marshals for the Territory and State of Idaho, 1861-99. RG 60. 9 rolls.

M685 Records Relating to Enrollment of Eastern Cherokees by Gaion Miller, 1908-1910. RG 75. 12 rolls.

M687 Letters of Application and Recommendation During the Administrations of Martin Van Buren, William Henry Harrison, and John Tyler, 1837-1845. RG 59. 35 rolls.

M688 U.S. Military Academy Cadet Application Papers, 1805-1866. RG 94. 242 rolls.

M689 Letters Received by the Office of the Adjutant General (Main Series), 1880-1889. RG 94. 740 rolls.

M690 Returns from Regular Army Engineer Battalions, September 1846-June 1916. RG 94. 10 rolls.

M691 Returns from Regular Army Coast Artillery Corps Companies, February 1901-June 1916. RG 94. 81 rolls.

M692 Compiled Service Records of Volunteer Union Soldiers Who Served in Organizations from the Territory of Utah. RG 94. 1 roll.

M693 Interior Department Appointment Papers: Idaho, 1862-1907. RG 48. 17 rolls.

M694 Index to Compiled Service Records of Volunteer Soldiers Who Served From 1784 to 1811. RG 94. 9 rolls.

M698 Index to General Correspondence of the Office of the Adjutant General, 1890-1917. RG 94. 1,269 rolls.

M701 Letters Sent by the Department of Justice: Instructions to U.S. Attorneys and Marshals, 1867-1904. RG 60. 212 rolls.

M704 Sixth Census of the United States, 1840. RG 29. 580 rolls.

M711 Registers of Letters Received, Office of the Adjutant General, 1812-89. RG 94. 85 rolls.

M721 The Territorial Papers of the United States. 16 rolls.

M725 Indexes to Letters Received by the Office of the Adjutant General (Main Series), 1846, 1861-1889. RG 94. 9 rolls.

M727 Returns from Regular Army Artillery Regiments, June 1821-January 1901. RG 94. 38 rolls.

M728 Returns from Regular Army Field Artillery Batteries and Regiments, February 1901-December 1916. RG 94. 14 rolls.

M732 Interior Department Appointment Papers: California, 1849-1907. RG 48. 29 rolls.

M742 Selected Series of Records Issued by the Commissioner of the Bureau of Refugees, Freedmen, and Abandoned Lands, 1865-1872. RG 105. 7 rolls.

M744 Returns from Regular Army Cavalry Regiments, 1833-1916. RG 94. 117 rolls.

M750   Interior Department Appointment Papers: Territory of New Mexico, 1850–1907. RG 48. 18 rolls.

M752   Registers and Letters Received by the Commissioner of the Bureau of Refugees, Freedmen, and Abandoned Lands, 1865–1872. RG 105. 74 rolls.

M754   Internal Revenue Assessment Lists for Alabama, 1865–1866. RG 58. 6 rolls.

M755   Internal Revenue Assessment Lists for Arkansas, 1865–1866. RG 58. 2 rolls.

M756   Internal Revenue Assessment Lists for California, 1862–1866. RG 58. 33 rolls.

M757   Internal Revenue Assessment Lists for Colorado, 1862–1866. RG 58. 3 rolls.

M758   Internal Revenue Assessment Lists for Connecticut, 1862–1866. RG 58. 23 rolls.

M759   Internal Revenue Assessment Lists for Delaware, 1862–1866. RG 58. 8 rolls.

M760   Internal Revenue Assessment Lists for the District of Columbia, 1862–1866. RG 58. 8 rolls.

M761   Internal Revenue Assessment Lists for Florida, 1865–1866. RG 58. 1 roll.

M762   Internal Revenue Assessment Lists for Georgia, 1865–1866. RG 58. 8 rolls.

M763   Internal Revenue Assessment Lists for the Territory of Idaho, 1865–1866. RG 58. 1 roll.

M764   Internal Revenue Assessment Lists for Illinois, 1862–1866. RG 58. 63 rolls.

M765   Internal Revenue Assessment Lists for Indiana, 1862–1866. RG 58. 42 rolls.

M766   Internal Revenue Assessment Lists for Iowa, 1862–1866. RG 58. 16 rolls.

M767   Internal Revenue Assessment Lists for Kansas, 1862–1866. RG 58. 3 rolls.

M768   Internal Revenue Assessment Lists for Kentucky, 1862–1866. RG 58. 24 rolls.

M769   Internal Revenue Assessment Lists for Louisiana, 1863–1866. RG 58. 10 rolls.

M770   Internal Revenue Assessment Lists for Maine, 1862–1866. RG 58. 15 rolls.

M771   Internal Revenue Assessment Lists for Maryland, 1862–1866. RG 58. 21 rolls.

M773   Internal Revenue Assessment Lists for Michigan, 1862–1866. RG 58. 15 rolls.

M774   Internal Revenue Assessment Lists for Minnesota, 1862–1866. RG 58. 3 rolls.

M775   Internal Revenue Assessment Lists for Mississippi, 1865–1866. RG 58. 3 rolls.

M776   Internal Revenue Assessment Lists for Missouri, 1862–1865. RG 58. 22 rolls.

M777   Internal Revenue Assessment Lists for Montana, 1864–1872. RG 58. 1 roll.

M779   Internal Revenue Assessment Lists for Nevada, 1863–1866. RG 58. 2 rolls.

M780   Internal Revenue Assessment Lists for New Hampshire, 1862–1866. RG 58. 10 rolls.

M782   Internal Revenue Assessment Lists for the Territory of New Mexico, 1862–1870. RG 58. 1 roll.

M784   Internal Revenue Assessment Lists for North Carolina, 1864–1866. RG 58. 2 rolls.

M787   Internal Revenue Assessment Lists for Pennsylvania, 1862–1866. RG 58. 107 rolls.

M788   Internal Revenue Assessment Lists for Rhode Island, 1862–1866. RG 58. 10 rolls.

M789   Internal Revenue Assessment Lists for South Carolina, 1864–1866. RG 58. 2 rolls.

M791   Internal Revenue Assessment Lists for Texas, 1865–1866. RG 58. 2 rolls.

M792   Internal Revenue Assessment Lists for Vermont, 1862–1866. RG 58. 7 rolls.

M793   Internal Revenue Assessment Lists for Virginia, 1862–1866. RG 58. 6 rolls.

M795   Internal Revenue Assessment Lists for West Virginia, 1862–1866. RG 58. 4 rolls.

M798   Records of the Assistant Commissioner for the State of Georgia, Bureau of Refugees, Freedmen, and Abandoned Lands, 1865–1870. RG 105. 36 rolls.

M799   Records of the Superintendent of Education for the State of Georgia, Bureau of Refugees, Freedman, and Abandoned Lands, 1865–1870. RG 105. 28 rolls.

M803   Records of the Education Division of the Bureau of Refugees, Freedmen, and Abandoned Lands, 1865–1871. RG 105. 35 rolls.

M804   Revolutionary War Pension and Bounty-Land Warrant Application Files. RG 15. 2,670 rolls.

M805   Selected Records from Revolutionary War Pension and Bounty-Land Warrant Application Files. RG 15. 898 rolls.

M808   Interior Department Appointment Papers: Colorado, 1857-1907. RG 48. 13 rolls.

M809   Records of the Assistant Commissioner for the State of Alabama, Bureau of Refugees, Freedmen, and Abandoned Lands, 1865-1870. RG 105. 23 rolls.

M810   Records of the Superintendent of Education for the State of Alabama, Bureau of Refugees, Freedman, and Abandoned Lands, 1865-1870. RG 105. 8 rolls.

M814   Interior Department Appointment Papers: Oregon, 1849-1907. RG 48. 10 rolls.

M815   Oregon and Washington Donation Land Files, 1851-1903. RG 49. 108 rolls.

M816   Registers of Signature of Depositors in Branches of the Freedman's Savings and Trust Company, 1865-1874. RG 101. 27 rolls.

M817   Indexes to Deposit Ledgers in Branches of the Freedman's Savings and Trust Company, 1865-1874. RG 101. 5 rolls.

M818   Index to Compiled Service Records of Confederate Soldiers Who Served in Organizations Raised Directly by the Confederate Government and of Confederate General and Staff Officers and Nonregimental Enlisted Men. RG 109. 26 rolls.

M821   Records of the Assistant Commissioner for the State of Texas, Bureau of Refugees, Freedmen, and Abandoned Lands, 1865-1869. RG 105. 32 rolls.

M822   Records of the Superintendent of Education for the State of Texas, Bureau of Refugees, Freedman, and Abandoned Lands, 1865-1870. RG 105. 18 rolls.

M826   Records of the Assistant Commissioner for the State of Mississippi, Bureau of Refugees, Freedmen, and Abandoned Lands, 1865-1869. RG 105. 50 rolls.

M829   U.S. Revolutionary War Bounty Land Warrants Used in the U.S. Military District of Ohio and Related Papers (Acts of 1788, 1803, 1806). RG 49. 16 rolls.

M830   Interior Department Appointment Papers: Wyoming, 1869-1907. RG 48. 6 rolls.

M831   Interior Department Appointment Papers: Wisconsin, 1849-1907. RG 48. 9 rolls.

M836   Confederate States Army Casualties: Lists and Narrative Reports, 1861-1865. RG 109. 7 rolls.

M841   Records of Appointment of Postmasters, 1832-September 30, 1971. RG 28. 145 rolls.

M843   Records of the Assistant Commissioner for the State of North Carolina, Bureau of Refugees, Freedmen, and Abandoned Lands, 1865-1870. RG 105. 38 rolls.

M844   Records of the Superintendent of Education for the State of North Carolina, Bureau of Refugees, Freedman, and Abandoned Lands, 1865-1870. RG 105. 16 rolls.

M845   Schedules of the Florida State Census of 1885. RG 29. 13 rolls.

M846   Schedules of the New Mexico Territory Census of 1885. RG 29. 6 rolls.

M847   Special Index to Numbered Records in the War Department Collection of Revolutionary War Records, 1775-1783. RG 93. 39 rolls.

M848   War of 1812 Military Bounty Land Warrants, 1815-1858. RG 49. 14 rolls.

M849   Interior Department Appointment Papers: Mississippi, 1849-1907. RG 48. 4 rolls.

M850   Veterans Administration Pension Payment Cards, 1907-1933. RG 15. 2,539 rolls.

M851   Returns of the Corps of Engineers, April 1832-December 1916. RG 94. 22 rolls.

M852   Returns of the Corps of Topographical Engineers, November 1831-February 1863. RG 94. 2 rolls.

M853   Numbered Record Books Concerning Military Operations and Service, Pay and Settlement of Accounts, and Supplies in the War Department Collection of Revolutionary War Records. RG 93. 41 rolls.

M854   Minutes, Trial Notes, and Rolls of Attorneys of the U.S. Circuit Court for the Southern District of New York, 1790-1841. RG 21. 3 rolls.

M859   Miscellaneous Numbered Records (The Manuscript File) in the War Department Collection of Revolutionary War Records, 1775-1790's. RG 93. 125 rolls.

M860   General Index to Compiled Military Service Records of Revolutionary War Soldiers [Sailors, and Members of Army Staff Departments]. RG 93. 58 rolls.

M861   Compiled Records Showing Service of
        Military Units in Confederate Organizations.
        RG 109. 74 rolls.

M863   Compiled Service Records of Volunteer
        Soldiers Who Served During the Mexican War
        in Organizations from the State of Mississippi.
        RG 94. 9 rolls.

M869   Records of the Assistant Commissioner for the
        State of South Carolina, Bureau of Refugees,
        Freedmen, and Abandoned Lands, 1865–1870.
        RG 105. 44 rolls.

M871   General Index to Compiled Service Records
        of Volunteer Soldiers Who Served During the
        War with Spain. RG 94. 126 rolls.

M872   Index to Compiled Service Records of
        Volunteer Soldiers Who Served During the
        Philippine Insurrection. RG 94. 24 rolls.

M873   Letters of Application and Recommendation
        During the Administrations of James Polk,
        Zachary Taylor, and Millard Fillmore,
        1845–1853. RG 59. 98 rolls.

M879   Index to Compiled Service Records of
        American Naval Personnel Who Served
        During the Revolutionary War. RG 93. 1 roll.

M880   Compiled Service Records of American Naval
        Personnel and Members of the Departments
        of the Quartermaster General and the Com-
        missary General of Military Stores Who Served
        During the Revolutionary War. RG 93. 4 rolls.

M881   Compiled Service Records of Soldiers Who
        Served in the American Army During the
        Revolutionary War. RG 93. 1,096 rolls.

M886   Minutes and Rolls of Attorneys of the U.S.
        District Court for the Southern District of
        New York, 1789–1841. RG 21. 9 rolls.

M904   War Department Collection of Post-
        Revolutionary War Manuscripts. RG 94. 4 rolls.

M905   Compiled Service Records of Volunteer
        Soldiers Who Served From 1704 to 1811. RG
        94. 32 rolls.

M907   Index to Compiled Service Records of Volunteer
        Soldiers Who Served During the Cherokee
        Disturbances and Removal in Organizations
        from the State of Georgia. RG 94. 1 roll.

M908   Index to Compiled Service Records of
        Volunteer Soldiers Who Served During the
        Cherokee Disturbances and Removal in
        Organizations from the State of Tennessee and
        the Field and Staff of the Army of the
        Cherokee Nation. RG 94. 2 rolls.

M910   Virginia Half Pay and Other Related
        Revolutionary War Pension Application Files.
        RG 15. 18 rolls.

M918   Register of Confederate Soldiers, Sailors, and
        Citizens Who Died in Federal Prisons and
        Military Hospitals in the North, 1861–65.
        RG 92. 1 roll.

M920   Index to Compiled Service Records of
        Revolutionary War Soldiers Who Served With
        the American Army in Connecticut Military
        Organizations. RG 93. 25 rolls.

M925   Records of the Massachusetts Continental
        Loan Office, 1777–1791. RG 53. 4 rolls.

M929   Documents Relating to the Military and Naval
        Service of Blacks Awarded the Congressional
        Medal of Honor from the Civil War to the
        Spanish-American War. 4 rolls.

M931   Minutes of the U.S. Circuit Court for the
        District of Maryland, 1790–1911. RG 21.
        7 rolls.

M932   Minutes of the U.S. Circuit Court for the
        Eastern District of Pennsylvania, 1790–1844.
        RG 21. 2 rolls.

M940   Letters Received by the Department of Justice
        from the State of Louisiana, 1871–1884.
        RG 60. 6 rolls.

M947   Letters Received by the Department of Justice
        from the State of South Carolina, 1871–1884.
        RG 60. 9 rolls.

M950   Interior Department Appointment Papers:
        North Carolina, 1849–1892. RG 48. 1 roll.

M967   Letters of Application and Recommendation
        During the Administrations of Franklin Pierce
        and James Buchanan, 1853–1861. RG 59.
        50 rolls.

M968   Letters of Application and Recommendation
        During the Administration of Ulysses S. Grant,
        1869–1877. RG 59. 69 rolls.

M970   Letters Received by the Department of Justice
        from the State of Mississippi, 1871–1884.
        RG 60. 4 rolls.

M972   Computer-Processed Tabulations of Data from
        Seamen's Protective Certificate Applications
        to the Collector of Customs for the Port of
        Philadelphia, 1812–1815. RG 36. 1 roll.

M979   Records of the Assistant Commissioner for the
        State of Arkansas, Bureau of Refugees,
        Freedmen, and Abandoned Lands, 1865–1871.
        RG 105. 52 rolls.

M980   Records of the Superintendent of Education for the State of Arkansas, Bureau of Refugees, Freedman, and Abandoned Lands, 1865-1871. RG 105. 5 rolls.

M991   U.S. Naval Academy Registers of Delinquencies, 1846-1850 and 1853-1882, and Academic and Conduct Records of Cadets, 1881-1908. RG 405. 45 rolls.

M996   Letters Received by the Department of Justice from the State of Georgia, 1871-1884. RG 60. 5 rolls.

M999   Records of the Assistant Commissioner for the State of Tennessee, Bureau of Refugees, Freedmen, and Abandoned Lands, 1865-1869. RG 105. 34 rolls.

M1000   Records of the Superintendent of Education for the State of Tennessee, Bureau of Refugees, Freedman, and Abandoned Lands, 1865-1870. RG 105. 9 rolls.

M1002   Selected Documents Relating to Blacks Nominated for Appointment to the U.S. Military Academy During the 19th Century, 1870-1887. 21 rolls.

M1003   Case Files of Applications from Former Confederates for Presidential Pardons ("Amnesty Papers"), 1865-1867. RG 94. 73 rolls.

M1005   Records of the Connecticut, New Hampshire, and Rhode Island Continental Loan Offices, 1777-1789. RG 53. 2 rolls.

M1006   Records of the New Jersey and New York Continental Loan Offices, 1777-1790. RG 53. 2 rolls.

M1007   Records of the Pennsylvania Continental Loan Office, 1776-1788. RG 53. 3 rolls.

M1008   Records of the Delaware and Maryland Continental Loan Offices, 1777-1790. RG 53. 1 roll.

M1015   Central Treasury Records of the Continental and Confederation Governments Relating to Military Affairs, 1775-1789. 7 rolls.

M1017   Compiled Service Records of Former Confederate Soldiers Who Served in the 1st Through 6th U.S. Volunteer Infantry Regiments, 1864-1866. RG 94. 65 rolls.

M1021   Minutes of the U.S. Circuit Court for the District of Columbia, 1801-1863. RG 21. 6 rolls.

M1022   Interior Department Appointment Papers: New York, 1849-1906. RG 48. 5 rolls.

M1026   Records of the Superintendent of Education for the State of Louisiana, Bureau of Refugees, Freedman, and Abandoned Lands, 1864-1869. RG 105. 12 rolls.

M1027   Records of the Assistant Commissioner for the State of Louisiana, Bureau of Refugees, Freedmen, and Abandoned Lands, 1865-1869. RG 105. 37 rolls.

M1028   Compiled Service Records of Volunteer Soldiers Who Served During the Mexican War in Organizations from the State of Pennsylvania. RG 94. 13 rolls.

M1033   Interior Department Appointment Papers: Nevada, 1860-1907. RG 48. 3 rolls.

M1036   Military Operations of the Civil War: A Guide to the Official Records of the Union and Confederate Armies, 1861-1865, Volume 1, Conspectus. 1 roll.

M1048   Records of the Assistant Commissioner for the State of Virginia, Bureau of Refugees, Freedmen, and Abandoned Lands, 1865-1869. RG 105. 67 rolls.

M1049   The Territorial Papers of the United States: The Territory of Oregon, 1848-1859. 12 rolls.

M1050   The Territorial Papers of the United States: The Territory of Minnesota, 1849-1858. 19 rolls.

M1051   Index to Compiled Service Records of Revolutionary War Soldiers Who Served With the American Army in Georgia Military Organizations. RG 93. 1 roll.

M1053   Records of the Superintendent of Education for the State of Virginia, Bureau of Refugees, Freedman, and Abandoned Lands, 1865-1870. RG 105. 20 rolls.

M1055   Records of the Assistant Commissioner for the District of Columbia, Bureau of Refugees, Freedmen, and Abandoned Lands, 1865-1872. RG 105. 21 rolls.

M1056   Records of the Superintendent of Education for the District of Columbia, Bureau of Refugees, Freedman, and Abandoned Lands, 1865-1872. RG 105. 24 rolls.

M1058   Interior Department Appointment Papers: Missouri, 1849-1907. RG 48. 9 rolls.

M1062   Correspondence of the War Department Relating to Indian Affairs, Military Pensions, and Fortifications, 1791-1797. RG 107. 1 roll.

M1064 Letters Received by the Commission Branch of the Adjutant General's Office, 1864-70. RG 94. 527 rolls.

M1066 Registers of Vessels Arriving at the Port of New York from Foreign Ports, 1789-1919. RG 36. 27 rolls.

M1082 Records of the U.S. District Court for the Eastern District of Louisiana, 1806-1814. RG 21. 18 rolls.

M1086 Compiled Service Records of Volunteer Soldiers Who Served in Organizations From the State of Florida During the Florida Indian Wars, 1835-58. RG 94. 63 rolls.

M1087 Compiled Service Records of Volunteer Soldiers Who Served in the Florida Infantry During the War with Spain. RG 94. 13 rolls.

M1091 Subject File of the Confederate States Navy, 1861-1865. RG 45. 61 rolls.

M1098 U.S. Army Generals' Reports of Civil War Service, 1864-1887. RG 94. 8 rolls.

M1104 Eastern Cherokee Applications of the U.S. Court of Claims, 1906-1909. RG 123. 348 rolls.

M1105 Registers of the Records of the Proceedings of the U.S. Army General Courts-Martial, 1809-1890. RG 153. 8 rolls.

M1111 Records of the Territorial Court of Michigan, 1815-1836. RG 21. 9 rolls.

M1116 DC Building Permits, 1877-1949. RG 351. 854 rolls as of this date.

M1119 Interior Department Appointment Papers: Florida, 1849-1907. RG 48. 6 rolls.

M1125 Name and Subject Index to the Letters Received by the Appointment, Commission, and Personal Branch of the Adjutant General's Office, 1871-94. RG 94. 4 rolls.

M1131 Record of Appointment of Postmasters, October 1789-1832. RG 28. 4 rolls.

M1144 Case Files of Chinese Immigrants, 1895-1920, from District No. 4 (Philadelphia) of the Immigration and Naturalization Service. RG 85. 51 rolls.

M1164 Index to Naturalization Petitions of the United States District Court for the Eastern District of New York, 1865-1957. RG 21. 142 rolls.

M1168 Indexes to Naturalization Petitions to the U.S. Circuit and District Courts for Maryland, 1797-1951. RG 21. 25 rolls.

M1172 Index Books, 1789-1928, and Minutes and Bench Dockets, 1789-1870, for the U.S. District Court, Southern District of Georgia. RG 21. 3 rolls.

M1181 Minutes, Circuit and District Courts, District of South Carolina, 1789-1849, and Index to Judgments, Circuit and District Courts, 1792-1847. RG 21. 2 rolls.

M1183 Record of Admissions to Citizenship, District of South Carolina, 1790-1906. RG 21. 1 roll.

M1184 Minutes of the U.S. Circuit Court for the District of Georgia, 1790-1842, and Index to Plaintiffs and Defendants in the Circuit Courts, 1790-1860. RG 21. 3 rolls.

M1186 Enrollment Cards of the Five Civilized Tribes, 1898-1914. RG 75. 93 rolls.

M1192 Naturalization Records Created by the U.S. District Courts in Colorado, 1877-1952. RG 21. 79 rolls.

M1208 Indexes to Registers and Registers of Declarations of Intention and Petitions for Naturalization of the U.S. District and Circuit Courts for the Western District of Pennsylvania, 1820-1906. RG 21. 3 rolls.

M1213 Minute Books of the U.S. District Court for West Tennessee, 1797-1839, and of the U.S. District Court for the Middle District of Tennessee, 1839-1865. RG 21. 1 roll.

M1214 Minute Books of the U.S. Circuit Court for West Tennessee, 1808-1839, and of the U.S. Circuit Court for the Middle District of Tennessee, 1839-1864. RG 21. 4 rolls.

M1232 Indexes to Naturalization Records of the U.S. District Court for Western Washington, Northern Division (Seattle), 1890-1952. RG 21. 6 rolls.

M1233 Indexes to Naturalization Records of the King County Territorial and Superior Courts, 1864-1889 and 1906-1928. RG 21. 1 roll.

M1234 Indexes to Naturalization Records of the Thurston County (WA) Territorial and Superior Courts, 1850-1974. RG 21. 2 rolls.

M1235 Indexes to Naturalization Records of the Snohomish County Territorial and Superior Courts, 1876-1974. RG 21. 3 rolls.

M1236 Indexes to Naturalization Records of the Montana Territorial and Federal Courts, 1868-1929. RG 21. 1 roll.

M1237   Indexes to Naturalization Records of the U.S. District Court, Western District of Washington State, Southern Division (Tacoma), 1890-1953. RG 21. 2 rolls.

M1238   Indexes to Naturalization Records of the Pierce County Territorial and Superior Courts, 1853-1923. RG 21. 2 rolls.

M1241   Indexes to the Naturalization Records of the U.S. District Court for the District and Territory of Alaska, 1900-1929. RG 21. 1 roll.

M1242   Index to the Naturalization Records of the U.S. District Court for Oregon, 1854-1956. RG 21. 3 rolls.

M1245   Interior Department Appointment Papers: Alaska, 1871-1907. RG 48. 6 rolls.

M1248   Indexes to Naturalization Petitions to the U.S. Circuit and District Courts for the Eastern District of Pennsylvania, 1795-1951. RG 21. 60 rolls.

M1250   Letters Received by the Department of Justice from the State of Virginia, 1871-1884. RG 60. 4 rolls.

M1274   Case Files of Disapproved Pension Applications of Widows and Other Dependents of Civil War and Later Navy Veterans ("Navy Widows' Originals"), 1861-1910. RG 15. Ca. 8,500 microfiche.

M1279   Case Files of Approved Pension Applications of Widows and Other Dependents of Civil War and Later Navy Veterans ("Navy Widows' Certificates"), 1861-1910. RG 15. Ca. 40,000 microfiche.

M1283   Cross Index to Selected City Street and Enumeration Districts, 1910 Census. RG 29. 50 microfiche.

M1290   Alphabetical Card Name Indexes to the Compiled Service Records of Volunteer Soldiers Who Served in Union Organizations Not Raised by States or Territories, Excepting the Veteran Reserve Corps and the U.S. Colored Troops. RG 94. 36 rolls.

M1301   Applications for Enrollment of the Commission to the Five Civilized Tribes, 1898-1914. RG 75. 468 rolls.

M1320   Passenger and Crew Lists of Vessels (February 1929-February 1959) and Airplanes (April 1946-February 1959) Arriving at Bridgeport, Groton, Hartford, New Haven, and New London, Connecticut. RG 85. 13 rolls.

M1321   Passenger Lists of Vessels Arriving at Gloucester, Massachusetts, October 1906-March 1942. RG 85. 1 roll.

M1327   Letters Received by the Department of Justice from the State of Florida, 1871-1884. RG 60. 2 rolls.

M1328   Abstracts of Service Records of Naval Officers ("Records of Officers"), 1829-1924. RG 24. 18 rolls.

M1343   Applications for Enrollment and Allotment of Washington Indians, 1911-19. RG 75. 6 rolls.

M1344   Records Concerning Applications for Adoption by the Quinaielt Indians, 1910-19. RG 75. 5 rolls.

M1345   Letters Received by the Department of Justice from the State of North Carolina, 1871-1884. RG 60. 3 rolls.

M1350   Selected Records of the Bureau of Indian Affairs Relating to the Enrollment of Indians on the Flathead Reservation, 1903-8. RG 75. 3 rolls.

M1352   Letters Received by the Department of Justice from the State of Maryland, 1871-1884. RG 60. 2 rolls.

M1356   Letters Received by the Department of Justice from the State of Alabama, 1871-1884. RG 60. 7 rolls.

M1357   Index to Passenger Lists of Vessels Arriving at Galveston, Texas, 1896-September 1906. RG 85. 3 rolls.

M1358   Index to Passenger Lists of Vessels Arriving at Galveston, Texas, October 1906-1951. RG 85. 7 rolls.

M1359   Passenger Lists of Vessels Arriving at Galveston, Texas, 1896-1948. RG 85. 36 rolls.

M1362   Letters Received by the Department of Justice from the State of Kentucky, 1871-1884. RG 60. 2 rolls.

M1364   Lists of Chinese Passengers Arriving at Seattle (Port Townsend), Washington, 1882-1916. RG 85. 10 rolls.

M1365   Certificates of Head Tax Paid by Aliens Arriving at Seattle (Washington) from Foreign Contiguous Territory, 1917-1924. RG 85. 10 rolls.

M1368   Petitions and Records of Naturalization of the U.S. District Court and Circuit Courts of the District of Massachusetts, 1906-1929. RG 21. 330 rolls.

M1371 Registers and Indexes for Passport Applications, 1810-1906. RG 59. 13 rolls.

M1372 Passport Applications, 1795-1906. RG 59. 694 rolls.

M1373 Registers of Lighthouse Keepers, 1845-1912. RG 26. 6 rolls.

M1387 Minutes of Boards of Special Inquiry at the San Francisco Immigration Office, 1899-1909. RG 85. 2 rolls.

M1389 Indexes to Passenger Lists of Vessels Arriving at San Francisco, California, 1893-1934. RG 85. 28 rolls.

M1391 Lists of Navy Veterans for Whom There are Navy Widows' and Other Dependents' Disapproved Pension Files ("Navy Widows' Originals"), 1861-1910. RG 59. 15 microfiche.

M1395 Letters Received by the Appointment, Commission, and Personal Branch, Adjutant General's Office, 1871-94. RG 94. 1,693 microfiche.

M1398 Passenger Lists of Vessels Arriving at Seattle, Washington, 1949-1954. RG 85. 5 rolls.

M1399 Crew Lists of Vessels Arriving at Seattle, Washington, 1903-1917. RG 85. 15 rolls.

M1407 Barred and Disallowed Case Files of the Southern Claims Commission, 1871-1880. RG 233. 4,829 microfiche.

M1410 Passenger Lists of Vessels Arriving at San Francisco, 1893-1953. RG 85. 429 rolls.

M1411 Passenger and Crew Lists of Vessels Arriving at San Francisco, 1954-1957. RG 85. 19 rolls.

M1412 Customs Passenger Lists of Vessels Arriving at San Francisco, 1903-1918. RG 85. 13 rolls.

M1413 Registers of Chinese Laborers Returning to the U.S. Through the Port of San Francisco, 1882-1888. RG 85. 12 rolls.

M1414 Lists of Chinese Passenger Arrivals at San Francisco, 1882-1914. RG 85. 32 rolls.

M1416 Crew Lists of Vessels Arriving at San Francisco, 1905-1954. RG 85. 174 rolls.

M1417 Index (Soundex) to Passengers Arriving in New York, New York, 1944-1948. RG 85. 94 rolls.

M1418 Letters Received by the Department of Justice from the State of Arkansas, 1871-1884. RG 60. 5 rolls.

M1425 Minute Books, U.S. District Court, Eastern District of North Carolina, Albemarle Division at Edenton, 1807-70, and at Elizabeth City, 1870-1914. RG 21. 1 roll.

M1426 Minute Books, U.S. District Court, Eastern District of North Carolina, Cape Fear Division at Wilmington, 1795-96 and 1858-1911. RG 21. 2 rolls.

M1427 Minute Books, U.S. District Court, Eastern District of North Carolina, Pamlico Division at New Bern, 1858-1914. RG 21. 2 rolls.

M1428 Minute Books, U.S. Circuit Court, Eastern District of North Carolina, Raleigh, 1791-1866. RG 21. 2 rolls.

M1436 Admitted Alien Crew Lists of Vessels Arriving at San Francisco, 1896-1921. RG 85. 8 rolls.

M1437 Indexes to Vessels Arriving at San Francisco, 1882-1957. RG 85. 1 roll.

M1438 Passenger Lists of Vessels Arriving at San Francisco from Insular Possessions, 1907-1911. RG 85. 2 rolls.

M1439 Lists of U.S. Citizens Arriving at San Francisco, 1930-1949. RG 85. 50 rolls.

M1461 Soundex Index to Canadian Border Entries Through the St. Albans, Vermont, District, 1895-1924. RG 85. 400 rolls.

M1462 Alphabetical Index to Canadian Border Entries Through Small Ports in Vermont, 1895-1924. RG 85. 6 rolls.

M1463 Soundex Index to Entries into the St. Albans, Vermont, District Through Canadian Pacific and Atlantic Ports, 1924-1952. RG 85. 98 rolls.

M1464 Manifests of Passengers Arriving in the St. Albans, Vermont, District Through Canadian Pacific and Atlantic Ports, 1895-1954. RG 85. 639 rolls.

M1465 Manifests of Passengers Arriving in the St. Albans, Vermont, District Through Canadian Pacific Ports, 1929-1949. RG 85. 25 rolls.

M1471 Letters Received by the Department of Justice from the State of Tennessee, 1871-1884. RG 60. 4 rolls.

M1475 Correspondence of the Eastern Division Pertaining to Cherokee Removal, April- December 1838. RG 393. 2 rolls.

M1476 Lists of Chinese Applying for Admission to the United States Through the Port of San Francisco, 1903-1947. RG 85. 27 rolls.

M1478   Card Manifests (Alphabetical) of Individuals Entering Through the Port of Detroit, Michigan, 1906-54. RG 85. 117 rolls.

M1479   Passenger and Alien Crew Lists of Vessels Arriving at the Port of Detroit, Michigan, 1946-57. RG 85. 23 rolls.

M1481   Alphabetical Card Manifests of Alien Arrivals at Alexandria Bay, Cape Vincent, Champlain, Clayton, Fort Covington, Mooers, Rouses Point, Thousand Island Bridge, and Trout River, New York, July 1929-April 1956. RG 85. 3 rolls.

M1482   Soundex Card Manifests of Alien and Citizen Arrivals at Hogansburg, Malone, Morristown, Nyando, Ogdensburg, Roosevelt Town, and Waddington, NY, July 1929-April 1956. RG 85. 3 rolls.

M1483   Records of the New Orleans Field Offices, Bureau of Refugees, Freedmen, and Abandoned Lands, 1865-1869. RG 105. 10 rolls.

M1484   Customs Passenger Lists of Vessels Arriving at Port Townsend and Tacoma, Washington, 1894-1909. RG 85. 1 roll.

M1485   Passenger Lists of Vessels Arriving at Seattle from Insular Possessions, 1908-1917. RG 85. 1 roll.

M1490   Passport Applications, January 2, 1906-March 21, 1923. RG 59. 2,740 rolls.

M1494   Passenger Lists of Vessels Arriving at San Francisco from Honolulu, 1902-1907. RG 85. 1 roll.

M1500   Records of the Special Boards of Inquiry, District No. 4 (Philadelphia), Immigration and Naturalization Service, 1893-1909. RG 85. 18 rolls.

M1502   Statistical and Nonstatistical Manifests of Alien Arrivals at Brownsville, Texas, February 1905-June 1953, and Related Indexes. RG 85. 40 rolls.

M1503   Index and Manifests of Alien Arrivals at Roma, Texas, March 1928-May 1955. RG 85. 5 rolls.

M1504   Manifests of Alien Arrivals at San Luis, Arizona, July 24, 1929-December 1952. RG 85. 2 rolls.

M1505   Compiled Military Service Records of Michigan and Illinois Volunteers Who Served During the Winnebago Indian Disturbances of 1827. RG 94. 3 rolls.

M1509   World War I Selective Service System Draft Registration Cards. RG 163. 4,277 rolls.

M1514   Indexes of Vessels Arriving at Brownsville, Texas, 1935-1955; Houston, Texas, 1948-1954; and at Port Arthur and Beaumont, Texas, and Lake Charles, Louisiana, 1908-1954. RG 85. 1 roll.

M1522   Naturalization Petitions for the Eastern District of Pennsylvania, 1795-1931. RG 21. 369 rolls.

M1523   Proceedings of U.S. Army Courts-martial and Military Commissions of Union Soldiers Executed by U.S. Military Authorities, 1861-1866. RG 94. 8 rolls.

M1524   Naturalization Records of the United States District Court for the Southern District of California, Central Division, Los Angeles, 1887-1940. RG 21. 244 rolls.

M1525   Naturalization Index Cards of the United States District Court for the Southern District of California, Central Division, Los Angeles, 1915-1976. RG 21. 14 rolls.

M1526   Naturalization Index Cards from the Superior Court of San Diego County, California, 1929-1956. 5 rolls.

M1528   Nonpopulation Census Schedules for Kentucky, 1850-1880. RG 29. 42 rolls.

M1535   Letters Received by the Department of Justice from the Territory of Dakota, 1871-1884. RG 60. 3 rolls.

M1537   Naturalization Petitions of the U.S. District Court, 1820-1930, and Circuit Court, 1820-1911, for the Western District of Pennsylvania. RG 21. 437 rolls.

M1538   Naturalization Records of the U.S. District Courts for the State of Montana, 1891-1929. RG 21. 3 rolls.

M1539   Naturalization Records of the U.S. District Courts for the State of Alaska, 1900-1924. RG 21. 5 rolls.

M1540   Naturalization Records of the U.S. District Court for the District of Oregon, 1859-1941. RG 21. 62 rolls.

M1541   Naturalization Records of the U.S. District Court for the Eastern District of Washington, 1890-1972. RG 21. 40 rolls.

M1542   Naturalization Records of the U.S. District Court for the Western District of Washington, 1890-1957. RG 21. 153 rolls.

M1543 Naturalization Records of the Superior Courts for King, Pierce, Thurston, and Snohomish Counties, Washington, 1850–1974. RG 21. 103 rolls.

M1545 Index to Naturalization Petitions and Records of the U.S. District Court, 1906–1966, and the U.S. Circuit Court, 1906–1911, for the District of Massachusetts. RG 21. 115 rolls.

M1547 Naturalization Records of U.S. District Courts in the Southeast, 1790–1958. RG 21. 106 rolls.

M1548 Index (Soundex) to the 1920 Federal Population Census Schedules for Alabama. RG 29. 159 rolls.

M1549 Index (Soundex) to the 1920 Federal Population Census Schedules for Arizona. RG 29. 30 rolls.

M1550 Index (Soundex) to the 1920 Federal Population Census Schedules for Arkansas. RG 29. 131 rolls.

M1551 Index (Soundex) to the 1920 Federal Population Census Schedules for California. RG 29. 327 rolls.

M1552 Index (Soundex) to the 1920 Federal Population Census Schedules for Colorado. RG 29. 80 rolls.

M1553 Index (Soundex) to the 1920 Federal Population Census Schedules for Connecticut. RG 29. 111 rolls.

M1554 Index (Soundex) to the 1920 Federal Population Census Schedules for Delaware. RG 29. 20 rolls.

M1555 Index (Soundex) to the 1920 Federal Population Census Schedules for the District of Columbia. RG 29. 49 rolls.

M1556 Index (Soundex) to the 1920 Federal Population Census Schedules for Florida. RG 29. 74 rolls.

M1557 Index (Soundex) to the 1920 Federal Population Census Schedules for Georgia. RG 29. 200 rolls.

M1558 Index (Soundex) to the 1920 Federal Population Census Schedules for Idaho. RG 29. 33 rolls.

M1560 Index (Soundex) to the 1920 Federal Population Census Schedules for Indiana. RG 29. 230 rolls.

M1561 Index (Soundex) to the 1920 Federal Population Census Schedules for Iowa. RG 29. 181 rolls.

M1562 Index (Soundex) to the 1920 Federal Population Census Schedules for Kansas. RG 29. 129 rolls.

M1563 Index (Soundex) to the 1920 Federal Population Census Schedules for Kentucky. RG 29. 180 rolls.

M1564 Index (Soundex) to the 1920 Federal Population Census Schedules for Louisiana. RG 29. 135 rolls.

M1565 Index (Soundex) to the 1920 Federal Population Census Schedules for Maine. RG 29. 67 rolls.

M1566 Index (Soundex) to the 1920 Federal Population Census Schedules for Maryland. RG 29. 126 rolls.

M1567 Index (Soundex) to the 1920 Federal Population Census Schedules for Massachusetts. RG 29. 326 rolls.

M1568 Index (Soundex) to the 1920 Federal Population Census Schedules for Michigan. RG 29. 291 rolls.

M1569 Index (Soundex) to the 1920 Federal Population Census Schedules for Minnesota. RG 29. 174 rolls.

M1570 Index (Soundex) to the 1920 Federal Population Census Schedules for Mississippi. RG 29. 123 rolls.

M1571 Index (Soundex) to the 1920 Federal Population Census Schedules for Missouri. RG 29. 269 rolls.

M1572 Index (Soundex) to the 1920 Federal Population Census Schedules for Montana. RG 29. 46 rolls.

M1573 Index (Soundex) to the 1920 Federal Population Census Schedules for Nebraska. RG 29. 96 rolls.

M1574 Index (Soundex) to the 1920 Federal Population Census Schedules for Nevada. RG 29. 9 rolls.

M1576 Index (Soundex) to the 1920 Federal Population Census Schedules for New Jersey. RG 29. 253 rolls.

M1577 Index (Soundex) to the 1920 Federal Population Census Schedules for New Mexico. RG 29. 31 rolls.

M1578 Index (Soundex) to the 1920 Federal Population Census Schedules for New York. RG 29. 885 rolls.

M1579 Index (Soundex) to the 1920 Federal Population Census Schedules for North Carolina. RG 29. 166 rolls.

M1580 Index (Soundex) to the 1920 Federal Population Census Schedules for North Dakota. RG 29. 48 rolls.

M1581 Index (Soundex) to the 1920 Federal Population Census Schedules for Ohio. RG 29. 476 rolls.

M1582 Index (Soundex) to the 1920 Federal Population Census Schedules for Oklahoma. RG 29. 155 rolls.

M1583 Index (Soundex) to the 1920 Federal Population Census Schedules for Oregon. RG 29. 69 rolls.

M1584 Index (Soundex) to the 1920 Federal Population Census Schedules for Pennsylvania. RG 29. 712 rolls.

M1585 Index (Soundex) to the 1920 Federal Population Census Schedules for Rhode Island. RG 29. 53 rolls.

M1586 Index (Soundex) to the 1920 Federal Population Census Schedules for South Carolina. RG 29. 112 rolls.

M1587 Index (Soundex) to the 1920 Federal Population Census Schedules for South Dakota. RG 29. 48 rolls.

M1588 Index (Soundex) to the 1920 Federal Population Census Schedules for Tennessee. RG 29. 162 rolls.

M1589 Index (Soundex) to the 1920 Federal Population Census Schedules for Texas. RG 29. 373 rolls.

M1590 Index (Soundex) to the 1920 Federal Population Census Schedules for Utah. RG 29. 33 rolls.

M1591 Index (Soundex) to the 1920 Federal Population Census Schedules for Vermont. RG 29. 32 rolls.

M1592 Index (Soundex) to the 1920 Federal Population Census Schedules for Virginia. RG 29. 168 rolls.

M1593 Index (Soundex) to the 1920 Federal Population Census Schedules for Washington. RG 29. 118 rolls.

M1594 Index (Soundex) to the 1920 Federal Population Census Schedules for West Virginia. RG 29. 109 rolls.

M1595 Index (Soundex) to the 1920 Federal Population Census Schedules for Wisconsin. RG 29. 196 rolls.

M1596 Index (Soundex) to the 1920 Federal Population Census Schedules for Wyoming. RG 29. 17 rolls.

M1597 Index (Soundex) to the 1920 Federal Population Census Schedules for Alaska. RG 29. 6 rolls.

M1598 Index (Soundex) to the 1920 Federal Population Census Schedules for Hawaii. RG 29. 24 rolls.

M1599 Index (Soundex) to the 1920 Federal Population Census Schedules for the Panama Canal Zone. RG 29. 3 rolls.

M1600 Index (Soundex) to the 1920 Federal Population Census Schedules for Military-Naval Districts. RG 29. 18 rolls.

M1601 Index (Soundex) to the 1920 Federal Population Census Schedules for Puerto Rico. RG 29. 165 rolls.

M1602 Index (Soundex) to the 1920 Federal Population Census Schedules for Guam. RG 29. 1 roll.

M1603 Index (Soundex) to the 1920 Federal Population Census Schedules for American Samoa. RG 29. 2 rolls.

M1604 Index (Soundex) to the 1920 Federal Population Census Schedules for the Virgin Islands. RG 29. 3 rolls.

M1605 Index (Soundex) to the 1920 Federal Population Census Schedules for Institutions. RG 29. 1 roll.

M1606 Index Cards to Overseas Military Petitions of the U.S. District Court for the Southern District of California, Central Division (Los Angeles), 1943-1945, 1954, 1955-1956. RG 21. 2 rolls.

M1607 Index to Naturalization Records of the U.S. District Court for the Southern District of California, Central Division, Los Angeles, 1887-1937. RG 21. 2 rolls.

M1608 Naturalization Index of the Superior Court for Los Angeles County, California, 1852-1915. 1 roll.

M1609 Index to Citizens Naturalized in the Superior Court of San Diego, California, 1853-1956. 1 roll.

M1611 Index to Naturalization Records of the U.S. District Court for the Eastern District of Tennessee at Chattanooga, 1888-1955. RG 21. 1 roll.

M1612 Index to Declarations of Intention in the Superior Court of San Diego County, California, 1853-1956. 1 roll.

M1613 Naturalization Records in the Superior Court of San Diego County, California, 1883-1958. 19 rolls.

M1614 Naturalization Records of the Superior Court of Los Angeles County, California, 1876-1915. 28 rolls.

M1615 Naturalization Records of the U.S. District Court for the Territory of Arizona, 1864-1915. RG 21. 5 rolls.

M1616 Naturalization Records of the U.S. District Court for the District of Arizona, 1912-1955. RG 21. 7 rolls.

M1626 Naturalization Petitions of the U.S. Circuit and District Courts for the Middle District of Pennsylvania, 1906-1930. RG 21. 123 rolls.

M1631 Internal Revenue Assessment Lists, Oregon District, 1867-1873. RG 58. 2 rolls.

M1633 U.S. Customs, Puget Sound District Log Books and Shipping Articles, ca. 1890-1937. RG 36. 68 rolls.

M1638 Immigration and Naturalization Service Case Files of Chinese Immigrants, Portland, Oregon, 1890-1914. RG 85. 15 rolls.

M1640 Naturalization Petitions of the U.S. District Court for the District of Maryland, 1906-1930. RG 21. 43 rolls.

M1643 Naturalization Petitions of the U.S. District Court for the Northern District of West Virginia, Wheeling, 1856-1867. RG 21. 2 rolls.

M1644 Naturalization Petitions of the U.S. District and Circuit Courts for the District of Delaware, 1795-1930. RG 21. 19 rolls.

M1645 Naturalization Petitions of the U.S. District Court for the Western District of Virginia (Abingdon), 1914-1929. RG 21. 2 rolls.

M1646 Naturalization Petitions of the U.S. District Court for the Western District of Virginia (Charlottesville), 1910-1929. RG 21. 1 roll.

M1647 Naturalization Petitions of the U.S. District Court for the Eastern District of Virginia (Richmond), 1906-1929. RG 21. 10 rolls.

M1648 Naturalization Petitions of the U.S. District Court for the Eastern District of Virginia (Alexandria), 1909-1920. RG 21. 5 rolls.

M1649 Index to Naturalization Petitions for the U.S. Circuit Court, 1795-1911, and District Court, 1795-1928, for the District of Delaware. RG 21. 1 roll.

M1650 Applications from the Bureau of Indian Affairs, Muskogee Area Office, Relating to Enrollment in the Five Civilized Tribes Under the Act of 1896. RG 75. 54 rolls.

M1658 Southern Claims Commission Approved Claims, 1871-1880: Georgia. RG 217. 761 microfiche.

M1659 Records of the Fifty-Fourth Massachusetts Infantry Regiment (Colored), 1863-1865. RG 94. 7 rolls.

M1674 Index (Soundex) to Naturalization Petitions Filed in Federal, State, and Local Courts in New York, New York, Including New York, Kings, Queens, and Richmond Counties, 1792-1906. RG 21. 294 rolls.

M1675 Alphabetical Index to Declarations of Intention of the U.S. District Court for the Southern District of New York, 1917-50. RG 21. 111 rolls.

M1676 Alphabetical Index to Petitions for Naturalization of the U.S. District Court for the Southern District of New York, 1824-1941. RG 21. 102 rolls.

M1677 Alphabetical Index to Petitions for Naturalization of the U.S. District Court for the Western District of New York, 1906-1966. RG 21. 20 rolls.

M1744 Index to Naturalization in the U.S. District Court for the Northern District of California, 1852-ca. 1989. RG 21. 165 rolls.

M1746 Final Revolutionary War Pension Payment Vouchers: Georgia. RG 217. 6 rolls.

M1747 Index to Records Relating to War of 1812 Prisoners of War. RG 94. 3 rolls.

M1754 Nonstatistical Manifests and Statistical Index Cards of Aliens Arriving at Eagle Pass, Texas, June 1905-November 1929. RG 85. 27 rolls.

M1755 Permanent and Statistical Manifests of Alien Arrivals at Eagle Pass, Texas, June 1905-June 1953. RG 85. 30 rolls.

M1756 Application for Nonresident Alien's Border Crossing Identification Cards Made at El Paso, Texas, ca. July 1945–December 1952. RG 85. 62 rolls.

M1757 Manifests of Aliens Granted Temporary Admission at El Paso, Texas, ca. July 1924–1954. RG 85. 97 rolls.

M1759 Nonstatistical Manifests and Statistical Index Cards of Aliens Arriving at Douglas, Arizona, July 1908–December 1952. RG 85. 4 rolls.

M1761 Index to Passenger Arrivals at San Diego, California, ca. 1904–ca. 1952. RG 85. 6 rolls.

M1763 Index to Passenger Lists of Vessels Arriving at San Pedro/Wilmington/Los Angeles, California, 1907–1936. RG 85. 7 rolls.

M1764 Passenger Lists of Vessels Arriving at San Pedro/Wilmington/Los Angeles, California, June 29, 1907–June 30, 1948. RG 85. 118 rolls.

M1766 Alphabetical Card Manifests of Alien Arrivals at Fort Hancock, Texas, 1924–1954. RG 85. 2 rolls.

M1767 Manifests of Alien Arrivals at San Ysidro (Tia Juana), California, April 21, 1908–December 1952. RG 85. 20 rolls.

M1768 Alphabetical Card Manifests of Alien Arrivals at Fabens, Texas, July 1924–1954. RG 85. 7 rolls.

M1770 Indexes and Manifests of Alien Arrivals at Rio Grande City, Texas, November 1908–May 1955. RG 85. 6 rolls.

M1771 Alphabetical Manifests of Non-Mexican Aliens Granted Temporary Admission at Laredo, Texas, December 1, 1929–April 8, 1955. RG 85. 5 rolls.

M1778 Passenger and Crew Lists of Vessels Departing the Trust Territory of the Pacific Islands for Arrival at Guam, 1947–1952, and Related Records. RG 85. 1 roll.

M1784 Index to Pension Application Files of Remarried Widows Based on Service in the War of 1812, Indian Wars, Mexican War, and Regular Army Before 1861. RG 15. 1 roll.

M1785 Index to Pension Application Files of Remarried Widows Based on Service in the Civil War and Later Wars and in the Regular Army after the Civil War. RG 15. 7 rolls.

M1786 Records of Invalid Pension Payments to Veterans of the Revolutionary War and the Regular Army and Navy, March 1801–September 1815. RG 15. 1 roll.

M1787 Compiled Service Records of Volunteer Union Soldiers Who Served in Organizations from the Territory of Nebraska. RG 94. 43 rolls.

M1788 Indexes to Naturalization Records of the U.S. District Court for the District, Territory, and State of Alaska (Third Division), 1903–1991. RG 21. 22 rolls.

M1789 Compiled Service Records of Volunteer Union Soldiers Who Served in Organizations from the Territory and State of Nevada. RG 94. 16 rolls.

M1791 Schedules of a Special Census of Indians, 1880. RG 29. 5 rolls.

M1792 Manufacturing Schedules Contained in the 1810 Population Census Schedules of New York State. RG 29. 1 roll.

M1793 Nonpopulation Census Schedules for the District of Columbia, 1850–1870: Agriculture, Industry, Mortality, and Social Statistics, and Nonpopulation Census Schedules for Worcester County, Maryland, 1850: Agriculture. RG 29. 1 roll.

M1794 Nonpopulation Census Schedules for the District of Columbia, Montana Territory, Nevada, and Wyoming Territory, 1880: Agriculture. RG 29. 1 roll.

M1796 Nonpopulation Census Schedules for Pennsylvania, 1870–1880: Industry and Manufacturing. RG 29. 9 rolls.

M1798 Nonpopulation Census Schedules for Vermont, 1850–1870: Agriculture and Industry. RG 29. 9 rolls.

M1799 Nonpopulation Census Schedules for Baltimore City and County, Maryland, 1850–1860: Agriculture, Industry, and Social Statistics. RG 29. 1 roll.

M1801 Compiled Military Service Records of Volunteer Union Soldiers Who Served with the United States Colored Troops: 55th Massachusetts Infantry (Colored). RG 94. 16 rolls.

M1802 Nonpopulation Census Schedules for Minnesota, 1860: Agriculture. RG 29. 1 roll.

M1803 Third Census of the United States, 1810: Population Schedules, Washington County, Ohio. RG 29. 1 roll.

M1804 Second Census of the United States, 1800: Population Schedules, Washington County, Territory Northwest of the River Ohio; and Population Census, 1803: Washington County, Ohio. RG 29. 1 roll.

M1805 Nonpopulation Census Schedules for North Carolina, 1850-1880: Mortality and Manufacturing. RG 29. 9 rolls.

M1806 Nonpopulation Census Schedules for Montana, 1870 and 1880. RG 29. 1 roll.

M1807 Nonpopulation Census Schedules for Utah Territory and Vermont, 1870: Mortality. RG 29. 1 roll.

M1808 Eighth Census of the United States for the Northern District of Halifax County, Virginia, 1860: Schedules of Free Inhabitants, Slave Inhabitants, Mortality, Agriculture, Industry, and Social Statistics. RG 29. 1 roll.

M1810 Nonpopulation Census Schedules for New Jersey, 1850-1880: Mortality. RG 29. 4 rolls.

M1811 First Territorial Census for Oklahoma, 1890. RG 29. 1 roll.

M1813 Kansas Territorial Censuses, 1855-1859. RG 29. 2 rolls.

M1814 1907 Census of Seminole County, Oklahoma. RG 29. 1 roll.

M1815 Military Operations of the Civil War: A Guide-Index to the Official Records of the Union and Confederate Armies, Volumes II-V. 18 microfiche.

M1816 Compiled Service Records of Volunteer Union Soldiers Who Served in Organizations from the State of Oregon. RG 94. 34 rolls.

M1817 Compiled Service Records of Volunteer Union Soldiers Who Served with the United States Colored Troops: 1st Through 5th United States Colored Cavalry, 5th Massachusetts Cavalry (Colored), 6th United States Colored Cavalry. RG 94. 107 rolls.

M1818 Compiled Military Service Records of Volunteer Union Soldiers Who Served with the United States Colored Troops: Artillery Organizations. RG 94. 299 rolls.

M1819 Compiled Military Service Records of Volunteer Union Soldiers Who Served with the United States Colored Troops: 1st United States Colored Infantry, 1st South Carolina Volunteers (Colored), Company A, 1st United States Colored Infantry (1 Year). RG 94. 19 rolls.

M1820 Compiled Military Service Records of Volunteer Union Soldiers Who Served with the United States Colored Troops: 2nd Through 7th Colored Infantry, Including 3rd Tennessee Volunteers (African Descent), 6th Louisiana Infantry (African Descent), 7th Louisiana Infantry (African Descent). RG 94. 116 rolls.

M1825 Proofs of Citizenship Used to Apply for Seamen's Protection Certificates at the Ports of Bath, Maine, 1833, 1836, 1839-50, 1853-65, 1867-68; and at Portsmouth, New Hampshire, 1857-58. RG 36. 3 rolls.

M1826 Proofs of Citizenship Used to Apply for Seamen's Protection Certificates for the Port of New Orleans, Louisiana, 1800, 1802, 1804-7, 1809-12, 1814-16, 1818-19, 1821, 1850-51, 1855-57. RG 36. 12 rolls.

M1827 Index to Naturalization Records of the U.S. Supreme Court for the District of Columbia, 1802-1909. RG 21. 1 roll.

M1829 Compiled Military Service Records of Maj. Uriah Blue's Detachment of Chickasaw Indians in the War of 1812. RG 94. 1 roll.

M1830 Compiled Military Service Records of Maj. McIntosh's Company of Creek Indians in the War of 1812. RG 94. 1 roll.

M1831 Miscellaneous Indian Removal Rolls, 1832-1846. RG 75. 1 roll.

M1832 Returns of Killed and Wounded in Battles or Engagements With Indians, British, and Mexican Troops, 1790-1848, Compiled by Lt. Col. J.H. Eaton (Eaton's Compilation). RG 94. 1 roll.

M1833 Revisions to the Wallace Rolls of Cherokee Freedmen and Delaware and Shawnee Cherokees, ca. 1890-96. RG 75. 1 roll.

M1834 Emergency Passport Applications (Passports Issued Abroad), 1877-1907. RG 59. 56 rolls.

M1838 Nonpopulation Census Schedules for Pennsylvania, 1850-1880: Mortality. RG 29. 11 rolls.

M1840 Passenger Lists of Aliens (1927-1939) and Citizens (1933-1939) Arriving in Panama City, Florida. RG 85. 1 roll.

M1842   Passenger Lists of Vessels Arriving at Georgetown, South Carolina, 1923-1939, and at Apalachicola, Boynton, Boca Grande, Carrabelle, Fernandina, Fort Pierce, Hobs Sounds, Lake Worth, Mayport, Millville, Port Inglis, Port St. Joe, St. Andrews, and Stuart, Florida, 1904-1942. RG 85. 1 roll.

M1844   Passenger Lists of Vessels Arriving at Tampa, Florida, November 2, 1898-December 31, 1945. RG 85. 65 rolls.

M1845   Card Records of Headstones Provided for Deceased Union Civil War Veterans, ca. 1879-ca. 1903. RG 92. 22 rolls.

M1848   Index to Passport Applications, 1850-52, 1860-80, 1881, 1906-23. RG 59. 61 rolls.

M1849   Manifests of Alien Arrivals at Yseleta, Texas, 1924-1954. RG 85. 7 rolls.

M1850   Index and Manifests of Alien Arrivals at Sasabe/San Fernando, Arizona, 1919-1952. RG 85. 3 rolls.

M1851   Index and Manifests of Alien Arrivals at Progreso/Thayer, Texas, October 1928-May 1955. RG 85. 6 rolls.

M1852   Records of Persons Held for Boards of Special Inquiry at the San Pedro, California, Immigration Office, November 3, 1930-September 27, 1936. RG 85. 1 roll.

M1853   Indians of California Census Rolls Authorized under the Act of May 18, 1928 (45 Stat. 602) as Amended, Approved May 16-17, 1933. RG 75. 1 roll.

M1858   Historical Register and Dictionary of the United States Army from its Organization, September 29, 1789, to March 2, 1903. 1 roll.

M1898   Compiled Military Service Records of Volunteer Union Soldiers Who Served with the United States Colored Troops: 54th Massachusetts Infantry Regiment (Colored). RG 94. 20 rolls.

M1959   Passenger Lists of Vessels Arriving at St. Petersburg, Florida, December 1926-March 1941. RG 85. 1 roll.

M1960   Compiled Service Records of Volunteer Union Soldiers Who Served in Organizations from the Dakota Territory. RG 94. 3 rolls.

M1961   Compiled Service Records of Volunteer Union Soldiers Who Served in Organizations from the State of Delaware. RG 94. 117 rolls.

M1973   Statistical Manifests of Alien Arrivals by Airplanes at San Antonio, Texas, May 17, 1944-March 1952. RG 85. 1 roll.

M2005   Crew Lists of Vessels Arriving at Ashland, Wisconsin, August 1922-October 1954. RG 85. 2 rolls.

M2007   U.S. Court of Claims Docket Cards for Congressional Case Files, 1884-1943. RG 123. 5 rolls.

M2008   Lists of Aliens Arriving at Laredo, Texas, from July 1903 to June 1907, via the Mexican National Railroad or the Laredo Foot Bridge. RG 85. 1 roll.

M2009   Work Projects Administration Transcript of Passenger Lists of Vessels Arriving at New Orleans, Louisiana, 1813-1849. 2 rolls.

M2010   Correspondence Relating to Enforcement of the "Passenger Acts," 1852-57. RG 60. 1 roll.

M2011   Indentures of Apprenticeship Recorded in the Orphans Court, Washington County, District of Columbia, 1801-11. RG 21. 1 roll.

M2014   Burial Registers for Military Posts, Camps, and Stations, 1768-1921. RG 92. 1 roll.

M2016   Alphabetical Index of Alien Arrivals at Eagle, Hyder, Ketchikan, Nome, and Skagway, Alaska, June 1906-August 1946. RG 85. 1 roll.

M2017   Lists of Aliens Arriving at Skagway (White Pass), Alaska, October 1906-November 1934. RG 85. 1 roll.

M2018   Lists of Aliens Arriving at Eagle, Alaska, December 1910-October 1938. RG 85. 1 roll.

M2019   Records Relating to War of 1812 Prisoners of War. RG 94. 1 roll.

M2021   Passenger Lists of Citizens (June 1924-August 1948) and Aliens (March 1946-November 1948) Arriving at Pensacola, Florida, and Passenger Lists of Vessels Departing from Pensacola, Florida (August 1926-March 1948). RG 85. 1 roll.

M2024   Indexes and Manifests of Alien Arrivals at Zapata, Texas, August 1923-September 1953. RG 85. 2 rolls.

M2027   Admitted Alien Crew Lists of Vessels Arriving at Pascagoula, Mississippi, July 1903-May 1935. RG 85. 1 roll.

M2030   Statistical and Nonstatistical Manifests, and Related Indexes, of Aliens Arriving at Andrade and Campo (Tecate), California, 1910-1952. RG 85. 5 rolls.

M2032 Passenger Lists of European Immigrants Arriving at Vera Cruz, Mexico, 1921–1923, and Related Correspondence, 1921–1931. RG 85. 1 roll.

M2037 Register of Cadet Applicants, 1819–67. RG 94. 5 rolls.

M2039 Correspondence, Field Notes, and the Census Roll of All Members or Descendants of Members Who Were on the Roll of the Ottawa and the Chippewa Tribes of Michigan in 1870 and Living on March 4, 1907 (Durant Roll). RG 75. 4 rolls.

M2040 Index to Manifests of Permanent and Statistical Arrivals at Eagle Pass, Texas, December 1, 1929–June 1953. RG 85. 2 rolls.

M2041 Temporary and Nonstatistical Manifests of Aliens Arriving at Eagle Pass, Texas, July 1928–June 1953. RG 85. 14 rolls.

M2042 Alphabetical Manifest Cards of Alien Arrivals at Calais, Maine, ca. 1906–1952. RG 85. 5 rolls.

M2061 Military Academy Registers, 1867–94. RG 94. 3 rolls.

M2062 Southern Claims Commission Approved Claims, 1871–1880: Alabama. RG 217. 36 rolls.

M2064 Alphabetical Manifest Cards of Alien and Citizen Arrivals at Fort Fairfield, Maine, ca. 1909–April 1953. RG 85. 1 roll.

M2071 Alphabetical Manifest Cards of Alien Arrivals at Vanceboro, Maine, ca. 1906–December 24, 1952. RG 85. 13 rolls.

M2074 Index to Naturalization [Records] in the U.S. District Court for the District of Hawaii, 1900–1976. RG 21. 23 rolls.

M2075 Record of Appointment of Substitute Clerks in First- and Second-Class Post Offices, 1899–1905. RG 28. 1 roll.

M2076 Index and Registers of Substitute Mail Carriers in First- and Second-Class Post Offices, 1885–1903. RG 28. 1 roll.

M2077 Indexes to Rosters of Railway Postal Clerks, ca. 1883–ca. 1902. RG 28. 1 roll.

M2079 Final Revolutionary War Pension Payment Vouchers: Delaware. RG 15. 1 roll.

P2257 Records of the U.S. House of Representatives; A: Consolidated Order of Claims; B: Summary Reports of the Commissions, 1871–1880. RG 233. 1 roll.

T9 Tenth Census of the United States, 1880. RG 29. 1,454 rolls.

T132 Minnesota Census Schedules for 1870. RG 29. 13 rolls.

T142 Selected Records of the Tennessee Field Office of the Bureau of Refugees, Freedmen, and Abandoned Lands, 1865–1872. RG 105. 73 rolls.

T227 Civil War Direct Tax Assessment Lists: Tennessee. RG 217. 6 rolls.

T275 Census of Creek Indians Taken by Parsons and Abbott in 1832. RG 75. 1 roll.

T279 Records of the 1820 Census of Manufactures. RG 29. 27 rolls.

T288 General Index to Pension Files, 1861–1934. RG 15. 544 rolls.

T289 Organization Index to Pension Files of Veterans Who Served Between 1861 and 1900. RG 15. 765 rolls.

T316 Old War Index to Pension Files, 1815–1926. RG 15. 7 rolls.

T317 Index to Mexican War Pension Files, 1887–1926. RG 15. 14 rolls.

T318 Index to Indian Wars Pension Files, 1892–1926. RG 15. 12 rolls.

T496 Census Roll of the Cherokee Indians East of the Mississippi and Index to the Roll, 1835. RG 75. 1 roll.

T498 Publications of the Bureau of the Census: 1790 Census, Printed Schedules. RG 29. 3 rolls.

T517 Index to Passenger Lists of Vessels Arriving at Ports in Alabama, Florida, Georgia, and South Carolina, 1890–1924. RG 85. 26 rolls.

T518 Index to Passengers Arriving at Providence, Rhode Island, June 18, 1911–October 5, 1954. RG 85. 2 rolls.

T519 Index to Passenger Lists of Vessels Arriving at New York, 1897–1902. RG 85. 115 rolls.

T520 Index (Soundex) to Passenger Lists of Vessels Arriving at Baltimore, Maryland, 1897–July 1952. RG 85. 42 rolls.

T521 Index to Passenger Lists of Vessels Arriving at Boston, Massachusetts, January 1, 1902–June 30, 1906. RG 85. 11 rolls.

T522 Index to Passengers Arriving at New Bedford, Massachusetts, July 1, 1902–November 18, 1954. RG 85. 2 rolls.

T523   Index to Passengers Arriving at Gulfport, Mississippi, August 27, 1904–August 28, 1954, and at Pascagoula, Mississippi, July 15, 1903–May 21, 1935. RG 85. 1 roll.

T526   Index (Soundex) Cards, Ship Arrivals at Philadelphia, Pennsylvania, January 1, 1883–June 28, 1948. RG 85. 60 rolls.

T527   Index to Passenger Lists of Vessels Arriving at New Orleans, Louisiana, 1853–1899. RG 36. 32 rolls.

T529   Final Rolls of Citizens and Freedmen of the Five Civilized Tribes in Indian Territory (as Approved by the Secretary of the Interior on or Before Mar. 4, 1907, With Supplements Dated Sept. 25, 1914). RG 48. 3 rolls.

T577   Index to Names of United States Marshals, 1789–1960. RG 60. 1 roll.

T612   Book Indexes to New York Passenger Lists, 1906–42. RG 85. 307 rolls.

T617   Index to Passenger Lists of Vessels Arriving at Boston, Massachusetts, July 1, 1906–December 31, 1920. RG 85. 11 rolls.

T618   Index to Passenger Lists of Vessels Arriving at New Orleans, Louisiana, 1900–1952. RG 85. 22 rolls.

T621   Index (Soundex) to Passenger Lists of Vessels Arriving at New York, New York, July 1, 1902–December 31, 1943. RG 85. 744 rolls.

T623   Twelfth Census of the United States, 1900. RG 29. 1,854 rolls.

T624   Thirteenth Census of the United States, 1910. RG 29. 1,784 rolls.

T625   Fourteenth Census of the United States, 1920. RG. 29. 2,076 rolls.

T655   Federal Mortality Census Schedules, 1850–1880 (formerly in the custody of the Daughters of the American Revolution), and Related Indexes. RG 29. 30 rolls.

T715   Passenger and Crew Lists of Vessels Arriving at New York, New York, 1897–1957. RG 85. 8,892 rolls.

T717   Records of the U.S. District Court for the Northern District of California and Predecessor Courts, 1851–1950. RG 21. 125 rolls.

T718   Ledgers of Payments, 1818–1872, to U.S. Pensioners Under Acts of 1818 Through 1858, From Records of the Office of the Third Auditor of the Treasury. RG 217. 23 rolls.

T734   Index (Soundex) to the 1880 Population Schedules for Alabama. RG 29. 74 rolls.

T735   Index (Soundex) to the 1880 Population Schedules for Arizona. RG 29. 2 rolls.

T736   Index (Soundex) to the 1880 Population Schedules for Arkansas. RG 29. 48 rolls.

T737   Index (Soundex) to the 1880 Population Schedules for California. RG 29. 34 rolls.

T738   Index (Soundex) to the 1880 Population Schedules for Colorado. RG 29. 7 rolls.

T739   Index (Soundex) to the 1880 Population Schedules for Connecticut. RG 29. 25 rolls.

T740   Index (Soundex) to the 1880 Population Schedules for Dakota Territory. RG 29. 6 rolls.

T741   Index (Soundex) to the 1880 Population Schedules for Delaware. RG 29. 9 rolls.

T742   Index (Soundex) to the 1880 Population Schedules for the District of Columbia. RG 29. 9 rolls.

T743   Index (Soundex) to the 1880 Population Schedules for Florida. RG 29. 16 rolls.

T744   Index (Soundex) to the 1880 Population Schedules for Georgia. RG 29. 86 rolls.

T745   Index (Soundex) to the 1880 Population Schedules for Idaho Territory. RG 29. 2 rolls.

T746   Index (Soundex) to the 1880 Population Schedules for Illinois. RG 29. 143 rolls.

T747   Index (Soundex) to the 1880 Population Schedules for Indiana. RG 29. 98 rolls.

T748   Index (Soundex) to the 1880 Population Schedules for Iowa. RG 29. 78 rolls.

T749   Index (Soundex) to the 1880 Population Schedules for Kansas. RG 29. 51 rolls.

T750   Index (Soundex) to the 1880 Population Schedules for Kentucky. RG 29. 83 rolls.

T751   Index (Soundex) to the 1880 Population Schedules for Louisiana. RG 29. 55 rolls.

T752   Index (Soundex) to the 1880 Population Schedules for Maine. RG 29. 29 rolls.

T753   Index (Soundex) to the 1880 Population Schedules for Maryland. RG 29. 47 rolls.

T754   Index (Soundex) to the 1880 Population Schedules for Massachusetts. RG 29. 70 rolls.

T755   Index (Soundex) to the 1880 Population Schedules for Michigan. RG 29. 73 rolls.

T756   Index (Soundex) to the 1880 Population Schedules for Minnesota. RG 29. 37 rolls.

T757   Index (Soundex) to the 1880 Population Schedules for Mississippi. RG 29. 69 rolls.

T758   Index (Soundex) to the 1880 Population Schedules for Missouri. RG 29. 114 rolls.

T759   Index (Soundex) to the 1880 Population Schedules for Montana. RG 29. 2 rolls.

T760   Index (Soundex) to the 1880 Population Schedules for Nebraska. RG 29. 22 rolls.

T761   Index (Soundex) to the 1880 Population Schedules for Nevada. RG 29. 3 rolls.

T762   Index (Soundex) to the 1880 Population Schedules for New Hampshire. RG 29. 13 rolls.

T763   Index (Soundex) to the 1880 Population Schedules for New Jersey. RG 29. 49 rolls.

T764   Index (Soundex) to the 1880 Population Schedules for New Mexico Territory. RG 29. 6 rolls.

T765   Index (Soundex) to the 1880 Population Schedules for New York. RG 29. 187 rolls.

T766   Index (Soundex) to the 1880 Population Schedules for North Carolina. RG 29. 79 rolls.

T767   Index (Soundex) to the 1880 Population Schedules for Ohio. RG 29. 143 rolls.

T768   Index (Soundex) to the 1880 Population Schedules for Oregon. RG 29. 8 rolls.

T769   Index (Soundex) to the 1880 Population Schedules for Pennsylvania. RG 29. 168 rolls.

T770   Index (Soundex) to the 1880 Population Schedules for Rhode Island. RG 29. 11 rolls.

T771   Index (Soundex) to the 1880 Population Schedules for South Carolina. RG 29. 56 rolls.

T772   Index (Soundex) to the 1880 Population Schedules for Tennessee. RG 29. 86 rolls.

T773   Index (Soundex) to the 1880 Population Schedules for Texas. RG 29. 77 rolls.

T774   Index (Soundex) to the 1880 Population Schedules for Utah Territory. RG 29. 7 rolls.

T775   Index (Soundex) to the 1880 Population Schedules for Vermont. RG 29. 15 rolls.

T776   Index (Soundex) to the 1880 Population Schedules for Virginia. RG 29. 82 rolls.

T777   Index (Soundex) to the 1880 Population Schedules for Washington Territory. RG 29. 4 rolls.

T778   Index (Soundex) to the 1880 Population Schedules for West Virginia. RG 29. 32 rolls.

T779   Index (Soundex) to the 1880 Population Schedules for Wisconsin. RG 29. 51 rolls.

T780   Index (Soundex) to the 1880 Population Schedules for Wyoming. RG 29. 1 roll.

T790   Book Indexes, Boston Passenger Lists, 1899-1940. RG 85. 107 rolls.

T791   Book Indexes, Philadelphia Passenger Lists, 1906-26. RG 85. 23 rolls

T792   Book Indexes, Providence Passenger Lists, 1911-34. RG 85. 15 rolls.

T793   Book Indexes, Portland, Maine, Passenger Lists, 1907-1930. RG 85. 12 rolls.

T825   Publications of the Bureau of the Census, 1790-1916. RG 29. 42 rolls.

T840   Passenger Lists of Vessels Arriving at Philadelphia, Pennsylvania, 1883-1945. RG 85. 181 rolls.

T843   Passenger Lists of Vessels Arriving at Boston, Massachusetts, 1891-1943. RG 85. 454 rolls.

T844   Passenger Lists of Vessels Arriving at Baltimore, Maryland, 1891-1909. RG 85. 150 rolls.

T905   Passenger Lists of Vessels Arriving at New Orleans, Louisiana, 1903-1945. RG 85. 189 rolls.

T928   Records of the U.S. District Court for the District of New Jersey and Predecessor Courts, 1790-1950. RG 21. 186 rolls.

T938   Crew Lists of Vessels Arriving at Boston, Massachusetts, 1917-1943. RG 85. 269 rolls.

T939   Crew Lists of Vessels Arriving at New Orleans, Louisiana, 1910-1945. RG 85. 311 rolls.

T940   Passenger Lists of Vessels Arriving at Key West, Florida, 1898-1945. RG 85. 122 rolls.

T941   Crew Lists of Vessels Arriving at Gloucester, Massachusetts, 1918-1943. RG 85. 13 rolls.

T942   Crew Lists of Vessels Arriving at New Bedford, Massachusetts, 1917-1943. RG 85. 2 rolls.

T943   Passenger Lists of Vessels Arriving at Savannah, Georgia, 1906-1945. RG 85. 4 rolls.

T944 Passenger Lists of Vessels Arriving at New Bedford, Massachusetts, 1902-1942. RG 85. 8 rolls.

T977 Muster Rolls of Officers and Enlisted Men of the U.S. Marine Corps, 1893-1940. RG 127. 461 rolls.

T985 Old Settler Cherokee Census Roll, 1895, and Index to Payment Roll, 1896. RG 75. 2 rolls.

T1030 Index (Soundex) to the 1900 Federal Population Census Schedules for Alabama. RG 29. 177 rolls.

T1031 Index (Soundex) to the 1900 Federal Population Census Schedules for Alaska. RG 29. 15 rolls.

T1032 Index (Soundex) to the 1900 Federal Population Census Schedules for Arizona. RG 29. 22 rolls.

T1033 Index (Soundex) to the 1900 Federal Population Census Schedules for Arkansas. RG 29. 135 rolls.

T1034 Index (Soundex) to the 1900 Federal Population Census Schedules for California. RG 29. 198 rolls.

T1035 Index (Soundex) to the 1900 Federal Population Census Schedules for Colorado. RG 29. 69 rolls.

T1036 Index (Soundex) to the 1900 Federal Population Census Schedules for Connecticut. RG 29. 107 rolls.

T1037 Index (Soundex) to the 1900 Federal Population Census Schedules for Delaware. RG 29. 21 rolls.

T1038 Index (Soundex) to the 1900 Federal Population Census Schedules for the District of Columbia. RG 29. 42 rolls.

T1039 Index (Soundex) to the 1900 Federal Population Census Schedules for Florida. RG 29. 62 rolls.

T1040 Index (Soundex) to the 1900 Federal Population Census Schedules for Georgia. RG 29. 214 rolls.

T1041 Index (Soundex) to the 1900 Federal Population Census Schedules for Hawaii. RG 29. 30 rolls.

T1042 Index (Soundex) to the 1900 Federal Population Census Schedules for Idaho. RG 29. 19 rolls.

T1043 Index (Soundex) to the 1900 Federal Population Census Schedules for Illinois. RG 29. 475 rolls.

T1045 Index (Soundex) to the 1900 Federal Population Census Schedules for Iowa. RG 29. 212 rolls.

T1046 Index (Soundex) to the 1900 Federal Population Census Schedules for Kansas. RG 29. 148 rolls.

T1048 Index (Soundex) to the 1900 Federal Population Census Schedules for Louisiana. RG 29. 146 rolls.

T1049 Index (Soundex) to the 1900 Federal Population Census Schedules for Maine. RG 29. 80 rolls.

T1050 Index (Soundex) to the 1900 Federal Population Census Schedules for Maryland. RG 29. 127 rolls.

T1052 Index (Soundex) to the 1900 Federal Population Census Schedules for Michigan. RG 29. 257 rolls.

T1053 Index (Soundex) to the 1900 Federal Population Census Schedules for Minnesota. RG 29. 180 rolls.

T1054 Index (Soundex) to the 1900 Federal Population Census Schedules for Mississippi. RG 29. 156 rolls.

T1055 Index (Soundex) to the 1900 Federal Population Census Schedules for Missouri. RG 29. 300 rolls.

T1056 Index (Soundex) to the 1900 Federal Population Census Schedules for Montana. RG 29. 40 rolls.

T1057 Index (Soundex) to the 1900 Federal Population Census Schedules for Nebraska. RG 29. 107 rolls.

T1058 Index (Soundex) to the 1900 Federal Population Census Schedules for Nevada. RG 29. 7 rolls.

T1059 Index (Soundex) to the 1900 Federal Population Census Schedules for New Hampshire. RG 29. 52 rolls.

T1061 Index (Soundex) to the 1900 Federal Population Census Schedules for New Mexico. RG 29. 23 rolls.

T1062 Index (Soundex) to the 1900 Federal Population Census Schedules for New York. RG 29. 768 rolls.

T1063   Index (Soundex) to the 1900 Federal Population Census Schedules for North Carolina. RG 29. 168 rolls.

T1064   Index (Soundex) to the 1900 Federal Population Census Schedules for North Dakota. RG 29. 36 rolls.

T1065   Index (Soundex) to the 1900 Federal Population Census Schedules for Ohio. RG 29. 397 rolls.

T1066   Index (Soundex) to the 1900 Federal Population Census Schedules for Oklahoma. RG 29. 42 rolls.

T1067   Index (Soundex) to the 1900 Federal Population Census Schedules for Oregon. RG 29. 54 rolls.

T1069   Index (Soundex) to the 1900 Federal Population Census Schedules for Rhode Island. RG 29. 49 rolls.

T1070   Index (Soundex) to the 1900 Federal Population Census Schedules for South Carolina. RG 29. 124 rolls.

T1071   Index (Soundex) to the 1900 Federal Population Census Schedules for South Dakota. RG 29. 44 rolls.

T1072   Index (Soundex) to the 1900 Federal Population Census Schedules for Tennessee. RG 29. 188 rolls.

T1073   Index (Soundex) to the 1900 Federal Population Census Schedules for Texas. RG 29. 286 rolls.

T1074   Index (Soundex) to the 1900 Federal Population Census Schedules for Utah. RG 29. 29 rolls.

T1075   Index (Soundex) to the 1900 Federal Population Census Schedules for Vermont. RG 29. 41 rolls.

T1076   Index (Soundex) to the 1900 Federal Population Census Schedules for Virginia. RG 29. 174 rolls.

T1077   Index (Soundex) to the 1900 Federal Population Census Schedules for Washington. RG 29. 69 rolls.

T1081   Index (Soundex) to the 1900 Federal Population Census Schedules for Military and Naval. RG 29. 32 rolls.

T1082   Index (Soundex) to the 1900 Federal Population Census Schedules for Indian Territory. RG 29. 42 rolls.

T1098   Index to Rendezvous Reports, Before and After the Civil War, 1846–1861 and 1865–1884. RG 24. 32 rolls.

T1099   Index to Rendezvous Reports, Civil War, 1861–1865. RG 24. 31 rolls.

T1100   Index to Rendezvous Reports, Naval Auxiliary Service, 1917–1918. RG 24. 1 roll.

T1101   Index to Rendezvous Reports, Armed Guard Personnel, 1917–1920. RG 24. 3 rolls.

T1118   Muster Rolls of the United States Marine Corps, 1798–1892. RG 127. 123 rolls.

T1128   Nonpopulation Census Schedules for Nebraska, 1860–1880. RG 29. 16 rolls.

T1130   Nonpopulation Census Schedules for Kansas, 1850–1880. RG 29. 48 rolls.

T1132   Nonpopulation Census Schedules for Virginia, 1850–1880. RG 29. 34 rolls.

T1133   Nonpopulation Census Schedules for Illinois, 1850–1880. RG 29. 64 rolls.

T1134   Nonpopulation Census Schedules for Texas, 1850–1880. RG 29. 59 rolls.

T1135   Nonpopulation Census Schedules for Tennessee, 1850–1880. RG 29. 39 rolls.

T1136   Nonpopulation Census Schedules for Louisiana, 1850–1880. RG 29. 15 rolls.

T1137   Nonpopulation Census Schedules for Georgia, 1850–1880. RG 29. 27 rolls.

T1138   Nonpopulation Census for Pennsylvania, 1850–1880: Agriculture. RG 29. 62 rolls.

T1156   Nonpopulation Census Schedules for Iowa, 1850–1880. RG 29. 62 rolls.

T1157   Nonpopulation Census Schedules for Pennsylvania, 1850–1860: Manufactures Schedules. RG 29. 9 rolls.

T1159   Nonpopulation Census Schedules for Ohio, 1850–1880. RG 29. 104 rolls.

T1163   Nonpopulation Census Schedules for Michigan, 1850: Mortality Schedules (in the custody of the State Library of Ohio). RG 29. 1 roll.

T1164   Nonpopulation Census Schedules for Michigan, 1850–1880 (in the custody of the Michigan State Archives). RG 29. 77 rolls.

T1175   Schedules of the Minnesota Territory Census of 1857. RG 29. 5 rolls.

T1196   Selected Pension Application Files Relating to the Mormon Battalion, Mexican War, 1846-1848. RG 15. 21 rolls.

T1204   Nonpopulation Census Schedules for Massachusetts, 1850-1880. RG 29. 40 rolls.

T1207   Private Land Grant Case Files in the Circuit Court of the Northern District of California, 1852-1910. RG 21. 28 rolls.

T1208   Internal Revenue Assessment Lists for Arkansas, 1867-1874. RG 58. 4 rolls.

T1209   Internal Revenue Assessment Lists for the Territory of Idaho, 1867-1874. RG 58. 1 roll.

T1210   Census Enumeration District Descriptive Volumes for 1900. RG 29. 10 rolls.

T1214   Index to Private Land Grant Cases, U.S. District Court, Northern District of California, 1853-1910. RG 21. 1 roll.

T1215   Index to Private Land Grant Cases, U.S. District Court, Southern District of California. RG 21. 1 roll.

T1216   Index by County to Private Land Grant Cases, U.S. District Court, Northern and Southern Districts of California. RG 21. 1 roll.

T1219   State Department Transcripts of Passenger Lists, ca. October 1819-ca. December 1832. RG 36. 2 rolls.

T1220   Selected Indexes to Naturalization Records of the U.S. Circuit and District Courts, Northern District of California, 1852-1928. RG 21. 3 rolls.

T1224   Descriptions of Census Enumeration Districts, 1830-1890 and 1910-1950. RG 29. 146 rolls.

T1234   Township Plats of Selected States. RG 49. 67 rolls.

T1259   Index (Soundex) to the 1910 Federal Population Census Schedules for Alabama. RG 29. 140 rolls.

T1260   Index (Soundex) to the 1910 Federal Population Census Schedules for Arkansas. RG 29. 139 rolls.

T1261   Index (Soundex) to the 1910 Federal Population Census Schedules for California. RG 29. 272 rolls.

T1262   Index (Soundex) to the 1910 Federal Population Census Schedules for Florida. RG 29. 84 rolls.

T1263   Index (Soundex) to the 1910 Federal Population Census Schedules for Georgia. RG 29. 174 rolls.

T1264   Index (Soundex) to the 1910 Federal Population Census Schedules for Illinois. RG 29. 491 rolls.

T1265   Index (Soundex) to the 1910 Federal Population Census Schedules for Kansas. RG 29. 145 rolls.

T1266   Index (Soundex) to the 1910 Federal Population Census Schedules for Kentucky. RG 29. 194 rolls.

T1267   Index (Soundex) to the 1910 Federal Population Census Schedules for Louisiana. RG 29. 132 rolls.

T1268   Index (Soundex) to the 1910 Federal Population Census Schedules for Michigan. RG 29. 253 rolls.

T1269   Index (Soundex) to the 1910 Federal Population Census Schedules for Mississippi. RG 29. 118 rolls.

T1270   Index (Soundex) to the 1910 Federal Population Census Schedules for Missouri. RG 29. 285 rolls.

T1271   Index (Soundex) to the 1910 Federal Population Census Schedules for North Carolina. RG 29. 178 rolls.

T1272   Index (Soundex) to the 1910 Federal Population Census Schedules for Ohio. RG 29. 418 rolls.

T1273   Index (Soundex) to the 1910 Federal Population Census Schedules for Oklahoma. RG 29. 143 rolls.

T1274   Index (Soundex) to the 1910 Federal Population Census Schedules for Pennsylvania. RG 29. 688 rolls.

T1275   Index (Soundex) to the 1910 Federal Population Census Schedules for South Carolina. RG 29. 93 rolls.

T1276   Index (Soundex) to the 1910 Federal Population Census Schedules for Tennessee. RG 29. 142 rolls.

T1277   Index (Soundex) to the 1910 Federal Population Census Schedules for Texas. RG 29. 262 rolls.

T1278   Index (Soundex) to the 1910 Federal Population Census Schedules for Virginia. RG 29. 183 rolls.

T1279   Index (Soundex) to the 1910 Federal Population Census Schedules for West Virginia. RG 29. 108 rolls.

The following entries are keyed to paragraph numbers, not to page numbers.
Entries do not include references to microfilm or other publications cited in the text.